Twenty-five Black African Filmmakers

Twenty-five Black African Filmmakers

A CRITICAL STUDY, WITH FILMOGRAPHY AND BIO-BIBLIOGRAPHY

Françoise Pfaff

Greenwood Press

New York • Westport, Connecticut • London

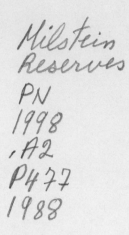

Library of Congress Cataloging-in-Publication Data

Pfaff, Françoise.
  Twenty-five Black African filmmakers.

  Bibliography: p.
  Includes index.
  1. Moving-picture producers and directors—Africa,
Subsaharan—Biography—Dictionaries. 2. Moving-
pictures—Africa, Subsaharan—Bio-bibliography.
I. Title.
PN1998.A2P477 1988   791.43′023′0922 [B] 87–15024
ISBN 0-313-24695-5 (lib. bdg. : alk. paper)

British Library Cataloguing in Publication Data is available.

Library of Congress Catalog Card Number: 87-15024
ISBN: 0-313-24695-5

First published in 1988

Greenwood Press, Inc.
88 Post Road West, Westport, Connecticut 06881

Printed in the United States of America

The paper used in this book complies with the
Permanent Paper Standard issued by the National
Information Standards Organization (Z39.48-1984).

10 9 8 7 6 5 4 3 2 1

Copyright Acknowledgements
The author and publisher gratefully acknowledge permission to reprint material from
the following copyrighted sources.
Françoise Pfaff. ''Toward a New Era in Cinema—Harvest 3,000 Years,'' *New Directions* 4, no. 3, July 1977.
Françoise Pfaff. ''Sarah Maldoror,'' *Black Art an International Quarterly* 5, no. 2,
1982.

Cet ouvrage est dédié à ma mère et à ma grand-mère avec toute ma gratitude.

Contents

PREFACE   ix

ACKNOWLEDGMENTS   xiii

Moustapha Alassane (1942–), Niger   1

Kwaw Ansah (1941–), Ghana   11

Ola Balogun (1945–), Nigeria   19

Timité Bassori (1933–), Ivory Coast   33

Moussa Bathily (1946–), Senegal   43

Souleymane Cissé (1940–), Mali   51

Jean-Pierre Dikongue-Pipa (1940–), Cameroon   69

Pierre-Marie Dong (1945–), Gabon   79

Henri Duparc (1941–), Ivory Coast   87

Désiré Ecaré (1939–), Ivory Coast   95

Kramo-Lanciné Fadika (1948–), Ivory Coast   107

Safi Faye (1943–), Senegal   115

Oumarou Ganda (1935–1981), Niger   125

Haile Gerima (1946–), Ethiopia   137

Med Hondo (1936–), Mauritania   157

Gaston Kaboré (1951–), Burkina Faso   173

Daniel Kamwa (1943–), Cameroon   185

Nana Mahomo (1930–), South Africa   195

Sarah Maldoror (1929–   ), France, Guadeloupe   205

Djibril Diop Mambety (1945–   ), Senegal   217

Ababacar Samb (1934–   ), Senegal   227

Ousmane Sembene (1923–   ), Senegal   237

Momar Thiam (1929–   ), Senegal   267

Mahama Johnson Traoré (1942–   ), Senegal   275

Paulin Soumanou Vieyra (1925–   ), Senegal   289

BIBLIOGRAPHY   305

INDEX   319

Preface

One of Africa's newest forms of art—and probably the least known in the Western world—is cinema. Although *Afrique sur Seine,* filmed in Paris in 1955 by a group of African students, is cited historically as the genesis of Black African cinema, most critics generally agree that Sub-Saharan Africa's cinema truly emerged in the early 1960s. The advent of indigenous Sub-Saharan African filmmaking coincided with the self-awareness and assertiveness generated at a time when most African countries were undergoing major political changes in the transition from years of colonial bondage to independence. In such a context, many African filmmakers felt the concurrent need to rectify images of themselves and their sociocultural environment through works that would be free of the one-dimensional and often derogatory stereotypes popularized by various non-Africans through the media, particularly cinema. For years, superficial and grossly distorted portrayals of Africa on the silver screen had mirrored the general paternalistic and contemptuous colonial ideology that regarded Africans as inferior beings seemingly "predestined" to peace and progress through European "salvation." Many European and American motion pictures set in Africa had resulted from such a racially biased outlook—one has only to mention the numerous escapist safari-melodramas manufactured on Hollywood's assembly lines since the turn of the century. In these alluring films, the African continent was but a mysterious, wild, exotic backdrop to the valiant deeds of Western adventurers and explorers. As expected, the bravery of these protagonists contrasted sharply with the blithesome and "uncivilized" simple-mindedness or cruel savagery of the natives, viewed in an unchanging and global perspective of lush landscapes and wild animals.

From its inception, Black African cinema has been largely envisioned as a functional art form. While redefining the portrayal of Africa on film, Black African filmmakers vehemently rejected alien stereotypes in favor of realistic images of Africa from an African perspective. Cognizant of the enormous power of film as a means of expression and communication, and realizing the extent to which this medium could benefit their predominantly illiterate compatriots,

Black African filmmakers generally conceived their work within a didactic framework. Although a few were later to orient themselves toward purely commercial entertainment, most Black African filmmakers remained faithful to their initial sociopolitical and cultural commitment. Their aim was to take an active part in national development by adapting film to the needs and aspirations of their new nations.

In a primarily serious mode not devoid of bitingly satirical and comical elements, Black African films depict Africa at its various historical, political, and social stages, express distinct cultural milieus and ideological trends, and reflect diverse geographic surroundings. Although a product of many cultures, this cinema offers an undeniable thematic homogeneity, for it emerges from countries which have had an analogous colonial past and similar preoccupations as newly independent nations. Thus, a great number of Sub-Saharan motion pictures illustrate the overall conflicting dichotomy between indigenous traditions and values inherited from the West. Frequently identifiable topics include such issues as the sociopolitical alienation some Africans may suffer in their society as well as the sociocultural estrangement they face as emigrants to foreign countries; the precariousness of village life and rural migration; increasing urban unemployment, poverty, and juvenile deliquency; prostitution; the power or weight of socioreligious traditions; and the inequities resulting from caste systems and tribalism. Other typical themes are the evolving condition of women; the exploitation of illiterate people by a corrupt elite or unscrupulous religious leaders; nepotism; misdeeds linked to colonialism and neocolonialism; political instability; and insufficient health care. Consequently, documentaries and feature films made by Black African directors have a twofold significance. For the African, they have depicted Africa's realities and served as a tool for progress through self-examination and self-actualization. At the same time, for the non-African, such movies are invaluable reflectors of Africa's changing societies, bringing about a new awareness in foreign thought and customs.

Until the present time, with but a few exceptions, most Black African motion pictures have been characterized by a slow-paced linear narrative and a style that is both straightforward and allegorical. Yet, in addition to drawing their thematic inspirations from African tales and legends, a growing number of cinéastes are making use of a film language deeply rooted in the techniques of traditional storytelling, thus forging an authentically African aesthetic that is instilling a unique flavor into their art. A similar adherence to their cultural heritage can be observed in an increasing preference for African vernaculars over such imported tongues as French, English, or Portuguese.

Made in countries for which cinema (because of its often critical and even subversive tone?) tends not to be a priority of national development, and in spite of attempts to establish such inter-African film structures as CIDC (Consortium Interafricain de Distribution Cinématographique), CIPROFILMS (Centre Interafricain de Production de Films), or the recently founded WAFCO (West African Film Corporation), Black African films have usually remained at the level of low-budget craftsmanship without yet being able to soar to the level of a true industry. Made more often than not on an independent basis, financed through bank loans, intermittent government funding, and, in the Francophone regions, frequent (now diminishing) financial support from the French Ministry of Cooperation, these films suffer acutely from a lack of sustained channels of production and distribution in areas of Africa where movie theaters are still supplied principally by foreign distribution companies that show more interest in mediocre Western and Asian motion pictures than in indigenous film products.

Although a number of works by Black African filmmakers have been shown on local television and in movie theaters with success, their distribution both throughout the continent and abroad is still limited. The screening of a number of these films has been restricted mainly to international festivals, particularly such biennial events as the Carthage film festival known as JCC (Journées Cinématographiques de Carthage) held in Tunisia, FESPACO (Festival Panafricain du Cinéma de Ouagadougou) in Burkina Faso, and more recently MOGPAFIS (Mogadishu Pan-African Film Symposium), organized in Somalia. In Western countries, African motion pictures remain items for festival or archival interest and are seen by specialized and limited audiences on the occasion of film series and scholarly colloquia. In the United States these are spearheaded by such organizations as universities, museums, the American Film Institute, the BenArena Film Society (Boston), the Black Film Institute (Washington, D.C.), Celebration of Black Cinema Inc. (Boston), Positive Productions (Washington, D.C.), Third World Moving Images Project (Amherst), and Third World Newsreel (New York). However, these films are rarely screened on television, and unfortunately have yet to be included in the lucrative video market.

Therefore, due to their sporadic and limited circulation, Black African films have, to date, generated a fair amount of reviews but only scarce in-depth and comprehensive publications, notably special issues of the journals *L'Afrique Littéraire et Artistique* ("Les Cinémas africains en 1972" and "Cinéastes d'Afrique noire," 1978) and *Cinémaction* ("Cinémas noirs d'Afrique," 1983) by Guy Hennebelle et al.; the books *Le Cinéma africain* (1975) by Paulin Soumanou Vieyra, *African Films: The Context of Production* (1982) by Angela Martin, and *Camera nigra, le discours du film africain* (1984), a collective work from CESCA (Le Centre d'Etude sur la Communication en Afrique). Other studies focusing on the cinema of individual African countries include *Le Cinéma au Mali* (1983), *Le Cinéma en Côte d'Ivoire* (1983), and *La Haute Volta et le cinéma* (1983) by Victor Bachy; *Le Cinéma au Nigéria* (1984) by Françoise Balogun; *Le Cinéma au Zaïre, au Rwanda et au Burundi* (1984) by Rik Otten; and a special issue of *Cinémaction* devoted to cinema in South Africa ("Le Cinéma Sud-africain est-il tombé sur la tête?" edited by Keyan Tomaselli, 1986).

Twenty-five Black African Filmmakers is designed to serve as a tool to explore further the realm of African film. Rather than presenting a comprehensive survey of all talented Black African directors (253 filmmakers from Sub-Saharan Africa and Madagascar are listed in "Cinémas noirs d'Afrique"), it highlights a selected group of representative cinéastes whose works have both significantly enriched African filmmaking and received substantial international exposure.

Each chapter of the book is devoted to an individual filmmaker, follows an identical format, and provides the reader with ample bio-bibliographical and filmographical information, including material gathered from personal interviews with the filmmakers, a thematic analysis of their motion pictures at realistic and symbolic levels, as well as critical responses to their works by both African and non-African critics. Such assessments include quotes from scholarly journals and books and also mass oriented publications so as to offer researchers a wide and diverse array of viewpoints (excerpts from interviews and publications in French were translated by the author). The volume includes an extensive general bibliography meant to reinforce and broaden its primary scope of investigation and research. A selection of related stills of representative films illustrates the text.

Twenty-five Black African Filmmakers constitutes a source of information that sheds much needed light and attention upon a too often neglected area of cinema studies. It is hoped that this book will prove useful to students, scholars, and anyone interested in the development of Third World cinema as well as African affairs and culture in general.

Acknowledgments

I owe special thanks to James H. Kennedy for his relentless support, constructive criticism, and precise proofreading throughout the writing of this book.

I would like to express my appreciation to James T. Sabin, Marilyn Brownstein, Maureen Melino, and William Neenan for spearheading and editing this work. I am grateful to Claire Méhat and Ruth Rhone for their assistance at various stages of the manuscript; Thomas Cripps, Abiyi Ford, and Lois Mailou Jones for their advice and encouragement over the years; the staff of the Library of Congress, in particular Laverne Page of the African and Middle Eastern Division, and the librarians of the Motion Picture, Broadcasting, and Recorded Sound Division for greatly facilitating my research; the organizers of FESPACO (Burkina Faso), the staff of the British Film Institute, the cinémathèque of the French Ministry of Cooperation, the Film Department of the New York Museum of Modern Art, the library of the Institut des Hautes Etudes Cinématographiques, and the American Film Institute in Washington, D.C., for their much appreciated help; Atria, Clément Tapsoba of *Carrefour Africain,* Mypheduh Films, and New Yorker Films for providing stills and other materials; Oumar Ba for conducting research in Dakar; Lloyd and Monique Mitchell for facilitating contacts in Senegal; Mamadou Diagne for his assistance in the translation of Wolof; most Black African filmmakers included in this book, and others, for favorably responding to my interviews, questionnaires, and requests for photos. Thanks are also extended to the Andrew Mellon Fund for its partial financial support of the final typing of the manuscript.

Twenty-five Black African Filmmakers

Moustapha Alassane (1942–)
Niger

BIOGRAPHY

Referred to as the "Méliès" *(Le Cinéma africain,* 1975, p. 139) and the "Douanier Rousseau" *(Afrique Contemporaine,* September-October 1975, p. 4) of African film, Moustapha Alassane is the pioneer of Niger's young cinema. Born around 1942 in N'Jougou, a village located in Benin, he is of Yoruba origin and Muslim extraction. The son of a polygamous tradesman, Alassane migrated with his family to Niger in 1953.

At an early age Alassane used to entertain his many siblings and friends by staging evening shadow-shows during which he would present animated visuals of his country's fauna. Later, as a young student at the lycée of Niamey (Niger's capital), Moustapha discovered he had a budding talent for drawing, which he eagerly cultivated from then on. Such skill subsequently allowed him to improve his evening spectacles, to the delight of his audience. In fact, he hand-painted color pictures on the transparent cellophane wrappings of cigarette packs, which he projected with a rudimentary projector of his own making. Unknowingly, Alassane had succeeded in re-creating the slow evolution of moving pictures from the ancient shadow shows of Asia to our forebears' magic lantern.

After finishing primary school and later obtaining his "brevet" (a ninth grade diploma awarded students in the French educational system), Moustapha Alassane worked as a mechanic's apprentice. Later he became a mechanic himself and within a few years purchased a truck with which he transported sundry merchandise on the Niamey-Abidjan route. By that time also he had become an assiduous viewer of urban film screenings at local movie theaters. Despite the fact that those films were more often than not second rate French and American products, which at that time flooded France's colonial screens, such films instilled in him a desire to explore further the technical facets of filmmaking. Expanding his previous endeavors, Alassane started hand-painting film with color dyes and thus singlehandedly created his first animated pictures of silhouettes of village life, namely, that of a canoe-paddler and of a woman pounding millet.

In his early twenties, Moustapha Alassane gave up truck-driving for a more sedentary occupation, that of a clerk at the IFAN (l'Institut Fondamental d'Afrique Noire, formerly known as l'Institut Français d'Afrique Noire), where his creative experiments, *Le Piroguier* (The Canoe-Paddler, 1962) and *La Pileuse de mil* (Woman Pounding Millet, 1962), were noticed by Jean Rouch, the French ethnologist and filmmaker, who was later to introduce Alassane to ethnographic filmmaking. Alassane remembers:

Jean Rouch had come to Niger as a civil engineer. He became seriously involved in ethnographic filmmaking after the Second World War. Since I was interested in film, I arranged to meet him, and I subsequently worked with him. It is with Jean Rouch that I acquired my basic training in filmmaking. This also explains why my early films had an ethnographic intent. (Alassane to author, Ouagadougou, 23 February 1987; undocumented quotations below are from the same interview.)

Simultaneously, Alassane's skills and inventiveness were encouraged by Jean-René Debrix, then head of the film division of the French Ministry of Cooperation, who was later to promote Alassane's early works such as *Aouré*, which was made in 1962, and received an award at the Saint-Cast Festival (France) and the Bronze Medal for short films at the Cannes Film Festival of that same year, and *La Bague du Roi Koda* (King Koda's Ring, 1964). In 1963–1964, upon Rouch's advice, the filmmaker undertook a nine-month training program in filmmaking at the Office National du Film (ONF) in Montreal, where he worked with Norman Mac Laren, the renowned specialist of hand-drawn cameraless film technique. After his trip to Canada, Alassane, who had previously studied ethnographic filmmaking in Paris (1962–1963), returned to Niger, where he worked for the IFAN. The cinéaste expounds: "I actively participated in the creation of the Niamey museum. I drafted its architectural plans and supervised its construction. I should say that I am a very good draftsman whenever I feel like putting my mind to it." Then, renewing his interest in hand-painted film, he made two short cartoons entitled *La Mort de Gandji* (Gandji's Death, 1965), which was to receive the Prize for Best Short Film at the 1966 Dakar Festival of Negro Arts, and *Bon voyage Sim* (1966), which was to receive a prize at the Annecy Film Festival (France). The year 1966 saw the release of Alassane's documentary *L'Arachide de Santchira* (Santchira Peanuts) as well as that of *Le Retour de l'aventurier* (The Adventurer's Return), the director's first middle-length feature film.

In 1968 Moustapha Alassane briefly ventured into the field of acting, holding a secondary role in Rouch's *Petit à petit ou Les Lettres persanes 1968*. In 1969 he shot a fiction film, *Les Contrebandiers* (The Smugglers), and participated in various symposia at the Mannheim Film Festival (Germany). The following year, he was invited to serve as a jury member at the Dinard Film Festival (France) and was also commissioned by the Centre des Traditions Orales of Niger to make a half-hour film *Deela* (1971). Also in 1971, Alassane shot *Jamya,* a documentary commissioned by the government of Niger. Subsequently, in 1972, Alassane completed *F.V.V.A.—Femmes, villa, voiture, argent* (Wives, Villa, Car, Money). This film, made on a $90,000 budget, was shot in twenty days and co-produced by government agencies of Niger and Burkina Faso (formerly Upper Volta). It received the OCAM (Organisation Commune Africaine et Mauricienne) Prize for Best Feature Length Film at the 1972 FESPACO (Pan-African Film Festival of Ouagadougou). That same year Alassane went to Nigeria where he made an ethnographic film *Sakhi,* for the French Musée de l'Homme. Shortly thereafter, Alassane co-directed with Anna Soehring *Toula ou le Génie des Eaux* (Toula or the Water Spirit, 1973), co-produced with a West German film company and based on works of Boubou Hama, a writer from Niger.

During the course of 1974 and 1975, besides making *Soubane,* a documentary commissioned by the government of Niger, Moustapha Alassane took to the wheel of a minibus to organize film screenings throughout Niger's countryside, reaching villages that had little or no exposure to cinematographic art forms. After this experience in itinerant film distribution, he resumed his career as a filmmaker and produced *Samba-le-Grand* (Samba the Great) in 1978, which was to be featured at the 1979 Pan-African Film Festival of Ouagadougou, Burkina Faso, and awarded a prize at the 1980 Carthage film festival (Prize for Best Short Film). He then made *Festival à Dosso* (Festival in Dosso) in 1979. Alassane's most recent feature film is *Kankamba* (1982), and his latest work to date is an animated film *Kokoa,* which was presented *hors concours* at the 1985 FESPACO (where Alassane was invited to serve as official judge). Like some of his other animated films, *Kokoa* has been shown extensively throughout West Africa, notably at French cultural centers. Since 1978, in addition to his cinematographic activities, Moustapha Alassane has been the owner of an open-air movie theater located in the city of Tahoua, Niger, where he presently lives with his two wives and ten children. Alassane is both a member of the Association des Cinéastes du Niger (ANC) and of FEPACI (Fédération Panafricaine des Cinéastes).

A folklorist and a moralist who has often worked in collaboration with griots (African storytellers and oral historians), Alassane untiringly pursues his career in filmmaking. His primary goal is to reach African audiences. He has no overwhelming concern for foreign markets, which explains why most of his films are shot in African vernaculars (Alassane speaks Djerma, Hausa, and Yoruba). Like most of his counterparts, Moustapha Alassane strongly believes in the didactic function of film and its capacity to initiate social change. He points out:

I consider cinema as a means of expression and communication. I usually write my own scripts. I believe African cinema should convey ideas. African filmmakers should participate in a struggle for mental and cultural liberation and bring about cultural awareness through works which should be meaningful and entertaining. To achieve such a goal, African filmmakers should draw their inspiration from the popular facets of Black Africa's oral tradition.

In the near future, Alassane intends to produce an animated feature length film based on a theater play by a well-known author whose name he will not yet disclose for fear of hampering current negotiations.

MAJOR THEMES

Moustapha Alassane's early endeavors in animated filmmaking, as exemplified in *Le Piroguier* and *La Pileuse de mil,* already show his interest in recording certain aspects of his compatriots' daily lives. His concern with rural lifestyle and traditional African customs is reflected furthermore in four other films: *Aouré, Jamya, Sakhi,* and *L'Arachide de Santchira,* an educational documentary about the commercialization of peanut crops.

As the voice-over narrator of his film *Aouré,* Alassane expounds with lyrical simplicity and misogynic humor the courtship and wedding rites of a Djerma village. In this love story, besides stressing the importance of the griot in traditional African societies, the filmmaker focuses on the collective participation of relatives and neighbors in the manifold stages of a seven-day marriage ceremony. *Jamya* describes a farmers' cooperative located in the Maradi region in eastern Niger. In *Sakhi,* Alassane depicts the investiture of the thirty-first Yoruba king of Sakhi, Nigeria, and his accreditation by local religious and political authorities. Both *Aouré* and *Sakhi* are disserved by technical drawbacks but remain interesting socioanthropological documents. Other films made by Alassane in the 1970s include *Soubane,* a documentary on family planning, and *Festival à Dosso,* which features the Dosso biennial youth festival.

One of Alassane's preoccupations is to use film as a means of preserving and revaluing his cultural heritage. This is shown in a number of works drawn from the African oral tradition. *La Bague du Roi Koda* uses narrative fiction to tell the story of a king who puts to the test one of his subjects, a fisherman. The king entrusts a ring to the fisherman, who is to return it three years later. On returning the ring, the fisherman is to be rewarded, but if he fails to do so he will be beheaded. Soon after having given the ring to the fisherman, the king approaches the fisherman's beautiful wife to induce her to betray her husband for monetary compensation. She accepts. Thus, having regained his ring, the king throws it in the river to insure its permanent disappearance. Three years later, as planned, the king calls the fisherman to his court to ask him for the ring. In awe, the fisherman discovers that it is missing. Yet, before being executed, the fisherman begs to feed his family for the last time. This request is granted by the king, and the fisherman goes to catch some fish. After having caught three fish, the fisherman sells two of them and takes the third fish home for his family's meal. As he cuts up the fish, the fisherman discovers the ring inside of it. The fisherman then rushes to the king to give the ring back to him. Having passed the test, the fisherman is not executed. Instead, as promised, the king generously offers him gold and half of his kingdom. The fisherman eventually realizes his wife's betrayal but forgives her, for "such is the duty of a true Muslim."

The verve, vivacity, and magic of African storytelling are also found in *Deela*, which describes the fate of an ungrateful young girl sheltered by a noble king. Adapted from a Hausa folk tale, the story of Deela is narrated in Hausa by a griot within the film (in which actors speak the same language) and in French by the filmmaker, who uses voice-over narration as an expository device. This ingenious blend of two styles respects the African verbal authenticity of the tale and renders the film accessible to both Hausa and French-speaking audiences— a technique that undoubtedly could be successfully applied to a number of other African films.

Toula ou le Génie des Eaux benefits, technically, from a higher budget than that of Alassane's other motion pictures. This film starts with a conversation between a young man and an elder concerning the drought that is devastating their country. Subsequently, the elder narrates the legend of Toula, and this constitutes the core of Alassane's plot. In this legend, a diviner attributes drought to the anger of a snake-god who demands a human sacrifice to appease its wrath. The king offers to sacrifice his own niece, Toula. To prevent her death, a young man who is in love with Toula sets forth to find a water-supply point. After having discovered a source, the young villager hurries back, only to find out that Toula has already been sacrificed to the snake-god. Should people appeal to supernatural powers (and risk death) to fight drought, or rather have recourse to modern technology? *Toula ou le Génie des Eaux* ends like a dilemma tale, the outcome of which should be debated and in a way decided by the film viewers. Stressing the political implications of his film, Moustapha Alassane once said:

I did not make *Toula* for the mere pleasure of adapting one of Boubou Hama's legends to the screen, but rather to draw attention to the agonizing problem of drought which could very well be solved if adequate measures were really taken. *(L'Afrique Littéraire et Artistique,* 3rd Quarter 1978, p. 17.)

In *Samba-le-Grand,* which shows some thematic similarities with *Toula ou le Génie des Eaux,* Alassane employs chatoyant dolls dressed in traditional African attire as well as attractive hand-painted sceneries to narrate the heroic deeds of a king's son who conquers kingdoms and kills an evil serpent (who rules over waters) to win a princess' heart.

Other films by Moustapha Alassane depict the dichotomy between African traditions and new values inherited from the West. In *Le Retour de l'aventurier,* which the director describes "not as an African western, but rather a parody of the western film genre"—with appropriate fistfighting, gunshooting, galloping, and saloon scenes, all of which is shot in Niger *(L'Afrique Littéraire et Artistique,* 3rd Quarter 1978, p. 15)—Alassane denounces the cultural alienation and adverse mimetism present among certain African youth engaged in a steady diet of cowboy movies. This film concerns a young man from Niger who comes back from the United States with cowboy outfits as gifts for his friends. Wearing cowboy clothes and carrying guns, he sets out as a gang leader and, with friends, starts to terrorize his and neighboring villages. Eventually, the gang's activities are ended by elders who succeed in dividing the gang and restoring traditional power over their delinquent, damaging, and even murderous misdeeds. It should be noted here that *Le Retour de l'aventurier* won popular acclaim in a number of West African countries.

It is sarcastically pointed out by many that the abbreviation "F.V.V.A.," which stands in French for "femmes, villa, voiture, argent" (wives, villa, car, money), has recently become a part of the vocabulary of Niger's postcolonial bourgeoisie. With the film *F.V.V.A.—Femmes, villa, voiture, argent,* Moustapha Alassane invites us to share the tribulations of Ali, a young clerk, as he passes from a modest but honest life to corruption and imprisonment. *F.V.V.A.— Femmes, villa, voiture, argent* attacks uncritical acculturation and arrivism, the presumptuousness of Africa's new establishment, arranged marriages, the exploitative power of some marabouts, the abuses of family solidarity, and the alleged disloyalty of modern African women. *Les Contrebandiers,* which denounces the illegal trade taking place at the Mali-Niger border, and *Kankamba,* a detective movie, belong to the same moralistic vein as *F.V.V.A.—Femmes, villa, voiture, argent.* Moustapha Alassane describes *Kankamba* as follows:

My film focuses on a taxi driver who accidentally hits a bike rider with his car, and the victim dies. This fatal accident occurs in an isolated area. Subsequently, fearing both police and justice, the taxi driver decides to make away with the cyclist's body. By the end of the film, the taxi driver's attempt to conceal the accident is discovered, and he will eventually have to face justice. What I wanted to show here was how human beings, for fear of reprisals, engage in unusual, fraudulent and pernicious deeds which are harmful to them and society. My aim was to illustrate an individual's reaction to social forces. The film, made for television, was only shown once. Intellectuals in Niger did not appreciate *Kankamba* which did not match familiar detective story criteria. They merely saw it as a commercial film and did not even try to understand why I had made my film.

Moustapha Alassane's latest motion picture, *Kokoa,* describes traditional wrestling using animated puppets.

The originality of Moustapha Alassane stems from his unique handling of social satire through animated cartoons. Best known among these are *La Mort de Gandji,* a political fable about a frog-king and his toady courtiers, and *Bon voyage Sim* (also with frogs as characters), a mockery of official state visits by contemporary African presidents. Thus, besides being an eclectic moralist, Moustapha Alassane will assuredly also be remembered as an irreverent satirist.

SURVEY OF CRITICISM

From the start, it is the inventiveness and the freshness of Alassane's works which have drawn the attention of film critics. In *Afrique Contemporaine* (July-October 1968, p. 10), Jean Debrix marvels at the ingenuity and the fertile imagination of the Niger filmmaker, who "entirely re-invents cinema, the African way." An African critic, D'Dée, endorses *Aouré* as a true expression of African authenticity *(La Vie Africaine,* October 1962, p. 50), while the French film critic Guy Hennebelle terms *La Bague du Roi Koda* a "naiviste" film *(L'Afrique Littéraire et Artistique,* 1st Quarter 1972, p. 235). At the Tours Film Festival (France) in 1966, Robert Benayoun was struck by the naturalness and "vivacity" of *La Mort de Gandji (Positif,* June 1966, p. 76). Also, Paulin Soumanou Vieyra*, the well-known African filmmaker and film historian, shows significant interest in the creative linguistical approach used by Alassane in *Deela (Présence Africaine,* 1st Quarter 1971, pp. 228–29).

Alassane's most widely reviewed works remain *Le Retour de l'aventurier, F.V.V.A—Femmes, villa, voiture, argent,* and *Toula ou le Génie des Eaux.* Wilson Mativo's opinion is as follows:

Le Retour de l'aventurier handles the question of cultural invasion in a manner likely to be misunderstood by the African and the African "masses," but a manner certainly understood by concerned people. . . . The fact that Moustapha uses the "Westerner" to illustrate his point is only too relevant in the sense that in the "Westerner" one is a hero by virtue of his ability to live at the expense of others. He kills in the guise of protecting somebody else from danger, but in the final analysis, this proves to be an act of selfishness, as this somebody else always becomes his follower, his possession. In an African context nothing is more abominable. *(UFAHAMU,* Winter 1971, p. 65)

In her article "Film in Niger," the Eastern European film critic Marie Benesova writes, "In this film, as in all of his work, Alassane avoids being influenced by Western films and seeks his own expression and voice." She states further: "The most distinctive features of his films are his visual impressionism, clear presentation of the story line, and sense of humor" *(Young Cinema and Theatre,* n. 1, 1975, p. 30). Such favorable comments are far from being shared by the French reviewer Jean Delmas, who deplores the style of *Le Retour de l'aventurier,* "where spluttering was intended as spontaneity" *(Jeune Cinéma,* December 1976–January 1977, p. 1). On the other hand, Guy Hennebelle finds the same film "delightfully satirical" in spite of its clumsiness and poor acting *(L'Afrique Littéraire et Artistique,* 1st Quarter 1972, pp. 235–36).

As is the case for *Le Retour de l'aventurier,* a number of reviewers feel uncomfortable with some of the technical flaws found in *F.V.V.A.—Femmes, villa, voiture, argent* (shoddy soundtrack, poor acting etc.). Jacques Binet regrets its lack of unexpectedness and drama but shows appreciation for the originality of its visual prologue, which stages animated frogs *(Afrique Contemporaine,* January-February 1976, p. 29).

Profiting from a much improved technical quality, *Toula ou le Génie des Eaux,* a moral tale with political implications, is hailed by many as Alassane's most accomplished work. However, Vieyra does not find the film convincing *(Présence Africaine,* 1st Quarter 1975, pp. 210–11), and Hennebelle even wonders if its excessively groomed pictorial beauty detracts from its authenticity *(Recherche, Pédagogie et Culture,* May-August 1975, pp. 7–9).

FILMOGRAPHY

Le Piroguier (The Canoe-Paddler), 16 mm, black and white, 2 min., 1962.
La Pileuse de mil (Woman Pounding Millet), 16 mm, black and white, 2 min., 1962.
Aouré, 16 mm, color, 30 min., 1962.
La Bague du Roi Koda (King's Koda's Ring), 16 mm, color, 30 min., 1964.
La Mort de Gandji (Gandji's Death), 16 mm, color, 7 min., 1965.
L'Arachide de Santchira (Santchira Peanuts), 16 mm, color, 25 min., 1966.
Le Retour de l'aventurier (The Adventurer's Return) 16/35 mm, color, 55 min, 1966.
Bon voyage Sim, 16 mm, black and white, 11 min., 1966.
Les Contrebandiers (The Smugglers), 16 mm, color, 1969 (intended as a feature length
    film, this motion picture has yet to be completed).
Deela, 16 mm, black and white, 30 min., 1971.
Jamya, 16 mm, black and white, 30 min., 1971.
F.V.V.A.—Femmes, villa, voiture, argent (Wives, Villa, Car, Money), 16/35mm, color,
    75 min., 1972.
Sakhi, 16 mm, color, 30 min., 1972.
Toula ou le Génie des Eaux (Toula or the Water Spirit), 16/35 mm, color, 90 min., 1973.
Soubane, 16 mm, color, 30 min., 1975.
Samba-le-Grand (Samba the Great), 16 mm, color, 14 min., 1978.
Festival à Dosso, 16 mm, color, 30 min., 1979.
Kankamba, 16 mm, color, 85 min., 1982.
Kokoa, 16 mm, color, 17 min., 1984.

BIBLIOGRAPHY

Interviews of Moustapha Alassane

Hennebelle, Guy, and Catherine Ruelle. "Alassane Mustapha." *L'Afrique Littéraire et
    Artistique,* n. 49, 3rd Quarter 1978, pp. 14–17.
Meideros, Richard de. "Dialogue à quelques voix." *Recherche, Pédagogie et Culture,*
    n. 17–18, May-August 1975, pp. 39–43.
Niandou, Harouna. "Un Pionnier: Moustapha Alassane." *Recherche, Pédagogie et Cul-
    ture,* n. 17–18, May-August 1975, pp. 55–56.

Film Reviews and Studies of Moustapha Alassane

Alain, Yves. "F.V.V.A. le film de Moustapha Alassane dénonce un certain laisser-
    aller." *Bingo,* n. 214, November 1970, pp. 48–49.
Benayoun, Robert. "A chacun son Tours." *Positif,* n. 76, June 1966, pp. 75–76.
Benesova, Marie. "Film in Niger." *Young Cinema and Theatre,* n. 1, 1975, pp. 28–
    30.
Binet, Jacques. "Cinéma Africain." *Afrique Contemporaine,* n. 83, January-February
    1976, pp. 27–30.

Boughedir, Ferid. "Le Cinéma nigérien: l'authenticité de l'autodidacte." *Cinéma Québec*, vol. 3, n. 9–10, August 1974, pp. 27–29.

Cluny, Claude-Michel. "Niger." *Cinéma 72*, n. 165, April 1972, p. 39.

D'Dée. "Enfin du vrai cinéma africain." *La Vie Africaine*, n. 29, October 1962, p. 50.

———. "Jeune cinéma d'Afrique noire." *L'Afrique Actuelle*, special issue, n. 15, 1967, pp. 1–40.

Debrix, Jean R. "Le Cinéma africain." *Afrique Contemporaine*, n. 38–39, July-October 1968, pp. 7–12.

———. "En direct . . . du Niger." *Recherche, Pédagogie et Culture*, n. 17–18, May-August 1975, pp. 54–55.

———. "Situation du cinéma en Afrique francophone." *Afrique Contemporaine*, n. 81, September-October 1975, pp. 2–7.

Delmas, Jean. "Situation du cinéma d'Afrique noire." *Jeune Cinéma*, n. 99, December 1976–January 1977, pp. 1–2.

Hennebelle, Guy. "Le Cinéma nigérien." *L'Afrique Littéraire et Artistique*, n. 20, 1st Quarter 1972, pp. 235–238.

———. "Le Cinéma nigérien, grand vainqueur à Ouagadougou." *L'Afrique Littéraire et Artistique*, n. 22, March 1972, pp. 98–100.

———. "Les Films africains en 1975." *Recherche, Pédagogie et Culture*, n. 17–18, May-August 1975, pp. 7–9.

———. *Guide des films anti-impérialistes*. Paris: Editions du Centenaire, 1975.

Lemaire, Charles. "Le Cinéma au Niger." *Unir Cinéma*, n. 7 (114), July-August 1973, pp. 3–4.

Mativo, Wilson. "Cultural Dilemma of the African Film." *UFAHAMU*, vol. 1, n. 3, Winter 1971, pp. 64–68.

"Mustapha Alassane réinvente le cinéma." *Bingo*, n. 201, October 1969, pp. 48–49.

Rivette, Jacques. "Le Retour d'un aventurier." *Cahiers du Cinéma*, n. 176, March 1966, p. 11.

Siclier, Jacques. "Le Recours aux légendes." *Le Monde*, 23 June 1978, pp. 1, 23.

Traoré, Biny. "Les Films africains." *L'Observateur*, n. 2038, 26 February 1981, pp. 1, 4–5.

———. "Cinéma africain et développement." *Peuples Noirs, Peuples Africains*, n. 33, May-June 1983, pp. 51–62.

Vieyra, Paulin S. "La Création cinématographique en Afrique." *Présence Africaine*, n. 77, 1st Quarter 1971, pp. 219–231.

———. "Les 5es Journées Cinématographiques de Carthage." *Présence Africaine*, vol. 93, 1st Quarter 1975, pp. 208–14.

Kwaw Ansah (1941–   )
Ghana

BIOGRAPHY

Author of the first independently produced and privately financed Ghanaian feature length film, Kwaw Paintsil Ansah was born on 17 July 1941 in Agona Swedru, Ghana. The son of an educated photographer married to three wives, Ansah has three sisters and two brothers. As he was growing up, the future filmmaker was greatly influenced by his father, who used to cultivate great dramatic flair in his everyday life: "He was a disciplinarian and being with my father was like being in hell. . . . being in hell does not say that he mistreated us but he had a sense of humor that was at times more painful than being lashed with a cane" (Kwaw Ansah at the African Studies Association (ASA) Conference, Washington, D.C., 5 November 1982). When he was but a boy, his father taught him that "life is not fun" (ASA Conference, 1982).

Thus, later, as an adolescent, Kwaw Ansah had little choice but to become a serious and hard-working student. It was at that time that he started manifesting abilities in drawing and painting, yet his father wanted him to engage in his trade. Ansah recalls: "He felt every child of his had to become a photographer. So, when I opted out he decided he would not pay my school fees and he meant it" (ASA, 1982). After secondary school, the young Ansah thus had to earn a living. Having noticed his promising talents as a draftsman, Ansah's brother-in-law introduced him to United Africa Company, a Unilever firm in Ghana. While working there, Kwaw Ansah acquired basic training in textile design. Shortly thereafter, as he was on the threshold of adulthood and ready to leave Ghana to further his studies in England, he was invited for the first time to share his father's meal, during which he received specific recommendations. On that occasion his father said to him:

There is a time when a father eats with his child. You have become of age, I am proud of you. You are going away but I want you to come back. Even though you are going to be among "civilized" people, I want you to come back not having forgotten where you come from. (ASA, 1982)

It was in England that Ansah's cousin, filmmaker Ato Yarney, spotted "some cinematic flair in him and brought him into the production of a short trial-film in London" (Production Press Kit, *Love Brewed in the African Pot*). After this first experience in filmmaking, Kwaw Ansah stayed for a while in London, where he studied theater design at the Regent Street Polytechnic School and took courses in drama at the American Musical and Dramatic Academy. There, Philip Burton (father of the late British actor Richard Burton), the principal of the American Musical and Dramatic Academy, advised him to get a grant to understudy film production at the RKO Studios in Hollywood. Having obtained a grant, Ansah went to California, where he understudied the TV series *Hogan's Heroes* and *The Fugitive*. In the United States, as he was familiarizing himself with the techniques of commercial filmmaking and television production, Kwaw Ansah became interested in playwriting and wrote two plays, *The Adoption* and *Mother's Tears*. *The Adoption* was produced off Broadway and then at Columbia University in New York. *Mother's Tears* appeared later in Ghana, where it met instant popular success.

Then came the time when Kwaw Ansah decided to go back to his country. He summarizes his stay overseas and his return to Ghana as follows: "So I went abroad to Britain, came to the States, went back home, and I was in film, an extension of photography. So my father said: "You did not run away after all, you are back home'" (ASA, 1982).

Subsequently, Ansah set out to put into practice what he had learned abroad, and for six months he worked as a production assistant for the Ghana Film Industry Corporation. Next he was employed for a few years as a film and radio producer by Unilever's Lintas Advertising and Target Advertising Services, which enabled him to produce several short films including documentaries and television advertisements. In 1977 Ansah set out to become a private film entrepreneur, and with a few friends he created Film Africa Limited, a production company based in Accra. To this day "the company aims at working to fill the vacuum created in the film industry in the African sector and will aspire through the medium to convey the untold story which is African and authentic" (Production Press Kit, *Love Brewed in the African Pot*).

Shortly after the founding of Film Africa Limited, Kwaw Ansah wrote the script of his first feature film, *Love Brewed in the African Pot*, which the new company was to produce. The filmmaker recollects:

It took me about six months to write this film. Then it came to finding the money for it. . . . Even though filmmaking had started as far back as in the fifties in Ghana, all productions were initiated by the Government Corporation. I was the first in the private sector to have attempted to come out with a full-length film and you can imagine what I went through in terms of financial matters. (ASA, 1982)

Since cinema is far from being considered a safe and profitable venture by most African businessmen and bankers, Kwaw Ansah had to spend an inordinate amount of time and show an indomitable determination to secure funding for his film. Eventually, by using the house given by his father-in-law as collateral, Ansah succeeded in obtaining a bank loan. Filmed with a crew of professional actors (such as Anima Misa, Reginald Tsiboe, George Wilson, Jumoke Debayo, and George Browne) at the Ghana Film Industry Corporation in Accra and other locations in Ghana, and edited by the Ghanaian filmmaker Bernard Odidja with Tony Palmer, *Love Brewed in the African Pot* was released in 1980. In January 1981 the film won the Jury's Special Peacock Award at the Eighth International Film Festival of India at New Delhi. Such an award recompensed "a genuine and talented attempt to find a national and cultural identity." The following month, *Love Brewed in the African Pot* entered competition at the Seventh Pan-African Film Festival of Ouagadougou, Burkina Faso, where it obtained the Oumarou Ganda Prize (an award named after the late filmmaker from Niger) "for a most remarkable direction and production in line with African realities." In August of that same year, the film received an award at the Commonwealth Television and Film Festival in Cyprus. In 1983 Ansah's work was included among the films presented at London's Festival of Third World Cinema. Then, in 1984, it was featured at the First Annual African and Black American Film Festival held in Los Angeles. Yet, even more significant is the fact that *Love Brewed in the African Pot* met a substantial commercial success in other African countries besides Ghana, among them Kenya, Zambia, and Sierra Leone; in the latter country it enjoyed an uninterrupted three-month run and broke box-office records.

Drawing conclusions from his own experience, Ansah strongly believes that the future of African film distribution should be envisioned within an inter-African framework:

African films can be marketed widely in other African countries. In fact *Love Brewed in the African Pot* was a tremendous success in East Africa and some of our films in Yoruba [one of Nigeria's main African languages] had a great success in other parts of Africa. What we are lacking so far are marketing techniques and distribution facilities . . . but we all realize that some of our countries are too small to be complete markets for a film. You cannot make a film in Upper Volta [now Burkina Faso] and hope to recover the budget of the film in Upper Volta alone. So, in the future, the key to an African film industry lies in the exploitation of the African market as a whole. (ASA, 1982)

Since 1984 Kwaw Ansah has been working on his new film, *Heritage,* which takes place during colonial times in Ghana. The film will be produced on a budget of over $2 million (a high budget in terms of African filmmaking), which the director hopes to gather from various sources, both local and foreign. Placing his future work in a perspective of "cultural revitalization" rather than terming it as "political," the Ghanaian filmmaker commented:

My aim is not for this film to make me a millionaire, but that a million people will have a change of heart, to improve the black situation in the world which has been so confused because of a lack of any faith we can relate to. *(West Africa,* 19 November 1984, p. 2319)

Having received part of his training in Hollywood, Ansah, unlike a number of other African filmmakers, has a perfect understanding of the mechanics of commercial cinema and thus does not discard the entertainment component of film. He says, "So what if someone laughed" (ASA, 1982).

Kwaw Ansah is open to criticism and even welcomes it: "As an artist I create for the public to appreciate. . . . we talk and show things about people and they have the right to tell us how it hits them. I think this is the only way we can improve upon our craft" (ASA, 1982).

A visual artist, Ansah is also endowed with musical talents. He has to his credit the musical theme of *Love Brewed in the African Pot,* which he composed with Sammy Lartey, and is furthermore the author of a few songs that have been quite successful in Ghana.

Kwaw Ansah has been married for nearly twenty years and has two teenaged children, Gyasiwa Paintsil Ansah and Nkwaye Paintsil Ansah. He is currently living and working in Accra. With Egbert Adjesu *(I Told You So,* 1970), King Ampaw *(They Call That Love,* 1972; *Kukurantumi—The Road to Accra,* 1983), Sam Aryete *(No Tears for Ananse,* 1968), Efua Sutherland *(Araba: The Village Story,* 1967), Bernard Odjidja *(Doing Their Thing,* 1971), and Kwate Nee-Owo *(You Hide Me,* 1971; *Struggle for a Free Zimbabwe,* 1974; *Angela Davis,* 1976), Ansah stands now as one of Ghana's best-known filmmakers. In 1985 Kwaw Ansah was invited to serve as one of the official judges at the Pan-African Film Festival of Ouagadougou (Burkina Faso).

MAJOR THEMES

Love Brewed in the African Pot, Ansah's only feature film to date, encompasses a number of themes related to one central issue: the clash between indigenous traditions and European influences in pre-independent Ghana (1951). As indicated through its humorously catchy title, this film is a love story *à l'africaine.* Here is how the director summarizes his plot:

A love affair between Aba, educated in a posh Cape Coast school and trained as a dressmaker, and Joe Quansah, a semi-literate auto mechanic [fitter] and son of a fisherman. Aba's father, a retired civil servant[,] wants her to marry Lawyer Bensah instead of Joe. Class consciousness, family and social pressures are brought to play on the lovers, in the process revealing the cultural conflicts existing within the African society. Eventually Joe runs away and Aba is driven from tragedy to the mental home. *(Synopsis of Love in the African Pot)*

Beyond the customary generation gap, the relationship between Kofi Appiah and his daughter Aba reveals the biases inherent in Ghanaian society. Although he also comes from a fisherman's family, Kofi Appiah seemingly discards his humble roots. Literate, he has moved up the social ladder and reached an "enviable" status, that of a clerk in the colonial administration. Having provided a good education for his children, Appiah expects Aba to marry a young man with a bright future. He is thus delighted when Mr. Bensah, the district chief clerk, asks for Aba's hand on behalf of his son, a promising lawyer. Unluckily, Kofi Appiah's great expectations will soon be shattered, as Aba insists on marrying Joe, the mechanic she loves. Angered and bitter, Appiah refuses to attend his daughter's tribal wedding and stays at home. At that precise moment, a dream sequence, handled in an incisively satirical manner by the director, describes the Westernized and pompous ceremony Appiah envisioned for his daughter had she accepted her lawyer suitor.

Far from being discouraged by Aba's marriage to Joe, the lawyer sporadically reappears to resume his courtship. Although Aba continually rejects the lawyer's offers, this awkward situation harbors grueling doubts and jealousy in Joe's mind. When Aba becomes pregnant, her husband questions her loyalty, rejects her, and leaves their home. Distraught and abandoned, Aba will have a miscarriage and be raped by an accountant who posed as a benevolent rescuer after Aba had, once more, managed to escape from the lawyer's assiduities. As Joe comes back to Aba, he discovers that she has been driven to insanity.

In his story, Kwaw Ansah presents a succession of crisis situations which oppose traditional values to Western ways and involve drastically diverse characters. Aba's determination greatly differs from her mother's whimpering submissiveness. Both the lawyer and the accountant, who represent Ghana's colonial elite, are, through their status and lifestyle, in sharp contrast with Joe, the humble fisherman's son. Likewise, the plot sheds light on the true hybrid nature of Aba's father. Claiming his complete adherence to Western culture, he will nonetheless resort to traditional healing (before modern medicine) in his desperate attempt to cure his daughter's mental illness. This meaningful episode illustrates how deeply ingrained traditional beliefs often remain in the psyche of Westernized Africans. It is that same cultural schizophrenia that will precipitate Aba's inner conflicts (although she demonstrates at first much more strength than her husband) and ensuing insanity—a fate which metaphorically serves to denounce the possible mental damage generated by acculturation, in this case a seemingly irremediable loss of one's prior self.

The theme of insanity which Ansah has chosen to illustrate in *Love Brewed in the African Pot* is infrequent in African cinema with the exception of a few films like *Sarzan* (Senegal, 1963) by Momar Thiam*; *Mouna ou le rêve d'un artiste* (Mouna, An Artist's Dream, Ivory Coast, 1969) by Henri Duparc*; *La Femme au couteau* (The Woman with a Knife, Ivory Coast, 1969) by Timité Bassori*; *Kodou* (Senegal, 1971) by Ababacar Samb*; or *Le Prix de la liberté* (The Price of Freedom, Cameroon, 1978) by Jean-Pierre Dikongue-Pipa*. Used as the narrative climax of the story in *Love Brewed in the African Pot,* this theme is less forcefully depicted than might have been expected. It is ill-served by overly melodramatic scenes such as that of the witch-doctor, whose authenticity would have benefitted from a less flamboyant and somewhat stereotypical treatment.

SURVEY OF CRITICISM

Love Brewed in the African Pot was a commercial success in Ghana and several other African countries and has received generally favorable reviews. In one of the first articles concerning *Love Brewed in the African Pot,* one of *West Africa*'s correspondents writes:

Apart from the general beauty of the colour, a good music score with two beautiful songs included, and several fine performances from the cast, the film's strongest point is its simplicity and accuracy. . . . It is this accuracy which puts the film beyond the reach of criticism arising from familiarity with the highly developed technique of Western film. Nor is this a celebration of "primitivism," an apologia for deficient film-making. *(West Africa,* 12 May 1980, p. 24)

Wondering why this film was met with such enthusiastic popular response at the Seventh FESPACO, Farida Ayari *(Adhoua,* April-September 1981, p. 6) concludes that it was "simply because Kwaw Ansah knew how to combine all the 'recipes' the Hollywood RKO Studios taught him." For Ayari *Love Brewed in the African Pot* is, to some extent, patterned after American, Egyptian, and Indian melodramas (also popular in Africa). Otherwise, this critic sees Ansah's work as a well-made film and approves of its effective directing and acting as well as its sagacious humor.

Ferid Boughedir also points out the Hollywood style of *Love Brewed in the African Pot (Jeune Afrique,* 11 March 1981, p. 63), while Raphael Bassan is inclined to compare its treatment of Africa's new urban bourgeoisie to that of Ousmane Sembene's* film *Xala (Afrique-Asie,* 17 January 1983, p. 55). Similar observations are interspersed in Vincent Canby's comments:

Mr. Ansah, who produced, wrote and directed this very good film, shifts from satire to comedy and then to melodrama in which the myths of the African past triumph over the borrowed manners of a precarious present. Like Ousmane Sembene, that very talented Senegalese filmmaker, Mr. Ansah takes a jaundiced view of black Africans who attempt to deny their heritage. He has a fine sense of humor, a perfectly natural appreciation for things supernatural, and an unsurprised sort of humanity I associate with Jean Renoir. *(New York Times,* 25 April 1981, p. 11)

Mosk, one of *Variety*'s film reviewers, considers *Love Brewed in the African Pot* "a bit simplistic in treatment" but concedes that it "does make its point with dramatic probity at times." The critic adds: "Technically passable, director Kwaw Ansah is definitely worth watching as he builds up his techniques and gives a deeper resonance to his committed attitude to film *(Variety,* 25 March 1981, p. 20).

A more in-depth analysis of *Love Brewed in the African Pot* is that of Mbye Baboucar Cham in his article covering West African film production from 1979 to 1981 *(Présence Africaine,* 4th Quarter 1982, pp. 172–76). Acknowledging Ansah's social and political "engagement" as a filmmaker, Cham finds that

there are, however, a few artistic and technical flaws which affect this film in terms of composition, progression and impact. The plot is overloaded with incidents which all too often seem contrived either to denounce explicitly aspects of Ghanaian social life which the director deems negative to the collective well-being, or to simply display on screen aspects of traditional beliefs and practices sometimes presented as antidotes to the crippling influences of a foreign mentality.

The Gambian film critic also reproves Ansah's choice of English as the language used in the film (rather than an African tongue). According to him, this "may have contributed to some of the flaws in the dialogue which tends to be trite at times or plain unconvincing, especially during the period of Joe's courtship of Abba *[sic].*" Yet, in spite of these reservations, Cham concurs with other reviewers in recognizing that Ansah's first feature length film shows undeniable skills and creative talent, and should be considered as a valuable contribution to the development of cinema in Ghana and the rest of Anglophone Africa.

FILMOGRAPHY

Several short films including documentaries and commercials.
Love Brewed in the African Pot, 35 mm, color, 125 min., 1980.

BIBLIOGRAPHY

Interview of Kwaw Ansah

Bentsi-Enchill, Niik. "Fair deal for film." *West Africa,* 19 November 1984, pp. 2319–20.

Film Reviews and Studies of Kwaw Ansah

Ayari, Farida. "Mélo de la Gold Coast." *Adhoua,* n. 4–5, April-September 1981, p. 6.
Bassan, Raphael. "La Dignité retrouvée." *Afrique-Asie,* n. 287, 17 January 1983, pp. 55–57.
Boughedir, Ferid. "Les Héritiers d'Oumarou Ganda." *Jeune Afrique,* n. 1053, 11 March 1981, pp. 62–63.
———. "Cinéma africain: le temps de l'immobilisme." *Les 2 Ecrans,* n. 42–43, February-March, 1982, pp. 15–19.
Canby, Vincent. "Film: Love Brewed . . . , on Middle-Class Ghana." *New York Times,* 25 April 1981, p. 11.

Cham, Mbye Baboucar. "Film Production in West Africa: 1979–1981." *Présence Africaine*, n. 124, 4th Quarter 1982, pp. 168–87.

Clayton, Sue. "Love Brewed in the African Pot." *City Limits*, n. 108, 28 October 1983, p. 44.

Kieffer, Anne. "Cinéma d'Afrique noire au Festival des Trois Continents." *Jeune Cinéma*, n. 149, March 1983, pp. 10–13.

Mosk. "Love Brewed in the African Pot." *Variety*, 25 March 1981, p. 20.

Nee-Owoo, Kwate. "Ghana: projets d'avenir." *Le Mondeo Diplomatique*, June 1981, p. 23.

"Relevant Love Story out of Ghana." *West Africa*, n. 3277, 12 May 1980, pp. 824–25.

Ola Balogun (1945–   )
Nigeria

BIOGRAPHY

A filmmaker, writer, playwright, and former diplomat, Ola Balogun is the most important single figure in Nigerian cinema. The son of a lawyer of Yoruba origin, Balogun was born in 1945 in Aba, located in the eastern part of Nigeria. After attending King's College in Lagos, where he received his O Level Certificate of Education, Ola Balogun took some French courses at the University of Dakar (Senegal) in 1962. Then he decided to go to France to continue his studies. He arrived in Paris in 1963 and subsequently enrolled at the Institute des Hautes Etudes Cinématographiques (the well-known IDHEC Film School), where he specialized in mise-en-scène, and at the University of Nanterre (near Paris), where he defended a doctoral dissertation on documentary films in 1970. While in France in 1966, he met Françoise, a young French woman who was to become his wife as well as his closest business associate.

In 1967 Balogun returned to Nigeria. In 1968–69 he worked for a few months as scriptwriter for the Federal Film Unit in Lagos before being appointed press attaché at the Nigerian embassy in Paris. Balogun explains this new orientation in his professional life as follows:

I became a diplomat by mere chance. . . . After the crisis which Nigeria underwent due to the secession of Biafra, my government showed an interest in me because of my knowledge of French. . . . Since I consider bureaucracy as the worst possible thing, I thought at first that I was going to suffocate. . . . Yet what I experience daily is most interesting and enriching, and I have become an ardent defender of Nigeria's unity. *(Bingo,* June 1971, p. 30)

In his own words, Balogun's political involvement served to destroy ''the myth according to which the artist is some kind of dreamer unable to do anything but to live in the clouds'' *(Bingo,* June 1971, p. 30). His first documentary, *One Nigeria* (1969), spawns from an ideological commitment which views Nigerian unity as a first step toward a future federation of Western African states. During his stay in Paris, Balogun also made a short documentary entitled *Les Ponts de Paris* (The Bridges of Paris, 1971).

Following this government assignment in France, Ola Balogun returned to Nigeria and in 1971 became a Research Fellow in Cinematography at Ife University's Institute of African Studies. Two years later he was put in charge of the creation of the audiovisual unit of his country's National Museum. Jointly with these occupations, he was able to complete his first fiction film *Alpha* (1972), with a cast including Daniel Kamwa* (at the time the film was shown at several private screenings in Paris), and to shoot a series of cultural documentaries *(Fire in the Afternoon,* 1971; *Thundergod,* 1972; *Nupe Mascarade,* 1972; *In the Beginning,* 1972; *Owuama, A New Year Festival,* 1973). In a political vein he made *Eastern Nigeria Revisited* (1973), which concerns the aftermath of Nigeria's civil war. Nonetheless, Ola Balogun felt that his involvement with both Ife University and the National Museum did not allow for the optimum expression of his creative talents. In 1973 he formed his own production company, Afrocult Foundation Ltd., which he also views as "a forum for discussion for the promotion of our culture not for mere rhetoric or adulterated culture" *(Daily Times,* 1 December 1973, p. 7). The following year saw the release of his middle-length picture *Vivre* (To Live), which depicts the plight of a paralyzed friend. Thus, with the founding of Afrocult began another phase in Balogun's career, that of an independent director and entrepreneur.

In 1975 Ola Balogun was commissioned to make *Nigersteel,* which describes Nigeria's renewed industrial progress. The first feature length film officially produced by Afrocult was *Amadi* (1975), a docudrama shot in Ibo, one of Nigeria's principal vernacular languages. This film was well received by the Nigerian public. The following year, Balogun undertook the making of a film in Yoruba (another indigenous tongue of Nigeria) with a well-known Nigerian Troupe director, Duro Lapido. Their collaborative effort resulted in the $250,000 *Ajani-Ogun* (written and produced by Balogun, with music and lyrics by Lapido), Black Africa's first musical comedy which became a local box-office success. Also in 1976, Balogun made *Muzik-Man,* a musical comedy in English (and pidgin English), starring the Cameroonian singer Georges Anderson (who also wrote the musical score), and co-produced with Nigeria Motion Pictures, an Indo-Nigerian distribution company. This film, which, unlike *Ajani Ogun,* did not feature well-known Nigerian theater actors, was not met with the same enthusiastic popular response as the previous one. Undaunted by the unspectacular release of *Muzik-Man,* the Nigerian filmmaker immediately set out to make his next film *Ija Ominira* (Fight for Freedom, 1977), shot in Yoruba, based on a novel by the Nigerian poet and dramatist Adebayo Faleti, and produced by Friendship Motion Pictures. Like *Ajani-Ogun,* this film borrows its style from the Yoruba theater and emerged from a cooperation between Ola Balogun and Ade Folayan, the director of the Ade Love Theatre. Such merging of stage and screen proved once more to be financially auspicious. *Ija Ominira* was later to be shown at the 1979 Moscow and London film festivals, as well as at the 1980

Los Angeles Film Festival. In 1978 Balogun embarked on an international co-production with a Brazilian production company, Magnus Films, which resulted in the film *A Deusa Negra* (Black Goddess), shot in Portuguese and filmed in Brazil and Nigeria. Although far from being commercially successful, this feature was appreciated by some film critics. *A Deusa Negra* won the Prize for Best Musical Score and the Prix de l'Office Catholique International du Cinéma (OCIC) at the 1978 Carthage Film Festival in Tunisia, and was shown in 1980 at the New Films/New Directors Film Festival at the New York Museum of Modern Art. Balogun was also later to present *A Deusa Negra* at an African film festival in Tokyo in 1984.

Shortly after his return from Brazil to Nigeria Ola Balogun was approached by Hubert Ogunde, whom many consider the father of Yoruba theater. Ogunde, who has been travelling with his itinerant theater for some forty years throughout Nigeria, requested that Balogun adapt one of his plays to the screen. Thus Balogun and Ogunde produced *Aiye* (in Yoruba), which, shot in five weeks and released in 1979, scored a rather significant commercial hit in Nigeria. In 1980 Ola Balogun went to Ghana, where he shot *Cry Freedom,* based on the novel *Carcase for Hounds* by the Kenyan writer Meja Mwangi and produced by Af-rocult Foundation. The cast of this film included Albert Hall, whose performance in *Apocalypse Now* had impressed Balogun. Shown in the festival circuit (it was, among others, featured at the 1981 London, Cannes, and Moscow film festivals as well as at the 1982 Brisbane Commonwealth Film Festival), this film proved to be rather unpopular among Nigerian movie fans. Renewing his ties with Yoruba theater, Balogun made *Orun Mooru* in 1982. This commercially suc-cessful film was co-produced with the stage director Moses Olaiya Adejume, on whose play it was based. Ola Balogun's last feature film to date is *Money Power* (1982), made with a $650,000 bank loan. In 1985 *Money Power* was presented at the Pan-African Film Festival of Ouagadougou (Burkina Faso) where, thanks to its leading actress, Clarion Chukruwah, it won the Prize for Best Female Interpretation. In the past few years, awaiting the opportunity to make a feature film, Balogun and Afrocult Foundation have mainly been involved in the pro-duction of commercials.

Examining Balogun's twenty-year career in cinema, it is interesting to note that his development as a filmmaker goes from the production of intellectual manifestos *(Alpha)* to that of popular cinema *(Ajani-Ogun, Aiye, Orun Mooru,* etc.) which draws its essence from Nigerian folklore and the Yoruba theater (inclusive of dances, songs, and special effects, and whose format is somewhat reminiscent of Indian melodramas). With most of his latest feature films, many of which are adaptations of already successful Nigerian plays, Ola Balogun has managed to address the Nigerian film market and build up a popular audience in a country of more than 80 million people and some 200 movie theaters at a time when other Black African filmmakers from much less populated countries do not benefit from such propitious local markets. Balogun states: ''All my films are progressions from a quest . . . for a popular audience in Nigeria without giving up a certain minimum of quality and artistic involvement'' *(Daily Star,* 22 January 1977, p. 13). Thus, unlike many of his Black African counterparts, Balogun now insists on stressing the entertainment aspect of film and opposes the kind of solely didactic work (often fringing on hermetism) with which, he says, foreign critics rather than local viewers can identify:

When you are talking about commercial feature films, basically you are talking about something which is a part of an entertainment industry. . . . One is not talking about abandoning the value of the content of the film, one is talking about mechanisms for making the film. . . . I have personally lost a huge amount of money trying to make films like *Cry Freedom* which our audience is not interested in seeing. . . . Film is entertainment. When you go to see a film like *Star Wars* do you think about the message it is conveying to humanity? . . . There is always tremendous pressure on African filmmakers to always be changing the world in each film they make. . . . If the audience does not feel entertained, it is not going to go to pay to watch the film. If the audience is not entertained you might not even succeed in conveying the message you want to convey. . . . we cannot always be preaching to people, we cannot be trying to carry out revolution through 90 minutes of film. We have to accept that film is entertainment. (Ola Balogun at the 1982 African Studies Association (ASA) Conference held in Washington, D.C.)

Linking the entertainment offered through film to that of Africa's oral tradition, Balogun adds:

When we sit down at home in Africa and people are telling us a folktale . . . it is funny, we laugh, our attention is caught, we are entertained. The reason why we absorb whatever ultimate philosophical meaning there is in the story is because we have been entertained and we have laughed. And, to make an audience laugh is not necessarily to lead it into silliness. (ASA, 1982)

A skillful craftsman, Balogun emphasizes the fact that Black African films should be well made (both technically and in terms of their social content) to compete efficiently with foreign films on the local and world market through adequate promotion and distribution:

We first have to master the instrument itself, we have to be able to make good films. . . . film has no frontier, it is an instrument, it is a technique . . . we can adopt and utilize to our benefit and advantage the means of expression that have been developed elsewhere. (ASA, 1982)

According to Balogun, ''Film production requires the mobilization of considerable capital and is by force an object of commercial exchange even though it is also an artistic medium. . . . film is a cultural medium which is inextricably grounded into an industrial, technological and commercial framework'' (ASA, 1982). To make his films Balogun prefers to rely on the financial returns of his previous motion pictures as well as private funding rather than rely on government support or foreign sources. He stresses:

Film budgets provided by non-commercial sources such as governments have, in many cases, the disadvantage of opening the door to some form of political pressure and censorship . . . and it may lead to favoritism and other forms of nepotism. . . . There are obvious dangers in relying on foreign sources for film finance, the danger of paternalistic influence. . . . I have seen some of my colleagues fall into inextricable contradictions. . . . how can you take money from the French government [in this case the French Ministry of Cooperation] to make films that denounce French colonial presence in Africa? At some stage you are bound to fall into a contradiction that you cannot surmount. Either the source of finance will dry out or you have to compromise too much to continue to get it. . . . The access to and the use of foreign sources can only be feasible if the filmmaker himself is so strong that he can impose his will on the source of finance or if he has a strong financial base which can lead to a co-production arrangement that gives him artistic freedom. (ASA, 1982)

Despite the countless difficulties that Black African directors have to face with respect to the financing and marketing of their films, Balogun expresses hopes regarding the future of an African cinema which will reflect the aesthetic, intellectual, and sociocultural preoccupations of Black people. He points out:

Film has not come to a continent devoid of aesthetic traditions. Africa has had a long history of civilization and art forms that have existed since the earliest times. . . . Art is vigorous in Africa, and there is no doubt that the challenge of new art forms like film will be taken up by artists fully capable of mastering them. *(The Education of the Filmmaker,* 1975, pp. 34–35)

A prolific practitioner of film and an articulate spokesman for Black African cinema, Ola Balogun is also a playwright and the author of a number of short stories. His play *Shango* was written in French and published in Paris, where it was read at the American Cultural Center in 1968. Exemplifying Balogun's perfect mastery of the French language, *Shango* concerns a fictitious African king, his despotic use of power, and his ensuing decline. Regarding his play, the cinéaste says, "It is not a political play, but it can generate political thoughts" *(Bingo,* June 1971, pp. 30–31). Balogun has also written two books, *The Tragic Years: Nigeria in Crisis 1966–70* on the Nigerian civil war and *Nigéria, du réel à l'imaginaire* (co-authored by B. Barbey), a lavishly illustrated work on Nigeria's history and lifestyles. Furthermore, a number of articles published in Africa and Europe reflect the broad scope of his interests, which encompass political concerns as well as artistic and cultural matters.

Serious-minded, soft-spoken, and courteous, Ola Balogun has been married for more than twenty years and is the father of two teenaged daughters. He is presently residing and working in Lagos. At the average rate of a film a year, he has directed a significant number of motion pictures (shorts as well as features) and has helped pave the way for a commercial cinema in Nigeria. He is also one of the founding members of the West African Film Corporation (WAFCO), a regional consortium for the production and distribution of African film created in 1985.

MAJOR THEMES

As would be expected from an artist sensitive to his country's vital issues, one of Balogun's first concerns was to reflect in film his country's sociopolitical aspirations and economic realities, elements seen in such documentaries as *One Nigeria, Eastern Nigeria Revisited* and *Nigersteel*.

Alpha (made in Paris), the Nigerian filmmaker's first feature film, is an experimental and somewhat hermetic work which deals with spiritual and artistic values while focusing on such themes as exile and cultural alienation. Apparently, *Alpha* is, in many respects, an autobiographical statement, that of an exiled African artist in search of his identity. In form and content, this film differs greatly from Ola Balogun's subsequent works. Its actions and dialogues are based on a motif provided by Balogun and collectively improvised by actors from Africa and the Black Diaspora. Breaking away from the customary narrative patterns of Western filmmaking, *Alpha* offers a series of interchangeable vignettes which can only come to an end with the title character's intended return to Africa, where he expects to realize his intellectual and mystical quest, hoping for acceptability in his own country.

In retrospect, Balogun feels that his stay in Europe reinforced his attachment to his people and culture *(Jeune Afrique,* 2 June 1981, p. 67). This statement is corroborated by a series of ethnographic documentaries concerning Nigeria's socioreligious traditions. Those documentaries include *Fire in the Afternoon* (concerning the Moreni festival, a Yoruba event which takes place annually in the city of Ife), *Thundergod* (dedicated to the worship of Shango, the Yoruba God of Thunder), *Nupe Mascarade* (on a traditional celebration in the Nupe region of Nigeria), *In the Beginning* (which focuses on the Yoruba myth of creation), and *Owuama, A New Year Festival* (in which the filmmaker attempts to translate the mood of animistic beliefs through the use of a special lens). With limited or even no commentary, these films faithfully witness ritualistic songs and dances and invite viewers to share directly a mystical experience without being distracted by the kind of overbearing and omniscient rigid explanatory narration that is frequently found in Western documentaries of a similar nature.

Amadi, Balogun's second feature, could be categorized as a didactic film belonging to the sociorealistic vein. Through the story of a young man who returns to his village after trying experiences in the city, the film advocates the introduction of modern agricultural techniques at the same time that it propounds the revival of Ibo cults—here the worship of Goddess Ala and that of her son Amadi-Oha.

Although religious sequences are found in such features as *Money Power* and others, Balogun's deep and sustained interest in the supernatural is reflected even more in three of his fiction works, namely, *A Deusa Negra, Aiye,* and *Orun Mooru.*

A Deusa Negra, written and directed by Balogun, is "a mystical story of reincarnation, with a cyclical movement that spans 200 years set against the background of slavery'' *(Daily Times,* 5 May 1979, p. 7). It opens with scenes of a tribal war between two African chiefs. The defeated prince, Oluyole, is made prisoner, enslaved, and deported to Brazil. The next sequence, which takes place in present-day Nigeria, shows an old man on his death bed. His wish is that his son go to Brazil in search of the descendants of his ancestor Oluyole, so as to accomplish a promise made earlier to Yemoja, the all-powerful Yoruba sea goddess. He tells his son: ''Your great grandfather returned from Brazil after the abolition of slavery. He promised to send one of his sons back but he never fulfilled the promise. You are my only son, Babatunde. Swear you will go to Brazil to get the rest of the family. . . . the Yemoja statue will guide you.'' Babatunde accepts his father's challenge, and such is the starting point of the initiatory and mystical quest that will lead him to Brazil. This will enable him to reestablish historical links between Africa and the Afro-Brazilian Diaspora. In Brazil, Babatunde meets Elisa, the daughter of a local diviner. It is in her company that he becomes acquainted with candomblé, a Brazilian variety of traditional Yoruba religion. In the course of a candomblé ritual, Elisa, in a state of trance, reveals to Babatunde that the object of his quest is to be found in Bahia, a city in northeastern Brazil, former center of the country's slave trade and currently noted for its vivid African cultural heritage. Therefore, Babatunde and Elisa set out on a journey to Bahia during which another revelation discloses that Babatunde is the reincarnation of Oluyole, while Elisa incarnates Amanda, whom Oluyole once loved. The film ends with a freeze frame of the two lovers as they walk away, forever reunited. In Balogun's words ''Babatunde has completed the cycle of life that was begun by his ancestor . . . owing to the intervention of Yemoja who has manipulated all this'' *(Daily Times,* 5 May 1979, p. 7).

Aiye (whose title is borrowed from a Yoruba word meaning ''world'' or ''existence'') is the screen adaptation of an original play by Hubert Ogunde. It illustrates—through the enactment of Yoruba metaphysics, nocturnal ceremonial rites, sundry metamorphoses, and the rising of a character from the kingdom of the dead, rendered with the help of a myriad of special effects—the universal and timeless Manichean struggle between benevolent and evil forces respectively embodied in a village diviner and a swarm of local witches:

The two antagonistic powers meet in the forest early in the film while Olori Awo [the diviner] is looking for herbs. Olori Awo implores the witch to cooperate with him to ensure a sorrow-free, peaceful world; the witch partially agrees but tells him that room must be left for some mischief. Therefore a series of human disasters caused by the witch bring her into an intense and protracted conflict with Olori Awo. . . . Meanwhile Olori Awo receives greater power from the gods, and evokes thunder and lightning on the witches who are struck dead one after another. *(West Africa,* 12 May 1980, p. 827)

As may be expected, the end of *Aiye* shows the triumphant victory of good over evil.

Balogun's film *Orun Mooru* (in Yoruba "Orun" means heaven and "Mooru" signifies hot) concerns the fate of Lamidi, a one-time successful businessman, who decides to commit suicide after having been robbed of his wealth by swindlers. As Lamidi undertakes his journey to the Kingdom of the Dead, he realizes that Death, Iku, is not yet ready for his coming. Therefore, Iku sends him to Ayo, the Spirit of Joy. Ayo entrusts Lamidi with two balls without telling him that the first ball represents wealth and the second ball contains death. Then, Ayo sends Lamidi back to earth, advising him to break the first ball immediately upon his return home and the second one fifty years later. Following Ayo's recommendation, Lamidi breaks the first ball and becomes instantly wealthy. Led by greed, Lamidi thinks he will get even richer by breaking Ayo's second ball. Yet, as he breaks it open, Lamidi finds himself confronted with death, from which he will, however, manage to escape.

This moralistic verve of the age-old African storytelling tradition is furthermore present in Balogun's *Ajani-Ogun, Musik-Man,* and *Ija Ominira,* all of which reflect in one way or another corruption, the greed for power and the unavoidable triumph of honesty.

Ajani-Ogun (Ogun is the Yoruba God of Iron, who protects man from evil) tells the story of a young hunter, Ajani-Ogun, who sets out to recover his late father's property which was misappropriated by a dishonest politician, Chief Abayomi. Ajani-Ogun is in love with a village beauty, Ajoke, whom Abayomi covets. After miscellaneous events, the young hunter regains his stolen property and prepares for a life of conjugal bliss with Ajoke. *Musik-Man* concerns the trials and tribulations of a musically gifted waiter who, overcoming corruption and adversity, succeeds in becoming a sought-after popular singer. And *Ija Ominira,* the plot of which takes place in the Middle Ages, details the victorious rebellion of an African village against the tyrannical rule of a despotic monarch.

Balogun's able use of mordant satire to denounce the faults and follies of man while tackling present-day social issues is best expressed in *Money-Power,* which offers "a penetrating look at the overpowering role of Naira currency in contemporary Nigerian society" (Afrocult Press Kit). The title of this film refers to the nickname given to Chief B. C. Ade, an unscrupulous aging businessman with political ambitions whose corruption and thuggery during an electoral campaign are brought to light by Jide, a young and handsome journalist. Jide's search for truth is greatly facilitated by Yemi, Ade's young secretary, whom the businessman had lustfully envisioned taking as his second wife against her will. Finally virtue wins over vice, and the film ends with Jide and Yemi hoping for a future of shared and everlasting happiness.

Thematically as well as stylistically, Balogun's *Cry Freedom* is radically different from his other features. According to the Nigerian director, this film is "the story of an uprising in an African country under colonial rule, leading to guerilla warfare" *(West Africa,* 12 May 1980, p. 82).

SURVEY OF CRITICISM

Due to limited local distribution and a general lack of distribution abroad, Balogun's early films have seldom been seen and have thus been neglected by both Nigerian and foreign film critics. One of the rare Nigerian journalists to have reviewed *Alpha* is Doyin Aboaba, who, analyzing its possible impact, writes the following:

In *Alpha* which can be said to be the starting point of a sequel of films, Dr. Balogun demonstrates . . . capability of reaching a wide audience without necessarily being "cheap" or of poor quality. With the combination of easy dialogues, songs and dance the audience can derive either aesthetically or symbolically from the film.

At the end the relevant point is that there is participation of the various ideas or even the appreciation of the colour, movement and arrangement of the film settings.

But mere momentary participation excludes identification either with the artist or the characters in the film. The problem of identification can be another stumbling block upsetting the artist's effort to establish a link with his audience. *(Daily Times,* 1 December 1973, p. 7)

Françoise Balogun includes in her book *Le Cinéma au Nigéria* what appear to be sincere and even candid comments concerning some of her husband's first works. For instance, she seems to regret the loosely structured style of *Alpha,* adding that the lack of popular response met by the film was undoubtedly linked to its "intellectual ramblings," which were "far from Nigerian realities" (p. 61). Then, while noting the "unexpected talent" of *Amadi*'s nonprofessional actors, she also deplores some of the deficiencies of this film, namely, the "clumsy" lighting of certain scenes shot inside village houses (p. 62), which she, however, attributes to a paucity of technical means rather than a directorial flaw. Also, Françoise Balogun appreciates the mystical and poetic qualities of *A Deusa Negra,* which, she stresses, the Nigerian public failed to recognize (p. 66).

Ajani-Ogun, which marked a turning point in Balogun's career, is a prime example of how a film may be divergently perceived in different cultural settings. Shunned by many foreign critics, *Ajani-Ogun* was quite favorably reviewed in Nigeria. Serge Daney (France) finds *Ajani-Ogun* "static," "boring," and over-eracted *(Cahiers du Cinéma,* December 1976, p. 46). Paulin Soumanou Vieyra (Senegal) views it as a "failure" because of the incoherence between its form and content *(Présence Africaine,* 1st and 2nd Quarter 1977, p. 232), and A. Chorfi (Tunisia) considers the film an abortive attempt at musical comedy in spite of some pleasant songs and dances *(L'Action,* 17 October 1976, p. 13). But in Nigeria, *Ajani-Ogun* proved to be a critics' favorite. In Nigeria's *Daily Times* (17 June 1976, p. 8), Willy Bozimo bids on the future success of *Ajani-Ogun* because it offers a blend of Yoruba folk theater, East Indian romantic melodrama, and "action-packed events reminiscent of Chinese karate films," all of which are popular among Nigerian moviegoers. Likewise, Chucks Okwuwa praises Balogun's effort "to bring indigenous films nearer to Nigerian cinema fans," while "combining . . . a measure of entertainment with a meaningful content," a device the critic associates with "the age-old African story-telling tradition" (*Nigerian Observer*, 19 June 1976, p. 7). These sentiments are shared by Eseoghene Barrett, who calls *Ajani-Ogun* "a moral fable" which "combines top flight entertainment with a simple but effective anti-corruption message." Barrett shows appreciation also for the "remarkable beauty of some of the visuals" and enjoys the comic relief scenes of *Ajani-Ogun (New Nigerian*, 19 June 1976, entertainment supplement).

Apparently, *Musik-Man*, *A Deusa Negra*, *Orun Mooru* (favorably reviewed for its comic appeal by Niyi Osundare in *West Africa*, 12 July 1982, p. 1821) have received little critical attention in comparison with Balogun's other works, namely *Ija Ominira*, *Aiye*, *Cry Freedom*, and *Money Power*.

The film reviewer Mosk, having viewed *Ija Ominira* at the 1979 Moscow Film Festival where it was featured, describes it as "a sprightly folk tale, replete with action, dancing and song" in which the actors have a tendency to overplay. Commenting on Balogun's skills, Mosk is convinced that "more film knowhow should make [the] director a man to watch on the Afro film scene" (*Variety*, 5 September 1979, p. 22). At the 1980 Los Angeles International Film Exposition, Linda Gross enthusiastically endorses *Ija Ominira*, stating that "this inflammatory and richly detailed cry for freedom is indigenous filmmaking at its best" (*Los Angeles Times*, 12 March 1980, part VI, p. 6).

In contrast with *Aiye's* popular appeal in Nigeria, Niyi Osundare, a faculty member at the University of Ibadan, offers a less than complimentary review of the film, arguing that it is inherently escapist and totally irrelevant to indigenous realities. Osundare feels that "the film has numerous flaws in terms of technical accomplishment and subject matter. One of the flaws arises from the problem of presenting the supernatural cinematographically." For the reviewer,

Aiye is a reinforcement of the destructive illogicalities, and collective paranoia that rule Nigerian life. The film takes us back several years, lures us into metaphysical chaos, and injects us with a dose of anaesthesia at a time when we should stand alert and ready to fight the myriad problems that besiege our existence. (*West Africa*, 12 May 1980, p. 828)

As is the case of *Ajani-Ogun*, *Cry Freedom* is judged differently by Western and African film critics. Mosk stresses its lack of originality (*Variety*, 29 July 1981, p. 26), and Mario Relich finds its surface treatment similar to a degree to that of "Hollywood heroics" (*West Africa*, 7 December 1981, p. 2907). The Algerian film critic Azzedine Mabrouki finds *Cry Freedom* a technically well-made film, with a meaningful content and balanced characterization (*Les 2 Ecrans*, June 1981, p. 32), while an Ivorian reviewer perceives it as a tribute paid to past and present African freedom fighters (*Fraternité Matin*, 20–21 February 1982, p. 15).

In his discussion of *Money Power*, Chuma Adichie *(Sunday Concord*, 8 January 1984, magazine section, p. 3) considers the film accurate in its true to life depiction of ''an obnoxious but universal culture called 'money culture,' '' shows interest in its trenchant characterizations, which provide ''symmetry and balance to the plot,'' but criticizes the length of some love scenes. While generally favorable to Balogun's depiction of easily recognizable types and situations found in contemporary Nigerian society, Nii K. Bentsi-Enchill would have wished for a more powerful plot *(West Africa*, 16 August 1982, p. 2094). Both critics vouch for the universal and commercial appeal of this film, and one wonders why Balogun's *Money Power* (in its abbreviated two-hour version) has not yet been more widely seen outside of Nigeria.

FILMOGRAPHY

One Nigeria, 16 mm, black and white, 10 min., 1969.
Les Ponts de Paris (The Bridges of Paris), 16 mm, black and white, precise length unknown, 1971.
Fire in the Afternoon, 16 mm, black and white, precise length unknown, 1971.
Thundergod, 16 mm, black and white, precise length unknown, 1972.
Alpha, 16 mm, color, 90 min., 1972.
Nupe Mascarade, 16 mm, color, 12 min., 1972.
In the Beginning, 16 mm, color, precise length unknown, 1972.
Owuama, A New Year Festival, 16 mm, color, 20 min., 1973.
Eastern Nigeria Revisited, 16 mm, black and white, precise length unknown, 1973.
Vivre (To Live), 16 mm, color, precise length unknown, 1974.
Nigersteel, 16 mm, color, precise length unknown, 1975.
Amadi, 16 mm, color, 90 min., 1975.
Ajani-Ogun, 16/35 mm, color, 120 min., 1976.
Musik-Man, 16 mm, color, precise length unknown, 1976.
Ija Ominira (Fight for Freedom), 35 mm, color, precise length unknown, 1977.
A Deusa Negra (Black Goddess), 35 mm, color, 150 min., 1978.
Aiye, 35 mm, color, precise length unknown, 1979.
Cry Freedom, 35 mm, color, 70 min., 1981.
Orun Mooru, 35 mm, color, 150 min., 1982.
Money Power, 35 mm, color, 210 min. in its original version, 150 min. in its abbreviated version, 1982.

BIBLIOGRAPHY

Writings by Ola Balogun

Balogun, Ola. *Shango*. Paris: J-P. Oswald, 1968.
———. ''Le Nigéria doit-il continuer à exister.'' *Jeune Afrique*, n. 468, 17 December 1969, p. 3.
———. *The Tragic Years: Nigeria in Crisis 1966–70*. Lagos: Ethiope Press, 1973.

————. "Ethnology and Its Ideologies." *Consequence* (journal of the Inter-African Council for Philosophy), n. 1, January-June 1974, pp. 109–126.

————. "Entertaining the People—Nigeria Deserves a Film Industry." *Daily Times*, 25 March 1975, p. 32.

————. "Decoding the Message of African Sculpture." *The UNESCO Courrier*, May 1977, pp. 12–16.

————. "Sekou Touré ou le piège du pouvior absolu." *Jeune Afrique*, n. 1232–1233, 15 August 1984, pp. 44–45.

————. "Cultural Policies as an Instrument of External Image-Building: A Blueprint for Nigeria." *Présence Africaine*, n. 133–134, 1st and 2nd Quarter 1985, pp. 86–98.

————, cont. *The Education of the Filmmaker*. Paris: The UNESCO Press, 1975.

————, and B. Barbey. *Nigeria, du réel à l'imaginaire*. Paris: Jeune Afrique Press, 1978.

Interviews of Ola Balogun

Aboaba, Doyin. "An Artist in Search of an Audience." *Daily Times*, 1 December 1973, p. 7.

Badday, Moncef S. "Que sera le théâtre africain?" *L'Afrique Littéraire et Artistique*, n. 15, 1971, pp. 55–59.

Egbuchulam, James. "The Film Industry: Has It any Hope in Nigeria?" *Daily Star*, 22 January 1977, p. 13.

"Film Art and Monetary Profit." *West Africa*, n. 3277, 12 May 1980, p. 828.

Moore, Carlos. "Le Cinéma africain n'existe pas encore." *Jeune Afrique*, n. 1065, 2 June 1981, pp. 66–67.

Noble, Peter. "Balogun: I Just Go from Film to Film." *Screen International*, n. 256, 30 August 1980, p. 25.

Ogan, Amma. "Ola Balogun's Black Goddess Revisited." *Daily Times*, 5 May 1979, p. 7.

Ruelle, Catherine. "Ola Balogun." *L'Afrique Littéraire et Artistique*, n. 49, 3rd Quarter 1978, pp. 22–24.

Sajoux, Thérèse. "Ola Balogun, dramaturge d'une civilisation oubliée." *Bingo*, n. 221, June 1971, pp. 30–31.

Reviews and Studies of Ola Balogun

"A Deusa Negra." *Guia de Filmes*, n. 79, 1979, p. 18.

Adichie, Chuma. "Money Power—A Celluloid Portrait." *Sunday Concord*, 8 January 1984, magazine section, p. 3.

Askelrad, Madeleine. "Ola Balogun." *L'Afrique Littéraire et Artistique*, 8 December 1969, pp. 26–27.

Bachy, Victor. "Le Cinéma au Nigéria." *OCIC INFO*, n. 5–6, November-December 1984, pp. 6–7.

Balogun, Françoise. "Un Cinéma au stade de l'adolescence." *Le Monde Diplomatique*, December 1981, p. 31.

————. *Le Cinéma au Nigéria*. Brussels: OCIC/L'Harmattan, 1984.

Barrett, Eseoghene. "Ajani-Ogun—A Film for All Seasons." *New Nigerian*, 19 June 1976, entertainment supplement.

Bentsi-Enchill, Nii K. "Money, Power and Cinema." *West Africa,* n. 3255, 16 August 1982, pp. 2093–94.

Boughedir, Ferid. "Le Plus Productif des cinéastes africains." *Jeune Afrique,* n. 1065, 2 June 1981, pp. 65–66.

———. "L'Effet Balogun." *Jeune Afrique,* n. 1138, 27 October 1982, p. 65.

Bozimo, Willy. "Ajani-Ogun Can Pull a Crowd." *Daily Times,* 17 June 1976, p. 8.

Cham, Mbye Baboucar. "Film Production in West Africa: 1979–1981." *Présence Africaine,* n. 124, 4th Quarter 1982, pp. 168–87.

Chorfi, A. "Ajani-Ogun (Nigeria)—un échec dans le cinéma musical." *L'Action,* 17 October 1976, p. 13.

Daney, Serge. "Carthage, an 10." *Cahiers du Cinéma,* n. 272, December 1976, pp. 43–49.

Gross, Linda. "Fight for Freedom." *Los Angeles Times,* 12 March 1980, part VI, p. 6.

Humblot, Catherine. "Cinémas d'Afrique: impasse ou mauvaise passe." *Le Monde,* 14 March 1985, p. 14.

J, K.K.M. "Pour la liberté d'Ola Balogun, le cinéma de libération." *Fraternité Matin,* 20–21 February 1982, p. 15.

Mabrouki, Azzedine. "Cry Freedom de Ola Balogun." *Les 2 Ecrans,* n. 35, June 1981, pp. 30–32.

Mosk. "Ija Ominira (Fight for Freedom)." *Variety,* 5 September 1979, p. 22.

———"Cry Freedom!" *Variety,* 29 July 1981, p. 26.

"Le Nouveau Film d'Ola Balogun fait rimer amour et humour . . . en langue Ibo." *Le Soleil,* 4 July 1975, p. 10.

Okwuwa, Chucks. "Fresh Hope for Nigerian Film Producers." *Nigerian Observer,* 19 June 1976, p. 7.

Opubor, Alfred E., and Onuora E. Nwuneli. *The Development and Growth of the Film Industry in Nigeria.* Lagos/New York: National Council for Arts and Culture/Third Press International, 1979.

Osundare, Niyi. "A Grand Escape into Metaphysics." *West Africa,* n. 3277, 12 May 1980, pp. 826–28.

———. "The King of Laughter." *West Africa,* n. 3388, 12 July 1982, p. 1821.

Relich, Mario. "From Glitter to Gore in the Film World." *West Africa,* n. 3358, 7 December 1981, pp. 2907–11.

Ricard, Alain. "Le Cinéma populaire nigérian." *Recherche, Pédagogie et Culture,* n. 58, July-September 1982, pp. 65–69.

Tchibinda, Claude Abdon. "Le Film nigérian Ajani-Ogun a drainé les foules au Komo." *L'Union,* 16 July 1978, p. 4.

"Traditional Yoruba Theatre." *West Africa,* n. 2093–2094, 3 December 1979, pp. 2226–27.

Traoré, Biny. "Jom et Money Power." *L'Observateur,* n. 2525, 9 February 1983, pp. 1, 4–5, 10.

Vieyra, Paulin Soumanou. "X⁰ anniversaire des Journées Cinématographiques de Carthage." *Présence Africaine,* n. 101–102, 1st and 2nd Quarter 1977, pp. 231–35.

——— "Carthage 78." *Présence Africaine,* n. 110, 2nd Quarter 1979, pp. 157–66.

——— "Le Festival du cinéma à Moscou—L'Afrique était aussi présente." *Le Soleil,* 18 September 1979, p. 10.

Timité Bassori (1933–   )
Ivory Coast

BIOGRAPHY

Timité Bassori is the first Ivorian to have formally studied filmmaking. He is an accomplished actor and a writer as well. He was born on 30 December 1933 in Aboisso, a small southeastern city located about 100 kilometers from Abidjan. Of Mandingo origin and Muslim extraction, he is the son of a literate and well-established coffee and cocoa planter. Although the number of Bassori's immediate relatives was limited, he was brought up in a large home amidst an extended traditional African family which counted no less than fifty people spread over three generations. His childhood was that of a dutiful Muslim child who attended both Koranic and primary school in his home town.

At the age of sixteen, Timité Bassori left Aboisso to enroll at the Collège Technique d'Abidjan (a vocational school), where he acquired basic business skills. As a teenager Bassori was a voracious reader. He recalls, ''I used to read everything that came to hand'' (Timité Bassori to author, Ouagadougou, February 1985). The adolescent's favorite readings ranged from the epics of ancient Greece, such as Homer's *Iliad* and *Odyssey,* to nineteenth-century Western adventure stories like Robert Louis Stevenson's *Treasure Island* and Théophile Gautier's *Le Capitaine Fracasse*. In 1952 Bassori obtained his Certificat d'Aptitude Professionnelle (CAP) and was graduated from the Collège Technique d'Abidjan. Next, he worked for a few years as a business clerk in Abidjan, where he spent a great deal of his leisure time watching second rate French and American motion pictures at local movie theaters. This steady film diet aroused a new orientation in the young man's professional aspirations. Bassori points out:

I had become acquainted with cinema around the age of eight because of the itinerant film showings that were taking place from time to time in small cities. Yet it is in Abidjan, where we had permanent film screenings, that I really discovered cinema. Thus in me grew a latent desire to become involved in cinema but I did not exactly know how. It was difficult at the time because in France's West Africa there was neither training nor openings in that area. With some schooling you could become a clerk in the colonial administration or work for a business firm. If you finished high school you could become a school teacher or a civil servant or else, the third possibility was to go to school in Dakar or Gorée where young Africans would be trained as medical doctors, veterinarians, high ranking school teachers or administrators. No training in the arts was available in Africa and an artistic career was unthinkable at the time. Yet, working as a clerk did not satisfy me and I felt I had to do something else. So I gathered my meager savings and set off for France. (Bassori to author, February 1985)

Timité Bassori arrived in Paris in 1956 and there enrolled at the Cours Simon, a well-known French school of dramatic arts. That same year he was privileged to attend the First Congress of Black Writers and Artists held at the Sorbonne. This international symposium—which gathered together writers, intellectuals, artists, social scientists, and scholars of the Black world—opened new horizons for the recently arrived Bassori, whose life had previously been spent solely in the Ivory Coast. Thus he was to mingle with some of the most prominent representatives of the Black Diaspora and to meet such young Africans and West Indians as Ababacar Samb*, Sarah Maldoror*, and the singer and actress Toto Bissainthe, with whom he engaged in a genuine and enduring friendship. A year later, after passing an entrance examination, Bassori joined his new young friends at the Centre d'Art Dramatique de la Rue Blanche, where they were studying. There, as had happened at the Cours Simon, Bassori was trained mainly in sundry classical plays of the French repertory. He reminisces:

We came to the realization that those classical French plays did not correspond to our personalities. The techniques we acquired were beneficial, we improved our diction and all, but our personalities were stiff and frozen in everything we were asked to play. (Bassori to author, February 1985)

So Bassori, Samb, Maldoror, and Bissainthe engaged in a kind of parallel theater practice that was closer to their aspirations as Black actors. Yet because of a lack of an extensive range of works written by African and Caribbean authors, they staged plays by Jean-Paul Sartre or Aleksandr Pushkin at various cultural centers, nursing homes, and students' hostels, where audiences were surprised and even amazed to see such plays performed by Black actors. Meanwhile, in 1957, the foursome (and others such as the West Indian actor Robert Liensol) had created their own troupe, the Compagnie d'Art Dramatique des Griots, whose most successful play was *Les Nègres* (The Blacks), a work the French playwright Jean Genêt had specifically intended for Black performers. Bassori nostalgically recalls: "This was a time of great expectation and passion, and we all believed that the future was ours. We came from different countries and we had met in Paris. We were like a family and we did a lot of things together" (Bassori to author, February 1985). Also at that time Bassori discovered the writings of such Negro-African and Caribbean writers as Leopold Senghor, Aimé Césaire, Jacques Roumain, and Nicolas Guillen, and avidly read works by the contemporary French writers Albert Camus, Jean-Paul Sartre, and André Malraux. After a while, Bassori decided to undertake film studies. He explains: "I had become aware of the limitations of theater. And, as an African stage actor in France I also had very little opportunity to find work" (Bassori to author, February 1985).

Thus, from 1958 to 1961, Bassori studied filmmaking at the Institut des Hautes Etudes Cinématographiques (IDHEC) in Paris. After his graduation from the film school, he worked briefly as an assistant director for French television.

In November 1962, Timité Bassori returned to his country, where he was to work intermittently for a newly founded production company, the Société Ivoirienne de Cinéma (SIC), until its foreclosure in 1979. In 1963 he actively participated in the creation of the state-owned Ivorian television station, for which he turned out three consecutive half-hour documentaries, namely *Les Forestiers* (The Foresters), *L'Abidjan-Niger,* and *Amédée Pierre*. While with the Ivorian television company, Bassori also initiated a film-related program entitled "Connaissance du Cinéma" and participated in the making of "Yao," an adventure series shot in the Ivory Coast. Then, in 1964, based on his own script, Bassori made his first short fiction film, *Sur la dune de la solitude* (On the Dune of Solitude), produced by the Ivorian television company. The motion picture was subsequently featured at the 1966 First International Festival of Negro Arts in Dakar. From 1965 to 1972, the cinéaste held a position at the SIC. It is during that time that he worked as assistant director during the shooting of Christian-Jaque's *Le Gentleman de Cocody* (1966), a Franco-Ivorian diamond-hunting adventure movie starring the famous French actor Jean Marais. Also in 1966, Timité Bassori made his first middle-length color documentary, *Le Sixième Sillon* (The Sixth Furrow), which was to be followed by a series of other short color films produced by the SIC or the Ivorian television company and primarily geared toward local audiences. Such films, portraying sociocultural, historical, and economic facets of the present-day Ivory Coast, include *Feux de brousse* (Bush Fires, 1967), *Abidjan, perle des lagunes* (Abidjan, the Lagoon Pearl, 1971), *Bondoukou, an 11* (Bondoukou, Year 11, 1971), *Odienné, an 12* (Odienné, Year 12, 1972), *Kossou 1* (1972), *Kossou 2* (1974), and *Les Compagnons d'Akati* (The Akati Fellows, 1974), a Franco-Ivorian co-production. Meanwhile, the cinéaste had also written, produced, and directed *La Femme au couteau* (The Woman with a Knife, 1968), which remains to this day his only venture in independent filmmaking. The film, in which he plays the leading role (allegedly to economize on the actors' salaries), was shot in one month and produced based on a budget of about $15,000. Bassori humorously stresses the miscellaneous problems he encountered in selecting nonprofessional female actors for *La Femme au couteau:*

Here [in the Ivory Coast] it is quite difficult to find a young woman willing to play a part in a film. People are not yet accustomed to seeing an African woman showing herself in front of a camera. They think right away that she is frivolous. Some women would like to act in a film but they are afraid of what people might think. . . . Sometimes relatives or a jealous fiancé interfere to prevent her from doing so. *(Fraternité Matin,* 14 January 1969, p. 7)

Timité Bassori's film was presented at the 1969 Pan-African Festival of Algiers, and a year later at the Carthage and Ouagadougou film festivals.

As director of the SIC from 1974 to 1978, Bassori co-produced with French and German film companies *La Victoire en chantant* (Black and White in Color, 1976)—an internationally successful satire concerning French and German colonialism during World War I—and produced *L'Herbe sauvage* (Weeds, 1978), a film by Henri Duparc.* Since 1979 he has been working as a film producer for Ivorian television.

Discussing the nature and role of African cinema, Bassori feels that

the language of the cinema is the expression of a country's proper cultural ambiance and a reproduction of life. . . . Cinema must help to make us aware of our realities and personalities and to better understand our problems. Therefore it will not be a cinema of leisure but one of reflection in complete freedom. *(Présence Africaine,* 2nd Quarter 1974, pp. 140–41)

Then, favoring individual artistry and free creativity over a strict adherence to the sociorealistic vein that prevails in African filmmaking, he emphasizes: "I am against imposing a particular trend [on] African cinema. A number of trends will take shape, and styles will emerge according to the personality of each filmmaker" *(Fraternité Matin,* 7 April 1970, p. 8). Therefore, although necessarily affected by the public's response to his work, Timité Bassori insists that "contrary to what people believe, the public is not always right. . . . I believe that what I have to say in my films is important, and all my efforts will be geared towards imposing my thoughts and style on the public" *(Fraternité Matin,* 7 April 1970, p. 8). As a filmmaker, Bassori does not pretend to solve any problem but rather poses questions for which he has no answers. Concerned with the overall quality of films, he devotes a large amount of time to the writing of his scripts and to the pre-production phase of his films. However, he does not systematically reject last minute changes whenever needed *(Fraternité Matin,* 14 January 1969, p. 7). Unlike many of his African counterparts, yet somewhat regretfully, Bassori generally favors the use of French in his films as a necessary linguistical vehicle in a country like the Ivory Coast in which more than a hundred languages and dialects are spoken *(Recherche, Pédagogie et Culture,* May-August 1975, p. 42).

Deploring the lack of extensive film structures in Africa, the Ivorian filmmaker, like most observers, foresees a viable future for African cinema in terms of inter-African agreements:

Our cinema needs to be industrially organized and can only blossom when political, administrative, financial and intellectual conditions permit it to produce films regularly and when films can freely circulate between countries. Only a continental market will guarantee its development at the production, distribution and exploitation levels. The coordination of these three sectors could be assisted by an institution created at the level of a group of states. *(Présence Africaine,* 2nd Quarter 1974, p. 140)

Otherwise Bassori regrets the limited number of African film critics who can judge African films within their indigenous frame of reference, and encourages African directors to find a film language that would avoid the imitation of Western models and criteria. His personal search for an original style deriving from both realism and symbolism probably explains why Ousmane Sembene* as well as Glauber Rocha, one of the leading representatives of Brazil's cinema novo, are to be counted among his favorite filmmakers.

Even though he has not made any films since 1974, Bassori remains optimistic as to the continued growth of African film. He observes: "I look at the future of African cinema in a very positive light, otherwise we [the first generation of African filmmakers] would have lived in vain" (Bassori to author, Ouagadougou, 1985).

Apart from being a filmmaker and an actor, Timité Bassori also shows talent as a writer. He is the author of *Les Bannis du village* (From the Village Banished, 1974), a collection of short stories, and has to his credit a number of other short stories which have appeared over the years in the Ivorian newspaper *Fraternité Matin.* Another of his short stories, "Les Eaux claires de ma source" (The Clear Waters of My Spring), was awarded the first prize at a literary competition organized by the French Ministry of Cooperation and Radio France Internationale in 1972. With the inclusion of his recent novel, *Grelots d'or* (Golden Anklet Bells, 1984), all of Bassori's writings reflect contemporary Ivorian lifestyles and sociocultural issues.

Calm, lucid, soft-spoken, and amiable, Timité Bassori has been from 1972 to 1987 president of the Association des Cinéastes Professionnels de la Côte-d'Ivoire (Ivorian Association of Professional Filmmakers) and as such has attended many film-related local and international colloquia. Besides heading the Abidjan bureau of CAC (Comité Africain des Cinéastes), he is also one of the founding members of the West African Film Corporation (WAFCO), a film consortium created in 1985. Timité Bassori now lives and works in Abidjan. He hopes, one day, to be able to resume his career as film director.

MAJOR THEMES

There are two orientations in Bassori's motion pictures: documentaries and fiction films. The former include a series of sociocultural and/or somewhat propagandist films celebrating the national sovereignty and the first achievements of the Ivory Coast since its independence from French rule in 1960. In such a vein both *Les Forestiers,* which deals with forest conservation, and *Feux de brousse,* which depicts the dangers of patch clearing through the use of fire, reflect ecological concerns. *L'Abidjan-Niger* focuses on the Ivorian train system,

Kossou 1 and *Kossou 2* describe the construction of a dam, and *Abidjan, perle des lagunes* depicts the diversified appeal of the capital of the Ivory Coast. *Le Sixième Sillon* illustrates the agricultural progress of Bassori's country during the first six years of its independence. *Bondoukou, an 11* and *Odienné, an 12* record on film the national Independence Day celebrations carried out in two Ivorian cities. In both cases these films provide an interesting look at the soci-oeconomic and cultural realities of the regions where Bondoukou and Odienné are located. *Amédée Pierre* offers a portrayal of a popular singer, while *Les Compagnons d'Akati* presents the activities of an Ivorian dance troupe.

More interesting from the point of view of artistic creativity, however, are Bassori's cinematographic explorations of fiction, in *Sur la dune de la solitude* and *La Femme au couteau*.

Sur la dune de la solitude draws its inspiration from the wealth of Africa's oral traditions. It is a modernized version of a legend widely known in Africa (and elsewhere), that of Mamy Watta, the seductive mermaid-like temptress who irremediably lures her human male captives into the depths of her deep-water realm. The black and white film opens on the glitter of Abidjan by night. Next, the camera trails a white European sportscar from a thoroughfare to a deserted beach. Subsequently Elia, a Westernized young man, comes out of the car and rids himself of tie and jacket before slowly walking onto the beach and into the night. Then he sits down and rests a short while before being awakened by the approach of a young woman. He stands up and follows her silently. After some reticence on her part they engage in conversation. As they come nearer to the sea, they evoke the legend of Mamy Watta, with whom the young woman playfully identifies. After bathing in the sea, Elia and his new friend lasciviously embrace and make love on the beach. In the morning, as he wakes up, Elia discovers that his companion has disappeared. Regretfully, he leaves the beach and goes back to his middle-class downtown apartment. Next, as he attends the wake for a friend's sister, Elia is awe-struck on discovering that the deceased woman (said to have been killed in a car accident the day before) is in fact the very woman with whom he has just spent the night. Who was this young woman? Was she real or a dream? Was she a living-dead? Was she Mamy Watta transiently embodied in the dead woman? *Sur la dune de la solitude* has the open-endedness found in traditional African tales, the outcome of which is debated and in a way decided by the spectators. In spite of blurred pictures, artificial and naive dia-logues, mediocre acting, and overall poor synchronization, *Sur la dune de la solitude* contains an irrefutable lyricism accentuated by an adept use of black and white light/shadow contrasts. It has some carefully photographed scenes which emphasize the lover's enticing physical beauty, and is also well-served by some forceful surrealistic compositions.

La Femme au couteau stands unquestionably as Timité Bassori's most ac-complished work. It focuses on the story of a young Westernized Ivorian who seeks appeasement for his existential anguish and hallucinatory sexual fears through traditional African healing and modern Western psychoanalysis. According to Bassori, the film is "a personal experience and the result of multifarious observations of life" *(Fraternité Matin,* 14 January 1969, p. 7).

La Femme au couteau is the cyclical interweaving of two stories which take place in a climate of psychological incertitude made to misdirect and puzzle viewers. The main plot concerns a young Ivorian bourgeois who suffers psychotic nightmares while enduring visual resurgences of a woman with a knife. The latter manifests herself sporadically, but particularly whenever the protagonist is about to engage in sexual intercourse. This schizophrenic ailment generates a seemingly incurable social and psychological estrangement. The subplot of this film revolves around an older African man wearing a tuxedo (no doubt a caricature of the solemn and artificial garb of Western civilization) who aimlessly strolls about the streets and bars of Abidjan. He lived for some time in France and finds it hard to reintegrate himself into his prior environment. A woman appears to him at night and declares herself "his wife from beyond." She gives him a copper bracelet which he can touch whenever he wishes to see her. The woman appears and disappears unnoticed by others, while the man with the tuxedo acts as if she were constantly in his company. His behavior soon arouses suspicion as to his sanity, and he ends up in a insane asylum, where his bracelet is confiscated. The man in the tuxedo metaphorically illustrates psychological and cultural alienation. He is but a reflection of the main protagonist, who also finds himself caught between traditional African mores and Western modernity. The final sequence of the film shows the young Ivorian freeing himself from his sexual inhibitions through the loving and tender care of a woman friend. At that point he realizes that the castrating woman with a knife who has so often appeared to him represents his own punitive mother who, when he was a child, caught him flirting rather innocently with a little village girl.

Describing *La Femme au couteau,* the filmmaker stresses:

It is not a standard scenario in the sense of having an introduction, an exposition and a conclusion. Rather it presents a central character who experiences overlapping situations, ambiances and moods. *(Fraternité Matin,* 14 January 1969, p. 7)

Insisting on the symbolic aspect of his work, Bassori states, *"La Femme au couteau* is old traditional Africa who feels abandoned by her children and becomes as peevish as a possessive mother who uses threat to retrieve her stray offspring" *(Fraternité Matin,* 15 February 1972, p. 8).

SURVEY OF CRITICISM

Apart from Catherine Ruelle's statement that *Sur la dune de la solitude* is but a "rough draft" characterized by a dragging pace and poor acting *(L'Afrique Littéraire et Artistique,* 3rd Quarter 1978, p. 133) and D'Dée's contrasting view of that same film as interesting poetic fiction where "enchantment mingles with everyday life" *(L'Afrique Actuelle,* n. 15, 1967, p. 10), reviews of Bassori's first fiction film are scarce. On the contrary, ample writing has been generated by *La Femme au couteau* because of its original style and unusual content, breaking away from the well-trodden paths of standard narrative cinema. As such, the film is sometimes severely criticized by some for its estrangement from African reality, while it is appreciated and even praised by others for its stylistic and thematic inventiveness. Gaoussou Kamissoko finds the protagonist of *La Femme au couteau* atypical of today's average African inasmuch as he has difficulty in communicating with people around him, and instead takes refuge and escapes into dream and unreality. Yet, Kamissoko approves of Bassori's masterful film language *(Fraternité Matin,* 14 April 1970, p. 2). Although she finds Bassori's treatment of insanity interesting, Béatrice Rolland deplores what she sees as his lack of social analysis and his ''clumsy'' representation of acculturation *(Positif,* February 1970, p. 88). Baffled by the style of *La Femme au couteau,* R. Atta Koffi (who candidly acknowledges his arriving late at the screening of the film) does not make any special effort to penetrate the intricacies of its story and jeers at the Freudian ''emasculation complex'' which the film director has chosen to illustrate *(Fraternité Hebdo,* 30 June 1972, p. 15). In a more serious study of the film, Wilson Mativo terms it ''a culmination of the African cultural dilemma'' *(UFAHAMU,* Winter 1971, p. 66). Claude Gérard is sensitive to the innovative construction of *La Femme au couteau* as well as to the judicious inclusion of John Coltrane's jazz music in its soundtrack *(Fraternité Matin,* 6 April 1970, p. 2). Although he regrets the actors' artificial handling of the French language, Paul-Louis Thirard accents Bassori's contribution to the universal realm of the surrealistic film genre *(Positif,* October 1969, p. 45). The most detailed and favorable review of *La Femme au couteau* is that of Madeleine Alleins, who applauds Bassori's work, in which the inner quest of the main character is acutely expressed within a universal, even ontological, framework. Furthermore, like Claude Gérard, she shows appreciation for the skillful and forceful musical score of the film, ''the haunting African rhythms which accompany the wanderings of the old madman or Coltrane's jazz which reflects the deep anguish of the soul.'' In her opinion, this motion picture is able to successfully compete on the international scene *(Lettres Françaises,* 1 October 1969, pp. 15, 16). Likewise, Guy Hennebelle favors Bassori's craftsmanship and agrees with Alleins on the international class of the film. He regretfully notes, however, that the actors' talent does not match the director's *(Jeune Afrique,* 17 December 1969, p. 13). Unfortunately, *La Femme au couteau* has had an extremely limited commercial run in the Ivory Coast. It has been seen primarily at film festivals and has not yet enjoyed the recognition it deserves.

FILMOGRAPHY

Les Forestiers (The Foresters), 16 mm, black and white, 30 min., 1963.
L'Abidjan-Niger, 16 mm, black and white, 30 min., 1963.
Amédée Pierre, 16 mm, black and white, 30 min., 1963.

Sur la dune de la solitude (On the Dune of Solitude), 16/35 mm, black and white, 32 min., 1964.
Le Sixième Sillon (The Sixth Furrow), 35 mm, color, 60 min., 1966.
Feux de brousse (Bush Fires), 35 mm, color, 25 min., 1967.
La Femme au couteau (The Woman with a Knife), 16/35 mm, black and white, 90 min., 1968.
Abidjan, perle des lagunes (Abidjan, the Lagoon Pearl), 16 mm, color, 30 min., 1971.
Bondoukou, an 11 (Bonkoudou, year 11), 35 mm, color, 11 min., 1971.
Odienné, an 12 (Odienné, year 12), 35 mm, color, 12 min., 1972.
Kossou 1, 35 mm, color, 35 min., 1972.
Kossou 2, 35 mm, color, 29 min., 1974.
Les Compagnons d'Akati (The Akati Fellows), 16 mm, color, 20 min., 1974.

BIBLIOGRAPHY

Writings by Timité Bassori

Bassori, Timité. "Un Cinéma mort-né?" *Présence Africaine,* n. 49, 1st Quarter 1964, pp. 111–16.
———. "The Problem of an Original Cinematographic Language." *Présence Africaine,* n. 90, 2nd Quarter 1974, pp. 140–41.
———. *Les Bannis du village.* Dakar/Abidjan: Les Nouvelles Editions Africaines, 1974.
———. *Grelots d'or.* Abidjan: Centre d'Edition et de Diffusion Africaine, 1984.

Interviews of Timité Bassori

"Le Cinéaste Timité Bassori et La Femme au couteau." *Fraternité Matin,* 15 February 1972, p. 8.
Gérard, Claude. "Avec Timité Bassori." *Fraternité Matin,* 14 January 1969, p. 7.
Hennebelle, Guy. "Côte d'Ivoire, Sénégal, Guinée: six cinéastes africains parlent. . . . *L'Afrique Littéraire et Artistique,* n. 8, 1969, pp. 58–70.
———. "Pour ou contre un cinéma engagé?" *L'Afrique Litteraire et Artistique,* n. 19, 1971, pp. 87–93.
Medeiros, Richard de. "Dialogue à quelques voix." *Recherche, Pédagogie et Culture,* n. 17–18, May-August 1975, pp. 39–42.
Ruelle, Catherine. "Timité Bassori." *L'Afrique Littéraire et Artistique,* n. 49, 3rd Quarter 1978, pp. 133–34.
Thirard, Paul-Louis. "Sur 'La Femme au couteau.' " *Positif,* n. 109, October 1969, pp. 44–47.
"Timité Bassori: faire un film actuellement, c'est déjà être engagé." *Fraternité Matin,* 7 April 1970, p. 8.

Film Reviews and Studies of Timité Bassori

Alleins, Madeleine. "Une Révélation: La Femme au couteau." *Lettres Françaises,* 1 October 1969, pp. 15–16.
Bachy, Victor. *Le Cinéma en Côte d'Ivoire.* Brussels: OCIC/L'Harmattan, 1983.
Binet, Jacques. "Cinéma africain." *Afrique Contemporaine,* n. 83, January-February 1976, pp. 27–30.

Bonneau, Richard. *Ecrivains, cinéastes et artistes ivoiriens, aperçu bio-bibliographique*. Abidjan-Dakar: Nouvelles Editions Africaines, 1973.

D'Dée. "Jeune Cinéma d'Afrique noire." *L'Afrique Actuelle*, Special Issue, n. 15, 1967, pp. 1–40.

Debrix, Jean-René. "Situation du cinéma en Afrique francophone." *Afrique Contemporaine*, n. 81, September-October 1975, pp. 2–7.

Gérard, Claude. "La Difficulté d'être." *Fraternité Matin*, 6 April 1970, p. 2.

Hennebelle, Guy. "La Femme au couteau par Bassori Timité." *Jeune Afrique*, n. 468, 17 December 1969, p. 13.

———. "Carthage." *Cinéma 71*, n. 154, March 1971, pp. 34–36.

———. "Le Cinéma ivoirien." *L'Afrique Littéraire et Artistique*, n. 20, 1st Quarter 1972, pp. 227–34.

Jusu, K.K. Man. "De la qualité des films africains." Fraternité Matin, 12 October 1982, p. 10.

Kamissoko, Gaoussou. "Abidjan et La Femme au couteau." *Fraternité matin*, 14 April 1970, p. 2.

Koffi, R. Atta. "La Femme au couteau . . . un coup d'épée dans l'eau." *Fraternité Hebdo*, 30 June 1972, p. 15.

Lory, Georges-Marie. "La Côte d'Ivoire ne peut encore se prévaloir que d'un modeste florilège cinématographique." *L'Afrique Littéraire et Artistique*, n. 63–64, 1982, pp. 115–17.

Mativo, Wilson. "Cultural Dilemma of the African Film." *UFAHAMU*, vol. 1, n. 3, Winter 1971, pp. 64–67.

Pedersen, Vibeke, and Viggo Holm Jensen. "Afrika, en kampande filmkontinent." *Chaplin 101*, n. 6, 1970, pp. 280–95.

Rolland, Béatrice. "Alger, juillet 1969, 1er festival panafricain." *Positif*, n. 113, February 1970, pp. 87–95.

"Venise à l'heure du tiers-monde." *Fraternité Matin*, 28 September 1969, p. 9.

Moussa Bathily (1946–   )
Senegal

BIOGRAPHY

I like telling a story and I am not the Messiah, the retainer of truth. I took up cinema because it gave me pleasure and not because it was a fulgurating means of reaching the masses. . . . [However,] it is difficult to make a film without taking into account the components of the society within which one lives, without considering current problems and preoccupations. The artist is some sort of a witness. One cannot live in the Senegal of 1985 without consciously or unconsciously depicting the circumstances that surround us. *(Waraango,* n. 10, 1st Quarter 1985, pp. 31–32)

This statement was made by Moussa Yoro Bathily, who, along with other Senegalese directors including Cheikh Ngaido Bah, Ousmane M'Baye, and Ben Diogaye Beye, belongs to what some critics call the new generation of Senegalese filmmakers *(Adhoua,* February-March 1981, p. 3).

Of Sarakholé origin and Muslim extraction, Bathily was born in 1946 near Bakel, an ancient fortified town overlooking the Senegal River and located in the easternmost region of Senegal. The son of a well-established landowner and regional governor, Moussa Bathily spent his childhood in Goudiry, a small town located near the Malian border, where he would occasionally attend outdoor screenings of both French and American films. Bathily remembers that the single most important influence on him during his childhood was that of his father, who, he says, was a well-balanced syncretism of tradition and modernity (Bathily to author, 29 December 1985).

After attending both Koranic and primary schools, Bathily went to high school at the lycée Lamine Gueye of Dakar, and then received his baccalauréat in 1968. As a young man, the filmmaker read not only writings by such authors as Diderot, Joseph Conrad, Céline, Antoine de Saint-Exupéry, and John Dos Passos, but also those of the twentieth-century Malian philosopher Amadou Hampaté Ba and works by the seventeenth-century philosopher Kocc Barma. Subsequently, Moussa Bathily undertook studies at the University of Dakar, where he earned an M.A. in history. His thesis focused on Blaise Diagne, the first Black representative at the French National Assembly. Next, he taught for three years at the lycée Abdoulaye Sadji in Rufisque. From 1971 to 1973, while teaching, Bathily wrote a film review column for *Le Soleil,* a Senegalese daily newspaper. Then, after resigning from the school system, Bathily came back to Dakar, where he regularly attended film screenings at the Dakar ciné-club. There he came into contact with young Senegalese filmmakers such as Djibril Diop Mambety* and Mahama Johnson Traore,* and started writing scripts. Hence, Bathily became increasingly impassioned with cinema, and soon his serious interest in film was noticed by Ousmane Sembene,* with whom he was to acquire on-the-job training as his assistant during the shooting of *Xala* (1974) and *Ceddo* (1976). In 1974 Bathily was entrusted with the direction of his first short film, *Fidak,* by the organizers of the Dakar International Fair. The year 1975 saw the release of *Ndakarou, impressions matinales* (Dakar, Morning Impressions), his documentary on Dakar, whose name in Wolof (the dominant vernacular language of Senegal) is Ndakarou. This film was financed by the now defunct Société Nationale de Cinéma under the tutelage of the Senegalese Ministry of Culture. The following year, Bathily made his third short, entitled *Des Personnages encombrants* (Cumbersome People). In 1978 the filmmaker went back to his native village to film *Tiyabu Biru,* his first feature length motion picture, which was shot in Sarakholé, a language commonly spoken in eastern Senegal. Subsequently, Bathily's reputation soared with this motion picture, which was to be featured at several international film festivals, among them the 1978 Cannes Film Festival, the Namur Festival of Francophone Cinema held in Belgium in 1978, and the 1979 Pan-African Film Festival of Ouagadougou (FESPACO) in Burkina Faso. It was later to be shown at the Racines Noires (Black Roots) festival held in Paris (1985). In 1981 the filmmaker shot *Siggi ou la poliomyélite* (Siggi or Poliomyelitis), a documentary produced by the United Nations, and *Le Certificat d'indigence* (The Certificate of Indigence), a fiction film financed by Le Fonds d'Aide à l'Industrie Cinématographique (a government-sponsored film fund created in 1978). *Le Certificat d'indigence* won the Prize for Best Short Film awarded by the International Catholic Organization for the Cinema at the 1983 FESPACO, and other recognitions that same year at the Cannes and Moscow film festivals. Bathily's latest film to date is *Des Sites et des monuments au Sénégal* (Senegalese Sites and Monuments), also financed by a Senegalese government agency.

In the fall of 1984 and the spring of 1985, the director engaged in the shooting of *Petits-Blancs au manioc et à la sauce gombo* (White Folks Served with Manioc and Okra Sauce), a fiction film whose title is barely translatable into English without removing parts of its culinary connotations and satirical overtones. The plot of this film revolves around the acculturation of five French technicians who are sent to an undetermined Sahelian village to install a solar pump. After the completion of their mission, four of them return to France, but one stays in Africa, apparently "devoured" by his love for a native woman. By the time this film is completed, it will probably have cost about $800,000, a substantial figure for an African production. It is Bathily's most ambitious venture, for which he achieved a budgetary tour de force by obtaining financing from varied sources including the French Ministry of Foreign Affairs, a German television station (WDR), and the newly created Société Nouvelle de Promotion Ciné-matographique (SNPC, Senegal). Unfortunately, the filming of *Petits blancs au manioc et à la sauce gombo* suffered a number of unforeseen mishaps, such as several crew strikes and the partial destruction of a complete clay village (built on location as the village in Sembene's *Ceddo)* as a result of torrential seasonal rains *(Afrique Nouvelle,* 9 January 1985, pp. 20–21). The delayed completion of this co-production should, however, be envisioned for 1987 or early 1988. Bathily's film projects include a fiction film entitled *L'Archer bassari* (The Bassari Archer) and a documentary on the Fangoune dance.

Apart from being a filmmaker, Moussa Bathily is also a writer. He has to his credit a number of short stories and has authored several newspaper articles, including essays on film. Primarily self-taught and with no formal training in the area of filmmaking, he has already demonstrated technical proficiency and directorial skills. Aspiring to be counted one day among the world's greatest filmmakers *(Waraango,* n. 10, 1st Quarter 1985, p. 34), Bathily appears un-doubtedly as an African director to watch. A member of the Cinéastes Sénégalais Associés (Senegalese Filmmakers' Association), he is now living and working in Dakar, where he heads EMEBE Diffusion Films, his own production company.

MAJOR THEMES

Several works by Moussa Bathily are commissioned promotional and/or ed-ucational motion pictures. *Fidak* (which stands for Foire Internationale de Dakar), for instance, concerns the 1974 Dakar International Fair. It has limited artistic merit, and its main purpose is to advertise the business appeal of the fair to potential exhibitors. Likewise, *Siggi ou la poliomyélite,* a health-oriented doc-umentary, advocates large-scale vaccination programs, and *Des Sites et des monuments au Sénégal* focuses on Senegal's touristic and cultural landmarks.

Bathily's *Des Personnages encombrants* is a fictional film, narrated by the Haitian poet Jean Brierre, in which a successful author is challenged by the characters he has created in his writings. These characters accuse him of having betrayed them and eventually kill the writer.

In *Ndakarou, impressions matinales,* which also reflects a personal outlook, the camera, skillfully handled by Georges Caristan (Sembene's favorite cam-eraman), lingers in the streets of Senegal's capital and witnesses its progressive awakening from dawn to mid-morning. The film is dedicated to "Henriette Bathily in homage to silent film." It has no commentary except for the overt implications contained in natural sounds such as the sonorous punctuation offered by the resonant "Allah Akbar"—celebrating God's greatness—of the muezzin calling for morning prayer. Hence the only narrative continuity of *Ndakarou, impressions matinales* is provided by ingenious editing, and the kora (a West African string instrument) music by S. Kouyaté which is included in its soundtrack. Otherwise its homogeneity is provided by shots of several characters whose actions evolve as the morning unfolds: several young female ballet dancers warming up for early practice, women fetching water from the communal fountain, and longshoremen at the Dakar harbor. Two of the film's unusual protagonists are a humorous couple played by Jacqueline and Lucien Lemoine (two Haitian stage actors and radio personalities well known on the Dakar cultural scene), whose gesticulatory interactions, mimicking a caricatural aborted courtship, are staged in an amusing fashion—seemingly to call to mind the exaggerated performing techniques used in early Western silent cinema, to which *Ndakarou, impressions matinales* pays tribute. In this film, Bathily paints with a keen, observant eye a series of vignettes of Dakar's matutinal life: empty bus and train stations, street cleaning, garbage collecting, little boys practicing Senegalese wrestling in the street, men's hasty breakfast on the precarious wooden stands of local restaurants, street corner newspaper vendors, a white couple walking their dog in front of the presidential palace, beggars, pupils lining up in front of a school, the winding, filthy waters of open air sewers followed by a shot of white swimmers in a nearby hotel swimming pool, the growing traffic of the first mass transit passengers, black and white worshippers as they leave Dakar's cathedral after morning mass, and finally (since time has now progressed) the intensified transactions of the variegated marketplace. Espousing the theme of Djibril Diop Mambety's *Contras City*— without, however, matching its visual inventiveness and wit —*Ndakarou, impressions matinales* is an honest film that reflects the pulse of Dakar's cosmopolitan and multireligious milieu. Without falling into the pitfall of miserabilism (beggars are only seen in passing), Bathily's work relies on a series of contrasting shots stressing the various inequities inherent in contemporary Senegalese urban society.

Tiyabu Biru's Sarakholé title refers to the shed *(biru)* of a village named Tiyabu where adolescents are made to retreat while undergoing collective circumcision. This documentary feature explores the socioreligious ritual of circumcision while questioning its practicability and relevance in Senegal's evolving agrarian communities.

Bathily's film opens with scenes of villagers feverishly preparing for the traditional ceremony of circumcision. Aziz and two other boys are too young to participate in its observance. Kept away, they decide to witness the ceremony furtively. Then, while preparing for the imminent festivities, the elders realize that the village can no longer afford the rising price of the sacrificial cattle. At this point Aziz and his friends secretly manage to steal the needed heads of cattle so that the circumcision may take place as is customary. Soon thereafter their misdeeds are discovered, and the owner of the cattle presses charges against the villagers, who are made to pay substantial damages. After these unpleasant dealings with local judiciary authorities, the villagers decide to give up their costly circumcision rites. An elder ponders, ''Our traditions are dying, we are facing new days." Subsequently, the three urchins are sent to school—which itself represents a step toward modernity. The film ends with a freeze frame of Aziz, pondering over his textbook. For him too a new life has started.

Moussa Bathily made this film in his own village, hence its lyrical visual allure is enhanced by a semi-autobiographical documentary-like authenticity. The filmmaker stresses, "I wanted to make this film as if I had never left my village" *(Adhoua,* January-March 1981, p. 4). But there is more to *Tiyabu Biru* than pastoral nostalgia; with penetrating insight and sociological accuracy the film illustrates the changing order experienced by traditional African rural societies.

Le Certificat d'indigence, like Sembene's *Mandabi,* depicts the obsessive tribulations of an illiterate individual balked by the intricacies and inadequacies of modern bureaucracy. This work denounces corruption, fatalism, and what the filmmaker calls the myth of African solidarity *(Afrique-Asie,* 10 October 1983, p. 55).

The plot of this film depicts the plight of a poor woman whose child is sick but who is denied access to the services of a hospital because she lacks the necessary "certificate of indigence" which would allow her to benefit from free medical care. Her dealings with the hospital staff reveal gross professional laxity and corruption, as well as the sundry deficiencies and inequities of an inadequate bureaucratic machinery. The woman is equally ill-treated at City Hall and other public service places where she attempts to obtain the necessary certificate and seek assistance. Finally, a commiserating motorist offers to take her back to the hospital and pay the fees. However, such belated efforts are in vain. The child dies upon arrival in the emergency room. In sorrow, but with no sign of indignation or anger, the woman leaves the building and silently merges into the street crowd. The last sequence of *Le Certificat d'indigence* shows another poverty stricken woman and her sick child approaching the same hospital, where she is expected to be caught in the same inextricable labyrinth.

Le Certificat d'indigence is based on a short article that was published in the current events section of *Le Soleil,* a Dakar newspaper. The film derives its power not only from its authentic settings but from its unadorned style, which shows an appreciable sense of visual realism. According to Derrick Knight, "The film—shown widely in Senegal—helped to change the law relating to free health care" *(New African,* April 1983, p. 43).

SURVEY OF CRITICISM

The motion picture by Bathily that has received the most critical attention is *Tiyabu Biru.* For N. Renaudin, a French critic, it is the first African film the story of which is seen through children's eyes *(Recherche, Pédagogie et Culture,* 1979, p. 103). The Algerian reviewer Azzedine Mabrouki sees it as "a very beautiful film" and adds:

It is a film which must appeal to champions of [African] authenticity like Sembene. At any rate, Bathily calls for resistance against the deterioration of culture and traditional lifestyle. . . . far from being "an ethnographic document" . . . *Tiyabu Biru* is . . . made with astonishing inner force and creativity by a filmmaker who is deeply concerned with the issues he raises. *(Les 2 Ecrans,* April 1979, p. 14)

The well-known Tunisian film critic Ferid Boughedir agrees with Mabrouki's overall comments but also praises Bathily for having achieved in his motion picture "a successful balance between an ethnographic document and a nostalgic evocation" *(Jeune Afrique,* 4 October 1978, p. 44). For Farida Ayari, another North African observer, *Tiyabu Biru* principally illustrates the role of children as the "symbolic guardians of tradition" and demonstrates the difficult transition of an old world inevitably permeated by new ways. This critic is particularly sensitive to the film's clear sociological implications as well as to its pictorial qualities, "enhanced by a very fine Soninké music of the Middle-Ages" *(Adhoua,* January-March 1981, p. 4). Jean de Baroncelli, one of the regular contributors to the French newspaper *Le Monde,* shows a more reserved appreciation for Bathily's skills. Yet, despite deploring the fact that the director's "mise-en-scène is more folkloric than convincing," Baroncelli seemingly approves of *Tiyabu Biru*'s content, which shows how "the power of money now corrupts ancestral customs" *(Le Monde,* 21 September 1978, p. 20).

Because short films are generally less frequently shown (and thus less reviewed) than features, Bathily's *Le Certificat d'indigence* has not been reviewed to the extent that *Tiyabu Biru* has. For Raphael Bassan, *"Le Certificat d'indigence* is a violent diatribe against local bureaucracy" *(Afrique-Asie,* 20 June 1984, p. 66). Nevertheless, Christine Delorme admires the strength of the film's evocative power *(Afrique-Asie,* 10 October 1983, p. 55). Both Bassan and Delorme concur on the undeniable talent of the Senegalese director.

FILMOGRAPHY

Fidak, 16 mm, color, 20 min., 1974.

Ndakarou, impressions matinales (Dakar, Morning Impressions), 16/35 mm, color, 16 min., 1975.

Des Personnages encombrants (Cumbersome People), 35 mm, color, 25 min., 1976.

Tiyabu Biru, 16 mm, color, 85 min., 1978.

Le Certificat d'indigence (The Certificate of Indigence), 16 mm, color, 35 min., 1981.

Siggi ou la poliomyélite (Siggi or Poliomyelitis), 16 mm, color, 40 min., 1981.

Des Sites et des monuments au Sénégal (Senegalese Sites and Monuments), 35 mm, color, 45 min., 1983.

BIBLIOGRAPHY

Writings by Moussa Bathily

Bathily, Moussa Yoro. "La Production du film de qualité en Afrique," in *FESPACO 1983,* pp. 33–41. Paris: Présence Africaine, 1987.

Interviews of Moussa Bathily

Delorme, Christine. "Certificat d'indigence." *Afrique-Asie,* n. 306, 10 October 1983, pp. 55–56.

Haffner, Pierre. "Jean Rouch jugé par six cinéastes d'Afrique noire." *Cinémaction,* n. 17, 1982, pp. 62–76.

Jean-Bart, Anne. "Certificat d'indigence de Moussa Yoro Bathily ou les complexités de l'administration." *Le Soleil,* 21 February 1983, p. 11.

Ruelle, Catherine. "Bathily Moussa." *L'Afrique Littéraire et Artistique,* n. 49, 3rd Quarter 1978, p. 26.

Savane, Vieux, and Idy-Caras Niane. "Moussa Yoro Bathily: Je veux être parmi les meilleurs cinéastes du monde." *Waraango,* n. 10, 1st Quarter 1985, pp. 31–35.

Film Reviews and Studies of Moussa Bathily

Ayari, Farida. "Jeune cinéma sénégalais: la parole à l'image." *Adhoua,* n. 3, January-March 1981, pp. 3–6.

Bachy, Victor. "Le Cinéma sénégalais." *La Revue du Cinéma, Image et Son,* n. 341, July 1979, pp. 38–43.

Baroncelli, Jean de. "Films francophones à Namur; tristes histoires du monde réel." *Le Monde,* 21 September 1978, p. 20.

Bassan, Raphael. "Un Sismographe." *Afrique-Asie,* n. 298, 20 June 1984, pp. 64–66.

Boughedir, Ferid. "L'Afrique à la une chez les francophones à Namur." *Jeune Afrique,* n. 926, 4 October 1978, pp. 44–45.

———. "Et maintenant que la fête commence." *Jeune Afrique,* n. 1151, 28 January 1983, pp. 53–55.

———. "Une Nouvelle vague de cinéastes." *Jeune Afrique,* n. 1156, 2 March 1983, pp. 78–80.

C. A. "Explorations Africaines." *L'Humanité,* 1 July 1978, p. 8.

Dia, Alioune Touré. "Cinema: Shadows over Senegalese Screens?" *Afrika,* vol. 24, n. 1, 1983, pp. 24–25.

Diedhiou, Djib. "Moussa Bathily au 'Soleil': Tiyabu Biru n'est pas un film ethnographique." *Le Soleil,* 2, 3, 4 June 1979, p. 2.

Euvrard, Michel. "Bathily Moussa." *L'Afrique Littéraire et Artistique,* n. 49, 3rd Quarter 1978, p. 25.

Jusu, K.K. Man. "De la qualité des films africains." *Fraternité Matin,* 12 October 1982, p. 10.

Kaboke, V. "Le Certificat d'indigence." *Unir Cinéma,* n. 23–24 (130–131), March-April and May-June 1986, p. 36.

Knight, Derrick. "African Films Turn on the Heat." *New African,* April 1983, pp. 42–43.

Lemaire, Charles. "Moussa Bathily en tournage: pour quelques millions de plus!" *Afrique Nouvelle,* n. 1853, 9 January 1985, pp. 20–21.

Mabrouki, Azzedine. "Senegal: Tiyabu de Moussa Yoro Bathily." *Les 2 Ecrans,* n. 12, April 1979, p. 14.

Martin, Angela. "Ouagadougou." *Framework,* Issue 10, Spring 1979, pp. 42–43.

Ouedraogo, Henri. "Les Africains étaient à Cannes." *Bingo,* n. 307, August 1978, pp. 51–52.

Renaudin, N. "Notes sur l'enfant dans le cinéma—l'enfant dans les films africains." *Recherche, Pédagogie et Culture,* n. 44, 1979, pp. 101–7.

Vieyra, Paulin Soumanou. *Le Cinéma au Sénégal.* Brussels: OCIC/L'Harmattan, 1983.

Souleymane Cissé (1940–)
Mali

BIOGRAPHY

Souleymane Cissé is, together with Ousmane Sembene*, now widely considered to be one of the leading figures of contemporary African cinema. This internationally known filmmaker was born on 21 April 1940 in Bamako, the capital of Mali. Raised in a large Muslim family, Cissé belongs to the Sarakholé ethnic group, known in West Africa for their business acumen and spirit of enterprise. His father started in life as a peddler and later became an established tailor.

It was at a very early age that the young Cissé discovered the magic of film in open air movie theaters. He remembers:

My brothers took me to the movies when I was six years old. I liked it so much that I would soon go to the movies by myself. I was quite young and the movie theater managers would let me get in for free; I used to spend all my evenings watching films. There were a lot of children at home. My father was working and had very little time to devote to us, and thus he would keep an eye chiefly on my sisters. I was on my own and I liked that kind of freedom which allowed me to do as I pleased. *(Calao,* May-June 1983, p. 4)

However, to be such a devotee of the Seventh Art apparently presented some drawbacks to Cissé's performance in primary school, from which he was eventually dismissed. Later, his parents moved to Dakar, Senegal, where the youngster resumed his studies at a local secondary school and his frequent attendance at movie theaters. The filmmaker remarks: "My favorite movie . . . was *High Noon.* I used to like Gary Cooper a lot. Then, I also enjoyed East Indian movies. I am very sensitive to minor social dramas. They used to bring tears to my eyes" *(Libération,* 20 April 1983, p. 19).

After the independence of Mali (1960), Cissé and his family returned to Bamako, where the young man's interest in cinema led him to organize student screenings, which proved to be a decisive step in his future career as a filmmaker. Cissé stresses:

At that time I was a member of a Malian youth group and I became a film projectionist. It was only in 1961 when I received a three-month scholarship to study this profession in the Soviet Union that I became fully cognizant of my love for the Seventh Art. After returning to Mali, I received another scholarship to study film camera work for a year in the Soviet Union. Later I requested, and received, a longer scholarship in the Soviet Union to study cinema. *(West Africa,* 7 May 1984, p. 973)

Cissé was trained as a projectionist from 1961 to 1962. It was in 1962, after seeing a film describing the incarceration and tragic death of Patrice Lumumba, one of Zaire's first leaders, that he decided to become a filmmaker. Subsequently, Cissé studied filmmaking from 1963 to 1969 at the VGIK, the State Institute of Cinema in Moscow, where he was given the opportunity to work under Mark Donskoi (a leading Soviet filmmaker who had also trained Ousmane Sembene a few years earlier), and other notable Soviet directors. Cissé recalls:

There was always contact in the school with the great artists of Soviet cinema. And there was always contact with the classic cinema of the entire world—there were two or three screenings of classic films a week followed by a discussion. Lastly there was a very good way of working—that is to say, the most practical way of making cinema. Really it was extraordinary. *(African Films: The Context of Production,* p. 89)

While in Moscow, Souleymane Cissé was introduced to Soviet socialist realism in film, a movement favoring straightforward social dramas. He states:

What I saw in Soviet films and what I experienced in Mali just after independence were largely similar. Soviet films, especially, concentrate on social questions, often on an everyday approach without grandiose scenarios and costly special effects. This really impressed me. Let's not ignore, either, that I was quite influenced by Italian neorealism of the post-war period. Here, too, was concern for the life of the small people in a realistic environment. *(West Africa,* 7 May 1984, p. 973)

Yet although the Malian filmmaker appears indebted to his training in the Soviet Union, he denies that it has had an overwhelming influence on his present methods of work and film language:

A film institute gives you a notion of film and the rest depends on the individual. The Soviets' vision of cinema matches their society. I studied how they made films but I also knew that it was impossible to make their kinds of films in the developing society in which I live. So, to be able to make films in Mali, I had to adapt to the socioeconomic realities of my country. (Souleymane Cissé, African Film and Filmmakers Lecture Series, Howard University, Washington, D.C., 16 September 1983)

Hence, according to Cissé, "The political conviction which permeates my films is generated by my country, Mali" *(Carrefour Africain,* 18 February 1983).

While studying in Moscow, Cissé made three films with African fellow students, namely, *L'Homme et les idoles* (Man and Idols, 1965), *Sources d'inspi-*

ration (Sources of Inspiration, 1966), and *L'Aspirant* (The Aspirant, 1968), for which VGIK awarded him a special mention.

In 1969, upon his return to Mali, Souleymane Cissé was hired to work as film director by the Service Cinématographique du Ministére de l'Information du Mali (SCINFOMA), for whom he produced (from 1970 to 1971) thirty newsreels and five documentaries on Malian subjects, including *Degal à Dialloubé* (Degal at Dialloubé, 1970) and *Fête du Sanke* (The Sanke Celebration, 1971). His first fiction film, *Cinq jours d'une vie* (Five Days in a Life), made with his own funds and shot in Bambara (Mali's most widely spoken vernacular language, also used in such other West African countries as Guinea and the Ivory Coast), was released in 1972. The following year, this film won the Third Prize ("Tanit de Bronze") at the Carthage Film Festival in Tunisia for its skillful technique and sensitivity. Also in 1973, Cissé completed a documentary entitled *Dixième anniversaire de l'OUA* (Tenth Anniversary of the Organization of African Unity). Subsequently, in 1974, with the help of the French Ministry of Cooperation, he made his first feature length film, *Den Muso* (The Young Girl), based on a budget of $50,000. *Den Muso* was to create for the Malian filmmaker a series of inextricable copyright difficulties with a Bamako ciné-club that had helped him to obtain the needed shooting permit. This legal dispute led to Cissé's imprisonment, which was fortunately brief due to the personal intervention of the Malian head of state. This controversy delayed the release of *Den Muso* until three years later. Nevertheless, in Cissé's own words:

This was the first Malian film to try to come to grips with daily life in our country. . . . It had a great impact on the Malian public and it confirmed my view that the African filmgoers were anxious to see more films mirroring their own existence and preoccupations. (*The Guardian*, 10 May 1984, p. 15)

Den Muso was to receive a prize in 1979 at the Nantes Three Continents Film Festival (France).

In 1976 and 1977, Cissé obtained a leave of absence from the Ministry of Information in order to film *Baara* (Work), which he had started writing while in prison. Financed in part by the French Institut National de l'Audiovisuel, based on a budget of $150,000, and shot in four months (instead of three weeks as planned), the motion picture was released in 1978 and attracted the attention of film critics both in Africa and abroad. That same year, *Baara* received the Grand Prize, and an award from the International Catholic Organization for the Cinema at the Pan-African Film Festival of Ouagadougou (FESPACO) in Burkina Faso. The film won, furthermore, the Second Prize "(Tanit d'Argent") and the Prize for Best Male Interpretation (awarded to its leading actor, Boubacar Keita) at the Carthage Film Festival. Otherwise, *Baara* obtained a number of other prizes at several film events, among them the Festival International du Film et des Echanges Francophone (FIFEF) held in Namur, Belgium (1978), and the Locarno Film Festival in Switzerland (1979). After some reservations during the first weeks it was shown in Bamako, *Baara* eventually met with considerable popular success in Mali, where it enjoyed a month and a half of uninterrupted showings in the capital city. Furthermore, Cissé's work was the first African film presented at prime time on a French television station (FR3), where it was seen by 1.6 million viewers in 1982. Two years later, in spite of its previous television screening, *Baara* was shown simultaneously for several weeks in three commercial Parisian movie theaters. In June 1985, *Baara* was featured at the third Festival Cinematografico Africano held in Perugia (Italy).

Cissé's most successful film to date is *Finyé* (1982), which was produced independently and shot in five months. Hampered by the French government's 1980 decision to discontinue its financial support of Francophone African cinema, Cissé had to rely on *Baara*'s returns and his own resources as well as on private investors and businessmen (among them his brother) to complete this $400,000 film, which was shot on location by a crew of Malian and French technicians, and subsequently processed and edited in Paris. Although *Finyé* illustrates student riots that actually took place in Mali in 1980 and denounces the abuse of military power, Cissé was allowed to make his film by the military government, which also gave him use of the military equipment and university buildings he needed. Subsequently, *Finyé* was seen in Mali by 100,000 viewers and had an equally successful run in such African countries as Senegal and the Ivory Coast. Then, in 1983, this film was shown commercially for six weeks in Paris. With its 400,000 viewers, *Finyé* proved to be the most popular Black African film ever presented on French movie screens. Now available in video cassettes (Films Cissé, BP 1236, Bamako), it is expected that Cissé's film will continue to broaden its viewership. Earlier, in 1982, Cissé's production had been presented at the Carthage Film Festival, where it won the Grand Prize ("Tanit d'Or"). In 1983 *Finyé* received the FESPACO Grand Prize and was featured at several international film festivals such as the Cannes Film Festival (where Cissé was invited to serve as jury member) and the London and New York film festivals. Also, during the fall of 1983, Souleymane Cissé was selected by the U.S. Information Agency and Operation Crossroad Africa to participate in a program entitled "Film as a Mirror of Contemporary Culture," which enabled him to tour the United States and discuss African cinema and his own work at such educational institutions as Howard University in Washington, D.C., and the University of California at Los Angeles. In 1984 Cissé was invited to participate in an international film festival held in India (Filmotsav). In the spring of 1985, he was an active participant at the Third Congress of the Fédération Panafricaine des Cinéastes (FEPACI) held in Ouagadougou at the same time as the Ninth FES-PACO. That same year, Cissé and his favorite cameraman, Etienne Carton de Grammont (who previously worked on *Baara* and *Finyé*), were engaged in the filming of *Yeelen* (The Light), a feature film about which Cissé was at the time rather secretive except to disclose that its setting was precolonial Mali. *Yeelen* was to be released two years later, and featured at the 1987 Cannes Film Festival where it received the Jury's Prize.

In spite of his international acclaim and the moral support he is able to draw from it, Souleymane Cissé still faces the same difficulties as other lesser known African directors and can barely expect to make a feature length film every four or five years. He says:

To make a film belongs to the realm of miracle. I have to do everything. I am in turn producer, cameraman and technician. I lend a hand in every area. There are no standard production facilities in Mali. . . . I am unable to screen the rushes of my films. . . . I have to go to Paris for processing because there are no adequate processing labs in [Black] Africa. . . . this lack of technical means is awful. It greatly burdens the budgets of films and restrains the filmmakers' creativity. *(Jeune Afrique,* 11 May 1983, p. 50)

Such scarcity of equipment even has a direct impact on the theme and style of his works. He observes: "My films take place in an urban context because I have limited means, and because I cannot afford shooting in the countryside where I would need generators and the kind of equipment which is not available to me" *(Le Magazine Littéraire,* May 1983, p. 44). Cissé offers as an example the fact that *Finyé* would have been a much better film had he benefitted from a higher budget and more adequate equipment:

In terms of its mise-en-scène I had to give up a lot of ideas because I had only one camera on tripod and limited lighting facilities. . . . Financing is always a big problem. I never think about it until my script is finished. I start shooting as soon as I have some money without knowing whether I'll be able to find adequate financing to complete my film. *(Les Nouvelles Littéraires,* 28 April 1983, p. 46)

An advocate of sociorealism, Cissé is as distrustful of blatant positive socialist film heroes as he is of Hollywood stardom. Thus, with the exception of Balla Moussa Keita (who plays the military governor in *Finyé* and the factory director in *Baara)* and Omou Diarra (who interprets the third wife of *Finyé*'s military governor as well as the wife of the young engineer in *Baara),* who have had some theatrical experience, the filmmaker does not customarily choose professional actors. For the sake of authenticity (and possibly budgetary constraints), Cissé favors the use of nonprofessional actors who come from the same sociocultural background as the characters they are to portray. He likes to emphasize that the young people who play in *Finyé* "have nothing to do with cinema and theater. I picked them up in the streets and I worked with them. Of course they were motivated and could thoroughly identify with the subject matter" *(Libération,* 18 May 1982, p. 5).

Although the Malian director, like a number of his African counterparts, started his career by making documentaries, he now shows a marked preference for fiction films, saying:

It's always more interesting, closer to people if you make a film of this genre, because they feel more concerned. If you make a documentary, for them it is like a newsreel. Whereas if it's a fiction film there are certain things which they may not have experienced but which could happen to them. So for me, it's quite normal in this context to make a fiction film so that the spectators can become more and more conscious of their role [in society]. *(Framework,* August 1979, p. 17)

In spite of being recognized as a talented filmmaker, Cissé maintains that he is still in search of a style and an original form of expression capable of illustrating the customs, the problems, and the aspirations of his society: "This quest is carried out based on my own culture and I am far from having found everything I am looking for" *(Cinéma 84,* November 1984, p. 38). He stresses furthermore that such faithfulness to his cultural heritage is essential, because "for want of returning to our own values we will remain alienated by those of others" *(Le Magazine Littéraire,* May 1983, p. 44).

"For me cinema is an art which is meant to have an impact on life" *(West Africa,* 7 May 1984, p. 973). An ardent supporter of didactic filmmaking in African countries with a largely illiterate population, Cissé strongly believes that his films should "address issues of the utmost concern and implication to his society, with the hope of positive change" *(West Africa,* 28 November 1983, p. 2728). For him, therefore, "an African filmmaker must first of all have a very high political awareness" (Howard University, 16 September 1983). He personally feels that "his mission as a filmmaker is to help a people to discover its identity" *(Le Monde,* 21 September 1978, p. 20). A humanist for whom "culture is as vital as rice" *(Jeune Afrique,* 11 May 1983, p. 51), Cissé sees himself as a man of culture and an artist rather than a political propagandist who chose film as a means of expression and communication.

Discussing the countless problems hampering African filmmaking, the Malian director points out:

I would say, above all, that African cinema is not properly understood by African leaders. . . . African businessmen have no notion of the possibilities of African cinema. . . . Our films are also poorly distributed in Africa and elsewhere around the world. A film which is not properly distributed cannot be profitable. This is a situation which must be overcome, though these problems do not mean that one should necessarily be pessimistic about the future of African cinema. *(West Africa,* 7 May 1984, p. 974)

Thus, for Cissé, the growth of film in Africa implies "a gradual breakaway from economic and technical dependence in the production, distribution and exhibition fields [and] encouraging the development of cinema based on our socioeconomic and cultural realities and aspirations" *(West Africa,* 7 December 1981, p. 2913).

Asked if one could presently delineate a specific African film language, the director responded:

Europe includes different countries which give birth to different cinemas. Likewise, in Africa we have a multitude of ethnic groups and each of them has its temperament. This is reflected through African cinema which is made of various styles and tendencies. (Cissé to author, Bamako, July 1983)

A scrupulous craftsman, Cissé deplores the technical deficiencies he noticed in a number of recent black African films: "What we see now is a bit depressing. . . . the new generation of cinéastes no longer master their art as would be wished for. In terms of style, nothing has changed in twenty years" *(Libération,* 15 March 1985, p. 30). For him this appears as a serious drawback to their competitiveness on the international scene. Furthermore, Cissé considers film as a universal language and, to him, one of the tests of his proficiency as a filmmaker is precisely the worldwide appreciation of his works beyond Third World film festivals or the Western university and museum film circuit *(Le Quotidien de Paris,* 26 April 1983, p. 34).

"Provided they show enough combativity" (Cissé to author, July 1983), Souleymane Cissé would encourage young Africans to become filmmakers. He thinks that African cinema will gradually assert itself in spite of the multitude of obstacles it still has to circumvent. Although he has now come to the fore as a leading independent African filmmaker, Cissé is still employed by the Malian Ministry of Information. He lives with his family in Bamako.

Outspoken when necessary but also somewhat unnecessarily temperamental (particularly when interviewed), the Malian director is "lighly built, sprite, full of vitality" *(Jeune Afrique,* 11 May 1983, p. 50) and is said to be "as slender as an adolescent, as wise as an elder" *(Le Monde,* 2 November 1982, p. 13). At any rate, he appears as a man of strong beliefs who has certainly wisely utilized his creative abilities and combative energies to gain due prominence in the area of Black African cinema. In 1985 Cissé participated in the creation of the West African Film Corporation (WAFCO), a consortium for the production and distribution of films in West Africa.

MAJOR THEMES

Part of his academic requirements at VGIK, Cissé's first shorts shot in the Soviet Union are not without interest and already indicate his skills and concerns as a filmmaker. *Sources d'inspiration,* for example, offers an interesting portrayal of the Malian painter Mamadou S. Coulibaly. Here scenes of the artist at work in his studio are interspersed with historical drawings of the slave trade, newsreel footage depicting important events and figures in the past and present of Africa and the Black Diaspora (African freedom fighters and Black American demonstrators of the 1960s, film clippings of Martin Luther King and Patrice Lumumba, etc.), rural African scenes, and shots of African masks and sculptures. Using newsreel collage in the manner of some Soviet and Cuban filmmakers, Cissé gathers yonder space and time, the painter's sources of inspiration. Punctuating the soundtrack of this film with excerpts of poems by Senghor (Senegal) and Césaire (Martinique) mingled with songs interpreted by Myriam Makeba (South Africa) and traditional African music, the filmmaker emphasizes the cultural role and the social function of the artist who, far from being secluded in an ivory tower, expresses on canvas his cultural roots as well as the struggles and hopes of Blacks beyond historical and/or geographic boundaries. In *L'Aspirant*, Souleymane Cissé compares modern Western medicine to traditional African healing through the experience of a young doctor (the son of a village diviner) who goes abroad to further his studies.

Besides short newsreels on Malian current affairs, Cissé has made several documentaries that focus on primarily sociocultural events and celebrate Mali's rich traditional patrimony. Among such films are *Degal à Dialloubé* and *Fête du Sanke*. *Degal à Dialloubé* depicts farmers' rituals that take place on the occasion of the yearly river crossing of cattle in search of new grazing pastures. *Fête du Sanke* illustrates the annual festivities of fishermen at San, a city located in the southeastern part of Mali.

Cinq jours d'une vie is a critical depiction of what Cissé views as the obsolete and unpractical education dispensed in today's Black African Koranic schools (a topic also treated by Mahama Johnson Traoré* in his film *Njangaan*). The motion picture also stresses the hardships (unemployment, vagrancy, petty larcenies, and imprisonment) suffered by displaced rural youth ill-prepared to cope with the demands of urban life, and advocates returning to the village environment for which they are better suited. The title of the film reflects the five main days of the protagonist's circular path of initiation from his first day of Koranic school to the day he decides to go back home and work after having been released from jail.

In *Den Muso*, Cissé shares with us the tragic destiny of an unwed pregnant girl in a Muslim urban surrounding, and explores Mali's social order. *Den Muso* is the story of Tenin, a deaf-mute girl from a middle-class family who discovers she is pregnant by Sekou, one of her father's former workers. A tragic sequence of events follows this disclosure: Tenin is rejected by her parents, her father dies of a heart attack, and Sekou denies having fathered the expected child. Angered by her lover's irresponsible attitude and then thoroughly distressed at finding him in bed with another woman, Tenin sets his hut on fire and commits suicide. Through showing how his female protagonist is "brutally confronted with the traditional and backward morals of her parents," Cissé wanted to depict a similar fate met by many urban girls who become alienated because they have "sinned" and are no longer wanted at home. According to the filmmaker, his choice of a mute character symbolizes the fact that in this society "women are not allowed to express opinions" *(Le Monde Diplomatique,* September 1978, p. 13).

Baara is the first Black African film to explore with some depth the status of the embryonic working class of developing Africa. *Baara* singles out the exploitation of the local labor force subjected to the whims, greed, and corruption of some of its post colonial mercantile elite. It also pinpoints the workers' awakening social awareness and subsequent struggle while highlighting the status of women, repressed by the same patriarchal bourgeoisie. Cissé insists that "nothing in the film is invented: the story is created on the basis of daily life" *(Framework,* August 1979, p. 17). However, to cautiously avoid total identification and possible court suits, the following words (in Bambara) appear on the screen at the beginning of his film: ''Any resemblance to any person living or dead is purely coincidental.''

The rather busy plot of *Baara* unfolds through the candid eyes of Balla Diarra, a young porter from the countryside who, like many others, comes to town looking for work in order to return later to his village. The film opens on an early morning scene, the awakening of several porters sharing a single room. Balla Diarra then starts his day in search of deliveries to make by means of his handpushed cart. This fortuitously leads him to witness a pregnant woman and her children being brutally ousted by her husband. Pitying her fate, Balla Diarra carries her belongings without making her pay. Next, he works for a market woman who will eventually cheat him. Finally, the porter runs an errand for Balla Traoré, a young engineer who befriends him and hires him to work in his textile factory. Subsequently, the democratically minded engineer (who nonetheless prevents his educated wife from working outside the home) sets out to reorganize his plant, lending a sympathetic ear to workers' demands. However, the engineer's initiatives are strongly disapproved by his corrupt boss, who has him beaten to death before killing his own unfaithful wife, Djenaba. *Baara* ends as an angry group of workers attempts to avenge the engineer by killing the boss; the latter is barely rescued by the police, who come to arrest him for having murdered Djenaba. *Baara*'s very last picture is the freeze frame of a shot which had already appeared at its beginning, that of Balla Traoré preceding Balla Diarra as they simultaneously walk (in slow motion) through a metaphorically purifying bushfire.

The necessary link to *Baara*'s multifaceted plot, purposely based on a somewhat disruptive editing, is provided through its musical score, composed by Lamine Konté, a noted West African composer and performer. Commenting on the soundtrack of his film, Cissé states:

It was a film I had conceived completely without music—that is, to be closer to reality. But the music in the film is part of that reality because it is used as folklore. . . . It's why there are these two or three themes linking the film. The music is taken from folklore and modernized by Lamine Konté. It's used like a dialogue because the words of the songs directly relate to the life of this porter. . . . the theme song of *Baara* reflects on how people must make contacts with the workers: instead of outlawing workers, mistreating them, people would do better to help them organize. *(Framework,* August 1979, p. 17)

From the start *Finyé* (The Wind)—with its opening epigraph, ''The wind awakens the thoughts of man,'' which suggests change and evolution—appears as both a sociocultural and political statement. ''The title of the film . . . is composed of ideograms in the Bambara language that represent the evident traces of a heritage to be preserved . . . or perhaps to be rediscovered.'' On a symbolic level, the wind refers to movement; it is ''the wind of the mind, the wind of history, a wind that sometimes disturbs and other times unifies. . . . A wind of change which effaces past errors . . . '' (both of the above quotations are from *Finyé*'s production press kit).

Although the film is shot in Bamako, the plot takes place in ''an African city today. A world where the social structures are disintegrating'' (press kit). Thematically, *Finyé* illustrates the conflict between modernity and tradition, the problems faced by urban youth in a changing African social milieu, corruption, the abuse of military power, polygamy, and the overall status and role of women in the Sahelian areas of Africa.

Finyé depicts the story of a forbidden love between Batrou and Bah, two socially divergent high school seniors. Batrou is the daughter of Sangaré, a corrupt and authoritative middle-aged polygamous military governor. Bah is the descendant of Kansaye, an elderly traditional chief whose land has been misappropriated by Sangaré. Both families disapprove of the relationship. Batrou will get in open conflict with her father as she decides to participate with Bah in a student protest triggered by a falsification of exam results. The students are brutally repressed by the military, which leads to the arrest and imprisonment of Bah and Batrou. Subsequently, in another effort to separate the two lovers, Sangaré orders Bah's deportation to a work camp. Yet, far from being weakened, the bond between the two is strengthened. Upon learning of Bah's fate, Kansaye goes to seek help from the spirits of the Sacred Wood, with whom he has a dialogue:

KANSAYE: I've come to plead for help, the chiefs have arrested my only hope, the last son of my race, help me so that he'll be safe and sound.

THE SPIRIT: I can see two stars darting across the sky. Between the stars, there shines a tiny star. It is coming towards us, it shines all over the planet . . . the sky is changing color. It is getting darker, that means that our knowledge escapes us. The divine forces have deserted us now, act according to your strength and what you know. Make offerings and go. From now on, act on your own instincts.

After receiving this answer, Kansaye goes to confront Sangaré. Protected by the spirits, Kansaye is able to evade the bullets of Sangaré, who attempts to kill him. Then, as he returns to his compound, Kansaye discovers that the soldiers have ransacked his home. Infuriated by their raid, Kansaye resorts no longer to supernatural powers but instead burns his amulets and his traditional attire before joining a group of student protestors, to whom he shouts: ''God bless you, what you are doing is without a price, our time is over, the world is yours. I will stand by you.'' Conscious of the magnitude and power of such mass demonstrations, the civil authorities order the release of the students, and Bah is freed. *Finyé*'s last scene continues its opening sequence, that of a young boy on a river bank. The film ends with a freeze frame of the child offering a gourd filled with water (a traditional symbol of communication and union) to an off-screen receiver.

Yeelen takes place in a rural setting among one of Mali's ethnic groups, the

Bambara. It is a timeless story which depicts the transmission of knowledge, as well as conflicts between father and son.

SURVEY OF CRITICISM

Many reviews and interviews concerning the works of Souleymane Cissé have appeared over the years in popular magazines and film periodicals. And, at an early stage, a number of film critics were prompt to notice signs of an encouraging talent in his first works. Among these were Paulin Soumanou Vieyra,* for whom *L'Aspirant* presents undeniable technical qualities *(Le Cinéma africain,* 1975, p. 122), and Ferid Boughedir, who is impressed by that same film's "sensitivity and accuracy" *(Cinéma Québec,* August 1974, p. 33). Otherwise, both Howard Schissel *(The Guardian,* 10 May 1984, p. 15) and Charles Tesson *(Cahiers du Cinéma,* February 1982, p. 40) offer favorable reviews of *Den Muso.*

Some of the most substantive comments concerning Cissé's film *Baara* are those of Azzedine Mabrouki, who writes:

Here is the kind of film many African filmmakers dream of making. A film which judiciously uses the resources of cinematic language, which situates itself so far from demagogy, from convention, from heavy and sterile discourse. It is first of all a profoundly authentic Malian film. . . . Everything is subtle and finished in the work of this filmmaker. His political project is located at the level of style. Cissé prefers detail which expresses many things, a fine continuous line, scrupulously careful framing and efficient rhythm to pretentious effects and talk. What a pleasure to see African actors avoiding verbiage and achieving this precise, studied and truthful acting. What strength and sensitivity is apparent in the smallest details of this work—as much as at the level of the scenario as in the directing." *(Les 2 Ecrans,* June 1978, pp. 34–35)

Likewise, Ferid Boughedir *(Jeune Afrique,* 4 October 1978, p. 44), Emmanuel Carrère *(Télérama,* 18 August 1982, p. 59), Biny Traoré *(Peuples Noirs, Peuples Africains,* May-June 1983, p. 56), Louis Marcorelles *(Le Monde,* 20 October 1984, p. 15), and Christian Bosseno *(La Revue du Cinéma, Image et Son,* November 1984, pp. 29–30) praise Cissé's work for its lucid depiction of the conflicts generated by the awakening social consciousness of Black Africa's incipient proletariat. Mosk *(Variety,* 23 August 1978, p. 36) concurs with these views, stressing that "Director Suleyman *[sic]* Cisse blocks out his characters knowingly as well as the underlying social problems . . ." adding that *Baara* "may still be too didactic in wrapping up its tale but still reveals a fine narrative sense, a feel for problems and human values. More suited for fests than for commercial changes abroad as yet, it still is another shaft of talent from Africa."

Stylistically, Paulin Soumanou Vieyra is struck by *Baara*'s disruptive film language, which, according to him, induces the viewers' pondering over what is shown and said *(Présence Africaine,* 2nd Quarter 1979, p. 164). Cherifa Benabdessadok notes its masterful intermingling of comical and tragic events—in particular when Djenaba's panic-stricken lover hops out of her bed upon the unexpected arrival of her husband, a scene almost immediately followed by her murder *(Afrique-Asie,* 3 December 1984, p. 64). Among other positive characteristics, Boughedir admires the style of *Baara,* which he holds as a true reflection of the pace and rhythm of African life *(Jeune Afrique,* 13 December 1978, p. 92). Moreover, G. Drabo *(Podium,* 31 May 1978, p. 6) and Rose Bastide *(L'Essor,* 21 December 1978, p. 4) concur on *Baara's* pictorial beauty as well as on the sober and natural performance of its actors. As for Angela Martin, she finds that "across a very busy plot, and with skillful direction, acting, camera work and editing, the film works through—without attempting to resolve—a number of important contradictions" *(Framework,* Spring 1979, p. 43).

Yet *Baara* has not been met solely with favorable criticism. Walter V. Addiego finds it "disappointingly . . . simplistic, slapdash and lacking in imagination," with a "contrived, melodramatic storyline" *(San Francisco Examiner,* 18 October 1980, p. A9). For Bernard Genin, the film is rather confusing, schematic, and somewhat scattered in spite of the effectiveness of its social content *(Télérama,* 20 October 1984, p. 42). On the contrary, Victor Bachy perceives *Baara* as a rich and dense motion picture but also acknowledges that it may be confusing for Western viewers *(La Revue du Cinéma, Image et Son,* July 1979, p. 51). Finally, Segun Oyekunle considers that "Cissé's *Barra [sic]* is too conclusive and optimistic" in suggesting that the engineer's death will indeed instigate social change *(West Africa,* 28 November 1983, p. 2729). His opinion is shared by Howard Schissel, according to whom *Baara's* "positive conclusion, in line with the socialist realism tradition, is probably overly optimistic" *(The Guardian,* 10 May 1984, p. 15).

Even more so than *Baara, Finyé* has won extensive international coverage. As in the case of *Baara,* it is primarily the keen realism and the definite sociopolitical orientation of its subject matter which have drawn most critical attention. According to Prairie:

The Wind is a frank, compassionate drama about a society in transition, and the conflicts that arise between people as they attempt to reconcile traditional values with modern customs, all the while seeking a fresh, meaningful outlook that is somehow a combination of the two. *(Daily World,* 5 October 1983, p. 9D)

Howard Schissel finds that "with shocking realism the film lashes out at the venal practices of African politicians and the brutal means used to crush all opposition to autocratic rule" *(The Guardian,* 10 May 1984, p. 15). For Anne Kieffer, *Finyé's* "incisive portrayal of an egotistic bourgeoisie" is somewhat reminiscent of Sembene's *Xala (Jeune Cinéma,* April 1983, p. 43). Ferid Boughedir calls *Finyé* "a striking meditation on today's Africa" *(Jeune Afrique,* 17 November 1982, p. 100) and praises Cissé's ability to make an innovative film based upon easily identifiable daily events *(Jeune Afrique,* 2 March 1983, p. 78). Liliane Larmoyer considers *Finyé* "a beautiful love story deeply rooted in contemporary Malian life" whose sociological and political implications are related in a tale-like fashion *(La Vie,* 5 May 1983, p. 21). Similarly, Paul-Bernard Chevillard sees it in turn as "a love story, a political satire, a Malian chronicle, a fairy-tale, a melodrama" *(La Croix,* 21 April 1983, p. 19), while Marcel Martin essentially perceives this "vigorous film" as a "political pamphlet" *(La Revue du Cinéma, Image et Son,* July-August 1982, p. 60). Although she shows an overall appreciation of *Finyé* (to which she nonetheless prefers *Baara),* Maryse Condé would have wished for more clarity in Cissé's ideological discourse. She remarks:

One must admire the courage of Souleymane Cissé who was bold enough to present such a film in a country ruled by the military. Yet aren't there limits to his accusation? We seemingly are invited to condemn the excess of a regime rather than its true nature. *(Afrique,* July 1982, p. 52)

Jacques Siclier *(Le Monde,* 15 May 1982, p. 24), Charles Tesson *(Cahiers du Cinéma,* July-August 1982, p. 22), and Paulo Antonio Paranagua *(Positif,* July-August 1982, p. 79) respectively view *Finyé* as soberly realistic, unconstrained, lyrical, and vivacious. Jean-Marie Gibbal observes that Cissé's sober work is stamped with an epic and at times farcical tone which calls to mind the narratives and *chansons de geste* of the Mandingo oral tradition *(Positif,* February 1983, p. 82). According to Janet Maslin:

Cissé's feeling for his characters is strong, and they are vividly drawn; his film works best when it approaches them individually, since the group scenes are sometimes indirect and mildly confusing. . . . The film's most impassioned sequence is a mystical one in which Ba's *[sic]* grandfather communes with a deity, praying for his grandson's future, and in a broader sense, that of his culture, *New York Times,* 24 September 1983, p. 11)

Didier Goldschmidt *(Cinématographe,* June 1982, p. 54) and Ginette Gervais *(Jeune Cinéma,* July-August 1982) are also sensitive to Cissé's use of allegory.

Apart from Anne de Gaspéri's rather far-fetched comparison of *Finyé's* young protagonists with James Dean and his tormented peers in the 1955 *Rebel Without a Cause (Le Quotidien de Paris,* 26 April 1983, p. 34), all film critics insist on *Finyé*'s Black African authenticity. Hence, says Holl, *"The Wind* scores as one of the most forceful pics to emerge from Africa thus far in this decade" *(Variety,* 26 May 1982, p. 19). A number of reviewers focus on Cissé's outstanding skills as director, and the amount of material available on him is an indication of his growing importance in the field of Sub-Saharan African cinema.

FILMOGRAPHY

L'Homme et les idoles (Man and Idols), 35 mm, color, 10 min., 1965.
Sources d'inspiration (Sources of Inspiration), 35 mm, black and white, 8 min., 1966.
L'Aspirant (The Aspirant), 35 mm, color, 20 min., 1968.
Degal à Dialloubé (Degal at Dialloubé), 35 mm, black and white, 20 min., 1970.
Fête du Sanke (The Sanke Celebration), 35 mm, black and white, 15 min., 1971.

Made thirty newsreel films and five documentaries produced by the Service Cinémato-
graphique du Ministère de l'Information du Mali (SCINFOMA), 1970–1971.
Cinq jours d'une vie (Five Days in a Life), 16 mm, black and white, 40 min., 1972.
Dixième anniversaire de l'OUA (Tenth Anniversary of the Organization of African Unity),
16 mm, black and white, 30 min., 1973.
Den Muso (The Young Girl), 16 mm, color, 90 min., 1974.
Baara (Work), 16/35 mm, color, 90 min., 1978.
Finyé (The Wind), 35 mm, color, 100 min., 1982.

BIBLIOGRAPHY

Writings by Souleymane Cissé

Cissé, Souleymane. "Mali: refléter la trame du quotidien."*Le Monde Diplomatique*,
September 1978, p. 13.
———. "La Chronique de Souleymane Cissé." *Libération*, 15–16 May 1982, p. 22.

Interviews of Souleymane Cissé

Barrat, Patrice. "Souleymane Cissé: V'la l'bon vent." *Les Nouvelles Littéraires*, 28 April
1983, p. 46.
Chevillard, Paul-Bernard. "C'est le vent." *La Croix*, 21 April 1983, p. 19.
Cressole, Michel. "L'Energie éolienne de Cissé." *Libération*, 20 April 1983, p. 19.
Dami, Samirou. "L'Important c'est le contact avec le public." *La Presse de Tunisie*,
26 November 1978, p. 5.
Hennebelle, Guy. "Vers un cinéma malien? Une interview de Souleymane Cissé."
Afrique-Asie, 14 May 1973, p. 46.
Martin, Angela. "Four Filmmakers from West Africa." *Framework*, Issue 11, Autumn
1979, pp. 16–21.
Mimoun, Mouloud, and Moulay, B. "Entretien avec Souleymane Cissé—'Le Vent,' cette
ouverture sur le monde." *Les 2 Ecrans*, n. 47–48, July-August 1982, pp. 20–22.
"Rencontre avec Souleymane Cissé" *Calao*, May-June 1983, pp. 3–5.
Ruelle, Catherine. "Bourrasques au Mali." *Le Magazine Littéraire*, May 1983, p. 44.
Ruelle, Catherine, and Andrée Tournes. "Cissé, Souleymane." *L'Afrique Littéraire et
Artistique*, n. 49, 3rd Quarter 1978, pp. 28–31.
Schidlow, Joshka. "Les Sources de Souleymane Cissé." *Télérama*, n. 1736, 20 April
1983, p. 34.
Schissel, Howard. "People's Film-maker." *West Africa*, 7 May 1984, pp. 973–74.
Stern, Yvan. "Interview: Souleymane Cissé." *Unir Cinéma*, n. 23–24 (130–131), March-
April and May-June 1986, pp. 44–45.
Tapsoba, Clément. "Souleymane Cissé: Nous, cinéastes et africains, ne devons pas fuir
nos responsabilités." *Carrefour Africain*, n. 766, 18 February 1983, pp. 18–19.
Tournes, Andrée. "Entretien avec Souleymane Cissé." *Jeune Cinéma*, n. 119, June
1979, pp. 16–17.

Film Reviews and Studies of Souleymane Cissé

Addiego, Walter V. "A Disappointing Film from Mali." *San Francisco Examiner*, 18
October 1980, p. A9.

Amiel, Mireille. "Baara de Souleymane Cissé." *Cinéma 84*, n. 311, November 1984, pp. 38–39.

Arthuys, Xavier d'. "Les Mensonges à peau d'éléphant." *Les Nouvelles Littéraires*, 28 April 1983, p. 47.

Aubert, Alain. "Ouagadougou." *Ecran 79*, n. 82, 15 July 1979, pp. 15–16.

Ayari, Farida. "Souleymane Cissé—un Sarakollé [sic] sur la Croisette." *Libération*, 18 May 1982, p. 5.

———. "Images de femmes." *Cinémaction*, n. 26, 1983, pp. 136–39.

Bachy, Victor. "Un (Relativement) Nouveau venu au cinéma: le Mali." *La Revue du Cinéma, Image et Son*, n. 341, July 1979, pp. 47–51.

———. *Le Cinéma au Mali*. Brussels: OCIC/L'Harmattan, 1983.

Baecque, Antoine de. "Balla le pousseur, Balla l'ingénieur." *Cahiers du Cinéma*, n. 366, December 1984, pp. 50–52.

Baroncelli, Jean de. "Films francophones à Namur; tristes histoires du monde réel." *Le Monde*, 21 September 1978, p. 20.

Bassan, Raphael, "Cannes 82: le tiers monde en force." *Afrique-Asie*, n. 269, 21 June 1982, pp. 54–56.

———. "Le Vent de l'esprit souffle sur le Mali." *Afrique-Asie*, n. 288, 31 January 1983, pp. 56–57.

———. "Le Vent." *La Revue du Cinéma, Image et Son*, n. 379, January 1983, p. 34.

Bastide, Rose. "Le Triomphe d'une oeuvre forte." *L'Essor*, 21 December 1978, p. 4.

Benabdessadok, Cherifa. "Baara: les héros du quotidien." *Afrique-Asie*, n. 336, 3 December 1984, pp. 63–64.

Binet, Jacques. "Le Cinéma africain." *Afrique Contemporaine*, n. 123, September-October 1982, pp. 5–8.

Bosséno, Christian. "Baara—les temps modernes de l'Afrique." *La Revue du Cinéma, Image et Son*, n. 399, November 1984, pp. 29–30.

Boughedir, Ferid. "Le Cinéma malien: premiers balbutiements." *Cinéma Québec*, vol. 3, n. 9–10, August 1974, p. 33.

———. "Le Cinéma africain hors des ghettos." *Jeune Afrique*, n. 791, 5 March 1976, pp. 43–45.

———. "L'Afrique à la une chez les 'francophones' à Namur." *Jeune Afrique*, n. 926, 4 October 1978, pp. 44–45.

———. "Carthage 78: pari tenu pour les Africains et les Arabes." *Jeune Afrique*, n. 936, 13 December 1978, pp. 91–93.

———. "A L'Est du nouveau. . . ." *Jeune Afrique*, n. 1088, 11 November 1981, p. 83.

———. "Le Vent en poupe." *Jeune Afrique*, n. 1141, 17 November 1982, pp. 100–01.

———. "Une Nouvelle Vague de cinéastes." *Jeune Afrique*, n. 1156, 2 March 1983, pp. 78–79.

———. "Des Films dans 'le vent.'" *Jeune Afrique*, n. 1172, 22 June 1983, pp. 76–77.

———. "Une Oasis en Somalie." *Jeune Afrique*, n. 1191, 2 November 1983, pp. 72–73.

———. "1982–83: de Carthage IX à Ouagadougou VIII—nouvelle génération, nouveaux espoirs." *Cinémaction*, n. 26, 1983, pp. 178–185.

Braudeau, Michel. "Rituels blancs et magie noire." *Le Monde*, 10–11 May 1987, p. 9.

Carrère, Emmanuel. "Baara." *Télérama*, n. 1701, 18 August 1982, p. 59.

Cervoni, Albert. "Explorations africaines." *L'Humanité,* 1 July 1978, p. 8.

——. "Le Vent." *Cinéma 82,* n. 283–84, July-August 1982, p. 42.

Chevallier, Jacques. "Le Vent." *L'Education Hebdo,* n. 28, 5 May 1983, p. 7.

Condé, Maryse. "Le Vent réveille la pensée des hommes." *Afrique,* n. 61, July 1982, p. 52.

Cressole, Michel. "Le Souffle de Souleymane Cissé." *Libération,* 20 April 1983, p. 19.

——. "Dans la chaleur de Ouaga." *Libération,* 15 March 1985, pp. 30–31.

"Developing Africa's Cinema." *West Africa,* n. 3358, 7 December 1981, pp. 2911–14.

Drabo, G. "Baara ou les ombres de la ville." *Podium,* 31 May 1978, p. 6.

Gaspéri, Anne de. "Cissé, un Malien dans le vent." *Le Quotidien de Paris,* n. 1062, 26 April 1983, p. 34.

Genin, Bernard. "Baara." *Télérama,* n. 1814, 20 October 1984, p. 42.

Gervais, Ginette. "Le Vent." *Jeune Cinéma,* n. 144, July-August 1982, p. 41.

Gibbal, Jean-Marie. "Le Vent." *Positif,* n. 264, February 1983, pp. 81–82.

Goldschmidt, Didier. "Finyé." *Cinématographe,* n. 79, June 1982, p. 54.

Guerrini, Pierre. "Le Vent de Souleymane Cissé." *Cinéma 83,* n. 293, May 1983, p. 41.

Holl. "Finyé." *Variety,* 26 May 1982, pp. 19, 24.

Ilboudou, Patrick, and Jacob Olivier. "Fespaco, l'autre regard du cinéma." *L'Observateur,* n. 2525, 9 February 1983, pp. 1, 6–7.

Jamet, Dominique. "Le Vent de Souleymane Cissé—du souffle." *Le Quotidien de Paris,* n. 1062, 26 April 1983, p. 34.

"Les Journées du Cinéma Africain au Québec." *Haiti-Observateur,* 3 May 1985, p. 6.

Kieffer, Anne. "Cinéma d'Afrique noire au festival des Trois Continents." *Jeune Cinéma,* n. 149, March 1983, pp. 10–13.

——. "Le Vent." *Jeune Cinéma,* n. 150, April 1983, pp. 42–43.

Larmoyer, Liliane. "Le Vent." *La Vie,* n. 2863, 5 May 1983, p. 21.

Mabrouki, Azzedine. "Baara." *Les 2 Ecrans,* n. 4, June 1978, pp. 34–35.

——. "L'An VI." *Les 2 Ecrans,* n. 12, April 1979, pp. 9–12.

Maiga, Mohammed. "Le Mali revient à l'écran." *Jeune Afrique,* n. 990–91, 26 December 1980, p. 81.

Marcorelles, Louis. "Baara, de Souleymane Cissé—l'Afrique d'une harmonie perdue." *Le Monde,* 20 October 1984, p. 15.

Martin, Angela. "Ougadougu [sic]." *Framework,* issue 10, Spring 1979, pp. 42–43.

——. *African Films: The Context of Production.* London: British Film Institute, 1982.

Martin, Marcel. "Afrique: présence de la vie quotidienne." *La Revue du Cinéma, Image et Son,* n. 374, July-August 1982, pp. 58, 60.

——. "Carthage: à la recherche de l'unité . . ." *La Revue du Cinéma, Image et Son,* n. 379, January 1983, pp. 86–87.

Maslin, Janet. " 'Wind' from Mali and 'Reassemblage' in Senegal." *New York Times,* 24 September 1983, p. 11.

Mativo, Kyalo. "Resolving the Cultural Dilemma of the African Film." *UFAHAMU,* vol. 13, n. 1, Fall 1983, pp. 134–46.

Mosk. "Baara." *Variety,* 23 August 1978, pp. 34, 36.

N, B. "Le Vent de Cissé." *Bwana,* May 1983, p. 24.

Oyekunle, Segun. "Africans in Hollywood." *West Africa,* 28 November 1983, pp. 2728–29.

P, S-L. "Vive 'Le Vent.' " *Libération,* 15–16 May 1982, p. 21.

Paranagua, Paulo Antonio. "Afrique noire." *Positif,* n. 257–258, July-August 1982, p. 79.

Peroncel-Hugoz, J-P. "Le Sacre de Souleymane." *Le Monde,* 2 November 1982, p. 13.

Peyrière, Marie-Christine. "Un Réalisateur à tout faire." *Jeune Afrique,* n. 1166, 11 May 1983, pp. 50–51.

Prairie. "Films Reveal Contrasting Objectives." *Daily World,* 5 October 1983, p. 9D.

Relich, Mario. "On Screen at the London Film Festival." *West Africa,* 19 December 1983, pp. 2940–41.

Sanchis, Vincente. "Yeelen." *Revista de Cine,* n. 148, June 1987, p. 36.

Schidlow, Joshka. "Les Ancêtres ne répondent plus." *Télérama,* n. 1736, 20 April 1983, p. 34.

Schissel, Howard. "Reel Time." *The Guardian,* 10 May 1984, p. 15.

Schoenberner, Gerhard. "Det svarta Africas filmer och deras regissörer." *Chaplin 166,* n. 1, 1980, pp. 10–15.

Siclier, Jacques. "Générations maliennes." *Le Monde,* 15 May 1982, p. 24.

Stern, Yvan. "Finyé." *Unir Cinéma,* n. 23–24 (130–131), March-April and May-June 1986, pp. 43–44.

Tesson, Charles. "La Route des Phillippines." *Cahiers du Cinéma,* n. 332, February 1982, pp. 39–43.

———. "Le Vent de Souleymane Cissé." *Cahiers du Cinéma,* n. 338, July-August 1982, pp. 22–23.

Touil, Hatem. "Giornate del Cinema Africano: Perugia città aperta." *Nigrizzia,* June 1985, p. 44.

Traoré, Biny. "Cinéma africain et développement." *Peuples Noirs, Peuples Africains,* n. 33, May-June 1983, pp. 51–62.

"Le Vent de Souleymane Cissé." *Révolution,* n. 169, 27 May 1983, p. 40.

Vieyra, Paulin Soumanou. "Carthage 78." *Présence Africaine,* n. 110, 2nd Quarter 1979, pp. 157–66.

———. "FESPACO 1979." *Présence Africaine,* n. 111, 3rd Quarter 1979, pp. 101–6.

———. "Présence africaine." *Le Soleil,* 24 June 1982, p. 19.

Yvoire, Jean d'. "Baara." *Jeune Cinéma,* n. 163, December 1984–January 1985, pp. 31–32.

Zongo, Célestin. "A mon avis." *Journal du 8ᵉ FESPACO,* n. 3, 13 February 1983, p. 7.

Jean-Pierre Dikongue-Pipa (1940–   )
Cameroon

BIOGRAPHY

Jean-Pierre Dikongue-Pipa was born on 20 October 1940 in Douala, Cameroon's main commercial center, located in the southwestern part of the country near the Gulf of Guinea. A Christian, Dikongue-Pipa is of Douala origin, which links him to a minority ethnic group of some 30,000 people in a nation that has close to 8 million inhabitants. His father was a literate man, well versed in the study of African legends and myths, whose nationalistic ideas were considered dangerous by the French authorities at a time when a part of Cameroon was under French colonial rule. He was subsequently arrested and deported during the Second World War. The filmmaker expounds:

When the Second World War began, it was discovered that some Cameroonians were exchanging letters with Germans to denounce French colonization. . . . My father was deported, my uncle was executed in my presence. I saw all of this through the eyes of a three-year-old child. I have not forgotten such a sight. . . . *(Actuel Développement, n. 25, 1978, p. 37)*

Thus, most of Dikongue-Pipa's early childhood was spent in the care of his mother. At the age of nine, young Jean-Pierre discovered cinema through the films of Charlie Chaplin, which were being shown in Douala's movie theaters. Soon, notwithstanding his parents' disapproval, he became a very assiduous film viewer who tried to re-create at home the magic of film by means of shadow shows. He now remembers:

I have always liked cinema . . . cinema somewhat brought to life the world of fables and legends which I had always been fed on as an African. I rediscovered on movie screens the fictitious world of the elders' tales. *(Ecran 76, 15 July 1976, p. 56)*

Yet, since in those days access to a camera for an African youth was an impossible dream, the adolescent sought compensation in the theater. At sixteen, with a few schoolmates, he created his own theater troupe, the ''Jeunesse artistique club'' (Artistic Youth Club), for which he wrote a few short plays that incorporated dance and pantomime. Subsequently, Dikongue-Pipa was sent to France, where he completed high school.

After some brief studies in the field of electrical engineering ''to please my father,'' and a budding career as a professional soccer player in Nice (1961–1962), Dikongue-Pipa decided to become seriously involved in cinema. Consequently, he registered at the Conservatoire Indépendent du Cinéma Français in Paris, where he was to be trained as a filmmaker from 1962 to 1964. There, while studying various film trends, he was particularly impressed by the works of Jean Renoir and Jean Cocteau, whom he admired for their poetic contribution to French cinema (Recherche, Pédagogie et Culture, May-August 1976, p. 56). After graduating from film school, Dikongue-Pipa supported himself by working as a substitute clerk for the Parisian municipal services while seeking opportunities to make films. With the help of the French Ministry of Cooperation, which provided him with some raw film stock, Dikongue-Pipa managed to film three documentaries entitled Un Simple (Down to Earth, 1965), Rendez-moi mon père (Give Me Back My Father, 1966), and Les Cornes (The Horns, 1966). All these films have yet to be provided a soundtrack and have only been privately screened.

Somewhat disappointed by his early attempts at filmmaking in France, in 1966 Dikongue-Pipa decided to return to Cameroon, where he started working for the Douala French Cultural Center. It was at this time that he created a new theater troupe, L'Avant-Garde Africaine, with which he was to stage no less than twenty-seven plays (including two of his own) over a ten-year period. Also in 1966, Dikongue-Pipa unsuccessfully submitted a $110,000 film proposal entitled ''Le Banc de Sable'' (Sand-bank) to the Cameroonian film bureau. A few years later, with that same project retitled Muna Moto (The Other's Child), the cinéaste obtained financial support from the French Ministry of Cooperation, which granted him $3,500, thereby acquiring exclusive noncommercial rights to the forthcoming film. With this meager budget and an additional loan from the Centre Audiovisuel International (CAI), a single 16 mm camera borrowed from the French Cultural Center, and an indomitable faith, Dikongue-Pipa ventured into filming his first feature length motion picture. Muna Moto's actors (including Dikongue-Pipa, who plays a police officer in the film) were for the most part recruited among the members of Dikongue-Pipa's theater troupe, and they agreed to work without salary with the understanding that they would be remunerated later if and when the film proved profitable. The director describes the esprit de corps that prevailed among his performers in the following words: ''We know each other well and we always work together. . . . While the film was being shot, all the actors felt personally involved. It was their film, our common project'' (Recherche, Pédagogie et Culture, May-August 1976, p. 54).

Because of a series of interruptions due to insufficient funding, the shooting of Muna Moto took nine months. The director recalls:

I had to pass the hat around, I had to beg left and right . . . some friends would lend me ten dollars or less to support my crew through the next day or to take a taxi to transport the equipment. The film was shot day by day. *(Recherche, Pédagogie et Culture,* May-August 1976, p. 54)

Yet, for Dikongue-Pipa another trial was to occur once the entire film had been shot. He recollects:

I had not been able to screen the rushes while shooting. And, in Paris at the editing stage, we discovered with sheer dread that the camera had been defective and that a part of what we had shot could not be used. As a consequence, crucial scenes are missing in the final version of the film. *(Ecran 76,* 15 July 1976, p. 57)

Such regrettable events came to a happy end, nevertheless. Once completed, *Muna Moto* was the first Cameroonian feature film to be both featured and acclaimed at several international film festivals. In 1975 *Muna Moto* was presented at the Moscow and Venice film festivals, won the First Prize at the Festival International du Film de l'Ensemble Francophone (FIFEF) held in Geneva and the Georges Sadoul Prize in France (jointly awarded to *Kaddu beykat* by Safi Faye* and *Nationalité immigrée* by Sidney Sokhona). The following year, *Muna Moto* was awarded the First Prize ("Etalon de Yenenga") at the fifth Pan-African Film Festival of Ouagadougou (Burkina Faso) and the Second Prize ("Tanit d'Argent") at the Carthage Film Festival (Tunisia). However, this black and white film, which employed unusual and complex editing to incorporate interspersed flashbacks and dream sequences, had an unspectacular commercial release in Cameroon, and was infrequently shown in other Sub-Saharan African countries. Thus, for his second feature film, *Le Prix de la liberté* (The Price of Freedom, 1978), which was financed through bank loans and made with the technical support of the Institut National de l'Audiovisuel (INA), Dikongue-Pipa opted for a more popular formula. Using standard narrative patterns, shot in color, and enhanced with a score by the well-known Cameroonian musician Manu Dibango, *Le Prix de la liberté* had a greater mass appeal but received much less critical endorsement than *Muna Moto*.

In 1982 Dikongue-Pipa shot *Histoires drôles, drôles de gens* (Funny Stories, Funny People), one of the rare sketch films of Black African cinema, followed in 1983 by two other feature-length pictures, *Courte Maladie* (Brief Illness) and *Music and Music,* also geared to popular audiences. Since 1983 Dikongue-Pipa has been involved in the making of *La Cicatrice* (The Scar), a semi-autobiographical film that addresses the colonization of Africa. With this film, his stated design is to facilitate the perception of certain painful past events in their historical context so as to instigate a genuine understanding between Black Africans and their former rulers. Dikongue-Pipa points out:

I deeply believe that only an unequivocal discussion will generate a true understanding between blacks and whites. This happened with the Germans in Europe after the Second

World War. . . . some people will probably view the film as being political. My aim is not to make a political film but only a dramatic one. I am interested in its characters rather than the promotion of my political ideas. *(Actuel Développement,* n. 25, 1978, p. 37)

Yet only the future will tell whether *La Cicatrice*'s delayed completion should be attributed solely to economic reasons or to the film's sensitive political implications as well.

In spite of his admiration for Ingmar Bergman, Luis Buñuel, Ousmane Sembene,* and Souleymane Cissé,* as well as some French and American filmmakers, Dikongue-Pipa says that he has not been strongly influenced by any of them and is still searching for an original means of expression that would reflect his sensitivity and allow him to communicate effectively with his African viewers. Based on this premise, and in spite of his sporadic use of Douala and Bassa (two of the African languages spoken in Cameroon) in *Muna Moto,* Dikongue-Pipa (unlike most of his counterparts who vouch for linguistical authenticity) shows a marked preference for the use of French in his films rather than an African language with subtitles, which could be read by but a few in a largely illiterate country. He states:

The characters in my films speak French because French is the most widespread vehicle for communication in Cameroon where 427 vernacular languages coexist. Take my own case for instance, I belong to the Douala ethnic group which has barely 30,000 people; if I made a film in Douala I would have to subtitle it in French and this would make its understanding even more difficult. *(Le Monde Diplomatique,* September 1978, p. 13)

Dikongue-Pipa maintains that the major problem presently faced by Black African filmmakers is that of inadequate local and foreign distribution of their films, a factor which considerably hampers their creativity. According to him, a number of African governments have until now used cinema as a convenient tool for propaganda and have shown limited interest in its growth as a part of their cultural, educational, and economical development policies, thus allowing the continued "cultural imperialism" exerted by foreign distribution companies in most Black African countries *(Fraternité Matin,* 6 November 1979, pp. 15–16). Nonetheless, in spite of such drawbacks and his own difficulties in completing his latest film project, Dikongue-Pipa has faith in the progress of Black African cinema. The Cameroonian director is now living and working in Douala, where he heads the Douala Office of the Comité Africain des Cinéastes (African Committee of Filmmakers), also known as CAC.

MAJOR THEMES

Technically, Dikongue-Pipa's first three documentaries merely appear as trial runs in his formative period as a filmmaker. Their themes, however, are not without interest. The cinéaste describes *Un Simple* as "an autobiographical evocation of an African's discovery of the Western world" *(La Revue du Cinéma, Image et Son,* June 1980, p. 92). *Rendez-moi mon père* depicts an African's fruitless search for the grave of his father, killed on the Verdun battlefield after having been drafted into the French army during the First World War. *Les Cornes* (entirely interpreted by European actors) is, according to its author, "a kind of ethnographic essay in reverse in which I tried to show how an African perceived the problem of conjugal infidelity within European society" *(Le Monde Diplomatique,* September 1978, p. 13).

To this day, Dikongue-Pipa's major film is *Muna Moto,* dedicated to his mother and children. At the opening of this work, the Cameroonian filmmaker invites his viewers to participate in the Ngongo celebration ("Ngongo" means navel in the Douala language), which takes place annually in Dikongue-Pipa's native city to commemorate its people's sociocultural roots. A voice-over specifies: "This year the Ngongo addresses the young who tend to lose touch with tradition." This statement appears as highly significant since the film's main goal is to denounce the corrupted facets of such tradition in the areas of dowry, forced marriage, women's status, and the omnipotent power of elders. In fact, *Muna Moto* illustrates an aborted rebellion against the abuses of tradition.

The plot of *Muna Moto* revolves around the story of Ngando, a young, hardworking villager who is in love with Ndomé, to whom he has been betrothed since their childhood. Yet the two are prevented from marrying because Ngando is unable to pay the required dowry, which amounts to $200—four cases of whisky, fifteen bottles of rum, one canoe, thirty yards of material, one hundred liters of palm oil, and several bars of soap—to Ndomé's parents. Amid relentless efforts to pay the bride-price, Ngando soon realizes that he cannot rely on the assistance of his rich uncle. The latter, Mbongo, covets Ndomé as his fourth wife since none of his other spouses has borne him a child. In an attempt to decrease the dowry and render it more accessible to Ngando, Ndomé renounces her "virginal value" by having sexual intercourse with her lover. Subsequently, Ndomé discovers that she is pregnant by Ngando, and therefore has strong hopes that Mbongo will reject her as a dishonored woman. On the contrary, far from repudiating Ndomé (who has proven her fecundity), the childless Mbongo, having already paid the dowry, insists on marrying her. Several years later, during the Ngongo, Ngando grabs his child from Ndomé's arms and manages to run away but is immediately arrested and imprisoned for having attempted to reclaim his own child.

Discussing the content of *Muna Moto,* Dikongue-Pipa emphasizes:

Through the dowry issue I am putting on trial a whole society whose values have become alienated. My film is concerned with a reflection on the question of power within the present Cameroonian society, mortgaged with such pernicious customs as tribalism. The public should realize that I am evoking an entire community through the despotic uncle's family. . . . I am evoking the whole issue of money by means of the young woman's fate.

Money has distorted the people's minds. . . . this reign of money was introduced here by colonialism. . . . Originally the dowry had only a symbolic significance and could amount to a cola nut. Since the advent of colonialism our bride-prices have undergone tremendous increases up to thousands of dollars. Money has devoured our culture. *(Ecran 76,* 15 July 1976, p. 57)

Dikongue-Pipa emphasizes that *Muna Moto* does not attack the custom of dowry per se, only its misuse:

As far as I am concerned, it is not the dowry custom which should be changed but the way in which it is practiced today. Formerly the dowry had practically no material value, it symbolized the union of two young people, the alliance between two families or two tribes. Nowadays everything is based on money: the young woman is sold to the highest bidder. . . . African customs are not necessarily bad but they have their negative sides. We should not give up our customs, but we should improve them. *(Télérama,* 26 May 1976, p. 86)

Similarly, *Le Prix de la liberté* has reformist intents and argues vigorously in favor of the emancipation of the African woman in an evolving society. Says Dikongue-Pipa:

I made a very simple film, using a basic linear structure. Yet the film lends itself to two levels of interpretation: on the one hand I show the story of a Cameroonian woman and how she relates to sexuality in a male-dominated society, on the other hand I present once more the individual confronting power because as soon as an individual holds a bit of power he uses it right away against the weakest. *(Le Monde Diplomatique,* September 1978, p. 13)

Le Prix de la liberté tells the story of Etée, a well-educated eighteen-year-old girl whose father intends to marry her to their middle-aged village chief. Etée refuses to fulfill her father's expectations and escapes to the city. There, after being propositioned by several suitors, she eventually finds a job as an air hostess and falls in love with Maka, a striving young musician. The two decide to live together. Shortly thereafter Etée discovers that she is pregnant. Their romance, however, will soon come to an end, for the resentful village chief comes to town to search for Etée and eventually has her lover killed. Etée plunges into insanity, which both modern medicine and traditional healing prove unable to cure. After being taken back to her village, she sets fire to the compound of the chief, who is finally killed in a rather confusing brawl. The film ends with a freeze frame of Etée and her child. Here, as in Sembene's *Niaye* (1964), the infant symbolizes hope in a new and fairer social order.

Dikongue-Pipa's other motion pictures focus on various aspects of Cameroonian life: *Histoires drôles, drôles de gens* humorously denounces the ills of his society; *Courte Maladie* concerns the making and downfall of a popular female singer; and *Music and Music* records on film performances by famous Cameroonian entertainers, among them Manu Dibango.

SURVEY OF CRITICISM

As could be expected, practically all critical writings pertaining to Dikongue-Pipa focus primarily on his prize-winning *Muna Moto,* which has been considered both as a touching love story and a virulent sociopolitical pamphlet by such film critics as Jean René Debrix *(Afrique Contemporaine,* September-October 1975, p. 6) and War Abdoul *(Cahiers du Cinéma,* December 1976, p. 62). Claude-Marie Trémois goes so far as to compare Ngando and Ndomé to "Tristan and Iseult in the Cameroonian forest" and is particularly sensitive to the filmmaker's lyrical and neorealistic rendition of their physical environment *(Télérama,* 26 May 1976, p. 86). Guy Hennebelle fully understands Dikongue-Pipa's goals in making his film and notes, *"Muna Moto* is not only an indictment against the dowry system but also, and perhaps above all, a study of the issue of power in Black Africa" *(Ecran 76,* 15 July 1976, p. 56). Hennebelle's view is shared by N. Renaudin, for whom "the film's main purpose is . . . to blame the violence of social institutions as well as the tragic coercion it exerts on people" *(Recherche, Pédagogie et Culture,* n. 44, 1979, p. 104). And Ferid Boughedir sees *Muna Moto* as "both a social testimony and a profoundly African work of art" *(Jeune Afrique,* 28 May 1976, p. 57).

Yet, even more so than its content, it is the structure of *Muna Moto* that has been stressed by most critics. Debrix finds that Dikongue-Pipa's use of flashbacks reveals "a keen understanding of cinematic language and drama" *(Afrique Contemporaine,* September-October 1975, p. 6); Abdelhafidh Bouassida praises his handling of editing *(L'Action,* 17 October 1976, p. 13); and Alexis Gnonlonfoun *(Afrique Nouvelle,* 18 February 1976, p. 14) as well as Victor Bachy *(La Revue du Cinéma, Image et Son,* June 1980, p. 92) is impressed by the pictorial beauty and stylistic inventiveness found in *Muna Moto.* Interestingly enough, Guy Hennebelle voices less favorable opinions. Attributing such characteristics to a lack of financial means, Hennebelle judges *Muna Moto's* film language to be uncertain *(Recherche, Pédagogie et Culture,* May-August 1975, p. 9), clumsy *(Ecran 76,* 15 July 1976, p. 56), and even confusing in its use of intermittent flashbacks and dream sequences (with Gérard Garreau, *L'Afrique Littéraire et Artistique,* 3rd Quarter 1978, p. 36). Moreover, Noureddine Ghali *(Cinéma 76,* January 1976, p. 25, and August-September 1976, p. 260) and Jean-Louis Pouillaud *(Positif,* September 1976, p. 68) deplore *Muna Moto's* ostentatious theatrical acting.

On the other hand, several film reviewers, among them Jacques Binet *(Afrique Contemporaine,* January-February 1976, p. 27) and Jean Delmas *(Jeune Cinéma,* December 1976–January 1977, p. 18), have been struck by the film's poetic mood and forceful evocative power. Finally, F. Maupin *(La Revue du Cinéma, Image et Son,* September 1976, p. 122) and Abdou Achouba *(Cinémarabe,* October-November 1976, p. 49) find that *Muna Moto* derives specifically from the timeless tradition of popular tales. "The film is not perfect but it undoubtedly reveals a gifted filmmaker"; such is Maupin's closing statement, which could assuredly be used to summarize the above. Unfortunately, *Le Prix de la liberté* and three other similarly disappointing commercial films did not live up to the critics' expectations *(Le Soleil,* 19 November 1979, p. 2). Let us hope that Dikongue-Pipa's talent will be confirmed by his forthcoming motion picture *La Cicatrice.*

FILMOGRAPHY

Un Simple (Down to Earth), 16 mm, black and white, 45 min., 1965.
Les Cornes (The Horns), 16 mm, black and white, 25 min., 1966.
Rendez-moi mon père (Give Me Back My Father), 16 mm, black and white, 18 min., 1966.
Muna Moto (The Other's Child), 16/35 mm, black and white, 110 min., 1974.
Le Prix de la liberté (The Price of Freedom), 16/35 mm, color, 100 min., 1978.
Histoires drôles, drôles de gens (Funny Stories, Funny People), 16 mm, color, 90 min., 1982.
Courte Maladie (Brief Illness), 16 mm, color, 90 min., 1983.
Music and Music, 16 mm, color, 90 min., 1983.
La Cicatrice (The Scar), 35 mm, color, 90 min., 1983–85.

BIBLIOGRAPHY

Writings by Jean-Pierre Dikongue-Pipa

Dikongue-Pipa, Jean-Pierre. "Cameroun: dénoncer les abus du pouvoir." *Le Monde Diplomatique,* September 1978, p. 13.

Interviews of Jean-Pierre Dikongue-Pipa

Bérimé, Jean Joseph. "La Parole à Dicongue-Pipa *[sic],* cinéaste camerounais." *Objectif,* n. 13, 25 January 1981, pp. 53–54.
Essola, N. S. "Le Cinéaste Dikongue-Pipa à Cameroon Tribune: Je prépare un film historique sur l'Afrique." *Cameroon Tribune,* 26 June 1975, p. 2.
Garreau, Gérard. "Dikongue-Pipa: un visionnaire." *Actuel Développement,* n. 25, 1978, pp. 33–38.
Hennebelle, Guy. "Muna Moto." *Ecran 76,* n. 49, 15 July 1976, pp. 55–57.
Jusu, Kinimo Man. "Dikongue-Pipa: Le cinéma africain est en progrès." *Fraternité Matin,* 6 November 1979, p. 15.
Saivre, Denyse de. "Entretien avec Dicongue-Pipa *[sic]." Recherche, Pédagogie et Culture,* n. 23–24, May-August 1976, pp. 54–57.

Film Reviews and Studies of Jean-Pierre Dikongue-Pipa

Abdoul, War. "Muna Moto." *Cahiers du Cinéma,* n. 272, December 1976, p. 62.
Achouba, Abdou. "Muna Moto." *Cinémarabe,* n. 4–5, October-November 1976, p. 49.
Ayari, Farida. "Images de femmes." *Cinémaction,* n. 26, 1983, pp. 136–39.
Bachy, Victor. "Le Cinéma au Cameroun." *La Revue du Cinéma, Image et Son,* n. 351, June 1980, pp. 87–94.

Belinga, Thérèse Baratte-Eno. *Ecrivains, Cinéastes et Artistes Camerounais: Bio-Bibliographie*. Yaoundé: Centre d'Editions et de Production pour l'Enseignement et la Recherche, 1978.

Binet, Jacques. "Cinéma africain." *Afrique Contemporaine*, n. 83, January-February 1976, pp. 27–30.

———. "Le Sacré, l'extase, la folie et leur expression dans les films." *Cinémaction*, n. 26, 1983, pp. 118–23.

Bouassida, Abdelhafidh. "Muna Moto ou l'art du silence musical." *L'Action*, 17 October 1976, p. 13.

Boughedir, Ferid. "Cameroun." *Cinéma Québec*, vol. 3, n. 9–10, August 1974, pp. 41–43.

———. "1975, l'année des grandes victoires." *Jeune Afrique*, n. 782–783, 2 January 1976, pp. 60–61.

———. "Le Cinéma africain hors des ghettos." *Jeune Afrique*, n. 791, 5 March 1976, pp. 43–45.

———. "Dans une Afrique d'opérette." *Jeune Afrique*, n. 803, 28 May 1976, pp. 56–57.

———. "Carthage 78: pari tenu pour les Africains et les Arabes." *Jeune Afrique*, n. 936, 13 December 1978, pp. 91–93.

———. "Cinéma africain—le temps de l'immobilisme." *Les 2 Ecrans*, n. 42–43, February-March 1982, pp. 15–19.

Daney, Serge. "Carthage, An 10." *Cahiers du Cinéma*, n. 272, December 1976, pp. 43–49.

D'Dée. "Jeune-Cinéma d'Afrique noire." *L'Afrique Actuelle*, n. 15, 1967, pp. 1–40.

Debrix, Jean-René. "Situation du cinéma en Afrique francophone." *Afrique Contemporaine*, n. 81, September-October 1975, pp. 2–7.

Delmas, Jean. "Muna Moto." *Jeune Cinéma*, n. 99, December 1976–January 1977, pp. 18–19.

Diedhiou, Djib. "Le Prix de la liberté—on pouvait mieux faire." *Le Soleil*, 19 November 1979, p. 2.

Ghali, Noureddine. "Festival International du Film de l'Ensemble Francophone." *Cinéma 76*, n. 205, January 1976, pp. 24–25.

———. "Muna Moto." *Cinéma 76*, n. 212–213, August-September 1976, pp. 259–60.

Gnonlonfoun, Alexis. "Ve Fespaco: qu'en penser?" *Afrique Nouvelle*, n. 1390, 18 February 1976, pp. 12–15.

Haffner, Pierre. "L'Esthétique des films." *Cinémaction*, n. 26, 1983, pp. 58–71.

Hennebelle, Guy. "Les Films africains en 1975." *Recherche, Pédagogie et Culture*, n. 17–18, May-August 1975, pp. 7–9.

———. "Muna Moto." *Ecran 76*, n. 49, 15 July 1976, pp. 55–57.

———, and Gérard Garreau. "Dikongue-Pipa, Jean-Pierre." *L'Afrique Littéraire et Artistique*, n. 49, 3rd Quarter 1978, pp. 36–41.

Marcorelles, Louis. "Le Prix Georges Sadoul 1975: l'Afrique et le Brésil au palmarès." *Le Monde*, 13 December 1975, p. 34.

Martin, Angela. *African Films: The Context of Production*. London: British Film Institute, 1982.

Maupin, F. "Muna Moto ou l'enfant de l'autre." *La Revue du Cinéma, Image et Son*, n. 308, September 1976, pp. 121–22.

"Muna Moto présenté au jury international du FIFEF." *Cameroon Tribune,* 3 October
    1975, p. 6.

Pouillaud, Jean-Louis. "L'Enfant de l'autre (Muna Moto)." *Positif,* n. 185, September
    1976, p. 68.

Renaudin, N. "Notes sur l'enfant dans le cinéma." *Recherche, Pédagogie et Culture,*
    n. 44, 1979, pp. 101–7.

Sumo, Honoré de. "Genèse et avenir du cinéma camerounais." *L'Afrique Littéraire et
    Artistique,* n. 39, 1976, pp. 59–62.

Trémois, Claude-Marie. "Muna Moto." *Télérama,* n. 1376, 26 May 1976, p. 86.

Pierre-Marie Dong (1945–   )
Gabon

BIOGRAPHY

Pierre-Marie Dong (also spelled N'Dong), one of the better-known Gabonese filmmakers, was born in 1945 in Libreville, the capital of Gabon. Dong spent his childhood and adolescence in an urban environment where he was exposed to a variety of commercial foreign films which caused him to become increasingly impassioned about cinema. After finishing high school in the mid-1960s, he embarked for France, where he studied filmmaking at the Institut des Hautes Etudes Cinématographiques (IDHEC) in Paris. After his graduation from this French film school, the young director returned to Libreville, where he started working for state-owned Gabonese television.

It is while working for television that Dong took a first stab at directing with *Carrefour humain* (Human Crossroads, 1969), *Gabon, pays de contraste* (Gabon, A Country of Contrasts, 1969), and *Lésigny* (1970). His first noted effort as a filmmaker was *Sur le sentier du requiem* (On the Requiem Path, 1971), which gained him some international notoriety on the festival circuit. The film won an award ("Prix d'Encouragement") at the Third Pan-African Film Festival of Ouagadougou (FESPACO), held in 1972 in Burkina Faso. That same year, Pierre-Marie Dong acted in *Il était une fois Libreville* (Once upon a Time, Libreville, 1972), a film by the Gabonese director Simon Augé. Then, also in 1972, with raw film stock left over from the production of *Les Tams Tams se sont tus* (Drums Stopped Playing, 1972) by his compatriot Philippe Maury, $10,000 allocated to him by the Gabonese president, Omar Bongo, and a team of mostly nonprofessional actors, Dong shot his first feature length film *Identité* (Identity), which received the African Authenticity Prize at the Fourth FESPACO (1973). After this recognition of his work, Pierre-Marie Dong was appointed general manager of the Gabonese television company. Eventually Dong's cinematic skills became increasingly noticed by the wife of the Gabonese head of state, Mrs. Josephine Bongo. Subsequently, Dong was asked to adapt two stories by Mrs. Bongo to the screen, and this resulted in the making of *Obali* (1975) and *Ayouma* (1977), co-directed with Charles Mensah, another Gabonese film-maker. Benefitting from adequate financing and proper equipment—a rare combination for Black films—*Obali* and *Ayouma* proved technically polished. Yet both movies were shunned by critics, who deplored their inconsequential plots and were not too impressed by their glossy pictorial beauty. *Obali* was even booed by African viewers at the 1977 Cabourg Film Festival in France. Nevertheless, it should be noted that both *Obali* and *Ayouma* enjoyed a respectable popular run in Gabon, and that *Ayouma* won the Audience Prize (awarded to the best film by public opinion) at the sixth FESPACO (1979). The two films were also presented at the Racines Noires Festival (Black Roots Festival) held in Paris in the spring of 1985.

After *Obali* and *Ayouma,* Pierre-Marie Dong was given another directing assignment by the Gabonese president himself. This resulted in Dong's latest film to date, *Demain, un jour nouveau* (Tomorrow, A New Day, 1978). Based on a script by Omar Bongo, shot with noted professional actors from Africa and the Black Diaspora (Doura Mane, Cathy Rozier, and Théo Légitimus), as well as a crew of foreign and local technicians, *Demain un jour nouveau* benefitted from a budget of more than $1 million—a record-breaking figure in terms of Black African cinema at the time. Notwithstanding rare festival screenings at FESPACO and Cannes in 1979, and at the 1985 Racines Noires Festival, this film, which is unabashedly propagandist of Bongo's rule, has been seen mainly in Gabon.

A member of Gabon's ruling party and of President Bongo's cabinet, Pierre-Marie Dong is presently living and working in Libreville, where he also heads the Organisme du Cinéma Gabonais (Gabonese Film Bureau).

MAJOR THEMES

Except for such films as *Gabon, pays de contraste,* which, as its title indicates, focuses on the geographic, ethnic, and cultural diversities of Gabon, Dong's basic themes center on the African's search for identity in a changing and conflicting world, caught between African traditions and new values inherited from the West.

Carrefour humain reflects the crisis of racial identity as well as the difficult social integration frequently experienced by people of mixed races. *Sur le sentier du requiem* is an innovative assemblage of highly contrasting scenes and newsreel footage accented by an intricate collage of sounds (including Bible verses, natural sounds of rural and city life, traditional and modern African music, pulsating heartbeats, etc.) intended to evoke the cultural dichotomy undergone by a young, aspiring filmmaker who perhaps is Dong himself.

Identité portrays an anguished protagonist's quest for the true essence of African life. The film starts with the return of Pierre, a young artist, to Gabon after completing his studies in France. At one point, he tells his friends: ''I traveled a lot and sometimes I feel lost in a labyrinth of civilizations.'' Next a discussion ensues about cultural alienation, and the clashes between traditional customs and Western mores. The following sequence shows four youths preparing for, and subsequently engaging in, the hold-up of a service station. Consequently, while fleeing from the scene of the crime, one of them, Felix, hides in Pierre's car and, threatening him with a knife, forces Pierre to drive away. As they reach Pierre's home, the artist invites the young delinquent for a drink and eventually, upon learning that Felix is an orphan, offers him temporary shelter in his house. Next, Pierre goes on a fruitless job hunt during which he encounters bureaucratic corruption and lackadaisical attitudes on the part of civil servants. In the meantime, Felix's hiding place is discovered by the police, who, while Pierre is away, circle his house to arrest Felix, who is shot in the ensuing skirmish. After witnessing the last moments of his repentant friend, Pierre decides to leave the city to "find himself and recover his true culture." To do so, Pierre (whose name indicates that he has been baptized in the Christian faith) goes to a distant village, where he undergoes the initiation rites of the Iboa religion amid unspoiled Eden-like pastoral surroundings. After this symbolic return to the sources of African authenticity, however, Pierre returns to the Westernized city.

In his own words, Dong's intent in making *Identité* was to show how

neo-colonialism uses culture, in the present case French culture, to penetrate and control our society. To remedy such [a] state of things one must fill the gap which exists between the masses who have remained close to traditional African culture, and the intellectuals who are largely acculturated. *(L'Afrique Littéraire et Artistique,* 3rd Quarter 1978, p. 54)

Asked once whether the ending of *Identité* advocates a return to nature as a possible cure for sociocultural alienation, the filmmaker stated:

I do not show traditional life in an idyllic light. For instance, I suggest that the status of the woman in the ancestral society is no longer acceptable today because it is based on her subjugation. Yet I do exalt . . . initiation. I underwent this process myself. I believe that it is . . . necessary if one wants to establish or reestablish links between the intellectuals and the masses . . . [yet] after being initiated my protagonist returns to modern life, drives a car, takes a plane etc. *(L'Afrique Littéraire et Artistique,* 3rd Quarter 1978, p. 53)

Dong's film *Obali* examines the "Obali" tradition according to which a widower has the right to demand a new wife from his in-laws as a replacement for his deceased spouse. Here, in the absence of any readily available woman, Ngondo, a young girl, is chosen as wife for the old village chief, who happens to be Ngondo's grandfather. Of course, Ngondo rebels against the Obali custom, all the more so since she is in love with a young and handsome villager. Interestingly enough, the incestuous aspect of the proposed union (blatant to any Western viewer) is never discussed by any of the characters. Next, Ngondo discovers that she is pregnant by her young lover. The latter proposes to marry Ngondo, but her family rejects him. Subsequently, Ngondo gives birth to a daughter. Shortly thereafter the infant becomes ill and cannot be cured through modern medicine. Therefore Ngondo's family resorts to a traditional healer (whom they had consulted before taking the child to a hospital), who attributes the child's illness to a vengeful spell cast by the old chief. Toward the end of the film, as another village girl agrees to become his wife, the old chief removes his spell. Seemingly, the Obali tradition is saved and, after sundry palavers and exorcism, Ngondo will be reunited with the man she loves, her child's father.

Ayouma, like *Obali,* focuses on the status of women within Gabonese society. The film centers on the story of Ayouma and Ndabouo. Ayouma, a spirited and successful car salesman, meets Ndabouo, a young and elegant secretary. Soon their friendship changes into love, and they decide to marry. Although they live in the city, both come from rural surroundings and wish to abide by tradition concerning the procedure of their marriage. As is customary, Ayouma goes to see Ntoungou, Ndabouo's father, to ask for Ndabouo's hand. Ntoungou, who had destined his daughter for a more affluent party, will eventually accept the marriage proposal since Ayouma proves able to pay for Ndabouo's dowry. Thus, Ayouma and Ndabouo marry and settle down in their new and comfortable suburban home. Shortly after his daughter's wedding, the recently widowed Ntoungou uses the money and goods received from Ayouma to marry Bakima, a young village woman. Ndabouo subsequently discovers that she is pregnant and later returns to her village for her delivery. As Ayouma visits his wife, he befriends Bakima. While Ayouma and Bakima are but friends, their relationship causes suspicion and jealousy in Ntoungou. One day, as he sees them joyously conversing in an isolated glade, Ntoungou kills Ayouma. Rather unexpectedly (and unconvincingly), the murder of Ayouma results in Ndabouo becoming a budding feminist: she addresses a congregation of villagers and vehemently advocates women's rights as a necessary step toward social progress in a society which, she argues, still considers women as mere "merchandise."

Demain, un jour nouveau depicts how a young, honest, and fearless Chief of Cabinet rids a fictitious country called Gamba of political and social corruption. After several attempts on his life and the raiding of his house by political opponents, he will eventually assume power upon the natural death of the aging head of state. The new president promises to implement a new order that will insure the prosperity and welfare of his country.

Due to Dong's status within Gabon's power structure, his films (with the exception of such early works as *Sur le sentier du requiem* and even *Identité*) are generally inherently different from most other Black African motion pictures (which often have subversive political overtones) in that they are only mildly critical of contemporary Gabonese society, when not overtly propagandistic, as is the case for *Demain, un jour nouveau*. (In *Obali* and *Ayouma,* for example, Dong attacks forced marriages and the subservient status of African women, but so does his scriptwriter, the president's wife.) Although they may at times provide interesting glimpses of Gabonese village life and customs, the filmmaker's recent works, particularly *Ayouma* and *Demain, un jour nouveau* (mainly shot in French, as is the case for his other motion pictures), espouse the escapist standards of commercial Western cinema and are stylistically conventional. As such, these films reflect the skill of a competent film technician rather than that of an imaginative director.

SURVEY OF CRITICISM

In an article appropriately subtitled "A la recherche d'une identité" (In Search of an Identity), the Tunisian film critic Ferid Boughedir explores the early productions of Gabonese cinema, including such works as *Carrefour humain, Sur le sentier du requiem* and *Identité*. He finds that the thematic content of these films focuses essentially on two elements: the antagonism between tradition and modernity, and the return to a serene and timeless Africa standing in sharp contrast with an alienating Western world. Hoping for more thematic originality in the future, Boughedir calls for "less tormented films" that would concern themselves with the majority of the Gabonese people instead of narcissistically depicting a minority of uprooted intellectuals *(Cinéma Québec,* August 1974, p. 35).

Both Guy Hennebelle and Claude-Michel Cluny are impressed with the style of *Sur le sentier du requiem*. Hennebelle praises its "often poetic editing" which, he writes, "foretells a filmmaker of great ability," provided Dong opts for more in-depth analysis in his forthcoming works *(L'Afrique littéraire et Artistique,* March 1972, pp. 93–94). Cluny also finds the film poetic as well as ambitious and intelligent, but he fears that its unusual construction may not appeal to general audiences *(Cinéma 72,* April 1972, p. 38).

In a brief review, Jacques Binet expresses mixed feelings about Dong's *Identité*. He finds it merely patterned after European motion pictures in its portrayal of a truly central character and cynical gangsters, as well as in its "love scene which is so remote from African respectability." The critic also regrets the film's thematic discrepancies in its treatment of the protagonist's initiatory quest, intermingled with the young gangster's repentance and self-awareness *(Afrique Contemporaine,* January-February 1976, p. 28). As for Noël Ebony, he apparently disapproves of Dong's attempt in *Identité* to solve social alienation through such individualistic means as religious initiation *(Fraternité Matin,* 10–11 February 1973, p. 11).

Although he readily acknowledges the glossy technical qualities of the high-budget *Obali,* Paulin Soumanou Vieyra* is highly critical of the film's ending, which, he says, fails to stress how in Black Africa tradition frequently delays the general process of economic and sociocultural progress *(Présence Africaine,* 4th Quarter 1978, p. 171).

The general reaction to *Ayouma* was not uniformly positive. While Jean de Baroncelli *(Le Monde,* 21 September 1978, p. 20) and Ferid Boughedir *(Jeune Afrique,* 4 October 1978, p. 44) term it a technically well-made and glowing melodrama with didactic overtones, Khemais Khayati *(Cinéma 78,* December

1978, p. 72) does not hesitate to call it "a horrible and silly film punctuated with whisky, Sylvaner wine, shady porches and late model cars." Victor Bachy shows interest in the theme of *Ayouma* but criticizes the flatness and the mediocrity of its dialogue. He also questions the authenticity of such a film, which, he says, imitates France's worst motion pictures *(Revue Belge du Cinéma*, October-November 1978, p. 37).

Demain, un jour nouveau was the subject of much controversy at the 1979 FESPACO, and only a few critics have reviewed it. Azzedine Mabrouki reports on its glamorous style and dreamlike, lavish settings, but shows little enthusiasm for its content *(Les 2 Ecrans*, April 1979, p. 16). Paulin Soumanou Vieyra views the film as a dangerous propagandistic work because of its uncritical glorification of an infallible charismatic leader. He also finds its approach and staginess so French that he wonders whether Dong's motion picture can indeed be called an African film *(Présence Africaine*, 3rd Quarter 1979, p. 104). Although Aly Kheury Ndaw also considers *Demain, un jour nouveau* an apology for President Bongo's regime, he supports Dong's film in the name of artistic freedom. Ndaw argues that all African directors should not necessarily be expected to make revolutionary motion pictures *(Le Soleil*, 5 March 1979, p. 2).

FILMOGRAPHY

Carrefour humain (Human Crossroads), 16 mm, black and white, precise length unknown, 1969.
Gabon, pays de contraste (Gabon, A Country of Contrasts), 16 mm, black and white, precise length unknown, 1969.
Lésigny, 16 mm, black and white, precise length unknown, 1970.
Sur le sentier du requiem (On the Requiem Path), 16 mm, black and white, 18 min., 1971.
Identité (Identity), 16/35 mm, color, 75 min., 1972.
Obali (co-directed with Charles Mensah), 35 mm, color, 120 min., 1975.
Ayouma (co-directed with Charles Mensah), 35 mm, color, 80 min., 1977.
Demain, un jour nouveau (Tomorrow, A New Day), 35 mm, color, 90 min., 1978.

BIBLIOGRAPHY

Interview of Pierre-Marie Dong

Hennebelle, Guy. "Dong Pierre-Marie." *L'Afrique Littéraire et Artistique*, n. 49, 3rd Quarter 1978, pp. 52–54.

Film Reviews and Studies of Pierre-Marie Dong

Bachy, Victor. "Ayouma." *Revue Belge du Cinéma*, n. 11, October-November 1978, p. 37.
———. "Le Cinéma gabonais." *Journal du 8ᵉ FESPACO*, n. 3, 13 February 1983, p. 10.

Baroncelli, Jean de. "Films francophones á Namur—tristes histoires du monde réel." *Le Monde,* 21 September 1978, p. 20.

Binet Jacques. "Cinéma africain." *Afrique Contemporaine,* n. 83, January-February 1976, pp. 27–30.

———. "La Nature dans le cinéma africain." *L'Afrique Littéraire et Artistique,* n. 39, 1976, pp. 52–58.

———. "Classes sociales et cinéma africain." *Positif,* n. 188, December 1976, pp. 34–42.

Boughedir, Ferid. "Ouagadougou." *Ecran 1973,* n. 15, May 1973, pp. 54–55.

———. "Le Cinéma gabonais: à la recherche d'une identité." *Cinéma Québec,* vol. 3, n. 9–10, August 1974, p. 35.

———. "L'Afrique à la une chez les francophones à Namur." *Jeune Afrique,* n. 926, 4 October 1978, pp. 44–45.

Cluny, Claude-Michel. "Gabon." *Cinéma 72,* n. 165, April 1972, p. 38.

Ebony, Noël. "Journée ivoirienne: triomphe pour nos réalisateurs." *Fraternité Matin,* 10–11 February 1973, p. 11.

Fanon, Josie. "Cannes sans l'Afrique." *Demain l'Afrique,* n. 27, 21 May 1979, p. 90.

Hennebelle, Guy. "Le Troisième Festival Panafricain du Cinéma de Ouagadougou." *L'Afrique Littéraire et Artistique,* n. 22, March 1972, pp. 88–95.

———. "Panorama des productions africaines et arabes." *Ecran 74,* n. 30, November 1974, pp. 39–46.

Khayati, Khemais. "L'Afrique sujet." *Cinéma 78,* n. 240, December 1978, pp. 72–73.

Mabrouki, Azzedine. "Gabon: Demain, un jour nouveau, de Pierre-Marie Dong (1978)." *Les 2 Ecrans,* n. 12, April 1979, pp. 16–17.

Ndaw, Aly Kheury. "Le Cinéma africain à Ouagadougou: IV—Demain un jour nouveau." *Le Soleil,* 5 March 1979, p. 2.

Pokam, Pierre Nguewa. "L'évocation du sacré." *Cinémaction,* n. 26, 1983, pp. 113–17.

Ruelle, Catherine. "Dong Pierre-Marie." *L'Afrique Littéraire et Artistique,* n. 49, 3rd Quarter 1978, p. 52.

Vieyra, Paulin Soumanou. *Le Cinéma africain.* Paris: Présence Africaine, 1975.

———. "Le 25ᵉ Festival International du Film de l'Ensemble Francophone." *Présence Africaine,* n. 108, 4th Quarter 1978, pp. 166–72.

———. "Fespaco 1979." *Présence Africaine,* n. 111, 3rd Quarter 1979, pp. 101–6.

Henri Duparc (1941–   )
Ivory Coast

BIOGRAPHY

Together with Timité Bassori* and Désiré Ecaré*, Henri Duparc belongs to what is now often called the first generation of Ivorian filmmakers. A Christian of African and Caucasian descent (his paternal grandfather was a French colonial administrator), Duparc was born on 25 December 1941 in the small inland town of Forécariah, Guinea, where he spent his early childhood with his six brothers and sisters. After attending primary school in his native town, the young adolescent continued his studies at Kindia, also in Guinea, from 1954 to 1958, and then in Paris, France, where his father (a banana plantation owner) sent him to complete high school.

It was primarily in Paris, as a student, that Henri Duparc developed a serious interest in cinema by haunting the movie theaters of the Latin Quarter and assiduously watching the world classics featured at the Cinémathèque Française. Then, the recipient of a scholarship, Duparc went to Yugoslavia in 1962, where he enrolled at the Belgrade Film School, and even participated in the shooting of *Marco Polo* (1963) by the noted French director Christian-Jaque. Nevertheless, shortly thereafter, Duparc abridged his stay and training in Belgrade and returned to Paris, where he was to transfer to the Institut des Hautes Etudes Cinématographiques (IDHEC) after briefly working as a bank clerk. While attending the IDHEC from 1964 to 1966, he started *Obs,* a film which to this day has not been completed. Next, he acted in two films whose plots center around the experiences of young uprooted African students in Paris, namely *Concerto pour un exil* (Concerto for an Exile, 1967) by Désiré Ecaré (who had been Duparc's schoolmate at IDHEC) and *Ame perdue* (Lost Soul, 1968) by Sekou Camara of Guinea. Yet Duparc insists that he never had any intention of engaging in an acting career.

It is only to help out these two friends that I agreed to play the role of a womanizer in both of these films. I had not received any training as an actor. I believe it suffices to remain natural in front of a camera to play a character part. This being said, I do not think I have a vocation for acting. *(Jeune Afrique,* 16 September 1969, p. 53)

In 1968, after briefly working for French television in Paris, Henri Duparc went to the Ivory Coast, where he was hired by the Société Ivoirienne de Cinéma (SIC). Seven months after his arrival in Abidjan, he made his debut as an independent director with *Mouna ou le rêve d'un artiste* (Mouna, An Artist's Dream, 1969), a low-budget fiction film shot in ten days. Duparc stresses:

Mouna ou le rêve d'un artiste is a medium length film which was intended to be a feature length film. I made it without any detailed script. While shooting, the actors, my wife and I were writing the dialogues as the plot unfolded. So we shot 2,000 meters of film footage amounting to one and a half hours of screening time, but unfortunately several sequences proved unusable at the editing stage. Therefore I chose to delete these sequences which represented ten minutes of screening time. *(Bingo,* June 1971, p. 58)

Mouna ou le rêve d'un artiste was based on a total budget of some $8,000. To make this film, Duparc benefitted from the free collaboration of friends (both technicians and actors) and financial help from SIC, but he also had to rely greatly on his own savings, as has been the case with most Black African filmmakers, especially when tackling their early works. *Mouna ou le rêve d'un artiste* was subsequently presented at the First Pan-African Festival held in Algiers in July 1969, and the following year it was featured at the Carthage Film Festival in Tunisia as well as at the Pan-African Film Festival of Ouagadougou (FESPACO) in Burkina Faso.

Also between 1968 and 1970, while working at SIC, Henri Duparc made seven documentaries (based on an average budget of $15,000 each) aimed at highlighting the history and the economic and touristic assets of the Ivory Coast. These films are *Récolte du coton* (Growing Cotton, in two parts), *Profil ivoirien* (Ivorian Profile), *Achetez ivoirien* (Buy Ivorian Products), *Tam-tam ivoire* (Ivorian Drums), *J'ai dix ans* (I Am Ten Years Old), and *Carnet de voyage* (A Traveller's Notes). Most of these motion pictures were shown on Ivorian television and in the course of itinerant film screenings throughout the Ivory Coast and several other West African countries.

Although it received some encouraging reviews, *Mouna ou le rêve d'un artiste* (with its dream sequences and unorthodox construction) did not appeal to mass audiences in the Ivory Coast or other African countries. Undaunted by the unspectacular reception of this film, Duparc decided to make a new movie that would be more commercially oriented and more accessible to large numbers of viewers. This resulted in Duparc's first feature length production, *Abusuan* (The Family), a carefully planned film based on his own script (co-written with Blaise Agui and Charles Goudou) and co-produced by SIC and the Société d'Exploitation Cinématographique (SECMA), one of the French monopolies which at the time controlled film distribution in Francophone West Africa. Provided with adequate financing, this film was shot in French (with only some village scenes in Agni, one of the indigenous languages of the Ivory Coast) by the French cameraman Christian Lacoste and a crew of both French and Ivorian technicians. *Abusuan* is interpreted by such professional African actors as Jean Baptiste Tiémélé and Léonard Groguhet as well as nonprofessional actors like Natou Koly, a librarian at the Abidjan Goethe Institute, who was then completing her B.A. in German. Made on a $75,000 budget, *Abusuan,* released in 1972, became an instant commercial hit in the Ivory Coast, and in Abidjan alone the film was seen by 150,000 viewers over a four-month period. In contrast, the film, a conventional yet technically well-made work replete with humorous action, went practically unnoticed at the 1973 FESPACO as well as at the 1974 Carthage Film Festival, where it was presented *hors compétition.*

In 1976 Duparc was commissioned to make *Les Racines de la vie* (The Roots of Life) to commemorate the International Year of the Woman. His latest film to date is *L'Herbe sauvage* (Weeds, 1977), made on a $100,000 budget, another color fiction film produced by SIC. Although Clementine Tikida, who plays the film's leading role, won the Prize for Best Female Interpretation at the 1978 Carthage Film Festival, *L'Herbe sauvage,* like *Abusuan,* received limited critical attention on the festival circuit. Nevertheless, with glossy photography by Christian Lacoste and a catchy musical score by the Cameroonian musician Manu Dibango, *L'Herbe sauvage,* a film distributed by the Consortium Interafricain de Distribution Cinématographique (CIDC), became a box-office success in the Ivory Coast, particularly in Abidjan, where it enjoyed three months of uninterrupted showings.

Much like Ola Balogun* and a few other Black African filmmakers, Henri Duparc has now ostensibly moved from obscure intellectualism *(Mouna ou le rêve d'un artiste)* to well-crafted and explicit cinema *(Abusuan, L'Herbe sauvage)* in the hope of reaching the bulk of Black African viewers, drawing them away from the Westerns, thrillers, Kung Fu films, Egyptian melodramas, and Indian sagas that still flood African screens *(Fraternité Matin,* 19 December 1972, p. 8). Yet, although Duparc increasingly views film as a product which must appeal to wide audiences, he by no means neglects its didactic potential, which he believes should contribute to the social progress of developing nations *(Fraternité Matin,* 6 February 1973, p. 7). He also considers cinema as a means of universal communication (Duparc to author, 2 July 1986).

Married and the father of three teenage daughters, Henri Duparc is presently living and working in Abidjan, where he heads Société Focale 13, his own film company. He is also one of the founding members of the Association des Cinéastes Professionnels de la Côte d'Ivoire, whose main goal is to work with the government toward the establishment and implementation of viable film structures in Black Africa. Although he has resided for some twenty years in the Ivory Coast, the filmmaker wishes one day to go back to Guinea.

MAJOR THEMES

Duparc's stay in Paris generated *Obs* (whose title stands for both "obsession" and "obscurantism"), a short fiction film which depicts the relationship between a young African man and a French woman—a theme rather infrequently found in Black African cinema. His subsequent documentaries are promotional and/or didactic pieces explaining various national development projects to the Ivorian public, or commemorating important sociohistorical events: *Récolte du coton* (with versions in French and several African vernaculars spoken in the Ivory Coast) encourages Ivorian farmers to engage in the growing of cotton; *Profil ivoirien, Tam-tam ivoire,* and *Carnet de voyage* highlight the economic resources, the cultural diversity, and the touristic appeal of the Ivory Coast; *Achetez ivoirien* promotes locally produced items over similar imported goods; *J'ai dix ans* celebrates the tenth anniversary of the independence of the Ivory Coast; *Les Racines de la vie* is an homage rendered to the African woman (particularly the Ivorian woman) because of the significant role she has always played in Black African societies.

Through the portrayal of a young Ivorian sculptor, *Mouna ou le rêve d'un artiste* shows how creativity may be debased by commercial pursuits. According to Henri Duparc, the film symbolizes the plight of many contemporary artists—sculptors, painters, and filmmakers alike *(Bingo,* June 1971, pp. 58–59).

Often deemed a somewhat autobiographical work, *Mouna ou le rêve d'un artiste* reveals the existential quest of Barba Bitty Moro (played by Jean Tapen), who seeks shelter in a visionary world to escape from the material contingencies of everyday worries. To make a living, Barba has to sell his masks to an Abidjan merchant specializing in the tourist trade of mass produced African masks and artifacts. Besides making inordinate profits off the artist's work, the latter also seduces Mouna, Barba's model and companion. The sculptor's inward agonies eventually result in hallucinations and sheer insanity. At the end of the film, commenting on the artist's tragic fate, one of his neighbors concludes, "He believed that life was a dream."

In *Abusuan* Henri Duparc condemns parasitism, in this case the abuse of family solidarity whenever it leads to the shameless exploitation by family members of individuals who show some financial success. The filmmaker emphasizes:

Here I chose a theme of concern to our present society because I knew that I would interest the public at large: which family has not had to house "brothers" or other acquaintances from the village? I did not make my film according to what audiences like but based on what affects them in real life. *(Fraternité Matin,* 19 December 1972, p. 8)

Consequently, *Abusuan* also addresses the issue of migration from village to town. Duparc explains: "The real problem is that of villagers who leave home . . . to come to a place where they will find nothing but unemployment" *(Fraternité Matin,* 19 December 1972, p. 8).

Abusuan, Duparc's first feature length film, depicts the story of Pierre Aka, a successful Ivorian architect who works for a government agency in charge of urban planning. His comfortable life is that of a member of the Westernized African elite, enjoying a plush modern-designed home and driving an expensive car. One day, after fifteen years of absence (which includes his formal training in France), Pierre decides to visit his relatives, who have stayed in his native village. He and his wife (a modern urban African woman) are warmly received by Pierre's family, who show considerable pride in his socioprofessional achievements. After a brief stay, Pierre and his wife return to Abidjan. Soon thereafter, upon a diviner's advice, Kwame, Pierre's cousin, comes to town with his two sons, whom he intends to commit to the care of the architect. Next, Pierre's sister, envious of Kwame's initiatives, sends her own offspring to her brother. Genuinely interested in the welfare of his family and in spite of his wife's recriminations, Pierre tries his best to provide his relatives with education and jobs. In the meantime, however, two of his wards become involuntarily involved in car theft and are arrested by the police. This last event instigates the family's return to the village, which, in the case of people ill-prepared for urban life, is presented as a more natural and favorable setting for human growth.

"Weeds destroy your crop when they spread over your field." Such is the Bambara proverb from which Duparc draws the title of *L'Herbe sauvage* (Weeds). In this film, weeds symbolize jealousy and the destructive impact it has on people. Like *Abusuan, L'Herbe sauvage* takes place among the postcolonial Ivorian bourgeoisie and highlights the role of both modern and traditional African women.

L'Herbe sauvage concerns a modern couple, both professionals in their thirties or early forties: she is a medical doctor at an Abidjan hospital; he is the manager of a palm tree plantation. He surrenders to the charms of his secretary, and his wife, on discovering her husband's unfaithfulness, envisions divorce. However, upon one of her female friends' advice, she goes to consult a diviner. The latter convinces her to seek reconciliation with her spouse, which she eventually does.

Stylistically, Duparc makes dexterous use of flashbacks and dream sequences in *L'Herbe sauvage* to emphasize the doctor's murderous feelings toward her husband and her husband's lover—as the credits unfold, and in the second half of the movie, the doctor is seen twice killing her husband and his secretary, which creates a dramatic uncertainty as to the actual ending of the film, where finally no one is killed. Thematically, in addition to a rather banal triangular love story, the director inserts in his film a very controversial social issue, namely, the ritual of clitoridectomy and its relevance in contemporary African societies.

SURVEY OF CRITICISM

In his perceptive article "Cultural Dilemma of the African Film," Wilson Mativo expresses some interest in *Mouna ou le rêve d'un artiste* because it "reveals the painful inward existence of an artist as a representation of the cultural position of the sensitive new African" *(UFAHAMU,* Winter 1971, p. 65). In a more detailed study of that same film, Claude Gérard praises its topic and finds the director's view of the world extremely pessimistic in that his characters (like Antonioni's) fail to communicate with one another and end up entrenched in loneliness and despair *(Fraternité Matin,* 6 April 1970, p. 2). Although he likes the subject matter of *Mouna ou le rêve d'un artiste,* Paulin Soumanou Vieyra is much less impressed by its loose construction and terms the film a failure *(Le Cinéma Africain,* 1975, p. 59).

Abusuan has received mixed reviews. On the one hand, Guy Kouassi *(Fraternité Matin,* 19 December 1972, p. 8), Noël Ebony *(Fraternité Matin,* 21 December 1972, p. 7), and Victor Bachy *(Le Cinéma en Côte d'Ivoire,* 1983, p. 45) endorse it as an honest and technically well-made film with a clear social message; but, on the other hand, Monique Hennebelle, while agreeing on the film's technical qualities, deplores *Abusuan*'s lack of political perspective. She writes:

It shows that the perennial nature of ancestral family traditions constitutes a drawback to the balance of modern society . . . [but] one could question the ideology contained in such a film. . . . Indeed, no moral lesson is going to bring a stop to a rural exodus caused by economic reasons. *(L'Afrique Littéraire et Artistique,* n. 34, 1974, p. 91)

Likewise, Paulin Soumanou Vieyra finds that *Abusuan* does not provide viewers with a serious look at social problems in the Ivory Coast. He adds: "As such, the film cannot lead to any new awareness. It merely tells a nice story taking place in a bourgeois milieu" *(Présence Africaine,* 1st Quarter 1975, p. 210).

Although *L'Herbe sauvage* is commonly gauged by critics as a conventional film replete with bourgeois clichés, Georges-Marie Lory *(L'Afrique Littéraire et Artistique,* n. 62–63, 1982, p. 116) approves nonetheless of its strong stand against female excision (clitoridectomy). As well, Paulin Soumanou Vieyra *(Peuples Noirs, Peuples Africains,* May-June 1983, p. 56) finds that *L'Herbe sauvage* presents interesting perspectives on development policies in contemporary Black African societies.

FILMOGRAPHY

Obs, 16 mm, black and white, 10 min., 1967.
Mouna ou le rêve d'un artiste (Mouna, An Artist's Dream), 16 mm, black and white, 55 min., 1969.
Récolte du coton (Growing Cotton), part one, 16 mm, color, 25 min., 1968.
Récolte du coton (Growing Cotton), part two, 16 mm, color, 25 min., 1968.
Profil ivoirien (Ivorian Profile), 16 mm, color, 25 min., 1969.
Achetez ivoirien (Buy Ivorian Products), 16 mm, color, 15 min., 1968.
Tam-tam ivoire (Ivorian Drum), 16 mm, color, 28 min., 1968.
J'ai dix ans (I Am Ten Years Old), 16 mm, color, 25 min., 1970.
Carnet de voyage (A Traveller's Notes), 16 mm, color, 30 min., 1969–1970.

Abusuan (The Family), 16/35 mm, color, 100 min., 1972.
Les Racines de la vie (The Roots of Life), 35 mm, color, 13 min., 1976.
L'Herbe sauvage (Weeds), 16/35 mm, color, 90 min., 1977.

BIBLIOGRAPHY

Interviews of Henri Duparc

Alain, Yves. "Mouna de Henri Duparc." *Bingo,* n. 221, June 1971, pp. 58–59.

"Le Cinéaste Henri Duparc et 'Mouna ou le rêve d'un artiste.' " *Fraternité Matin,* 22 February 1972, p. 8.

Hennebelle, Guy. "Comment devenir fou, entretien avec Henri Duparc." *Jeune Afrique,* n. 454, 16 September 1969, p. 53.

———. "Côte-d'Ivoire, Sénégal, Guinée: six cinéastes africains parlent. . . ." *L'Afrique Littéraire et Artistique,* n. 8, 1969, pp. 58–70.

Kane, Samba. "Quatre cinéastes ivoiriens à l'assaut de Ouaga." *Fraternité Matin,* 6 February 1973, p. 7.

Kouassi, Guy. "Le Cinéma ivoirien en marche: Henri Duparc tourne Abusuan." *Fraternité Matin,* 6 June 1972, p. 8.

———. "Abusuan, d'Henri Duparc: Qu'avons-nous fait pour eux?" *Fraternité Matin,* 19 December 1972, p. 8.

Ruelle, Catherine. "Duparc Henri." *L'Afrique Littéraire et Artistique,* n. 49, 3rd Quarter 1978, pp. 57–59.

Film Reviews and Studies of Henri Duparc

Bachy, Victor. *Le Cinéma en Côte d'Ivoire.* Brussels: OCIC/L'Harmattan, 1983.

Boughedir, Ferid. "Quinze jours ailleurs." *Ecran 1973,* n. 15, May 1973, pp. 54–55.

———. "Côte d'Ivoire." *Cinéma Québec,* vol. 3, n. 9–10, August 1974, pp. 30–32.

Cheriaa, Tahar. "Ouagadougou, un cinéma africain libre s'affirme." *Cinéma 73,* n. 175, April 1973, pp. 22–29.

Debrix, Jean-René. "Situation du cinéma en Afrique francophone." *Afrique Contemporaine,* n. 81, September-October 1975, pp. 2–7.

Ebony, Noël. "Abusuan—première ce soir au Rex." *Fraternité Matin,* 21 December 1972, p. 7.

———. "Journée ivoirienne: triomphe pour nos réalisateurs." *Fraternité Matin,* 10–11 February 1973, p. 11.

Gérard, Claude. "La Difficulté d'être." *Fraternité Matin,* 6 April 1970, p. 2.

Hennebelle, Guy. "Le Troisième Festival Panafricain du Cinéma de Ouagadougou." *L'Afrique Littéraire et Artistique,* n. 22, March 1972, pp. 88–95.

Hennebelle, Monique. "Carthage: un festival ouvert à tous les cinémas." *L'Afrique Littéraire et Artistique,* n. 34, 1974, pp. 79–93.

Lory, Georges-Marie. "La Côte d'Ivoire ne peut encore se prévaloir que d'un modeste florilège cinématographique." *L'Afrique Littéraire et Artistique,* n. 62–63, 1982, pp. 115–17.

Mativo, Wilson. "Cultural Dilemma of the African Film." *UFAHAMU,* vol. 1, n. 3, Winter 1971, pp. 64–68.

Pedersen, Vibeke, and Viggo Holm. "Afrika, en kampande filmkontinent." *Chaplin 101*, n. 6, 1970, pp. 280–95.

Traoré, Biny. "Cinéma africain et développement." *Peuples Noirs, Peuples Africains*, n. 33, May-June 1983, pp. 51–62.

Vieyra, Paulin Soumanou. *Le Cinéma africain*. Paris: Présence Africaine, 1975.

———. "Les 5èmes Journées Cinématographiques de Carthage." *Présence Africaine*, vol. 93, 1st Quarter 1975, pp. 200–14.

———. "Carthage 78." *Présence Africaine*, n. 110, 2nd Quarter 1979, pp. 159–66.

Désiré Ecaré (1939–   )
Ivory Coast

BIOGRAPHY

One of the early practitioners of Ivorian cinema is Désiré Ecaré, a Christian of Akan origin (this ethnic group lives principally in the southeastern region of the Ivory Coast) who was born on 15 April 1939 in Treichville, a working-class suburb of Abidjan. Describing his family background, the filmmaker expounds:

I come from a close Catholic family. I had a happy and rather uneventful childhood. My father was a civil servant and my mother a housewife who has always been extremely devoted to her family. We were ten kids at home, and we all went to school. Most of my siblings are now engaged in professional careers. (Désiré Ecaré to Christine Delorme, Paris, May 1985)

After having attended primary and secondary school at Catholic educational institutions, Désiré Ecaré enrolled at the Centre d'Art Dramatique in Abidjan, where he acted in such plays as *Papa Bon Dieu* by Louis Sapin. After he successfully staged *Noé* by André Obey in 1960, Ecaré was granted a scholarship by the Ivorian government to further his theater studies in France.

On 19 September 1961 the aspiring actor and stage director thus left the Ivory Coast for Paris, where he registered at the Centre d'Art Dramatique de la rue Blanche from which he was graduated two years later with a second prize in dramatic art after brilliant performances such as that of the lead role in Shakespeare's *Othello*. Yet, being an actor did not fully satisfy Ecaré, whose inner wish was to become a stage director so as to exert more control over his artistry. Thus, after failing the entrance examination to the renowned French Conservatoire d'Art Dramatique, Ecaré opted to explore the realm of cinema. In 1964 he was admitted to the Institut des Hautes Etudes Cinématographiques (IDHEC) in Paris, where he studied filmmaking for two years. There he fell in love with a fellow student specializing in editing, whom he was to marry shortly thereafter. Ecaré stresses:

I was all the more inclined to stick to my studies after I had met my wife, Marjietta, a Finnish woman who gave me two sons (they are now 16 and 20 years old). We are now divorced. However . . . she remains the only woman I ever married. (*Jeune Afrique Magazine,* July 1985, p. 68)

Even as a film student, however, Ecaré did not sever his ties altogether with the stage. He joined Jean-Marie Serreau's troupe Le Toucan, and, with such African actors as Douta Seck, he performed in a number of plays, including *La Tragédie du Roi Christophe* and *Une Saison au Congo* by the Martiniquan poet and playwright Aimé Césaire as well as in *The Exception and the Rule* by Bertolt Brecht.

After graduating from IDHEC in 1966, Désiré Ecaré, who had decided to spend a few more years in Paris, found it difficult to find a job that would put to proper use his recently acquired skills. Instead, he had to work at odd jobs to help support his wife and newborn son. Consequently, he elected to form his own production company, Les Films de la Lagune, and decided to undertake the making of his own motion picture, based on his wife's idea to illustrate on film the psychological and sociocultural alienation of Africans living in Paris. He recalls:

I said to myself that the best way to learn how to swim was to jump into the water. We tried to gather some raw film here and there and we tried to borrow a camera. Yet, I must say that at the beginning our major assets were our enthusiasm and our desire to make a film. (*Cahiers du Cinéma,* August 1968, p. 21)

Hence, it was with ten cans of film provided by J-R Debrix, who at that time was head of the film division of the French Ministry of Cooperation, and very limited capital—partly resulting from selling his own car—that Désiré Ecaré set out to shoot the first sequences of what was to become *Concerto pour un exil* (Concerto for an Exile). After viewing the early footage, Anatole Dauman, manager of Argos Films, provided Ecaré with sufficient funds to complete his work. The film was based on a loosely structured script intended to stimulate actors' contributions through improvisation. This method proved successful since, with the exception of Claudie Chazel, *Concerto pour un exil* was interpreted by nonprofessional actors whose roles were very close to their own life experiences as Black students exiled in Paris. The film's technical crew also consisted of friends whose willingness and dedication compensated for certain unexpected mishaps. In this respect, Henri Duparc* (one of Ecaré's IDHEC classmates) as well as the director's wife were given parts in the film to substitute for actors who, for one reason or another, failed to appear for shooting. *Concerto pour un exil* was released in 1967, and soon afterwards the filmmaker saw his relentless determination amply rewarded. In 1968 the film won a number of awards at the Hyères (France), Oberhausen (Germany), Carthage (Tunisia), Tashkent (USSR), and Cannes film festivals. Subsequent to such international exposure, *Concerto pour un exil* was broadcast by television stations in Germany and the Scandinavian countries, and was featured at the San Francisco Film Festival.

Ecaré's second film, *A nous deux, France* (Beware of France, 1970), whose total cost was a mere $20,000, was shot in French in Paris and edited in three months. Produced by Les Films de la Lagune and Argos Films, *A nous deux, France* premiered in Abidjan on 16 June 1970, during the course of a gala evening sponsored by the Société Ivoirienne de Cinéma (SIC). This event included a recital by the Black American musician and composer Memphis Slim, who had composed the film's musical score. That same year, *A nous deux, France* received the Jury's Special Prize at the Hyères Film Festival. *A nous deux, France* as well as *Concerto pour un exil* was shown at the Racines Noires (Black Roots) festival in Paris (1985).

Désiré Ecaré returned to the Ivory Coast in 1972, and because of limited opportunity in cinema in Abidjan, the director chose to become a civil servant. He was appointed counsellor at the Ministry of Tourism and the Ministry of Culture to delineate the impact the tourist industry was having on his country's cultural heritage. However, eagerly wishing for a return to filmmaking, Ecaré left his sedentary government job and in 1973 shot a few promotional pieces for real estate and agricultural companies. At this time he started *Visages de femmes* (Faces of Women), which was almost immediately interrupted for want of adequate financing. Then, upon the advice of a friend, Ecaré decided to establish himself financially by raising hogs, but was unsuccessful. In 1980 the indefatigable Ecaré undertook a campaign to be elected as representative, but this bid at political life also resulted in failure. Disappointed by these fruitless attempts, Desiré Ecaré bought a restaurant in Burkina Faso. In retrospect, he stresses humorously:

Now people say that I am a restaurant keeper because I own "Le Maquis" in Ouagadougou. I kind of like this label anyway. To tell you the truth I got this place in Ouagadougou because this city has become the capital of Black African cinema. Many filmmakers come to Ouagadougou for the Panafrican Film Festival (FESPACO) or stop there when they travel in this part of Africa. I lived there for a while and increased the number of customers. We cook nice dishes . . . but let's face it, the profits from this business will never allow me to finance a film. (Désiré Ecaré to Christine Delorme, May 1985)

In 1983 Ecaré returned to Abidjan with the intention of completing *Visages de femmes*, which he had started ten years earlier. This time, through bank loans backed by his real estate collateral, he succeeded in raising enough capital to add new sequences to his film as well as process and edit it. *Visages de femmes* (shot in French and such Ivorian vernaculars as Baoulé, Jula, and Bété), based on a total budget of $280,000 and produced and directed by Ecaré and distributed by Gerick Films, was released in 1985. Selected to be a part of the Critics'

Week at the 1985 Cannes Film Festival, the film received the International Film Critics' Award as well as the CITC Prize offered by the International Council of Television and Cinema (Conseil International de la Télévision et du Cinéma). A month later, accompanied by substantial press coverage, *Visages de femmes* opened in Paris, where it was simultaneously shown in as many as eight local movie houses and seen by 150,000 viewers. The film was also presented commercially and shown on television in several European countries, and featured at film festivals in London, Glasgow, New York, Los Angeles, San Francisco, Chicago, Washington D.C., and Montreal, and in 1987 at FESPACO (where Mme. Cissé Roland, who plays the role of Bernadette, was awarded the Prize for Best Female Interpretation). Yet, paradoxically, because of its explicit love scenes, *Visages de femmes* was censored for a while in Ecaré's country. As expected, the filmmaker bitterly resented such a ban (the first ever applied to an Ivorian film), which he denounced as an abusive attempt to limit his freedom of expression *(Libération,* 28 June 1985, p. 31). Ecaré's irritation with his government's position regarding *Visages de femmes* is all the more understandable since he has always made a point of not being an overtly subversive director. Of himself and other Black African directors he once said:

I think that we all have a pretty clear idea of what we want to do, but we have to learn how to express it in a simple and effective way. We must all beware of the demagogy which is presently stirring our continent. I also think that African cinema must provide our viewers with emotional and intellectual nourishment in accordance with our temperament. Finally, I feel that one must not nip African cinema in the bud by taking too blunt a stand, because this would alarm our leaders, who are already rather sensitive in matters concerning their political options. In my opinion, one can remain pleasant while being subversive. One can say terrible things with a disarming smile. *(L'Afrique Littéraire et Artistique,* n. 4, 1968, p. 81)

Ecaré considers cinema "a double-edged sword" which can "caress" or hurt depending on the way it is used *(Cahiers du Cinéma,* August 1968, p. 22). This explains, he says, the distrust African governments have of such a medium, hence their lack of support of the film industry. He suggests, however, that such a situation could be viably compensated by networks of privately funded coproductions. Ecaré also deplores the small number of African films shown on local television in the Ivory Coast and observes:

It is shameful to watch television for two hours and see films with heartbroken people driving cars on a Bach musical score whereas we, as Africans, have equally interesting things to show to African and foreign audiences. *(Fraternité Matin,* 11 March 1968, p. 7)

In general Ecaré favors thought-provoking films concerned with mankind and the complexities of life. For him, cinema is a universal means of expression, a sociocultural reflector which should inspire self-awareness as well as facilitate a better understanding among human beings. Although he does not believe himself to have been influenced by them, he admires such filmmakers as François Truffaut, Jean-Luc Godard, Orson Welles, Max Ophüls, Kenji Mizoguchi, and Carl Theodor Dreyer. In the field of Black African cinema, Ecaré appreciatively quotes works by Ousmane Sembene* (in particular *Mandabi)*, adding: ''I like what he does but I do not want to follow in his footsteps. I must invent my own film language. He has a linear narrative style, I don't'' *(L'Afrique Littéraire et Artistique,* n. 4, 1968, p. 81). Ecaré furthermore shows admiration for Med Hondo* *(Soleil O)* as well as Souleymane Cissé* *(Le Vent)* and Gaston Kaboré* *(Wend Kuuni),* both of whom he praises for their ability to re-create innovatively the African reality.

One could say that, on the whole, Ecaré's ironic films offer a rather critical and corrosive view of society. His elliptic film style differs from that of most of his African counterparts in that he outlines characters and situations without fully defining them. Désiré Ecaré now lives and works in Abidjan. It is to be hoped that his latest film, *Visages de femmes,* will provide sufficient returns for him to produce *Affaires Africaines* (African Stories), whose scenario he wrote several years ago.

MAJOR THEMES

Concerto pour un exil, A nous deux, France, and *Visages de femmes* are part of an ongoing film series entitled ''Castigare ridendo mores,'' which Ecaré views as a sort of *comédie humaine* aimed at correcting social ills through laughter.

Concerto pour un exil, whose title, significantly, refers to a musical composition, sketches in an ironic tone, rather than vehemently, the disillusionment of African youths living in Paris. According to Ecaré, it is neither a political tract nor a social document:

I did not want to make an ethnographic film on exile. I wanted to create an ambiance. I would like to have been a musician. At the beginning I did not know how my film would evolve. I only knew that it would have four protagonists. I detest linear narratives and this is why I conceived my film as a farandole within which my protagonists would come and go. *(L'Afrique Littéraire et Artistique,* n. 4, 1968, p. 76)

Although Ecaré acknowledges having experienced situations identical to those depicted in *Concerto pour un exil,* he denies that it is an autobiographical film:

My film concerns the dual estrangement of a whole generation of students. Here are people who earned diplomas that are rather important for Africa because our underdevelopment is largely due to a lack of trained professionals. We waste a great part of our national product to send them to school abroad. Yet, after the completion of their studies they prefer to stay in France . . . instead of returning to Africa to find their country ruled by people who are ill-prepared to head a modern state. *(Télérama,* 12 October 1969, p. 60)

Composed of vignettes, *Concerto pour un exil* focuses on Hervé, a disenchanted student union leader; his wife, who cures her loneliness with tranquillizers and the prospect of an extramarital affair; Doudou, a womanizer whose hunting grounds know no ethnic frontiers; and Yao, a recently arrived streetsweeper. They all frequently meet and/or sleep at Hervé's overcrowded quarters, a situation which eventually leads to the couple's eviction from their apartment building. The film closes on a freeze frame of the two lost amid an anonymous crowd. On being asked if they are on their way back to Africa, Ecaré says: "I don't think so but I don't know. I purposely left them in the street. The end of the film is open" *(L'Afrique Littéraire et Artistique,* n. 4, 1968, p. 77).

A nous deux, France also focuses on alienation. The film's title, "Beware of France," which could also be translated as "Let's get to grips, France" alludes to both the country and the name of one of its French female characters. Here this title should almost be taken as a war-cry uttered by young African women as they come to France to conquer the heart of Ivorian students living in Paris. According to Ecaré:

A nous deux, France stemmed from a real story. In 1946 our current president, Houphouet-Boigny, sent to France young men who were to become the first post-colonial government executives of the Ivory Coast. But most of them were marrying European women. So, Houphouet-Boigny decided to dispatch to Paris planeloads of young Ivorian women to marry these men. The end result was not the one that had been expected. But the women did take advantage of this new freedom to "evolve." *(Jeune Afrique Magazine,* July-August 1985, p. 69)

In *A nous deux, France,* such an "evolution" is satirically depicted through portraits of Black women wearing blond wigs and sporting the latest fashions of Paris. One of them has been living there for ten years with a seemingly financially secure Frenchman, who at one time had promised to launch her into a singing career; by the end of the motion picture his thirst for exoticism will be quenched by a newly arrived and younger African woman. The film's protagonist is Tarzan, who bears no resemblance whatsoever to his mythical namesake. He wears a derby hat and is dressed in a tuxedo; speaking of his attire, he states: "One must remain dignified in order not to display one's misery." Tarzan stands as a starched and stifled jobless wanderer, meant as a caricature of Western acculturation. Married to France, by whom he has a child, his legal status does not in the least prevent him from having affairs with Black women—an alleged attempt to recover his own Africanness! At one point he recites to one of his African lovers verses from "Black Woman," a love poem by Leopold Sedar Senghor that glorifies African women. After Tarzan's lyrical rendition, the woman says, "He could marry us instead of singing our beauty," a derisive reference to Senghor's having married a white woman. This innuendo and other ironical allusions to Senghor's "negritude" (a philosophy that praises the values and essence of Negro African civilization) caused *A nous deux, France* to be banned in Senegal during Senghor's regime.

Other characters in Ecaré's film include an anonymous Black dancer who steps in and out of the frame, providing a syncopated leitmotiv to the nonlinear plot. Asked why he is always dancing, he mockingly replies (with an American accent) that he is merely performing the role that was given to him. Significantly, one finds him again in the final sequence of the film, dancing away in a shanty town inhabited by African migrant workers while words such as "where shall I go from here" are heard in the soundtrack—which in itself stresses the despair and loneliness of Ecaré's protagonists, irremediably caught in a merry-go-round of broken hopes and aborted dreams.

Visages de femmes follows some of the stylistic patterns found in Ecaré's previous films. Like *A nous deux, France,* it is rhythmically constructed around a dance which punctuates the motion picture and from which characters are made to emerge to perform in given situations. Says Ecaré:

This dance is a joyous celebration which originated in the South of the Ivory Coast. . . . I devised the first part of *Visages de femmes* as a series of impressions. It is a celebration which bursts out in front of you and in which one notices various characters . . . these characters mingle with the crowd and disappear in the dance from which they sprang. (*Libération,* 28 June 1985, p. 31)

Shot in Abidjan and in Ecaré's family village, *Visages de femmes* could be termed a multifaceted comedy of manners which depicts the changing conditions of women in the Ivory Coast. In the filmmaker's words, "It shows that for 25 years, in post-colonial Ivory Coast, women have always participated in development efforts" (*Afrique-Asie,* 29 July 1985, p. 57). Here is how Désiré Ecaré summarizes his plot:

In Treichville . . . Bernadette, a fishmonger . . . tries to expand her business. . . . she has to switch from a barter economy to a money-based society. . . . The bankers' attitude, . . . family traditions . . . the reactions of businessmen who are not ready to accept a woman in their midst, as well as her own ignorance of the mechanics of large-scale business considerably reduce her chances for success.

At the village of Koffikro, one witnesses N'Guessan's tragic fate as she refuses to be her husband's object in order to conquer her own right to love. . . . Fanta strives to escape men's whims and idiosyncrasies by learning karate. Her aim is to challenge men through force, a means men have always used. . . .

They [African women] all want to escape male domination . . . yet the means they bring into play contradict their initial goal. (Pressbook, *Visages de femmes,* 1985)

These means have seemingly been used by women since the beginnings of time. To illustrate such a theme, Ecaré stages here the most explicit love scene in the whole history of Black African cinema, whose prudishness has now become legendary. While *Concerto pour un exil* contained restrained eroticism and *A nous deux, France* showed a scene where Tarzan is strumming France's naked body, *Visages de femmes* offers views of a sin-spared African Eden in which bronze bodies dive and merge lasciviously in the luscious bed of a nearby river.

SURVEY OF CRITICISM

Concerto pour un exil was generally well received by film critics. G. Kamissoko hails it as one of the most sophisticated works of Black African cinema *(Fraternité Matin,* 23 June 1970, p. 7), and Guy Hennebelle writes:

It is indubitably Désiré Ecaré who has best probed the ambiguity of the emigration of intellectuals with his "Concerto pour un exil." I do not agree with my nonetheless friend Jean-Pierre Choisey who considers in *Young Cinema and Theatre* n. 41 that the author has bypassed the real problems. Ecaré has only outlined the specific drama of the sub-proletariat it is true! But as concerns students, who generally come from well-off families, his incisive serenity and his rejection of any peevishness must be appreciated. *(Young Cinema and Theatre,* vol. 3, 1970, p. 27).

Claude-Jean Philippe notes:

With remarkable skill, Désiré Ecaré films what he knows and what he has experienced.
. . .

Désiré Ecaré is a born filmmaker. . . . His film teems with observations which he aptly organizes in a motion picture structured in a flexible yet rigorous manner. *(Télérama,* 12 October 1969, p. 60).

Likewise, Marcel Martin is impressed by the quality of Ecaré's first effort as a filmmaker: "Désiré Ecaré has a good eye. . . . he depicts wandering characters whose . . . resignation prevents them from falling into despair. These characters form a lively and truthful microcosm" *(Cinéma 68,* August-September 1968, p. 75).

Other reviewers, like Michel Ciment *(Positif,* Summer 1968, p. 32) and Michel Capdenac *(Les Lettres Françaises,* 1 October 1969, p. 14), point out the derisive mood and vivid spontaneity of Ecaré's film, and Claude Gérard *(Fraternité Matin,* 27 August 1968, p. 7) draws attention to its rhythmic and quasi-musical format.

Georges-Marie Lory defines *A nous deux, France* as a "humorous analysis of acculturation" *(L'Afrique Littéraire et Artistique,* n. 63–64, 1982, p. 116). Yet, more than its content, it is primarily the film's style that has drawn the critics' attention. After establishing a parallel between Ecaré's irony and that of Jonathan Swift, Claude Gérard states:

A nous deux, France carries further the aesthetic and thematic concerns found in *Concerto pour un exil. A nous deux, France* demonstrates the maturity of a director who is now in full command of his film language . . . who has invented his own style . . . a style which is both easily identifiable and original. *(Fraternité Matin,* 26 April 1971, p. 4)

Mireille Amiel likes Ecaré's "Voltaire-like" use of satire and favors Memphis Slim's musical score which, she says, is in perfect harmony with the film's syncopated pace *(Cinéma 71,* January 1971, p. 139). For Louis Seguin, the Ivorian filmmaker is an "African Lubitsch" who knows how to treat a serious subject matter without falling into the pitfalls of didactism *(Positif,* Summer 1970, p. 42). According to Guy Hennebelle, with *Concerto pour un exil* and *A nous deux, France* "Ecaré has introduced humour into African films. . . . No doubt he is one of the best hopes of the continent's cinema" *(Young Cinema and Theatre,* vol. 3, 1970, p. 29).

Olivier Séguret describes *Visages de femmes* as "a cyclical motion picture made of three parts which are autonomous and complementary. Each part concerns the life of a particular African woman. . . . *Visages de femmes* does not resemble any film one has been given to see" *(Libération,* 28 June 1985, p. 31). Anne de Gaspéri remarks:

Désiré Ecaré observes the changing women of a new society with subtlety, insolence, and a certain degree of seriousness even though he does so with humor and cheerfulness. . . . in the manner of Marivaux and Molière, Désiré Ecaré depicts Ivorian women as they are and not as they should be. *(Le Quotidien de Paris,* 29 June 1985, p. 24)

Cherifa Benabdessadok is equally appreciative of *Visages de femmes'* satirical tone and visual beauty. However, he regrets what he calls the film's "systematically negative portrayals of men," and finds its overall message confusing, wondering which female characteristics the director is really praising *(Afrique-Asie,* 29 July 1985, p. 57).

As expected, various comments are made about *Visages de femmes'* nude scene, but none of the film critics judges it to be distasteful. Catherine Humblot *(Le Monde,* 30 June 1985, p. 11) sees it as "audacious" but adds that it is "neither pornographic nor truly erotic. It is more a pantheistic love scene." Both Claude-Marie Trémois *(Télérama,* 29 June 1985, p. 27) and Catherine Humblot stress some of *Visage de femmes'* structural deficiencies, but seem more interested in the film's narrative pattern, which they link to the African oral tradition. The latter comments: "Here, like in African storytelling, one shifts from symbol to reality, from what is told to what is shown. A celebration opens and concludes the story which closes on a morale as happens in tales." Thus, as far as Catherine Humblot is concerned, Désiré Ecaré should be considered a moralist rather than a political advocate.

FILMOGRAPHY

Concerto pour un exil (Concerto for an Exile), 16/35 mm, black and white, 42 min., 1968.
A nous deux, France (Beware of France), 16/35 mm, black and white, 52 min., 1970.
Visages de femmes (Faces of Women), 35 mm, color, 105 min., 1985.

BIBLIOGRAPHY

Writing by Désiré Ecaré

Ecaré, Désiré. "Film: Visages de femmes." *Unir Cinéma*, n. 18 (125), May-June 1985, pp. 10–12.

Interviews of Désiré Ecaré

Aumont, Jacques. "En marge de Hyères: entretien avec Désiré Ecaré." *Cahiers du Cinéma*, n. 203, August 1968, pp. 21–22.
Chemla, Max. "Désiré Ecaré." *Film Critica*, n. 193, December 1968, pp. 530–31.
Ciment, Michel. "Entretien avec Désiré Ecaré." *Positif*, n. 97, Summer 1968, pp. 33–36.
Delorme, Christine. "Un Cinéaste du regard." *Libération*, 28 June 1985, p. 31.
Hennebelle, Guy. "Naissance d'un cinéma ivoirien: Concerto pour un exil—Opus 1 de Désiré Ecaré." *L'Afrique Littéraire et Artistique*, n. 4, 1968, pp. 75–81.
———. "Désiré Ecaré." *Jeune Cinéma*, n. 34, November 1968, pp. 4–9.
———. "Entretien avec Désiré Ecaré." *Ciné 71*, n. 152, January 1971, pp. 138–40.
———. "Ecaré Désiré." *L'Afrique Littéraire et Artistique*, n. 44, 3rd Quarter 1978, pp. 60–62.
Morellet, Jean-Claude. "Désiré Ecaré—beaucoup de sympathie et pas d'argent." *Jeune-Afrique*, n. 386–387, 27 May 1968, p. 69.
"Visage africain du cinéma d'aujourd'hui—Avec Désiré Ecaré." *Fraternité Matin*, 11 March 1968, p. 7.

Film Reviews and Studies of Désiré Ecaré

Amiel, Mireille. "A nous deux, France." *Cinéma 71*, n. 152, January 1971, pp. 138–40.
"Après le Sénégalais Sembène Ousmane, l'Ivoirien Désiré Ecaré voit son talent consacré à Cannes. . . ." *Fraternité Matin*, 11 June 1968, p. 7.
Bachy, Victor. *Le Cinéma en Côte d'Ivoire*. Brussels: OCIC/L'Harmattan, 1983.
———. "Dossier—Visages de femmes." *Unir Cinéma*, n. 19 (126), July-August 1985, pp. 11–14.
Benabdessadok, Cherifa. "Visages de femmes." *Afrique-Asie*, n. 353, 29 July 1985, p. 57.
Ben Yahmed, Danielle, and Michel Servet. "Gros plan sur Désiré Ecaré." *Jeune Afrique Magazine*, n. 18, July-August 1985, pp. 68–69.
Boughedir, Ferid. "Le Cinéma ivoirien: de riches possibilités." *Cinéma Québec*, vol. 3, n. 9–10, August 1974, pp. 31–32.
———. "Femmes, humour et militantisme." *Jeune Afrique*, n. 1260, 27 February 1985, p. 61.
Canby, Vincent. "Film: 'Faces,' Two Ivory Coast Tales." *New York Times*, 13 February 1987, p. C22.
Capdenac, Michel. "Stridences japonaises et nostalgies africaines." *Les Lettres Françaises*, n. 1302, 1 October 1969, pp. 13–14.
"Concerto pour un exil (découpage in extenso)." *Avant-Scène Cinéma*, n. 134, March 1973, pp. 41–49.

"Débat-Forum: une séquence érotique du film 'Visages de femmes' polarise l'attention." *Sidwaya,* 27 February 1987, p. 8.

Debrix, Jean-René. "Situation du cinéma en Afrique francophone." *Afrique Contemporaine,* n. 81, September-October 1975, pp. 2–7.

"Désiré Ecaré: encore un nouveau film!" *Fraternité Matin,* 4 February 1969, p. 7.

Devalière, François. "Désiré Ecaré: un désir égaré sur des visages de femmes?" *Relais* (Bulletin des agents en coopération et à l'étranger), n. 2, April 1986, pp. 14–15.

Ferrari, Alain. "Le Second Souffle du cinéma africain." *Téléciné,* n. 176, January 1973, pp. 2–9.

France, Francine. "Une Cabale de mauvais coucheurs." *Le Matin,* 2 July 1985, p. 27.

Gaspéri, Anne de. "Les Joyeuses Mutantes de Désiré Ecaré." *Le Quotidien de Paris,* 29 June 1985, p. 24.

Gérard, Claude. "Le XXIIᵉ festival du cinéma français: un enrichissement général." *Fraternité Matin,* 27 August 1968, p. 7.

———. "Venise à l'heure du Tiers-Monde." *Fraternité Matin,* 29 September 1969, p. 9.

———. "A nous deux, France." *Fraternité Matin,* 26 April 1971, p. 4.

"Grande première de gala des films de Désiré Ecaré." *Fraternité Matin,* 16 June 1970, p. 7.

Hennebelle, Guy. "Concerto pour un exil et Cabascabo." *Jeune Afrique,* n. 458, 8 October 1969, pp. 18–19.

———. "L'Afrique noire francophone." *Cinéma 70,* n. 142, January 1970, pp. 87–98.

———. "Côte d'Ivoire: A nous deux, France." *Jeune Afrique,* n. 488, 12 May 1970, pp. 40–41.

———. "Socially Committed or Exotic." *Young Cinema and Theatre,* vol. 3, 1970, pp. 24–33.

———. "Carthage." *Cinéma 71,* n. 154, March 1971, pp. 34–36.

———. "Le Cinéma ivoirien." *L'Afrique Littéraire et Artistique,* n. 20, 1st Quarter 1972, pp. 227–34.

———. *Guide des films anti-impérialistes.* Paris: Editions du Centenaire, 1975.

Hoberman, J. "It's a Mad, Mad World." *Village Voice,* 17 February 1987, p. 67.

Humblot, Catherine. "Visages de femmes, de Désiré Ecaré—la condition africaine." *Le Monde,* 30 June 1985, p. 11.

Jusu, K.K. Man. "De la qualité des films africains." *Fraternité Matin,* 12 October 1982, p. 10.

———. "Le 18ème FESPACO à Ouagadougou—des avis partagés sur 'Visages de femmes.' " *Fraternité Matin,* 27 February 1987, p. 9.

Kamissoko, G. "Désiré Ecaré, un grand Ivoirien." *Fraternité Matin,* 23 June 1970, p. 7.

Kauffmann, Stanley. "Stanley Kauffmann on Films." *The New Republic,* 16 February 1987, p. 24.

Lory, Georges-Marie. "La Côte d'Ivoire ne peut encore se prévaloir que d'un modeste florilège cinématographique." *L'Afrique Littéraire et Artistique,* n. 63–64, 1982, pp. 115–17.

Marcorelles, Louis. "Deux films africains." *Le Monde,* 30 September 1969, p. 17.

Mardore, Michel. "Renoir en Afrique." *Le Nouvel Observateur,* n. 1077, 28 June 1985, p. 18.

Martin, Marcel. "Concerto pour un exil de Désiré Ecaré." *Cinéma 68,* n. 128, August-September 1975, pp. 75–76.

Mativo, Wilson. "Cultural Dilemma of the African Film." *UFAHAMU,* vol. 1, n. 3, Winter 1971, pp. 64–68.

Maurin, François. "Originalité d'un cinéma africain." *L'Humanité,* 27 September 1969, p. 8.

Meda, Yirzada. "Visages de femmes, vrai ou faux." *Sidwaya,* 27 February 1987, p. 6.

N, H., and Z. Y. "Interviews express à propos de Visages de femmes." *Sidwaya,* 2 March 1987, p. 9.

"Une Nouvelle Étape dans le cinéma africain: la victoire au festival d'Hyères du réalisateur ivoirien Désiré Ecaré." *Fraternité Matin,* 7 May 1968, p. 7.

Pedersen, Vibeke, and Viggo Holm Jensen. "Afrika, en kampande filmkontinent." *Chaplin 101,* n. 6, 1970, pp. 280–95.

Perez, Michel. "Visages de femmes de Désiré Ecaré." *Le Matin,* 2 July 1985, p. 27.

Philippe, Claude-Jean. "Les Africains n'ont pas confiance en leurs cinéastes. Ils ont tort." *Télérama,* n. 1030, 12 October 1969, pp. 59–61.

Placca, Jean-Baptiste. "La Consécration d'un non-conformiste." *Jeune Afrique,* n. 1278, 3 July 1985, pp. 60–61.

Seguin, Louis. "Hyères en 1970." *Positif,* n. 118, Summer 1970, pp. 40–51.

Séguret, Olivier. "Visages de femmes." *Libération,* 28 June 1985, p. 31.

Tessier, Max. "Hyères, aujourd'hui et demain?... A nous deux France! de Désiré Ecaré." *Cinéma 70,* n. 147, June 1970, pp. 21–22.

Trémois, Claude-Marie. "Visages de femmes." *Télérama,* n. 1850, 29 June 1985, pp. 25, 27.

Vieyra, Paulin Soumanou. *Le Cinéma africain.* Paris: Présence Africaine, 1975.

Welsh, Henry. "La Semaine de la critique." *Jeune Cinéma,* n. 168, July-August 1985, pp. 27–28.

Kramo-Lanciné Fadika (1948–)
Ivory Coast

BIOGRAPHY

We cannot allow ourselves the luxury of using cinema as pure entertainment. African cinema should have a didactic role and address the many problems Africans have to face in their societies. I strongly believe that our cinema must be socially-oriented or else I would not have taken up filmmaking. I do not want to make "digestive films," the type you watch after dinner and before going to bed. For me, cinema is another means of communication which should be geared towards educating the masses.

Such a vigorous and uncompromising statement was made on 9 November 1982 by Kramo-Lanciné Fadika as he presented his film *Djeli* at the Howard University School of Communications, Washington, D.C., during his visit to the United States sponsored by the African Studies Association (ASA).

Kramo-Lanciné Fadika belongs with directors such as Jean-Louis Koula and Mory Traoré to what is commonly called the "new wave" of Ivorian filmmakers. Of Malinke origin and Muslim extraction, Fadika was born in 1948 in Danané, located in the western region of the Ivory Coast. He was brought up in a large polygamous family with thirteen children. His father was a tradesman, and his mother was a housewife as well as a fruit and vegetable vendor. After completing high school at the Lycée of Bingerville in 1969, Kramo-Lanciné Fadika studied modern literature at the University of Abidjan, from which he earned in 1970–1971 a university degree in literary studies (Diplôme Universitaire d'Etudes Littéraires, also known as DUEL). In October 1971, Fadika went to Paris, where he attended the Louis Lumière Film School for three years. In 1975 he returned to Abidjan, where he obtained a position at the Office National de la Promotion Rurale, a government agency in charge of rural development whose services were terminated in 1981. This job enabled him to produce and direct several pedagogical documentaries aimed at spearheading certain government policies in the area of agriculture, education, and health.

It was while working as a civil servant that Fadika managed to save enough money to begin filming *Djeli,* a feature length film based on his own scenario. He stresses: "*Djeli* did not have any specific source of financing. It was basically through my own resources and the input of some members of my family that I was able to make this film" (Howard University, 9 November 1982).

Although the shooting of *Djeli* started during the filmmaker's vacation in 1978, it was to be completed only in 1980. The director explains:

It took me two and a half years to finish the film. I would shoot whenever I had money, but I had to stop each time my money ran out. The extras were paid daily but the other actors and technicians had to wait for the film to make some profit to get their salary. These and other factors explain how I was able to keep *Djeli*'s budget down to a mere $100,000. (Howard University, 1982)

Except for some specific village scenes, *Djeli* was shot mostly in French by a crew of Ivorian and French technicians, among them Christian Lacoste, who had previously participated in *Abusuan* and *L'Herbe sauvage,* two feature films by Henri Duparc*, another director from the Ivory Coast. *Djeli* is interpreted entirely by nonprofessional actors such as the villagers of Kouto (located in the northern part of the Ivory Coast), whom the filmmaker had befriended during former field trips while working for the Office National de la Promotion Rurale. Fadika emphasizes:

The people you see in the film never acted before. Having had some experience working in the countryside before, I was able to gauge pretty much their reactions and I knew how to approach them. So, when I went to see them to discuss my film project, I filmed the villagers on video. Then we screened and discussed the video footage together. It is through such a process that we selected those who eventually were to act in the film. (Howard University, 1982)

Released in 1981, *Djeli* was extremely well received by most critics to the extent that Kramo-Lanciné Fadika became the first Ivorian director to win the Grand Prize, the International Film Critics Prize, and an award from the International Catholic Organization for the Cinema (OCIC) at the Seventh Pan-African Film Festival of Ouagadougou (FESPACO) in Burkina Faso. That same year, *Djeli* was featured at the Locarno Film Festival and subsequently has done rather well on the festival circuit. As well, Kramo-Lanciné Fadika was to present *Djeli* at an African film festival held in Tokyo (1984). *Djeli* has also been presented in France, England, Italy, Canada, and the United States, among other places. Yet, more important for a filmmaker who essentially addresses his works to his fellow Africans, *Djeli* became a commercial success in the Ivory Coast and a number of other West African countries, where it often drew larger audiences than Western and Asian movies at the time (as happened in the Ivory Coast and Niger). It should be noted that *Djeli* is now available on video cassette, a distribution channel which should be more frequently used by independent Black African filmmakers.

Unfortunately, *Djeli*'s successful local runs and international recognition have not secured sufficient means for Kramo-Lanciné Fadika to shoot *Le Gros Lot* (Jackpot), a satirical motion picture (with a projected budget of $170,000) concerning the impact of money on the Ivorian society. Fadika has been working on *Le Gros Lot* since 1982. The director points out:

Presently, there are no production infrastructures in the Ivory Coast, and cultural policies pertaining to cinema remain rather enigmatic all over Black Africa; either our leaders have not yet understood the impact of film or they have understood it too well. (Howard University, 1982)

And for the Ivorian filmmaker, these poor working conditions, more than any other factor, together with a similarity of themes, constitute the common ground of Black African cinema. According to him:

Black African cinema could be defined through certain common denominators. For instance, all Black African filmmakers have to face difficult work conditions. Also one could say that our cinema is characterized from the point of view of theme rather than style. One cannot speak of Black African cinema from an aesthetic point of view because we are all looking for ways of expressing ourselves. Some of us tend to adopt Western film styles and others try to pattern their films after the African oral tradition. Let us hope that one day we will be able to find an African way of filming ourselves. (Howard University, 1982)

In the course of the 1981 FESPACO, the search for an authentically African film language (including the preeminence of imagery over standard narrative patterns), along with the need for sharing technical resources, led such young filmmakers as Kramo-Lanciné Fadika, Idrissa Ouedraogo of Burkina Faso, and Cheikh Ngaido Bah, Ousmane William M'Baye, and Ben Diogaye Beye of Senegal to create L'Oeil Vert (Green Eye), an inter-African film cooperative whose very name is intended to symbolize hope and new perspectives. Like most African directors, Fadika is a member of the Fédération Panafricaine des Cinéastes (FEPACI). After completing *Le Gros Lot*, Fadika plans to film *Abidjan City*, a feature-length musical comedy which he is currently trying to stage. His present activities include professional photography and video. Kramo-Lanciné Fadika is single and lives and works primarily in Abidjan.

MAJOR THEMES

Djeli examines the social inequities resulting from the survival in contemporary societies of a timeless caste system which forbids conjugality between a man of griot origin and a woman of noble lineage. "Djeli" is a Malinke word which means bloodline. It also designates a caste of people, also called griots, who specialize in storytelling, reciting legends, or recounting the valiant deeds of a family's or country's forebears. The Ivorian director explains:

The griots are basically a caste of musicians, shoemakers and blacksmiths. They tell stories and represent a historical and cultural continuity between the past, present and future. . . . Their social status is very complex because on the one hand they play a very important role as intermediaries between the nobles and other castes in society but, on the other hand they are not allowed to marry outside their caste and other people look down upon them with some type of contempt. (Howard University, 1982)

From the beginning, *Djeli* invites viewers to penetrate the magic realm of African storytelling. Its initial scene takes place in the cozy living room of a well-off household where the whole family is gathered to listen to a Malinke legend narrated by three griots. This legend appropriately explains the griots' fealty to nobility. The following sequence is rendered through sepia-hued images meant to accent the mythical origin of griots and to separate it from the rest of the film (in standard colors), which illustrates present-day reality. The film tells a story within a story, that of two men who set out on a long journey in the countryside. After walking for days, they run out of food, and one of them collapses of total exhaustion. At this point the other man cuts flesh from his own side and offers it to his companion to eat. This generous act saves the failing man's life. The latter feels forever indebted and tells him: "You fed me with your blood and flesh, so from now on my descendants will pledge allegiance to yours. I am now your griot and your own blood." This is why, says the legend, griots have remained noblemen's vassals and sing their praises. Next, the credits of the film unfold on the screen over a panoramic view of contemporary Abidjan. What ensues is "a modern tale" (such is also *Djeli*'s subtitle) concerning modern Ivorian society.

The plot of the film focuses on the story of Fanta and Karamoko. Both come from the same village but now live in Abidjan, where their friendship has changed into love. She has just graduated from high school, and he is a college student. When the two return home for vacation, Fanta's graduation is warmly celebrated by her family. However, this festive mood soon falters as she announces to her parents her intention to marry Karamoko. Her father forbids such a union because Fanta is of noble extraction and Karamoko is a griot's son. Fanta vehemently rebels against her father's decision, and her mother laments that she has become "as stubborn as a goat." Yet the young girl also refuses to go to the city and marry, as one of her girlfriends suggests, arguing that a marriage against tradition and her parents' will would make an outcast of her and prevent her from coming back to her native village. In the meantime, the relationship between Fanta's parents deteriorates, and her father repudiates his wife, whom he holds responsible for their daughter's insubordination. Upon his older brother's plea for clemency, Fanta's father reconsiders his decision but obstinately refuses to change his mind concerning his daughter's marriage. Inextricably caught between the dictates of tradition and her own feelings, Fanta decides to commit suicide. Rushed to an emergency room, Fanta will be saved. Fanta's father and Karamoko meet at the hospital. The film ends on a freeze frame as the two men forcefully look at each other.

With the exception of a few films like *Niaye* (1964) and *Black Girl* (1966), both by Ousmane Sembene*, *Saitane* by Oumarou Ganda*, (1973) or *Suicides* (1982) by the Cameroonian director Jean-Claude Tchuilen, suicide has rarely been illustrated in Black African films, mainly because it is infrequently found in traditional Sub-Saharan societies. Here Fadika chooses to include such a theme in his film precisely to emphasize the unmistakable changes that have taken place in those societies. He stresses: "Suicides are very rare in our traditional societies but now their rate tends to increase because our traditions have been perturbed. Therefore, Fanta's attempted suicide in the film should be given a highly symbolic value" (Howard University, 1982). Thus, logically, Fadika is equally interested in probing the many facets of such social transformations. He points out:

Although on one level the film may present a love story, my intention was to do something more and to show how a young African, like myself, perceives certain problems which are still prevalent in African societies. I was primarily interested in analyzing the fact that people's thought patterns have not matched other changes. . . . I should emphasize that the film is also based on total contradiction because the young people who advocate change are also attached to tradition. They listen to traditional music and respect the customs of their forefathers. . . . The elders' standpoint is also ambiguous. Fanta's father refuses to let his daughter marry a griot's son, yet he encourages her to further her studies in contrast to what was done before. Moreover, Fanta's grandmother [disapproves of] girls' schooling but shows pride in her granddaughter's scholastic achievements. All of this demonstrates our contradictions. In *Djeli,* I tried to dramatize the oppositions existing between tradition and modernity while showing both the constructive and destructive aspects of tradition. (Howard University, 1982)

SURVEY OF CRITICISM

To this day, Kramo-Lanciné Fadika remains the only filmmaker in the history of Black African cinema to have received, for his first feature film, the FESPACO Grand Prize as well as several other awards at the same festival. Therefore, as can be expected, substantial press coverage salutes this distinction.

An article published in the Ivorian daily *Fraternité Matin* (10 March 1981, p. 16) presents engaging comments from filmmakers and film critics, recorded in Ouagadougou immediately after *Djeli* was acclaimed at the Seventh FES-PACO. Ousmane Sembene says of Fadika: "Here is a man who has substance. . . . There are some filmmakers who do nothing but illustrate stories. He is an authentic storyteller." Sarah Maldoror* states: "This film impressed me a lot and I told Fadika Kramo-Lanciné that he reminded me of Oumarou Ganda; both are sensitive and show great respect for human beings." Moreover, the French critic Pierre Haffner praises the director for his sensitive and refreshing look at traditional life, whereas previous Ivorian filmmakers had essentially focused on plots taking place in urban settings.

In their respective film reviews, Frédéric Grah-Mel compliments *Djeli* for its pictorial beauty and intelligent thematic treatment *(Fraternité Matin,* 2 March 1981, p. 28), while Mario Relich writes that "next to *The Exile* [by Oumarou Ganda], it was the most impressive African film in the festival [Seventh FES-PACO]," adding: "Kramo Lanciné surpasses, and this is only his first film, even Ousmane Sembene's probing depiction of neighborhood life, and use of non-professional actors, in *The Money Order" (West Africa,* 7 December 1981, p. 2909). For Ferid Boughedir:

Djelli [sic] is a particularly brilliant work. . . . the strength of the film is to avoid any caricatural schematism by clearly presenting the motivations of the elders for whom the rejection of tradition equates self-denial. Yet, the cause of the young is pleaded by an old man who realizes that the world has changed. The actors are not would-be villagers as can be found in so many African films. They play their own role so well that, in comparison, the acting of the two students (who are unfortunately made to speak French) seems artificial. *(Jeune Afrique,* 11 March 1981, p. 62)

Both Anne Samson *(La Croix,* 19 March 1981, p. 17) and Charles Tesson *Cahiers du Cinéma,* February 1982, p. 40) favor *Djeli*'s simplicity and sincerity. For Georges-Marie Lory, the film draws its inspiration from the universal Romeo and Juliet theme and should be remembered mainly for its interesting depiction of village life in the north of the Ivory Coast *(L'Afrique Littéraire et Artistique,* n. 63–64, 1982, p. 116).

A somewhat lukewarm appraisal of *Djeli* is that of the American film critic Mosk, who writes:

Director Fadika Kramo-Lancine . . . has told his tale with some ethnic insights which could slant it for specialized fests and seminars. However, despite good intentions it [Djeli] remains a bit sluggish in tempo though its depiction of village and country life develops interest. A worthwhile attempt that will still have more force on African grounds, and word is it scored at various Afro fests, with more informative than untoward chances in other climes. Technically acceptable. *(Variety,* 26 August 1981, p. 24)

Finally, beyond its thematic connotations with the African oral tradition, *Djeli* has also been stylistically influenced by this tradition, as observed by Farida Ayari, who notes that "Fadika Kramo-Lanciné has chosen an open ending for his film, thus complying with the structure of the traditional tale whose social usefulness is to trigger a discussion rather than to propose a solution" *(Adhoua,* April-September 1981, p. 7). Likewise, *Le Soleil*'s film reviewer, D. D., draws similarities between *Djeli*'s narrative structure and that of traditional African storytelling *(Le Soleil,* 9–10 October 1982, p. 8). Such tale-like style could undoubtedly be seen as Fadika's initial steps toward a truly African film language.

FILMOGRAPHY

Several short documentaries on agricultural issues for L'Office National de la Promotion Rurale.

Djeli, 16/35 mm, color, 90 min., 1981.

BIBLIOGRAPHY

Film Reviews and Studies of Kramo-Lanciné Fadika

Ayari, Farida. "Djeli, de Fadika Kramo-Lanciné (Côte d'Ivoire): la légende au présent." *Adhoua,* n. 4–5, April-September 1981, pp. 7–8.

———. "Images de femmes." *Cinémaction,* n. 26, 1983, pp. 136–39.

Bachy, Victor. *Le Cinéma en Côte d'Ivoire.* Brussels: OCIC/L'Harmattan, 1983.

Bosséno, Christian. "Fêtes biennales des cinémas d'Afrique." *Recherche, Pédagogie et Culture,* n. 53–54, May-August 1981, pp. 69–73.

Boughedir, Ferid. "Les Héritiers d'Oumarou Ganda." *Jeune Afrique,* n. 1053, 11 March 1981, pp. 62–63.

———. "L'Année des dupes." *Jeune Afrique,* n. 1095, 30 December 1981, pp. 166–69.

———. "FEPACI, fais pas ça." *Jeune Afrique,* n. 1107, 24 March 1982, pp. 58–59.

Cham, Mbye Baboucar. "Film Production in West Africa: 1979–1981." *Présence Africaine,* n. 124, 4th Quarter 1982, pp. 168–87.

D. D. "Djeli: Contre le système des castes." *Le Soleil,* 9–10 October 1982, p. 8.

Grah-Mel, Frédéric. "La Côte d'Ivoire arrache le Grand Prix du 7ᵉ Fespaco." *Fraternité Matin,* 2 March 1981, p. 28.

———. "L'Honneur et le devoir." *Fraternité Matin,* 3 March 1981, p. 25.

———. "Fespaco—un Accueil très favorable au film ivoirien Djeli." *Fraternité Matin,* 10 March 1981, p. 16.

Lory, Georges-Marie. "La Côte d'Ivoire ne peut encore se prévaloir que d'un modeste florilège cinématographique." *L'Afrique Littéraire et Artistique,* n. 63–64, 1982, pp. 115–17.

Mosk. "Djeli—Conte d'aujourd'hui." *Variety,* 26 August 1981, p. 24.

Relich, Mario. "From Glitter to Gore in the Film World." *West Africa,* n. 3358, 7 December 1981, pp. 2907–11.

Samson, Anne. "La Fête africaine du cinéma." *La Croix,* 19 March 1981, p. 17.

Sidibé, Ladji. "Les Cinéastes ivoiriens déclarent: nous ne sommes pas aidés." *Fraternité Matin,* 7–8 March 1981, p. 5.

Tapsoba, Clément. "Concilier le public africain et son cinéma." *Carrefour Africain,* n. 767, 25 February 1983, pp. 19–20.

Tesson, Charles. "La Route des Philippines." *Cahiers du Cinéma,* n. 332, February 1982, pp. 39–43.

Traoré, Biny. "Djeli ou le mariage impossible." *L'Observateur,* n. 2039, 27–28 February 1981, pp. 6–8.

———. "Cinéma et développement." *Peuples Noirs, Peuples Africains,* n. 33, May-June 1983, pp. 51–62.

Safi Faye (1943–)
Senegal

BIOGRAPHY

Presently the only active independent female Black African-born filmmaker, Safi Faye was born in Dakar in 1943. Her parents come from Fad'jal, a small village located about 100 kilometers south of Dakar. Faye is of Serer origin. This ethnic group, which constitutes about 20 percent of the Senegalese population, lives primarily in the Thiès and Sine-Saloum regions. Mainly sedentary farmers tending peanut crops, the Serers have traditionally remained strongly attached to their cultural heritage and lived somewhat isolated from other ethnic groups. Yet, through recent migrations to Dakar and other Senegalese cities, some Serers are now gradually merging into the prevailing Wolof culture and urban lifestyle.

Born into the household of a polygamous village chief and businessman, Faye is the second of her mother's seven children and has thirteen half brothers and sisters as well. Although Faye's mother is illiterate, both parents expected their sons and daughters to be well educated. Many of their children are now engaged in such fields as medicine and teaching. However, Faye recalls that she and her siblings were given more freedom, as they were growing up, than other Senegalese youth. Benefitting from the care, warmth, and solidarity of an extended family and nurtured by the tales of a rich oral tradition, the childhood of the Senegalese cinéaste was extremely happy. To this day, she has maintained close ties with her relatives whom she affectionately portrayed in her film *Kaddu beykat* (Peasant Letter).

After primary school, Faye attended the Rufisque normal school and, at the precocious age of nineteen, obtained her teacher's certificate. In 1963 she started working for the Dakar school system, where she was to remain for six years. She liked teaching, and her stay in Senegal's capital enabled her to enjoy its varied cultural events. Among these was the 1966 Dakar Festival of Negro Art, for which she was selected to serve as an official hostess and guide to foreign guests. During this festival she met Jean Rouch, the noted French ethnologist and filmmaker who, apparently, encouraged her serious interest in cinema, particularly ethnographic filmmaking. However, it was as an actress that she first entered the realm of cinema. Rouch chose her, along with Damouré Zira Lam, Ibrahima Dia, and Mustapha Alassane*, to play in *Petit à petit ou Les Lettres persanes 1968* (Little by Little or the 1968 Persian Letters), whose title alludes to Montesquieu's *Persian Letters* about the coming of two Persians to Paris and their ironic comments concerning their new lifestyle. With an approach somewhat similar to that of the eighteenth-century French philosopher, Rouch's loosely structured film records the discoveries of a young man from Niger faced with contemporary Parisian life. The shooting of this film enabled Faye to leave Senegal temporarily and travel to Paris, Switzerland, the Ivory Coast, and Niger. More significantly, however, *Petit à petit ou Les Lettres persanes 1968* allowed her to become acquainted with Rouch's technique of cinéma-vérité (an unobtrusive camera eye, spontaneous shooting, improvised nonprofessional acting, and mostly single takes), which was to influence her greatly in the course of her future career as a filmmaker. Yet, in retrospect, Safi Faye dislikes this film, questions its significance, and expresses severe criticism as to her own performance in it *(Cinémaction,* n. 17, 1982, pp. 63–64). After *Petit à petit ou Les Lettres persanes 1968,* Safi Faye returned to Dakar, where she resumed her teaching, but her brief experience in the film world had a lingering effect on her mind. A year later she abandoned her teaching activities and went to Paris, where she registered at the Ecole Pratique des Hautes Etudes to study ethnology and at the Louis Lumière Film School in 1972. For several years, Faye led the life of a student, also engaging in modelling and film dubbing in order to support herself. This was a time of hard work and cultural estrangement during which she occasionally relaxed to the tunes of European pop singers and those of Wilson Pickett and Aretha Franklin. In 1972, still a film student, she used her meager savings to make her first film, *La Passante* (The Passerby). The following year, after participating with other fellow students of the Louis Lumière Film School in the making of a collective film, *Revanche* (Revenge), she spent her summer at home, conducting research on Serer religions. She began shooting her first feature length docudrama, *Kaddu beykat,* with a crew of three, including a French cameraman and her uncle, who worked briefly as a soundman. This film, made on a shoestring budget of $20,000 with the money she earned from *La Passante* and financial support from the French Ministry of Cooperation, was completed in 1974 at about the time she graduated from the Louis Lumière Film School. Subsequently, in 1975, Safi Faye pursued her studies in ethnology at the Sorbonne. That same year, *Kaddu beykat* (which she had started in 1972) was released and well received by most critics. It was presented at the Cannes Film Festival and won an award at the Festival International du Film de l'Ensemble Francophone (FIFEF) held in Geneva. In 1975–1976 this film obtained the Georges Sadoul Prize in France and a special award at the Fifth Pan-African Film Festival of Ouagadougou (FESPACO) in Burkina Faso, and won the International Film Critics Award at the Berlin Film Festival (FIPRESCI). Two years later (1978) *Kaddu beykat* was to be shown in the retrospective of Senegalese films presented at the New York Museum of Modern Art. Among other film events, the motion picture was to be included in the Racines Noires (Black Roots) film festival held in Paris from 18 March to 8 April 1985 and in 1986 in an ''African Mini-Series'' at the Biograph, a commercial movie theater located in Washington, D.C. Also in 1976, Safi Faye gave birth to a daughter, Zeiba. Faye received a diploma in ethnology from the Sorbonne in 1977 and was invited to serve as one of the official judges of FIFEF. Involved in both filmmaking and academic pursuits, she received a Ph.D. in ethnology from the University of Paris VII in 1979, and her research on the Serer peasantry culminated in two new films: *Fad'jal* (Come and Work) and *Goob na ñu* (The Harvest is In). The $70,000 *Fad'jal,* produced by Safi Faye, the French Ministry of Cooperation, and ZDF (a German television station), was featured at the 1979 Cannes Film Festival and was to receive an award at the 1980 Carthage Film Festival. During the academic year 1979–1980, Faye joined the faculty of the Free University of Berlin as a guest lecturer and studied video production in Berlin, during which time she shot *3 ans 5 mois* (3 Years 5 Months, filmed in 1979 and edited in 1983), a video film produced by a German cultural association, Deutsche Akademische Austansch Dienst (also known as DAAD). In Germany she became interested in the fate of expatriate African students, about whom she made the $30,000 budget *Man Sa Yay* (I, Your Mother, 1980), co-produced with ZDF. The year 1981 saw the release of *Les Ames au soleil* (Souls under the Sun), a $50,000 documentary commissioned by the United Nations. A year later, Faye completed *Selbé et tant d'autres* (Selbe and So Many Others), co-produced by UNICEF and Faust Films Production (Munich). The film won a special prize at the 1983 Leipzig Festival (Germany).

In November 1982, along with such African filmmakers as Kwah Ansah*, Ola Balogun*, and Haile Gerima*, Safi Faye participated in symposia on African cinema during the annual African Studies Association (ASA) Conference held in Washington, D.C. At that conference she discussed her sociopolitical commitment as an independent African director as follows: ''Independent African filmmakers are anxious to fight against all forms of foreign domination. In dealing with social conditions, they stress the economic aspect of life and focus on problems which are directly affecting our people.'' Describing her filmmaking techniques, the Senegalese cinéaste added:

I do not work single-handedly but rather through and with other people. I go to talk to the farmers in their village, we discuss their problems and I take notes. Even though I may write a script for my films, I basically leave the peasants free to express themselves in front of a camera and I listen. My films are collective works in which everybody takes an active part. . . . I have never made a fiction film. I am mainly interested in film as a research tool.

Favoring the direct portrayal of real characters and true events, Faye focused her lenses in 1984 on various ethnic restaurants located in Paris. This project resulted in *Ambassades nourricières* (Culinary Embassies), produced by INA (Institut National de l'Audiovisuel) and FR3, a French television station. In 1984, as well, Faye travelled to India and Japan to take part in film festivals. The following year she was again hired by FR3 to make a ten-minute documentary film on Racines Noires (Black Roots), a multimedia cultural festival held in Paris and dedicated to the cinema, poetry, and painting of Africa and the Black Diaspora. Also in 1985, Safi Faye attended a number of film events. She served as one of the official judges at the Tenth International Film Festival of India (3– 17 January 1985) held in New Delhi, and was invited to participate in the Second Festival Internacional de Cinema, TV e Video de Rio de Janeiro (21 November- 1 December 1985) in Brazil, where she presented her film *Kaddu beykat*.

Although in 1963 a Cameroonian journalist by the name of Thérèse Sita Bella distinguished herself by making a half-hour documentary entitled *Tam Tam à Paris* (African Drums in Paris), and in spite of playwright Efua Sutherland's brief try at cinema with *Araba: The Village Story,* a docudrama produced by ABC and shot in Ghana in 1967, Black African cinema still remains a male-dominated sphere. Although a few African women are engaged in television productions, Safi Faye is today the only independent African-born woman director of Black African filmmaking. Asked how she felt about this, Faye stated:

I do not make any difference between male and female African directors. My problems are the same as those faced by my male counterparts. They struggle to make films and so do I. My films are not primarily focusing on women. As a filmmaker I am equally concerned with the fate of all Senegalese peasants, both men and women. (ASA Conference, 1982)

A strong-minded and outspoken yet amiable woman possessing a keen sense of humor, Safi Faye is presently living in Paris, where she divides her time between raising her daughter and working assiduously on a number of film projects. In the near future, the Senegalese director plans to undertake the making of her first fiction film, entitled *Negu Jaargon* (Cobweb), which will be based on a $1 million budget.

MAJOR THEMES

Although touching on one of Faye's familiar themes, exile, *La Passante* diverges considerably from her other films. It was shot by the American cameraman Kal Muller and interpreted by Faye, the Cameroonian actor and filmmaker Daniel Kamwa*, and Philippe Luzuy. In *La Passante* Safi Faye plays the role of a young African woman living in France. Walking down the streets of Paris, she draws the attention, respectively, of a French and an African man. The film in essence expresses the two men's perception of the young woman. On one hand, the European suitor dreams of taking her to visit the city and dine while discussing intellectual matters, after which he would take her to bed. On the other hand, the African admirer imagines that they would go to his room and dance lasciviously. Then, nostalgic for the spices and flavors of his native land, he would ask her to prepare an African dish. In this film no words are spoken, and only music and three lines of poetry are recorded on its soundtrack. Even though the depth of *La Passante* is debatable, its good-humored and light-hearted tone and sexual inferences were at the time in sharp contrast with the serious and somewhat puritanical works of most of Safi Faye's male counterparts. Faye says of her film:

The female protagonist of *La Passante* is a foreigner who arouses a certain curiosity among the people of the country in which she is presently residing. She lives in a country where she is neither integrated nor assimilated. She is in Europe but her thoughts are in Africa. I am just like her, I define myself as a "passerby." (Faye to author, Paris, Winter 1985)

La Passante was but a trial run. So was *Revanche,* a short film which narrates the story of a madman who wants to climb the Pont Neuf, one of Paris' oldest bridges. Faye's first major work, in which she describes the daily life of villagers, is *Kaddu beykat,* dedicated to her own grandfather, who died a few days after the shooting of the film was completed. *Kaddu beykat* (Wolof for "The Voice of the Peasant") was literally meant to "give a voice" to Senegalese peasants so that they might debate among themselves as well as delineate to others the socioeconomic and political facets of their agricultural problems. Purposely shot at a slow pace to reflect the lyrical intimacy of man and nature as well as the ritualistic aspect of farming, the film condemns the precariousness of rural life based on the whims of peanut monoculture. Introduced in the eighteenth century under French colonialism, such monoculture is still largely practiced in Senegal, where farmers are subject to dramatic fluctuations in the price of peanuts on the world market. *Kaddu beykat* is a soberly poetic yet politically effective black and white fictionalized documentary which denounces what Faye sees as the inadequate measures taken by her government to cure the ills of the Senegalese peasantry. About the political content of such a film as *Kaddu beykat* (which has been banned in Senegal), Faye stresses:

It is all too easy and convenient to place the blame for Africa's present ills uniquely on the past or on outside forces. . . . It is without a doubt more important to explore the continent's present problems in terms of the policies of those in power, for putting the spotlight exclusively on extraneous forces is an alibi. *(The Guardian,* July 9, 1980, p. 7)

Shot in three weeks during the busy rainy season, Faye's unadorned film, which through her own voice-over takes the structural form of a letter to a friend, is interpreted by nonprofessional actors, who were given much freedom to play their own roles. Her camera witnesses village life from dawn to dusk: its awakening, collective work on dusty fields, domestic tasks, family meals, children's games, work songs, the timeless custom of courting and marriage, traditional medicine practices, and the daily evening meetings of elders under the "palaver tree," where they regretfully recall a bountiful past while expressing fears in the face of a most uncertain future. Here the filmmaker depicts such life not merely as a detached observer but as an intrinsic part of her society. Although Safi Faye shows mainly collective concerns, she also takes the time to narrate an individual story, that of a young villager who is forced to migrate temporarily to Dakar (where he faces the ruthless exploitation of some of Senegal's new middle class) to work at odd jobs to purchase his fiancée's dowry. The film ends on a freeze frame of the dignified face of an old man (Faye's own grandfather) who questions the audience with a forceful look as Faye, through voice-over, closes her work on a solemn note with the brief yet powerful statement: "This is the voice of the peasant—Kaddu beykat." In this manner the filmmaker lends her film larger significance, for as she told film critic Paulin S. Vieyra*: "This story . . . could take place in any other African country as well; I shot it in Senegal because, as a Senegalese, it was easier for me to do it there" (Le Cinéma africain, 1975, p. 190).

Fad'jal (which bears the name of Faye's Serer village) provides us with an analysis of the sociocultural realities of her rural community. Using in her film the quote by the well-known Malian philosopher Hampaté Ba, according to which "in Africa, whenever an old man dies, it is as though a library has burnt down," Faye's goal here is to show how collective memory is transmitted by the elders to the younger generations through the oral tradition. Again, with a camera perfectly integrated in the environment she chooses to describe, Faye focuses on the loss of old values as she depicts the changes occurring within the Senegalese peasantry due to government reforms and the migration of farmers to urban centers and foreign countries. With the exception of some staged scenes like the grandfather's narration to the village children, the filmmaker successfully uses direct cinema as a privileged means of expression.

Kaddu beykat and Fad'jal exemplify Safi Faye's ethnographic and socioanthropological approach to film and indicate the overall direction of her subsequent works. Goob na ñu is, thus, a documentary that concerns itself with agricultural issues, and Man Sa Yay, structurally reminiscent of Kaddu beykat, is based on an exchange of letters between an exiled Senegalese student and his mother at home. With Man Sa Yay, Faye also illustrates the isolation of guest workers in a compelling film where "West Berlin itself becomes an anonymous mass of glass and concrete" (West Africa, 16 August 1982, p. 2112). 3 ans 5 mois, which focuses on Faye's own daughter, shows the ease with which young children adapt to foreign culture. Les Ames au soleil stresses the problems related to drought, health, and development and how they affect women and children in remote rural areas. Selbé et tant d'autres describes the fate of village women left behind after men have migrated to urban centers in search of work to support their families. Ambassades nourricières is an original attempt to penetrate specific cultures through their culinary rites. It contains interviews of African, Armenian,

Asiatic, Hungarian, Italian, and Latin American restaurant owners who have established themselves in Paris. These interviews provide specific insights into their past historical, sociocultural, and political milieu as well as topics concerning emigration and acculturation.

SURVEY OF CRITICISM

Asked once for whom she made such a film as *Fad'jal*, Safi Faye responded: "First of all, for Africa, for African people—those who know what Africa is and those who don't know although they think they do. And then for the rest" *(Framework,* Fall 1969, p. 17).

Unfortunately, Faye's films, which are often severely critical of Senegal's policies, have not yet been allowed for official public viewing in that country. As a consequence, her films have been principally viewed by non-African audiences and, with but a few exceptions, have been reviewed only by Western critics. Louis Marcorelles, for instance, praises Faye's affectionate but precise consideration of village life in *Kaddu beykat (Le Monde,* 13 December 1975, p. 34), while Jacques Grant credits her for avoiding the pitfalls of exoticism *(Cinéma 77,* January 1977, p. 93). Ali Kheury N'Daw likes the film's introspective qualities, lucidity, and sensitivity *(Le Soleil,* 12 April 1977, entertainment section). The African-American film critic Clyde Taylor finds this work to be

a disarming, satisfying film. Its story is familiar in the new, independent African cinema, but it is told with a serene, authoritative touch that made me think something new was being brought to African visual art. *(The Black Collegian,* May-June 1979, p. 95)

After having uttered some reservations concerning the technical quality of *Kaddu beykat*'s pictures, Christian Bosséno enthusiastically writes:

The first feature length film of the young woman director Safi Faye is exemplary. It discusses with sensitivity, simplicity and effectiveness the major problem of Third World economy subjected to the hazards of monoculture. . . . the film calls for an awareness of and a resistance against an economic system which is aberrant for the future of the country. *Revue du Cinéma, Image et Son,* October 1977, p. 157)

In *Variety,* Holl foresees that *Kaddu beykat* "will draw the attention on the fest circuit and elsewhere as a prominent helmer." He describes this film as "a fiction docu" which "gives more than just facts." The reviewer adds:

Faye's quiet approach to her subject in an idyllic, meditative manner commands respect and attention. Camera angles are set at a convenient distance from the action and the rest follows without show or emphasis. The graphic account of a woman's sickness, the witch-doctor treatments and cleansing rituals in soft shadows, underscores a compassionate individual's pleading for traditional ways in a changing, neo-colonial world. *(Variety,* 14 July 1976, p. 25)

Holl's views are confirmed by Janick Arbois, who urges French audiences to see this film if they want to view Africa with the heart and the eyes of an African woman *(Télérama,* 20 October 1976, p. 87).

Termed "a visual tale" *(Des femmes en Mouvement,* 4 April 1980, p. 6) by some, *Fad'jal*'s construction, seen as a mixture of documentary genre and historical re-creation, is not as convincing for others *(Positif,* July-August 1979, p. 55), although all critics agree on the originality of its approach. Here, in Marcel Martin's words, Safi Faye "avantageously combines an ethnographic and social perspective" *(Ecran 79,* 15 July 1979, p. 22). Deploring its lack of "narrative thread," Mosk finds the film repetitive and "more ritualistic than clarifying," concluding, however, that *Fad'jal* "does give a fine surface picture of village life" *(Variety,* 6 June 1979, p. 22).

With the exception of Mario Relich's review of *Man Sa Yay* as a "compelling film" in spite of some "contrived" scenes *(West Africa,* 16 August 1982, p. 2112) and of Raphael Bassan's commendation of *Ambassades nourricières (Afrique-Asie,* 31 December 1985, p. 129), comparatively few writings have been devoted to Faye's other films. As reflected in reviews of her films, Safi Faye's international reputation is due primarily to *Kaddu beykat* and *Fad'jal.* Even though both films have been criticized sporadically for some technical deficiencies and their stylistic wavering between documentary and fiction, most observers agree that they unmistakably represent a most significant breakthrough in the area of African ethnographic filmmaking.

FILMOGRAPHY

La Passante (The Passerby), 16 mm, color, 10 min., 1972.
Revanche (Revenge), 16 mm, black and white, 15 min., 1973.
Kaddu beykat (Peasant Letter), 16 mm, black and white, 95 min., 1975.
Fad'jal (Come and Work), 16 mm, color, 108 min., 1979.
Goob na ñu (The Harvest is In), 16 mm, color, 30 min., 1979.
3 Ans 5 mois (3 Years 5 Months), videofilm, color, 30 min., 1979–1983.
Man Sa Yay (I, Your Mother), 16 mm, color, 60 min., 1980.
Les Ames au soleil (Souls under the Sun), 16 mm, color, 27 min., 1981.
Selbé et tant d'autres (Selbe and So Many Others), 16 mm, color, 30 min., 1982.
Ambassades nourricières (Culinary Embassies), 16 mm, color, 58 min., 1984.

BIBLIOGRAPHY

Interviews of Safi Faye

Bernard, Jean. "Safi Faye comme elle se dit." *Afrique Nouvelle,* n. 1372, 15 October 1975, pp. 17–18.
Eichenberger, P. "Safi Faye—une africaine derrière la caméra." *Unir Cinéma,* n. 69, October-November 1976, pp. 1–2 (supplement).

Haffner, Pierre. "Jean Rouch jugé par six cinéastes d'Afrique noire." *Cinémaction*, n. 17, 1982, pp. 62–76.

Mangin, Marc. "J'aime filmer sur un rythme africain." *Droit et Liberté*, n. 389, March 1980, pp. 35–36.

Martin, Angela. "Four Filmmakers from West Africa." *Framework*, n. 11, Fall 1969, pp. 16–21.

Maupin, Françoise. "Entretien avec Safi Faye." *La Revue du Cinéma, Image et Son*, n. 303, February 1976, pp. 76–80.

Ruelle, Catherine. "Faye Safi." *L'Afrique Littéraire et Artistique*, n. 49, 3rd Quarter 1978, pp. 63–65.

Traoré, Moussa. "La Passion selon Safi Faye." *Bingo*, n. 319, August 1979, pp. 28–29.

Vasudev, Aruna. "When the Festival Is Over, Everyone Returns to His Corner." *Festival News* (Tenth International Festival of India), n. 13, 15 January 1985, pp. 1–3.

Welsh, Henry. "Entretien avec Safi Faye." *Jeune Cinéma*, n. 99, December 1976–January 1977, pp. 9–12.

Film Reviews and Studies of Safi Faye

Arbois, Janick. "Lettre paysanne." *Télérama*, n. 1397, 20 October 1976, p. 87.

Bachy, Victor. "Festivals et rencontres: les Journées Cinématographiques de Carthage 1980." *Revue Belge du Cinéma*, n. 20, 1981, pp. 35–36.

Bassan, Raphael. "Quand nourriture rime avec culture." *Afrique-Asie*, n. 338, 31 December 1985, p. 129.

Beye, Ben Diogaye. "Safi Faye, vedette du film *Petit à petit ou les Lettres persanes 1968.*" *Bingo*, n. 192, January 1969, pp. 26–27.

———. "Après le Festival de Royan, une réelle dialectique dans le dialogue des cultures." *Cinéma 77*, n. 221, May 1977, pp. 64–68.

Binet, Jacques. "Cinéma africain." *Afrique Contemporaine*, n. 83, January-February 1976, pp. 27–30.

Bosséno, Christian. "Lettre paysanne." *Revue du Cinéma, Image et Son*, n. 320–321, October 1977, pp. 157–58.

———. "Paysans." *Cinémaction*, special issue, 1982, pp. 188–195.

Courant, Gérard. "Fad'jal." *Cinéma 79*, n. 247–248, July-August 1979, p. 27.

"Fad'jal." *Le Film Français*, n. 1768, 4 May 1979, p. 23.

Ghali, Noureddine. "Festival international du film de l'ensemble francophone." *Cinéma 76*, n. 205, January 1976, pp. 24–25.

Grant, Jacques. "Lettre paysanne, carnet de notes pour la paysannerie africaine." *Cinéma 77*, n. 217, January 1977, pp. 93–94.

Haffner, Pierre. "Sénégal." *Cinémaction*, special issue, 1982, pp. 157–160.

Hoberman, J. "Inside Senegal." *Village Voice*, 6 February 1978, pp. 42, 48.

Holl. "Kaddu beykat." *Variety*, 14 July 1976, p. 25.

Kettelhack, Angelika. "Kaddu beykat." *Frauen und Film*, n. 9, October 1976, p. 57.

Marcorelles, Louis. "Le Prix Georges Sadoul 1975—l'Afrique et le Brésil au palmarès." *Le Monde*, 13 December 1975, p. 34.

Martin, Marcel. "Fad'jal." *Ecran 79*, n. 82, 15 July 1979, p. 22.

Moustapha, Mahama Baba. "Lettre paysanne de Safi Faye." *Cinémarabe*, n. 6, March-April 1977, p. 36.

Mosk. "Fadjal." *Variety*, 6 June 1979, p. 22.

N'Daw, Ali Kheury. "Des Paysans bien de chez nous." *Le Soleil,* 12 April 1977, entertainment section.

P., J-L. "Lettre paysanne." *Positif,* n. 188, December 1976, p. 72.

Paranagua, Paulo-Antonio. "Fad'jal de Safi Faye (Sénégal)." *Positif,* n. 220–221, July-August 1979, p. 55.

"La Passante religieuse." *Jeune Afrique,* n. 607, 26 August 1972, pp. 60–61.

"Les Pasionarias n'étaient pas au rendez-vous." *Jeune Afrique,* n. 792, 12 March 1976, p. 56.

Relich, Mario. "Chronicle of a Student." *West Africa,* n. 3393, 16 August 1982, p. 2112.

"Safi Faye: Profile of a Filmmaker." *Playback—A Family Bulletin on Audiovisual Matters,* n. 3, 1981, pp. 6–7.

Schissel, Howard. "Africa on Film: The First Feminine View." *The Guardian,* 9 July 1980, p. 7.

Sylviane and Marie-Aude. "Un Conte visuel qui, à travers des images en écho, transmet l'histoire d'un village." *Des Femmes en Mouvement,* n. 22–23, 4 April 1980, p. 6.

Taylor, Clyde. "The Screen Scene." *The Black Collegian,* vol. 9, n. 5, May-June 1979, pp. 94–96.

Vaugeois, Gérard. "Lettre paysanne." *Ecran 76,* n. 53, 15 December 1976, p. 66.

Vieyra, Paulin Soumanou. *Le Cinéma africain.* Paris: Présence Africaine, 1975.

———. *Le Cinéma au Sénégal.* Brussels: OCIC/L'Harmattan, 1983.

Oumarou Ganda (1935–1981)
Niger

BIOGRAPHY

Of Djerma origin and Muslim extraction, Ganda was born in 1935 in Niamey, the capital of Niger. He was raised in a modest and caring family, whose evenings were often devoted to storytelling, thus giving rise to Ganda's lifelong interest in the African oral tradition.

After attending primary school in Niamey, Ganda enrolled in the French army (Niger was then under French tutelage) at the age of seventeen, pretending to be nineteen to have a better chance of being considered for enlistment. As an artillery man, he received basic training in his native city and was later stationed in Mali before being sent to Indochina (now Vietnam), where he fought for two years in the French expeditionary force against the Indochinese freedom fighters. After France's memorable defeat in Dien Bien Phu in 1955 Ganda was discharged and returned to Niger, where he faced a difficult adjustment into his former surroundings. Embittered by unemployment, the young veteran decided to try his luck elsewhere. He subsequently went to the Ivory Coast, where he met Jean Rouch, the French ethnologist and filmmaker, who was to play an essential part in Ganda's future professional life. Here is Ganda's recollection of this encounter:

I was working in the Ivory Coast as a surveyor-statistician. . . . At that time Jean Rouch was conducting a survey on the emigrants from Niger who were then residing in the Ivory Coast. He finally decided to make a film on one of these people. He wanted as his protagonist an emigrant from Niger who would symbolize his expatriated countrymen living in the Ivory Coast. This is how I ended up playing the role. (*Bingo,* August 1979, p. 29)

Thus, in 1958, without any training as an actor, Oumarou Ganda played the part of a jobless army veteran traumatized by his experiences at the front in Rouch's *Zazouman de Treichville* (named after Abidjan's working-class suburb), which depicts the problems faced by the Ivorian subproletariat. Primarily intended as a fourteen-minute documentary, this motion picture grew into a seventy-minute film and was eventually retitled *Moi, un Noir* (I, A Black Man). In 1959, *Moi, un Noir,* both a docudrama and a psychodrama, was awarded the Louis Delluc Prize and was praised by Jean-Luc Godard and other French New Wave proponents for the director's innovative and spontaneous approach to filmmaking. Ganda himself was less enthusiastic concerning Rouch's work. He once said: "I personally did not like this film very much . . . it rang false at some point; in addition I felt the film should have been made in an entirely different way" *(Cinémaction,* 1982, p. 70). Ganda readily acknowledged, nevertheless, the positive sides of being exposed to Jean Rouch's direct cinema:

The shooting of *Moi, un Noir,* showed me that cinema could be used to reflect life . . . in various areas of the world. I also realized that, on a large scale, cinema was the most effective means of expression. *(L'Afrique Littéraire et Artistique,* n. 4, 1968, p. 71)

On another occasion Ganda emphasized:

For me it was a decisive experience. I discovered an aspect of film that I had never perceived before. I realized that films could also serve to reflect reality instead of distorting it as happens in most of the foreign films which are massively distributed throughout Africa. *(Les Lettres Françaises,* 4 June 1969, p. 18)

Yet, after this first encounter with the world of film, Oumarou Ganda continued working as a surveyor-statistician in Abidjan. In 1962, however, he participated in the making of Rouch's *Rose et Landry* (Rose and Landry), a black and white film illustrating Abidjan youth caught in the clash between traditional customs and modern values. Impressed by Ganda's aptitude and interest in film, Rouch advised him to seek formal film training. Following Rouch's suggestion, Ganda subsequently returned to Niamey, where a team of French cinéastes had been sent to initiate young Africans into the art of film.

In the latter half of the 1960s, after having learned basic filmmaking techniques, Ganda became an assistant director in the cinema department of the Niamey French Cultural Center. Soon thereafter, he entered a script-writing competition and won the first prize for best film project. This provided him with $5,000 and the technical means to start *Cabascabo* (1968)— produced by Argos Film and the Consortium Audio-visual International—his first film shot by the French cameraman Gérard de Battista, in which Ganda also played the main role. Noted for its simplicity and documentary-like authenticity, this largely autobiographical black and white fiction film was selected for the Critics' Week at the Cannes Film Festival in 1969. Of particular importance is the fact that, in 1969 as well, *Cabascabo* received the Special Jury Award at the Moscow Film Festival, the Critics' Prize at the Malaga Film Festival in Spain, and the Third Prize ("Tanit de Bronze") at the Carthage Film Festival in Tunisia. In Niger, where it was widely shown, the film was well received by both urban and rural audiences. Also in 1969, Oumarou Ganda participated in a filmmakers' roundtable at the Mannheim Film Festival (Germany). Meanwhile, besides his activities as a filmmaker, Oumarou Ganda cultivated his interest in the oral tradition by initiating on Radio-Niger "L'Heure du Conte" (the storytelling hour), a weekly program in Djerma (one of Niger's local languages) during which he would tell traditional legends and tales as well as stories of his own invention.

In 1970 Ganda directed his second feature film, *Le Wazzou polygame* (The Polygamist's Morale), produced by Argos Film with partial financing from the French Ministry of Cooperation. *Le Wazzou polygame* was shot in three weeks in the Djerma language by a crew of African technicians and Gérard de Battista. The following year this color motion picture won the International Film Critics Award at the Dinard Film Festival in France as well as the First Prize ("Etalon de Yenenga") at the third Pan-African Festival of Ouagadougou (FESPACO) in Burkina Faso. After the success of *Le Wazzou polygame,* Ganda invested his own funds in the making of *Saitane* (Satan), which took three years to complete due to occasional financing difficulties and the sporadic availability of film technicians and equipment. Eventually Ganda's perseverance was rewarded, for *Saitane* won a special award at the Fifth FESPACO, held in 1976 in Burkina Faso. It should also be noted that two years earlier Oumarou Ganda had already received special recognition from FESPACO's official judges for "the remarkable continuity and undeniable quality of his inspiration." Both *Le Wazzou polygame* and *Saitane* were featured at the Racines Noires (Black Roots) festival held in Paris in the spring of 1985.

In addition to his feature films, Ganda made several documentaries, including *Cock, cock, cock* (1973). The director's fourth and last feature film is *L'Exilé* (The Exiled, 1980), a $75,000 production co-funded by the French Ministry of Cooperation and the government of Niger (by way of a grant allocated to an association of local filmmakers). *L'Exilé* was featured at the 1980 Carthage Film Festival and the 1981 London Film Festival.

Oumarou Ganda was working on a historical film project entitled *Gani Kouré, le vainqueur de Gourma* (Gani Kouré, The Conqueror of Gourma) when he suddenly died of a heart attack on 1 January 1981.

From his first motion picture, *Cabascabo,* which was shot in Hausa, Djerma, and Songhai (three of the local languages spoken in Niger) and released with French subtitles, Ganda firmly asserted that the African reality was better expressed in a local vernacular rather than an alien tongue inherited from the West. This attitude comes as no surprise since the director's primary concern was to make films for African audiences.

Although Ganda's favorite filmmakers included Jean Rouch (whose spontaneous techniques undoubtedly influenced *Cabascabo*'s film language), Jean-Luc Godard, François Truffaut, Mustapha Alassane*, and Ababacar Samb*, he showed a marked preference for Ousmane Sembene*. Like Sembene, Ganda felt that the African filmmaker was but a modern griot, the bard, historian, and moralist of his society. He once stated: "In our countries cinema must be a means of education and entertainment. However, it will also concern itself with issues that will make our political leaders think" *(L'Afrique Littéraire et Artistique,* n. 4, 1968, p. 74).

In spite of his early death at the age of forty-five, Oumarou Ganda has left an indelible imprint in the history of Black African cinema, as well as in the minds of filmmakers and film critics alike, who remember him as a discreet, sincere, sensitive, and talented individual *(Adhoua,* January-March 1981, p. 6). Consequently, a special homage was posthumously rendered to the director at the 1981 FESPACO, where the Oumarou Ganda Prize was instituted to acknowledge "the first work of a film director whose creative efforts are particularly noteworthy and deserve encouragement." Moreover, a bust of Oumarou Ganda was erected in Niamey to honor the memory of the late filmmaker, whose works, like the stories of the griot, are the repository of Africa's traditions and cultural values.

MAJOR THEMES

After interpreting the role of a former conscript in the Indochinese War in Jean Rouch's *Moi, un Noir,* a docudrama largely drawn from Ganda's experiences on the front, Oumarou Ganda decided to make a film that would present his own account of such experiences. This resulted in *Cabascabo,* the straightforward and moving story of a veteran who returns home and attempts to reestablish himself in a society from which he has been physically and psychologically estranged.

Cabascabo (whose title means "the tough guy" in local vernacular) opens with images of a military parade. The camera soon focuses on a row of veterans with military medals pinned on their *boubous* (long robes customarily worn by men in many West African countries). A man, also dressed in traditional attire and carrying with him a kora (a West African string instrument), leaves the crowd of spectators. His musical instrument, which he will adeptly play, suggests that he is a griot and that as such he may have just witnessed an event which might serve as a source of inspiration for future oral renditions. The griot now reaches a bar where a group of men are discussing their past military exploits. Among them is Cabascabo, who reminisces about the Indochinese War. Here the picture blurs into a flashback: Cabascabo squats motionless in a rice field while clenching a machine gun. The following sequence shows Indochinese freedom fighters killed in an ambush by a battalion of African soldiers. Thereupon, Cabascabo questions his fighting such a colonial war and vehemently stresses his wish to return home. A verbal altercation between Cabascabo and his African sergeant ensues, which will cause the private to serve a week of military detainment for "insults and threats to a non-commissioned officer." The viewer is now brought back to the local bar, where the griot recalls Cabascabo's homecoming; a subsequent flashback illustrates the former soldier's own recollection.

Returning to his former urban neighborhood, Cabascabo is enthusiastically greeted as a local military hero by his friends. Inviting them to rounds of drinks, Cabascabo inexhaustibly recounts his life overseas. Soon a griot (the same one seen at the beginning of the film) joins the lively group of avid listeners and improvises a praise song dedicated to Cabascabo's valor. The next day, after spending the night with a prostitute, Cabascabo is awakened by a group of well-wishers to whom he generously distributes some of his belongings. His young friend warns him: "Cabascabo, beware of these friends, they are only interested in your money." However, Cabascabo, who trusts that his service in the army will easily grant him some government job, disregards such advice. And indeed, day in and day out, a seemingly endless series of so-called friends relentlessly visit him to benefit from his generosity. As expected, Cabascabo's military savings dribble away, and only when he is completely broke and unable to pay his rent does he look for work. But, as he applies for a job in the police force (and although his country is now officially freed from colonial tutelage), Cabascabo is turned away because of an unfavorable report from the French army. Consequently, everywhere the veteran applies for work, he finds himself turned down as a potential troublemaker. Forced to seek manual labor, Cabascabo is eventually hired to work on a construction site. However, this low-paying job is soon brought to an end as he engages in a fistfight with a foreman who insulted him.

We are now back at the bar, where Cabascabo has just related the above account of his recent past. A few days later, the disillusioned war veteran chooses to return to his village, where he is expected to lead a more meaningful life. Yet, as Ganda once said to an interviewer: "I send him back to where he came from! I do not say however that he will stay there" *(Afrique-Asie,* 15 May 1972, p. 50). Ganda's second feature film, *Le Wazzou polygame,* owes its present title to an erroneous translation. The director clarified this mistake as follows:

In Djerma . . . "wazzou" means "morale." The credits of the film stipulate that "wazzou" is synonymous with "El Hadj" (a Muslim title conferred upon a man who has gone on a pilgrimage to Mecca): the title was mistranslated by the producer. In fact, the title should be "Le Wazzou du polygame," that is to say "The Polygamist's Morale." *(Afrique-Asie,* 15 May 1972, p. 50)

Le Wazzou polygame centers on polygamy and the issue of forced marriage while alluding to the theme of rural exodus. Here the filmmaker uses explicit, pointed satire to illustrate the tragedy caused by a hypocritical religious devotee who preaches loquaciously on religion, but at the same time resorts to trickery in his attempts to win a young girl as his third wife. Ganda once stated:

I am against polygamy. The story I tell in "le Wazzou polygame" is drawn from a real event which took place in Niamey in 1969. A tailor had a quarrel with his wife and told her his intention to take a second wife. His first wife warned him that if such a thing ever happened, she would kill both him and his new wife. The husband did not take her seriously and married. The first wife carried out her threat, but mistakenly killed the bridesmaid. The first wife was arrested and is still in jail today. I was struck by this tragic story and decided to make a film of it to make my compatriots think. *(Afrique-Asie,* 15 May 1972, p. 50)

The film's main character is Saley, a well-off merchant with two wives. Upon his return from Mecca (and probably to add to the prestige this journey has provided him), Saley, a middle-aged man, decides to marry Satou, a young village girl. But Satou is in love with Garba, to whom she has been betrothed for three years. Their marriage has been delayed because Garba has not yet been able to pay for Satou's dowry. As she learns of Saley's proposal, Satou adamantly refuses to marry him. However, impressed by Saley's wealth and gifts, Satou's father bestows his daughter on him. A griot confirms the forthcoming union by announcing: "Saley paid the dowry, the other suitors must withdraw."

Infuriated by her husband's design, Saley's second wife goes to see the village diviner (played by Oumarou Ganda) to seek advice and occult means of preventing the marriage. In exchange for forty kola nuts and a chicken, the diviner assures her that the wedding will not take place. Yet, in spite of these predictions, Saley carries out his marriage plans.

On the wedding night, however, Satou refuses to share her husband's couch. Early the following morning, this news is spread all over the village. Meanwhile, after Saley has left the house, his second wife stealthily penetrates into Satou's room, where she and her bridesmaid are still sleeping, and inadvertently kills the bridesmaid instead of Satou. Awed by the murder of her childhood friend, Satou flees from the village to go to Niamey. Affected by Satou's departure, Garba in turn leaves for Ghana. With limited marketable assets in the city, Satou becomes a prostitute.

Saitane, whose protagonist is interpreted by Oumarou Ganda, is a humorous, incisive parable attacking the power of local marabouts (here diviners and/or healers familiar with the handling of magic forces within the framework of traditional African religions). The film has the freshness and flavor of tales deeply rooted in African oral traditions. According to the filmaker:

It is the story of a young couple whose lives are upset when the woman has a love affair. The people of the neighborhood become involved. Thereupon, the father of the young woman appears and decides to take his daughter and her baby back to his house as is customarily done here. Yet, the husband also wants to keep the child. . . . The title of the film, *Saitane* ("Satan" in French), alludes to the marabout who is accused of having led the young woman astray. *(Afrique-Asie,* 15 May 1972, p. 50)

And, indeed, it is Zima, the venal marabout, whom people contact for a variety of purposes (such as seeking advice, good health, personal advantages, etc.), who has used his occult ascendancy over people to "arrange" the relationship between Safi (the young woman) and her lover, who also happens to be one of Zima's regular customers. . . . But soon Zima's exploitation of people's credulity

will come to an end. One day, as he recites incantations in front of a sacred
tree, a voice responds ''A Salam Alleykum,'' a Muslim greeting which means
''May the blessings of God be on you.'' Terrified by what he holds to be a
supernatural manifestation, the diviner runs away. While he escapes, loud and
sarcastic laughter is heard, that of a hunter hidden in the sacred tree. Subsequently, this man jovially tells his friends how he tricked Zima. Following this
disclosure, Zima's credibility is questioned and his reputation is progressively
ruined. Unable to bear the stigma of having become a public laughing stock,
Zima terminates his life by jumping from the top of a cliff. In the meantime,
after vivacious negotiations, Safi has safely returned to her husband's home.

The film *L'Exilé*, also bearing the mark of Africa's oral tradition, is a story
within a story, narrated by a former African ambassador (somewhat stiffly played
by Oumarou Ganda) exiled in Switzerland. For Ganda, the theme of exile contained in the film goes beyond the diplomat's fate:

I think that we [Westernized Africans] are all exiled. To be in exile is to be cut off from
one's natural milieu. . . . [However] whatever risks may be involved, whoever is politically
exiled must stay in his own country and fight. *(Sahel,* 15 September 1980, p. 18)

Ganda's film illustrates the sacredness of the given word:

My film is fictional and my intention was to highlight the importance of the word. I think
that in Africa (as happens elsewhere in the world), the spoken word has lost its importance
to the advantage of the written word. One often says things without feeling tied to
promises. . . . In traditional Africa, the spoken word had much more value. . . . To give
one's word was sacred even if one had to incur death to keep it. *(Sahel,* 15 September
1980, p. 18)

One of *L'Exilé*'s opening sequences takes place in a cosy living room where
a group of friends has gathered. Among them is the former African ambassador.
His European wife cryptically explains; ''My husband had no other choice but
to resign from his post.'' A discussion on Africa ensues. At this point the diplomat
offers to narrate a traditional African tale whose plot unfolds on the screen.

Once upon a time, many years ago, there was a bountiful African country
where people honored their gods and respected the spoken word. The people
there were happy and lived peacefully. One day, fascinated by the beauty of the
king's daughters, Sadou and his brother incautiously declared that they would
be willing to give up their heads in exchange for one night with the princesses.
The king took them at their word and married his daughters to the young men.
The two couples led a very happy life. A year later, the king reminded the two
husbands of their earlier statement. Thus, in order to keep his word, Sadou's
brother submitted to the executioner's sword. On the other hand, Sadou's wife
pledged that she would kill herself after his death, and Sadou decided to flee.
For weeks, the two journeyed further and further away until they reached a

country of which Sadou would eventually become king. One day, the diviner came to him to announce that a long and severe drought would affect the region unless his wife were sacrificed to the gods. So, to spare his wife's life and save his people from devastating famine, Sadou offered his own life to the demanding gods. Hence, as critic Mario Relich stated, he had "not escaped his fate after all, nor the consequences of failing to keep his word" *(West Africa*, 7 December 1981, p. 2907).

The final part of the motion picture takes us back to the European living room where the listeners' faces (shot in close-ups) indicate their appreciation of the diplomat's story. Shortly afterwards, the former ambassador is killed by an anonymous gunman. In resigning from his post as ambassador, he too had failed to honor his commitment.

SURVEY OF CRITICISM

With but a few exceptions, Ganda's works have been approvingly endorsed by film critics. Claude-Jean Philippe's appreciation of *Cabascabo* is expressed as follows: "Oumarou Ganda tells the story of *Cabascabo*, his own story. He does so with great simplicity and sincerity" *(Télérama*, 12 October 1969, p. 61). In an article devoted to the "cultural dilemma of the African film," Wilson Mativo states:

Oumarou Ganda's *Cabascabo* is one illustration of this dilemma. It is a question of choosing between living a "civilized," empty life in town and a humble existence in the countryside. False appearances of a good life victimize a man whose naiveté dictates an imitation of life rather than its interpretation. He finds a somewhat satisfying solution by refusing to smoke or drink; in fact, he literally walks out of this habit and returns to lead a country life. This metaphorical visualization of a personal dilemma is only the more painful because we know that it is not easy to walk out of it spotless and at will. *(UFAHAMU*, Winter 1971, p. 64)

Likewise, Marie Benesova is of the opinion that

the film touches on several specifically African problems and, through its psychological portrait of the main character, criticizes the passivity of the African, just as Sembene does in his film *The Money Order [Mandabi]*. The story-line is treated lyrically, and the film is quite sophisticated stylistically. With its high level of intellectual and artistic achievement, it ranks among the best works of the African cinema, alongside the Senegalese films and those from the Ivory Coast. *(Young Cinema and Theatre*, 1975, p. 29)

Such a comparison between Ganda's films and Sembene's early works (particularly *Mandabi)* is also present in the writings of other reviewers. Struck by the "placid boldness" of its topic, Guy Hennebelle connects *Cabascabo*'s subversive implications with those more overtly contained in Sembene's motion pictures *(Cinéma 69*, June 1969, pp. 95–96). Jean-Louis Comolli links the magic and maleficent power of money soberly described in *Cabascabo* to an identical trait found in *Mandabi (Cahiers du Cinéma,* June 1969, p. 16). Referring also to Sembene, Michel Capdenac stresses Cabascabo's finesse, discreet lyricism, and insightful glimpses of the African persona *(Lettres Françaises,* 1 October 1969, p. 14).

Le Wazzou polygame has received generally favorable reviews. Jean de la Guerivière *(Le Monde Diplomatique,* April 1973, p. 21) and Maxime Scheifeingel *(Avant-Scène du Cinéma,* 1 April 1981, p. 39) point out its freshness and adept treatment of universal themes. Claude-Michel Cluny praises its visual charm and cutting humor *(Cinéma 72,* April 1972, p. 39), while Ferid Boughedir stresses the film's "poetry and humor" *(Ecran 1973,* May 1973, p. 55). As far as Guy Hennebelle is concerned:

Le Wazzou polygame is more striking because of the impact of its subject matter than because of its stylistic qualities . . . .the rapport between content and form is not fully satisfying. The script should undoubtedly have been more polished. However, even if *Le Wazzou polygame* is less coherent than *Cabascabo,* it is a work of undeniable strength. *(L'Afrique Littéraire et Artistique,* March 1972, p. 100)

In a brief overview of African films, Ferid Boughedir cites *Saitane* as an example of the cultural vein of African cinema whose essential aim is the revaluation of traditional mores *(Filméchange,* Fall 1978, p. 77). For Tahar Cheriaa, *Saitane* is a "sarcastic comedy shot with unimpeded pertness" *(Cinéma 73,* April 1973, p. 22), while Alexis Gnonlonfoun is impressed by both its truthfulness and simplicity *(Afrique Nouvelle,* 25 February 1976, p. 13).

Farida Ayari perceives *L'Exilé* as a legendary tale which takes on allegorical dimensions and present-day significance *(Le Continent,* 19 November 1980, p. 12). Abdoulaye Boureima sees it as "a hymn to ancestral Africa" *(Sahel,* 10 September 1980, p. 4). Many of these views are shared by Mario Relich, who concludes:

It is not so much the actual story which grips one. Rather, it is the densely-textured images of chieftains, priests and mounted retainers conjuring up a vanished, feudal world whose glitter was indeed gold because truth was highly-prized. It is not the apparent exoticism of these images that matters—and indeed they do not seem so exotic in Niger— but their underlying truth. *(West Africa,* 7 December 1981, p. 2907)

Indeed, with *L'Exilé,* Ganda advocates in an epic tone the rediscovery of African identity.

FILMOGRAPHY

Cabascabo, 35 mm, black and white, 45 min., 1968.
Le Wazzou polygame (The Polygamist's Morale), 35 mm, color, 50 min., 1970.
Saitane (Satan), 16 mm, color, 64 min., 1973.

Cock, cock, cock, 16 mm, color, 1973.
L'Exilé, (The Exiled) 35 mm, color, 80 min., 1980.

BIBLIOGRAPHY

Interviews of Oumarou Ganda

Haffner, Pierre. "Entretien avec Oumarou Ganda." *Septiéme Art,* n. 42, Summer 1981, pp. 16–19.
———. "Jean Rouch jugé par six cinéastes d'Afrique noire." *Cinémaction,* n. 17, 1982, pp. 62–76.
Hennebelle, Guy. "Un Nouveau Cinéaste nigérien: Oumarou Ganda de Moi, un Noir à Cabascabo." *L'Afrique Littéraire et Artistique,* n. 4, 1968, pp. 70–74.
———. "Oumarou Ganda (Cabascabo): Moi, un Noir . . . c'est moi." *Les Lettres Françaises,* n. 1286, 4 June 1969, p. 18.
———. "Le Wazzou polygame, un film d'Oumarou Ganda contre le mariage forcé." *Afrique-Asie,* n. 4, 15 May 1972, pp. 49–50.
———. "Ganda Oumarou." *L'Afrique Littéraire et Artistique,* n. 49, 3rd Quarter 1978, pp. 66–67.
Ibricheck. "A bâtons rompus avec Oumarou Ganda. L'Exilé: une aventure." *Sahel,* n. 240, 15 September 1980, p. 18.
Medeiros, Richard de. "Dialogue à quelques voix." *Recherche, Pédagogie et Culture,* n. 17–18, May-August 1975, pp. 39–42.
"Menaces sur le cinéma nigérien—Oumarou Ganda, le premier explique pourquoi." *Bingo,* n. 319, August 1979, pp. 29–30.

Film Reviews and Studies of Oumarou Ganda

Ayari, Farida. "Deux films africains présentés au festival de Carthage." *Le Continent,* 19 November 1980, p. 12.
———. "Ouagadougou 81." *Adhoua,* n. 4–5, April-September 1981, pp. 4–5.
Benesova, Marie. "Film in Niger." *Young Cinema and Theatre,* n. 1, 1975, pp. 28–30.
Binet, Jacques. "Le Cinéma africain." *Afrique Contemporaine,* n. 123, September-October 1972, pp. 5–8.
———. "Cinéma africain." *Afrique Contemporaine,* n. 83, January-February 1976, pp. 27–30.
Bouassida, A. "Les Manifestations marginales des J.C.C." *L'Action,* 17 October 1976, p. 12.
Boughedir, Ferid. "Quinze jours ailleurs." *Ecran 1973,* n. 15, May 1973, pp. 54–55.
———. "Le Cinéma nigérien: l'authenticité de l'autodidacte." *Cinéma Québec,* vol. 3, n. 9–10, August 1974, pp. 27–29.
———. "Le Cinéma africain a quinze ans." *Filméchange,* n. 4, Fall 1978, pp. 75–80.
———. "Les Héritiers d'Oumarou Ganda." *Jeune Afrique,* n. 1053, 11 March 1981, pp. 62–63.
Boureima, Abdoulaye. "L 'Exilé de Oumarou Ganda—un hymne à l'Afrique profonde." *Sahel,* 10 September 1980, p. 4.

Capdenac, Michel. "Stridences japonaises et nostalgies africaines." *Lettres Françaises*, n. 1302, 1 October 1969, pp. 13–14.

Cheriaa, Tahar. "Ouagadougou—un cinéma libre s'affirme." *Cinéma 73*, n. 175, April 1973, pp. 22–29.

Cluny, Claude-Michel. "Niger." *Cinéma 72*, n. 165, April 1972, p. 39.

Comolli, Jean-Louis. "Cabascabo (Oumarou Ganda)." *Cahiers du Cinéma*, n. 213, June 1969, p. 16.

Debrix, Jean-René. "En direct . . . du Niger." *Recherche, Pédagogie et Culture*, n. 17–18, May-August 1975, pp. 54–55.

Delahaye, Michel. "D'une jeunesse à l'autre: classement élémentaire de quelques notions et jalons." *Cahiers du Cinéma*, n. 197, December 1967–January 1968, pp. 78–81.

Gnonlonfoun, Alexis. "En suivant la caméra." *Afrique Nouvelle*, n. 1391, 25 February 1976, pp. 12–15.

Godard, Jean-Luc. "L'Afrique vous parle de la fin et des moyens." *Cahiers du Cinéma*, n. 94, April 1959, pp. 19–22.

Guerivière, Jean de la. "Le Dénuement des citadins et la misère des villageois, vus par Oumarou Ganda." *Le Monde Diplomatique*, April 1973, p. 21.

Hennebelle, Guy. "Cabascabo d'Oumarou Ganda (Niger)." *Cinéma 69*, n. 137, June 1969, pp. 95–96.

———. "Concerto pour un exil et Cabascabo." *Jeune Afrique*, n. 458, 8 October 1969, pp. 18–19.

———. "Africains à vos marks!" *Jeune Afrique*, n. 460, 22 October 1969, pp. 57–58.

———. "Le Cinéma nigérien, grand vainqueur à Ouagadougou." *L'Afrique Littéraire et Artistique*, n. 22, March 1972, pp. 98–100.

———. *Guide des films anti-impérialistes*. Paris: Editions du Centenaire, 1975.

Kaboke, V. "Saitane." *Unir Cinéma*, n. 23–24 (130–131), March-April and May-June 1986, pp. 33–34.

———. "Le Wazzou Polygame." *Unir Cinéma*, n. 23–24 (130–131), March-April and May-June 1986, p. 34.

Kara, Ki el. "VIIᵉ FESPACO: c'est parti." *L'Observateur*, n. 2035, 23 February 1981, pp. 1, 13–14.

Lemaire, Charles. "Le Cinéma au Niger." *Unir Cinéma*, n. 7 (114), July-August 1983, pp. 3–4.

Marcorelles, Louis. "Deux films africains." *Le Monde*, 30 September 1969, p. 17.

———. "Une Chance pour le cinéma africain." *Le Monde*, 21 January 1982, pp. 1, 12.

Martin, Angela. *African Films: The Context of Production*. London: British Film Institute, 1982.

Mativo, Wilson. "Cultural Dilemma of the African Film." *UFAHAMU*, vol. 1, n. 3, Winter 1971, pp. 64–68.

Maurin, François. "Originalité d'un cinéma africain." *L'Humanité*, 27 September 1969, p. 8.

Petersen, Vibeke, and Viggo Holm Jensen. "Afrika, en kampande filmkontinent." *Chaplin 101*, n. 6, 1970, pp. 280–95.

Philippe, Claude-Jean. "Les Africains n'ont pas confiance en leurs cinéastes. Ils ont tort." *Télérama*, n. 1030, 12 October 1969, pp. 59–61.

"Qui est Oumarou Ganda?" *Télérama*, n. 1646, 29 July 1981, p. 19.

Relich, Mario. "From Glitter to Gore in the Film World." *West Africa*, n. 3358, 7
    December 1981, pp. 2907–11.
Rouch, Jean. "Hommage à Oumarou Ganda." *Le Monde*, 10 January 1981, p. 21.
Scheifeingel, Maxime. "Cabascabo, un film de Oumarou Ganda." *Avant-Scène du Cin-
    éma*, n. 265, 1 April 1981, pp. 39–50.
Schoenberner, Gerhard. "Det svarta Afrikas filmer och deras regissorer." *Chaplin 166*,
    n. 1, 1981, pp. 10–15.
Traoré, Biny. "Cinéma africain et développement." *Peuples Noirs, Peuples Africains*,
    n. 33, May-June 1983, pp. 50–62.
Vieyra, Paulin Soumanou. *Le Cinéma africain*. Paris: Présence Africaine, 1975.
Z, O. "Niger: Semaine Ganda Oumarou." *Unir Cinéma*, n. 23–24 (130–131), March-
    April and May-June 1986, pp. 17–18.

Haile Gerima (1946–)
Ethiopia

BIOGRAPHY

"To me, being Black is inherent. I would say that I'm an Ethiopian filmmaker residing for many historical reasons here in the United States. I would say, really, that I'm a Third World independent filmmaker" *(The Journal of the University Film and Video Association,* Spring 1983, p. 60). Such is Haile Gerima's definition of himself. He is, to date, not only the best-known Ethiopian director but also one of the most creative representatives of Black African cinema.

Haile Gerima was born on 4 March 1946 in the small town of Gondar, near Lake Tana in northwest Ethiopia. He recalls that his paternal grandfather was at one time secretary to Emperor Theodoros, a legendary historical figure who united Ethiopia in the nineteenth century. In his own words, Gerima belongs to the literate Ethiopian lower middle class.

During his childhood, Gerima and his nine siblings were strongly influenced by their immediate home environment. He remembers:

My father was an orthodox priest, a teacher, a historian and a playwright. He wrote plays of resistance to mobilize people during the Italian invasion of Ethiopia. He then joined a nationalist movement that brought him in direct conflict with his own church which collaborated with the Italians. Thus, from then on he denounced religion. My mother was educated by Catholic missionaries, and so she raised us in the Catholic faith. She taught home economics in a vocational school. . . . Both my mother and my grandmother were wonderful storytellers and as kids we used to spend many evenings, gathered around a fire, listening to the legends and tales of the Ethiopian oral tradition. (Gerima to author, Washington, D.C., 14 November 1985)

As an adolescent, Gerima was initiated by his father into theater art:

Every summer, when he was not teaching, my father headed an itinerant theater troupe which performed across the country. He staged his own plays, and I had the opportunity to act in all of them. My father directed his actors in a very traditional way. He composed the music for his plays and then would teach it to young people. It is to pay tribute to my father that I included two of his songs in my film *Harvest: 3,000 Years*. He is also the one who sings the song in the film. Working with my father provided me with a major training ground. It is as if a legacy was handed down to me, and this explains why the Ethiopian theater tradition was to play such an important role in the development of my storytelling skills. (Gerima to author, 14 November 1985)

Yet, at the same time that he was exposed to traditional dramatic art, the young Haile worked as a ticket boy in a local movie house during his free time from school and became increasingly exposed to foreign films and Western movie heroes:

In fact, as kids, we tried to act out the things we had seen in the movies. We used to play cowboys and Indians in the mountains around Gondar . . . identifying with cowboys conquering the Indians. . . . Even in Tarzan movies . . . whenever Africans sneaked up behind Tarzan, we would scream our heads off, trying to warn him that "they" were coming! It was the politically and psychologically damaging exploitation of my very being. *(Framework,* Spring 1978, p. 32)

Soon, because of the foreign values reflected in such films, the adolescent reached the point of questioning his traditions and grew to look down on his own culture. He became an awkward cultural hybrid of sorts, feeling uneasy with aspects of both societies.

After high school, Gerima moved to Ethiopia's capital city, Addis Ababa, where he studied drama and interpreted parts in radio plays to earn a livelihood. During his studies in Addis Ababa, he came into contact with Peace Corps volunteers who encouraged him to seek further training in the United States. Thus, in 1967, Haile Gerima embarked for Chicago, where he enrolled at the Goodman School of Drama to study acting. Shortly thereafter, Gerima's experiences at this school generated a deep sense of sociocultural alienation. In discussing this point, he stresses:

I took classes in an attempt to lose my accent. They were drilling me to fit in a box and they almost succeeded. It is only later that I realized that I should keep my identity and my accent as long as I was able to communicate efficiently. I was Ethiopian. Why did I have to force myself to speak like an American? (Gerima to author, Washington, D.C., 16 April 1976)

Moreover, Gerima points out:

I was totally unproductive in Chicago because of the whole cultural issue. I was a Third World person at a school oriented towards Western culture. I was being trained as an actor through Greek tragedies and modern Western plays. This whole culture was not speaking to me, and there was no way I could really develop in this context. (Gerima to author, Washington, D.C., 11 May 1983)

Coming to the United States was also a decisive step in the shaping of Gerima's sociopolitical consciousness and the rediscovery of his cultural heritage. Having been raised in a society where caste and class were more significant than the shade of one's skin, he became profoundly affected by the issue of racism in the United States and increasingly shared the problems and aspirations of the African-American community. At this time he began reading the writings of Malcolm X and other black militants of the 1960s, and came to identify with their struggle. Interestingly, it is through their search for African roots that Gerima reasserted his own Africanness:

The movies that I had seen in Ethiopia had led me to believe that America was a white Anglo-Saxon world. I discovered the Black American community when I came to Chicago, and later the African-American social movement played a major role in reorienting me back to my own heritage, making me accept not only my father but my people and the legitimate aesthetic criteria they had transmitted to me. (Gerima to author, 11 May 1983)

In 1969 Haile Gerima transferred to UCLA (University of California at Los Angeles) in the hope of finding a drama school that would be more responsive to his needs. Yet, again he was made to perform subservient roles in Western plays. Thus, both to express his sociopolitical concerns and compensate for the scarcity of meaningful Black roles in the Western theater, Gerima engaged in play writing. This was not his first attempt at writing plays. Gerima had written his first play, concerning a father who dies while fighting the Italians, when in eighth grade, and later had authored a few one-act plays based on Ethiopian morality tales while working for a radio station in Addis Ababa. The plays he wrote in the late sixties and early seventies include *Chief* (1969–1970), a symbolic play concerning slavery and Black militancy, and *Awful Pit* (1970–1971), which depicts the growing political awareness of an African-American shoe shiner. Describing the content of his plays, Gerima stresses: "All the themes I illustrate are related to political and social oppression and they can be broadened to a universal scope." He adds that his "explosive" play *Chief* has received two awards, but he points out that "nobody has ever taken the risk of staging it!" *(Positif,* October 1977, p. 54).

It was in 1970 that, on discovering the power of cinema as a means of expression and communication, Gerima decided to become a filmmaker:

I found that I had to control what I would do. As an actor I didn't have much power. I was looking for a [medium] that would make me control what I'd say. I also chose cinema because it reaches more people and has the fastest style. Images are the simplest way to communicate, especially with African audiences. *(New Directions,* July 1977, p. 29)

At UCLA, Gerima read works by Frantz Fanon, W.E.B. Du Bois, Amilcar Cabral, and Che Guevara, and acquainted himself with the newly emerging Third World cinema. He remembers: "At that time, I was part of a group of students at UCLA who fought to bring to the school films from Africa, South and Central America'' (Gerima to author, 11 May 1983). Regarding African film in particular, Gerima readily acknowledges the significant role played by Ousmane Sembene* and Med Hondo* in the development of his own film language:

I think that Sembene . . . is a forerunner because of the kinds of choices he has made. He is the kind of person who has tried to communicate through his culture. . . . He says to us ''be yourself and be proud of your culture.'' He has given me courage, confidence, and encouragement. I think he has had an impact on me and on a lot of African filmmakers although they may, egotistically, not admit it. *(The Cinema of Ousmane Sembene, A Pioneer of African Film,* 1984, p. 195)

Speaking about Med Hondo, the Ethiopian filmmaker states: ''I identify more with Med Hondo in terms of anger and I share his obsession with history and self-reliance'' (Gerima to author, 11 May 1983). Among other filmmakers that have had a lasting influence on him, Gerima cites Vittorio de Sica *(The Bicycle Thief,* Italy, 1949), Luis Buñuel *(The Young and the Damned,* Mexico, 1951), Fernando Solanas *(The Hour of the Blast Furnaces,* Argentina, 1967), Humberto Solas *(Lucia,* Cuba, 1968), Tomas Gutierrez Alea *(Memories of Underdevelopment,* Cuba, 1969), and Jorge Sanjines *(Blood of the Condor,* Bolivia, 1970).

Gerima eagerly explored the technical, artistic, and political facets of film and became rapidly fascinated by the medium. ''For me, cinema represented some sort of technological miracle'' *(Positif,* October 1977, p. 54), he says. Therefore, at the same time that he was studying film and taking history and sociology courses, Gerima saved $500, which he used in the making of his first film *Hourglass* (1971), a thirteen-minute experimental film.

I had to find my own identity as a filmmaker. . . . I just plunged into my first film in super 8 and I started to discover certain things. Before I learned about editing I started to establish certain ways of editing. And when the traditional teachers saw the final product and opposed it, there were also people who began to like it. This clash of points of view gave me more confidence to continue the process of discovering how I could speak better, sharpening my skills. *(Framework,* Spring 1978, p. 32)

In 1972, with fellow students, Haile Gerima shot *Child of Resistance,* a $5,000 medium-length color film which associates the art of film with that of the theater. This early motion picture, superbly interpreted by the Black American actress Barbara O. Jones, remains to this day one of the most stylistically daring films of Black African cinema.

Two years later, during his summer vacation, Gerima underwent what he termed ''a kind of [cultural] rehabilitation process'' through the filming of *Harvest: 3,000 Years,* a 150–minute black and white docudrama on the Ethiopian peasantry. It was made on a $20,000 budget (Gerima's own funds saved from working at odd jobs) with a small team of friends and a group of mostly nonprofessional actors. *Harvest: 3,000 Years* was shot in Ahmaric, the principal language of Ethiopia, in August 1974 during the slow takeover of power by the army after the overthrow of Emperor Haile Selassie. According to Gerima:

This was the only short period of time in Ethiopia in which the film could be made. . . . A month earlier, the bureaucrats of Haile Selassie would have stopped the film or forbidden the shooting. A month later, after the military had consolidated their power, things would have been crippled as well. . . . I had prepared the crew before leaving America that if the famine was still happening, we would make a film about that, because *Harvest* could be made another time. This, I thought, was the right political decision. But if Ethiopia is erupting and if conditions are about to burst, then we abandon the famine-project and make a film about the political conditions. *(Framework,* Spring 1978, p. 34)

This prospect of political change necessitated, as cameraman Elliot Davis calls it, a "guerilla-type production efficiency" based on light equipment and a limited but highly energetic crew. He points out:

Considering the fact that we were shooting in the midst of a military takeover, our top priority in every aspect of the production was to shoot in the most mobile and expedient manner possible. . . . we made the peasants the dominant criteria for what the camera would do. The film was not set up in shots but rather in scenes. The camera remained as fluid as possible. . . . We used the camera in as inconspicuous a way as possible, keeping a very low profile. We moved all around the peasants, giving them as much freedom as we could by not trying to make them feel like they were performing. . . . The theory of non-interference worked very satisfactorily. With the long lens, it appeared that the peasants had forgotten about us. *(Filmmakers Newsletter,* April 1975, p. 18)

Harvest: 3,000 Years was filmed in two weeks, but it took Gerima more than a year to edit it in the United States. Shot in 16 mm, the motion picture was blown into 35 mm so as to fit the criteria of Ethiopian movie houses. Yet this film, primarily intended for Ethiopian audiences, has to this day never been shown in that country. *Harvest: 3,000 Years* has baffled a number of American critics by its slow pace, and was received with mixed reactions after its 1976 premiere in the New Directors/New Films series held at the Museum of Modern Art in New York. Gerima remarks:

Harvest: 3,000 Years was to be presented in New York. The same thing happens when you fix local dishes. People want you to adapt the food to their tastes, rather than adapt their tastes to your food and try to understand how our food relates to us. If people cannot appreciate it, they should not ask us to adapt it for them because in such case it is no longer Ethiopian food, it's acculturated food. *(New Directions,* July 1977, p. 28)

Although it received the 1976 Oscar Micheaux Award for Best Feature Film from the Black Filmmakers Hall of Fame in Oakland, California, *Harvest: 3,000 Years* has undoubtedly fared better on European film festival circuits than in the United States. That same year it was awarded the George Sadoul Prize from the French Critics Association, the Outstanding Film Award at the London Film

Festival, and two grand prizes, at the Locarno International Film Festival in Switzerland and the Festival International de Dinema, Figueira da Foz, Portugal, respectively. In the subsequent years *Harvest: 3,000 Years* was to be extensively shown in Algeria, Angola, Mozambique, and Cuba. More recently, in March 1986, *Harvest: 3,000 Years* was featured in an "African Mini-Series" at the Biograph, one of Washington, D.C.'s, local movie theaters.

The year 1976 saw as well the release of Gerima's UCLA master's thesis, *Bush Mama,* a film he had started as early as 1973 but had discontinued to allow for the completion of *Harvest: 3,000 Years*. This $50,000 feature-length black and white motion picture was made with a production grant from the National Endowment for the Arts. Deftly filmed by Charles Burnett, an independent Black American filmmaker who was at the time one of Gerima's schoolmates, *Bush Mama* depicts the plight of a ghetto mother, played by Barbara O. Jones.

Finally, that same year, Haile Gerima was invited to join the faculty of Howard University, a historically Black institution located in Washington, D.C., where he still teaches filmmaking and the aesthetics of Third World cinema. Commenting on his work at Howard, the filmmaker emphasizes:

Howard is my last stopover before I return to Africa. I teach a body of internationally diversified students from Third World countries. I tell them to become self-reliant and organize themselves in order to fight Hollywood's monopoly. They have to build their own audiences. . . . and in order to survive, young Black filmmakers should follow the example of early Black American directors like Oscar Micheaux. Even if one is critical about the content of his films, one should learn from him. He was an excellent businessman and knew how to propose his motion pictures to various organizations. He knew how to hustle, make and distribute his films. We should learn from the experiences of early Black independent filmmakers in this country. We should analyze and know why they failed in order to avoid making the same mistakes. Independent film practitioners have to be disciplined and this goes from work to lifestyle. A film tells a lot about who you are and it also extends to the ideology of the group these filmmakers represent. I teach my students to respect the people they address and thoroughly study the subject matter of their film projects. (Gerima to author, Washington, D.C., 15 April 1977)

The Ethiopian director finds pleasure in teaching and feels he has the responsibility of training independent Black filmmakers who will provide positive and realistic portrayals of Black life on the screen:

I prefer teaching in the process of production. Throughout my career I have tried to use as few professionals as possible, save for cinematography and sound. All along the majority of my crews were made up of people who wanted to become filmmakers— students and community people. I combine them with professionals so that they can learn the craft. *(The Journal of the University Film and Video Association,* Spring 1983, p. 63)

Faithful to his word, Gerima involved the Black American community, as well as Howard students, in the production of his subsequent motion pictures. From

1976 to 1978, he shot and edited *Wilmington 10–USA 10,000,* a two-hour color documentary on political prisoners in the United States. Here is how the film-maker explains the production of his motion picture:

Wilmington 10–USA 10,000 was mostly funded by community organizations, among them the Wilmington 10 Defense Committee. Ninety-nine percent of the crew was made [up] of students from Howard University who donated their labor. The students were very professional. They made mistakes tied to people's development but they were committed and the awareness of the injustices within the judiciary system alone added to their maturity. It was a filming experience where people could learn and study while the film was being made. (Gerima to author, Washington, D.C., 29 September 1978)

To facilitate the production and the distribution of *Wilmington 10–USA 10,000,* Gerima initiated the creation of Positive Production, a nonprofit film collective which still plays a significant role in the funding, promotion, and exhibition of independent films. *Wilmington 10–USA 10,000* premiered at Hunter College in New York on 11 November 1978 during ''an evening in solidarity with Zimbabwe and the Wilmington 10'' sponsored by the Mozambique Film Project in asso-ciation with the Commission for Racial Justice of the United Church of Christ. *Wilmington 10–USA 10,000* was also presented at other such events held in Boston, Philadelphia, San Francisco, and a number of other major U.S. cities. For this documentary and his previous works, Gerima received in 1979 the Freedom Journalist Award. Also in 1979, he was granted a fellowship by the John Simon Guggenheim Memorial Foundation to sponsor his research for forth-coming film projects.

In 1981 the cinéaste completed *Ashes and Embers,* a $100,000 color feature film that took almost four years to make. Shot by Augustin E. Cubano, Elliot Davis, and Charles Burnett, with music by Brother Ah and The Sounds of Awareness, this film about a Black Vietnam War veteran was financed through production grants from the National Endowment for the Arts and the Washington, D.C., Commission for the Arts, loans, and Gerima's own resources (part of his teaching salary as well as profits generated by exhibitions of his former films). *Ashes and Embers* premiered in 1982 at the Oscar Micheaux Theater of Buffalo in New York State.

In addition to having been included in several U.S. film festivals, *Ashes and Embers* was shown abroad at the 1982 ''Journées cinématographiques contre le racisme et pour l'amitié entre les peuples'' (an international anti-racism film series) in Amiens, France, as well as at the 1983 Pan-African Film Festival of Ouagadougou (FESPACO) in Burkina Faso. Gerima's work won the Grand Prize at the 1982 Lisbon International Film Festival. In 1983 it received an Outstanding Production Award at the London Film Festival, the Fipresci Film Critics Award at the Berlin Film Festival, and the International Critics Award at the Festival des Trois Continents in Nantes, France. Also in 1983, the Ethiopian director served as one of the official judges at FESPACO. The following year, a retrospective of Gerima's films was presented in France at the La Rochelle Film Festival. Also in 1984, Gerima was invited to participate in two international film festivals held in Japan and India.

Haile Gerima's most recent film is *After Winter: Sterling Brown* (1985), a low-budget, hour-long color documentary which, funded by Howard University, honors the Black American poet, essayist, and literary critic. Says Gerima:

It was a class project and a cultural experience because the students not only learned of their heritage through their interaction with one of the strongest links in Black culture, the students had to come up with written research material about Sterling Brown, and so they had to learn about the Harlem Renaissance, Alain Locke, Langston Hughes, and Carter G. Woodson. This film is my own interpretation of Sterling Brown but the students played a major role in directing. I only interfered to avoid disasters. (Gerima to author, 14 November 1985)

Gerima is optimistic about the future of *After Winter: Sterling Brown* which, he believes, should do well in the university, library, and museum film circuits.

Gerima's immediate film project is a two-hour color fiction film, *Nunu*. Based on an $800,000 budget, this work (the script of which was undertaken ten years ago) is now at an advanced preproduction stage. *Nunu* will take place on a sugar plantation in the South of the United States just prior to the Civil War. Later, the director looks forward to completing *The Death of Tarzan, Donald Duck and Shirley Temple,* which will document the nature and role of African cinema. After these two films, Gerima plans to make *In the Eye of the Storm*, a film concerning the advent of European colonialism in Africa.

From the time he became a filmmaker, Haile Gerima has always vehemently discarded what he defines as the "escapist" Hollywood approach to film in favor of a socially and politically oriented independent cinema that would provide a "realistic and meaningful" portrayal of Africa and the Black Diaspora:

You don't have to fit the criteria and the definition of Hollywood. A film can be 15 minutes, 20 minutes or 10 hours long. People should consider their economic realities as predominant factors. It is important not to pretend. We should only make a color film when we really want to do it and when we are able to. You should invest what you have, even 30 or 40 dollars and you should get your film to the people. You should not be desperate to make a film every year but make a film when you have something to say. *(New Directions, July 1977, p. 30)*

Likewise, Gerima does not believe in portraying individual heroes for quick and convenient audience identification, as is customary in commercial cinema. He likes to deal with anti-heroes or collective heroes because he is convinced that movie heroes merely work as substitutes for people's frustrations. In general, he favors the use of nonprofessional actors:

Most actors have a unified set of expressions. . . . Actors have become almost like man-ufactured goods. Their physical and psychological gestures are virtually uniform. To work with professional actors, I'd have to break them down into reality, to take them away from this star dream they have. . . . Non-professional actors have that uniqueness and quality that I must have. . . . For me, in low budget filmmaking, it would be too expensive and take too long to break an actor into a character you want. . . . I'm in search of new aesthetics not only in my shots and composition, but in the expressions of characters. For a Third World filmmaker, the people you cast are tremendously important in terms of capturing reality. *(The Journal of the University Film and Video Association,* Spring 1983, p. 63)

Making ample use of fragmented editing, colliding images, dream sequences, and striking sound effects, Gerima likes to challenge conventional film norms as part of his 'awakening' process addressed to both audiences and film critics *(Cahiers du Cinéma,* September-October 1976, p. 64). Furthermore, he strongly feels that ''the African cinema should concentrate on inventing rather than im-itating.'' He further adds that such a cinema should also be

a collective and communal experience . . . an effective catalyst bringing about dialogue between people . . . benefiting the entire social network, including artists. . . . It is entirely appropriate to perceive cinema as being symbolic of the fire—the central point of life, earth and energy. . . . I am advocating a cinema of electricity that affirms our great civilizations, our history of resistance; a cinema with a profound realistic passion for humanity, a cinema of boundless human vision. *(Filmfaust,* May-June 1984, p. 54)

Since he uses the medium of film to create interaction, whenever possible Gerima likes to discuss his films with audiences and learn from people's remarks and suggestions.

Money is an incessant worry for independent filmmakers, and Haile Gerima is no exception:

It's very rare that I resort to grants and more and more I'm trying to be truly ''inde-pendent.'' Most of the financing comes from me, my labor. . . . Friends who believe . . . in the people put their time, energy and creativity into the project. We believe that the existing system fails to respond to our cultural needs. . . . Declaring independence means equally economic, political, and cultural independence. The issue is not to make a statement. The issue is do you control your statement—the aesthetics and the benefit of that product. *(Journal of the University Film and Video Association,* Spring 1983, p. 61)

An impassioned advocate of economic self-reliance, the enterprising film di-rector now heads Mypheduh Films Inc., a company located in Washington, D.C., which distributes Black American as well as African films, and organizes film symposia and other intercultural exchanges, such as the participation of a dozen U.S.-based Black filmmakers and film critics in the 1985 FESPACO, where they discussed, with African directors, cooperative production, distribu-tion, and marketing devices. Moreover, Gerima is a member of CAC (Comité

Africain de Cinéastes), an African filmmakers' collective which spearheads the international exhibition of Black African motion pictures.

"As an independent filmmaker I do not make motion pictures to earn money but to express ideas," insists Gerima *(Positif,* October 1977, p. 56), who disclaims any adherence to a definite social ideology, stressing:

I don't like political labels, it is too alienating. I am constantly growing and challenging. I am very suspicious of all politicians, I think they have short-range objectives. I am more interested in denouncing sociopolitical contradictions through film. (Gerima to author, 11 May 1983)

Nevertheless, although he wishes his films to be agents for social change, he also wisely recognizes that "no film has ever triggered a revolution" (Gerima to author, 15 April 1977).

"I belong both to Ethiopia and Black America" *(Le Monde,* 7 July 1984, p. 11), declares Gerima, who one day hopes to return to Africa. He is now residing in Washington, D.C., with his wife Shirikiana (an African-American filmmaker whom he married in 1983) and their three children. Quick-tempered, endowed with unharnessed energy and boundless creativity, Gerima has asserted himself both as a gifted craftsman and as an articulate film theorist whose work and thought are establishing new bridges between Africa and the Black Diaspora.

MAJOR THEMES

Less than a year after enrolling in UCLA's film school, Haile Gerima's early ventures in the realm of cinema resulted in *Hourglass,* a short motion picture which already reflects some of the thematic concerns found in his later works. Here is how he summarizes his film:

It's about a young guy who is raised in a foster home, in an Anglo-Saxon culture, and how much he is alienated from his own cultural essence. As a result he ends up playing basketball at a university, but he is not a normal participant of the sport and soon realizes that he's the new modern gladiator. That is the arrival point. He finally leaves this densely white school as a gladiator and goes into the community, where he needs to go for his own peace and security. That is a constant and very insistent theme in my work: transformation, change, realization. *(Cineaste,* vol. 14, n. 1, 1985, p. 29)

Transformation through political awareness is also at the very core of *Child of Resistance,* the cinematographic illustration of a dream Gerima had about Angela Davis, to whom he dedicates his work. Made in black and white (scenes of the Black female inmate's reality) and color sequences (depicting a stylized outside world where people are victims of abusive consumerism, drugs, and prostitution), *Child of Resistance* is an eruptive film rich in surrealistic decor and bold imagery. The director emphasizes:

This film is about a Black woman who is in jail because of her political beliefs. It's about any Black intellectual who is analyzing the conditions of his or her people. The movie character has dreams and nightmares at the same time. I deal with symbols on a very sophisticated level: crosses, television sets with no picture. People are glued to a television with no message coming out of it. Those people are just paying attention to an empty screen. . . . My film is criticizing Black men who are not playing the role they should be playing right now. *(New Directions,* July 1977, p. 30)

Bush Mama shows a Black welfare mother's steps from frustration and anger to political consciousness. Her man is in jail for a crime he did not commit. She then discovers that she is pregnant. Her social worker advises her to have an abortion but she refuses to abide by what she perceives as genocide. She will be arrested for having killed a white policeman who attempted to rape her daughter.

Harvest: 3,000 Years is Gerima's only film to take place in his native country, within a sterile environment from which some have to flee to survive—here physical and political realities metaphorically coincide, and both call for change. *Harvest: 3,000 Years* is a superbly composed and stylistically sophisticated docudrama in which are revealed Gerima's deep feelings for his downtrodden compatriots. The title is meant to reflect the 3,000 years that the Ethiopians have spent in feudal bondage. The filmmaker defines his work as follows: "I would say that it's about a peasant family, their hard work, their dignity in relation to a symbolic, unproductive landlord" *(New Directions,* July 1977, p. 28).

Wilmington 10–USA 10,000, whose musical score is vividly enhanced by protest songs interpreted by Sweet Honey in the Rock, concerns political imprisonment, and is based on the case of the Wilmington Ten, the now liberated group of ten civil right activists (led by Ben Chavis, a Black minister) who were convicted in 1972 for allegedly committing arson in Wilmington, North Carolina. This documentary does not focus only on the above prisoners; it also presents striking portrayals of their relatives and friends. Says Gerima:

Wilmington 10–USA 10,000 contains interviews, demonstrations and church activities— the way some people carry out demonstrations through churches, and the kind of awareness reached by certain human beings. It's about the moral transformation of people. (Gerima to author, Washington, D.C., 29 September 1978)

Constructed in a nonlinear format with a forceful sound mix, *Ashes and Embers* offers an impressionistic account of a Black American Vietnam veteran's tormented homecoming. His geographic and psychological journey from war to his previous environment—in which he now feels totally alienated—results in anguish and anger. Yet, after interactions with friends and primarily with his grandmother, the protagonist is expected to achieve self-realization. Gerima points out:

I felt that the black youth . . . in the film should make a profound and concrete linkage with his grandmother. . . . Without understanding the grandparents, we cannot take a single step in dealing with all the contradictions we experience every day. *(Cineaste,* vol. 14, n. 1, 1985, p. 39)

After Winter: Sterling Brown (the title is taken from one of Brown's poems) also explores the sociocultural legacy of Black Americans, and pays tribute to the knowledge and wisdom of the elderly. Here the eighty-year-old Sterling Brown appears as a witty griot (the storyteller and historian of the African oral tradition) whose contribution is associated, through montage, with that of Harriet Tubman, Frederick Douglass, W.E.B. Du Bois, Malcolm X, and others. Quietly puffing his pipe, Sterling Brown, who taught for many years at Howard University, defines himself as "a minor poet and a major teacher." He tells his listeners: "Be prepared, be productive, never forget where you came from." Seated at home, chatting in a jazz club, and lecturing in an academic setting, Brown, a gifted raconteur, talks about jazz, literature, and his life experiences, and reads his own poetry (including his well-known poem "Strong Men") with an unforgettable incantatory voice.

SURVEY OF CRITICISM

It is *Child of Resistance* that first revealed Gerima's creative potential to the viewing public. The African-American scholar and film critic Clyde Taylor recalls:

The first time I saw Haile Gerima's "Child of Resistance" I was rocked back on my heels. Less than an hour long, this film is a cinematic, symbolic projectile of rage out of the consciousness of the sixties, but with an artfulness seldom reached in that decade. *(The Black Collegian,* May-June 1979, p. 94)

Another American reviewer terms it "an angry film" *(Cineaste,* vol. 14, n. 1, 1985, p. 29), while a Third World film specialist, Raphael Bassan, calls attention to *Child of Resistance*'s subversive surrealism *(Afrique-Asie,* 13 August 1984, p. 61).

Gerima's reputation as a filmmaker grew with *Bush Mama.* Kalamu Ya Salaam enthusiastically remarks:

There has been no commercial movie made that prepares us for the experience of "Bush Mama".... the film is daring in conception and execution. It exudes not simply a documentary peek at Black life, but rather delves into the depths of Black working women rising up angry, fighting back.... This is a film of revolutionary optimism based in the reality of social transformation. *(The Black Collegian,* May-June 1977, p. 63)

A similar opinion is expressed by Célestin Monga, who views *Bush Mama* as one of the most faithful portrayals of Black American life ever made *(Jeune Afrique,* 25 July 1984, p. 59). Both Christine de Montvalon *(Télérama,* 7 July 1984, p. 29) and Gabriel Gibus *(Afrique-Antilles,* September 1984, p. 46) praise the film's unorthodox style. Although he finds this motion picture "poorly constructed and wildly uneven," J. Hoberman concurs that *"Bush Mama* smashes the tenets of polite naturalism." He states:

It's a film that takes chances and projects an urgent sense of personal necessity. Gerima has too much to say and an admirable impatience with standard means of film exposition. His raw, fragmented study of a Watts welfare mother's political awakening mixes on-the-street documentary footage with flashbacks, instant replays, and violent fantasies, to achieve a constant all over motion. . . . An exceptional cast assumes various political and apolitical postures, which, even at their most self-deceiving, shed a harsh illumination on the quality of their oppression. . . . the film has a jarring forcefulness which cannot be denied. *(Village Voice,* 24 September 1979, p. 57)

Reporting on the opening of the Alternative Film Festival held at the Miya Gallery in Washington, D.C., a film reviewer (for whom *Bush Mama* is reminiscent of Roberto Rossellini's *Open City)* writes:

Haile Gerima's "Bush Momma" *[sic]* is not a slick film, nor even smooth. It is too long. The sound is harsh and often garbled. The storyline is sometimes confusing, sometimes overstated.

But "Bush Momma" is a picture that must be seen. The chronicle of a black woman in the Los Angeles Watts area who is driven to discover her identity and pride, this film crackles with energy. Fury shakes the very frame. *(Washington Post,* 27 January 1977, p. C9)

Harvest: 3,000 Years established Gerima as a director of international standing. Ahmed El Maanouni *(Cinémarabe*, March-April 1977, p. 34) and Gilles Colpart *(Cinéma 77,* August-September 1977, p. 178) see it as a striking and harrowing testimony about Ethiopia's social reality. Robert Grelier *(La Revue du Cinéma, Image et Son,* October 1977, p. 233) is particularly sensitive to the director's ethnographic concerns and his inherent respect for traditional Ethiopian music as expressed throughout the film's soundtrack. Albert Cervoni *(L'Humanité,* 19 May 1976, p. 8) feels that *Harvest: 3,000 Years'* social content is unequivocally matched by its plastic beauty. Louis Marcorelles *(Le Monde,* 21 April 1977, p. 33) likes its original oneiric components and symbolic sound editing and favors its elaborate formal composition, which he compares to that found in the works of such Russian directors as Sergei M. Eisenstein, Vsevolod I. Pudovkin, and Alexander P. Dovzhenko. Furthermore, Michel Ciment *(Positif,* July-August 1976, p. 90) stresses the film's "irony, revolt, lyricism" which, he says, echoes cinema novo. Clyde Taylor expounds on Gerima's use of imagery:

Some of his strongest metaphors are lodged in his film. A peasant girl dreams of her family being yoked like oxen to a plough and driven to death by the landlord. In a later scene she drowns in swift currents, trying desperately to save the landlord's ox. Both images carry the alienation suffered by the downtrodden in the name of property. *(Africa Now,* December 1983, p. 81)

Likewise, Mbye B. Cham emphasizes that "In *Harvest,* . . . dreams and hallucinations constitute two of the most effective techniques employed by Gerima to underscore the inhumanity and beastly nature of feudal exploitation and the inevitability of change" *(Présence Africaine,* 1st Quarter 1984, p. 85).

Describing the film's lyrical camera work, Steve Howard finds that "the hypnotic images of fields and valleys, and the slow panning shots of the land and sky, evoke a sense of viewing an epic silent documentary or a moment from Mizoguchi" *(Cineaste,* vol. 14, n. 1, 1985, p. 29).

Very few negative comments concerning *Harvest: 3,000 Years* can be found in print. Some, however, are included in articles such as one by Lawrence Van Gelder, who points out:

Both as a movie and as an exercise in consciousness-raising with an eye toward rebellion, its principal flaws—a far too languorous pace, born of an unwillingness or inability to impose concision on its material; an absence of subtlety—. . . are not likely to be overlooked by audiences familiar with more sophisticated and urgently manipulative techniques.

On the other hand, its exotic setting, its unfamiliar language . . . its fascinating faces, its vivid sound and excellent photography mitigate the excessive length. . . .

Unfortunately, drama and conflict are not the strengths of "Harvest: 3,000 years." . . . And, while showing more than need be seen, it explains less than should be known *(New York Times,* 6 April 1976, p. 27)

It remains true that *Harvest: 3,000 Years* has been overwhelmingly acclaimed as a landmark in the search for an original African film aesthetic. This view is shared by Louis Marcorelles *(Le Monde,* 19 May 1976, p. 21) and Jean-Luc Douin *(Télérama,* 27 April 1977, p. 91), while Marcel Martin *(Ecran 1976,* 15 May 1976, p. 3, and *Ecran 77,* 15 May 1977, p. 61), Evelyne Malnic *(Jeune Afrique,* 18 June 1976, p. 51), and Michel I. Makarius *(Jeune Afrique,* 25 June 1976, p. 107) place it in a more universal scope, and consider it a crucial event in the realm of world cinema.

In comparison with *Bush Mama* and *Harvest: 3,000 Years, Wilmington 10– USA 10,000* received little critical attention. Discussing its content, Margaret Tarter notes that "the powerful, beautifully photographed documentary is about the history of black people in America, and how the oppression of the African slaves in the U.S. persists today in their descendants' lives" *(Bay State Banner,* 17 May 1979, p. 19), whereas Janice L. Berry writes: "It's not a fact-packed documentary full of dull statistics. It's an honest portrayal of the faces and emotions of Americans wronged by injustice" *(The New Communicator,* 8 February 1979, p. 3). Tony Safford and William Triplett stress Gerima's use of "folk dialogue" and his close adherence to "Black oral tradition" *(The Journal of the University Film and Video Association,* Spring 1983, p. 59), and E.

Fullman finds that Gerima "successfully documents the plight of political prisoners and the intense hardships incarceration has caused them and their families" *(The Hilltop,* 17 November 1978, p. 1).

Gerima's award-winning fiction film *Ashes and Embers* has been mostly well received by critics with the exception of a few like Janet Maslin, who reports:

It's a rambling, almost dreamlike film that drifts between Washington, where Ned Charles, its protagonist, (played by John Anderson) wanders past ghetto streets and war memorials; Los Angeles, where he hopes to find his future, and instead winds up in police custody; and the rural setting of his grandmother's farmhouse. . . .

There is a lot of talk in "Ashes and Embers," and it is better focused at some times than at others. Some of this is attributable to poor sound recording, and some is a result of Mr. Gerima's impassioned but sprawling style. The film's concerns emerge as heartfelt even when they aren't clearly expressed. On those occasions when clarity prevails the style becomes emphatic and tough, but at other times it tends to preach and to wander. But the rarity of new films about Blacks in America is reason enough to overlook some of the haziness of this one. *(New York Times,* 17 November 1982, p. C30)

On the contrary, Ferid Boughedir offers only favorable statements about *Ashes and Embers (Jeune Afrique,* 21 December 1983, p. 54). Said Ould Khelifa appreciates the film's militancy and plastic beauty *(Afrique-Asie,* 12 April 1982, p. 59). Catherine Arnaud *(Les 2 Ecrans,* November 1982, p. 28) is impressed by its images and elaborate sound score, and links Gerima's lyricism to that of the Egyptian filmmaker Youssef Chahine. Similarly, J. Hoberman fully endorses *Ashes and Embers:*

Opening with a scream and concluding with an invocation of the Second Coming, Haile Gerima's angry, ambitious *Ashes and Embers* is a . . . sort of horror film, a two-hour excursion through the personal hell of a black Vietnam vet. . . . Gerima churns up the screen for three-quarters of the movie with his solipsistic protagonist's visceral anguish, then abruptly shifts gears for some didactic consciousness raising. . . . The frenzied, discombobulated structure parallels Charles's own overwrought confusion. . . .

The film includes an exceptional performance by Evelyn Blackwell as Charles's venerable toothless grandmother and a triumphantly dense sound mix. *(Village Voice,* 23 November 1982, p. 62).

Concluding that same article, the critic asserts that *"Ashes and Embers* establishes Gerima as among the most interesting and original narrative filmmakers on the current scene."

After viewing *After Winter: Sterling Brown,* Kathy Elaine Anderson comments: "It is not without minor technical blemishes. Nonetheless, it is an important film because it documents so well the life and work of one of the pivotal figures in Afro-American literature" *(Black Film Review,* Winter 1985, p. 6). Future critical accounts of this motion picture will probably judge that it lacks the inventive creativity present in the filmmaker's earlier works.

FILMOGRAPHY

Hourglass, super 8, color, 13 min., 1971.
Child of Resistance, 16 mm, color/black and white, 47 min., 1972.
Bush Mama, 16 mm, black and white, 98 min., 1976.
Harvest: 3,000 Years, 16 mm, black and white, 150 min., 1976.
Wilmington 10–USA 10,000, 16 mm, color/black and white, 120 min., 1978.
Ashes and Embers, 16 mm, color, 120 min., 1981.
After Winter: Sterling Brown, 16 mm, color, 60 min., 1985.

BIBLIOGRAPHY

Writings by Haile Gerima

Gerima, Haile. "Fireplace-Cinema (Gathering, Warming, Sharing)." *Filmfaust,* n. 39,
    May-June 1984, pp. 44–55.
———. "Visual Footprint—The Battle for the Film Frame," in Renee Tajima, ed.
    Journey Across Three Continents, pp. 26–27. New York: Third World Newsreel,
    1985.

Interviews of Haile Gerima

Anderson, Kathy Elaine. "The Filmmaker as Storyteller: An Interview with Haile
    Gerima." *Black Film Review,* vol. 2, n. 1, Winter 1985, pp. 6–7, 19.
Daney, Serge. "Rencontre avec Haile Gerima (Une Moisson de 3.000 ans)." *Cahiers
    du Cinéma,* n. 270, September-October 1976, pp. 63–64.
Lardeau, Yann, and Serge Le Péron. "Entretien avec Haile Gerima: du cinéma indé-
    pendant et de l'importance d'une perspective historique." *Les 2 Ecrans,* n. 50,
    November 1982, pp. 34–36.
Marcorelles, Louis. "Haile Gerima: J'appartiens à la fois à l'Ethiopie et à l'Amérique
    noire." *Le Monde,* 7 July 1984, p. 11.
Martin, Marcel." Entretien avec Haile Gerima." *Ecran 77,* n. 58, 15 May 1977, p. 62.
Mimoun, Mouloud. "Entretien." *L'Afrique Littéraire et Artistique,* n. 49, 3rd Quarter
    1978, pp. 70–72.
Pfaff, Françoise. "De quelle moisson s'agit-il?—dialogue avec Haile Gerima, auteur du
    film La Récolte de 3,000 ans." *Positif,* n. 198, October 1977, pp. 53–56.
Safford, Tony, and William Triplett. "Haile Gerima: Radical Departure to a New Black
    Cinema." *The Journal of the University Film and Video Association,* vol. 35, n.
    2, Spring 1983, pp. 59–65.
Willemin, Paul. "Interview with Haile Gerima on 3,000 Year Harvest." *Framework,* n.
    7–8, Spring 1978, pp. 31–35.

Film Reviews and Studies of Haile Gerima

Anderson, Kathy Elaine. "After Winter, a Loving Portrait of Sterling Brown." *Black
    Film Review,* vol. 2, n. 1, Winter 1985, pp. 6, 9, 17.
Arnaud, Catherine. "Cinéastes noirs américains à Amiens." *Les 2 Ecrans,* n. 50, No-
    vember 1982, pp. 27–28.

Bassan, Raphael. "La Saga du cinéma des noirs américains." *Afrique-Asie*, n. 279, 11 October 1982, pp. 54–56.

———. "Un Film phare." *Afrique-Asie*, n. 320, 23 April 1984, p. 51.

———. "La Rochelle: le sceau Patil-Gerima." *Afrique-Asie*, n. 328, 13 August 1984, pp. 60–61.

Berry, Janice L. "Wilmington Ten Chronicled in Wilmington 10,000." *The New Communicator*, vol. 4, n. 1, 8 February 1978, p. 3.

Berthomé, Jean-Pierre. "Le Festival des Trois Continents." *Positif*, n. 277, March 1984, p. 47.

Boughedir, Ferid. "A Cannes, le tiers monde est présent." *Jeune Afrique*, n. 802, 21 May 1976, pp. 56–57.

———. "Le Septième Art entre deux mondes." *Jeune Afrique*, n. 808, 2 July 1976, pp. 56–57.

———. "Et maintenant que la fête commence!" *Jeune Afrique*, n. 1151, 26 January 1983, p. 53.

———. "La Bobine en solitaire." *Jeune Afrique*, n. 1198, 21 December 1983, pp. 54–55.

Cervoni, Albert. "Pour la première fois, l'Ethiopie." *L'Humanité*, 19 May 1976, p. 8.

———, and Bo Torp Pedersen. "Den Afro arabiska filmen." *Chaplin 166*, n. 1, 1980, pp. 19–21.

Cham, Mbye Baboucar. "Art and Ideology in the Work of Sembène Ousmane and Haile Gerima." *Présence Africaine*, n. 129, 1st Quarter 1984, pp. 79–91.

Ciment, Michel. "Harvest: 3,000 Years (Moisson, 3.000 ans) de Haile Gerima." *Positif*, n. 183–184, July-August 1976, p. 90.

Colpart, Gilles. "La Récolte de trois mille ans." *Cinéma 77*, n. 224–225, August-September 1977, p. 178.

Davis, Elliot. "The Making of Harvest. "*Filmmakers Newsletter*, vol. 8, n. 6, April 1975, pp. 18–19.

Delmas, Jean. "Harvest." *Jeune Cinéma*, n. 96, July-August 1976, p. 39.

Douin, Jean-Luc. "La Récolte de 3.000 ans." *Télérama*, n. 1424, 27 April 1977, p. 91.

Fieschi, Jacques. "Harvest: 3,000 Years de Haile Gerima (Ethiopia)." *Cinématographe*, n. 19, June 1976, p. 30.

Fullman, E. "Wilmington 10–USA 10,000 Makes Its World Premiere." *The Hilltop*, 17 November 1978, pp. 1, 8.

Gabriel, Teshome. *Third Cinema in the Third World—The Aesthetics of Liberation*. Ann Arbor, Mich.: UMI Research Press, 1982.

Gibus, Gabriel. "Bush Mama d'Haile Gerima." *Afrique-Antilles*, n. 64, September 1984, p. 46.

Grelier, Robert. "La Récolte de 3.000 ans." *La Revue du Cinéma, Image et Son*, n. 320–321, October 1977, p. 233.

Hennebelle, Guy. "Gerima Haile." *L'Afrique Littéraire et Artistique*, n. 49, 3rd Quarter 1978, p. 68.

Hoberman, J. "Declaration of Independents." *Village Voice*, 24 September 1979, p. 57.

———. "Ashes and Embers." *Village Voice*, 23 November 1982, p. 62.

Howard, Steve. "A Cinema of Transformation: The Films of Haile Gerima." *Cinéaste*, vol. 14, n. 1, 1985, pp. 28–29, 39.

Kernan, Michael. "Bush Momma *[sic]*: Realities." *Washington Post*, 27 January 1977, p. C9.

Khelifa, Said Ould. "Journées d'Amiens: la preuve par l'image." *Afrique-Asie*, n. 263, 12 April 1982, pp. 58–59.

Kieffer, Anne. "Tiers monde à Nantes." *Jeune Cinéma*, n. 159, June 1984, pp. 36–37.

Lardeau, Yann. "Cinéma des racines et histoires du ghetto." *Cahiers du Cinéma*, n. 340, October 1982, pp. 48–52.

Maanouni, Ahmed El. "Ethiopie: An 3.000 de Haile Gerima." *Cinémarabe*, n. 6, March-April 1977, p. 34.

Makarius, Michel I. "Kébébé le fou ou l'Ethiopie millénaire." *Jeune Afrique*, n. 807, 25 June 1976, p. 107.

Malnic, Evelyne. "Un Document dramatique." *Jeune Afrique*, n. 806, 18 June 1976, p. 51.

Marcorelles, Louis. "L'Ethiopie millénaire à la Semaine de la critique." *Le Monde*, 19 May 1976, p. 21.

———. "La Récolte de 3.000 ans d'Haile Gerima. Un très long voyage dans le passé du monde." *Le Monde*, 21 April 1977, p. 33.

———. "Bush Mama, la vie et la menace." *Le Monde*, 7 July 1984, p. 11.

Martin, Angela. *African Films: The Context of Production*. London: British Film Institute, 1982.

Martin, Marcel. "Harvest: Three Thousand Years de Haile Gerima." *Ecran 1976*, n. 47, 15 May 1976, p. 3.

———. "La Récolte de 3.000 ans." *Ecran 77*, n. 58, 15 May 1977, pp. 61–62.

Maslin, Janet. "Screen: Ashes and Embers." *New York Times*, 17 November 1982, p. C30.

Monga, Célestin. "Leçon de courage." *Jeune Afrique*, n. 1229, 25 July 1984, pp. 58–59.

Montvalon, Christine de. "Bush Mama." *Télérama*, n. 1799, 7 July 1984, p. 29.

Pfaff, Françoise. "Ethiopia's 3,000 Year Harvest: Toward an African Cinema." *Washington Newsworks*, 29 April 1976, p. 26.

———. "Toward a New Era in Cinema." *New Directions*, vol. 4, n. 3, July 1977, pp. 28–30.

———. *The Cinema of Ousmane Sembene, A Pioneer of African Film*. Westport, Conn.: Greenwood Press, 1984.

Said, Abdulkadir N. "Sterling Brown . . . The Film." *New Directions*, vol. 13, n. 1, January 1986, p. 31.

Salaam, Kalamu Ya. "Bush Mama." *The Black Collegian*, May-June 1977, p. 63.

Scarupa, Harriet Jackson. "Filmmakers at Howard." *New Directions*, vol. 10, n. 2, April 1983, pp. 4–11.

Sublett, Scott. "Black Filmmakers Start to Flourish." *Washington Times*, 17 September 1982, pp. 4C-5C.

Tarter, Margaret. "Wilmington 10–USA 10,000? Chronicles Age-Old Racism." *Bay State Banner*, 17 May 1979, pp. 19, 22.

Tate, Gregory S. "Positive Productions." *Palavra*, Fall 1981, p. 6.

Taylor, Clyde. "The New Black Cinema Comes Home." *First World*, May-June 1977, pp. 46–47.

———. "Shooting the Black Woman." *The Black Collegian*, vol. 9, n. 5, May-June 1979, pp. 94–96.

———. "Haile Gerima: Firestealer." *Africa Now*, December 1983, p. 81.

Van Gelder, Lawrence. "Harvest: 3,000 Years Is Elementary Film." *New York Times,*
     6 April 1976, p. 27.
Yearwood, Gladstone L., ed. *Black Cinema Aesthetics, Issues in Independent Black
     Filmmaking.* Athens, Ohio: Ohio University Center for Afro-American Studies,
     1982.

Med Hondo (1936–   )
Mauritania

BIOGRAPHY

The son of a Senegalese father and a Mauritanian mother, Abid Mohamed Medoun Hondo, better known as Med Hondo, was born on 4 May 1936 in Ain Ouled Beni Mathar, located in the Atar region of Mauritania. Describing his background, he says: "My forefathers were slaves. My ancestors were Sudanese, my family undertook a long migratory journey which led them to Mauritania" (*Jeune Cinéma*, September-October 1974, p. 29). Since his family members are permanently settled as cultivators, Hondo spent his childhood and early adolescence in an oasis on the borders of the Saharan desert.

In 1954 Med Hondo was sent to Rabat, Morocco, to be trained for four years as a cook at a hotel management school. As a chef, he wished to expand his gastronomic savoir-faire, and thus embarked for France in 1959. This is how he summarizes his first experiences on French soil:

When you are an immigrant, the diplomas you may have don't have any weight. Before being able to work in the kitchen of a restaurant, I had to work as a dock-worker and then I picked citrus fruits on farms. What a disillusionment! Eventually I was hired to work for a Marseille restaurant. . . . It was hard work but the most trying part was my relationship with some of the people I worked with. My boss, who had hired me at substandard wages, was ashamed of me. So, he relegated me to the back of his kitchen until he noticed that, with my chef's cap, I was providing an exotic flair to his establishment. (*Télérama*, 18 April 1979, p. 88)

Shortly thereafter, Hondo worked in a restaurant in Vittel, a thermal health resort located in eastern France. Says the Mauritanian filmmaker:

These various jobs allowed me to learn a lot about the French proletariat. When I came to Paris in 1962, I worked at Les Halles [Paris' central market at the time] as a Swiss cheese delivery man. Then, I became a waiter, and later I worked for two years at the famous La Reine Pédauque restaurant. In both cases I learned a lot about the French bourgeoisie just by watching them eat. (Hondo to author, Paris, Summer 1979)

In 1965, at the same time that he was working, Med Hondo took drama courses under the late Françoise Rosay, a well-known French stage and screen actress whom he describes as "an extraordinary lady who knew how to keep in touch with reality" *(Le Monde,* 20 September 1979, p. 19). Yet, in spite of valuable and intense training as a stage actor, Hondo soon felt culturally alienated by the roles he was asked to play. He reminisces:

I became involved in drama because I felt a need to express myself and because I had a great deal of naïvete. As I saw actors on the stage, they reminded me of the griots and the palaver trees under which African people debate their problems. I thought that by way of the theater I could tell what I had been enduring and what I felt. My assumptions proved to be wrong. While studying drama I had to learn parts from plays by Molière, Racine and Shakespeare. They did not illustrate the experience I had sought to express. Moreover, there were few parts Black actors could play on the French stage. Classical theater did not answer my needs. (Hondo to author, Summer 1979)

Thus, in 1966, in order to explore a repertory of plays closer to his own concerns, Hondo decided to create a theater ensemble, which he eloquently named Shango, after the Yoruba God of Thunder:

The troupe consisted of African and West Indian friends. We staged plays by the Mar-tiniquan poet and playwright Aimé Césaire, by Afro-American authors such as Imamu Baraka and by many unknown African and South American playwrights. We performed in small theaters and cultural centers all over France but the public at large had little interest in our productions. We realized that it was very hard to break through the established structures of French theater, and that we were not more welcome on the stage than anywhere else. (Hondo to author, Summer 1979)

A few years later, Hondo's troupe merged with Les Griots, a theater company headed by the Guadeloupean actor and stage director Robert Liensol. The new theater company, named Griot-Shango, staged a number of works on Black topics written in French, among them plays by René Depestre (Haiti), Guy Monga (Congo), and Daniel Boukman (Martinique). In addition to being a stage director, Hondo interpreted parts in plays by Anton Tchecov, Kateb Yacine, Bertolt Brecht, and William Hanley. He also played in Césaire's *La Tragédie du Roi Christophe* under the direction of the late Jean-Marie Serreau. He performed as well in *Les Verts Pâturages* (Green Pastures), adapted for French television by Jean-Christophe Averty, and played the role of an Amazonian Indian in a French TV series. Moreover, after working as an extra in various films, Hondo was offered parts in movies such as *Un Homme de trop* (Shock Troops, 1967) by Costa-Gavras, *A Walk with Love and Death* (1969) by John Huston, and *Tante Zita* (Zita, 1968) by Robert Enrico.

After having entered film as an actor, Med Hondo soon became fascinated with the camera. Therefore, with the intention of learning all he could about cinema, Hondo started working on various sets as assistant director. This led to another phase in his career, that of filmmaker. He stresses: "I did not go to any film school. I used to go to see films two or three times in a row during my leisure time and I would do my own critique. This is how I familiarized myself with the seventh art" *(Cinémaction,* Summer 1979, p. 82). He also claims: "If one is able to speak and to express oneself, one is capable of making a motion picture" *(Jeune Cinéma,* June-July 1970, p. 32).

Med Hondo's first efforts as a filmmaker were two black and white shorts, *Balade aux sources* (Ballad to the Sources, 1969) and *Partout ou peut-être nulle part* (Everywhere, Nowhere Maybe, 1969). Yet, it is with *Soleil O* (O Sun, 1969) that he really began to make a name for himself in cinema. As early as 1965 Med Hondo had written the film's scenario, which took him six months to complete:

When I wrote my script I did not have any audience in mind. . . . I was living in France with the sense of being a minority and I needed to literally throw up the things I had on my chest. . . . I had to yell and free myself. *(Cinémaction,* Summer 1979, p. 82)

In another interview, Hondo states:

Once the script was written, I gathered a crew of technicians and a team of African actors. Then, I went to see some film processing companies and told them: "Here I am, I don't have a penny in my pocket but I want to make a film . . . lend me some raw film. . . . I will reimburse you on an installment plan, and if I fail to do so you can put me in jail." They agreed. The film cost $30,000 . . . and was shot in a year because my actors were not always available. . . . It was completed in August 1969. *(Les Lettres Françaises,* 6 May 1970, p. 17)

Soleil O, whose protagonist was portrayed by Robert Liensol, was selected to be shown at the International Critics' Week during the 1970 Cannes Film Festival. It won the Golden Leopard Award at the 1970 Locarno Film Festival (Switzerland) and received the International Critics' Prize at the 1971 Pan-African Film Festival of Ouagadougou (FESPACO) held in Burkina Faso. In 1972, *Soleil O* was awarded the Human Rights Prize in Strasbourg, France. Probably because of its pointed attacks on African rulers and its sharp criticism of colonialism and neocolonialism, *Soleil O* has rarely been seen in Sub-Saharan African nations. It has, however, been shown in such countries as Algeria, where it was well received by varied audiences. Hondo remarks:

There are different perceptions of an image. *Soleil O* is crystal-clear and is neither intellectual nor sophisticated. It has often happened that those who understood it best were illiterate. This film was shown in Algeria. There, because they were completely able to identify with the film, the proletarians explained it to the intellectuals. (Hondo to author, Summer 1979)

The year 1973 saw the release of Hondo's subsequent motion picture, entitled *Les Bicots-nègres, vos voisins* (Arabs and Niggers, Your Neighbors). Like *Soleil*

O, Les Bicots-nègres, vos voisins examines the life of Black and Arab workers in France. Says Hondo: ''I cannot help but show the lot of Africans in Paris because it is a reality which hurts and torments me'' *(Télérama,* 16 October 1974, p. 77). In *Les Bicots-nègres, vos voisins,* migrant workers were not only made to play their own roles on the screen, but were also directly involved in the creative process of the film by making suggestions as to its content. The director emphasizes:

Since my aim was to make a film that would reflect the concerns of migrant workers, I wanted to work with them instead of using traditional creative methods. It is not a collective work, but rather a dialectical film whose various stages were assessed by all those involved in its making. *(Cinéma-Québec,* April 1975, p. 37)

In 1974 *Les Bicots-nègres, vos voisins* won the Grand Prize (''Tanit d'Or'') at the Carthage Film Festival (Tunisia), as well as the International Film Critics' Prize in Toulon (France). Mainly shown in France at film festivals, ciné-clubs, cultural centers, or to migrant workers' associations, Hondo's film was seen by some 50,000 people at the time. To date, and presumably for the same reasons as in the case of *Soleil O,* the film has rarely been screened in Sub-Saharan Africa.

Subsequently, Med Hondo made two color documentaries concerning the freedom fighters of the Western Sahara (the Polisario). These films are *Nous aurons toute la mort pour dormir* (We'll Sleep When We Die, 1977), on a budget of $75,000, and *Polisario, un peuple en armes* (Polisario, A People in Arms, 1979). Another work by Hondo is *West Indies,* shot in Creole and French in 1979, and based on *Les Négriers* (The Slavers), a play by Daniel Boukman which Hondo had produced three times on the legitimate stage (in 1972, 1974, and 1976).

In terms of Black African cinema *West Indies* should be considered a high-budget film since it reached a production cost of some $800,000, including a $200,000 slave ship built by set designer Jacques Saulnier in an abandoned car factory. According to film reviewer Maryse Condé *(Demain l'Afrique,* 12 March 1979, p. 69), Med Hondo refused a $2.5 million offer from an American film producer because the latter wanted him to use noted Black American actors instead of a lesser known West Indian cast. So, to insure the film's financing as well as to protect his own creative prerogatives, Hondo turned to investors from Mauritania, Senegal, and the Ivory Coast. He sought the technical backing of Algerian television as well, and obtained some funds ($85,000) from the French National Cinema Center (CNC). Eventually, with both professional and nonprofessional actors, seventy dancers (most of whom are West Indian performers), ballets staged by the Black American choreographer Linda Dingwall, and a musical score composed by Frank Valmont of Martinique, Hondo crafted a musical epic that illustrates the main stages of the history of the French West Indies. The filmmaker points out:

I wanted to free the very concept of musical comedy from its American trade mark. I wanted to show that each people on earth has its own musical comedy, its own musical tragedy and its own thought shaped through its own history. *(Ecran 79,* 15 June 1979, p. 25)

Benefitting from extensive press coverage, *West Indies* opened simultaneously in eight Gaumont movie theaters in Paris, but soon proved to be a commercial failure. Apparently this film has had a much better career on the festival circuit: it was chosen to inaugurate the 1979 Venice Film Festival and received a ten-minute standing ovation at the 1979 Montreal Film Festival. The following year, Hondo's film was awarded the Special Jury Prize at the Carthage Film Festival and the Golden Eagle at the International Festival of Francophone Countries. At the 1981 FESPACO, *West Indies* won the Prize of the Seventh Art, awarded to a film director who has shown great mastery of film language in his or her work. More recently, the motion picture was featured at the "Celebration of Black Cinema IV," a film festival organized in Boston (30 April-2 May 1986).

Med Hondo insists that he does not make films for art's sake but to convey ideas. For him "cinema is not a vocation; it is part of a self-awareness process" *(Télérama,* 18 April 1979, p. 88). He stresses:

I make films to show people the problems with which they are confronted every day. I hope my films will help them fight these problems. I also decided to make films to bring some Black faces to the lily-white French screens which have been ignoring us for years. In France little is said about the Black contribution to the world. . . . People have to stop considering us as a homogeneous swarm of grasshoppers and acknowledge our ethnic differences. . . . For three centuries, due to historical circumstances, a whole people has been led to believe that it was superior to the people it had colonized. Such an ideology has not been eradicated in the past 20 years in spite of the independence of African countries. People should be educated about the richness of the African heritage and the discrimination faced by immigrants in France. I hope my films explain Africa and the crucial and burning issues faced by Black people in Africa and abroad. (Hondo to author, Summer 1979)

Hondo's philosophy of cinema is connected with the functional aspect of most African art forms. He believes that "African cinema has an important role to play in education, in raising the consciousness of African moviegoers as well as in the shaping of the new African" *(Les 2 Ecrans,* May 1979, p. 26). Accordingly, he deplores that in Africa "most politicians don't understand the importance of cinema as a factor of development" *(Screen International,* 23 February 1985, p. 16).

As can be anticipated, Hondo is against escapist films—which he calls "opium cinema"—and rejects the patterns of commercial Western movie-making in favor of an alternative film language which would more adequately reflect the Black experience. He explains:

Our languages and the richness of our history must convey a certain uniqueness to our films. This is why I often say that African cinéastes must beware of mimicking. When one has a specific history, a people with its particular way of walking, shaking hands, looking at one another and eating rice, one should film this in a different manner, and impose a distinct film language. *(Cinémaction,* Summer 1979, p. 95)

Consequently, Hondo once said: "Why am I involved in a kind of cinema which dismantles the narrative and psychological mechanisms of traditional dramaturgy? Because, as an African filmmaker, I have something uniquely African to express" *(Cinematografo,* August-September 1975, p. 359).

Med Hondo has a very personal film style, and the content of his motion pictures is usually his sole responsibility. Except for *West Indies,* he has written all of his scripts and has directed, produced, and distributed his films on an independent basis, limiting his budgets by using basic crews and equipment.

Although he is now an internationally recognized filmmaker, Hondo still feels "displaced both culturally and morally" *(Framework,* Spring 1978, p. 29) as an immigrant. Yet, he also acknowledges that his exile might have been a determining factor in his becoming a film director:

First, if I had stayed in my country, I probably would have never made any films. Furthermore, assuming that I could have managed to get involved in cinema, I probably would have never made *Soleil O* or *Les bicots-nègres, vos voisins* because I would have been in an entirely different environment; I might have made a film concerning the peasantry or perhaps I would have been throttled or muzzled like many of my counterparts who are unable to make films. I might have become an unemployed worker among thousands; I would have stayed in my village washing floors. *(Jeune Cinéma,* September-October 1974, pp. 30–31)

A talented actor, a skillful stage director, and a forceful filmmaker, Med Hondo is equally known as a relentless and vivid spokesman for the cause of Black African cinema. An artist with entrepreneurial abilities, Hondo created his own film company, Soleil O, as early as 1970. In 1982 he spearheaded the founding of CAC (Comité Africain de Cinéastes), or African Committee of Filmmakers, an organization which promotes and distributes African motion pictures on an international scale. More recently, in 1985, with such filmmakers as Ola Balogun*, Timité Bassori*, Ousmane Sembene*, and Paulin Soumanou Vieyra*, Med Hondo participated in the creation of the West African Film Corporation (WAFCO), an organization which will also facilitate the production and commercialization of African motion pictures.

Med Hondo recently made his most ambitious film yet, *Sarraounia* (1986), a $2.5 million historical film, with 800 extras, shot over a twelve-week period in Burkina Faso and co-produced by the government of Burkina Faso, and Hondo's film company Soleil O. The motion picture premiered in Paris in November 1986, won the Grand Prize ("Etalon de Yennenga") at the Tenth FES-PACO held in Burkina Faso from 21 February to 28 February 1987, and was subsequently featured at a number of international film festivals such as FILM-FEST D.C. in Washington D.C. (22 April - 3 May 1987).

Hondo spends a lot of his time in Paris. Apart from his film-related activities, the Mauritanian filmmaker is frequently involved in acting, dubbing, and directing French language versions of foreign films.

MAJOR THEMES

Med Hondo uses film as a privileged means of expression "to say what bothers me in the world, what makes me ill and prevents me from breathing" *(Positif,* September 1970, p. 25). It is thus hardly suprising that his first motion picture, *Balade aux sources,* would reflect his immediate concerns as an exiled African. According to him, it "tells the story of an African who lives in France. Compelled to ponder over his condition, he decides to return to his country. Unemployed, he finds himself wandering on an African beach and meditates on the choice he has made" *(Cinémaction,* Summer 1979, p. 82). Hondo outlines *Partout ou peut-être nulle part* as "the story of a white bourgeois couple seen through my eyes, those of an African. . . . it ended with the suicide of the man, who had proven unable to act concretely, seeking gratification by way of abstract intellectual talks" *(Positif,* September 1970, p. 22).

Soleil O (O Sun) owes its title to an old song African slaves used to sing in Haiti to express their dramatic estrangement from their native land. Hondo symbolically links their fate to that of contemporary Black workers in France. The opening scene of *Soleil O,* which serves as background to the credits, is very indicative of the content and tone of Hondo's film. Here he uses a cartoon showing an African put into power by foreign military intervention, but whose leadership is subsequently terminated by those who had formerly helped him. The filmmaker thereby announces that his film will be a pamphlet against foreign imperialism in Africa from the slave trade to neocolonialism. This theme expands itself through a subsequent sequence in which the cross of recently baptized Africans becomes a sword with which they proceed to kill one another under the watchful eye of a white officer.

Soleil O is a succession of forceful tableaus describing the illusions and miseries of African migrant laborers. Their plight is reflected through that of a nameless African who comes to Paris with the hope of securing a job as an accountant. During his relentless search for work and decent housing, the accountant has to face a variety of racially based rejections. Med Hondo stresses:

My main character could be a garbage collector, a student or a teacher. His status does not prevent him from being affected in the same manner by the general conditions of history within a racist society. To be a Black expatriate is an identity. If I am to take the subway today, I will have to encounter the same problems migrant workers have to face. You might be stopped in the subway by the police asking to check your identity papers or your alien card. Whatever his job or diploma, any Black or Arab living in France may be confronted with racism on a daily basis. (Hondo to author, Summer 1979)

As the film evolves, the alienation to which the young accountant is subjected generates an existentialist quest for self. Estranged from the Western world, he will go through different phases of anguish and near insanity. The last sequence of *Soleil O* shows him in a forest. Invited to share a meal with a French family vacationing at their country home, he is shocked by their waste as the children playfully step over the food set on the lunch table. Disgusted and revolted by acts so strongly opposed to his own values and deprivation, the protagonist abruptly stands up, leaves the family, and proceeds to walk deeper into the forest. There he starts to run. Breathless, he falls at the bottom of a tree, where he has visions of Third World figures such as Patrice Lumumba, Malcolm X, and Che Guevara. At this point, while cracking machine guns resound in his mind, his painful experience becomes collective and universal. Images of a new self amid a new world flash before him at the very moment he has collapsed at the roots of a womblike trunk of a tree—his metaphorical cultural matrix. It is through these roots that he will reconcile the various parts of his severed self and regain his inner identity as an African.

Soleil O's eruptive tone and nonlinear format have often been associated with European "avant-garde" dramatic techniques. Med Hondo vehemently denies such a comparison by saying:

Soleil O derives from the African oral tradition. It depicts a unique reality. There is no dichotomy between style and content; here it is the content which imposes a style. I wanted to describe several people through one person instead of using a group of people. In my country, when people talk about a specific issue, they may digress and come back to their initial topic. Black cultures have a syntax which has nothing to do with Cartesian logic or that of other civilization. (Hondo to author, Summer 1979)

In a style identical to that of *Soleil O, Les Bicots-nègres, vos voisins* calls for the unity of the oppressed. It underscores the importation of cheap labor into capitalistic societies and denounces the subhuman living conditions of expatriate workers in France. *Les Bicots-nègres, vos voisins* also includes a significant prologue which addresses the nature and role of Black African cinema in view of the cultural imperialism exerted in most of Africa through Western films.

Nous aurons toute la mort pour dormir (which received an award from the International Catholic Organization for the Cinema in 1977, Berlin) and *Polisario, un peuple en armes* document the Polisario's struggle against the Mauritanian and Moroccan armed occupation of the Western Sahara, which started in 1975, after the end of Spanish rule in that area. In both films, Hondo depicts the agonies of war, illustrates the harsh daily reality of refugee camps, and interviews a number of freedom fighters concerning their most pressing sociopolitical issues.

West Indies is a vast musical fresco which covers nearly 400 years in the history of the French West Indians from their enslavement to their present-day displacement in France for want of adequate work in the Islands. As happened in most of Hondo's previous works, *West Indies* tells of colonial exploitation, exile, and the struggle led by people to achieve their freedom.

Hondo's epic *Sarraounia*, adapted from a novel by Abdoulaye Mamani (based on real events), with a musical score by Pierre Akendengué, depicts the valiant deeds of a West African queen who opposed French colonial troops at the end of the 19th century.

SURVEY OF CRITICISM

In spite of two earlier motion pictures, it is with *Soleil O* that Med Hondo established his credentials as a film director with personal vision. Guy Hennebelle salutes *Soleil O* as one of the most original films screened during the International Film Critics' Week at the 1970 Cannes Film Festival *(Les Lettres Françaises,* 6 May 1970, p. 17). Notwithstanding what he calls "construction flaws" and "an often jolting style," Michel Ciment is highly impressed by the strength and acuteness of Hondo's first feature length movie *(Positif,* September 1970, p. 18). Jean-Louis Bory sees it as a vigorous and intelligent film which is both a dramatic parable and a commanding psychodrama *(Le Nouvel Observateur,* 4 December 1972, p. 81). Claude-Michel Cluny likes *Soleil O*'s thematic richness and stylistic inventiveness *(Cinéma 1973,* January 1973, pp. 128–29). Although he finds the film repetitive, Mosk likes its "dynamic mixture of symbolism" as well as its "rugged flair" *(Variety,* 6 May 1970, p. 20). Jerry Oster writes:

"Soleil O" . . . is most effective in its cinema verite photography of dismal working class sections of Paris and least effective when it tries to join these visual essays together by means of a series of fictional confrontations between black and white, poor and rich, oppressed and oppressor.

"Soleil O" is notable for its unusually imaginative use of sound and music as counterpoint to its stark, grainy images. *(Daily News,* 15 March 1973, p. 93)

Film critic A.H. Weiler stresses Hondo's efficient use of elliptical symbolism and "stream-of-consciousness approach" but considers his "dramatization of injustice . . . open-ended and inconclusive" *(New York Times,* 15 March 1973, p. 55). For Archer Winsten:

Director Med Hondo loses no chance to drive home the hypocrisies, the vicious racism and the handicaps that face the black in France. He has chosen his blacks well for the favorable impression, his whites equally well to be downgraded in most cases. Even so, it is not an indictment that can be shrugged off. There is much truth and a corroding bitterness in the picture. Essentially it is documentary rather than fiction. It is an argument by one who has been hurt deeply and is hitting back. It is a picture with something to say, and Med Hondo says it with plain, hard power. *(New York Post,* 15 March 1973, p. 50)

Also, because of *Soleil O*'s original style and uncompromising content, Bernard Trémege encourages viewers concerned with Africa and/or cinema to see it *(Jeune Cinéma,* December 1972–January 1973, p. 39).

Like *Soleil O, Les Bicots-nègres, vos voisins* has generated varied comments. Jean-Luc Douin notes its ''impassioned, sarcastic and aggressive tone'' as well as its stylistic audacities and concludes: ''Here is an important work not only in the history of African film but also in that of political cinema'' *(Télérama,* 16 October 1974, p. 77). For Monique Hennebelle, *Les Bicots-nègres, vos voisins* is ''a very important document on the immigration of Arab and African workers to France'' but, she adds, ''this film is far from matching the inner coherence and the stylistic brilliance of *Soleil O*'' *(L'Afrique Littéraire et Artistique,* n. 34, 1974, p. 84). Jean-Patrick Lebel values Hondo's work because it provides a thorough analysis of immigration as related to imperialism, colonialism, and neocolonialism *(La Nouvelle Critique,* December 1974–January 1975, p. 125). Pascal Kane approves of the film's clarity but questions its validity as testimony of migrant workers *(Cahiers du Cinéma,* July-August 1974, p. 78). Likewise, Thérèse Giraud wonders about Hondo's ability, as an intellectual, to reflect adequately the workers' plight *(Cahiers du Cinéma,* December 1974–January 1975, p. 42).

For a number of film critics such as Jean-Luc Douin *(Télérama,* 30 March 1977, p. 104), Louis Marcorelles, *(Le Monde,* 30 March 1977, p. 22), Paul-Louis Thirard *(Positif,* May 1977, pp. 73–74), and Guy Fichet *(Lutte Ouvrière,* 16 April 1977, p. 23), *Nous aurons toute la mort pour dormir* is an arresting motion picture which eloquently heralds a people's war for freedom. Gilles Colpart praises its accuracy, lack of demagogy, and visual beauty *(La Revue du Cinéma, Image et Son,* October 1977, p. 192). In another review, Colpart judges Hondo's work to be didactic and informative and further defines it as ''a poem to the glory of human dignity'' *(Cinéma 77,* July 1977, p. 103). On one hand, Marcel Martin approves of its rigorous ideological analysis, plastic qualities, and epic tone *(Ecran 77,* 15 May 1977, p. 50); on the other hand, Guy Hennebelle would have wished for a film with a more explicit political demonstration. In addition, Hennebelle considers *Nous aurons toute la mort pour dormir* to be too long and repetitive *(Ecran 77,* 15 May 1977, p. 51). In contrast with *Nous aurons toute la mort pour dormir,* little material, if any, seems readily available on *Polisario, un peuple en armes*.

West Indies engendered a mixed critical response. Despite its inventive mise-en-scène, Philippe Carcassonne does not find the film totally convincing *(Cinématographe,* October 1979, p. 49). Jacqueline Nacache stresses the contrived performances of its actors, but regrets even more that *West Indies* lacks homogeneity, a fact which she attributes to Hondo's constant wavering between political didactism and the musical epic *(Cinéma 79,* n. 251, 1979, p. 101). Farida Ayari views the film as a ''didactic discourse which ends up being boring because it is too repetitive'' *(Jeune Afrique,* 19 September 1979, p. 67). Ina Césaire, the daughter of the Martiniquan poet and politician Aimé Césaire, points out:

"The film does not provide any solution. Perhaps it expresses the confused feeling that in the immediate future the people of Martinique will not be ready to go out into the street and take up arms. The film does not go beyond the present" *(Demain l'Afrique,* 27 August 1979, p. 74).

Among the favorable reviews of *West Indies* is that of Ben Gibson, who shows a good understanding of the filmmaker's intentions:

West Indies . . . takes as its subject the life of an island in the Caribbean. But rather than accept any of the Hollywood-Caribbean legacy against which it might be set, full of languourous island beauties, pirates with black eye-patches and carefree Calypso singers, Hondo chooses to construct a story for the people of the Antilles which presents the islanders' problems as a continuing struggle against the same enemies, however mutable their form(s). At once deconstructive of traditional forms and associations and ideologically based on the concept of popular history . . . the film blends past and present . . . through the central image of an enormous ship.

Against this epic backcloth—with its own popular structure represented through from *[sic]* the Commandant's cabin, second and third classes, and the hold—the lowest level inhabited by the majority of the people—are pictured the transformations of colonial exploitation and Caribbean (mis)government from the 17th century to the present. The ship, in itself a reference to the infamous "slavers" . . . as well as the modern ships which carry tourists and unemployed islanders in opposite directions, houses all the action. . . .

A project of the size and scope of *West Indies* . . . represents a remarkable breakthrough for the economically restricted African cinema. *(Framework,* Autumn 1979, p. 21)

Likewise, Maryse Condé observes:

For too long a time, African cinema has been conceived as a destitute cinema, a cinema of approximations where techniques did not match ideas . . . . *West Indies* . . . presents itself quite differently: it uses the contribution of both technical and financial means. Its visual sumptuousness is not gratuitous. It proves that a militant film can be beautiful and reach viewers by other means than dry political argumentation. . . . Indeed *West Indies* . . . is no more a West Indian film than an African film. . . . It is a film which summons all people whose past is marked by oppression, whose present results from aborted promises and whose future is left to be conquered. *(Demain l'Afrique,* 27 August 1979, pp. 72, 74)

Edouard J. Maunick calls *West Indies* a daring motion picture *(Demain l'Afrique,* 27 August 1979, p. 70), Marcel Martin terms it a "lucid and corrosive work" *(Ecran 79,* 20 October 1979, p. 64), and Louis Marcorelles appreciates its lyricism, impertinence, and vengeful irony *(Le Monde,* 20 September 1979, p. 19). For Jean Wagner, *West Indies* is "lyrical imagery" and a "history lesson" taught within the somewhat surrealistic setting of a slaveship *(Télérama,* 12 September 1979, p. 101). Although he acknowledges the film's theatrical overtones, B. Abdou favors Hondo's mingling of varied genres, such as ballet and opera, in "a creative symbiosis which leads to a resplendent and arresting spectacle" *(Les 2 Ecrans,* November 1979, p. 47). Likewise, Jean-Louis Pouillaud shows appreciation for *West Indies'* stylized and expressionistic stage devices because they render "its historical vision even more meaningful" *(Positif,* December 1979, p. 76).

Sarraounia was well received by a number of film critics. Rich notes: "Hondo displays impressive production skills in executing the long march and battle sequences. The scenario is also stiletto-sharp in its satirical slicing of the cruel French colonial personality and the craveness of the invaders' African lackeys. . . . Performances are effective. . . . The musical score is wonderful, and a soundtrack LP could help sell 'Sarraounia abroad" *(Variety,* 10 September 1986, p. 19). For Francoise Balogun, *Sarraounia* "is a rehabilitation of African history, it is a hymn to the sense of dignity and it is a positive portrait of an African woman, a queen" *(West Africa,* 17 November 1986, p. 2406). Manny Shirazi believes that *"Sarraounia* will remain a classic film on resistance to colonialism." *(West Africa,* 23 March 1987, p. 558) And Claude Wauthier does not hesitate to hail the motion picture as "the first great epic film of Black African cinema" *(Le Monde,* 26 November 1986, p. 16).

FILMOGRAPHY

Balade aux sources (Ballad to the sources), 16 mm, black and white, 25 min., 1969.
Partout ou peut-être nulle part (Everywhere, Nowhere Maybe), 16 mm, black and white, 30 min., 1969.
Soleil O (O Sun), 16/35 mm, black and white, 100 min., 1969.
Les Bicots-nègres, vos voisins (Arabs and Niggers, Your Neighbors), 16 mm, color, 130 min., 1973.
Nous aurons toute la mort pour dormir (We'll Sleep When We Die), 16 mm, color, 160 min., 1977.
Polisario, un peuple en armes (Polisario, A People in Arms), 16 mm, color, 60 min., 1979.
West Indies, 35 mm, color, 110 min., 1979.
Sarraounia, 35 mm, color, 120 min., 1986.

BIBLIOGRAPHY

Writings by Med Hondo

Hondo, Med. "What Is Cinema for Us?" *Framework,* Issue 11, Autumn 1979, pp. 20–21.
————. "Cinémas africains, écrans colonisés." *Le Monde,* 21 January 1982, p. 12.
————. "Le Cinéaste africain à la conquête de son public," in *FESPACO 1983*, pp. 27–32.

Interviews of Med Hondo

Ciment, Michel, and Paul-Louis Thirard. "Entretien avec Med Hondo." *Positif,* n. 119, September 1970, pp. 22–26.
Delati, Abdou Achouba. "Interview de Med Hondo." *Ecran 74,* n. 30, November 1974, p. 81.

Delmas, Jean. "Med Hondo: Soleil O." *Jeune Cinéma,* n. 48, June-July 1970, pp. 32–38.

Dura, Madeleine. "Entretien avec Med Hondo." *Jeune Cinéma,* n. 121, September-October 1979, pp. 21–28.

Ghali, Nourredine. "Med Hondo: Je suis un immigré." *Jeune Cinéma,* n. 81, September-October 1974, pp. 29–31.

Head, Anne. "Africa: Towards a National Cinema." *Screen International,* n. 485, 23 February 1985, p. 16.

Hennebelle, Guy. "Med Hondo: Dans Soleil O, je dénonce les nègres-blancs. . . . " *Les Lettres Françaises,* n. 1333, 6 May 1970, p. 17.

———. "Med Hondo: Mon film est un vomissement." *Cinémaction,* n. 8, Summer 1979, pp. 82–85.

Ilboudo, Patrick, and Jacob Olivier. "Il n'y a pas de cinéma africain." *L'Observateur,* n. 2524, 8 February 1983, pp. 1, 4–5.

"Intervista con Med Hondo." *Cinematografo,* n. 8–9, August-September 1975, pp. 359–62.

Lemaire, Charles. "Med Hondo répond." *Afrique Nouvelle,* n. 1863, 20 March 1985, p. 16.

Martin, Marcel. "Brève rencontre . . . avec Med Hondo." *Ecran 79,* n. 81, 15 June 1979, pp. 25–26.

"Med Hondo." *Le Film Française,* n. 2131, 6 March 1987, p. 47.

Merzak, M. "Entretien avec . . . Med Hondo." *Les 2 Ecrans,* n. 13, May 1979, pp. 24–26.

Ranvaud, Don. "Interview with Med Hondo." *Framework,* n. 7–8, Spring 1978, pp. 28–30.

Reid, Mark. "Med Hondo Interview: Working Abroad." *Jump Cut,* n. 31, 1986, pp. 48–49.

Rivel, Moune de. "Un Mauritanien tourne l'histoire des Antilles. Med Hondo parle de son film." *Bingo,* n. 319, August 1979, pp. 35–36.

Ruelle, Catherine. "Med Hondo: Quand on a une histoire particulière on doit filmer autrement." *Cinémaction,* n. 8, Summer 1979, pp. 94–95.

Wagner, Jean. "Med Hondo tourne West Indies." *Télérama,* n. 1527, 18 April 1979, pp. 88–89.

"Wir werden den Tod haben um zu schlafen." *Filmfaust,* n. 5, September-October 1977, pp. 91–99.

Film Reviews and Studies of Med Hondo

Abdou, B. "Le ballet des opprimés—West Indies, les nègres marrons de la liberté." *Les 2 Ecrans,* n. 18, November 1979, pp. 46–47.

Arosio, Mario. "Cinema Arabo e Africano." *Cinematografo,* n. 8–9, August-September 1975, p. 358.

Arthuys, Xavier d'. "Les Mensonges à peau d'éléphant." *Les Nouvelles Littéraires,* 28 April 1983, p. 47.

Ayari, Farida. "Négriers d'hier et d'aujourd'hui." *Jeune Afrique,* n. 976, 19 September 1979, p. 67.

Bachy, Victor. "Les Journées Cinématographiques de Carthage 1980." *Revue Belge du Cinéma,* n. 20, 1981, pp. 35–36.

Balogun, Françoise. "A Hymn to Dignity." *West Africa,* 17 November 1986, pp. 2406–7.

Binet, Jacques. "Cinéma africain." *Afrique Contemporaine*, n. 83, January-February 1976, pp. 27–30.

Bory, Jean-Louis. "Les Pièges du catéchisme." *Le Nouvel Observateur*, n. 421, 4 December 1972, p. 81.

———. "Le Cri des africains." *Le Nouvel Observateur*, n. 521, 4 November 1974, p. 82.

Braucourt, Guy. "Carthage." *Ecran 75*, n. 33, February 1975, pp. 9–11.

"The Cannes Film Festival and Africa." *Africa*, n. 73, September 1977, pp. 88–89.

Carcassonne, Philippe. "West Indies." *Cinématographe*, n. 51, October 1979, p. 49.

Cavoignat, Jean Pierre. "Sarraounia." *Première*, n. 116, November 1986, p. 25.

Cervoni, Albert. "Un Film rive gauche." *Cinémaction*, n. 8, Summer 1979, pp. 81–82.

Chevallier, Jacques. "Sarraounia." *La Revue du Cinéma, Image et Son*, no. 422, December 1986, pp. 25–26.

Ciment, Michel. "Soleil O." *Positif*, n. 119, September 1970, pp. 18–22.

"Cinema in Africa." *Africa*, n. 42, February 1975, pp. 54–56.

Cluny, Claude-Michel. "Soleil O—la vraie jungle est en Europe." *Cinéma 73*, n. 172, January 1973, pp. 127–29.

———. *Dictionnaire des nouveaux cinémas arabes*. Paris: Sindbad, 1978.

Colpart, Gilles. "Nous aurons toute la mort pour dormir." *Cinéma 77*, n. 223, July 1977, p. 103.

———. "Nous aurons toute la mort pour dormir." *La Revue du Cinéma, Image et Son*, n. 320–321, October 1977, p. 192.

Condé, Maryse. "Quatre siècles d'oppression." *Demain l'Afrique*, n. 22, 12 March 1979, pp. 68–70.

———. "Med Hondo ouvre une ère nouvelle." *Demain l'Afrique*, n. 33–34, 27 August 1979, pp. 72–74.

Delmas, Jean. "Nous aurons toute la mort pour dormir." *Jeune Cinéma*, n. 102, April-May 1977, p. 51.

Douin, Jean-Luc. "Les Bicots-nègres, nos voisins." *Télérama*, n. 1292, 16 October 1974, p. 77.

———. "Nous aurons toute la mort pour dormir." *Télérama*, n. 1420, 30 March 1977, p. 104.

"L'Etalon du Yennenga ā la Sarraounia." *Balafon*, n. 82, May-June 1987, pp. 46–47.

F, M. "West Indies . . . Esclavage moderne." *Adhoua*, n. 3, January-February-March 1981, pp. 23–25.

Fanon, Josie. "Cannes sans l'Afrique." *Demain l'Afrique*, n. 27, 21 May 1979, p. 30.

———. "Point de vue d'Ina Césaire. "*Demain l'Afrique*, n. 33–34, 27 August 1979, p. 74.

Fichet, Guy. "Nous aurons toute la mort pour dormir." *Lutte Ouvrière*, n. 450, 16 April 1977, p. 23.

Flor, Paola, and Luigi Elongi. "Sarraounia une reine africaine." *Afrique-Asie*, n. 389, 15 December 1986, p. 54.

Gervais, Ginette. "Hier et aujourd'hui, même combat." *Jeune Cinéma*, n. 121, September-October 1979, p. 21.

Gibson, Ben. "West Indies Story." *Framework*, n. 11, Autumn 1979, p. 21.

Giraud, Thérèse. "Parler de, ou parler d'eux. . . . " *Cahiers du Cinéma*, n. 254–255, December 1974–January 1975, pp. 41–43.

Gnonlonfoun, Alexis. "V^e fespaco: qu'en penser?" *Afrique Nouvelle*, n. 1390, 18 February 1976, pp. 12–15.

Hennebelle, Guy. "Le Cinéma mauritanien." *L'Afrique Littéraire et Artistique*, n. 20, 1st Quarter 1972, pp. 189–93.

———. "Les Bicots-nègres, vos voisins." *Ecran 74*, n. 30, November 1974, pp. 79–80.

———. Où vont les cinémas africains?" *Ecran 74*, n. 30, November 1974, pp. 36–46.

———. *Guide des films anti-impérialistes*. Paris: Editions du Centenaire, 1975.

———. "Nous aurons toute la nuit pour dormir." *Ecran 77*, n. 58, 15 May 1977, pp. 50–51.

———. "Hondo, Med." *L'Afrique Littéraire et Artistique*, n. 49, 3rd Quarter 1978, pp. 73–74.

———. "Le Hurlement d'une révolte—1970: Soleil O de Med Hondo." *Cinémaction*, n. 8, Summer 1979, pp. 80–81.

Hennebelle, Monique. "Carthage: un festival ouvert à tous les cinémas." *L'Afrique Littéraire et Artistique*, n. 34, 1974, pp. 79–93.

Huleu, Jean-René, and Pascal Kane. "Rencontres du jeune cinéma à Toulon." *Cahiers du Cinéma*, n. 251–252, July-August 1974, p. 77.

Hunter, Mark. "Films of War, Catholic Cliché and Classic Comedy." *International Herald Tribune*, 3–4 January 1987, p. 5.

Kaboré, Mouni Etienne. "Les Derniers Débats-forums [includes a review of Sarraounia]." *Sidwaya*, 2 March 1987, p. 9.

Kane, Pascal. "Bicots-nègres, vos voisins de Med Hondo." *Cahiers du Cinéma*, n. 251–252, July-August 1974, pp. 77–78.

Lebel, Jean-Patrick. "Bicots-nègres, vos voisins." *La Nouvelle Critique*, n. 79–80, December 1974–January 1975, pp. 125–26.

Lemaire, Charles. "Fépaci—s'unir ou mourir." *Afrique Nouvelle*, n. 1863, 20 March 1985, pp. 15–16.

———. "Sarraounia, une revue africaine." *Afrique Nouvelle*, n. 1941, 1 October 1986.

Manceau, Jean-Louis. "Sarraounia." *Cinéma 86*, n. 377, 19 November 1986, p. 4.

Marcorelles, Louis. "Nous aurons toute la mort pour dormir d'Abib Med Hondo." *Le Monde*, 30 March 1977, p. 22.

———. "West Indies, un film de Med Hondo: la galère de l'histoire." *Le Monde*, 20 September 1979, p. 19.

———. "Le colloque de Niamey—une chance pour le cinéma africain." *Le Monde*, 21 January 1982, p. 1.

———. "Rencontre avec Med Hondo—le point de vue de l'Afrique." *Le Monde*, 15 May 1982, p. 24.

Martin, Angela. *African Films: The Context of Production*. London: British Film Institute, 1982.

Martin, Marcel. "Nous aurons toute la mort pour dormir." *Ecran 77*, n. 58, 15 May 1977, p. 50.

———. "West Indies." *Ecran 1979*, 20 October 1979, pp. 63–64.

Maunick, Edouard J. "West Indies, les nègres marrons de la liberté." *Demain l'Afrique*, n. 33, 27 August 1979, p. 70.

"Med Hondo: Film-maker." *West Africa*, 6 June 1983, pp. 1348–49.

Mirmont, Roger. "Impressions d'Afrique." *Première*, n. 112, July 1986, pp. 87–91, 112–16.

Mosk. "Soleil O." *Variety*, 6 May 1970, p. 20.

Nacache, Jacqueline. "West Indies." *Cinéma 79*, n. 251, 1979, p. 101.

Ndaw, Aly Kheury. "L'Etalon de Yennenga à Med Hondo." *Le Soleil*, 2 March 1987, p. 10.

"Nos teremos a morte inteira para dormir." *Versus*, August 1978, p. 7.

Oster, Jerry. "Black's Plight in Paris Told." *Daily News*, 15 March 1973, p. 93.

Pâquet, André. "Carthage et les cinémas africains—l'avance des cinémas arabes." *Cinéma Québec*, vol. 4, n. 2, April 1975, pp. 34–39.

Pfaff, Françoise. "Films of Med Hondo—An African Filmmaker in Paris." *Jump Cut*, n. 31, 1986, pp. 44–46.

Pouillaud, Jean-Louis. "West Indies." *Positif*, n. 225, December 1979, p. 76.

Rich. "Sarraounia." *Variety*, 10 September 1986 pp. 15, 19.

"Sarraounia." *Le Technicien du Film*, n. 535, 15 December 1986, p. 58.

"Sarraounia, un appel ã l'unité." *Balafon*, n. 81, March-April 1987, pp. 48–49.

"Sarraounia: une vrae coopération franco-africaine." *Le Film Français*, n. 2114, 7 November 1986, p. 4.

Schidlow, Joshka. "Sarraounia." *Télérama*, n. 1923, 22 November 1986, p. 41.

Schoenberner, Gerhard. "Det svarta Afrikas filmer och deras regissorer." *Chaplin 166*, n. 1, 1980, pp. 10–15.

Thirard, Paul-Louis. "Nous aurons toute la mort pour dormir." *Positif*, n. 193, May 1977, pp. 73–74.

Trémege, Bernard. "Soleil O." *Jeune Cinéma*, n. 67, December 1972–January 1973, p. 39.

Vast, Jean. "Sarraounia." *Unir Cinéma*, n. 135, January-March, pp. 14–17.

Vieyra, Paulin. "Les 5èmes Journées Cinématographiques de Carthage." *Présence Africaine*, vol. 93, 1st Quarter 1975, pp. 200–214.

———. *Le Cinéma africain*. Paris: Présence Africaine, 1975.

Wagner, Jean. "West Indies." *Télérama*, n. 1548, 12 September 1979, p. 101.

Wauthier, Claude. " 'Sarraounia' de Med Hondo: Lépopeé africaine." *Le Monde*, 26 November 1986, p. 16.

Weiler, A. H. "Screen: Vivid Soleil O." *New York Times*, 15 March 1973, p. 55.

Winsten, Archer. "Soleil O." *New York Post*, 15 March 1973, p. 50.

Yvoire, Christophe d'. "Sarraounia." *Première*, n. 112, July 1986, p. 86.

1. Bernadette Sanou, the Burkinabè Minister of Culture (2d from r.) and Filippe Sawadogo (1st from r.), the Secretary General of FESPACO, inaugurate the 10th FESPACO, held in Ouagadougou, Burkina Faso from 21 to 28 February 1987. (Courtesy Boly Djage.)

2. Timité Bassori (1st from l., front row), Mustapha Alassane (3rd from l., front row), and Ousmane Sembene (1st from r.) in conversation with Claude Prieux (French Cultural Officer in Dakar) at the 10th FESPACO. (Courtesy Boly Djage.)

3. Director of photography José Medeiros (l.) observes Ola Balogun (c.) as he directs Shina Peters in a scene from *Money-Power*. (Courtesy Ola and Françoise Balogun.)

4. Clarion Chukwurah in *Money-Power*. (Courtesy Ola and Françoise Balogun.)

5. Albert Hall and Jorge Coutinho in *Cry Freedom*. (Courtesy Ola and Françoise Balogun.)

6. Timité Bassori opposite Mary Vieyra in a scene from *La Femme au couteau*. (Courtesy Timité Bassori.)

7. Moussa Bathily (c.) talks to cameraman Bara Diokhane during the shooting of *Des Personnages encombrants*, with Jean Brierre (r.). (Courtesy Moussa Bathily.)

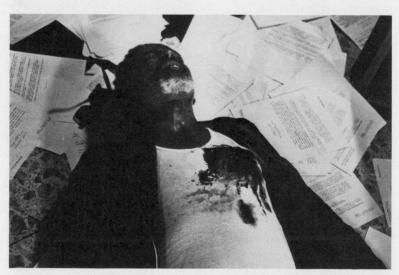

8. The tragic end of the writer (played by Jean Brierre) in *Des Personnages encombrants*. (Courtesy Moussa Bathily.)

Mamoutou et Dany

dans

'' **den muso** ''

(la fille)

un film de *Souleymane Cissé*

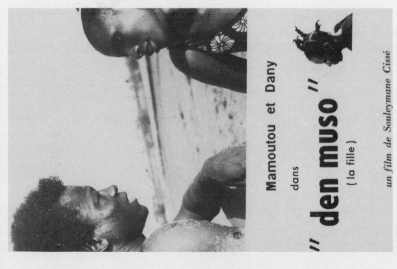

9. Mamoutou Sanogo (l.) opposite Dany Coulibaly in *Den Muso*. (Courtesy Souleymane
Cissé.)

10. Souleymane Cissé. Photo by Françoise Pfaff.
(Author's collection.)

12. Francesca in *L'Herbe Sauvage*. (Courtesy Henri Duparc.)

11. Jean-Pierre Dikongue-Pipa at the 9th FESPACO held in Ouagadougou, Burkina Faso from 23 February to 2 March 1985. Photo by Françoise

13. *L'Herbe Sauvage*. Viviane Toure and Donaldo Fofana. (Courtesy Henri Duparc.)

14. *Faces of Women*. Bernadette (c., in traditional attire), a fishmonger played by Eugénie Cissé Roland, visits her business site. (Courtesy Geric Film.)

15. Désiré Ecaré. (Courtesy Geric film.)

16. Kramo-Lanciné Fadika (l.) directing Joachim Ouatara and Fatou Ouatara in *Djeli*. (Courtesy Kramo-Lanciné Fadika.)

17. *Djeli*. Kramo-Lanciné Fadika (l.) and Etienne Amouzou interpreting one of the scenes which portrays the legendary origin of the Malinke griot. (Courtesy Kramo-Lanciné Fadika.)

18. Safi Faye. (Courtesy Safi Faye.)

19. *Kaddu Beykat*. Maguette Gueye as Coumba, the young villager's fiancée. (Courtesy Safi Faye.)

20. Haile Gerima (c.) during the shooting of *Harvest: 3,000 Years*. (Courtesy Mypheduh Films.)

21. This dream sequence from *Harvest: 3,000 Years* symbolizes the plight of hardworking peasants oppressed by their ruthless feudal landlord. (Courtesy Mypheduh Films.)

22. Med Hondo (with hat, at r.) during the shooting of *West Indies*. (Courtesy Med Hondo.)

23. A scene from *West Indies*. (Courtesy Med Hondo.)

24. Gaston Kaboré at the 10th FESPACO. (Courtesy Boly Djage.)

25. *Wend Kuuni*. Rosine Yanogo as Pognere, the protagonist's adopted sister. (Courtesy Mypheduh Films.)

26. Marthe Odome-Ewane (as Rose) and Daniel Kamwa (as Pousse-Pousse) in *Pousse-Pousse*. (Courtesy Daniel Kamwa.)

27. L. to r.: Stanislas Awana as Mbarga, Daniel Kamwa as André, the presidential advisor, and Berthe Mbia as Charlotte, in *Notre fille*. (Courtesy Daniel Kamwa.)

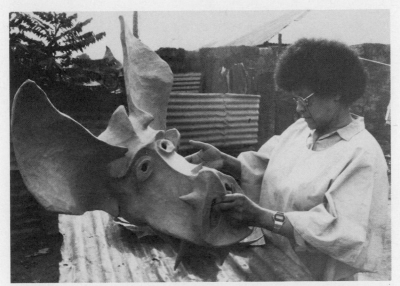

28. Sarah Maldoror during the shooting of *Un carnaval dans le Sahel*. Photo by Chris Marker. (Courtesy Sarah Maldoror.)

29. A scene from *Un carnaval dans le Sahel*. Photo by Chris Marker. (Courtesy Sarah Maldoror.)

30. Cheik Doukoure (l.) and Sidiki Bakaba in *Un dessert pour Constance*. Photo by C. Doucé. (Courtesy Sarah Maldoror.)

31. *Sambizanga*. Maria (Elisa Andrade) leaves the prison after being informed of her husband's death. (Courtesy New Yorker Films.)

33. Magaye Niang (l.) and Myriam Niang on a poster for *Touki-Bouki*. (Courtesy Djibril Diop Mambety.)

32. *Sambizanga*. Domingos (Domingos Oliviera) is shown here in his prison cell after being questioned and beaten by the Portuguese authorities concerning his anti-colonial underground activities. (Courtesy New Yorker Films.)

34. Djibril Diop Mambety at the 10th FESPACO.
Photo by Françoise Pfaff. (Author's collection.)

35. Ababacar Samb. (Courtesy Mypheduh Films.)

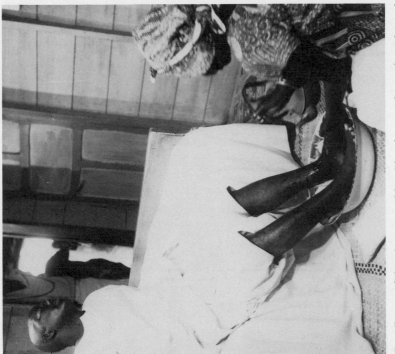

36. *Jom.* Dumi Sene as Koura Thiaw, the socially-conscious dancer and singer. (Courtesy New Yorker Films.)

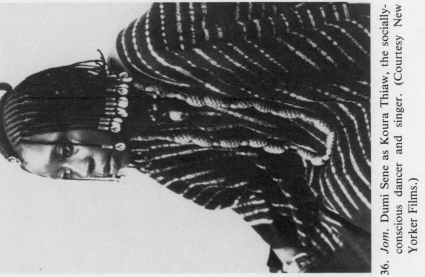

37. All-powerful at home, rushing his wives to domestic tasks and prayer, Ibrahima Dieng at the outset does not arouse the viewer's sympathy. Mamadou Gueye (l.) in *Mandabi.* (Courtesy Ousmane Sembene.)

38. A scene of *Xala*'s wedding party. (Courtesy New Yorker Films.)

39. Douta Seck (c., standing) as Gorgui, the beggars' blind leader, in one of *Xala*'s final scenes. (Courtesy New Yorker Films.)

40. *La Noire de*. Thérèse M'Bissine Diop as Diouana. (Courtesy New Yorker Films)

41. *Emitai*. The villagers prepare to bury their chief, who died while fighting the French colonial troops. (Courtesy New Yorker Films.)

42. *Emitai*. A villager is tied up and forced to sit in the scorching sun to disclose where the rice is hidden. (Courtesy New Yorker Films.)

43. Momar Thiam during the shooting of *Bouki Cultivateur*. (Courtesy Films Momar.)

44. Maleye Thiam (l.) as "Bouki the hyena," Sophie Thiam as "the hare" and Youssouph Biteye as the shepherd in *Bouki cultivateur*, a film for children. (Courtesy Films Momar.)

45. *Njangaan*. A koran-study class at Mame's school. (Courtesy New Yorker Films.)

46. Mame is reassured by his mother (Fatim Diagne) in a scene from *Njangaan*. (Courtesy New Yorker Films.)

47. Paulin Soumanou Vieyra (r.). Photo by Françoise Pfaff. (Author's collection.)

48. Oumarou Ganda (r.) as the village diviner in a scene from *Le Wazzou poly-game*. (Courtesy CAC.)

49. Lounès Tazairt and Anne Caudry in a scene from *Le Passager du Tassili* Photo by R. Picard. (Courtesy Sarah Maldoror.)

Gaston Kaboré (1951–)
Burkina Faso

BIOGRAPHY

A leading figure in his country's emerging cinema, Gaston Kaboré was born on 23 April 1951 in the city of Bobo Dioulasso, located in the southwestern part of Burkina Faso (formerly Upper Volta). The fifth of ten children of an upper-class Catholic family of Burkina Faso's dominant ethnic group, the Mossi, Gaston Kaboré came to his country's capital, Ouagadougou, at the age of three. The son of a well-educated district chief who retired from government service in 1970, the young Kaboré began his education at a primary school in Ouagadougou and finished his secondary studies at a Catholic boarding school in Toussiana, sixty kilometers from Bobo Dioulasso. Although he spent most of his formative years in an urban environment, Kaboré was reared in a family that kept close ties with its rural origins. He recalls:

I have never lived in a village but my father taught me a lot of things. In spite of the fact that he had left his village at the age of ten to go to school, he kept an intimate relationship with his native environment, which he transmitted to me. For instance, he has always been closely attached to land. These are things that he never mentions but which are expressed in his comportment. *(Libération,* 8 March 1984, p. 32)

In 1970, after graduating from high school, Kaboré enrolled at the Centre d'Etudes Supérieures d'Histoire de Ouagadougou, which he attended for two years. Then, in 1972, he went to Paris in order to pursue his studies at the Sorbonne, where he earned a master's degree in history. Although he had already developed a liking for cinema as an urban youngster, it is mainly as a student in Paris that Gaston Kaboré took a serious interest in film. Kaboré remembers:

I loved cinema and I would spend a large part of my scholarship to go to see movies! One day, when I saw Sembene Ousmane's [Ousmane Sembene*] *Xala* at the Champollion movie theater, I realized that the camera could be used as a tool to express African culture. *(Libération,* 8 March 1984, p. 32)

Thus, concurrent with his work on a Ph.D. thesis on the relationship between Islam and state in the kingdoms of Upper Volta, and with the primary intention of using film as a research instrument in the area of history, Kaboré decided to acquire training in filmmaking. In 1974 he registered at a French film school, l'Ecole Supérieure d'Etudes Cinématographiques (ESEC), from which he graduated two years later. By then, Gaston Kaboré had totally given up his career in history, and his main concern was to assert his skill as filmmaker.

In 1976 Kaboré returned to Burkina Faso, where he was appointed director of his country's Centre National du Cinéma (CNC). The following year, while holding this executive position in the government, he began teaching filmmaking and script writing at the then newly founded Institut Africain d'Etudes Cinématographiques (INAFEC). This development in Kaboré's professional career resulted in his first film, *Je viens de Bokin* (I Come from Bokin, 1977), which he shot with a crew of INAFEC students. The production was financed by a $10,000 grant awarded by UNESCO. Subsequently, Kaboré directed a series of commissioned documentaries: *Stockez et conservez les grains* (Stock and Keep Grain, 1978), *Regard sur le VIème FESPACO* (A Look at the Sixth FESPACO, 1979), and *Utilisation des énergies nouvelles en milieu rural* (The Use of New Energies in Rural Environments, 1980). *Stockez et conservez les grains* is an educational motion picture based on a $3,500 budget and financed by the Communauté Economique de l'Afrique de l'Ouest (CEAO). *Regard sur le VIème FESPACO* was made at a total cost of $15,000, with technical and financial support from INAFEC and the CNC. As reflected in its title, *Utilisation des énergies nouvelles en milieu rural* focuses on development issues. Its $17,500 budget was also provided by CEAO.

Gaston Kaboré made his debut as a feature director with *Wend Kuuni* (1982), the title of which means ''the gift of God'' in Moré, one of the two major African languages spoken in Burkina Faso. Kaboré had written the very first draft of the script for *Wend Kuuni* as early as 1975, while a student in Paris. The film was shot from 15 October 1981 to 13 February 1982 by a crew of technicians from the CNC, and the production's $115,000 budget was provided by the Fonds de Promotion et d'Extension de l'Activité Cinématographique, a national film fund which draws its subsidies from a 15 percent tax on all movie tickets sold in the country. Although processed and edited in Paris, *Wend Kuuni* is the first feature film to have been entirely produced by the state of Burkina Faso.

For *Wend Kuuni,* as has been the case for a great number of other Black African films, Kaboré elected to use nonprofessional actors. He emphasizes:

The man who plays the role of Tinga, the adoptive father, teaches natural science in high school; the two mothers are executive secretaries, and my nephews play the part of Wend Kuuni at the ages of 9 and 11. Working with them was easy but it required an extended period of time. We would shoot on Thursday afternoons, Saturdays and Sundays; we adapted ourselves to the actors' availability. The village in which the film was made is located 30 kilometers from Ouagadougou and the film's plot takes place before the colonial era. *(Jeune Cinéma,* March 1983, p. 15)

Wend Kuuni was first released on 22 September 1982 in Burkina Faso, where it was then viewed by a total of 200,000 people—a rather significant number in a country which has only fourteen movie theaters and a total population of less than 7 million inhabitants. The film opened on 7 March 1984 in Paris, where it was simultaneously shown in three commercial movie theaters and was met with widespread critical acclaim. In August 1982, it was awarded a prize at the Locarno Film Festival in Switzerland. It received the Second Prize ("Tanit d'Argent") and a special commendation for the originality of its musical score at the 1982 Carthage Film Festival in Tunisia. Moreover, the film reaped four prizes at the 1983 FESPACO, namely, the Special Jury Prize, the Prize for Best Actress (awarded to eleven-year-old Rosine Yanogo, who boasted an impressive performance as Wend Kuuni's adoptive sister), the Golden Camera Prize, awarded to Issaka Thiombiano and Sekou Ouedraogo for their skillful camera work, and an award from the International Catholic Organization for the Cinema. That same year *Wend Kuuni* won the First Prize at the International Ecological Film Festival (France) and the Osiris Prize awarded in Rome by the Food and Agriculture Organization (FAO), and was presented at a number of film festivals, including the London Film Festival and various yearly cinematographic events held in such French cities as Orleans, Nantes, Poitiers, and Amiens. In 1984 Kaboré was invited to present his film at an African film festival held in Tokyo. Then, on 2 March 1985, his work won the Cesar Award for Best Francophone Film. *Wend Kuuni* was featured at the Third Festival Cinematografico Africano held in Perugia (Italy) from 14 to 20 April 1985, and on 22 April 1985 the film was selected to open the Montreal festival devoted to African cinema. In January 1986, the motion picture won the highest award at the Festival de Films du Tiers-Monde (Third World Film Festival) held in Fribourg, Switzerland. In March of that same year, *Wend Kuuni* was included in an "African Mini-Series" at the Biograph, a commercial movie theater located in Washington, D.C. Then Kaboré presented his motion picture at the "Celebration of Black Cinema IV," a film festival organized in Boston (30 April-2 May 1986).

   Presently Gaston Kaboré is working on a film project whose plot, according to the filmmaker,

concerns problems raised by urbanism in Ouagadougou. Yet, it is a fiction film and not a documentary. The plot revolves around a man who owns land on the edges of town and refuses to sell it to developers. I will show how urban life endangers the balance between man and nature. . . . The film includes a journalist who witnesses this mutation and denounces the injustices resulting from social change. Then, from its very beginning, the film also features a musician, playing a string instrument, who tells the story and comments upon it as is customarily done in our societies. (Kaboré to author, Washington, D.C., 3 May 1985)

Asked why he became a filmmaker, Kaboré responds by saying:

I like to tell stories and to listen to people. I do both in my films. Honestly, I do not
believe that I received a special call. I make films to reflect people's relationships, their
feelings and emotions, as well as their way of life. I also like to investigate the forces
at work in a given society. Of course in doing so I may take a stand, but my films are
not meant to be political essays. (Kaboré to author, 3 May 1985)

However, a supporter of his present head of state, Captain Thomas Sankara,
Kaboré believes in the social usefulness of cinema as a mass-oriented means of
information and education, whose goal is to participate in the development,
dignity, and cultural independence of Burkina Faso (*Afrique-Asie,* n. 319, 9
April 1984, p. 57).

Kaboré feels that it is yet premature to delineate with precision the stylistic
components of Black African cinema:

Black African cinema is rather young and it is difficult to define it in aesthetical terms.
Black African cinema is still a generic name. It bears historical connotations because it
emerged at the time when most African nations acquired their independence. As such,
Black African films present certain similarities: they are instruments which allow us to
affirm our identity, to fight cultural imperialism as well as economic and political oppression. . . . However, those films have also significant differences due to the filmmakers'
individual political choices and/or the governmental structures of the nations in which
they are made. . . . A few Black African films have purely commercial aims but I think
that most of them show genuine sociopolitical concerns. (Kaboré to author, 3 May 1985)

Gaston Kaboré is deeply convinced that Black African cinema must use its own
dynamics to achieve self-reliance and flourish. Like most of his counterparts,
he acknowledges that its progress and assertiveness have been severely impeded
by inadequate production and distribution, a situation he proposes to remedy
through such steps as the establishment of inter-African agreements that would
spearhead film co-productions and enable an increased circulation of African
motion pictures throughout the continent; the propagation of national film funds
which would draw their budget from taxes levied on the gross earnings of both
foreign and African films; governmental implementation of tax laws which would
encourage investors and facilitate the importation of film-related equipment; and
the development of sound indigenous film infrastructures, including the construction of new movie houses, to increase the input of cinema in the economic
life of African nations (Kaboré to author, 3 May 1985).

A highly regarded representative of the younger generation of Black African
filmmakers, a dedicated teacher, as well as a convincing advocate of African
cinema, Gaston Kaboré has been director of the National Cinema Center of
Burkina Faso for several years. He was also appointed general secretary of the
Fédération Panafricaine des Cinéastes (FEPACI) in 1985. Married since 1982,
Kaboré currently resides with his family in Ouagadougou. Few would deny that

the stylistic flair of *Wend Kuuni* has contributed much to the international recognition of Burkinabè cinema. More examples of Kaboré's proven cinematographic abilities will no doubt soon materialize.

MAJOR THEMES

The short films of Gaston Kaboré address several current issues. *Je viens de
Bokin* concerns itself with the topic of migration from village to town. *Stockez
et conservez les grains* as well as *Utilisation des énergies nouvelles en milieu
rural* promotes the use of new agricultural techniques. And *Regard sur le VIème
FESPACO* covers the various events that occurred at the 1979 Pan-African Film
Festival of Ouagadougou.

Thematically, *Wend Kuuni* differs from the majority of Black African motion
pictures, whose plots are generally set in contemporary environments. Kaboré,
whose early training was in history, points out:

Wend Kuuni takes place in pre-colonial times . . . [but] its exact time frame is not important. It could be 1420 or 1850 because the sociocultural reality which I depict remained
unchanged for years. Besides, the colonial and post-colonial eras have been amply illustrated by African cinema. Moreover, I did not want *Wend Kuuni* to be labelled a film
on the emancipation of women, the conflict between tradition and modernity, traditional
hospitality or other traditional values. Tradition is often contrasted with modernity, but
for people with an autonomous culture . . . there is no such opposition. All of this brought
me to choose a past and autonomous society with its own oppressive forces and inner
contradictions, a community which I did not regard as an ideal African society. (Kaboré
to author, 3 May 1985)

Although based on Kaboré's original script, *Wend Kuuni* derives its general
mood from African oral tradition, which the filmmaker views as "a cultural
testimony of African history" (Kaboré to author, 3 May 1985). The story of
Wend Kuuni takes place at the time that the Mossi empire was at the height of
its power and splendor. One day a peddler found a child lying unconscious at
the foot of a tree. He then discovered that the young boy was mute and could
not reveal his past. Soon thereafter, the child was adopted by a weaver and his
family. They called him Wend Kuuni, which means "the gift of God." Henceforth, Wend Kuuni was lovingly raised by his foster parents. He developed a
touching friendship with Pognéré, his young adoptive sister, who was able to
relate to him in spite of his impairment. Wend Kuuni shared village life and
became a shepherd. Suddenly, the idyllic serenity of Wend Kuuni's new community was disrupted by a woman who boisterously accused her aging husband
of impotence. Unable to bear this public shame, the husband put an end to his
life by hanging himself. Upon the emotional shock of discovering the dead man's
body, Wend Kuuni regained his power of speech. Finally able to tell his own
story, he explained that he had become mute from the trauma of having seen
his mother die in the bush after being banned from her village as a witch because,

hoping for the return of her husband who had disappeared while hunting, she had refused to abide by tradition and remarry.

Told in a tale-like fashion, *Wend Kuuni* is beautifully photographed, and its timeless pastoral simplicity is universalized by René Guirma's musical score, in which Mossi melodies (recorded in Paris) are uniquely rendered through such classical Western instruments as the piano, cello, and oboe.

SURVEY OF CRITICISM

Presented in a number of film festivals and movie theaters, *Wend Kuuni*'s international exposure has generated a rather substantial amount of critical accounts, most of which fully support Kaboré's first feature length screen work. Christian Bosséno enthusiastically reports:

Wend Kuuni's beauty and freshness will take the most blasé film viewers by surprise. . . . For more than one good reason it is a clear and fascinating film. It is first a faithful chronicle of village life. . . . It is also an honest and well-made film on childhood. . . . For a long time we had not seen on the screen two children as spontaneous and credible as Wend Kuuni and his young friend Pognéré. . . . Finally, it is a superb poem . . . to the glory of nature. . . . In this film . . . Gaston Kaboré gives evidence . . . of extraordinary sensitivity.

From the start, he has the makings of a confirmed cinéaste worthy of being included with his elders, Ousmane Sembene or Souleymane Cissé[*], among the most fertile creators of African cinema. *(La Revue du Cinéma, Image et Son,* February 1984, p. 26)

A Burkinabè reviewer, Clément Tapsoba, approves of Kaboré's choice of a past setting for his film. He asks: "Isn't it by studying our past that we will be able to better grasp our future?" *(Carrefour Africain,* 18 February 1983, p. 14). Similarly, the Tunisian filmmaker and critic Ferid Boughedir shows interest in the time period of *Wend Kuuni* and considers the film as both "a meditation on past Africa" and a "visually narrated African tale." He writes:

Its film language succeeds in rediscovering the poetry, the simplicity and the structure of traditional [African] storytelling. . . .

In this adult world, the child is not given the right to speak, like Wend Kuuni whose dumbness has metaphorical connotations. He must observe and listen in order to acquire wisdom. *(Jeune Afrique,* 28 July 1982, p. 56)

Likewise, Raphael Bassan *(Afrique-Asie,* 17 January 1983, p. 55), Vincent Canby *(New York Times,* 27 March 1983, p. 55), Kyalo Mativo *(UFAHAMU,* Fall 1983, p. 136), Louis Skorecki *(Libération,* 8 March 1984, p. 32), Jean Roy *(L'Humanité,* 10 March 1984, p. 8), Françoise Audé *(Positif,* March 1984, p. 70), Charles Tesson *(Cahiers du Cinéma,* April 1984, p. 44), Jay Carr *(The Boston Globe,* 2 May 1986, p. 43), and Anne Kieffer link *Wend Kuuni* to Africa's lyrical and timeless oral tradition. Although the film is set in a given society, Anne Kieffer also sees it as a universal tale. She expounds:

Its tale-like format overlays the socioeconomical analysis of a precolonial rural community. But Gaston J.M. Kaboré does not consider this community a lost paradise. If men and women live in harmony with nature, social laws punish any deviation from the established order. Two women are bold enough to transgress the patriarchal law of polygamy, one elects to remain for too long a time a widow, and the other rejects publicly her old husband. Both bring about punishment: Wend Kuuni becomes mute, and the old Bila hangs himself. Yet, this tragic situation leads to Wend Kuuni's regaining his speech. Old ways remain attached to Bila's tree while the voice of a new Africa is bestowed on Wend Kuuni. At this point the metaphor fulfills itself. *(Jeune Cinéma,* March 1983, p. 10)

Using somewhat identical arguments, Michel Pérez insists that *Wend Kuuni* is not an "ecological paradise" because it contains violence and stresses the inequities faced by women at the time" *(Le Matin,* 15 March 1984, p. 29). Also, Joelle Fontaine, for whom *Wend Kuuni*'s pace is reminiscent of Pier Paolo Pasolini's *Il Fiore delle Mille e Una Notte* (A Thousand and One Nights, 1974), sees Kaboré's work as the portrayal of an "untouched Africa" but also stresses that its "harmony is not totally exempt from conflicts" *(Le Matin,* 9 March 1984, p. 30). And for Louis Skorecki, the film calls to mind some of Robert Bresson and Yasujiro Ozu's motion pictures *(Libération,* 8 March 1984, p. 32).

Commenting on *Wend Kuuni*'s stylistic characteristics, J-P. Péroncel-Hugoz praises its visual beauty *(Le Monde,* 2 November 1982, p. 13), while Paulin Soumanou Vieyra* likes its simplicity and fluidity *(Le Soleil,* 24 June 1982, p. 19). Segun Oyekunle favors the film's structure because it transcends linguistical boundaries:

Wend Kuuni by Gaston Kaboré . . . could be understood without understanding the languages used. It becomes most urgent therefore that African film-makers become more conscious of their scripting, film narrative and the use of dramatic images and common symbols and colour perspectives in such a way as to make their films effectively break language barriers. *(West Africa,* 21 March 1983, p. 726)

Kaboré's sensitive vision and skillful craftsmanship have also been recognized by American film critics. Luis Francia observes that he is

a filmmaker wise enough not to indulge cleverness. In *Wend Kuuni* . . . he deftly sidesteps the pitfalls of so many beginners. He avoids kinetic fireworks: Kaboré has no need to discover the celluloid wheel. He has a simple tale to tell, and he tells it simply, in the manner of a Mossi folktale. . . .

The movie's rustic sentiment is tugged at by sentimentality but resists its pull. The folksy portrait of the villagers' way of life is on one hand charming and naive enough to be pastoral, and on the other, comes with enough everyday texture to be believable. . . .

But what best reveals the director's adroit handling of cinematic Yin and Yang is the poetic irony that gives the film its unity. . . . Viewers who are used to being sucked rather than drawn in will need some time to adjust to the film's Ozu-like tempo. Kaboré's a slow hand and a sure one. *(Village Voice,* 29 March 1983, p. 55)˙

For Edna, *Wend Kuuni*

is a surprisingly successful combination of African narrative style and Western technical know-how. . . .
   The prevalent mood throughout is one of a folk tale, with the charm and the candor implied. . . .
   Editing is neat, even if the pace will seem slow to Western audiences, and most surprising of all, the score is entirely occidental, African themes played on classical instruments, without even one drum roll for local color. As a matter of fact Guirma's soundtrack is closest to modern chamber music of the European tradition, which makes for an unexpected effect, when juxtaposed with the pure African landscape. *(Variety,* 25 August 1982, p. 15)

Another *Variety* reviewer, Yung, remarks:

Made as a children's picture, *Wend Kuuni* . . . is a simple, slow moving parable. . . . The picture has charm and simplicity but space-age kids schooled on tv and E.T. may find the lack of action dull. . . .
   The little boy and girl, both very fetching, dominate the tale. But the real, ham star is René B. Guirma's original music, a repeated melody said to be inspired by "tradition" but sounding incongruously European Medieval to most ears. A little might have been a nice accompaniment; a lot becomes uncomfortable early on and adds a note of inauthenticity to pic, just the opposite of what it aims to achieve. In compensation, lensing of the bush "where no white man trod" is lovely, as is the reconstruction of a tribal village. *(Variety,* 17 November 1982, p. 26)

Interestingly enough, Guirma's musical score has also been diversely appreciated by other critics. Françoise Audé finds it "rather irritating" *(Positif,* March 1984, p. 70). Segun Oyekunle feels the Western instrumentation of Mossi folk music is "perhaps inappropriate" but adds that it "is intended for, and succeeds in attracting foreign audiences" *(West Africa,* 28 November 1983, p. 2729). But Joshka Schidlow *(Télérama,* 7 March 1984, p. 32), Catherine N'Diaye *(Jeune Afrique,* 28 March 1984, p. 59), and Catherine Taconet *(Cinéma 84,* April 1984, p. 57) like *Wend Kuuni*'s innovative music, which punctuates Kaboré's poetic microcosm in a striking fashion.

FILMOGRAPHY

Je viens de Bokin (I Come from Bokin), 16 mm, color, 38 min., 1977.
Stockez et conservez les grains (Stock and Keep Grain), 16 mm, color, 22 min., 1978.
Regard sur le VIéme FESPACO (A Look at the Sixth FESPACO), 16 mm, color, 40 min., 1979.

Utilisation des énergies nouvelles en milieu rural (Use of New Energies in Rural Environments), 16 mm, color, 40 min., 1980.
Wend Kuuni, le don de Dieu (Wend Kuuni, the Gift of God), 35 mm, color, 75 min., 1982.

BIBLIOGRAPHY

Writings by Gaston Kaboré

Kaboré, Gaston, and Rasmane Ouedraogo. "Irremplaçable FEPACI." *Afrique-Asie,* n. 346, 22 April 1985, pp. 66–67.
Kaboré, Gaston. "Qu'est-ce qu'un film africain?" *Unir Cinéma,* n. 20–21, December 1986, p. 35.

Interviews of Gaston Kaboré

Benabdessadok, Cherifa. "Wend Kuuni, le don de Dieu." *Afrique-Asie,* n. 319, 9 April 1984, pp. 55–57.
———. "La Baraka cinématographique—un entretien avec Gaston Kaboré et Paul Zoumbara." *Afrique-Asie,* n. 331, 24 September 1984, pp. 60–61.
Delorme, Christine. "J'ai essayé d'éclater toutes les barrières." *Le Matin,* 9 March 1984, p. 30.
Kieffer, Anne. "Préserver l'esprit du conte—un entretien avec Kaboré." *Jeune Cinéma,* n. 149, March 1983, pp. 15–17.
Lemaire, Charles, and Dellwendé. "Entretien avec Gaston Kaboré." *Unir Cinéma,* n. 5, March-April 1983, p. 10.
Ouedraogo, Nicolas. "Coup de manivelle au Sud." *Voix de l'INAFEC,* February 1985, pp. 7–9.
Roy, Jean. "Mon imagination est née de la culture de mon peuple." *L'Humanité,* 10 March 1984, p. 8.
Skorecki, Louis. "Gaston Kaboré: Je n'ai pas besoin de certitude ou de suspense." *Libération,* 8 March 1984, p. 32.
Tapsoba, Clément. "Gaston Kaboré, réalisateur de Wend Kuuni." *Carrefour Africain,* n. 744, 17 September 1982, pp. 21–22.
"Wend Kuuni de Gaston Kaboré." *Calao,* n. 59, September-October 1984, pp. 6–7.

Film Reviews and Studies of Gaston Kaboré

Audé, Françoise. "Wend Kuuni, le don de Dieu." *Positif,* n. 277, March 1984, p. 70.
Bachy, Victor. *La Haute-Volta et le Cinéma.* Brussels: OCIC/L'Harmattan, 1982.
Bamouni, Babou Paulin. "Regard rétrospectif sur le cinéma voltaique." *Journal du 8ème FESPACO,* n. 1, 5 February 1983, pp. 3–4.
———, and B. Hubert Pare. "Regard rétrospectif sur le cinéma burkinabè et perspectives d'avenir." *Carrefour Africain,* n. 871, 22 February 1985, pp. 18–22.
Bassan, Raphael. "La Dignité retrouvée." *Afrique-Asie,* n. 287, 17 January 1983, pp. 55–57.
Ben Idriss, Z. "VIIème FESPACO—Jour J." *L'Observateur,* n. 2034, 20 February 1981, pp. 1, 8, 11.

Bosséno, Christian. "A Carthage: l'entente arabo-africaine." *Afrique-Asie*, n. 283, 22 November 1982, pp. 52–53.

———. "Le Don de Dieu—les enfants du Sahel." *La Revue du Cinéma, Image et Son*, n. 391, February 1984, pp. 25–26.

Bossy, Magda. "Le Communiqué officiel du jury (Festival de Films du Tiers-Monde)." *Unir Cinéma*, n. 23–24 (130–131), March-April and May-June 1986, pp. 29–30.

Boughedir, Férid. "Le Conte de l'enfant muet." *Jeune Afrique*, n. 1125, 28 July 1982, pp. 56–57.

———. " 'Le Vent' en poupe." *Jeune Afrique*, n. 1141, 17 November 1982, pp. 100–101.

———. "Et maintenant, que la fête commence!" *Jeune Afrique*, n. 1151, 26 January 1983, pp. 53–54.

———. "Une Nouvelle Vague de cinéastes." *Jeune Afrique*, n. 1156, 2 March 1983, pp. 78–80.

———. "1982–83: de Carthage IX à Ouagadougou VIII—nouvelle génération, nouveaux espoirs." *Cinémaction*, n. 26, 1983, pp. 178–85.

———. "FESPACO 85: l'impossible décollage du cinéma africain." *Jeune Afrique*, n. 1262, 13 March 1985, pp. 50–52.

———. "Les Grandes Dates du cinéma africain." *Jeune Afrique*, n. 1303–1304, 25 December 1985, p. 89.

Canby, Vincent. "Screen: Wend Kuuni." *New York Times*, 27 March 1983, p. 55.

Carr, Jay. "Kaboré's Wend Kuuni: Sensitive Tale of Africa." *The Boston Globe*, 2 May 1986, p. 43.

"Carthage Film Festival." *New African*, n. 207, December 1984, p. 34.

Dellwênde, and Charles Lemaire. "Fiche de film africain: Wend Kuuni." *Unir Cinéma*, n. 3, November-December 1982, pp. 15–16.

Edna. "Wend Kuuni." *Variety*, 25 August 1982, p. 15.

Fall, Elimane. "Cinema: plus de colloques que de films." *Jeune Afrique*, n. 1303–1304, 25 December 1985, pp. 87–89.

Fontaine, Joelle. "L'Afrique intacte de Gaston Kaboré." *Le Matin*, 9 March 1984, p. 30.

Francia, Luis, "New Directors: From Upper Volta to Staten Island." *Village Voice*, 29 March 1983, p. 55.

Guirma, Bélemsida René. "La Musique du film voltaique Wend Kuuni." *Unir Cinéma*, n. 4, January-February 1983, pp. 5–6.

Humblot, Catherine. "Cinémas d'Afrique: impasse ou mauvaise passe?" *Le Monde*, 14 March 1985, p. 14.

Ilboudo, Patrick, and Jacob Olivier. "FESPACO, l'autre regard du cinéma." *L'Observateur*, n. 2525, 9 February 1983, pp. 1, 6–7.

"Les Journées du Cinéma Africain au Québec." *Haiti-Observateur*, 3 May 1985, p. 6.

Kieffer, Anne. "Cinéma d'Afrique Noire au Festival des Trois Continents." *Jeune Cinéma*, n. 149, March 1983, pp. 10–13.

Knight, Derrick. "African Films Turn on the Heat." *New African*, April 1983, pp. 42–43.

Lemaire, Charles. "FEPACI—s'unir ou mourir." *Afrique Nouvelle*, n. 1863, 20 March 1985, pp. 15–16.

Martin, Marcel. "Carthage: A la recherche de l'unité . . . " *La Revue du Cinéma, Image et Son*, n. 379, January 1983, pp. 86–87.

Mativo, Kyalo. "Resolving the Cultural Dilemma of the African Film." *UFAHAMU*, vol. 13, n. 1, Fall 1983, pp. 134–46.

N'Diaye, Catherine. "La Parole retrouvée." *Jeune Afrique*, n. 1212, 28 March 1984, p. 59.

Oyekunle, Segun. "Films for the Future." *West Africa*, 21 March 1983, pp. 725–26.

———. "Africans in Hollywood." *West Africa*, 28 November 1983, pp. 2728–29.

Pérez, Michel. "Wend Kuuni de Gaston J.M. Kaboré, une jolie parabole africaine." *Le Matin*, 15 March 1984, p. 29.

Péroncel-Hugoz, J-P. "La Fin des Journées de Carthage." *Le Monde*, 2 November 1982, p. 13.

Relich, Mario. "On Screen at the London Film Festival." *West Africa*, 19 December 1983, pp. 2940–41.

Roy, Jean. "Partage de l'amour, la parole perdue et retrouvée." *L'Humanité*, 10 March 1984, p. 8.

Schidlow, Joshka. "Wend Kuuni, l'enfant trouvé." *Télérama*, n. 1782, 7 March 1984, p. 32.

Skorecki, Louis. "Wend Kuuni: le secret de l'enfant trouvé." *Libération*, 8 March 1984, p. 32.

Stern, Yvan. "Le Cinéma avec passion." *Journal du 8ème FESPACO*, n. 3, 13 February 1983, p. 9.

Taconet, Catherine. "Wend Kuuni de Gaston Kaboré." *Cinéma 84*, n. 3045, April 1984, p. 57.

Tapsoba, Clément. "Aperçu sur le prochain FESPACO du 5 au 13 février 1983: trois films voltaiques seront probablement présentés." *Carrefour Africain*, n. 740–741, 20 August 1982, p. 18.

———. "8ème édition du FESPACO: la Haute-Volta en sort auréolée." *Carrefour Africain*, n. 766, 18 February 1983, pp. 13–15.

———. "Concilier le public africain et son cinéma." *Carrefour Africain*, n. 767, 25 February 1983, pp. 19–20.

Tesson, Charles. "Lorsque l'enfant parle." *Cahiers du Cinéma*, n. 358, April 1984, pp. 44–45.

Touil, Hatem. "Giornate del Cinema Africano: Perugia Città Aperta." *Nigrizzia*, June 1985, p. 44.

Traoré, Biny. "La Technique cinématographique dans Wend-Kuuni." *L'Observateur*, n. 2436, 1–3 October 1982, pp. 8–9.

Vieyra, Paulin Soumanou. "Présence africaine." *Le Soleil*, 24 June 1982, p. 19.

"Wend Kuuni, le don de Dieu." *Ciné-Revue*, n. 10, 8 March 1984, p. 8.

Yung. "Wend Kuuni." *Variety*, 17 November 1982, p. 26.

Daniel Kamwa (1943–   )
Cameroon

BIOGRAPHY

Because of the popular appeal of his feature films, Daniel Kamwa is one of the better known Cameroonian filmmakers. The third of five children of a Bamileke coffee plantation owner, Kamwa was born on 14 April 1943 in Nkong-samba, located in western Cameroon, 135 kilometers north of Douala. He grew up in a large and caring Christian family who, he says, continued the practice of traditional African religion (Kamwa to author, 15 December 1986). Kamwa recalls that he had a very happy childhood. He was a boy scout, spent much time outdoors, and practiced several sports, including judo, karate, swimming, and horseback riding. Daniel Kamwa attended primary school in his native city and high school at the lycée Joss of Douala. After graduating from high school, he went to Paris to study economics, but soon took film courses at the University of Paris VIII, studied dance at the Académie Internationale de la Danse in that same city, and subsequently worked with Peter Brook at the Paris Centre International de la Recherche Théâtrale. Besides the performing arts, Kamwa also acquired further training in karate.

Daniel Kamwa is a stage actor by training (he studied at the Actor's Studio from 1967 to 1968). And, in spite of his having taken some theoretical university cinema studies, one could say that he is primarily a self-taught director. Here is his explanation of the various steps of his career as a filmmaker:

At home, in Cameroon, movies were the only source of entertainment besides family evening gatherings. So, like everybody else, I went to see films to identify myself with movie heroes. Then, I wanted to get involved in cinema. I went to France to study, but I did not attend any specialized school. I wanted to become a stage actor but in Europe black actors have had a hard time finding roles to play. Thus, rather than waiting for an offer that would enable me to express myself, I decided to become a stage director and then I became a film director. I got bits of training here and there. I learned about editing and how to do it, and then I read books about it. The IDHEC Film School did not interest me at the time because its courses were very theoretical. I also had to make a living.

Therefore, I trained myself on the job, which is the best way of doing it because one is immediately confronted with practice. *(L'Afrique Littéraire et Artistique,* n. 33, 1974, p. 69)

Kamwa's experiences as a stage actor are eclectic and range from roles in Shakespeare's *Othello* and *The Merchant of Venice* to performances in modern French theater. In addition, he interpreted parts in *Une Saison au Congo* and *La Tragédie du Roi Christophe,* both by the Martiniquan poet and playwright Aimé Césaire. In 1969 Daniel Kamwa performed with the American actress Marpessa Dawn in Lanford Wilson's *Home Free,* which Kamwa translated and then successfully staged at the Kaleidoscope, a Left Bank Parisian theater *(Bingo,* September 1969, p. 45). A few years later, Kamwa interpreted the role of Christ in one of Max Fritsch's plays presented at the Théâtre National de Belgique.

In 1972 Daniel Kamwa's first endeavors in the area of cinema resulted in *Boubou-Cravate* (which literally means Tie and African Attire, but whose official English title is *Cross-Breed),* an $18,000 comedy which he was able to produce through his newly founded company, DK7–Communications, with financial support from the Consortium Audiovisuel International. *Boubou-Cravate,* interpreted by Daniel Kamwa, Marpessa Dawn, and James Campbell, is based on the filmmaker's script adapted from a short story by the Cameroonian musician and writer Francis Bebey. This film received a Quality Award from the French Centre National du Cinéma (CNC) in 1973, but enjoyed only a limited commercial run.

In 1974 Daniel Kamwa won the Prize for Best Screenplay ($45,000), annually awarded by the French Ministry of Cooperation, for his film project *Pousse-Pousse* (Tricycle Man). This award and a substantial grant from the Cameroonian government allowed Kamwa to complete the $460,000 motion picture. *Pousse-Pousse,* whose main role is also played by Kamwa, was shot in four weeks (in 1974) by African and French technicians on location in Cameroon. The film was made in French. In a multilingual country such as his, the filmmaker explains this choice of language as follows:

In order to please myself, I could make my actors speak Bamiléké, but only 20% of Cameroon's population speaks that language, and I want my films to reach as large an audience as possible. . . . To resort to subtitles is not a feasible solution in today's Africa because of illiteracy. So, between authenticity and efficacy I am sorry to say that I choose efficacy. *(L'Afrique Littéraire et Artistique,* n. 33, 1974, p. 73)

After having been featured in the 1979 Pan-African Film Festival of Ouagadougou (FESPACO), and having received the Best Screenplay Award at the 1979 Festival International du Film et des Echanges Francophones (FIFEF) held in Nice (France), *Pousse-Pousse* was nonetheless shunned by several critics. But due to its straightforward story line, comical elements, and a catchy musical score by André-Marie Tala, the motion picture had tremendous appeal in fourteen

West African countries, where it was seen by 700,000 moviegoers. Moreover, *Pousse-Pousse* was shown in the Soviet Union as well. Kamwa says of this:

I have purposely chosen to use a humoristic narrative tone because I have noticed that, until now, most African and Arab films tend to favor drama and some of them are quite hermetic. I have attended the screening of films with popular audiences and I have observed that they were not well received by viewers, which is a problem in the case of films whose intent is to arouse people's consciousness. I think that African cinema should diversify itself. I am not saying that I am necessarily on the right track, but I want to try a different approach. . . . At the risk of being accused of having made a commercial film, I have chosen to turn to a kind of easily accessible humor which entertains people while making them think. In so doing I place myself in the line of the traditional African culture in which ideas are transmitted through tales and sketches at evening gatherings." *(L'Afrique Littéraire et Artistique,* n. 49, 1978, p. 82)

The year 1980 saw the release of Kamwa's second feature length film, *Notre fille* (Our Daughter), based on *Notre fille ne se mariera pas* (Our Daughter Must Not Marry), a play by the popular dramatist and short story writer Guillaume Oyono-Mbia—which had won the 1969 Inter-African theater competition sponsored by Radio-France Internationale. The $580,000 motion picture, whose sound score was also composed by André-Marie Tala, was financed by a Cameroonian government film fund (Fonds de Développement de l'Industrie Cinématographique, also known as FODIC), the French Institut National de l'Audiovisuel (INA), and DK7–Communications. It was shot in French with interspersed sequences in African languages. *Notre fille* was screened at the Twentieth Marché du Film during the 1980 Cannes Film Festival, received a best Actor Award at the 1980 Carthage Film Festival (Journées Cinématographiques de Carthage) held in Tunisia, and was featured at the 1981 Moscow Film Festival as well as at the Museum of Modern Art in New York. It was also selected by the Academy of Motion Pictures, Arts and Sciences to compete for its Best Foreign Film Award in 1981. After having been presented in various West African countries, *Notre fille* opened in Paris on 4 November 1981, where it was simultaneously shown in two movie theaters. Also, it was successfully shown in the USSR, where it was dubbed in several regional languages. Although it has not matched *Pousse-Pousse*'s popular success, *Notre fille* has had a notable international run.

Besides his fiction films, Daniel Kamwa has made a number of documentaries (some of them were commissioned by the airline and hotel industries) meant to highlight traditions and economic development in Cameroon. These films are the $25,000 *La ligne du coeur* (Line of the Heart, 1978), $25,000 *Akum* (1979), $21,000 *Novotel* (1979), $6,000 *Danse, automate, danse* (Dance, Automaton, Danse, 1979), $7,500 *Messe à Melen* (Mass at Melen, 1980), *Cam-Air, dix ans d'essor* (Cameroon Airlines, A Decade of Flight, 1981), $40,000 *Nous les fous du volant* (Such Crazy Driving, 1982), and $83,000 *Les Fleurs du terroir* (Flowers of the Soil, 1983). Some of these motion pictures have had a varied viewership. *Akum* was screened in local movie theaters, *Nous les fous du volant* and *Les Fleurs du terroir* were featured by Cameroonian television and movie theaters, and *Danse, automate danse* and *Messe à Melen* were shown commercially in both Cameroon and France.

For Daniel Kamwa, Black African films should reflect significant social issues and should be viewed as "palaver trees, those century-old agoras, in the privileged shade of which collective discussion brings men and women together" *(Le Monde Diplomatique*, September 1980, p. 12). Accordingly, as Kamwa vehemently stressed during the 1980 Carthage Film Festival, Black African cinema should also be judged within an African frame of reference rather than by a set of pre-established foreign criteria *(Revue Belge du Cinéma*, n. 20, 1981, p. 36).

Kamwa offers the following definition of the African filmmaker:

Whether he comes from Africa or from any other continent, a filmmaker is like any artist. He should be intellectually free to choose the role he wants to fulfill according to the current context, his environment and his present preoccupations. However, he must always remain deeply aware of the fact that whatever he does, and whether he wants it or not, both his African and non-African audiences view him as a privileged witness, a highly sensitive human being who is able to see, understand and translate past, present and future social phenomena through the magic mirror of the movie camera. (Kamwa to author, 15 December 1986)

As a film director, Kamwa values his stage experiences:

Being an actor helps me understand the difficulties faced by the actors I direct. Yet this can also be a drawback if, while guiding them you try to make them act in the very same way you would. As you help actors get a feel for the characters they interpret, experience teaches you how to take into consideration their sensitivities and personalities. (Kamwa to author, 15 December 1986)

In an interview Daniel Kamwa made the following statement concerning the future of African films:

African cinema should find its own course through films which will be both useful and entertaining. Yet, in the near future, its main problem lies in the relationship between filmmakers and African governments. I am afraid that there is a misunderstanding between intellectuals and politicians. Politicians believe filmmakers always want to attack them. . . . The problems faced by African cinema are primarily economic. I do not know whether nationalization [of film structures] is a solution but I am convinced that distribution is a key question. It is absolutely essential for a [better] distribution of African films both in and outside of Africa. *(L'Afrique Littéraire et Artistique*, n. 33, 1974, p. 73)

Through DK7–Communications, Kamwa is presently involved in the production of commercials, promotional audiovisual programs, and commissioned documentaries. He is also actively seeking funds for his next feature length film,

Daisy Kiss, based on his own script set in South Africa. Another film project is *Mort d'un Empire* (Death of an Empire), a historical film which will take place in northern Cameroon.

Kamwa is the father of two daughters and a son. His activities, as both a filmmaker and an actor (he still works occasionally as both a film and stage actor), keep him commuting between Douala (the economic center of Cameroon) and Paris. He is today one of the most commercially successful representatives of Cameroonian cinema. Often criticized for the commercial orientation of his films, Kamwa has nonetheless the merit of having brought some comic relief to a largely stern and often austere African screen. In addition, his search for a popular African film language (which one could compare to that of Ola Balogun*) might, one day, lead to very interesting results.

MAJOR THEMES

The title of Kamwa's first film, *Boubou-Cravate*—which refers to the fact that its protagonist will wear both a traditional African gown *(boubou)* and a Western tie *(cravate)*—is in itself a symbolic illustration of its main theme, that of cultural alienation. The film's epigraph stipulates: ''I do not want doors and windows to be closed for I want various cultures to enter, yet I do not wish to become uprooted.''

Boubou-Cravate takes place in an urban African setting. Gilbert, the main character, is a diplomat who leads an apparently untroubled European lifestyle with Angèle, his Westernized African wife. Yet, occasionally Gilbert has to endure the mockeries of his loquacious manservant, who tells him that he eats and behaves like a white man. One day, to prove his servant wrong, Gilbert decides to sport African attire—but with a tie. This accoutrement only provokes further sly comments from his European secretary. That same evening, Gilbert (dressed in a tuxedo) and his wife give an elegant cocktail party at their house. While the couple is mingling with their guests against a background of classical European music, the servant invites some of his friends to eat and celebrate in the kitchen. Soon drums are heard and a masquerade leads the servant's friends from the kitchen into the dining room. There they rid Gilbert of his tie and make him wear a traditional necklace. The film closes on a frantic African dance in the course of which Gilbert is metaphorically reinserted into tribal life.

Like *Muna Moto,* by the Cameroonian director Jean-Pierre Dikongue-Pipa*, *Pousse-Pousse* examines the traditional African custom of dowry and the abuses it entails in an increasingly money-oriented society. It furthermore presents amusing vignettes of Douala's trading quarter. Here Pousse-Pousse, the eponymous central character, is a striving Bamiléké delivery man who aspires to marry Rose, a young Douala woman he has secretly been courting. Now that he has some savings, Pousse-Pousse officially asks for Rose's hand. This will cause humorous yet seemingly endless transactions between the father of Pousse-Pousse and that of Rose, who keeps increasing the bride-price. Faced with such greediness, Pousse-Pousse and Rose decide to get married without the consent of Rose's father. A number of farcical scenes take place on their wedding day, including the bride-to-be's last minute escape from her family compound while her sister, working as an accomplice, tricks their father into drunkenness to prevent him from further delaying the young couple's happiness.

La Ligne de coeur literally means "heart line," but here it is also intended to signify an airline. The film, primarily a documentary, is meant to promote Cameroon Airlines, the nation's varied population and fauna, and its general touristic appeal. The country is seen through the eyes of a young Cameroonian boy who vividly introduces his land to a European friend. The film includes a number of breathtaking aerial views of Cameroon's multifaceted landscapes. An identical promotional intent is reflected through *Cam-Air, dix ans d'essor, Novotel,* which focuses on Cameroon's expanding hotel industry, *Les Fleurs du terroir,* which highlights the country's agricultural resources, and *Akum,* which describes the annual fertility rites (a syncretism of African and Christian religions) in Akum, a village located near Bamenda, in northwest Cameroon. Such a symbiosis of African traditions and Western religious rituals is also present in *Messe à Melen,* filmed in a populous neighborhood of the country's capital, Yaoundé. *Danse, automate, danse* follows the steps of a young local street puppeteer, and *Nous les fous du volant* is a short fictional film which promotes safe driving in Cameroon.

Kamwa's latest feature film is *Notre fille,* which centers on the conflictive dichotomy between Western values and ancestral African traditions. Its story is that of a rural family of humble means, living on the outskirts of Yaoundé, which has sent a daughter, Nicole, to France to complete her university studies. Now the family anxiously waits to share in the expected benefits of her education: a high-paying job and a wealthy husband. Yet, instead of fulfilling her family's expectations, Nicole starts to work as a modest civil servant who plans to marry a penniless suitor. In an attempt to remind his daughter of her family responsibilities, her father, Mbarga, and his wives come to town, giving rise to a series of comical mishaps. Their efforts prove vain, but the film offers a light-hearted ending in which love triumphs over family pressures. The final sequence of this Cameroonian vaudeville of sorts includes a merry dance during which a female protagonist drops her Western wig, thus symbolically regaining her Africanity, as happens in the closing scene of *Boubou-Cravate* with the removal of the protagonist's tie.

SURVEY OF CRITICISM

Because they have had wider exposure than his documentaries, Kamwa's fiction films are those which have elicited the most critical response. Noël Ebony notes that "in spite of the film's intellectual subject matter" *Boubou-Cravate* has been well received by Ivorian moviegoers *(Fraternité Matin,* 10–11 February 1973, p. 11). Ferid Boughedir finds *Boubou-Cravate* "promising" *(Jeune Af-*

rique 28 May 1976, p. 56), but Paulin Soumanou Vieyra* *(Le Cinéma africain,* 1975, p. 46) and Jacques Binet *(Afrique Contemporaine,* January-February 1976, p. 27) are somewhat disappointed by its limited analysis of acculturation.

It is interesting to note that *Pousse-Pousse,* a commercially successful motion picture, has generated primarily lukewarm reviews. Berkati Brahim deplores its superficial thematic treatment and adds, "Let us hope that the next time D. Kamwa will address us in Bamiléké, and show us more than a 'pretty' shanty town" *(Cinémarabe,* October-November 1976, p. 50). Jean-Louis Pouillaud calls *Pousse-Pousse* "a Punch-and-Judy show in the Molière tradition" and regrets its lack of true sociopolitical concerns *(Positif,* September 1976, p. 70). Jacqueline Lajeunesse wonders whether the film's commercial intents contributed to the paucity of its content *(La Revue du Cinéma, Image et Son,* June-July 1976, p. 106). Ferid Boughedir finds *Pousse-Pousse*'s comical devices complacently conventional and views its characters as stereotypical *(Jeune Afrique,* 28 May 1976, p. 56). Jean René Debrix terms *Pousse-Pousse* a somewhat unconvincing "comédie à l'italienne," but favors its colorful depiction of Douala's population *(Afrique Contemporaine,* September-October 1975, pp. 6–7). Similar comments are made by the Cameroonian reviewers Fame Ndongo and Arthur Si Bita *(Cameroon Tribune,* 10 June 1975, p. 6). Louis-Marie Barbarit judges Kamwa's film to be entertaining and feels it offers a clear illustration of the problems dowry may cause in present-day Africa *(Télérama,* 28 April 1976, p. 88).

Like *Pousse-Pousse, Notre fille* has triggered mixed comments on the part of film critics. Yann Lardeau stresses its theatrical effects and appealing characters (which he links to Molière's comedies) but has qualms about its lack of depth *(Cahiers du Cinéma,* January 1982, p. 57). Mouldi Fehri endorses Kamwa's technical abilities and his handling of irony, but he also emphasizes the filmmaker's sketchy depiction of social dichotomy, as well as his noncommittal views concerning such women's issues as polygamy *(Adhoua,* January-March 1981, pp. 19–20). While they are pleased with Kamwa's engaging portrayal of the Cameroonian milieu (its customs, human warmth, and sensuous landscapes), Christine de Montvalon *(Télérama,* 4 November 1981, p. 33) and Eric de Saint-Angel *(Le Matin,* 11 November 1981, p. 26) also underscore the actors' stagy and clumsy performances and question Kamwa's excessive and ambiguous use of caricature which, they say, could instigate racially oriented and stereotypical responses from non-African viewers. In a more detailed study of *Notre fille,* Ferid Boughedir observes that Kamwa should not be considered a class-conscious political filmmaker but a moralist who intends to fight social evils in a light-hearted tone. In addition, Boughedir criticizes Kamwa's overly caricatural characters (a trait he attributes to the filmmaker's experiences on the legitimate stage) and wishes for more "comical dosage" in his future works *(Jeune Afrique,* 2 December 1981, pp. 78–79). Ginette Gervais shows appreciation for *Notre fille's* clarity and well-intentioned satirical mood but stresses its thematic superficiality and the hesitant and theatrical rendition of its actors *(Jeune Cinéma,* December

1981, pp. 48–49). Françoise Audé makes similar remarks concerning Kamwa's players, and she deplores his "ambivalent argumentation" about polygamy *(Positif,* January 1982, pp. 85–86). In spite of its static sequences, François Lechat likes *Notre fille,* which he calls a "mischievous, tender-hearted and sensitive comedy" *(Cinéphilia,* 4 October 1981, p. 18). For Christian Bosséno, *Notre fille* is a "savory family chronicle" which is not without interest, but he also feels that its realism and naturalness would have greatly benefitted from the use of African languages rather than French *(La Revue du Cinéma, Image et Son,* December 1981, p. 54).

FILMOGRAPHY

Boubou-Cravate (Cross-Breed), 16 mm, color, 30 min., 1972.
Pousse-Pousse (Tricycle Man), 16/35 mm, color, 90 min., 1975.
La Ligne de coeur (Line of the Heart), 16 mm, color, 25 min., 1978.
Akum, 16 mm, color, 15 min., 1979.
Novotel, 16 mm, color, 15 min., 1979.
Danse automate, danse (Dance, Automaton, Dance), 16 mm, color, 15 min., 1979.
Messe à Melen (Mass at Melen), 16 mm, color, 15 min., 1980.
Notre fille (Our Daughter), 16/35 mm, color, 100 min., 1980.
Cam-Air, dix ans d'essor (Cameroon Airlines, A Decade of Flight), 16 mm, color, 40 min., 1981.
Nous les fous du volant (Such Crazy Driving), 16 mm, color, 18 min., 1982.
Les Fleurs du terroir (Flowers of the Soil), 16 mm, color, 30 min., 1983.

BIBLIOGRAPHY

Interviews of Daniel Kamwa

Essola, Donat. "Rencontre avec le réalisateur et un acteur de Pousse-Pousse." *Cameroon Tribune,* 12 June 1975, p. 2.
Hennebelle, Guy. "Kamwa Daniel." *L'Afrique Littéraire et Artistique,* n. 49, 3rd Quarter 1978, pp. 80–83.
Hennebelle, Monique. "Daniel Kamwa, lauréat du meilleur scénario 1974 décerné par l'agence de coopération culturelle et technique: 'Dans Pousse-Pousse, je dénoncerai la pratique de la dot au Cameroun." *L'Afrique Littéraire et Artistique,* n. 33, 1974, pp. 69–73.
Mouasso-Priso, S. "Je ne fais pas de l'exotisme, nous confie Daniel Kamwa, réalisateur de 'Pousse-Pousse.' " *Cameroon Tribune,* 6 June 1975, p. 7.
Ramonet, Ignacio. "Comme des arbres à palabres." *Le Monde Diplomatique,* September 1980, p. 12.

Film Reviews and Studies of Daniel Kamwa

"African Films at the Cannes Film Festival." *West Africa,* n. 3279, 26 May 1980, pp. 918–19.
Aubert, Alain. "Ouagadougou." *Ecran 79,* n. 82, 15 July 1979, pp. 15–16.

Audé, Françoise. "Notre fille." *Positif*, n. 250, January 1982, pp. 85–86.

Bachy, Victor. "Le Cinéma au Cameroun." *La Revue du Cinéma, Image et Son*, n. 351, June 1980, pp. 87–94.

———. "Festivals et rencontres." *Revue Belge du Cinéma*, n. 20, 1981, pp. 35–36.

Barbarit, Louis-Marie. "Pousse-Pousse." *Télérama*, n. 1372, 28 April 1976, p. 88.

Belinga, Thérèse Baratte-Eno. *Ecrivains, cinéastes et artistes camerounais: bio-bibliographie*. Yaoundé: Centre d'Edition et de Production pour l'Enseignement et la Recherche, 1978.

Binet, Jacques. "Cinéma africain." *Afrique Contemporaine*, n. 83, January-February 1976, pp. 27–30.

Bosséno, Christian. "Fêtes biennales des cinémas d'Afrique." *Recherche, Pédagogie et Culture*, n. 53–54, May-October 1981, pp. 69–73.

———. "Notre fille." *La Revue du Cinéma, Image et Son*, n. 367, December 1981, p. 54.

Boughedir, Ferid. "Ouagadougou." *Ecran 1973*, n. 15, May 1973, pp. 54–55.

———. "Cameroun." *Cinéma Québec*, vol. 3, n. 9–10, August 1974, pp. 41–43.

———. "Dans une Afrique d'opérette." *Jeune Afrique*, n. 803, 28 May 1976, pp. 56–57.

———. "Sept films africains à Cannes." *Jeune Afrique*, n. 1009, 7 May 1980, p. 71.

———. "La Petite Soeur de Boubou-Cravate." *Jeune Afrique*, n. 1091, 2 December 1981, pp. 78–79.

———. "Les Grandes Dates du cinéma africain." *Jeune Afrique*, n. 1303–1304, 25 December 1985, pp. 87–89.

Brahim, Berkati. "Pousse, Pousse . . . Pouce." *Cinémarabe*, n. 4–5, October-November 1976, p. 50.

Cham, Mbye-Baboucar. "Film Production in West Africa: 1979–1981." *Présence Africaine*, n. 124, 4th Quarter 1982, pp. 168–87.

"Daniel Kamwa, un talentueux camerounais." *Bingo*, n. 200, September 1969, p. 45.

Debrix, Jean-René. "Situation du cinéma en Afrique francophone." *Afrique Contemporaine*, n. 81, September-October 1975, pp. 2–7.

Dikongue-Pipa, Jean-Pierre. "Cameroun: dénoncer les abus de pouvoir." *Le Monde Diplomatique*, September 1978, p. 13.

Ebony, Noël. "Journées ivoiriennes: Triomphe pour nos réalisateurs." *Fraternité Matin*, 10–11 February 1973, p. 11.

Fehri, Mouldi. "Notre fille de Daniel Kamwa (Cameroun)—Le choc de deux civilisations." *Adhoua*, n. 3, January-March 1981, pp. 18–20.

Gervais, Ginette. "Notre fille." *Jeune Cinéma*, n. 139, December 1981, pp. 48–49.

Haffner, Pierre. "Le Cinéma indien en Afrique noire ou les vertus pédagogiques de l'imaginaire cinématographique."

Filméchange, n. 21, Winter 1982–83, pp. 21–25.

Kieffer, Anne. "Cinéma d'Afrique noire au Festival des Trois Continents." *Jeune Cinéma*, n. 149, March 1983, pp. 10–13.

Lajeunesse, Jacqueline. "Pousse-Pousse." *La Revue du Cinéma, Image et Son*, n. 307, June-July 1976, pp. 104–6.

Lardeau, Yann. "Notre fille." *Cahiers du Cinéma*, n. 331, January 1982, p. 57.

Lechat, François. "Notre fille." *Cinéphilia*, n. 2, 4 October 1981, p. 18.

M, J-P. M. "Le Tournage du film de Kamwa vient de commencer à Douala." *Cameroon Tribune*, 9–10 November 1974, p. 5.

Matchet. "Cameroon in Films." *West Africa,* n. 3141, 19 September 1977, p. 1921.

Montvalon, Christine de. "Notre fille." *Télérama,* n. 1660, 4 November 1981, p. 33.

Ndaw, Aly Kheury. "Pousse-Pousse de Daniel Kamwa." *Le Soleil,* 11 December 1975, p. 8.

Ndongo, Fame. "Pousse-Pousse—la banalité et après?" *Cameroon Tribune,* 10 June 1975, p. 6.

"Notre fille." *Ciné Revue,* n. 45, 5 November 1981, p. 44.

Pouillaud, Jean-Louis. "Pousse-Pousse." *Positif,* n. 185, September 1976, p. 70.

Saint-Angel, Eric de. "Notre fille de Daniel Kamwa." *Le Matin,* 11 November 1981, p. 26.

Schoenberner, Gerhard. "Det svarta Afrikas filmer och deras regissorer." *Chaplin 166,* n. 1, 1980, pp. 10–15.

Si Bita, Arthur. "Pousse-Pousse, maturité culturelle." *Cameroon Tribune,* 10 June 1975, p. 6.

Soyer, Chantal. "Afrique noire: un cinéma étranger à son propre monde." *Film-action,* n. 2, February-March 1982, p. 10–11.

Sumo, Honoré de. "Genèse et avenir du cinéma camerounais." *L'Afrique Littéraire et Artistique,* n. 39, 1976, pp. 59–62.

Vieyra, Paulin Soumanou. *Le Cinéma africain.* Paris: Présence Africaine, 1975.

Nana Mahomo (1930–)
South Africa

BIOGRAPHY

A member of the Suto ethnic group whose family originated in Lesotho, Nana Mahomo was born in 1930 in Johannesburg, South Africa. He was one of seven children, and both of his parents were schoolteachers by profession. Mahomo's father was also a minister whose household closely followed the ethics of the Christian faith. Young Nana was reared in a segregated part of town, and attended both primary and secondary school in his native city. He recalls:

My siblings and I experienced the abuses of apartheid, but because our parents were schoolteachers we had a better start in life than most of our contemporaries. By the time I went to school, I could already read and write, which was not the case of my peers. And unlike many others, our parents were able to provide us with adequate food and stable shelter. (Mahomo to author, Washington, D.C., 16 January 1985)

As an adolescent, and unlike most African urban youth outside of South Africa, Nana Mahomo would infrequently use movie-going as a form of relaxation. He emphasizes:

For Blacks in South Africa, going to the movies is another experience of apartheid. Not only do they have to go to segregated theaters, but they are restricted to viewing certain types of films. You saw cowboy films and motion pictures which did not show interaction between Whites and Blacks or if they did they would show White people in full command of the situation. There was nothing which would show both groups on an equal footing and in any case nothing that would indicate a mixing of races amongst males and females. (Mahomo to author, 16 January 1985)

After high school, Nana Mahomo left Johannesburg and went to college in Cape Town. He says:

I was going to go to law school and become a lawyer. I went to a White university with but a few Black students. In the year that I was there, there were 12,000 students and a half dozen Blacks. Blacks and Whites were in the same classrooms, but I know for a fact that my grades were based on a different assessment because I tested it out on two or three occasions. I always managed to get a D if my name was on the paper. Otherwise I got a B+ or an A when I used another name. I am not saying that this was done by all professors but it certainly happened with some. . . . No matter who you are or what your qualifications may be, nobody ever judges you on the basis of these qualifications. What counts in South Africa is that you are Black. (Mahomo to author, 16 January 1985)

Thus, increasingly angered by South Africa's racial policies, which perniciously permeate all facets of socioeconomic, political, and cultural life, Mahomo joined the newly formed Pan-Africanist Congress (PAC) led by Robert Sobukwe, and engaged in sustained anti-apartheid activities. This new involvement was to become a decisive factor in the orientation of Mahomo's future professional life. He stresses:

I was in my fourth year of law school when I was asked to leave South Africa by Sobukwe to represent the PAC abroad. I left South Africa before taking my law degree. I thought the task I had ahead of me was important enough to intrude on my legal studies. (Mahomo to author, 16 January 1985)

Nana Mahomo arrived in England in 1960. There he started organizing support for the Black liberation movement in South Africa. As a member of the Executive Committee of the Pan-Africanist Congress, he was invited to participate in the 1969 Pan-African Festival of Algiers, and was made to tour a number of European countries to deliver lectures. It is after such experiences that he became interested in film as a medium which could illustrate South African reality from a Black perspective, and counteract the pro-apartheid propaganda films produced with significant financial means by the South African Information Service. Mahomo remarks:

My preoccupation for a long time had nothing to do with films because I was going to be a hot shot lawyer. I didn't really think much about film, which I considered as a means of entertainment, and I never thought in terms of my active participation in such an area. I started thinking about film because of my involvement in politics. The more I described to people what apartheid is, the more I felt they did not believe me. What I was saying was so incredible that it was hard for them to really agree that certain things do happen, that they can exist. . . . I got to a stage where I felt that it was imperative for me to say this in a more concrete fashion. This led me to consider making documentary films. (Mahomo to author, 16 January 1985)

Hence, without any formal training in the area of filmmaking, Mahomo and a group of South Africans in exile, in collaboration with English associates who had been students at the London Film School, founded the London-based production company Morena Films, with the intention of making motion pictures explaining the conditions under which South African Blacks live. Another goal of the new company was to use any profits generated by those films in support of the PAC cause. Their first film, *End of the Dialogue*, marks the beginning of Mahomo's career as a director. This low-budget documentary financed through British bank loans was shot secretly in South Africa in 1969 and edited in London the following year. The present forty-seven-minute version of *End of the Dialogue* stems from a total footage of four hours. Mahomo reminisces about the production of this film.

When we embarked on this operation it was shrouded in mystery. Everybody we approached about filmmaking and the problems involved made it sound very mysterious, very complicated, something requiring extraordinary abilities and financing. . . . we didn't have money, but we thought we could acquire the necessary know-how. . . . You will acquire more skills by going out in the field and doing what you have to do than by the theoretical knowledge you may acquire in a classroom. . . . When we consulted people on the possibility of making a 45–minute documentary with a budget of less than $15,000, they thought we were crazy. We didn't have $15,000, we didn't even have $1,000 to start with . . . but we rented a Beaulieu [portable French-made camera], we acquired film stock and we began shooting.
   Then the next problem came—how do we develop the film? When we went to the lab, we discovered that we would have to pay cash on delivery. So we said, OK, some of us will work for two months until we have the money to pay for the development. *(Cineaste*, Fall 1976, pp. 18–19)

It should also be noted that because of insufficient financial means, *End of the Dialogue*, intended to be totally shot in color, includes some black and white footage out of sheer necessity, although some critics have been prompt to attribute it to the director's wish for increased dramatic impact *(UFAHAMU*, vol. 7, n. 1, 1976, p. 103). When released in 1970, *End of the Dialogue* received an Emmy Award after being shown on CBS in the United States. It was also presented by the BBC in England and broadcast by a number of European television stations in such countries as the Netherlands, Sweden, and Denmark. It was featured as well at the Brno Film Festival in Czechoslovakia.

Nana Mahomo's second film is the $70,000 *Last Grave at Dimbaza*, made during 1973–1974. Like *End of the Dialogue*, this work was filmed illegally in South Africa (where rigid laws concerning film shooting permits would not have allowed for such a motion picture to be made) and smuggled out. *Last Grave at Dimbaza* was shot by an eight-member team: three white film technicians went from London to South Africa, where they joined efforts with a five-member local Black crew. Mahomo recalls that a Black African cameraman could walk about quite easily with film apparatus, because South African authorities did not suspect that he was actively participating in the making of a film:

One asset in our favor is that normally white South Africans don't see black people, and if a black person is carrying a camera, he is regarded just as a laborer, carrying it for his white master. We were helped by the fact that people have become accustomed to seeing American and Japanese tourists carrying a lot of camera equipment. Sometimes the ordinary still camera equipment which they carry is more impressive than the movie camera that we used. *(The Black Scholar,* May 1976, p. 31)

After such unfortunate mishaps as the damaging of five hours of film footage by a London processing laboratory, *Last Grave at Dimbaza* was completed in 1974. It has since received worldwide exposure and remains to this day one of the most forceful cinematic indictments of apartheid. Among other official recognitions, *Last Grave at Dimbaza* won prizes at the Grenoble International Short Film Festival in France (for the film's quality as a social documentary and the strength of its political message) and at the Mannheim Film Festival (Germany) in 1974. That same year it was presented at the Carthage Film Festival. Also in 1974, Mahomo's work was presented in England by the BBC and included in television programs in many European countries. In 1975 *Last Grave at Dimbaza* received a Cannes Film Festival award in the documentary area. It was aired in the United States by PBS on 27 October 1976. To this day the film has been extensively shown on noncommercial film circuits and has frequently been used by diverse political groups to spearhead campaigns against South Africa's racial policies. Mahomo points out:

We had several problems in that some groups used the film before we even gave them permission to do so. The film has been videotaped by certain groups. Such groups have been using the film for their own purposes. We have not unfortunately gotten any remuneration for that kind of use. It would take a brilliant detective to trace all those videotape copies of *Last Grave at Dimbaza.* We want as many people as possible to see the film, but unless we can keep going, keep going in terms of selling film, there is no possibility of our continuing our work. *(UFAHAMU,* vol. 7, n. 1, 1976, p. 101)

According to reviewer Patrick O'Meara, the impact of *Last Grave at Dimbaza* was such that the South African government produced *Black Man Alive* in 1975, a film which "promotes an idealized form of synthetic primitivism (visually, in the commentary, and in the musical background) and emphasizes cultural diversity and separate development" *(Jump Cut,* n. 18, August 1978, p. 8). Interestingly, a similar approach was later used by the white South African director Jamie Uys in his film *The Gods Must Be Crazy,* made in the early 1980s.

Last Grave at Dimbaza was not primarily intended for use in South Africa, but rather outside of that country to inform world opinion and decision makers. As expected, the motion picture has never been shown overtly in South Africa. O'Meara points out that "its only official showing was in the Hendrik Verwoerd Office Building in Cape Town to government officials, Cabinet ministers and members of the Senate and House Assembly" *(Jump Cut,* n. 18, August 1978, p. 7).

Although to date he has been involved only in the making of documentaries, Nana Mahomo welcomes the idea of producing a feature film: "If there was a possibility of making a feature length film on a political theme but in a more popular manner for commercial purposes, I might consider it, particularly if it would pay for the resistance movement in South Africa'' *(Cineaste,* Fall 1976, p. 19).

The main concern of the South African filmmaker has been to make politically oriented films. An unabashed admirer of the Senegalese director Ousmane Sembene* (see *The Black Scholar,* May 1976, p. 32), Mahomo feels that Third World filmmakers ''need to present films with an awareness of their social responsibility, of their commitment to enlightening the audience or focusing on a particular social problem, so that it isn't just entertainment'' *(Cineaste,* Fall 1976, p. 19). However, the South African director does not believe in restricting his activities solely to cinema. He states:

Primarily I want to be an instrument for change. I would like to see myself contributing in as many fields as possible for one man to contribute. I want to feel that I have acquired or I am acquiring skills which will be used for the betterment of people in Africa, or, in South Africa in particular. . . . I don't just see myself spending my life making films. I would like to be more involved in active participation, either in the liberation struggle or in a role similar to that. *(The Black Scholar,* May 1976, p. 33)

Faithful to such considerations, Mahomo is currently working with the AFL-CIO, an American trade union which was among the first to call for the end of apartheid in the 1950s, and is now offering assistance to Black trade unions in South Africa. Like Lionel N'Gakane (a talented Black South African director, and also a representative of the African National Congress now residing in London), Nana Mahomo has spent more than twenty-five years in exile, except for two clandestine visits to his native country, because he is on South Africa's banned list. He is presently living and working in Washington, D.C.

MAJOR THEMES

We are fighting to reestablish the position of the black man there [South Africa] in terms of his human work, in terms of his dignity. We are trying to make sure that the inhumanity which is being paraded under the cloak of apartheid is absolutely understood by each and every one so that the issues are clear and it can only be done through more and more people knowing what the issues are in Southern Africa. *(UFAHAMU,* vol. 7, n. 1, 1976, p. 106)

In accordance with this statement by Nana Mahomo, both *End of the Dialogue* and *Last Grave at Dimbaza* depict facets of South Africa's reality. *End of the Dialogue* (whose title itself calls for action) illustrates the life of the inhabitants of Soweto, an overpopulated Bantu township which was to attract worldwide attention in 1976 because of the brutal repression of youth demonstrations, during which a number of high school students were killed under police gunfire. In this Black shanty town, whose population provides nearby Johannesburg's cheap commuting labor force, mine workers are grossly underpaid at 5 pounds a month (while White South Africans enjoy one of the highest standards of living in the world), the average life expectancy is thirty-four years, and many children die before they reach the age of five. At the same time that it quotes these shattering figures, *End of the Dialogue* delves into the repressive and unjust sociopolitical conditions under which Blacks are forced to live in South Africa.

Last Grave at Dimbaza could be considered a sequel to *End of the Dialogue*. Its title refers to Dimbaza, a township located in a "bantustan" or "homeland," an area developed by South Africa's government as a settlement where Blacks are relegated. *Last Grave at Dimbaza,* a vivid, graphic portrayal of apartheid in urban as well as rural settings, contrasts affluent white lifestyles with the miserable living conditions of most Blacks in a country where 18 million Blacks are controlled by a white minority of under 4 million owning 87 percent of the land (the rest of South Africa's 28 million population consists of less than a million Asians and a large segment of "colored"—people of mixed races). Among other facts, the motion picture underscores the destructive influence of the migratory labor system (regulated by the notoriously ignominious passbook, the lack of which leads to arrest and imprisonment) has on families whenever Black workers are forced to be separated from wives and children, whom they are allowed to visit once a year. Black laborers' wives and children have been defined by a South African official as merely "superfluous appendages" liable to impede industrial productivity. And besides, as a former minister of Bantu Affairs puts it in the film: "African males from the homelands have no rights whatsoever in South Africa, they are only in South Africa to sell their labour." Furthermore, *Last Grave at Dimbaza* emphasizes the division of labor based on racial lines, and condemns subsequent discrepancies in wage policies (in the mining industry white workers earn sixteen times as much as Blacks). Next, one learns that while education is free for Whites and not for Blacks, the South African government spent (in 1970) eighteen times more money for the education of a White child than it did for a Black one. The film also discloses that due to inadequate health care facilities, some homelands are plagued with tuberculosis and a devastating rate of mortality among very young children. In this factual and well-documented denunciation of apartheid, Mahomo also indicts the complicity of foreign industrial companies that, established in South Africa, profit from such a system, which supplies them with cheap manpower. Two sequences of the motion picture have a particularly gruesome significance: one shows a healthy White child spoon-fed by his Black nanny, whose own son has died of malnutrition; the other features a garbage collection during which Black laborers with full cans in their arms run after a truck whose White driver won't stop. The filmmaker emphasizes: "He could, of course, but he prefers to express his contempt for them–and he is allowed to *(Variety,* 13 November 1974, p. 39). At the end of the motion picture, the viewer is personally drawn into South Africa's world when told:

During the hour you have been watching this film, in South Africa . . . six Black families have been thrown out of their homes, sixty Blacks have been arrested under the Pass Laws, sixty Black children have died of the effects of malnutrition and, during the same hour the Gold Mining companies have made a profit of thirty-five thousand pounds. *(UFAHAMU,* vol. 7, n. 1, 1976, p. 96)

Last Grave at Dimbaza concludes with laconic and painful images of a cemetery (with instances of wooden signs and plastic feeding bottles as grave markers) where a number of lots have already been dug to cope with rampant infant mortality. In centering on the conditions and consequences of apartheid, Mahomo's work willfully fails to describe Black resistance movements in South Africa. The filmmaker points out: "You have to realize that if you are making a film which touches on an underground movement, then there is no longer an underground movement" *(UFAHAMU,* vol. 7, n. 1, 1976, p. 100).

SURVEY OF CRITICISM

End of the Dialogue, which has been more rarely seen than Mahomo's second documentary, has produced favorable comments. David Wilson says of the film:

It is a grim catalogue, but irrefutably accurate and here set out without slant or emotion; as in Resnais' *Night and Fog,* it is the very absence of emotion which generates it. This is a technique basic to propaganda film, and the makers of *End of the Dialogue* apply it with shattering effect. Their use of juxtaposition is equally classic, and equally legitimate for their purpose: African children carry shopping baskets for white women, a white tennis player is intercut with blacks rolling a cricket pitch, the camera moves from whites occupying park benches to focus on Africans squatting in the pavement dirt. The emotive power of the visual image is exploited without reservation; and if the method sometimes involves a juxtaposition that seems facile, like the final roll-call of political prisoners and the repetition of the words "sentenced to death," its effect is its own justification. . . . *End of the Dialogue* is an eloquent, angry testament. *(Monthly Film Bulletin,* March 1971, p. 56)

According to Ken Gay:

End of the Dialogue . . . set out not to be a personal statement by a great film director but an argument against something politically despised. It achieves art in its successful communication. . . . The narration moves slowly round the social spectrum . . . making a creative treatment of actuality, placing the film in the tradition of social documentary, saying "this is what I the film maker sees!" Angry white South African supporters argue the film is biased; but documentary is always biased and selective: what was filmed was there for selection. What is most important is not the art but the communication and the effect. We become involved in mankind. *(Films and Filming,* March 1971, p. 80)

A number of critics have shown appreciation primarily for *Last Grave at Dimbaza.* After previewing the film, Dave Pirie declares:

The film is gripping, terrifying, shattering and wholly incredible—technically excellent and faultlessly constructed. I would be tempted to call it the horror movie of the year except for one thing: every frame and every event in it is real. . . . The film examines in detail the white population's stratospheric standard of living, which is greatly improved by using their victims as we use machines. . . . The film continually juxtaposes the two communities of South Africa to ghostly effect, and the cold statistics of its commentary are unbearable. Everyone knows that conditions in South Africa are bad. This film presents proof that they are genocidal. *(Time Out,* 28 June 1974, p. 30)

Likewise, Monique Hennebelle *(L'Afrique Littéraire et Artistique,* n. 34, 1974, p. 92), André Pâquet (Cinéma-Québec, April 1975, p. 39), and Verina Glaessner *(Monthly Film Bulletin,* May 1975, p. 109) praise the forceful exactness of its demonstration, and Mack calls *Last Grave at Dimbaza* "a trenchant piece of film journalism, though marred somewhat by drowning, rhetorical narration" *(Variety,* 26 March 1975, p. 32). For Kay Gardella it is "an accusing and devastating film" *(Daily News,* 27 October 1975, p. 64). Arthur Unger writes:

Certainly Nana Mahomo's controversial film uses crudely simplistic methods, ironic juxtaposition of scenes, shrewd manipulation of facts to make its points. Certainly there is no attempt to show more than one side of apartheid. But the film was obviously made out of frustration . . . and total commitment. It has a point to make—that the enforced separation of the races as practiced in South Africa results in a depressed and demeaning status for non-whites. *(Christian Science Monitor,* 24 October 1975, p. 26)

In turn, Susan J. Hall points out:

It is a powerful film—calculated to shock viewers who know little about the country, strengthen the resolve of those dedicated to righting injustices, and rouse the ire of the system's defenders. Serious and depressing, it will shake the apathy of the most quiescent. *(Film Library Quarterly,* vol. 9, n. 1, 1976, p. 15)

Clyde Taylor's only reservation concerning Mahomo's work is as follows: "If there is any drawback to *Last Grave,* it is that its wrenching exposure makes no mention of the struggles of Black South Africans to throw off this unbending domination" *(The Black Collegian,* February-March 1981, p. 14). Taylor's opinion reflects that of Monique Hennebelle *(L'Afrique Littéraire et Artistique,* n. 34, 1974, p. 92) and Serge Toubiana *(Cahiers du Cinéma,* January 1976, p. 125).

FILMOGRAPHY

End of the Dialogue, 16 mm, black and white with parts in color, 47 min., 1969.
Last Grave at Dimbaza, 16 mm, color, 40 min., 1974.

BIBLIOGRAPHY

Interviews with Nana Mahomo

Anthony, David H. "The Black Scholar Interviews Mahomo." *The Black Scholar*, vol. 7, n. 8, May 1976, pp. 30–35.
———. "Clandestine Filming in South Africa: An Interview with Nana Mahomo." *Cineaste*, vol. 7, n. 3, Fall 1976, pp. 18–19, 50.
———. "Mahomo, Nana." *L'Afrique Littéraire et Artistique*, n. 49, 3rd Quarter 1978, pp. 84–85.
Chenu, François. "La Fin du dialogue." *L'Afrique Littéraire et Artistique*, n. 20, 1st Quarter 1972, pp. 270–75.

Film Reviews and Studies of Nana Mahomo

Fraser, C. Gerald. "Dimbaza, Film Smuggled Out of South Africa, Won Aid of Church and Labor." *New York Times*, 27 October 1975, p. 52.
Gabriel, Teshome H. "Let Their Eyes Testify." *UFAHAMU*, vol. 7, n. 1, 1976, pp. 96–113.
Garcia, Jean-Pierre, Marc Mangin, and René Prédal. "Afrique du Sud." *Cinémaction Tricontinental*, January 1982, pp. 86–88.
Gardella, Kay. *"Last Grave at Dimbaza."* *Daily News*, 27 October 1975, p. 64.
Gay, Ken. "Documentary." *Films and Filming*, vol. 17, n. 6, March 1971, pp. 80–81.
Glaessner, Verina. "Last Grave at Dimbaza." *Monthly Film Bulletin*, vol. 42, n. 496, May 1975, p. 109.
Hall, Susan J. "A Critique of Last Grave at Dimbaza." *Film Library Quarterly*, vol. 9, n. 1, 1976, pp. 15–18.
Hennebelle, Guy. *Guide des films anti-impérialistes*. Paris: Editions du Centenaire, 1975.
Hennebelle, Monique. "Carthage: un festival ouvert à tous les cinémas." *L'Afrique Littéraire et Artistique*, n. 34, 1974, pp. 79–93.
"How Mike and Chris Shot an Illegal Film." *Cinema TV Today*, 22 June 1974, p. 11.
Maanouni, Ahmed El. "La Dernière Tombe à Dimbaza." *Cinémarabe*, n. 6, March-April 1977, p. 37.
Mack. "Last Grave at Dimbaza." *Variety*, 26 March 1975, pp. 22, 32.
Millar, Gavin. "Conscience." *The Listener*, vol. 93, n. 2400, 3 April 1975, p. 449.
O'Connor. "Last Grave at Dimbaza Was Filmed Illegally." *The New York Times*, 27 October 1975, p. 52.
O'Meara, Patrick. "Films on South Africa." *Jump Cut*, n. 18, August 1978, pp. 7–8.
Pâquet, André. "Carthage et les cinémas africains: l'avance des cinémas arabes." *Cinéma-Québec*, vol. 4, n. 2, April 1975, pp. 34–39.
Pirie, Dave. "The Real Nightmare." *Time Out*, n. 226, 28 June 1974, p. 30.
———. "David Pirie Reports On: A Truncated Version of Last Grave at Dimbaza (BBC 2, Thursday)." *Time Out*, n. 249, 6 December 1974, p. 26.
———. "Last Grave at Dimbaza." *Time Out*, n. 459, 2 February 1979, p. 45.
"Secretly Made Black Labor Pic in Ottawa; So. Africa Protests." *Variety*, 13 November 1974, p. 39.
Taylor, Clyde. "South Africa: Images of Struggle." *The Black Collegian*, vol. 11, n. 4, February-March 1981, pp. 14–22.

Toubiana, Serge. "Dimbaza." *Cahiers du Cinéma*, n. 262–263, January 1976, p. 125.
Unger, Arthur. "Controversial Look at South Africa." *Christian Science Monitor*, 24 October 1975, p. 26.
Wilson, David. "Phela-Ndaba (End of the Dialogue)." *Monthly Film Bulletin*, vol. 38, n. 446, March 1971, p. 56.

Sarah Maldoror (1929–)
France, Guadeloupe

BIOGRAPHY

Although she is not an African by birth, because of her ethnic origins, her work, and her dedication to the cause of Africa, Sarah Maldoror is commonly given a privileged place in comprehensive analysis of Black African cinema.

When asked to define herself, Maldoror responded as follows:

I feel at home wherever I am. I am from everywhere and from nowhere. My ancestors were slaves. In my case it may sometimes be difficult to define myself. The West Indians blame me for not having lived in the West Indies, the Africans say I was not born in Africa and the French blame me for not being like them. *(Black Art,* vol. 5, n. 2, 1982, p. 31)

Of African descent, Sarah Maldoror (her real name is Sarah Ducados; she chose the name Maldoror after reading *Les Chants de Maldoror* by the nineteenth-century French writer Count de Lautréamont) was born in 1929 in a small town in southern France of a West Indian father (from Guadeloupe) and a French mother. After high school, Maldoror envisioned becoming a stage actress and went to Paris to study drama at the Centre d'Art Dramatique de la Rue Blanche. In subsequent years she interpreted minor roles in various plays, but soon became aware of the limited repertoire available to Black actors on the French stage. In 1956, discontent with playing subservient roles, she and three friends, the Haitian singer Toto Bissainthe, Timité Bassori*, and Ababacar Samb*, decided to create their own troupe, the Compagnie d'Art Dramatique des Griots. Unfortunately, for lack of sustained financial backing, these efforts were short-lived. However, the troupe succeeded in interpreting such plays as *No Exit* by the French writer Jean-Paul Sartre and *La Tragédie du Roi Christophe* by the Martiniquan playwright and poet Aimé Césaire. Says Maldoror: "I first learned acting, and then with The Griots I became involved in stage managing. I believe this experience was most fruitful because one must know about acting and theater rules in order to make films" (Maldoror to author, Washington, D.C., 1 April 1981).

In the late 1950s, Sarah Maldoror abandoned the legitimate stage to become actively involved in the struggle for African liberation. At that time, many African militants were exiled in Paris. Among them was the Angolan writer Mario de Andrade, one of the leaders of the Popular Movement for the Liberation of Angola (MPLA), whose life Maldoror was to share for a number of years. It is with him that she subsequently went to Guinea-Conakry, where she came to realize that in Africa cinema was the most appropriate medium that could be used to raise the political awareness of the masses of people, many of whom were and still are illiterate. At that point Sarah Maldoror set out to become a filmmaker. Awarded a scholarship by the Soviet Union, she went to Moscow to study filmmaking in 1961 and 1962. There, together with Senegalese director Ousmane Sembene*, she studied at the Gorki Studio under Sergei Gerassimov and Mark Donskoy, who introduced her to the techniques and ideology of Soviet cinema. Both Maldoror and Sembene worked as assistants on Donskoy's film *Hello Children* (1962).

In 1963 Sarah Maldoror stayed in Morocco for a short time and then went to reside for some time in Algeria, where she became Gillo Pontecorvo's assistant during the filming of *The Battle of Algiers*. This 1966 film, which illustrates the bloody confrontations between the Algerian freedom fighters and French paratroopers in 1957 and 1958, now stands as a classic of militant cinema. Maldoror also worked for the Algerian filmmaker Ahmed Lallem while he was shooting *Elles*, a documentary on Algerian school girls. It was also in Algeria that she made her first motion picture, *Monangambee*, in 1970. The film's script (written by Sarah Maldoror in collaboration with Serge Michel) is based on a short story by the white Angolan writer and political activist Luandino Vieira, who had been sentenced by the Portuguese colonial regime to serve a fourteen-year term at the camp of Tarrafal in Cape Verde. Maldoror remarks: "I don't mind whether the writer is black or white . . . if I am satisfied with the story. The cinema has no borders. It is the only art which has no boundaries" *(Bulletin,* 10 April 1981, p. 14).

Except for the prison guard, played by the Algerian actor Mahamed Zinet, *Monangambee* is interpreted by nonprofessional actors. It was produced with financial support ($7,000) and technical help from the Algerian government. *Monangambee* was shot in three weeks near Algiers. When released, the film received a prize at the Dinard Film Festival (France), won the International Critics' Prize at the Carthage Film Festival (Tunisia), and was selected to be presented at the third Pan-African Film Festival of Ouagadougou (FESPACO) in 1972.

After *Monangambee,* in 1971, Maldoror went to film *Des Fusils pour Banta* (Guns for Banta) among Amilcar Cabral's freedom fighters in the bush of Guinea-Bissau. Financed by the Algerian government and produced by liberation movements of Angola, Mozambique, and Guinea-Bissau, *Des Fusils pour Banta* was made with a crew of Algerian technicians and a team of underground resistants who play their own role in the film. Maldoror recalls:

For three months we experienced life on a military post (ten wooden compounds hidden in the bush) by following the fighters in all of their movements. Each time an enemy plane spotted the village we were bombed for hours. Everybody sought shelter in trenches. . . . Then we had to leave, move the whole village, take women and children away and build a school and a hospital 30 kms from there . . . they [the freedom fighters] did not consider acting a game. They probably did not understand why it was necessary to shoot ten times the same scene, but they were well aware that the goal of the film was to provide world exposure to their cause. All the action sequences, such as military attacks, were faithfully filmed according to their instructions. I had to bring constant changes to the script. I realized that . . . war had until then been a very abstract concept for me. There I "felt" things: the insecurity, the plight of the wounded who would die for lack of medicine, the children who would eat but once a day. *(Jeune Afrique,* 6 November 1971, pp. 62–63)

Yet, subsequently and for some unclear reasons (Maldoror cites a verbal confrontation she had with a high-ranking Algerian officer), *Des Fusils pour Banta,* intended as a 105–minute film, never went beyond the editing stage.

Maldoror spent the following year in France, where she made three commissioned films, namely *Saint-Denis-sur-Avenir* (The Future of Saint-Denis), *La Commune, Louise Michel et nous* (The Commune, Louise Michel and Us), and *Et les chiens se taisaient* (And the Dogs Fell Silent). Also in 1971, Sarah Maldoror received $45,000 from the French Centre National du Cinéma and a subsidy from the French Ministry of Cooperation, which helped her to finance *Sambizanga,* produced by Isabelle Films; its total cost approached $100,000. The film's screenplay was adapted by Mario de Andrade, Maurice Pons, and Sarah Maldoror from *A Vida Verdadeira de Domingos Xavier* (The True Life of Domingos Xavier), a novel published in 1961 by Luandino Vieira. Maldoror stresses:

I was faithful to the novel. When he [Vieira] had a white engineer who helped the blacks, or a mulatto who was a torturer, I respected the story. Naturally in making a film you have a political option. I make a film according to my political ideas. I made the choice when I picked the novel to film. *(Bulletin,* 10 April 1981, p. 14)

Sambizanga was shot in the People's Republic of Congo by a crew of mostly French technicians (including cameraman Claude Agostini), and interpreted by a cast of performers recruited mainly from PAIGC (African Party for the Independence of Guinea and the Cape Verde Islands) and MPLA militants who, according to their ethnic origin, express themselves in such languages as Portuguese and the African vernaculars Lingala and Lari. Maldoror explains:

We shot the film in seven weeks in the outskirts of Brazzaville. . . . It took ten weeks to edit the film in Paris. The actors are non-professional. The male protagonist is a tractor operator. I found him by chance on a construction site. The heroine, Elisa de Andrade, is an economist. She lives in Algiers and had already played a part in *Monangambee.* *(Ecran 73,* May 1973, p. 71)

Sambizanga received the Grand Prize ("Tanit d'Or") at the Carthage Film Festival in 1972 and the International Catholic Film Office Award at FESPACO in 1973. In the past fifteen years, *Sambizanga* has been shown at a number of film festivals in many countries. In the United States it has been featured at such festivals as the African Woman Series (New York, 1979), the Black Women Film Festival (Washington, D.C., 1980), and the First Baltimore Women's Film and Video Festival (University of Maryland, 1983).

In spite of the recognition she gained from *Sambizanga,* Sarah Maldoror had to wait until 1976 to make a short documentary entitled *La Basilique de Saint-Denis* (The Saint-Denis Basilica). In 1977 she filmed *Un Homme, une terre: Aimé Césaire* (A Man, a Land; Aimé Césaire). This work, focusing on her favorite poet, Aimé Césaire, was produced and broadcast by French television. Next, from 1977 to 1979, Maldoror shot a series of shorts for the French Ministry of Foreign Affairs, among them *Paris, le cimetière du Père Lachaise* (Paris, the Père Lachaise Cemetery), *Un Masque à Paris: Louis Aragon* (A Mask in Paris: Louis Aragon), and *Miro.* Far from looking down upon what some might consider minor undertakings, Maldoror insists that such concise films allow her both to sharpen her skills and earn a living. Also in 1979, she shot two documentaries for the government of Cape Verde: *Fogo, l'île de feu* (Fogo, Island of Fire) and *Un Carnaval dans le Sahel* (A Carnival in the Sahel).

In 1981 Sarah Maldoror made *Un Dessert pour Constance* (A Dessert for Constance), a $160,000 medium-length film, based on Maurice Pons' adaptation of a short story by French writer Daniel Boulanger and co-produced by Antenne 2 (a French television station) and Top Films, a French motion picture company. The cast included several noted African and French actors such as Sidiki Bakaba, Cheik Doukouré, Jean Bouise, and Bernard Haller. Maldoror's latest fiction works are the $500,000 *L'Hôpital de Léningrad* (The Leningrad Hospital, 1982) and the $700,000 *Le Passager du Tassili* (The Tassili Passenger, 1986), both of which were also produced by Antenne 2. *L'Hôpital de Léningrad,* whose aging protagonist is played by veteran stage and screen actor Roger Blin, was drawn from *The Tropic and the North,* a short story written in 1932 by Russian-born author Victor Serge. *Le Passager du Tassili,* whose main role is played by the Algerian actor Lounès Tazaïrt, is based on the novel *Les A.N.I. du Tassili* (The Unidentified Arab Passengers of the Tassili Liner) by Akli Tadjer, a young French writer of Algerian descent. Also in 1986, Maldoror engaged in the making of several short motion pictures produced by FR3, a French television station. One of them, *Portrait de Madame Diop,* focuses on Christiane Diop, who heads Présence Africaine, a publishing company which is primarily concerned with works by writers from Africa and the Black Diaspora.

Sarah Maldoror has several film projects in store. She would like to adapt Césaire's *La Tragédie du Roi Christophe* for a film which would not only focus on past historical events (King Christophe's coming to power in nineteenth-century Haiti), but also incorporate them into a contemporary setting to examine why some African nations are still subjected to various forms of neocolonialism after having obtained their independence almost three decades ago. Maldoror's other plans include a film about Angela Davis and another focusing on Harlem.

Sarah Maldoror enjoys Soviet and Japanese cinema. In addition to Donskoy, Eisenstein, and Kurosawa, she admires such French filmmakers as Alain Resnais, Jean-Luc Godard, Chris Marker, and Agnès Varda. Regarding Black African cinema, her preferences go to Ousmane Sembene, Med Hondo*, Djibril Diop Mambety*, Timité Bassori, and Mustapha Alassane*. Like most of them, she is primarily interested in the sociopolitical and cultural aspects of film. She states:

I make films because I am deeply interested in both cinema and African history. I believe that we, as blacks, have a moral responsibility to present a fair account of African history. If we want to eradicate racism, we will have to study our culture very thoroughly in order to present it to the world. . . . If only Westerners make films about Africa, people will only see Africa through their eyes. . . . When Americans made films about Africa, they made westerns transposed in Africa! These films were remarkably well done, but their African characters were, more often than not, stupid and ignorant. . . . In my films, I mainly strive to present issues of importance to Africa or the Black Diaspora from a Black perspective. This does not mean that only Blacks can make those kinds of films or that I should only be limited to Black themes. Culture is an exchange and a mixing of ideas. Whenever culture is limited it stagnates. I strongly believe that tomorrow's culture will be largely based on images and this is why filmmakers have such an important role to play in their society. *(Black Art,* vol. 5, n. 2, 1982, pp. 31–32)

Maldoror strongly believes that Black African films should be of high technical quality so as to successfully compete on an international scale. Although she does not altogether reject purely didactic works, Maldoror feels that African motion pictures should be devised so as to be universally accessible without, however, losing their unique African components. In this respect, she considers feature films more effective than documentaries. Maldoror emphasizes: "I think one has better chances to interest people by telling them a story" *(Ecran 73,* May 1973, p. 71).

Sarah Maldoror believes that it is still too early to delineate a stylistic orientation within Black African cinema. She explains:

I think people are searching for a film language that would reflect African cultures, but this takes time. Black African cinema is merely 25 years old, which is still very young as compared to others. The French New Wave, for instance, came out of a film tradition; these people had a film library from which to study and they benefitted from a lot of things filmmakers have never had in Africa. (Maldoror to author, Paris, Summer 1985)

She also insists that the growth of Black African cinema depends to a very large extent on the implementation of new cultural policies at the national level that would solve the many problems which are presently impeding the production and distribution of African films.

Except when she makes films in special circumstances (as happened in Guinea-Bissau), Maldoror generally uses a very precise method of work. As a rule she spends a great deal of time finding suitable locations before the actual shooting of the film. A careful planner, she also carries out multiple rehearsals with her actors, but allows for script changes whenever deemed necessary. Unlike most African filmmakers, Sarah Maldoror infrequently participates in scriptwriting. She stresses: "I am not a writer, therefore, I adapt short stories or novels. I need for other people to provide me with stories on which to base my films. I can translate everything into pictures, but please do not ask me to describe a chair in writing" *(Black Art,* vol. 5, n. 2, 1982, p. 32).

Sarah Maldoror appears as a politically committed filmmaker who sides with the oppressed and struggles against all forms of injustice. Maldoror says that she is not actively involved in any women's movement, though she strongly supports those who are. Furthermore, the filmmaker does not feel that her career has been hampered by the fact that she is a woman, but she has at times found it difficult to combine work and family life. The mother of two college-age daughters, Maldoror maintains her residence and works in Paris. She is a frequent speaker at film related symposia. It was on the occasion of such an event, as she was presenting her films at a number of universities and cultural institutions throughout the United States, that Ethiopian director Haile Gerima* (referring to *Sambizanga)* hailed Maldoror as "one of the forerunners of African film" (Howard University, Washington, D.C., 1 April 1981).

MAJOR THEMES

Monangambee (whose title means "porter" and by extension any lower-class Black in Angola), shot in the late 1960s, depicts Portuguese ignorance of Angolan culture and the cruel treatment and imprisonment of people actively opposed to colonialism. The film narrates the story of an African imprisoned for political reasons. His wife is allowed to visit him in jail. As they part, she promises to have a "fato completo" (which denotes a "suit" in Portuguese) sent to him. A guard reports this conversation to prison officials, who proceed to interrogate the prisoner as to why he would need a suit. Has he been told he would soon appear in court? As the prisoner refuses to divulge any further information, he is severely beaten and whipped by his jailers. The last sequence of the motion picture shows the prisoner back in his cell. After having regained his consciousness he tells another inmate: "These fools will never understand anything: for us a 'fato completo' is a local fish dish and not a suit."

Sarah Maldoror's second film, *Des Fusils pour Banta,* depicts the militancy of a woman from Guinea-Bissau who, after having spearheaded armed resistance against Portuguese rule, dies before the struggle of national liberation actually begins.

Maldoror's best-known work, *Sambizanga* (named after a Black working-class suburb of Luanda, Angola's capital), is based on events that took place in 1961, fourteen years prior to Angola's independence. The motion picture starts shortly before Domingos, an Angolan construction worker belonging to an anticolonial underground network, is arrested and jailed by the Portuguese authorities. He will eventually be tortured to death for persistently refusing to disclose the name of other members of his resistance movement. Parallel to Domingos' tragic fate, the film shows the plight and determination of his wife, Maria, who sets out on foot in search of her husband: arriving at the Luanda prison, she is informed of his death. *Sambizanga* ends as Black militants discuss the forthcoming assault on the Luanda prison, the long-hated symbol of Portuguese oppression.

Instead of depicting an open rebellion, *Sambizanga* centers on events that led to consciousness awakening and armed uprising. As such, the film radiates an intimate tone and a meditative lyricism which one is not generally accustomed to seeing in comparable films. Maldoror states:

Some people have blamed me for not having made a film with tanks and guns. But *Sambizanga* is by no means a war film as, for instance, American cinema would regard it. The film intends to describe a real story which occurred in the 1960s at the beginning of anti-colonial resistance in Angola. I show how people try to organize a resistance movement. People have blamed me . . . for selecting actors who, they say, are too beautiful: Well, there are indeed Black people who are beautiful and that's all. . . . In terms of the rhythm of the film, I tried to recreate the slow pace which characterizes African life. Nothing is invented. Everything I show in the film springs from my own perception of such a reality. *(Ecran 73,* May 1973, p. 71)

Maldoror's next feature film, *Un Dessert pour Constance,* intends to illustrate in a somewhat light-hearted manner the friendship and solidarity among African migrant workers in Paris:

Un dessert pour Constance centers around two street sweepers and occasional garbage collectors who memorize the recipes of a French cookbook they found in some trash. They do so in order to win the cash prize of a TV game show, and this prize will entitle one of their [terminally ill] friends to go back to Africa to die in his ancestors' land. . . . Her parable ends with a sad comment reflected in one of the protagonists' final words: "The main thing is never to come to work in loneliness and contempt." *(Black Art,* vol. 5, n. 2, 1982, p. 31)

Uncharacteristically, *L'Hôpital de Leningrad,* shot in Paris in an abandoned match factory, does not focus on a topic related to either Africa or the Black Diaspora. It denounces the arbitrary political arrests and "psychiatric" confinements perpetrated in the Soviet Union under Stalin's government. With *Le Passager du Tassili,* nevertheless, the cinéaste returns to prior concerns and mirrors the sociocultural alienation suffered by young French people of Algerian descent.

Finally, Maldoror's documentaries cover a variety of subject matters. *Et les chiens se taisaient* is a cinematographic rendition of a poem by Césaire amid the African masks of a Parisian museum. *Saint-Denis-sur-Avenir* describes the problems faced by workers in one of Paris' working-class suburbs. *La Commune, Louise Michel et nous* stresses the participation of women in the 1870 Paris uprisings. *La Basilique de Saint-Denis* recounts the history of the medieval abbey. *Un Homme, une terre, Aimé Césaire* presents Césaire in his home environment on the occasion of the official visit of President Leopold Senghor to Martinique. *Paris, le cimetière du Père Lachaise* features various facets of Paris' best known historical graveyard. *Un Masque à Paris: Louis Aragon* is dedicated to one of France's major twentieth-century writers. *Miro* highlights the works of Spain's internationally known abstract painter. *Fogo, l'île de feu* reflects the geographic aridity of one of Cape Verde's volcanic islands, as well as its ethnic and cultural diversity and the industriousness of its people. *Un Carnaval dans le Sahel* touches a number of themes already found in *Fogo, l'île de feu*, but here popular celebration is interspersed with images of a PAIGC political rally.

SURVEY OF CRITICISM

Due to scarce screenings, *Monangambee* has been reviewed by a limited number of film critics. Guy Hennebelle finds it poorly photographed and says it reflects an "unconvincing stylistic practice" *(L'Afrique Littéraire et Artistique,* March 1972, p. 88), but Nadja Kasji (quoted by Sylvia Harvey) favors the work's impressionistic mood. She comments:

Maldoror does not only allow the direct development of the story to unfold; she does not simply describe the game the colonial henchman plays with his victim. She recreates the atmosphere under which the suffering takes place and the estrangement people feel in a colonial society. *(Women and Film,* vol. 1, n. 5–6, 1974, p. 74)

Maldoror's best-known film is unquestionably *Sambizanga*. As can be expected, it has drawn widespread critical attention. Michael Kerbel notes:

Sambizanga, an affecting first feature by Sarah Maldoror . . . is often awkward (as in the cross-cutting between Maria's struggle and Domingos's imprisonment) but Maldoror does have a remarkable talent for expressive closeups. She creates a feeling of intimacy with the characters, and in the scenes within the couple's tiny home and Domingos's prison, a palpable claustrophobia. The bewilderment, and increasing militancy of the people are conveyed through an accumulation of memorable closeup portraits: one remembers especially Domingos's fellow prisoners chanting over his body; the Angolans looking on in confusion and in unexpressed resentment, as Maria screams in agony; the group of revolutionaries reacting to the news of Domingos's death—deeply sorrowful but also exultant in his spiritual triumph and martyrdom . . .

Therein is expressed the film's central revolutionary theme. Progress is no longer possible for individuals: only by collective action can the people succeed. *(Village Voice,* 6 December 1973, p. 85)

In spite of a style which, he says, wavers from lyricism to political didactism, Guy Hennebelle is struck by *Sambizanga*'s smooth editing qualities and overall aesthetic value. He concludes: *"Sambizanga* is made in a rather conventional manner, but it reveals a talented filmmaker whose work is a significant contribution to Black African cinema" *(Ecran 73,* May 1973, p. 70). Alain Labrousse praises Maldoror for having underscored the silent heroism of an unknown militant as well as the workings of an underground network, rather than more overt episodes of Angola's struggle for independence. He also feels that *Sambizanga*'s tone and rhythm are perfectly suited to its theme *(Le Monde Diplomatique,* April 1973, p. 21). Paulin Soumanou Vieyra* is impressed by the film's technical qualities but much less so by its ending (an outdoor ball during which militants honor Domingos's memory), which he considers lengthy and weak *(Le Cinéma africain,* 1975, p. 42). For Linda Gross:

Sambizanga is an excellent and impassioned film about solitude and political solidarity ... Sarah Maldoror ... possesses stunning pictorial techniques and the ability to evoke mood and atmosphere. She imparts a strong sense of community and also conveys the gradual changes that take place in people forced by circumstances to take courageous stands. *(Los Angeles Times,* 23 September 1977, p. 14)

Mosk is pleased with *Sambizanga*'s poignant plot and "technical flair" *(Variety,* 25 April 1973, p. 18), and Clyde Taylor shows appreciation for Maldoror's "fine directorial work" and the "excellent performances" of her nonprofessional actors *(The Black Collegian,* May-June 1979, p. 95). However, for Claude-Michel Cluny, *Sambizanga* lacks political depth for, in his opinion, it is anecdotic, complacent, and disappointing *(Cinéma 73,* n. 178–179, 1973, p. 308). While she favors the film's visual metaphors, Sylvia Harvey also deplores its political superficiality. According to her:

These images of closeness, collective responsibility and sharing, rather than any speeches ... form the semantic substance of the film. Just as the images of the water foaming and crashing on the rocks at the beginning of the film are more than an indication of physical geography, but part of the spiritual geography of resistance and struggle....
    What the film does not show are the levels of colonial oppression; it shows the surface manifestations of brutality but not the causes of that brutality which lie in the economic relationship between Portugal and its colonies. Neither does the film show how the developing consciousness of the woman is translated into political action. What is important, however, is that it shows the beginnings of that change in consciousness. *(Women and Film,* vol. 1, n. 5–6, 1974, p. 71)

More recently, Mario Relich underlined the timelessness of Maldoror's feature by saying:

Originally intended to publicize the anti-colonial struggle in Angola, *Sambizanga* has lost none of its impact, though originally released ten years ago. Its aesthetic qualities, however, are now more sharply evident, so that Maldoror's political views and her vision of life merge indissolubly.... Maldoror's film is permeated with a strong sense of life quite opposed to anything doctrinaire. *(West Africa,* 21 June 1982, p. 1850)

Un Dessert pour Constance, whose style and tone are drastically different from those found in Maldoror's previous works, generated mixed reviews on the part of film critics. In an article entitled ''Maldoror Turns Her Coat,'' Maryse Condé questions the satirical nature of the film and its overall impact which, she implies, might very well reinforce certain preexisting racial biases regarding Blacks *(Afrique,* May 1981, p. 47). Hélène also finds *Un Dessert pour Constance* disappointing and calls it a ''secular Christmas tale'' whose African protagonists are reminiscent of Harriet Beecher Stowe's Uncle Tom *(Libération,* 12 February 1981, p. 21). Philippe Nourry finds Maldoror's work uneven both in style and content *(Le Figaro,* 16 February 1981, p. 26). For Catherine Humblot, *Un Dessert pour Constance* is ''a light-hearted comedy which depicts, between two peals of laughter, the somewhat incredible tribulations of two migrant workers in Paris,'' as well as a ''burlesque and poetic tale'' which makes some pertinent and even fierce comments concerning race relations within French society. Yet the critic is also disturbed by the film's ambiguous humor *(Le Monde,* 8 February 1981, p. 9).

Yet, other film reviewers, like Christian Bosséno *(Cinémaction,* Supplement to *Tumulte,* n. 7, 1982, p. 69), approve of Maldoror's use of comedy in treating serious subject matter. Similarly, Jérôme Garcin considers *Un Dessert pour Constance* ''a little masterpiece of humor and poetry'' *(Les Nouvelles Littéraires,* 12 February 1981, p. 41), and Jean Barenat mentions that its comic plot should not be viewed as a farce because it releases ''a very healthy draft of fresh air'' which underlines ''the shameful and malign facets of our society.'' He also favors the performance of its two main African actors *(L'Humanité,* 13 February 1981, p. 2). Anne Calvet writes:

This film . . . is not a thesis on the working conditions of migrant laborers. With inimitable good fortune and gracefulness, Sarah Maldoror has managed to avoid this pitfall as well as ponderous rhetoric and moralizing laments. Her weapons are the humor, derision, freshness and spontaneity with which she handles caricature, and these owe more to African storytelling than socioeconomic discourses. *(Humanité Dimanche,* 8 February 1981, radio/television insert)

No critical evaluations are available on Maldoror's documentaries. At the time of this writing, only scarce reviews of *Le Passage du Tasili* (reflecting mixed reaction) are available, precluding assessment of the critical evaluation of this work.

FILMOGRAPHY

Monangambee, 35 mm, black and white, 20 min., 1970.
Des Fusils pour Banta (Guns for Banta), 35 mm, black and white, 105 min., 1971.
Saint-Denis-sur-Avenir (The Future of Saint Denis), color, 13 min., 1971.
La Commune, Louise Michel et nous (The Commune, Louise Michel and Us), color, 13 min., 1971.

Et les chiens se taisaient (And the Dogs Fell Silent), color, 13 min., 1971.
Sambizanga, 16/35 mm, color, 102 min., 1972.
La Basilique de Saint-Denis (The Saint-Denis Basilica), 16 mm, color, 5 min., 1976.
Un Homme, une terre: Aimé Césaire (A Man, a Land: Aimé Césaire), 16 mm, color, 51 min., 1977.
Paris, le cimetière du Père Lachaise (Paris, the Père Lachaise Cemetery), 16 mm, color, 5 min., 1977.
Un Masque à Paris: Louis Aragon (A Mask in Paris: Louis Aragon), 16 mm, color, 13 min., 1978.
Miro, 16 mm, color, 5 min., 1979.
Fogo, l'île de feu (Fogo, Island of Fire), 16 mm, color, 13 min., 1979.
Un Carnaval dans le Sahel (A Carnival in the Sahel), 16 mm, color, 13 min., 1979.
Un Dessert pour Constance (A Dessert for Constance), 16 mm, color, 51 min., 1980.
L'Hôpital de Leningrad (The Leningrad Hospital), 16 mm, color, 51 min., 1982.
Le Passager du Tassili (The Tassili Passenger), 16 mm, color, 90 min., 1986.
Portrait de Madame Diop (Portrait of Mrs. Diop), 16 mm, color, 10 min., 1986.

BIBLIOGRAPHY

Interviews of Sarah Maldoror

Condé, Maryse. "Entretien avec Sarah Maldoror." *Recherche, Pédagogie et Culture,* February-March 1981, pp. 56–58.
Harvey, Sylvia. "Third World Perspectives: Focus on Sarah Maldoror." *Women and Film,* vol. 1, n. 5–6, 1974, pp. 71–75, 110.
Hennebelle, Guy. "Sarah Maldoror, cinéaste guadeloupéenne auteur de Monangambee nous déclare." *Jeune Afrique,* n. 469, 24 December 1969, p. 45.
———. "Pour ou contre un cinéma engagé?" *L'Afrique Littéraire et Artistique,* n. 19, October 1971, pp. 87–93.
———. "Entretien avec Sarah Maldoror." *Ecran 73,* n. 15, May 1973, pp. 70–71.
———. "Maldoror Sarah." *L'Afrique Littéraire et Artistique,* n. 49, 3rd Quarter 1978, pp. 88–91.
Hennebelle, Monique. "Sambizanga: un film de Sarah Maldoror sur les débuts de la guerre de libération en Angola." *L'Afrique Littéraire et Artistique,* n. 28, April 1973, pp. 78–87.
Maillet, Dominique. "Sarah Maldoror." *Cinématographe,* n. 3, Summer 1973, pp. 41–42.

Film Reviews and Studies of Sarah Maldoror

Aubert, Alain. "Ouagadougou." *Ecran 79,* n. 82, 15 July 1979, pp. 15–16.
B, C. "Avant-première, Un dessert pour Constance." *La Croix,* 12 February 1981, p. 18.
Barenat, Jean. "Une Histoire d'Africains." *L'Humanité,* 13 February 1981, p. 2.
Bosséno, Christian. "Sur deux films récents: Ali au pays des Mirages et un dessert pour Constance." *Cinémaction,* Supplement to *Tumulte,* n. 7, 1982, pp. 68–69.
Calvet, Anne. "Un Dessert pour Constance." *Humanité Dimanche,* 8 February 1981, radio/television insert.

Cluny, Claude-Michel. "Sambizanga." *Cinéma 73*, n. 178–179, 1973, p. 308.

Condé, Maryse. "Maldoror change de veste." *Afrique*, n. 47, May 1981, p. 47.

Ferrari, Alain. "Le Second Souffle du cinéma africain." *Téléciné*, n. 176, January 1973, pp. 2–9.

Garcin, Jérôme. "Réalisateurs, les nouvelles de Daniel Boulanger vous tendent leurs pages!" *Les Nouvelles Littéraires*, 12 February 1981, p. 41.

Gross, Linda. "Africa's Xala and Sambizanga." *Los Angeles Times*, 23 September 1977, pp. 14, 15.

Hélène. "Le Dessert des Wolofs." *Libération*, 12 February 1981, p. 21.

Hennebelle, Guy. "Le Cinéma et les guerillas africaines." *L'Afrique Littéraire et Artistique*, n. 20, 1972, pp. 267–78.

———. "Le Troisième Festival panafricain de cinéma de Ouagadougou." *L'Afrique Littéraire et Artistique*, n. 22, March 1972, pp. 88–95.

———. "Sambizanga." *Ecran 73*, n. 15, May 1973, pp. 70–71.

———. *Guide des films anti-impérialistes*. Paris: Editions du Centenaire, 1975.

Humblot, Catherine. "Tableau de la France raciste." *Le Monde*, 8 February 1981, p. 9.

Jacques, Paula. "Guinée-Bissau: le mythe et la réalité." *Jeune Afrique*, n. 565, 6 November 1971, pp. 62–63.

Kerbel, Michael. "Angola: Brutality and Betrayal." *Village Voice*, 6 December 1973, p. 85.

Knorr, Wolfram. "Sambizanga." *Jugend Film Fernsehen*, n. 3, 1973, pp. 155–56.

Labrousse, Alain. "Sambizanga ou la naissance d'une révolution." *Le Monde Diplomatique*, April 1973, p. 21.

Maillet, Dominique. "Sambizanga." *Cinématographe*, n. 3, Summer 1973, p. 42.

Martin, Angela. *African Films: The Context of Production*. London: British Film Institute, 1982.

Moran, Marty. "Sambizanga: Powerful Story of the Angolan Revolution." *Bulletin*, 10 April 1981, p. 14.

Mosk. "Sambizanga." *Variety*, 25 April 1973, p. 18.

Navas, Christiane. "Le Passage du Tasili." *Télérama*, 1 August 1987, p. 67.

Nourry, Philippe. "Pousse-au-crime et pause-café." *Le Figaro*, 16 February 1981, p. 26.

Pearson, Lyle. "Four Years of African Film." *Film Quarterly*, vol. 26, n. 3, Spring 1973, pp. 42–47.

Pfaff, Françoise. "Sarah Maldoror." *Black Art*, vol. 5, n. 2, 1982, pp. 25–32.

Relich, Mario. "Africa's Women Film Makers." *West Africa*, 21 June 1982, p. 1850.

Schmidt, Nancy J. "African Literature on Film." *Research in African Literatures*, vol. 13, n. 4, Winter 1982, pp. 518–28.

Schoenberner, Gerhard. "Det svarta Afrikas filmer och deras regissörer." *Chaplin 166*, n. 1, 1980, pp. 10–15.

Taylor, Clyde. "Shooting the Black Woman." *The Black Collegian*, May-June 1979, pp. 94–96.

Vieyra, Paulin Soumanou. *Le Cinéma africain*. Paris: Présence Africaine, 1975.

Djibril Diop Mambety (1945–)
Senegal

BIOGRAPHY

Of Wolof origin and Muslim extraction, Djibril Diop Mambety was born in 1945 in Dakar, the capital city of Senegal. Since he has granted only a few interviews, little is known about his early childhood and adolescence except that, as a schoolboy, he liked to attend shows at local movie theaters and would playfully re-create the films at his parents' house. Reflecting on this aspect of his childhood, Mambety says: "I used to gather at home a few friends for whom I would stage shadow-shows. . . . Everyone would bring something, a lump of sugar or other things. It was a very successful enterprise which many young Africans have experienced" (*L'Afrique Littéraire et Artistique,* 3rd Quarter 1978, p. 42).

After high school, Mambety studied drama in his native city, where he then worked as a stage actor. He also interpreted parts in motion pictures including *Pour ceux qui savent* (For Those Who Know, 1970), by his compatriot Tidiane Aw. He remembers:

I acted for three years at the National Daniel Sorano Theater in Dakar. I had the opportunity to play important roles and even to work as stage director. . . . I could have continued my career in the area of theater but, in 1969, I was forced to make a move by being dismissed for indiscipline from the Sorano theater. I took this as a challenge and within three months I gathered enough money to shoot a small color film entitled *Contras' City.* (*L'Afrique Littéraire et Artistique,* 3rd Quarter 1978, pp. 42–43)

With a meager budget of under $10,000 provided by Senegalese investors, Mambety shot *Contras' City* in six days while he was secretary of the Dakar ciné-club. Although he had not had any formal training in filmmaking, the director believes that he met no major hardship while making his first motion picture. The film was featured at the First Pan-African Festival held in Algiers (1969) where, in an ensuing debate, some viewers accused Mambety of lacking political depth (*Positif,* February 1970, p. 89). After making *Contras' City,*

Mambety was invited to participate in a filmmakers' roundtable at a retrospective of African films held at the Mannheim Film Festival (Germany) from 6 to 11 October 1969.

With *Badou Boy,* released in 1970, Djibril Diop Mambety further established his talent as a filmmaker. It should be mentioned that the cinéaste had previously shot a black and white version of *Badou Boy* in 1966. Yet, dissatisfied with the technical shortcomings of this version, he decided to produce a color motion picture based on the same theme with the same nonprofessional actors he had used earlier. In its new format, *Badou Boy* won the second prize (''Tanit d'Argent'') at the 1970 Carthage Film Festival, but to date the film has received more critical recognition than popular acclaim. Mambety observes:

The film was not overly successful because the film language and style which I selected were not popular. One has to choose between engaging in stylistic research or the mere recording of facts. I feel that a filmmaker must go beyond recording facts. Moreover, I believe that we [Africans], in particular, must reinvent cinema. It will be a difficult task because our viewing audience is used to a specific film language, but a choice has to be made: either one is very popular and one talks to people in a simple and plain manner, or else one searches for an African film language that would exclude chattering and focus more on how to make use of visuals and sounds. (*L'Afrique Littéraire et Artistique,* 3rd Quarter 1978, p. 43)

In 1973, with financial support from the Senegalese government, Mambety produced his first feature length film, *Touki-Bouki* (The Hyena's Journey), shot by the Senegalese cameraman Pap Samba Sow. Based on Mambety's script, the film was made with a $30,000 budget and a team of nonprofessional actors, and was edited in both Rome and Paris. In *Touki-Bouki,* Djibril Diop Mambety further developed the original film style of his prior works. That same year, this motion picture won the Special Jury's Award at the Moscow Film Festival and was selected to be a part of the Filmmakers' Fortnight at the Cannes Film Festival (France). In subsequent years, the work was shown in Senegal and featured at a number of film events, among them the Senegalese film series organized by the New York Museum of Modern Art in 1978. In 1984 *Touki-Bouki* was presented during a special screening at the Carthage Film Festival. The following year, it was shown at the Racines Noires (Black Roots) festival held in Paris. In 1986 the film was finally ''discovered'' by distributors, who gave it its first commercial run in France thirteen years after its initial release.

Unlike many African filmmakers, Djibril Diop Mambety is not a proponent of didactic films made in an essentially serious mode. In the same way that he advocates artistic diversity, he also believes in artistic freedom. And, although his works are not devoid of social criticism, Mambety refuses to use the film medium as a tool that would reflect its author's overt political orientation. He explains: ''I think that we, as African filmmakers, must not all embark on the same track. . . . By nature I do not like to make revolutionary statements'' (*L'Afrique Littéraire et Artistique,* n. 8, 1969, p. 67).

A meticulous film practitioner, Djibril Diop Mambety also vigorously promotes high standards of technical sophistication:

Each time a foreign critic stresses a construction flaw or a shortcoming in an African film, the filmmaker rides his high horse and proclaims it is a stylistic component related to his African personality. . . . I want to be judged through my works without people taking into account the fact that I am either Black or African. I want to be judged like any other filmmaker. If I have, as I am convinced I do, a Black or an African temperament, such a temperament should transpire through my works and not solely through my statements. *(L'Afrique Littéraire et Artistique,* n. 8, 1969, p. 68)

Commuting between Senegal and Europe, Mambety has led a somewhat dilettantish and bohemian life in France, Germany, and Italy during the past fifteen years. He is now said to be at work on a film project entitled *Hyènes* (Hyenas) based on a play by Friedrich Durrenmatt—a trilogy on power and insanity. The first part of this film should be shot in June 1987 *(Black,* n. 28, 15 March 1986, p. 7). This motion picture will, it is hoped, confirm the talent and creativeness he has expressed in his prior works.

Unfortunately, Mambety has not yet received the recognition he deserves. If this situation can undoubtedly be linked to his long estrangement from filmmaking, it is also due to the fact that the films he made at an early stage in his professional career did not follow the aesthetic and narrative patterns customarily found in Black African cinema at the time. Not only can one expect that his personal style will be fully understood and appreciated in the future, but many already concur that his works—especially *Touki-Bouki*— will stand the trial of time and be counted among the classics of Sub-Saharan African film.

MAJOR THEMES

Characteristically, the films of Djibril Diop Mambety are satirical and iconoclastic. They all illustrate, in various degrees, the clashes that exist between African traditions and new values inherited from the West.

As suggested by its title, *Contras' City* depicts the sociocultural dichotomies of Dakar. They are portrayed through George Brachet's carefully composed shots and an elaborate soundtrack, which includes infrequent but derisive statements (at one point Diop even imitates President Senghor's voice) over a symbolic montage of French classical music and tunes from the indigenous kora (a West African string instrument). In so doing, the film presents viewers with a succession of vivid impressionistic sequences: the presidential palace (former residence of the French governor), imposing high-rises, overcrowded slums, picturesque outdoor barbers, tailors, and street vendors, interesting close-ups of women standing in line at public water fountains, Muslim devotees filling streets during Friday's midday prayer, African and European Catholics gathering outside the cathedral after Sunday's Mass, crippled beggars asking for alms, traders and customers bargaining at the marketplace, and swarms of travellers mingling at Dakar's train station, whose building is also reminiscent of colonial times. In sum, *Contras' City* offers an ironic look at Dakar's colonial architectural legacy and the multifaceted aspects of its bustling cosmopolitan life.

Djibril Diop Mambety pursues his sarcastic portrayal of Senegal's capital city through *Badou Boy,* about which the filmmaker says: *"Badou Boy* reflects a part of my youth, but many Senegalese and Africans can identify with it. Badou Boy is a slightly amoral street urchin who resembles me a lot" *(L'Afrique Littéraire et Artistique,* 3rd Quarter 1978, p. 43).

In a sensitive, humorous, and surrealistic fashion, *Badou Boy* underscores the conflict that may exist between individuals and the repressive forces of society. It does so through the vagrancies of a cunning urban youth who uses his wits to escape from a stupid, bow-legged, and overweight policeman.

"Touki-Bouki was conceived at the time of a very violent crisis in my life. I wanted to make a lot of things explode," says Mambety while discussing his major work *(Adhoua,* January-March 1981, p. 3). The film is, in both content and form, an autobiographical statement intended to disrupt the rules of conventional narrative African cinema and denounce the sociocultural alienation suffered by young Africans.

Touki-Bouki, which means "the hyena's journey" in Wolof (a language spoken by most of Senegal's population), draws its title from the West African oral tradition, which includes a number of tales involving the hyena, an animal accused of greed and mischievousness. This scavenger with an unpleasant odor and repulsive physical characteristics also symbolizes trickery and social marginality, and it is accordingly that the animal is used by Mambety in his story, which again opposes nonconventional individuals to the established mores and laws of society.

Touki-Bouki portrays the wanderings of Mory, a former shepherd who now lives in Dakar. There he meets Anta, a young university student, with whom he soon shares his dream of going to France. Consequently, both join wits in devising a series of unlawful schemes intended to secure the financial means to undertake this journey. One of these schemes consists of robbing the gate-money at a wrestling contest, only to discover that the stolen coffer contains only a skull and an amulet—possibly a contestant's fetish. Subsequently, Mory decides to pay a call on Charlie, a well-off and corpulent homosexual who had formerly propositioned him. As expected, Charlie is delighted by Mory's visit and invites him into his house; here the song "Plaisir d'amour," interpreted by the French singer Mado Robin, leaves no doubt as to the true nature of Charlie's intentions. Next, while Charlie is taking a seemingly endless shower, Mory proceeds to steal Charlie's costly wardrobe. In the meantime, Anta, who mingles with people outside of Charlie's house, robs a wallet from one of Charlie's guests. The two meet as Mory hurriedly exits from the house. Mory and Anta manage to flee and succeed in purchasing two boat tickets with a stolen check. At the last minute, however, Mory decides to stay ashore, and Anta goes off, the only one to fulfill their common dream.

Touki-Bouki contains a number of interesting thematic juxtapositions and metaphors which cannot be adequately rendered in a linear summary. Here, "the hyena's journey" can be interpreted as both physical and psychological. Mory travels from a quiet pastoral life with its cattle, slow pace, and open spaces to an urban setting with its speed, violence, and the roaring of its engine-powered vehicles—at the film's beginning, the gentle and idyllic tune of a shepherd's flute is briskly covered by the loud hum of Mory's motorcycle. Although he now lives in the city, Mory rides his motorcycle (the handlebars of which are adorned with a zebu's skull and horns) through both traditional and modern areas of Dakar: animated streets, the marketplace, the university, the Fass arenas where traditional Senegalese wrestling takes place, modern villas, low-class neighborhoods, and the harbor. But the real purpose of Mory's odyssey is to go to France, beyond the sea, his ultimate boundary. Mory's vagrancies also parallel his psychological journey, which is aptly reflected on the screen through the young man's memory of a serene, rural past (shown as a Paradise Lost) and dream (that of going to France, viewed as a Land of Enchantment). Thus, his voyage within time and space is both an escape from a rather hostile urban environment and a frantic pursuit of the means to fulfill a dream.

Djibril Diop Mambety's motion picture also contains obsessive and anguishing illustrations of the theme of death. The film opens and closes with haunting images and sounds of a slaughterhouse for cattle, repeatedly presents the butchering of a sheep, and shows at various intervals the nightmarish scene of a vociferous and threatening woman brandishing a knife, somewhat calling to mind the castrating female of *La Femme au couteau* (The Woman with a Knife, 1968) by the Ivorian director Timité Bassori*. Yet, intermingled with the theme of death is that of life and love. At one point, for example, Anta undresses on the beach, but the scene is unexpectedly interrupted as she prepares to lie down. This scene is followed by images of a sheep, perhaps symbolically sacrificial, being slaughtered, and a full shot of foaming waves. A subsequent close-up of Anta's fingers clenching a dogon cross—a symbol of fertility—on the rear of Mory's motorbike, accompanied by off-screen orgasmic sounds, finally reveals that Anta has actually lain with Mory and that the viewer has actually witnessed a love scene.

The topic of social alienation is omnipresent throughout Mory's frantic obstacle race, which is at times strikingly accented by excerpts from "Paris, Paris," a song by Josephine Baker, a Black American entertainer who spent most of her life exiled in France. Social alienation is also at the core of the two protagonists' marginal activities as they engage in a succession of larcenies. In addition, it is expressed through Anta's androgynous look (she has very short hair, her budding breasts are covered with an ample man's shirt, and she usually wears pants), which is in sharp contrast with standard Senegalese female attire. A forceful scene shows class divisions amid urban youth as Mory is tied up to a jeep by Anta's schoolmates in her absence. Else, a strange Tarzan-like character, appears sporadically in *Touki-Bouki* and embodies another type of alienation, that of a Westerner who has lost touch with the evolving world and proves unable to make proper use of its modern technology: the ape-man steals Mory's motorcycle, but his joy ride tragically ends in an accident.

Although it does not follow the clear linear progression of African storytelling, *Touki-Bouki* includes thematic elements commonly found in African tales. Mory is the trickster type frequently described in the oral tradition, which portrays as well a number of protagonists leaving their village to venture in an unknown land. Like a folk hero, Mory has to overcome obstacles and triumph over adversity. In so doing, he performs a rite of passage from tradition to modernity, and from adolescence to adulthood. His odyssey is an initiatory rite resulting in new knowledge. As he reaches the liner's desk, visions of cattle tied and ready to be slaughtered cross his mind. Soon the bellowing of cattle becomes the sound of the boat's deafening siren. Equating his departure with a form of death, Mory briskly leaves the boat and chooses to remain ashore. Here *Touki-Bouki* grows into both a morality and a dilemma tale. The moral of Mory's story suggests that exile is but another form of alienation. Although the film ends with a freeze frame of young Mory riding a zebu (an identical shot was presented during the film's opening sequence), implying that the protagonist might go back to his rural roots, nothing definite is said concerning his future. Mory's destiny is left to the viewer's imagination, and as such Mambety's plot calls to mind the open-endedness of African dilemma tales. As in African oral stories, and despite the director's opposition to outward message films, *Touki-Bouki* espouses a didactic function: Mory's quest for a dream is indeed a self-searching journey.

The dynamic pulse of *Touki-Bouki* relies on a constant movement between opposite poles (e.g., realistic scenes versus oneiric and/or surrealistic sequences), its elaborate editing (fragmented time, visual leitmotivs, parodic and allegorical juxtapositions), and its creative use of sound as an added storytelling device. *Touki-Bouki* requires the viewers' ceaseless participation in the reconstruction of a deconstructed reality, a device also found in Western literature and cinema (e.g., Jean-Luc Godard's films). And its apparent hermetism may startle and/or confuse filmgoers, especially non-African viewers unaware of the specific sociocultural codes and visual metaphors that lie at the heart of Mambety's work.

SURVEY OF CRITICISM

It is interesting to observe that Djibril Diop Mambety's first film, *Contras' City* already reveals his highly personal film style. Guy Hennebelle is struck by the film's use of "biting irony" in its criticism of Senegalese society (*L'Afrique Littéraire et Artistique,* 1st Quarter 1972, p. 210), and Catherine Ruelle hails it as one of the first comic films of African cinema (*L'Afrique Littéraire et Artistique,* 3rd Quarter 1978, p. 42). Paulin Soumanou Vieyra* calls the work ''a critical essay on Dakar's life,'' and is pleased with its nonchalant tone and innovative stylistic characteristics *(Le Cinéma africain,* 1975, p. 182). Jacques Binet notes *Contras' City's* intellectual irony, skillful construction, and plastic beauty *(Afrique Contemporaine,* January-February 1976, p. 30). Louis Marcorelles thinks that the director uses cinema as some sort of "magic toy," but deplores the fact that the film's irreverence is somewhat weakened by its excessive picturesqueness *(Le Monde,* 20 August 1969, p. 10). Beatrice Rolland concurs with Marcorelles' view and regrets *Contras' City's* political superficiality *(Positif,* February 1970, p. 89).

Badou Boy was generally well received by film critics. Hannes Kamphausen terms it "a brilliant slapstick film" *(Cineaste,* Summer 1972, p. 35), Alain Ferrari praises its innovative vivaciousness *(Téléciné,* January 1973, p. 3), and Jacques Binet favors its incisive humor and nonlinear film style *(Afrique Contemporaine,* January-February 1976, p. 30). Guy Hennebelle finds *Badou Boy* appealing, but stresses its uneven comic traits *(L'Afrique Littéraire et Artistique,* 1st Quarter 1972, p. 210). For Paulin Soumanou Vieyra, the motion picture provides a sensitive, lyrical, and acutely critical look at Senegalese society *(Le Cinéma au Sénégal,* 1983, p. 74).

As is to be expected, *Touki-Bouki* has generated a fair amount of film reviews. Because of its creativeness, it is to date the only Black African film to which a book-length frame by frame analysis has been devoted (André Gardies' *Description et analyse filmique: Touki-Bouki,* published in Abidjan in 1982). Also impressed by its new film language, Abdou Aziz Sy calls it "a masterpiece" *(Unir Cinéma,* January-February 1985, p. 27), and so does Louis Skorecki *(Libération,* 19 March 1986, p. 32), while Paulin Soumanou Vieyra considers the work an overwhelming event in the history of Senegalese filmmaking *(Le Cinéma au Sénégal,* 1983, p. 82). For Ferid Boughedir, *Touki-Bouki* exemplifies the "intellectualistic trend" of African cinema in which "the director aims at expressing his personal universe through avant-garde stylistic research" *(Filméchange,* Fall 1978, p. 77). Moreover, Boughedir includes the work in a listing of thirteen films which he judges landmarks of African cinema *(Jeune Afrique,* 25 December 1985, p. 89). Jean-René Debrix sees it as "an impressive marqueterie full of original finds" in spite of its "affected film style" *(Afrique Contemporaine,* September-October 1975, p. 3). For Catherine Ruelle, *Touki-Bouki* is an impetuous, inventive, and irreverent "surrealistic poem" *(L'Afrique Littéraire et Artistique,* 3rd Quarter 1978, p. 42). Albert Cervoni views it as a vivid and colorful surrealistic chronicle of Senegalese life *(Cinéma 73,* June 1973, p. 39). Rolf Luapa praises the film's "freshness, poetry, musicality" *(Afrique-Asie,* 19 May 1986, p. 78). Jacques Binet terms it an unwonted "initiatory journey" *(Cinémaction,* 1982, p. 36). Xavier Villetard *(Libération,* 5 November 1984, p. 33) draws a comparison between *Touki-Bouki* and Jean-Luc Godard's *Pierrot-le-Fou* (1965), and Pierre Haffner points out:

Touki-Bouki is . . . a film about youth, dreams, love, alienation, justice and fears. . . . It is an extremely complex motion picture which to this day probably stands as the most fascinating work of Black African cinema. . . . disconcerting . . . provocative, even insolent and blasphemous yet compassionate and generous, *Touki-Bouki* appears as the most profound incursion into the psyche of a Senegalese youth traumatized by colonization and urban aggressions. *(Cinémaction-Tricontinental,* Special Issue, 1982, p. 158)

And, indeed, the fact that *Touki-Bouki* was even better received by film critics when shown at the 1984 Carthage Film Festival, eleven years after its first release *(Libération,* 5 November 1984, p. 33), is additional proof of its classic quality and timeless visual beauty.

FILMOGRAPHY

Contras' City (A City of Contrasts), 16 mm, color, 16 min., 1969.
Badou Boy, 16 mm, color, 60 min., 1970.
Touki-Bouki (The Hyena's Journey), 35 mm, color, 90 min., 1973.

BIBLIOGRAPHY

Interviews of Djibril Diop Mambety

Hennebelle, Guy. "Côte d'Ivoire, Sénégal, Guinée: six cinéastes africains parlent. . . .
     " *L'Afrique Littéraire et Artistique,* n. 8, 1969, pp. 58–70.
Ruelle, Catherine. "Diop-Mambety Djibril." *L'Afrique Littéraire et Artistique,* n. 49,
     3rd Quarter 1978, pp. 42–44.

Film Reviews and Studies of Djibril Diop Mambety

Ayari, Farida. "Le Jeune Cinéma sénégalais: la parole à l'image." *Adhoua,* n. 3, January-
     March 1981, pp. 3–6.
———. "Carthage: la morosité." *Afrique-Asie,* n. 335, 19 November 1984, pp. 138–
     40.
Bachy, Victor. "Panoramique sur les cinémas sud-sahariens." *Cinémaction,* n. 26, 1983,
     pp. 23–43.
Bassan, Raphael. "Comment filmer l'Afrique?" *Afrique-Asie,* n. 320, 24 April 1984,
     pp. 50–52.
Beye, Ben Diogaye. "Après le festival de Royan, une réelle dialectique dans le dialogue
     des cultures." *Cinéma 77,* n. 221, May 1977, pp. 64–68.
Binet, Jacques. "Cinéma africain." *Afrique Contemporaine,* n. 83, January-February
     1976, pp. 27–30.
———. "Migrations d'Afrique Noire." *Cinémaction,* Supplement to *Tumulte,* n. 7,
     1982, pp. 35–38.
———. "Langage des cinéastes africains." *Cinémaction,* n. 26, 1983, pp. 84–89.
Boughedir, Ferid. "Le Cinéma africain a quinze ans." *Filméchange,* n. 4, Fall 1978,
     pp. 75–80.
———. "Les Grandes Dates du cinéma africain." *Jeune Afrique,* n. 1303–1304, 25
     December 1985, p. 89.
Cervoni, Albert. "Touki-Bouki." *Cinéma 73,* n. 177, June 1973, p. 39.

Debrix, Jean-René. "Situation du cinéma en Afrique francophone." *Afrique Contemporaine*, n. 81, September-October 1975, pp. 2–7.

Faye, Paloma. "Touki-Bouki: le talent de Djibril Diop Mambety." *Black*, n. 28, 15 March 1986, p. 7.

Ferrari, Alain. "Le Second Souffle du cinéma africain." *Téléciné*, n. 176, January 1973, p. 3.

Gardies, André. *Description et analyse filmique: Touki-Bouki*. Abidjan: Université Nationale de Côte d'Ivoire, Centre d'Enseignement et de Recherche Audio-Visuels, 1982.

Haffner, Pierre. "Sénégal." *Cinémaction-Tricontinental*, Special Issue, 1982, pp. 157–60.

Hennebelle, Guy. "Vers un tiers cinéma africain?" *Jeune Afrique*, n. 452, 2 September 1969, p. 40.

———. "Djibril Diop-Mambety." *L'Afrique Littéraire et Artistique*, n. 20, 1st Quarter 1972, p. 210.

———. "Carthage." *Cinéma 71*, n. 154, March 1971, p. 35.

Kamphausen, Hannes. "Cinema in Africa: A Survey." *Cineaste*, vol. 5, n. 3, Summer 1972, pp. 29–38.

Luapa, Rolf. "Touki Bouki, treize ans après." *Afrique-Asie*, n. 374, 19 May 1986, p. 78.

Marcorelles, Louis. "L'Afrique noire au rendez-vous d'Alger." *Le Monde*, 20 August 1969, p. 10.

Pokam, Pierre Nguewa. "L'Evocation du sacré." *Cinémaction*, n. 26, 1983, pp. 113–17.

Rolland, Béatrice. "Alger, juillet 1969—ler festival panafricain." *Positif*, n. 113, February 1970, pp. 87–95.

Skorecki, Louis. "L'histoire rouge et noire de Touki Bouki." *Libération*, 19 March 1986, p. 32.

Sy, Abdou Aziz. "Lecture de film: Touki-Bouki." *Unir Cinéma*, n. 16 (123), January-February 1985, pp. 27–29.

———. "Lecture de film: Touki-Bouki." *Unir Cinéma*, n. 17 (124), March-April 1985, pp. 25–26.

———. "Lecture de film: Touki-Bouki." *Unir Cinéma*, n. 18 (125), May-June 1985, pp. 14–15.

"Touki Bouki offert aux enfants d'Afrique. "*Afrique-Asie*, n. 397, 6 April 1987, p. 57.

Toureh, Fanta. "Nature et décors." *Cinémaction*, n. 26, 1983, pp. 131–35.

Vieyra, Paulin Soumanou. *Le Cinéma africain*. Paris: Présence Africaine, 1975.

———. *Le Cinéma au Sénégal*. Brussels: OCIC/L'Harmattan, 1983.

Villetard, Xavier. "Touki-Bouki: aimé mais pas distribué." *Libération*, 5 November 1984, p. 33.

———. "Djibril Diop Mambety n'a pas vieilli." *Libération*, 19 March 1986, p. 32.

Ababacar Samb (1934–   )
Senegal

BIOGRAPHY

According to film critic Farida Ayari *(Adhoua,* January-March 1981, p. 3), Ababacar Samb-Makharam, commonly called Ababacar Samb, belongs to the second generation of Senegalese filmmakers. A Muslim of Lebou origin, Samb was born in Dakar on 21 October 1934 into a family of fishermen and farmers. He went to primary school in his native city and, after obtaining the Certificat d'Etudes Primaires and working at odd jobs, by 1953 managed to gather enough funds to go to Paris, where he enrolled at a vocational school and took up electrical engineering (1954–1955). In 1956 he received a French government scholarship, which enabled him to register at the Centre d'Art Dramatique de la rue Blanche, where he studied drama at the same time as Timité Bassori* and Sarah Maldoror*, who were later to engage in new careers as filmmakers. With Bassori, Maldoror, and the Haitian singer Toto Bissainthe, Samb was a member of the Compagnie d'Art Dramatique des Griots, a Black theater group which staged primarily plays by African and West Indian playwrights as well as contemporary French authors. During this period, he acted in several productions, including Abdou Anta Ka's *La Fille des dieux* (The Gods' Daughter), Jean-Paul Sartre's *No Exit,* and Louis Sapin's *Papa Bon Dieu.* He also appeared in a few films, among them John Berry's *Tamango* (1958) and Claude Bernard Aubert's *Les Tripes au soleil* (1958), which focuses on the psychological and physical violence generated by racial prejudice. In 1958 Ababacar Samb gained a scholarship that allowed him to study filmmaking at the Centro Sperimentale in Rome, Italy, from 1959 to 1962. After a short trip to the United States, Samb returned to France, where he worked as an assistant director for French television (1962–1963).

On returning to Senegal in 1964, Samb was hired by the Ministry of Information to produce a literary radio program. He then worked as a cameraman for Senegalese television's news program. In 1965 he made his screen debut with *Et la neige n'était plus* (There Was No Longer Snow), based on his own script and shot in French by Ousmane Sembene's* favorite cameraman, Georges Caristan. This low-budget black and white film, featuring a cast of nonprofessional actors, was made with Samb's savings as well as some technical and financial support from the Senegalese government. The following year, although it had generated some unfavorable criticism from young Senegalese intellectuals, *Et la neige n'était plus* won the Prize for Best Short Film at the Dakar Festival of Negro Arts and the Prize for Best Fiction Film at the African and Malagasy Film Festival held in Saint-Cast (France). Among other such film events, the motion picture was subsequently presented at the African Film Week organized by the French Cinémathèque (14–22 April 1967). Later it was featured at the Senegalese film series held at the Museum of Modern Art in New York in 1978.

After the recognition he received for his first work, Ababacar Samb was invited to serve as a jury member at the 1969 Mannheim Film Festival (Germany). Next, in 1971, Samb was made secretary general for the Fédération Panafricaine des Cinéastes (Pan-African Federation of Filmmakers, also known as FEPACI), an inter-African organization whose aim is to promote the production, distribution, and exhibition of African films. That same year saw the release of *Kodou*, adapted from an unpublished short story by the Senegalese journalist and poet Annette M'Baye d'Enerville. Samb was able to make the film after winning the $15,000 Prize for Best Scenario awarded in 1970 by the French Ministry of Cooperation. In addition, Samb benefitted from a grant from the French National Cinema Center (CNC). The film was shot in Wolof (Senegal's main African language) and in five weeks (from March to April 1971), by a mostly Senegalese crew including cameraman Baidy Sow. *Kodou* received the Georges Sadoul Prize (France, 1971) and the International Critics' Award at the Third Pan-African Film Festival of Ouagadougou (FESPACO, 1972). Moreover, Samb's film was shown at the 1973 New Directors/New Film Series in New York and the Royan Film Festival (France, 1977), and was selected to be a part of the Senegalese film festival that took place at the New York Museum of Modern Art (1978).

As a filmmaker and secretary general of FEPACI, Ababacar Samb travelled extensively, and as such was invited to participate in the Festival International des Films de l'Ensemble Francophone (FIFEF) held in 1972 in Dinard, France. He also took part in a month-long U.S. government-sponsored tour of the United States during which he had the opportunity to meet with such Black American film figures as Gordon Parks, as well as Hollywood executives (1973). As secretary general of FEPACI, Samb organized a film-related symposium in Algiers (1975) so that Black African filmmakers could debate their common problems. Next, in 1976, he saw his administrative duties extended on being elected president of the Cinéastes Sénégalais Associés (Association of Senegalese Filmmakers). In 1977, judging that his film career was hampered by such joint responsibilities, Samb resigned from his post as FEPACI's secretary general, but was to remain for a few more years at the head of the Senegalese filmmakers' association.

Ababacar Samb needed two years of sustained archival research in both Senegal and France to weave the historical components of his third motion picture, entitled *Jom, ou l'histoire d'un peuple* (Jom, or The Story of a People, 1981). The film, based on a screenplay written in collaboration with the Senegalese sociologist Babacar Sine, was made with a mixed crew of Western and African technicians, and a team of both nonprofessional and professional actors including Oumar Seck and Issa Niang of the Dakar National Daniel Sorano Theater. Shot in Wolof, with a musical score by the noted Senegalese musician and composer Lamine Konté, *Jom* was produced by Samb's company, Baobab Film, and Zweites Deutschen Fernsehen (ZDF), a German television station. The production's $180,000 budget was in part provided through a loan from the Senegalese government. In 1982, although noncompeting, the film was reviewed during the Critics' Week at the Cannes Film Festival and screened at the International Third World Film Festival held in Paris. The following year, *Jom* was presented at the Mogadiscio Pan-African Film Festival (Mogpafis) in Somalia and obtained an International Catholic Film Office Award at the Eight FESPACO. In Senegal, *Jom* was generally appreciated by film-goers, and since its release the film has fared rather well on the international film festival circuit. It was shown (with Samb's *Kodou)* at the Racines Noires (Black Roots) festival held in Paris in 1985. In the United States it has, among others, been featured in a 1986 Senegalese film series sponsored by the American Film Institute at the Kennedy Center in Washington, D.C.

When asked why he became a filmmaker after having started his professional career as a stage actor, Samb answers:

I came to filmmaking because of a passion which I am unable to either rationalize or explain through words. I think that if I had not grown into a filmmaker, I would have continued my career in drama. I have a need to communicate with others and the film medium enables me to do so. From an ideological viewpoint, I think that cinema is a weapon. It can be used as a means of promotion and information, and help the development of our countries. (Samb to author, Dakar, Summer 1978)

Ababacar Samb, interestingly, compares the Black African filmmaker to the sculptor of yesteryear:

Depending on people's opinions, a filmmaker can be an educator or an artist, but he should in any case be viewed as a conscious member of a society as sculptors used to be in traditional African societies. Their masks had an aesthetic value but they had a function in rituals and festivals. Likewise, our films have both an artistic and a sociopolitical significance. Furthermore, I feel that there is no such thing as non-political cinema; even commercial and escapist films are political. (Samb to author, Summer 1978)

Although he admires such filmmakers as Vittorio De Sica, Charlie Chaplin, and Ingmar Bergman, Samb feels that Black African directors should not necessarily follow the pattern of Western filmmaking, but use a style that would reflect an African culture and the specific sociogeographic context from which they have emerged. Samb's comments concerning film and culture are as follows:

What determines culture? It is its physical environment . . . the climate, the savannah, the mountain, the forest in which we live. Culture is the way we deal with the world around us: how we look for food, how we react in the face of joy or fear. . . . We [Senegalese] do not yet have a film school. But we have a stylistic approach which matches what we have just described. I believe that a slow pace characterizes Senegalese films, even African films. . . . It would be very easy for us to speed up our films through editing but I don't think we should make concessions. . . . By continuing to make films which serve our own needs, I believe that we will reach a point when our works will assert themselves universally. A film has to stem from its deepest [cultural] roots. I do not want to quote any names, but each time an African has indiscriminately used European criteria to make a film, it has always resulted in a flop. Yet each time the filmmaker linked his work to his roots and made a film for his own people, he was able to better communicate with them and by the same token, he also reached non-African viewers. *(Cinéma-Québec,* July-August 1972, p. 30)

Thus, contrary to some other Black African directors, Samb would gladly offer foreign language versions of his motion pictures: "I do not see why I would not dub my films in another language than Wolof to facilitate their distribution. I do not feel this would betray their authenticity" (Samb to author, Summer 1978).

Samb also believes that filmmakers should be given total freedom of expression *(L'Afrique Littéraire et Artistique,* n. 1, 1968, p. 58), and accordingly the director does not overtly abide by any given political ideology:

As far as I am concerned, I place myself in a category which I cannot define because I make it a matter of principle that no ideology attempting to imitate what occurs elsewhere, in socialist as well as capitalistic countries, will succeed in helping us to solve our own problems (which does not mean that I do not have my own political options). (Cited in *Canadian Journal of African Studies,* 1980, p. 384)

An independent filmmaker as well as a tireless promoter of Black African cinema, Ababacar Samb is presently living and working in Dakar, where he still single-handedly runs his own production company. He is married and the father of two children.

MAJOR THEMES

"My films, like most Black African films, deal with the issue of cultural alienation and assimilation," observes the Senegalese director (Samb to author, Summer 1978). A case in point, *Et la neige n'était plus* treats the readjustment problems of exiled Africans as they return to their prior environment. Here is how Samb describes his first work:

Critics have said that my film has autobiographical overtones because it tells the story of a young man who has lived for a long time in Western countries. . . . The theories and the ideas he received in Europe are in direct contradiction to what he sees in his country. The African world to which he goes back is both traditional and oriented towards the systematic imitation of the West. He is caught between two worlds, but in the end he will remain faithful to the African tradition. He will be able to retain traditional values and at the same time accept progressive changes. (Samb to author, Summer 1978)

In *Et la neige n'était plus* (whose title refers to Europe's snowy winters), a young intellectual undergoes a crisis of consciousness from the very moment he lands at Dakar's airport, dressed in a tailored Western suit. An off-screen voice reflects his inner thoughts as he reaches his former neighborhood: "Have you changed? And yet you so anxiously waited for the day of your return. . . . Will your large family still accept you? Are you a tourist in search of exoticism?. . . . Wouldn't you be alien to the society you wish to reintegrate?. . . . Have you become a foreigner?" Soon the young man notices that his own society has evolved and been permeated with European mores. Will he also become a member of the young Westernized elite? The film ends after he meets a young village woman with whom he falls in love. Through this idyllic encounter the filmmaker suggests that the protagonist will eventually discover his true self, and serenity, by going back to traditional African values.

Unlike *Et la neige n'était plus,* which takes place in an urban setting, *Kodou* illustrates aspects of tribal life. Its plot centers around Kodou, the film's eponymous character, an adolescent who appears to be on the threshold of adulthood. One day, without her parents' consent or any preparatory stages, the young girl decides to undergo the traditional female lip tattooing which, in her society, is equated with courage and maturity. But, as she is being tattooed, Kodou is unable to stand the pain and runs away. Her failure to go through with the ritual generates derision by her peers and brings shame to her family. Ababacar Samb explains:

She escapes and is then rejected by the group. . . . This young girl eventually becomes insane and mute. She is taken to the European doctors who cannot find any cure for her illness, which is cultural. She is then taken to the village healer who, through various rituals, reintegrates her into her social group. (Samb to author, Summer 1978)

In this film, Samb duly explores Kodou's traumatized psyche (she has fantasies of having been raped by a horseman), depicts the psychotherapy afforded patients at the Fann Psychiatric Hospital in Dakar, and presents viewers with stunning scenes of the "Ndepp" ritual used to cure Kodou of her insanity.

Ababacar Samb defines the title of his last motion picture, *Jom,* as follows:

Jom is a Wolof word which has no equivalent in French or in English. "Jom" means dignity, courage, respect. . . . It is the origin of all virtues. It somehow means an elegance in the way one lives. Fidelity toward one's involvements. Respect toward others and oneself.

"Jom" guides the lives and behavior of thousands of people in West Africa. For them, it is "jom" which makes a man, and not his family origins or his wealth. "Jom" protects us against the absurdity of life. It keeps us away from lies and cowardice. It saves us from humiliations and offenses. . . . "Jom" is beyond God and beyond evil." (Production Press Kit, *Jom)*

Thus, faithful to such a meaning, *Jom*'s plot transcends both time and class divisions. Khali, a griot, tells listeners the story of Dieri Dior Ndella, a legendary turn-of-the-century prince who was led to kill a French colonial administrator to safeguard his honor. As a reprisal for his action, Dieri is ambushed by Canar Fall, who is also a member of Senegal's feudal aristocracy. Rather than surrender to his foe, Dieri chooses to die in dignity by taking his own life. Dieri's courage and character will be remembered by a present-day striker, who encourages other factory workers to show strength and solidarity in their fight for better wages and the reinstatement of laid-off workmen. Next, Khali praises Koura Thiaw, a celebrated dancer and singer of the 1940s who publicly sided with socially oppressed maids. She did so while performing for their employers. The film ends by taking us back to the factory site, where some laborers are secretly given money to act as strike breakers. Yet, most of the workers will show "jom" and remain uncorrupted. It is expected that their story will in turn become a part of Senegal's collective memory.

SURVEY OF CRITICISM

Ababacar Samb's early endeavors in the area of cinema drew some rather mixed critical attention. D'Dée's makes the following remarks concerning *Et la neige n'était plus*: "This film states with frankness, courage and some humor, the problems faced by contemporary African youth" *(L'Afrique Actuelle,* n. 15, 1967, p. 16). Guy Hennebelle shows interest in the thematic components of *Et la neige n'était plus,* but seems to regret its unilateral condemnation of Western influence in African societies. Hennebelle also describes the film as verbose and commonplace *(L'Afrique Littéraire et Artistique,* 3rd Quarter 1978, p. 108). Paulin Soumanou Vieyra* likes its visual appeal, but finds it overly didactic (in spite of well-grounded social comments) and judges its ending unconvincing *(Le Cinéma africain,* 1975, pp. 173–76).

Slightly more extensive critical coverage followed the release of *Kodou.* Paulin Soumanou Vieyra writes:

If *Kodou* suffers a bit from its mediocre photography, it appears however as one of the most accomplished African films at the level of mise en scène. The author's technical skills are remarkable when one takes into consideration that it is his first feature length film. *(Le Cinéma africain,* 1975, p. 178)

Using a Fanonian approach, Guy Hennebelle terms it a "political allegory" on the fate of present-day Africa caught between African traditions and a Western lifestyle. He also favors its mise-en-scène, served by an adequate slow pace, but deplores its technical deficiencies at the level of photography *(L'Afrique Littéraire et Artistique,* 1st Quarter 1972, p. 216). Hannes Kamphausen notes:

The message of *Kodou* is that the deeper African problems cannot be cured by turning to European ways. Original solutions are to be found that do not disregard tradition. On the other hand, Samb is far from giving an overharmonious picture of traditional life. *(Cineaste,* Summer 1972, p. 33)

Jacques Binet *(Afrique Contemporaine,* January-February 1976, p. 30) and Ben Diogaye Beye *(Cinéma 77,* May 1977, p. 67) respond favorably to *Kodou*'s plot, which aptly documents the issue of mental disorders in a traditional African context. Likewise, Pierre Haffner states:

Kodou. . . . is a very thorough film on insanity because it explores its causes, manifestations and therapy. . . . the quality of this motion picture not only comes from the fact that the filmmaker succeeded in depicting mental disorders, but that he was able to avoid giving a simplistic and schematic solution to the crucial problem of cultural traumatism, a recurrent theme in many Senegalese films. *(Cinémaction-Tricontinental,* Special Issue, 1982, p. 158)

Jom, Samb's latest picture to date, has generated several unenthusiastic comments. Gaston Haustrate reacts unfavorably to it because he feels that the filmmaker failed in his intention to convey a sociopolitical message through the use of storytelling devices. In addition, he dislikes *Jom*'s conventional style, thinks poorly of the actors' "amateurish" performance, and wonders whether the film had enough merit to be featured at the 1982 Cannes Film Festival *(Cinéma 82,* July-August 1982, p. 45). For Alain Philippon, *Jom* is a "half success" with some vivid sequences but too much didactism *(Cahiers du Cinéma,* July-August 1982, p. 28). From an almost similar viewpoint, Ferid Boughedir calls *Jom* "an honorable failure" *(Cinémaction,* n. 26, 1983, p. 182).

Positive reviews of Samb's films, nevertheless, have by far outnumbered the negative ones. Louis Marcorelles feels that *Jom* expresses "[Senegalese] national sensibility in its purest and noblest sense" throughout an unassuming but convincing narrative *(Le Monde,* 14–15 March 1982, p. 11). Although he feels that the film's contemporary protagonists could have been more acutely described, Paulo Antonio Paranagua favors *Jom*'s plastic beauty and the human warmth which emanates from the griot and a number of lively, energetic, and forceful female characters *(Positif,* July-August 1982, p. 79). Charles Lemaire enjoys *Jom*'s simple (yet not simplistic) plot which, according to him, should appeal to popular African audiences. In addition, he stresses the film's imagery, which "skillfully avoids the pitfall of exoticism," and likes Samb's use of storytelling techniques, but makes some reservations concerning the acting by saying: "The actors' performance is generally good except for a few details which can prove irritating. One neither kills nor dies in movies the way one does on the stage" *(Unir Cinéma,* July-August 1982, p. 14). Biny Traoré calls *Jom* "a beautiful Senegalese film" and appreciates its straightforward and timeless moralistic content *(L'Observateur,* 9 February 1983, p. 5). Janet Maslin writes that Ababacar Samb narrates his story through "vivid pageantry, and with a passion and intensity that reflect considerable "jom" of his own" *(New York Times,* 28 March 1983, p. 9), and Mosk praises the filmmaker's deft handling of "imagery, movement and historical perspective" *(Variety,* 26 May 1982, p. 17). Pantelis Karakasis sees *Jom* as both a "lyrical and colorful work" *(Film Faust,* May-June 1984, p. 39). Finally, after alluding to *Ceddo,* another Senegalese film by Ousmane Sembene, J. Hoberman establishes an interesting comparison between Samb's movie and Brazilian cinema:

Like *Ceddo, Jom* mixes past and present. And like *Ceddo* as well, it sets up traditional African values as a bulwark against the moral confusion of the post-colonial era. . . . Although *Jom* also includes a lengthy ritual performance—the most electrifying sequence in the movie—tradition here is a backbeat to class struggle. The film's meat is the story of a strike and "jom" . . . is identified equally with resistance to European colonization and resistance to the blandishments of the Senegalese ruling class.

Subtitled "The Story of a People," *Jom* resembles the early films of the Brazilian cinema novo in that it is an explicit political-aesthetic manifesto. . . .

Although didactic, *Jom* eschews the warmed-over Clifford Odets agitprop of Brazilian filmmaker Leon Hirszman's similar strike story, *They Don't Wear Black Tie.* Samb is less interested in representing individual psychologies than rehabilitating collective archetypes; *Jom* is at least as metaphysical as it is political. Although in some ways the film is even more two-dimensional than *They Don't Wear Black Tie,* its stilted compositions need to be seen in the context of an overwhelmingly oral culture. Images as well as narrative are here at the service of the word. *(Village Voice,* 13 September 1983, p. 46)

FILMOGRAPHY

Et la neige n'était plus (There Was No Longer Snow), 16/35 mm, black and white, 22 min., 1965.
Kodou, 35 mm, black and white, 110 min., 1971.
Jom, ou l'histoire d'un peuple, (Jom, or The Story of a People), 35 mm, color, 80 min., 1981.

BIBLIOGRAPHY

Interviews of Ababacar Samb

Dia, Alioune Touré. "Jom ou la dignité, le Sénégalais Ababacar Samb parle de son dernier film." *Bingo,* n. 333, October 1980, pp. 58–59.

Hennebelle, Guy. "Rencontre à Dinard avec des responsables de la Fédération Panafricaine des Cinéastes." *L'Afrique Littéraire et Artistique*, n. 24, August 1972, pp. 92–97.

———. "Samb-Makharam Babacar." *L'Afrique Littéraire et Artistique*, n. 49, 3rd Quarter 1978, pp. 109–10.

Pâquet, André. "Ababacar Samb, Codou [sic], et le cinéma au Sénégal." *Cinéma-Québec*, vol. 1, n. 10, July-August 1972, pp. 28–31.

———. "Babacar Samb-Makharam: de la notion d'universalisme." *Cinéma-Québec*, vol. 2, n. 6–7, March-April 1973, pp. xviii–xx.

Saint-Mathieu, Diane de. "Brève rencontre avec Ababacar Samb, Secrétaire Général de la Fédération Panafricaine des Cinéastes." *Ecran 75*, n. 33, February 1975, pp. 12–14.

Film Reviews and Studies of Ababacar Samb

Alain, Yves. "Codou d'Ababacar Samb, un film que l'on n'attendait plus." *Bingo*, n. 217, February 1971, pp. 58–59.

———. "Jom." *Le Film Français*, n. 1901, 7 May 1982, p. 90.

Ayari, Farida. "Jeune cinéma sénégalais: la parole à l'image." *Adhoua*, n. 3, January-March 1981, pp. 3–6.

Bassan, Raphael. "Cannes 82: le tiers monde en force." *Afrique-Asie*, n. 269, 21 June 1982, pp. 54–56.

Beye, Ben Diogaye. "Après le festival de Royan: une réelle dialectique dans le dialogue des cultures." *Cinéma 77*, n. 221, May 1977, pp. 64–68.

Binet, Jacques. "Cinéma africain." *Afrique Contemporaine*, n. 83, January-February 1976, pp. 27–30.

———. "Le Cinéma africain." *Afrique-Contemporaine*, n. 123, September-October 1982, pp. 5–8.

Boughedir, Ferid. "Présence africaine." *Recherche, Pégagogie et Culture*, n. 17–18, May-August 1975, pp. 43–45.

———. "Cinéma africain: le temps de l'immobilisme." *Les 2 Ecrans*, n. 42–43, February-March 1982, pp. 15–19.

———. "Et maintenant, que la fête commence!" *Jeune Afrique*, n. 1151, 26 January 1983, pp. 53–54.

———. "1982–83: de Carthage IX à Ouagadougou VIII: nouvelle génération, nouveaux espoirs." *Cinémaction*, n. 26, 1983, pp. 179–85.

———. "Une Oasis en Somalie." *Jeune Afrique*, n. 1191, 2 November 1983, pp. 72–73.

D'Dée. "Jeune cinéma d'Afrique Noire." *L'Afrique Actuelle*, n. 15, 1967, pp. 1–40.

G, R. "Jeune cinéma d'Afrique Noire." *Revue du Cinéma, Image et Son*, n. 212, January 1968, pp. 16–18.

Gervais, Ginette. "Jom." *Jeune Cinéma*, n. 144, July-August 1982, pp. 40–41.

Greenspun, Roger. "Screen: New Directors." *New York Times*, 11 April 1973, p. 39.

Haffner, Pierre. "Sénégal." *Cinémaction-Tricontinental*, Special Issue, 1982, pp. 157–60.

Haustrate, Gaston. "Jom, film sénégalais de Ababacar Samb." *Cinéma 82*, n. 283–284, July-August 1982, p. 45.

Hennebelle, Guy. "Africains, à vos marks." *Jeune Afrique*, n. 460, 22 October 1969, pp. 57–58.

———. "Babacar Samb-Makharam." *L'Afrique Littéraire et Artistique*, n. 20, 1st Quarter 1972, pp. 216–19.

———. "Le Troisiéme Festival Panafricain du Cinéma de Ouagadougou." *L'Afrique Littéraire et Artistique*, n. 22, March 1972, pp. 88–95.

———. "Samb-Makharam, Babacar." *L'Afrique Littéraire et Artistique*, n. 49, 3rd Quarter 1978, pp. 108–9.

Hoberman, J. "Paradise Now." *Village Voice*, 13 September 1983, p. 46.

Johnson, Rudy. "African Film Makers Seek Aid Here." *New York Times*, 2 May 1973, p. 42.

Kamphausen, Hannes. "Cinema in Africa: A Survey." *Cineaste*, vol. 5, n. 3, Summer 1972, pp. 29–37.

Karakasis, Pantelis. "Afrikanische Filme." *Film Faust*, n. 39, May-June 1984, p. 39.

Lemaire, Charles. "Jom ou l'histoire d'un peuple." *Unir Cinéma*, n. 1 (108), July-August 1982, pp. 13–14.

Makédonsky, Erik. "Route étroite pour le jeune cinéma sénégalais." *L'Afrique Littéraire et Artistique*, n. 1, 1968, pp. 54–62.

Marcorelles, Louis. "Jom d'Ababacar Samb Makharam. Le sens africain de l'honneur." *Le Monde*, 14–15 March 1982, p. 11.

Martin, Angela. *African Films: The Context of Production*. London: British Film Institute, 1982.

Martin, Marcel. "Afrique: présence de la vie quotidienne." *Revue du Cinéma, Image et Son*, n. 374, July-August 1982, pp. 58–60.

Maslin, Janet. "Screen: Senegalese Jom." *New York Times*, 28 March 1983, p. 9.

Medjigbodo, Nicole. "Afrique cinématographiée, Afrique cinématographique." *Canadian Journal of African Studies*, vol. 13, n. 3, 1980, pp. 371–87.

Mosk. "Jom." *Variety*, 26 May 1982, p. 17.

Ndaw, Aly Kheury. " 'Jom,' prochain film d'Ababacar Samb." *Le Soleil*, 27 May 1980, p. 2.

Oyekunde, Segun. "Films for the Future." *West Africa*, 21 March 1983, pp. 725–26.

Paranagua, Paulo Antonio. "Afrique Noire." *Positif*, n. 257–58, July-August 1982, p. 79.

Philippon, Alain. "Jom de Ababacar Samb Makharam." *Cahiers du Cinéma*, n. 338, July-August 1982, p. 28.

Rouch, Jean. "Codou par Ababacar Samb." *Jeune-Afrique*, n. 565, 6 November 1971, pp. 54–55.

Schoenberner, Gerhard. "Det svarta Afrikas filmer och deras regissörer." *Chaplin 166*, n. 1, 1980, pp. 10–15.

Traoré, Biny. "Jom et Money Power." *L'Observateur*, n. 2525, 9 February 1983, pp. 1, 4–5, 10.

Vieyra, Paulin Soumanou. *Le Cinéma africain*. Paris: Présence Africaine, 1975.

———. Le Cinéma au Sénégal. Brussels: OCIC/L'Harmattan, 1983.

Ousmane Sembene (1923–   )
Senegal

BIOGRAPHY

Reflecting upon Sembene's dense and varied career, Aimé Césaire, the Martiniquan poet and playwright, once said of him:

He symbolizes the accomplishment of the African who, thanks to constant individual effort, has succeeded in attracting the attention of the world by the indisputable quality of his artistic creation, the truthfulness of the picture which it gives of the way people live and by the honesty of his African vision. *(Young Cinema and Theatre, n. 1, 1968, p. 41)*

A major African writer as well as Black Africa's best known filmmaker, Ousmane Sembene was born on 1 January 1923 in the city of Ziguinchor, located in Casamance, the fertile southernmost region of Senegal. Of Lebou origin and Muslim extraction, Sembene was born into a family of fishermen. After his parents' divorce, the young Ousmane divided his early years between living with his father and grandmother (a midwife and expert storyteller) in Casamance, and his uncles in other regions. Sembene gratefully acknowledges the influence of Abdou Rahmane Diop, his mother's oldest brother, a Marsassoum school teacher and devout Muslim, who instilled in him a pride in African culture and traditions. At the age of eight, Ousmane Sembene was sent to Koranic school. Following Diop's death in 1935, Sembene was sent to live with another member of his family in Dakar. There he pursued his education in a French school. Yet, as he was preparing for the Certificat d'Etudes (a diploma for completion of primary studies in the French educational system), after having a physical altercation with his school principal, the youth abandoned his studies at the age of fourteen. Faced with the necessity of becoming self-sufficient, the adolescent had to seek employment. Sembene recalls: "I worked at odd jobs in order to earn some money. I became a mechanic, then a carpenter, but masonry is the trade I really learned" (Sembene to author, Dakar, Summer 1978). At that time, he would spend most of his leisure hours with a group of friends, going to local movie theaters, participating in the activities of an amateur theater troupe, and attending performances of neighborhood griots, who told him about Senegal's rich epic past and familiarized him with traditional storytelling techniques that would later be reflected in his literary and cinematographic works.

In 1938 Sembene experienced what his close friend Paulin Soumanou Vieyra* calls "a mystical period" *(Sembène Ousmane cinéaste,* 1972, p. 13). Rediscovering Islam, Sembene momentarily found in religion the ferment necessary to his idealism. But, shortly thereafter, Sembene took some evening classes and had his first contacts with labor union leaders, who played an essential role in redirecting Sembene's devotion from God to the fate of mankind within an atheistic framework.

At the age of nineteen, Sembene joined the French colonial troops, with whom he fought for four years in both Africa and Europe. After his military discharge in Dakar, Sembene participated in the Dakar-Niger railroad strike for better wages and improved working conditions. This strike, which lasted from October 1947 to March 1948, was to provide Sembene with the thematic fabric of his major novel, *God's Bits of Wood.*

Since in the postwar period Senegal had limited job opportunities to offer its youth, in 1948 Sembene embarked as a stowaway aboard a ship bound for France. There he was employed for three months as a factory worker at the Citroen auto factory near Paris. He then moved to Marseilles, where he became a longshoreman and a labor organizer. Sembene reminisces: "I was a member of the General Confederation of Workers (CGT), a union affiliated with the communist party, and this helped to increase my political awareness" (Sembene to author, Summer 1978). In that same period, Sembene started to take a vehement stand against the French colonial presence in Indochina. Consequently, in the early 1950s, Sembene participated in a three-month dockworkers' strike aimed at hampering the shipment of arms to Indochina (Cinémaction, n. 34, 1985, p. 21). Sembene was instrumental as well in the creation of l'Association des Travailleurs Sénégalais en France, a Senegalese workers' organization.

When he was not involved in union related activities, Ousmane Sembene searched for means to best express his inner feelings and thoughts. Thus, he started writing poetry, painted, and took part in the political and cultural movements of African students. He subsequently developed a growing interest in African, African-American, and Caribbean writers such as Cheik Anta Diop, Richard Wright, and Claude McKay. His readings included the works of Black Francophone authors like Aimé Césaire, René Maran, and Jean Brierre. Before long, Sembene too began to write, keeping records of his varied experiences as an African worker in France. His first novel, *Le Docker noir* (The Black Dockworker), published in 1956, is an outgrowth of these writings. That same year, Sembene attended the First International Congress of Black Writers and Artists held in Paris. In 1957 he wrote *O pays, mon beau peuple* (O My Country, My Beautiful People), a novel about a Senegalese war veteran who, with his French wife, returns to his native village and subsequently embarks on a self-imposed mission of organizing the peasants and modernizing their farming techniques. Also in 1957, Sembene travelled to the USSR. Moreover, a 1958 encounter with W.E.B. Du Bois at the First Congress of African and Asiatic Writers in Tashkent was to leave an indelible mark on the young writer's mind. Shortly thereafter, Sembene was invited to go to China and North Vietnam to meet with artists, writers, and political leaders.

In 1960 Sembene published *Les Bouts de bois de Dieu* (God's Bits of Wood), an epic novel considered by many to be Sembene's literary masterpiece. Henceforth recognized as a talented writer, Sembene was given the opportunity to meet with Roger Martin du Gard, Louis Aragon, Simone de Beauvoir, and Jean-Paul Sartre, the leftist elite of French authors. They were all fervent advocates of the writer's sociopolitical commitment, an ethic to which Sembene himself had already subscribed. Likewise, Sembene continued to mingle with members of the Black intelligentsia, of which he had become an influential part, among them Léon Damas, David Diop, Camara Laye, Mongo Beti, Bernard Dadié, Ferdinand Oyono, and others. He also paid frequent visits to Présence Africaine, a publishing house headed at the time by Alioune Diop, and also a meeting place for Black intellectuals in Paris.

In 1961, while travelling extensively in West Africa, Ousmane Sembene came to realize the limited distribution of African literature there. It was this experience which led him to the conclusion that film could indeed be a more effective means of reaching out to the largely illiterate African masses. For this reason he decided to embrace a career in film. Thus, in 1962, after the publication of a collection of short stories, *Voltaique* (Tribal Scars), Sembene went to Moscow for a year's training in filmmaking under the tutelage of Mark Donskoy and Sergei Gerassimov, who acquainted him with Soviet sociorealism.

After his stay in the Soviet Union, Ousmane Sembene returned to Africa, where he was commissioned by the government of Mali to make a short documentary entitled *L'Empire Sonhrai* (The Sonhrai Empire, 1963). Next, he shot his first significant motion picture, *Borom Sarret,* for the production of which he founded his own company, Domirev ("the country's child" in Wolof, Senegal's major African language). Filmed by three people, with a group of nonprofessional actors, and postsynchronized in French, *Borom Sarret* was awarded the First Film Award at the 1963 Tours Film Festival (France). The following year, Sembene authored another book, *L'Harmattan,* published in Paris. The novel interweaves the lives and experiences of numerous characters in a fictitious African country. The plot unfolds amid a political upheaval which closely parallels De Gaulle's 1958 referendum in France.

The year 1964 saw the release of *Niaye,* which, like *Borom Sarret,* was made with minimal financial resources and basic film equipment. In 1965, *Niaye* won an award at the Tours Film Festival and an Honorable Mention at the Locarno Film Festival (Switzerland). The film has, to date, never been commercially distributed. Yet, Sembene's growing involvement in filmmaking apparently did not alter his output as a writer: his short story "Vehi Ciosane ou Blanche Genèse"

(Vehi Ciosane or White Genesis) and novel *Le Mandat* (The Money Order) were published in one volume by Présence Africaine in 1965, and acclaimed as the best work by an African writer at the First International Festival of Negro Arts in Dakar (1966).

In 1966 Sembene produced *La Noire de* (Black Girl), a $20,000 production shot by the French cameraman Christian Lacoste (who had already worked with Sembene on *Borom Sarret)* in twenty days, and based on a story from *Voltaique*. This first Sub-Saharan feature film, which is now considered one of the landmarks of early Black African cinema, obtained a number of awards the year of its release, namely, the Jean Vigo Prize (France), the Silver Antelope Award at the First International Festival of Negro Arts, and the First Prize (''Tanit d'Or'') at the Carthage Film Festival (Tunisia). *La Noire de* was screened, moreover, during the Critics' Week at the 1966 Cannes Film Festival. Now a confirmed filmmaker, Sembene was invited to serve as one of the official judges at the 1967 Cannes Film Festival.

Sembene's second feature length film is *Mandabi* (The Money Order, 1968), the screen adaptation of his novel *Le Mandat,* which was shot in six weeks by Georges Caristan and Paul Soulignac. The film required three months of preparation, including several weeks of rehearsals by nonprofessional actors, many of whom agreed to perform without remuneration. *Mandabi,* which benefitted from a $60,000 grant from the French government film fund and cost a total of $300,000 to produce, was a co-production of the Comptoir Français du Film and Domirev. Almost banned in Senegal for its "disrespect of Islam" *(La Revue du Cinéma, Image et Son,* November 1977, p. 178), *Mandabi* was eventually distributed in that country, where it was met with unprecedented commercial success. It enjoyed, furthermore, a commercial run in France and has been a favorite on the film festival circuit since it premiered at the 1968 Venice Film Festival, where it won the International Critics' Prize. Also in 1968, *Mandabi* was featured at the Tashkent Film Festival, and there was awarded the Soviet Filmmakers' Prize. A year later, it was shown at the London Film Festival and chosen as Best Foreign Film at the Atlanta Film Festival. Shot in two versions, one in French and one in Wolof, this work encouraged many other Black African directors to produce their films in African vernaculars.

In 1969 Sembene made his first trip to the United States to attend the New York Film Festival, in the course of which he presented *Mandabi*. That same year, he participated in the Pan-African Festival of Algiers and made two films (on unemployment and Senegal's history, respectively) for two European television stations. In 1970, with funds provided by American sponsors (the Broadcasting Film Commission and the National Council of the Church of Christ), Ousmane Sembene shot a short color film, *Taw,* which won him the Golden Lion at the 1971 Asmara Film Festival in Ethiopia. His third feature length motion picture, *Emitai* (God of Thunder), was also completed in 1971 after two years of research and preparation. This $200,000 color film, based on Sembene's script (which he rewrote three times), was shot in seven weeks in the Diola language, which is widely spoken in Casamance. *Emitai* was given a Silver Medal at the 1971 Moscow Film Festival, and screened a year thereafter at the Berlin, Cannes, and Carthage film festivals. Yet, because of its anti-French stand, *Emitai* faced difficult distribution (when not an outright ban) in several West African countries. It was finally presented in France six years after its initial release.

In the early 1970s, Sembene, a fervent advocate of the use of African languages, was instrumental in the creation of *Kaddu* (The Voice), a Dakar newspaper in Wolof. In that same period, he was also elected president of the Association des Cinéastes Sénégalais, an organization whose aim is the promotion of Senegalese film. In 1972 the filmmaker was chosen to participate in the production of a documentary on the Twentieth Olympic Games. Interviewed on location, Sembene declared:

I am filming the activities of the Senegalese basketball team, but more important than that, I am trying to document the meeting between black Africans and Afro-Americans and Afro-Europeans who are participating in the games. *(American Cinematographer,* November 1972, p. 1322)

Also in 1972, the director visited the campus of the University of Wisconsin, Madison, where he presented *Emitai* and participated in several lively discussions with faculty and students.

Ousmane Sembene published a new novel, *Xala,* in 1973. A year later, he married Carrie Moore, an African American woman who had written her Ph.D. dissertation on his literary works. In 1974 Sembene completed his film *Xala,* based on his book. This motion picture, produced by Domirev and the Senegalese Société Nationale de Cinéma (SNC), which provided $80,000 toward its financing, necessitated two years of preparation and three months of steady rehearsals from a dedicated team of nonprofessional actors. The film was shot in five weeks on location in both French and Wolof. When completed, *Xala* was frowned upon by the Senegalese Board of Censors, who demanded that the film be cut at ten different places before it could be officially released in Senegal. Once released, the motion picture became an instant box-office success in Senegal. *Xala* was commercially distributed in Paris and the United States and in 1975 was shown at the Rotterdam, Locarno, New York, and Cannes film festivals. A year later, it was screened at the Bombay Film Festival and the Moscow Film Festival (noncompeting), and won the special Jury's Prize at Karlovy Vary (Czechoslovakia) as well as the Silver Medal at the Festival Figueira da Foz (Portugal).

Ceddo, Sembene's latest film to date, was produced by Domirev in 1976 at a cost of $500,000, with an $80,000 loan from the Senegalese government added to the director's profits from his previous motion pictures. Requiring two years of preproduction work, *Ceddo* was shot in ten weeks by Sembene's favorite cameraman, Georges Caristan, with Moussa Bathily* and Ousmane M'Baye working as assistant directors. This film about Catholic and Muslim imperialism in seventeenth-century Africa was banned for eight years in Senegal. The reason given for its rejection was that its title did not follow government regulations concerning the spelling of "Ceddo," which officials insist should only have one "d." More plausibly, the film was probably censored for religious and political reasons, given the fact that Senegal's Muslims are said to represent from 70 to 80 percent of that country's population. Before its release in Senegal, *Ceddo* had been widely shown at various film events. Sembene presented it in person to American audiences during a 1978 tour of the United States. Also in 1978, *Ceddo* was awarded the Paul Robeson Prize in Los Angeles, California. That same year, almost all of Sembene's films (with the exception of *L'Empire Sonhrai*) were shown at a film series entitled "Senegal: Fifteen Years of an African Cinema, 1962–1977" held at the New York Museum of Modern Art from 26 January to 27 February.

Pursuing his career as a writer, Ousmane Sembene published in 1980 a two-volume novel entitled *Le Dernier de l'Empire* (The Last of the Empire), about a constitutional coup d'état organized by a fictitious Senegalese president. In the spring of 1981, Sembene lectured in London on the occasion of a retrospective of his works held at the British Film Institute. Another retrospective of his films was part of the Nantes Festival des Trois Continents (France). That same year Sembene was selected to be chairman of the New Delhi Film Festival (India). In 1982 the filmmaker went to Niamey to join jurists, economists, government representatives, and film professionals in a colloquium concerning development policies for cinema in Africa. He travelled also to Mexico to attend the UNESCO World Conference on Cultural Policies. In 1983 Sembene presided over the jury of the Eighth Pan-African Film Festival of Ouagadougou (FESPACO). Also in 1983, the director was selected to be among the official judges of the Venice Film Festival. A year later, Sembene was invited to participate in other film events in Japan and Brazil, and as president of the Dakar Pen Club, he paid tribute to the former Senegalese head of state, Leopold S. Senghor, a renowned writer with whom he had had a number of political and cultural divergences over the years. In 1984 as well, Sembene and Raymond Hermantier adapted the novel *Les Bouts de bois de Dieu* to the stage at the Dakar Daniel Sorano Theater. In 1985 Ousmane Sembene was made president of the Société Nouvelle de Promotion Cinématographique (SNPC), a post formerly held by Mahama Johnson Traoré*. That same year, he participated in a symposium at the Racines Noires (Black Roots) festival in Paris, where most of his films were shown. From 27 January to 17 February 1986, seven of Sembene's motion pictures were presented by the American Film Institute at the Kennedy Center (Washington, D.C.) in a series entitled "Senegal and Sembene: The Birth of Black African Cinema." In May 1986, the Senegalese filmmaker came to New York to participate in the United Nations General Assembly's special session on Africa. The following year, at the tenth FESPACO, Sembene received the Médaille de Bronze du Nahouri (Nahouri Bronze Medal) from the government of Burkina Faso for his outstanding contribution to African cinema. Also in 1987, Sembene published *Niiwam*, a collection of short stories.

Ousmane Sembene is presently considered by literary and film critics alike as one of Africa's most prolific contemporary creators. Once asked which medium he favored as a means of expression, he responded: "I prefer literature because I find it a bit more rich than film—a richer medium for expressing oneself. You can go more deeply into things" *(American Cinematographer,* November 1972, p. 1322). But Sembene also recognizes that film has a broader popular impact than literature. He stresses: "If I'm lucky, maybe I could sell 10,000 copies of one of my novels but I reached millions of people with *Xala*" *(Washington Post,* 17 June 1976, p. B4). This concern for touching an optimum number of people explains both the stylistic and thematic clarity of most of Sembene's works. He observes:

I'm a storyteller in as simple a manner as possible. I want to be understood at different cultural levels. I select my subjects with social and political implications. I detail and narrate my stories in my own way. I speak to the housewife just as I speak to the philosophy professor. If I am not understood by the masses I will consider myself a failure. *(Film World,* March 1979, p. 69)

Sembene has unswervingly described Africa's need for a cinema of awareness and assertiveness that would reflect its cultural, sociopolitical, and economic reality. He expounds:

What interests me is exposing the problems confronting my people. I consider the cinema a means of political action. Nevertheless I don't want to make "poster films." Revolutionary films are another thing. Moreover, I am not so naive as to think that I could change Senegalese reality with a single film. But I think that if there were a whole group of us making films with that same orientation, we could alter reality a little bit. *(Young Cinema and Theatre,* n. 3, 1970, p. 27)

Accordingly, Sembene relentlessly advocates a kind of cinema that would inform, instruct, and raise the African viewers' comprehension of their environment, thus achieving an initiatory learning process comparable to the one commonly found in the African oral tradition. In the filmmaker's words: "African cinema is a useful instrument for change, born out of social necessity" *(Essence,* July 1978, p. 24), which "is in the process of becoming the most important tool for the fertilization of a new African culture" *(Africa,* July 1977, p. 80).

As he thinks that film should have a social function, Sembene believes that the African director should be free and honest so as to establish a durable relationship between the moral and aesthetic facets of his work and broader ethical values. Thus, he denounces the influence that may be exerted on filmmakers in countries where the government is directly involved in the film process. He points out: "We want the government to help us but we also want to be free to criticize the government. This is one among the many contradictions film-makers have to face'' (Sembene to author, Summer 1978).

After its thirty years of existence, Ousmane Sembene believes that Black African cinema is on its way to reaching an original film language. He stresses: ''Our way of making films is different from that of French, American, Japanese or Italian directors'' *(Ecran 76,* 15 January 1976, p. 49). Sembene is not merely a theoretician of African film. He has pragmatically applied his views throughout his career as a filmmaker. As one of the founding members of the Fédération Panafricaine des Cinéastes (FEPACI) and of the West African Film Corporation (WAFCO) created in 1985 with such filmmakers as Ola Balogun*, Timité Bas-sori*, Souleymane Cissé*, and Paulin Soumanou Vieyra*, he has constantly sought, with his counterparts, solutions to the many difficulties encountered by African cinema. Yet, in spite of problems of production and distribution that still impede its full growth, Sembene shows unyielding optimism concerning the future of Black African filmmaking.

A socially committed writer, a provocative director, a social activist and critic, and an internationally recognized spokesman for Sub-Sahara's Black artistry, Sembene is presently residing in Yoff, near Dakar, with his two sons, Alain and Moussa. Since 1982 he has been actively working on a film project, *Samori* (focusing on Samori Touré, the nineteenth-century resistant to French colonial imperialism in West Africa), a historical epic which he envisions as a three-part motion picture of two hours each, as well as a television series. This motion picture, which has been on Sembene's mind for the past twenty years, will be co-produced by several African and European countries. Its budget will reach an estimated $18 million, a figure commonly cited in Hollywood circles, but barely dreamed of in the realm of Black African film. Says Sembene: ''If I am able to make my film on Samori, I shall give up filmmaking and dedicate all my time to writing. With *Samori,* I shall have given the best of myself'' (Sembene to author, Atlanta, 11 November 1979). However, before *Samori* and during the summer of 1987, the director plans to co-direct with Thierno Faty Sow *Le Camp de Thiaroye* (The Thiaroye Camp), based on tragic historical events which took place in French-ruled Senegal during the Second World War. The motion picture will be entirely produced by the Société Nouvelle de Promotion Ciné-matographique (SNCP) with an estimated budget of over $1 million.

MAJOR THEMES

Sembene's films, which are both realistic and symbolic, are commentaries on Senegal's changing society and often focus on such sensitive and/or controversial themes as sociocultural alienation; colonialism; neocolonialism; the difficulties common people face because of poverty and illiteracy; the vulnerability of av-erage citizens to intricate and rigid bureaucracies; the corruption of the elite; the changing condition of women and of the family; abuses committed in the name of religion; the question of freedom; authority; and the role of the community in individuals' lives. While some of his works illustrate present-day situations, others rediscover history from an African perspective.

L'Empire Sonhrai, Sembene's very first motion picture, concerns an Islamized group of people who occupy the middle reaches of the Niger River in what is now called Mali. The work describes the historical significance of the city of Timbuctu, the Sonhrai's resistance to French colonialism, and finally the decline and fall of the Sonhrai empire due to a succession of internal dissensions and foreign invasions.

Borom Sarret, whose title is a common Wolof expression designating the owner of a cart, narrates the frustrating day of a Dakar cart driver. His last passenger, waving bills and assuring him that he has "pull," asks to be taken downtown, where carts are prohibited. There the cartman is stopped by the police, who confiscate his vehicle while the seemingly well-off customer runs off without paying his fare. Deprived of his means of livelihood and penniless, the protagonist reaches home in a state of deep despair. Consequently his wife leaves their child with him and quietly goes out into the street, saying: "I promise you, we will eat tonight." Here the director skillfully ends his film—leaving the audience free to draw its own conclusion.

Contrary to *Borom Sarret,* whose crisis situation develops in an urban setting, *Niaye* delves into a traditional rural world in which a thirteen-year-old girl is found to be pregnant. As can be expected, such a revelation causes dismay among the villagers, especially when they discover that it is the village chief who has impregnated his daughter. A tragic sequence of events follows. The father is killed by his son, a former soldier in the French army who has lost his sanity, and the young girl's mother commits suicide. The young girl and her new born child are subsequently rejected by the community, whose honor has been tarnished. Yet the village, anxious to safeguard its dignity, does not disclose these tragedies to the French administrator. These events, based on a true story, are related by the village griot (storyteller).

La Noire de recounts the life of a young Diola maid hired by a French couple in Senegal. They take her to France, where she is ill-treated. Her linguistic isolation (she understands but does not speak French) and her cultural alienation away from her extended African family lead her to suicide. Here again, Sembene's plot stems from a true story.

Mandabi is a bittersweet comedy which reflects the quixotic tribulations of Ibrahima Dieng, an illiterate and seemingly unemployed middle-aged Muslim with two wives and seven children. Following the receipt of a $100 money order from his nephew, a migrant worker living in Paris, Dieng is caught in a series of misadventures where his efforts to cash the money order are frustrated by bureaucracy and dishonesty. At the end of the story, he is more in debt and poorer than ever, but such poverty is largely compensated by his new knowledge of the corruption of some civil servants and his own vulnerability.

The plot of *Taw* (which means the oldest of the family in Wolof) unfolds in one of the working-class neighborhoods of Dakar. Its eponymous character is twenty and still lives at his father's house. Although he has received some schooling, the young man is unable to find employment, a situation that his authoritarian father attributes to laziness. Step by step, Sembene's camera follows Taw's fruitless search for work. One day, Taw's girlfriend announces to him that she is pregnant. After first denying paternity, Taw decides to face his responsibilities. He will leave his parents' home and start a new life for himself and his family to be.

Emitai, whose title refers to the Diola God of Thunder, takes place during the Second World War. It details the rebellion of a Casamance village controlled by African myths and traditions against a heavy rice tax imposed by the French colonial administration. The villagers' tragic final action is spearheaded by its women, who defiantly protest the increasing demands of the French, who seek men and foodstuffs in their overseas colonies to help sustain France's war efforts in Europe.

Xala, which means "temporary impotence" in Wolof, describes the sexual and social impotence of El Hadji Abdoukader Beye, a middle-aged polygamous Dakar businessman. He discovers his ailment on his wedding night, after having married his third wife. Beye believes that a spell has been cast upon him and goes to consult with various local healers for help. His sexual impotence soon parallels his business bankruptcy. Impoverished and accused of embezzlement, Beye ends up in social disgrace, and most of his luxurious possessions are confiscated. Finally he discovers that he has been cursed by a blind beggar in revenge for Beye's past misappropriation of his land. The beggar promises Beye the recovery of his manhood if he will strip and be spat upon by him and other beggars. The former businessman feels that he has no choice but to surrender to the beggar's request in the hope of regaining his virility. Sembene intends for Beye's story to serve as a satirical parable illustrating the fate of Senegal's new elite, which hides its inherent powerlessness under the cloak of ostentatious lifestyles.

Ceddo, a stylized motion picture whose impressionistic musical score is the work of Cameroonian composer Manu Dibango, starts with the kidnapping of Princess Dior, the king's daughter, by an insubordinate villager (a "ceddo"), who thereby protests against the monarch's political weakness and the increasing penetration of Islam. After the king dies a mysterious death, the imam (Muslim priest) rises to power, brutally forces the villagers to convert to Islam, and rescues the princess with the intention of marrying her. The film ends as the princess unexpectedly grabs and slays the imam in front of his followers. Although *Ceddo*'s time frame is unspecified in the film, it is said to take place in the seventeenth century (at the time of the slave trade) when traditional African rule was being threatened by Muslim imperialism, European mercantilism, and the introduction of Christianity in West Africa.

SURVEY OF CRITICISM

Widely acknowledged as the leading force in Black African cinema, Sembene has had substantial international press coverage since the early stages of his film career. *Borom Sarret* was the first of Sembene's films to be reviewed. For D'Dée, the film is based on a worthwhile subject and calls to mind Italian neorealism. The critic feels that *Borom Sarret* is effective in spite of some deficiencies in sound quality *(L'Afrique Actuelle,* n. 15, 1967, p. 14). Michel Capdenac finds the work interesting because it is the first African film to depict the life of the African proletariat *(Les Lettres Francaises,* 30 September 1970, p. 29). Paulin Soumanou Vieyra hails the film as a dense and sincere motion picture which adequately reflects the fate of the deprived *(Sembène Ousmane cinéaste,* 1972, p. 45). Robert A. Mortimer remarks:

It is a tribute to the director's skill that in his rather short footage, Sembene is able to convey the heavy weight of poverty, the growing demoralization of an unproductive day, the frustration of the struggle to survive in a setting marked by the gap between the rich who make the law and the poor who suffer its inequities. The cart-driver tries his best to support his family only to have his wife thrown back upon her own resources at the end. The mood of the film is one of pathos, not of revolution, but the impact of the story is strong and troubling. *(African Arts,* Spring 1972, p. 64)

For Roy Armes, "the film owes much to its well observed detail and neat characterization" *(Cine Tract,* Summer-Fall 1981, p. 74). Also, in retrospect, a number of film critics see *Borom Sarret* as a significant film which announces some of the thematic and stylistic directions of Sembene's subsequent works. This opinion is shared by Ferid Boughedir *(Ecran 76,* 15 January 1976, p. 42), Guy Hennebelle *(L'Afrique Littéraire et Artistique,* 3rd Quarter 1978, p. 111), Catherine Ruelle *(Actuel Développement,* January-February 1982, p. 44), Mbye Baboucar Cham *(American Journal of Islamic Studies,* August 1984, p. 16), and Maxime Scheinfeigel *(Cinémaction,* n. 34, 1985, p. 32).

Because of its theme, D'Dée places *Niaye* in the wake of ancient Greek tragedies. He is impressed by some of its visual compositions but regrets the mediocre quality of its sound score, as well as its somewhat unstructured mise-en-scène *(L'Afrique Actuelle,* n. 15, 1967, p. 15). Mortimer describes *Niaye* as "a stark vision of the disintegration of traditional rural life under the dual pressure of outmoded authority relationships and colonial interference" *(African Arts,* Spring 1972, p. 65). René Gardies terms it a "moral fable" told through the voice of a griot *(La Revue du Cinéma, Image et Son,* January 1968, p. 17). In the same vein, Jean-René Debrix *(Afrique Contemporaine,* July-October 1968, p. 11) and Béatrice Rolland *(Positif,* February 1970, p. 88) establish a direct link between *Niaye* and the African oral tradition. Paulin Soumanou Vieyra regrets the work's uncinematic style (due to Sembene's adaptation of his own literary work) as well as its polemical and moralizing tone *(Le Cinéma africain,* 1975, p. 161). Jean Rouch terms it a mysterious hieratic story and one of Sembene's most beautiful films *(Cinémaction,* n. 34, 1985, p. 89).

After attending the screening of *La Noire de,* during the Critics' Week at the Cannes Film Festival, Jacques Bontemps stated: "To put on the very weak film of a young Senegalese director is a disastrous and paternalistic attitude; it can only bring harm to the young Senegalese who are starting to make films'' *(Cahiers du Cinéma,* June 1966, p. 48). On the contrary, *La Noire de*, pleased D'Dée, who considers it a well-constructed, sober, and lucid motion picture *(L'Afrique Actuelle,* n. 15, 1967, p. 14). René Gardies maintains a similar opinion *(La Revue du Cinéma, Image et Son,* November 1967, p. 133). Jean Delmas terms it a sensitive African work with universal overtones *(Jeune Cinéma,* April 1967, p. 22). Paulin Soumanou Vieyra hails the film as a multifaceted work which marks an important date in the history of Black African cinema *(Le Cinéma africain,* 1975, p. 162). For Udayan Gupta ''the terse, stark style of the film and the nature of the narrative make it one of the major anti-colonial documents from Africa'' *(N.Y. Amsterdam News,* 11 February 1978, p. B12). But Jean Copans sees it as neither realistic nor Senegalese but merely a ''vengeful act'' addressed to the West *(Afrique-Asie,* 6 February 1978, p. 49). In spite of structural and technical flaws, Guy Hennebelle sees *La Noire de* as an important document on neocolonialism *(Guide des films anti-impérialistes,* 1975, p. 18). J. Hoberman finds that it ''has the terse spirituality of a film by Bresson or Hanoun'' *(Village Voice,* 6 February 1978, p. 42), and Ferid Boughedir favors its ''quasi-Brechtian restraint'' *(Ecran 76,* 15 January 1976, p. 42). Marsha Landy points out Sembene's interesting use of ''self-reflexivity, satire, irony, and experimentation with cinematic structural components, such as montage.'' According to Landy, Sembene ''blends traditional African storytelling devices with experimental film language. He fuses a form of neorealism with a critique of the real'' *(Jump Cut,* n. 27, 1982, p. 23). Lieve Spass stresses that *''La Noire de*'s visual composition exploits the obvious black/white dichotomy'' and details further in his article how ''the black-and-white cinematography provides the formal and semantic basis of the film'' *(Jump Cut,* n. 27, 1982, p. 26). For Bernard Cohn *(Positif,* October 1966, p. 96), Claude Pennec *(Arts et Loisirs,* 5 April 1967, p. 52), Marie-Claude Veysset *(Jeune Cinéma,* November 1968, p. 10), Michel Capdenac *(Les Lettres Françaises,* 27 November 1968, p. 22), and Susan Hall *(Africa Report,* January-February 1977, p. 15), *La Noire de* is a provocative and poignant film. M-C. Ropars-Wuilleumier provides an interesting study of the theme of dispossession presented at various levels in the film *(Recherche, Pédagogie et Culture,* May-August 1975, pp. 10–15). In her thorough analysis of *La Noire de,* Landy stresses:

Diouana's suicide has multiple significance. . . . Her refusal to continue in a condition of servitude is representative of the necessary refusal of other Africans, equally uneducated and imbued with false illusions, to identify with the white oppressor. Her death symbolizes the desired destruction of this old way of life as Sembene diagnoses it. Sembene has identified Diouana's lusting after European culture as suicidal. *(Jump Cut,* n. 27, 1982, p. 24)

Nancy J. Schmidt notes that

Sembene has skillfully adapted a short story that is primarily one person's reflection upon her unfortunate status in life into a film that is a character study of three persons, Diouana and her employers. The characters are well cast and effectively portray the conflicts in cultural background and expectations that are central to the story's major themes of human exploitation and suffering. *(Research in African Literatures,* Winter 1982, pp. 525–26)

In commenting on both *Borom Sarret* and *La Noire de,* A. H. Weiler concludes: "The films . . . are not landmarks of technique. But they put a sharp, bright focus on an emerging, once dark African area and on a forceful talent with fine potentials" *(New York Times,* 13 January 1969, p. 31).

Like *Niaye* and *La Noire de, Mandabi* is based on Sembene's writings. As she compares the film to the book, Schmidt observes that the film offers a better characterization, a more vivid setting, and a more acute criticism of Islam than the novella *(Research in African Literatures,* Winter 1982, p. 524). Pierre Pommier devotes a rather large portion of his book to a detailed study of *Mandabi,* which he considers a significant example of Black African cinema *(Cinéma et développement en Afrique noire francophone,* 1974, pp. 114–39). Ferid Boughedir inscribes *Mandabi,* along with *Borom Sarret* and *La Noire de,* in his listing of the landmarks of African cinema *(Jeune Afrique,* 25 December 1985, p. 89). Jean Devin writes:

This is a truly mature, wise and beautiful work. Its creator . . . observes and describes the most banal daily events in order then to be able to place them in the fuller context of the crisis which rules Senegalese society today,—a moral, family and religious crisis aroused by the change in the socioeconomic structure . . . *The Money Order* is a profound film with obvious intentions, showing that special conglomeration of colonial capitalism, along with archaic rituals, superstitions and bureaucratic corruption which took the European example as its model yet often carried it to the point of absurdity. The film is exciting, among other things because of its poetic style and detail in depicting everyday, day-to-day problems. *(Young Cinema and Theatre,* n. 2, 1969, pp. 26–27)

Mortimer calls *Mandabi* "a political film lightly disguised as a farce" *(African Arts,* Spring 1972, p. 66). For Mbye Baboucar Cham, "Mandabi is also an invitation to positive political action" *(Présence Africaine,* 1st Quarter 1984, p. 85). On the contrary, Roy Armes finds that "though *Mandabi* ends with a muted plea for change, it is a richly coloured social study rather than a work of political intent" *(Cine Tract,* Summer-Fall 1981, p. 75). Janick Arbois *(Téléciné,* February 1969, p. 29), Mohand Ben Salama (Hennebelle et al., *Ecran 76,* 15 January 1976, p. 43), and Jacques Binet *(Afrique Contemporaine,* January-February 1976, p. 30) favor Sembene's lucid, vivid, and realistic critical portrayal of Dakar life. In this respect, Guy Gauthier compares Sembene's skills to those of the French playwright and filmmaker Marcel Pagnol, whose works reflect the authentic flavor of southern France *(La Revue du Cinéma, Image et Son,* January 1969, p. 99). Nigel Andrews says, "Sembene's story . . . has the force of a Jonsonian satire in which society is seen as a vast network of greed, with the opportunists and self-seekers eternally thriving at the expense of the gullible innocents'' *(Monthly Film Bulletin,* February 1973, p. 30). Michel Capdenac *(Les Lettres Françaises,* 27 November 1968, p. 22), Vieyra *(Le Cinéma africain,* 1975, p. 168), J. Hoberman *(Village Voice,* 6 February 1978, p. 42), and Guy Hennebelle *(L'Afrique Littéraire et Artistique,* 3rd Quarter 1978, p. 112) are impressed with Sembene's sensitive approach and sarcastic verve. In contrast, Michel Ciment finds Sembene's chronicle ''timorous'' *(Positif,* December 1968– January 1969, p. 45), and Richard Combs thinks that its ''surface flummery . . . is overindulged. . . . *The Money Order* is too heavily padded with weary folk comedy'' *(The Times,* 26 October 1973, p. 15). According to Margaret Tarratt, *Mandabi* is

a fable built around the frustrations engendered by petty bureaucracy. Unlike *Death of a Bureaucrat* which comes to mind at once when seeing this film, its interest is more sociological than cinematic. . . . This film . . . remains static and theatrical . . . an exercise in laboured and predictable political irony not conceived with the screen in mind. *(Films and Filming,* January 1974, pp. 45–46)

As for Louis Marcorelles, he does not hesitate to say that *Mandabi* is ''one of the most profound films of this era'' *(Les Lettres Françaises,* 6 November 1968, p. 19). Equally as complimentary in opinion, John Frazer points out:

It appears likely that for the time being, Ousmane Sembene will speak for Africa to European and American audiences, just as Satyajit Ray has spoken for the Indian sub-continent.

In this third film, *Mandabi* (The Money Order), Sembene reveals himself as an artist of talent, commitment and unselfconscious simplicity . . . the film resembles a French farce. . . . In scene after scene the unhurried pace of the film allows time for a full understanding of both action and reaction. As in the films of Ozu, the important events are reactions and the mute comments of objects. *(Film Quarterly,* Summer 1970, p. 48)

Shortly after the film's initial release, the Senegalese film reviewer Bara Diouf remarkably foresaw that *''Le Mandat* (Mandabi), . . . a plea for progress and development, should do well and establish its director as the staunchest representative of the young African cinema'' *(Dakar-Matin,* 7 December 1968, p. 8).

Made for an American religious organization, the National Council of the Church of Christ, *Taw* has been screened primarily in U.S. festival and academic film circuits. For this reason and the fact that it cannot be counted among Sembene's major works, *Taw* has apparently been neglected by most film critics except a few like Hennebelle, who finds the work a pertinent depiction of unemployment in a developing country and places the film in the neorealist vein *(Guide des films anti-impérialistes,* 1975, p. 99).

For Tewfik Farès, *Emitai* is a masterpiece which clearly presents an implacable examination of the very nature of colonialism as well as the revolutionary awakening of the colonized *(Jeune Afrique,* 22 July 1972, p. 66). In his article entitled

"Emitai: or Africa Arisen,'' Moktar Diack considers that Sembene's film ''represents the treatment by a great film-maker of one of the most glorious chapters in the history of the Senegalese resistance'' *(Young Cinema and Theatre,* n. 4, 1972, p. 27). Like Farès and Diack, but with some reservations concerning the work's static dialectics, Jean-Louis Pouillaud terms *Emitai* a forceful and poignant film *(Positif,* July-August 1977, pp. 120–21). On the other hand, Daniel Serceau calls it a failure from a narrative standpoint *(Cinémaction,* n. 34, 1985, p. 43). After reviewing the motion picture at the Paris Palais de Chaillot, Mosk notes: ''Sembene shows a good technical knowhow and the film holds interest in its look at pre-war Africa and emerging nationalism.'' Nevertheless, the critic stresses that *Emitai* ''appears mainly for specialized showing abroad but its objectivity could interest more popular marts, if well placed and handled, primarily in the growing black mart'' *(Variety,* 12 July 1972, p. 28). Although he underscores a number of inaccuracies in Sembene's illustration of Diola cosmology and mores, J. David Sapir concludes:

Emitay [sic] is a brilliant film. It is a well conceived, well structured, and well acted film. It is certainly Sembene at his best. For these reasons, it must be seen by anyone who takes an active interest in the creative efforts of modern African artists. What it might lack in ethnographic and historical verismilitude is more than compensated by its artistry and clear presentation of one African's vision of the form true independence must take. *(American Anthropologist,* September 1974, p. 697)

Vieyra sees *Emitai* as an epic film which denounces colonialism as well as certain aspects of traditional African societies *(Le Cinéma africain,* 1975, p. 172). Hennebelle likes its construction and notes (contrary to the filmmaker's previous works) Sembene's exaltation of a collective African hero in a motion picture which stigmatizes an event of the colonial era. From a thematic and stylistic perspective, Hennebelle suggests further study of *Emitai* based on a comparison with some of Jorge Sanjines' films *(Ecran 76,* 15 January 1976, p. 44). For Héléne Dury:

Emitai is a militant film which shows that neither credulity nor submission to religious beliefs nor passive resistance could be taken as efficacious weapons. One may regret the slow pace of the plot which somewhat muffles its dramatic impact. *(Lutte Ouvrière,* 14 May 1977, p. 20)

According to Lyle Pearson, ''Sembene's *Emitai* can be related to Sophocles' Antigone in its story, but not to any film in its style'' *(Film Quarterly,* Spring 1973, pp. 46–47). William F. Van Wert's opinion is that in *Emitai* ''Sembene has never been more in control of his camera'' *(Quarterly Review of Film Studies,* Spring 1979, p. 216), but Armes thinks that the film ''lacks the tight dramatic unity and flow of *Mandabi''* *(Cine Tract,* Summer-Fall 1981, p. 75). Jacques Chevallier examines *Emitai*'s varied genres: realism, humor, irony, revolutionary lyricism, and dramatic climaxes. For him, if not faultless, such a stylistic blend attests to Sembene's original and audacious film language *(La Revue du Cinéma, Image et Son,* October 1977, p. 97).

Xala received significant critical appraisals. For John Ngara:

The film rightly deserves to be classed as much an epoch-making event as the subject which it so unsparingly satirises. . . . *Xala*'s success derives largely from the fact that it is told in the authentic fashion of the African folklore. Both its structure and substance give it an unmistakable Africanness. . . . *Xala* is capable of reaching virtually anyone because its message is simple, straight-forward and succinct.

The film is a scathing revelation of the true nature of the political independence of many African states. In consistently depicting the Europeanised style of living side by side with the ubiquitous poverty and neglect, Ousmane succeeds in locating the central issue which many African nations have still to get to grips with. *(Africa,* December 1976, p. 51)

Tom Dowling believes that

few if any Third World movies have made so bold as to express a disgust of such unrelieved, one might almost say overdone, ferocity with the cultural heritage and social values of their native land. . . . there is enough unexpected bite in an African filmmaker bitterly tearing into his own country's roots to allow one's fascination with the subject matter to overcome one's impatience with all the film's technical deficiencies. *(Washington Star,* 28 September 1977, pp. B1, B4)

Udayan Gupta sees *Xala* as "a magnificent critique of the neo-colonial structures that have sprouted from the ruins of colonialism" *(N.Y. Amsterdam News,* 11 February 1978, p. B12). Teshome H. Gabriel emphasizes: "*Xala* is on one level a comedy. . . . On another level, however, the film offers a poignant satire about Africa's neo-colonial leaders" *(Jump Cut,* n. 27, 1982, p. 31). Kathleen McCaffrey notes: "Besides mocking the new black bourgeoisie in Senegal, *Xala* is a condemnation of polygamy" *(Africa Report,* March-April 1981, p. 57). Linda Gross remarks: "Xala is an outrageously funny comedy of manners that suddenly turns into a serious parable of corruption" *(Los Angeles Times,* 23 September 1977, p. 14, part IV). Likewise, Archer Winsten writes:

Actually it's an amusing fable and one that must carry more literal truth than Senegal would like exported. Sembene is a film artist, doubling as writer-director, of exceptional crude force. *(New York Post,* 6 October 1975, p. 23)

For Jill Forbes, *Xala* succeeds essentially by witty observation rather than statement" *(Monthly Film Bulletin,* December 1976, p. 261). Moreover, Sembene's storytelling techniques and handling of satire are praised by Richard Eder *(New York Times,* 1 October 1975, p. 62), David Wilson *(Sight and Sound,* Fall 1975, p. 213), Abdou Achouba Delati (Hennebelle et al., *Ecran 76,* 15 January 1976, p. 45), Janick Arbois *(Télérama,* 10 March 1976, p. 82), Jean Delmas *(Jeune*

Cinéma, March 1976, p. 30), Noureddine Ghali *(Cinéma 76*, April 1976, p. 94), Danièle Dubroux *(Cahiers du Cinéma*, May 1976, p. 72), David Robinson *(The Times*, 5 November 1976, p. 9), and Lucy Fisher in her in-depth article entitled "Xala: A Study in Black Humor" *(Millennium*, Fall-Winter 1980–1981, pp. 165–72). Gilles Dagneau finds *Xala*'s protagonist reminiscent of some of Jean Renoir's characters who also wear the mask of a class to which they do not inherently belong *(La Revue du Cinéma, Image et Son*, April 1976, p. 102). While favoring the film, Alain Masson compares Sembene's excessive and ferocious humor to that of Aristophanes, and considers *Xala*'s final scene (that of the beggars spitting on the businessman) an imitation of Luis Buñuel's 1961 *Viridiana (Positif*, June 1976, p. 56). In contrast, judging the filmmaker's work within its own cultural milieu (a method which should indeed be more often used in the criticism of Black African film), Harriet D. Lyons draws a revealing parallel between *Xala*'s businessmen and the hyena-men of West Africa's folklore *(Canadian Journal of African Studies*, vol. 18, n. 2, 1984, pp. 321–23). Holl feels that there is no reason why *Xala* should not reach an international audience. The reviewer adds:

The style of the film is pinned to the narrative, without subtle dependence on symbols or visual gimmicks, and the slowness of this narrative at times (the wedding and the beggars' march) seems casually deliberate. The last scene might send the meek headed for the doors . . . but the laughs all along the way balance things out nicely. The pic deserves a broad audience, not just an intellectual one. *(Variety*, 20 August 1975, p. 19)

For Hennebelle this motion picture confirms the international scale of Sembene's talent *(Recherche, Pédagogie et Culture*, May-August 1975, p. 7), while Jack Kroll goes as far as saying that *"Xala* is the work of one of the most remarkable artists in the world" *(Newsweek*, 13 October 1975, p. 103).

Apart from these glowing reviews, nevertheless, *Xala* also incurred a few negative comments. Olivier Serre finds the film is not as well made as *Mandabi (Téléciné*, April 1976, p. 24). Because of excessive caricature, dualistic over-schematization (rich vs. poor, evil vs. good) and what he calls a technically botched ending, Ferid Boughedir views *Xala* as the least convincing of Sembene's films to date *(Jeune Afrique*, 2 April 1976, p. 57). In spite of its "amusing premise and a reassuring professional appearance," Gary Arnold (who obviously does not understand the far-reaching symbolism of the film's last sequence) suggests that *Xala* "should end several scenes earlier" *(Washington Post*, 29 September 1977, p. D9). Finally, Anne-Marie Engelibert and Françoise Martin *(Aujourd'hui l'Afrique*, n. 3, 1975, pp. 36–40) as well as Nancy Schmidt *(Research in African Literatures*, Winter 1982, pp. 527–28) offer comparisons between Sembene's film and the novel on which it is based.

Sembene's *Ceddo* has generally been hailed for both its daring topic and original film style. For Udayan Gupta:

Ceddo looks at the role of black leaders in the enslavement of their own people and examines the destructive effects of the imposition of Islam on Africans. . . .

Unlike lavish Hollywood re-creation of other historical periods, *Ceddo* is spare and simple. . . . Unlike *Roots,* it depicts the slave trade not in simple moralistic and racial terms, as an atrocity committed by bad whites against good blacks, but as a function of class as welll. *(Seven Days,* 10 March 1978, p. 25)

Mbye Baboucar Cham views *Ceddo* as "the most irreverent attack on Islam by a Senegalese artist" *(American Journal of Islamic Studies,* August 1984, p. 18). Jean-Claude Bonnet terms the work "a great political film . . . a great African film" *(Cinématographe,* June 1977, p. 44). According to Tom Allen:

Sembene's cinema is cast in pageant form, in which the raw forces of culture, politics, and religion clash on an uncluttered stage. . . . *Ceddo* has the deceptive simplicity of a medieval morality play. . . . As in the Greek plays, the format lends itself naturally to debates between opposing power blocs and the selection of individual champions as the spokesmen for each point of view . . . Sembene, with wondrous simplicity, achieves an operatic orchestration of raw forces similar to Eisenstein's *Alexander Nevsky* and Kurosawa's *Seven Samurai.*

From another aspect, *Ceddo*, like *Padre Padrone,* seizes small details of the present and expands them into awesome portents of the future. *(Village Voice,* 20 February 1978, p. 40)

Emmanuel Decaux describes *Ceddo* as "an ancient Greek tragedy" *(Cinématographe,* October 1979, p. 48). Azzedine Mabrouki *(Les 2 Ecrans,* April 1979, p. 18) and Fabienne Pascaud *(Télérama,* 18 July 1979, p. 72) favor *Ceddo*'s forceful denunciation of imperialistic alien intrusion. Furthermore, Ayi Kwei Armah notes that the film "is no mere historical document. Nor is it just a work of art using history to clarify the present. It is an exquisitely framed meditation on the theme of liberation" *(West Africa,* 8 October 1984, p. 2031). For James Leahy, "This magnificent film is a history for Africans and in African terms. It is a work of great organisational and thematic complexity, beautifully staged, mainly in depth, and displaying extraordinary kinetic grace and rhythmic control" *(Monthly Film Bulletin,* January 1982, p. 5). Louis Marcorelles feels that *Ceddo* is "quite simply magnificent" and states: "This work is probably the most important African film to date. Because of its scope, mise en scène and lyricism—a kind of lyricism its author never expressed before, *Ceddo* reminds one of a Glauber Rocha film" *(Le Monde,* 7 May 1977, p. 33). Barthelemy Amengual also compares *Ceddo* to Brazilian cinema novo but primarily establishes links between the film and Sembene's own cultural matrix *(Positif,* July-August 1977, p. 83). Mireille Amiel *(Cinéma 77,* July 1977, p. 75), Sheila Smith Hobson *(N.Y. Amsterdam News,* 11 February 1978, p. B12), Michel Boujut *(Les Nouvelles Littéraires,* 12 July 1979, p. 28), Raphael Bassan *(Ecran 79,* September 1979, p. 63), and Madior Diouf *(Le Soleil,* 10 July 1984, p. 7) stress Sembene's use of rich and commanding metaphors. Serge Daney *(Cahiers du Cinéma,* October 1979, pp. 51–53), Vieyra *(Le Cinéma au Sénégal,* 1983, p. 97), and Robert Cancel *(A Current Bibliography on African Affairs,* vol. 18, n. 1, 1985–86, pp. 3–19) relate *Ceddo* to traditional African oral epics. Christian Bosséno is pleased with the film's sustained rhythm, its rigorous editing and beautiful visuals, as well as the actors' hieratic gestures and gait *(La Revue du Cinéma, Image et Son,* September 1972, p. 116).

Interspersed with these highly supportive critiques, however, are some less enthusiastic responses to Sembene's *Ceddo.* For instance, Mosk writes:

Sometimes the pic is too talky and the fable-like quality and actions not always incisive or effective enough to stave off a certain heaviness in narration. . . . An item of festival and archive interest but more difficult for commercial chances. *(Variety,* 1 June 1977, p. 18)

From an almost identical viewpoint, Jerry Oster states:

Because most of his actors are amateurs, or have only a little experience, Sembene makes many of his points more broadly than a Western viewer would like. The camera work is often clumsy and the cutting abrupt. The result is a rigidity that works against Sembene's narrative. *(New York Tribune,* 17 February 1978, p. 28)

According to Vincent Canby:

"Ceddo" is a folk tale presented as the kind of pageant you might see enacted at some geographic location made famous by history and now surrounded by souvenir stands. It's not cheap or gaudy, but it's an intensely solemn, slightly awkward procession of handsomely costumed scenes designed to pass on a lot of information as quickly and efficiently as possible. . . . There are no characterizations in the film, only rather grand impersonations. Most of "Ceddo" has been photographed in the sort of medium-long shot from which one might observe an outdoor theatrical. Only twice, in fantasy sequences, does Mr. Sembene allow himself the imaginative film maker's freedom to distort history to achieve some kind of dramatic truth. The rest is picturesque. *New York Times,* 17 February 1978, p. C8)

Finally, Mireille Amiel dislikes Manu Dibango's "manipulative music," questions Sembene's use of the Princess' nudity, deplores the overcaricatural portrayal of the imam, and regrets what she terms *Ceddo*'s simplistic manicheism *(Cinéma 79,* September 1979, pp. 92–93).

FILMOGRAPHY

L'Empire Sonhrai (The Sonhrai Empire), 35 mm, black and white, length unknown, 1963.
Borom Sarret, 35 mm, black and white, 20 min., 1963.
Niaye, 35 mm, black and white, 35 min., 1964.
La Noire de (Black Girl), 35 mm, black and white, 60 min., 1966.

Mandabi (The Money Order), 35 mm, color, 105 min., 1968.
Taw, 16 mm, color, 24 min., 1970.
Emitai (God of Thunder), 35 mm, color, 95 min., 1971.
Xala, 35 mm, color, 116 min., 1974.
Ceddo, 35 mm, color, 120 min., 1976.

BIBLIOGRAPHY

Writings by Ousmane Sembene

Sembene, Ousmane. *Le Docker noir*. Paris: Nouvelles Editions Debresse, 1956.
————. *O pays, mon beau peuple*. Paris: Amiot, 1957.
————. "La Mère" (short story). *Présence Africaine*, n. 17, December 1957–January 1958, pp. 111–12.
————. *Les Bouts de bois de Dieu*. Paris: Amiot Dupont, 1960. Published in English as *God's Bits of Wood*. New York: Doubleday, 1962; London: Heinemann, 1970.
————. "The Negro Woman of . . ." (short story). *Présence Africaine*, n. 36, 1961, pp. 103–19.
————. *Voltaïque*. Paris: Présence Africaine, 1962. Published in English as *Tribal Scars and Other Stories*. London: Heinemann, 1973.
————. *L'Harmattan*. Paris: Présence Africaine, 1964.
————. *Vehi Ciosane ou Blanche Genése*, suivi du *Mandat*. Paris: Présence Africaine, 1965. Published in English as *The Money Order, with White Genesis*. London: Heinemann, 1972.
————. "L'Image cinématographique et la poésie en Afrique," in Paulin Soumanou Vieyra, *Sembene Ousmane cinéaste*. Paris: Présence Africaine, 1972.
————. *Xala*. Paris: Présence Africaine, 1973. Published in English as *Xala*. Westport, Conn.: Lawrence Hill and Co., 1976.
————. "Influence de la révolution d'octobre et réflexion sur le cinéma d'Afrique noire." Unpublished lecture delivered at a film-related conference held in Moscow, 21–30 July 1977.
————. *Le Dernier de l'Empire*. 2 vols. Paris: L'Harmattan, 1981. Published in English as *The Last of the Empire*. London: Heinemann, 1983.

Interviews of Ousmane Sembene

A, B. "Sembene Ousmane: les cinéastes ne sont pas des martyrs." *Fraternité Matin*, 13–14 March 1982, p. 16.
"African Cinema Seeks a New Language—Sembene Ousmane, Writer and Film Director (Senegal)." *Young Cinema and Theatre*, n. 3, 1983, pp. 26–28.
Arbois, Janick. "Ousmane Sembene: L'indépendance ca sert à quoi?" *Télérama*, n. 987, 15 December 1968, p. 54.
Armes, Roy. "Ousmane Sembene: Question of Change." *Cine Tract*, Summer-Fall 1981, pp. 71–77.
Arora, K. L. "Africa Speaks Out." *Film World*, vol. 16, n. 3, March 1979, pp. 67–69.
Berruer, André. "Un Cinéaste africain: Ousmane Sembene." *Pas à Pas*, n. 142, March 1964, pp. 31–34.

Bonnet, Jean-Claude. "Ousmane Sembene." *Cinematographer*, n. 28, June 1977, pp. 43–44.

Bosséno, Christian. "Entretien avec Ousmane Sembene." *La Revue du Cinéma, Image et Son*, n. 342, September 1979, pp. 116–18.

Cheriaa, Tahar. "Ousmane Sembene, Carthage et le cinéma africain." *Cinéma-Québec*, vol. 3, n. 9–10, August 1974, pp. 51–52.

———. "Problématique du cinéaste africain: l'artiste et la révolution." *Cinéma-Québec*, vol. 3, n. 9–10, August 1974, pp. 13–17.

———. "Ousmane Sembene: Carthage et le chemin de la dignité africaine et arabe." *Cinémarabe*, n. 4–5, November 1976, pp. 15–17.

———, and Férid Boughedir. "Jeune Afrique fait parler Sembene Ousmane." *Jeune Afrique*, n. 795, 2 April 1976, pp. 54–55.

Delmas, Jean, and Ginette Delmas. "Ousmane Sembene: 'Un film est un débat.' " *Jeune Cinéma*, n. 99, December 1976–January 1977, pp. 13–17.

Diedhiou, Djib. "Sembene Ousmane—mon prochain film: Samory." *Le Soleil*, 4 July 1984, pp. 2–3.

———. "Ceddo de Sembene Ousmane: un pas de plus vers Samory." *Le Soleil*, 7–8 July 1984, p. 7.

Dury, Hélène. "Un Entretien avec Sembene Ousmane." *Lutte Ouvrière*, n. 454, 14 May 1977, p. 20.

Fanon, Josie. "Au nom de la tolérance—un entretien avec Sembene Ousmane." *Demain l'Afrique*, n. 32, 30 July 1979, pp. 72–73.

"Film-makers and African Culture." *Africa*, n. 71, July 1977, p. 80.

Fiofori, Tam. "Film Realities. "*West Africa*, 27 April 1987, p. 820.

Ghali, Noureddine. "Ousmane Sembene." *Cinéma 76*, n. 208, April 1976, pp. 83–95.

Gregor, Ulrich. "Interview with Ousmane Sembene." *Framework*, n. 7–8, Spring 1978, pp. 35–37.

Grelier, Robert. "Ousmane Sembene." *Revue du Cinéma, Image et Son*, n. 322, November 1977, pp. 74–80.

Gupta, Udayan, Deborah Johnson, and Nick Allen. "Seven Days Interview: Sembene." *Seven Days*, 10 March, 1978, pp. 26–27.

Haffner, Pierre. "Eléments pour un autoportrait magnétique." *Cinémaction*, n. 34, 1985, pp. 20–24.

Hennebelle, Guy. "Ousmane Sembene." *Jeune Cinéma*, n. 34, November 1968, pp. 4–9.

———. "Ousmane Sembene: Pour moi le cinéma est un moyen d'action politique, mais . . . " *L'Afrique Littéraire et Artistique*, n. 7, 1969, pp. 73–82.

———. "Ousmane Sembene: En Afrique noire nous sommes gouvernés par des enfants mongoliens du colonialisme." *Les Lettres Françaises*, n. 1404, 6 October 1971, p. 16.

———. "Pour ou contre un cinéma africain engagé?" *L'Afrique Littéraire et Artistique*, n. 19, October 1971, pp. 87–93.

———. "Sembene Ousmane." *L'Afrique Littéraire et Artistique*, n. 49, 3rd Quarter 1978, pp. 114–26.

———. "Sembène parle de ses films." *Cinémaction*, n. 34, 1985, pp. 25–29.

"J.A. fait parler Sembene Ousmane." *Jeune Afrique*, n. 976, 19 September 1979, pp. 72–75.

James, Emile. "Je n'utilise pas de vedettes ça coûte trop cher." *Jeune Afrique,* n. 499, 28 July 1970, pp. 39–42.

Jensen, Monika. "Interview with Ousmane Sembene." *Arts in Society,* vol. 10, n. 2, Summer-Fall 1973, pp. 220–25.

Lemoine, Jaqueline. "Sembene: le théâtre est un accouplement de tous les soirs." *Le Soleil,* 1 March 1984, pp. 4–5 (arts and letters section).

Mabrouki, Azzedine. "Entretiens avec Sembene Ousmane." *Les 2 Ecrans,* n. 12, 1979, pp. 19–21.

Marcorelles, Louis. "Ousmane Sembene, romancier, cinéaste poète." *Les Lettres Françaises,* n. 1177, 6 April 1967, p. 24.

Medeiros, Richard de. "Dialogue à quelques voix." *Recherche, Pédagogie et Culture,* n. 17–18, May-August 1975, pp. 39–42.

Morellet, Jean-Claude. "Sembène Ousmane: pour un congrès des cinéastes africains." *Jeune Afrique,* n. 386–387, 27 May 1968, p. 70.

NAP. "Sembène Ousmane nous dit: j'ai été témoin d'un drame, dans un village sénégalais. J'ai voulu en faire un roman . . . et puis ce fut un film." *Dakar-Matin,* 1 March 1966, p. 4.

Ndaw, Aly Kheury. "Sembene Ousmane et l'impuissance bourgeoise." *Jeune Afrique,* n. 694, 7 April 1974, p. 20.

"Ousmane Sembene at the Olympic Games." *American Cinematographer,* vol. 53, n. 11, November 1972, pp. 1276, 1322.

Pâquet, André, and Guy Borremans. "Ousmane Sembene: les francs-tireurs sénégalais." *Cinéma-Québec,* vol. 2, n. 6–7, March-April 1973, pp. vii–xii.

Perry, G. M., and Patrick McGilligan. "Ousmane Sembene: An Interview." *Film Quarterly,* vol. 26, n. 3, Spring 1973, pp. 36–42.

Pfaff, Françoise "Entretien avec Ousmane Sembène: à propos de Ceddo." *Positif,* n. 235, 1980, pp. 54–57.

Prelle, François. "Ousmane Sembene à bâtons rompus." *Bingo,* n. 222, July 1971, pp. 56–60.

Ramonet, Ignace de. "Ousmane Sembene: retrouver l'identité africaine." *Le Monde Diplomatique,* March 1979, p. 29.

V, C. "Un Film dont on parle et dont on parlera longtemps: Le Mandat de Ousmane Sembene." *Bingo,* n. 195, April 1969, pp. 41–42.

Weaver, Harold D. "Film-makers Have a Great Responsibility to Our People—An Interview with Ousmane Sembene." *Cineaste,* vol. 6, n. 1, 1973, pp. 27–31.

Film Reviews and Studies of Ousmane Sembene

Allen, Tom. "The Third World Oracle." *Village Voice,* 20 February 1978, p. 40.

———"Pleasure over Pain: The Good, Better, and Best." *Village Voice,* 1 January 1979, p. 39.

Amengual, Barthelemy. "Ceddo, de Sembene Ousmane (Senegal)." *Positif,* n. 195–96, July-August 1977, p. 83.

Amiel, Mireille. "Ceddo de Ousmane Sembene (Sénégal)." *Cinéma 77,* n. 223, July 1977, p. 75.

——— "Ceddo, Ousmane Sembene." *Cinéma 79,* n. 249, September 1979, pp. 92–93.

Amuka, Peter. "Some Uses of Sex-Relations in the Writings of Sembene Ousmane." Unpublished paper, 1979, pp. 1–16.

Andrews, Nigel. "Le Mandat (The Money Order)." *Monthly Film Bulletin,* vol. 40, n. 469, February 1973, pp. 30–31.

Arbois, Janick. "Le Mandat." *Télérama,* n. 987, 15 December 1968, p. 57.

——— "Le Mandat." *Téléciné,* February 1969, p. 29.

——— "Xala." *Télérama,* n. 1365, 10 March 1976, p. 82.

Armah, Ayi Kwei. "Islam and Ceddo." *West Africa,* 8 October 1984, p. 2031.

Arnold, Gary. "Xala: The Curse of Storytelling Impotence." *Washington Post,* 29 September 1977, p. D9.

Aumont, Jacques, and Sylvie Pierre. "Huit fois deux." *Cahiers du Cinéma,* n. 206, November 1968, p. 30.

B, A. J. "Xala, Ceddo et les autres. . . ." *Le Soleil,* 4 July 1984, p. 3.

B, F. "Le Mandat." *Le Film Français—La Cinématographie Française,* n. 1270, 13 December 1968, p. 17.

Bass. "Je ne milite dans aucun parti, je milite à travers mon oeuvre, nous affirme Ousmane Sembene." *Dakar-Matin,* 11–12 April 1966, p. 1.

Bassan, Raphael. "Ceddo." *Ecran 79,* n. 83, September 1979, pp. 62–63.

——— "Comment filmer l'Afrique?" *Afrique-Asie,* n. 320, 24 April 1984, pp. 50–52.

Billard, P. and M. Martin. "La Cinquième Semaine Internationale de la Critique au prochain Festival de Cannes." *Cinéma 66,* n. 106, May 1966, p. 89.

Binet, Jacques. "Cinéma africain." *Afrique Contemporaine,* n. 83, January-February 1976, pp. 27–30.

Bogle, Donald. *Toms, Coons, Mulattoes, Mammies and Bucks.* New York: Viking Press, 1973.

Bonitzer, Pascal. "L'Argent-fantôme." *Cahiers du Cinéma,* n. 209, February 1969, pp. 57–58.

Bonnet, Jean-Claude. "Ceddo." *Cinématographe,* n. 28, June 1977, p. 44.

Bontemps, Jacques. "Semaine de la critique à Cannes: La Noire de . . . de Ousmane Sembène." *Cahiers du Cinéma,* n. 179, June 1966, p. 48.

Bory, Jean-Louis. "Le Mandat," in *Dossiers du cinéma, films I,* pp. 137–139. Paris: Casterman, 1971.

Bosséno, Christian. "Ceddo." *La Revue du Cinéma, Image et Son,* n. 342, September 1979, pp. 114–16.

Boughedir, Ferid. "The Blossoming of the Senegalese Cinema." *Young Cinema and Theatre,* n. 4, 1974, pp. 14–20.

———. "Le Cinéma sénégalais: le plus important d'Afrique noire." *Cinéma-Québec,* vol. 3, n. 9–10, August 1974, pp. 24–26.

———. "Une Parabole des privilégiés." *Jeune Afrique,* n. 795, 2 April 1976, pp. 56–58.

——— "Les Grandes Dates du cinema africain." *"Jeune Afrique,* n. 1303–1304, 25 December 1985, p. 89.

Boujut, Michel. "Ceddo de Sembène Ousmane, film sénégalais." *Les Nouvelles Littéraires,* n. 2695, 12 July 1979, pp. 28–29.

Broz, Martin. "The Birth of African Cinema." *Young Cinema and Theatre,* n. 1, 1968, pp. 37–43.

"Caméra et fusil—Ousmane Sembène." *Cinéma 72,* n. 162, January 1972, p. 20.

Canby, Vincent. "Film: Ceddo, a Pageant from Sembene's Africa." *New York Times,* 17 February 1978, p. C8.

Cancel, Robert. "Epic Elements in Ceddo." *A Current Bibliography on African Affairs,* vol. 18, n. 1, 1985–86, pp. 3–19.

Capdenac, Michel. "Le Mandat, film sénégalais de Sembene Ousmane." *Les Lettres Françaises,* n. 1259, 27 November 1968, p. 22.

———. "Les Damnés de la terre." *Les Lettres Françaises,* n. 1353, 30 September 1970, pp. 28–29.

Cervoni, Albert. "Le Mandat, si Dakar m'était conté." *Cinéma 69,* n. 134, March 1969, pp. 119–21.

———, and Bo Torp Pederson. "Den Afroarabiska filmen." *Chaplin 166,* n. 1, 1980, pp. 19–21.

Cham, Mbye Baboucar. "Ousmane Sembene and the Aesthetics of African Oral Traditions." *Africana Journal,* vol. 13 n. 1–4, 1982, pp. 24–39.

———. "Art and Ideology in the Work of Sembene Ousmane and Haile Gerima." *Présence Africaine,* n. 129, 1st Quarter 1984, pp. 79–91.

———. "Islam and the Creative Imagination in Senegal." *American Journal of Islamic Studies,* August 1984, pp. 1–22.

———. "The Creative Artist, State and Society in Africa." *A Current Bibliography on African Affairs,* vol. 17, n. 1, 1984–85, pp. 17–28.

Chauvet, Louis. "Le Mandat." *Le Figaro,* 4 December 1968, p. 28.

Chevallier, Jacques. "Emitai, Dieu du Tonnerre." *La Revue du Cinéma, Image et Son,* n. 320–21, October 1977, p. 97.

Chevrier, Jacques. "Sembène Ousmane, écrivain." *Cinémaction,* n. 34, 1985, pp. 12–16.

Ciment, Michel. "Mandabi." *Positif,* n. 100–101, December 1968–January 1969, p. 45.

Cluny, Claude-Michel. "Emitai de Sembène Ousmane." *Cinéma 72,* n. 165, April 1972, pp. 40–42.

Coad, Malcom. "Ousmane Sembene and Ceddo." *Index on Censorship,* vol. 10, n. 4, August 1981, pp. 32–33.

Cohn, Bernard. "Une Semaine de Critique en 1966 à Cannes." *Positif,* n. 79, October 1966, p. 96.

Combs, Richard. "Jodorowsky's Carnival of Cruelty. *"The Times,* 26 October 1973, p.15

Copans, Jean. "Non à l'ethnocinéma." *Afrique-Asie,* n. 155, 6 February 1978, pp. 48–49.

——— "Entre l'histoire et les mythes." *Cinémaction,* n. 34, 1985, pp. 57–59.

Cyclope, Le. "Xala, Rut Barre d'Ousmane Sembene." *Le Soleil,* 27 February 1975, p. 11.

Dagneau, Gilles. "Xala." *La Revue du Cinéma, Image et Son,* n. 305, April 1976, pp. 102–5.

Dahmani, Abdelaziz. "Samory ou le couronnement." *Jeune Afrique,* n. 1045, 14 January 1981, p. 68.

Daja, Allarabaye. "Efferverscence dans le cinéma sénégalais." *Unir Cinéma,* n. 20–21 (127–128), September-December 1985, pp. 31–32.

"Dakar: Sembene's Railway Strike on Stage." *Afrika,* vol. 25, n. 8–9, 1984, p. 40.

Daney, Serge. "Ceddo (O. Sembene)." *Cahiers du Cinéma,* n. 304, October 1979, pp. 51–53.

D'Dée. "Jeune cinéma d'Afrique noire." *L'Afrique Actuelle,* n. 15, 1967, pp. 1–40.

Debrix, Jean-René. "Le Cinéma africain." *Afrique Contemporaine*, n. 38–39, July-October 1968, pp. 7–12.

Decaux, Emmanuel. "Ceddo." *Cinématographe*, n. 15, October 1979, pp. 48–49.

Delmas, Jean. "Jeune cinéma d'Afrique et de Yougoslavie." *Jeune Cinéma*, n. 22, April 1967, pp. 20–22.

———. "Xala." *Jeune Cinéma*, n. 93, March 1976, pp. 30–32.

———. "Sembène Ousmane." *L'Afrique Littéraire et Artistique*, n. 49, 3rd Quarter 1978, pp. 111–13.

Devin, Jean. "A Senegalese Film, and French-Algerian Cooperation." *Young Cinema and Theatre*, n. 2, 1969, pp. 26–27.

Diack, Moktar. "Emitai or Africa Arisen." *Young Cinema and Theatre*, n. 4, 1972, pp. 27–29.

Diédhiou, Djib. "Raymond Hermantier: la passion du peuple." *Le Soleil*, 1 March 1984, p. 3 (arts and letters section).

Dione, Sakhewar. "Ceddo—recouvrer l'héritage négro-africain." *Le Soleil*, 19 July 1984, p. 8.

Diop, Abdoulaye Bara. "La Polygamie au Sénégal." *Cinémaction*, n. 34, 1985, pp. 51–54.

Diouf, Bara. "Le Mandat, film d'Ousmane Sembene." *Dakar-Matin*, 7 December 1968, p. 8.

———. "Ceddo ou la résistance à l'islamisation." *Le Soleil*, 10 July 1984, p. 7.

Dowling, Tom. "Two New Movies: The Impotence of a Groom and His Country." *Washington Star*, 28 September 1977, pp. B1, B4.

Dubroux, Danièle. "Exhibition (Xala)." *Cahiers du Cinéma*, n. 266–267, May 1976, pp. 72–74.

Dury, Hélène. "Emitai de Sembene Ousmane." *Lutte Ouvrière*, n. 454, 14 May 1977, p. 20.

Duvigneau, Michel. "La Noire de." *Téléciné*, n. 134, August-September 1967, p. 46.

Echemin, Kester. "Sembene Ousmane et le mythe du peuple messianique." *L'Afrique Littéraire et Artistique*, n. 46, 1978, pp. 51–59.

Eder, Richard. "Film Festival: Cutting, Radiant Xala." *New York Times*, 1 October 1975, p. 62.

Enagnon, Yénoukoumé. "Sembène Ousmane, la théorie marxiste et le roman." *Peuples Noirs, Peuples Africains*, n. 11, September-October 1979, pp. 92–127.

Engelibert, Anne-Marie, and Françoise Martin. "Sembene Ousmane: une oeuvre, deux moyens d'expression." *Aujourd'hui l'Afrique*, n. 3, 1975, pp. 36–41.

Farès, Tewfik. "Les Gris-gris de Ousmane Sembene." *Jeune Afrique*, n. 602, 22 July 1972, p. 66.

Fisher, Lucy. "Xala: A Study in Black Humor." *Millennium*, n. 7–9, Fall-Winter 1980–1981, pp. 165–72.

Flatley, Guy. "Senegal Is Senegal, Not Harlem." *New York Times*, 2 November 1969, p. D17.

Forbes, Jill. "Xala." *Monthly Film Bulletin*, vol. 43, n. 515, December 1976, pp. 260–61.

Frazer, John. "Mandabi." *Film Quarterly*, vol. 23, n. 4, Summer 1970, pp. 48–50.

Gabriel, Teshome. "Xala: A Cinema of Wax and Gold." *Jump Cut*, n. 27, 1982, pp. 31–33.

Gardies, René. "La Noire de. . . . " *La Revue du Cinéma, Image et Son*, n. 210, November 1967, pp. 132–33.

———. "Jeune cinéma d'Afrique noire." *La Revue du Cinéma, Image et Son*, n. 212, January 1968, pp. 16–18.

Gauthier, Guy. "Le Mandat." *La Revue du Cinéma, Image et Son*, n. 224, January 1969, pp. 99–100.

Ghali, Noureddine. "Emitai, la vraie nature du colonialisme." *Cinéma 76*, n. 208, April 1976, p. 94.

———. "Xala, histoire symbolique d'une déchéance." *Cinéma 76*, n. 208, April 1976, p. 95.

Gross, Linda. "Africa's Xala and Sambizanga." *Los Angeles Times*, 23 September 1977, pp. 14–15, part IV.

Gueye, A. Mactar. "Spelling It Out." *Index on Censorship*, vol. 8, n. 4, July-August 1979, pp. 57–58.

Gupta, Udayan. "The Watchful Eye of Ousmane Sembene." *N.Y. Amsterdam News*, 11 February 1978, p. B12.

———. "Banned in Senegal." *Seven Days*, 10 March 1978, p. 25.

———. "Ceddo." *Cinéaste*, vol. 8, n. 4, Summer 1978, pp. 37–38.

Haffner, Pierre. *Palabres sur le cinématographe*. Kinshasa: Les Presses Africaines, 1978.

———. "Radiographie du cinéma sénégalais." *Filméchange*, n. 18, Spring 1982, pp. 41–48.

———. "Sandy et Bozambo—Entretien avec Jean Rouch sur Sembène Ousmane." *Cinémaction*, n. 34, 1985, pp. 86–94.

Hall, Susan. "African Women on Film." *Africa Report*, January-February 1977, pp. 15–17.

Hennebelle, Guy. "Vers un tiers cinéma africain?" *Jeune Afrique*, n. 452, 2 September 1969, p. 40.

———. "Socially Committed or Exotic? Films from French-Speaking Africa." *Young Cinema and Theatre*, n. 3, 1970, pp. 24–33.

———. "Ousmane Sembene." *L'Afrique Littéraire et Artistique*, n. 20, 1st Quarter 1972, pp. 202–8.

———. "Les Films africains en 1975." *Recherche, Pédagogie et Culture*, n. 17–18, May-August 1975, pp. 7–9.

———. *Guide des films anti-impérialistes*. Paris: Editions du Centenaire, 1975.

———, Ferid Boughedir, Mohand Ben Salama, and Abdou Achouba Delati. "Le Cinéma de Sembene Ousmane." *Ecran 76*, n. 43, 15 January 1976, pp. 41–50.

Hill, Allan. "African Film and Filmmakers." *Essence*, July 1978, pp. 18–24.

Hinxman, Margaret. "So Many Children. . . . " *Sunday Telegraph*, 1 July 1973, p. 18.

Hoberman, J. "Inside Senegal." *Village Voice*, 6 February 1978, pp. 42–48.

Hobson, Sheila Smith. "Ceddo: An Epic Masterpiece." *N.Y. Amsterdam News*, 11 February 1978, p. B12.

———. "In the Senegalese filmmaker's Will to Succeed, a Lesson for All." *N.Y. Amsterdam News*, 11 February 1978, p. B12.

Holl. "Xala (Impotence)." *Variety*, 20 August 1975, p. 19.

Huannou, Adrien. "Sembene Ousmane, cinéaste et écrivain sénégalais." *L'Afrique Littéraire et Artistique*, n. 31, 1975, pp. 24–28.

Ijere, Muriel. "Victime et bourreau: l'Africain de Sembene Ousmane." *Peuples Noirs, Peuples Africains*, n. 35, September-October 1983, pp. 67–85.

"Institution d'un prix de la Fondation Léopold Sédar Senghor." *Le Soleil,* 25 October 1982, p. 5.

Jacob, Haruna Jiyah. "The Voice of the People?" *West Africa,* 27 May 1985, pp. 1045–46.

Jouvet, Pierre. "Emitai." *Cinématographe,* n. 27, May 1977, p. 40.

Kakou, Antoine. "La Thématique." *Cinémaction,* n. 34, 1985, pp. 16–19.

———. "Les Gris-gris d'un conteur." *Cinémaction,* n. 34, 1985, pp. 62–65.

Kamphausen, Hannes. "Cinema in Africa: A Survey." *Cineaste,* vol. 5, n. 3, Summer 1972, pp. 29–37.

Kebzabo, Salek. "Ceddo ou l'homme du refus." *Jeune Afrique,* n. 812, 30 July 1976, pp. 60–61.

Klain, Stephen. "Senegal's Astonishing Film Industry." *Variety,* 1 February 1978, p. 7.

Kroll, Jack. "The World on Film." *Newsweek,* 13 October 1975, pp. 103–4.

Landy, Marsha. "Politics and Style in Black Girl." *Jump Cut,* n. 27, 1982, pp. 23–25.

Leahy, James. "Ceddo." *Monthly Film Bulletin,* vol. 49, n. 576, January 1982, p. 5.

Losse, Deborah N. "The Beggar as Folk Character in African Literature of French Expression." *Ba Shiru,* vol. 10, n. 1, pp. 14–19.

Lyons, Harriet D. "The Uses of Ritual in Sembene's Xala." *Canadian Journal of African Studies,* vol. 18, n. 2, 1984, pp. 319–29.

Mabrouki, Azzedine. "Ceddo—période négrière et pénétrations religieuses." *Les 2 Ecrans,* n. 12, April 1979, p. 18.

———. "Londres: un hommage à Ousmane Sembene." *Les 2 Ecrans,* n. 35, June 1981, pp. 33–34.

Maiga, Mohamed. "La Nouvelle École du films sénégalais." *Jeune Afrique,* n. 998, 20 February 1980, p. 64.

Makédonsky, Erik. "Route étroite pour le jeune cinéma sénégalais." *L'Afrique Littéraire et Artistique,* n. 1, 1968, pp. 54–62.

Malcolm, Derek. "Xala." *The Guardian,* 4 November 1976, p. 10.

"Le Mandat." *Avant-Scène Cinéma,* n. 90, March 1969, pp. 147–50.

Marcorelles, Louis. "Le Mandat, Sénégal." *Les Lettres Françaises,* n. 1256, 6 November 1968, p. 19.

———. "Les Vérités premières de Sembène Ousmane." *Le Monde,* 7 May 1977, pp. 1, 33.

Martin, Angela. "Ousmane Sembene." *National Film Theatre,* April 1981, pp. 6–7.

———. *African Films: The Context of Production.* London: British Film Institute, 1982.

Masson, Alain. "Mascarade à Dakar." *Positif,* n. 182, June 1976, pp. 54–56.

Mbengue, Papa Wongué. "Essai d'une lecture de l'espace dans Ceddo." Unpublished paper, 1984, pp. 1–5.

———. "Le Cinéma de Sembene Ousmane: thématique et écriture." Unpublished paper, 1984, pp. 1–7.

McCaffrey, Kathleen. "African Women on the Screen." *Africa Report,* vol. 26, n. 2, March-April 1981, pp. 56–58.

Ms. L. "Le Premier Festival de Carthage." *Cahiers du Cinéma,* n. 187, February 1967, p. 13.

Mortimer, Robert A. "Ousmane Sembene and the Cinema of Decolonization." *African Arts,* vol. 5 n. 3, Spring 1972, pp. 26, 64–68, 84.

Mosk. "Emitai." *Variety,* 12 July 1972, p. 28.

———. "Ceddo." *Variety,* 1 July 1977, p. 18.

Nave, Bernard. "Ceddo." *Jeune Cinéma,* n. 104, July-August 1977, pp. 43–44.

Ndaw, Aly Kheury. "Ousmane Sembene tel qu'en lui-même: I—Cinéaste proche du peuple." *Le Soleil,* 24 July 1984, p. 8.

———. "Ousmane Sembene tel qu'en lui-même: II—Plaidoyer du militant." *Le Soleil,* 25 July 1984, p. 12.

———. "Sembene Ousmane tourne 'Le Camp de Thiaroye.' "*Le Soleil,* 24 March 1987, p. 10.

———. "Thiaroye ã l'écran." *Le Soleil,* 22 April 1987, pp. 1, 13.

Ngara, John. "Xala—An Allegory on Celluloid." *Africa,* n. 64, December 1976, p. 51.

N'Noruka, M. "Une Lecture de Xala de Sembène Ousmane." *Peuples Noirs, Peuples Africains,* n. 36, November-December 1983, pp. 57–76.

Nwagboso, Maxwell. "West African Film Festival: Sembene Rides High." *Africa Now,* June 1985, p. 63.

Ode, Okore. "The Film World of Ousmane Sembene." Ph.D. dissertation, Columbia University, 1982.

Oster, Jerry. "African Portrait: Ceddo—Film from Senegal." *New York Tribune,* 17 February 1978, p. 28.

Pascaud, Fabienne. "Ceddo." *Télérama,* n. 1540, 18 July 1979, p. 72.

Pearson, Lyle. "Four Years of African Films." *Film Quarterly,* vol. 26, n. 3, Spring 1973, pp. 42–47.

Pedersen, Vibeke, and Viggo Holm Jensen. "Afrika, en kampande filmkontinent." *Chaplin 101,* n. 6, 1970, pp. 280–95.

Pennec, Claude. "La Noire, d'Ousmane Sembene." *Arts et Loisirs,* n. 80, 5 April 1967, p. 52.

Peters, Jonathan. "Aesthetics and Ideology in African Film: Ousmane Sembene's Emitai," in Eileen Julien et al. eds., *African Literature in Its Social and Political Dimensions,* pp. 69–75. Washington, D.C.: Three Continents Press, 1986.

Pfaff, Françoise. "Film and the Teaching of Foreign Languages and Cultures." *CLA Journal,* vol. 22, n. 1, September 1978, pp. 24–30.

———. "Notes on Cinema." *New Directions,* vol. 6, n. 1, 1979, pp. 26–29.

———. "Ousmane Sembene: His Films, His Art." *Black Art,* vol. 3, n. 3, 1979, pp. 29–36.

———. "Myths, Traditions and Colonialism in Ousmane Sembene's Emitai." *CLA Journal,* vol. 24, n. 3, March 1981, pp. 336–46.

———. "Three Faces of Africa: Women in Xala." *Jump Cut,* n. 27, 1982, pp. 27–31.

———.*The Cinema of Ousmane Sembene, a Pioneer of African Film.* Westport, Conn.: Greenwood Press, 1984.

———. "Ceddo," in Frank N. Magill, ed., *Magill's Survey of Cinema: Foreign Language Films,* pp. 492–496. Englewood Cliffs, N.J.: Salem Press, 1985.

Pommier, Pierre. *Cinéma et développement en Afrique noire francophone.* Paris: Pédone, 1974.

Pouillaude, Jean-Louis. "Emitai." *Positif,* n. 195–196, July-August 1977, pp. 120–121.

Prédal, René. "La Noire de . . . : premier long métrage africain." *Cinémaction,* n. 34, 1985, pp. 36–39.

Randal, Jonathan C. "An African Director Reaching the People." *Washington Post,* 17 June 1976, pp. B1, B4.

Richter, Rold. "Ich will mit meinem Volk reden-Gesprach mit Ousmane Sembène." *Film und Fernsehen,* n. 2, 1978, pp. 32–34.

Robertson, Nan. "Xica and African Films." *New York Times*, 12 August 1983, p. C3.

Robinson, David. "The Nasty Spell of Success." *The Times*, 5 November 1976, p. 9.

Rolland, Béatrice. "Alger, juillet 1969, ler festival panafricain." *Positif*, n. 113, February 1970, pp. 87–95.

Ropars-Wuilleumier, MC. "A propos du cinéma africain: la problématique culturelle de La Noire de. . . . " *Recherche, Pédagogie et Culture*, n. 17–18, May-August 1975, pp. 10–15.

Rouch, Jean. "L'Afrique entre en scéne." *Le Courrier de l'Unesco*, n. 3, 1962, pp. 10–15.

Ruelle, Catherine. "Sembène Ousmane, un cinéaste hors du commun." *Actuel Développement*, n. 46, January-February 1982, p. 44.

———. "La Place de la femme." *Cinémaction*, n. 34, 1985, pp. 80–83.

Sapir, T. David. "Emitay." *American Anthropologist*, vol. 76, n. 3, September 1974, pp. 693–97.

Scheinfeigel, M. "Borom Sarret, un film de Ousmane Sembene—Découpage intégral et dialogues." *L'Avant-Scène*, n. 229, June 1979, pp. 35–42.

———. "Borom Sarret: la fiction documentaire." *Cinémaction*, n. 34, 1985, pp. 32–34.

Schissel, Howard. "Sembene Ousmane: Film-maker." *West Africa*, 18 July 1983, pp. 1665–66.

Schmidt, Nancy J. "African Literature on Film." *Research in African Literatures*, vol. 13, n. 4, Winter 1982, pp. 518–29.

Schoenberner, Gerhard. "Det svarta Afrikas filmen och deras regissorer." *Chaplin 166*, n. 1, 1980, pp. 10–15.

"Sembene Ousmane and the Censor." *Africa*, n. 86, October 1978, p. 85.

"Senegalese Filmmaker Sembene Premieres on Cable T.V." *New York Amsterdam News*, 19 June 1982, p. 29.

Serceau, Daniel. "Emitai: l'échec d'une transposition dramatique." *Cinémaction*, n. 34, 1985, pp. 43–45.

———. "Ceddo: la barbarie à visage divin." *Cinémaction*, n. 34, 1985, pp. 54–57.

——— "La Recherche d'une écriture." *Cinémaction*, n. 34, 1985, pp. 66–72.

Serceau Michel "Niaye: l'Afrique sans masque." *Cinémaction*, n. 34, 1985, p. 35.

———. "Le Mandat: un film catalyseur des relations sociales." *Cinémaction*, n. 34, 1985, pp. 40–42.

———. "Xala: une fable sur la bourgeoisie africaine." *Cinémaction*, n. 34, 1985, pp. 46–50.

———. "Du masque au mandat: tradition et modernité." *Cinémaction*, n. 34, 1985, pp. 72–79.

Serre, Olivier. "Xala." *Téléciné*, n. 207, April 1976, p. 24.

Sevastakis, Michael. "Ousmane Sembene's Five Fatalistic Films—Neither Gangsters nor Dead Kings." *Film Library Quarterly*, vol. 6, n. 3, Summer 1973, pp. 13–23, 40–48.

Spass, Lieve. "Female Domestic Labor and Third World Politics in La Noire de. . . . " *Jump Cut*, n. 27, 1982, pp. 26–27.

Tarratt, Margaret. "The Money Order." *Films and Filming*, vol. 20, n. 4, January 1974, pp. 45, 48.

Taylor, Clyde. "Shooting the Black Woman." *The Black Collegian*, vol. 9, n. 5, May-June 1979, pp. 94–96.

————. "Two Women," in Renee Tajima ed., *Journey Across Three Continents, Film and Lecture Series*, pp. 28–31. New York: Third World Newsreel, 1985.

Tesson, Charles. "Si l'Afrique nous était contée." *Cahiers du Cinéma*, n. 64, July-August 1986, p. 5.

Timossi, Jorge. "Entrevista con Ousmane Sembene." *Cine Cubano*, n. 60–62, 1969, pp. 89–93.

Torres, Miguel. "Con Ousmane Sembene en el Festival Internacional de Moscu 1969." *Cine Cubano*, n. 58–59, 1969, pp. 89–93.

Turvey, Gerry. "Xala and the Curse of Neo-colonialism." *Screen*, vol. 26, n. 3–4, May-August 1985, pp. 75–87.

Van Wert, William F. "Ideology in the Third World Cinema: A Study of Sembene Ousmane and Glauber Rocha." *Quarterly Review of Film Studies*, vol. 4, n. 2, Spring 1979, pp. 207–26.

Vast, Jean. "Ousmane Sembene et Maxence Van der Nerech: même combat pour la justice." *Unir Cinéma*, n. 18 (125), May-June 1985, pp. 4–5.

Veysset, Marie-Claude. "Un Film, deux visions." *Jeune Cinéma*, n. 34, November 1968, pp. 10–11.

Vieyra, Paulin Soumanou. "Le Deuxième Festival Cinématographique de Tachkent." *Présence Africaine*, n. 83, 1972, pp. 86–91.

————. *Sembène Ousmane cinéaste*. Paris: Présence Africaine, 1972.

————. *Le Cinéma africain*. Paris: Présence Africaine, 1975.

————. *Le Cinéma au Sénégal*. Brussels: OCIC/L'Harmattan, 1983.

————. "Silence, on (dé) tourne!" *Africa*, n. 178, December 1985, pp. 36–38.

Vignal, D. "Le Noir et le Blanc dans Voltaïque de O. Sembène." *Peuples Noirs, Peuples Africains*, n. 36, November-December 1983, pp. 96–116.

Vogel, Amos. *Film as a Subversive Art*. New York: Random House, 1974.

Weaver, Harold. "Interview with Ousmane Sembene." *Issue*, vol. 2, n. 4, Winter 1972, pp. 58–64.

Weiler, A. H. "Screen: 2 from Senegal." *New York Times*, 13 January 1969, p. 31.

Wilson, David. "Locarno." *Sight and Sound*, vol. 44, n. 4, Fall 1975, pp. 212–13.

Winsten, Archer. "Xala—A Senegalese Fable." *New York Post*, 6 October 1975, p. 23.

X. "Ceddo ou le poids des mystifications en Afrique." *Peuples Noirs, Peuples Africains*, n. 12, November-December 1979, pp. 37–46.

Momar Thiam (1929–   )
Senegal

BIOGRAPHY

Momar Thiam is one of the early Senegalese film practitioners. A practicing Muslim of Wolof origin (the Wolof constitute Senegal's major ethnic group), Thiam was born on 24 September 1929 into the family of a traditional jeweler. Thiam went to Koranic school and then received his primary and secondary education in Dakar, his native city.

In the early 1950s, after working for nine years as an accountant in Dakar, Momar Thiam went to Paris, where he studied still photography. There he soon acquired some additional training in the area of filmmaking. Thiam stresses:

I started with photography, then I learned how to handle a movie camera and I subsequently got involved in editing. From the start I wanted to familiarize myself with all the practical aspects of cinema, so I furthered my training at the Boulogne and St Maur film studios, which are located just outside of Paris. I ended up spending a total of 18 months in France. (Thiam to author, Dakar, Summer 1978)

Shortly thereafter, Thiam returned to Senegal, where he set out to put into practice what he had learned abroad. Consequently, he started working for the film service of the Senegalese Ministry of Information. It was in 1963, with *Sarzan,* based on a $10,000 budget, that Thiam began his career as a cinematographer. The film, made in French and adapted by Momar Thiam and Lamine Diakité from a short story by the Senegalese writer Birago Diop, was shot with leftover black and white footage from *Liberté 1,* a 1961 Franco-Senegalese co-production directed by French filmmaker Yves Ciampi. *Sarzan,* financed primarily by Thiam with some technical and financial support from the Senegalese Ministry of Information, was performed by drama students from the Dakar Daniel Sorano Theater.

In 1964–1965, Momar Thiam participated, as production manager, cameraman, and editor, in the making of *N'Dakarou* (Dakar's name in the Wolof language), a $16,000 collective motion picture based on a script by the Senegalese painter Papa Ibra Tall. Next, 1967 saw the release of *La Malle de Maka Kouli* (The Maka Kouli Trunk), a short black and white fiction film which presents similarities with Thiam's first film in that it is drawn from a short story by Birago Diop and also interpreted by student stage actors. The film, which cost $16,000, was featured and well received at the Verona Film Festival (Italy, 1970). Subsequently, Thiam undertook the filming of two documentaries, namely, *Luttes casamançaises* (Casamance Wrestling, 1968) and *Simb, le jeu du faux lion* (Simb, or the False Lion's Game, 1969), whose budgets amounted to $20,000 and $14,000, respectively.

In 1971 Momar Thiam produced his first feature length movie, *Karim*, transposed into a modern day setting from a 1948 novel by his countryman Ousmane Socé Diop. Commenting on the production, the director points out:

I must say that I had been dreaming of adapting this book to the screen since I started my career as a filmmaker. The author gave me permission to use his book in 1959. I was interested in depicting the life of a young Senegalese . . . in the 1930s. However, I ended up using a contemporary context. In fact the antagonism between young people attached to traditional life . . . and intellectuals bewitched by Western ways still exists today. . . . if young men no longer dream of emulating the "Samba-Linguères" (our noble warriors of yesteryear), they still like to waste money and display their riches. If they no longer dispense their money to griots, they spend it in night clubs, which amounts to the same thing. Senegalese women are still in the habit of asking for more and more money from the men who are courting them. . . . Even working women have kept such a mentality. (*L'Afrique Littéraire et Artistique*, 3rd Quarter 1978, p. 131)

Based on a budget of $44,000, *Karim* was made possible thanks to the understanding of both technicians and actors, who agreed to be paid after the film would bring in some profits. Shot in Wolof and French, and distributed by the Société d'Exploitation Cinématographique Africaine (SECMA), *Karim* received the Special Jury's Award at the 1971 Dinard Film Festival (France).

In 1974 Thiam completed *Baks* (Cannabis). This $88,000 motion picture, produced by the director's own film company and the now defunct Senegalese Société Nationale de Cinéma (SNC), was snubbed at several film festivals but enjoyed long and successful commercial runs in Senegal. The following year, Momar Thiam was made treasurer general of the Fédération Panafricaine des Cinéastes (FEPACI), a post he was to hold for ten years. At the beginning of 1978, several of Thiam's films (*Luttes casamançaises, Karim, Simb, le jeu du faux lion,* and *Baks*) were part of a film series organized by the New York Museum of Modern Art, "Senegal: Fifteen Years of an African Cinema, 1962–1977."

After *Baks*, which essentially focuses on a present-day topic, Thiam went back to illustrating facets of Senegal's traditions by making the $115,000 *Sa Dagga-Le M'Bandakatt* (The Griot, 1981–1982), adapted from a story by Birago Diop (whose major source of inspiration is West African storytelling) and shot by Cheikh Dieng (who had already worked as cameraman for *Karim),* and *Bouki cultivateur* (Bouki the Farmer, 1983), whose total cost amounted to less than $20,000.

In general, Momar Thiam aims at directing straightforward, didactic motion pictures accessible to the average Senegalese viewer. Accordingly, he likes to capture on film the timeless African oral tradition and make use of contemporary topics with which the Senegalese can identify. In his own words, "The Senegalese filmmaker must inform people and tell them the truth" (Thiam to author, Summer 1978).

Momar Thiam, who is more a sincere cinéaste than an innovative craftsman, currently lives and works in Dakar. While a filmmaker, Thiam also works as a still photographer for the Dakar Musée Dynamique and heads a photo shop in that same city. With his daughter and son, Tope Thiam and Moussa Thiam (who worked, respectively, as editor and camera operator in *Bouki cultivateur),* the filmmaker is now engaged in the making of two motion pictures, entitled *Le Procès du pilon* (The Pestle Trial), based on a work by Ousmane Goudiam, and *Buur Tileen,* a ninety-minute production which he plans to shoot in the spring of 1987.

MAJOR THEMES

"All my films show that I am not against tradition. I view myself as a conservative," observes Thiam. He once humorously stated as well: "The other Senegalese film-makers are already busy building the future: let me be nostalgic about the past!" *(Young Cinema and Theatre,* n. 4, 1974, p. 18). Indeed, without always offering a clear-cut viewpoint, Thiam's films tend to underscore the importance of traditional values in a society that is increasingly pervaded with Western ways.

Sarzan (a phonetic distortion of the word "sergeant") tells the story of Moussa, a veteran discharged from his military duties in the French colonial army, who returns home after fifteen years of absence. Unable to readjust to a community from which he has been culturally estranged, Moussa plans to "civilize" the inhabitants of his native village, and vehemently rejects their traditions for the sake of Westernization. In so doing, he goes as far as destroying the religious altars of the Sacred Wood, which entails exclusion from his social group. The former sergeant is subsequently driven to insanity, but the road he advocated will eventually be built. The filmmaker expounds: "Moussa became insane because he was on the edge of two worlds and wanted to alter tradition abruptly. He thus became socially and psychologically alienated" (Thiam to author, Summer 1978).

N'Dakarou illustrates the theme of rural exodus. Enticed by a friend's nostalgic and dreamlike visions of Dakar, a villager decides to migrate to town. Yet, ill-prepared for urban life, the young man is soon involved in delinquency, which leads to his arrest and imprisonment. Luckily, an influential Senegalese intervenes in his favor and the protagonist is released from jail. After such trying experiences in the city, the young villager is brought to a new awareness: he chooses to leave Dakar and return to his rural environment.

La Malle de Maka Kouli has the freshness of African tales. In this film a young man, Seydou, wishes to marry Aminata, his childhood sweetheart, but lacks the means to pay for her dowry. At this point Seydou's mother reveals to him that, before his death, his father entrusted Malik Gueye, a personal friend, with some possessions to be given to his son when the latter would come of age. Upon Gueye's refusal to restore Seydou's inheritance, the young man brings his case to the local elder, who respectively orders Malik and his wife, as well as Seydou and his mother, to carry a heavy trunk around the village limits. After this test is carried out, two boys unexpectedly emerge from the trunk. Based upon conversations they overheard, the elder is able to ascertain Malik's dishonesty. Good triumphs over evil: Seydou will recover his father's estate and marry Aminata.

Luttes casamançaises depicts the various facets of a type of wrestling that originated in southern Senegal (Casamance). In this interesting and much appreciated sport, the fighter has to win twice to be proclaimed the victor. *Simb, le jeu du faux lion* illustrates a traditional activity which is also highly popular in Thiam's country. Says the filmmaker: "Here the main protagonist is a man said to have been wounded by a lion and who subsequently imitates his aggressor. This game is organized by the women" (Thiam to author, Summer 1978).

Karim (whose title is also the main character's name) illustrates the fate of a young Senegalese bureaucrat who splurges his money in order to win the heart of Marième, also courted by her cousin Badara. Both suitors engage in the "Diamale," a traditional contest during which the two opponents shower the desired woman with monetary displays and gifts. Karim, proclaimed the loser of this competition, leaves Saint-Louis (Senegal's former capital) for Dakar, where he hopes to forget Marième. There he meets young intellectuals and succumbs to the charms of Aminata, a divorcee whose taste for the better things in life drives him into debt and the loss of his job. Subsequently, Karim decides to return to Saint-Louis, where he learns that his rival, Badara, has been arrested for embezzlement. Karim is thus free to marry Aminata and thereafter may lead a happy life as predicted by the diviner.

Baks describes some of Senegal's current social problems, particularly rural migration and juvenile delinquency as reflected through the story of Idrissa, a school boy who plays truant and joins in the petty crimes of a gang of drug pushers. After his arrest, the boy is put in his parents' custody. *Baks'* optimistic ending suggests hope for the boy's permanent rehabilitation.

In *Sa Dagga-Le M'Bandakatt,* Thiam examines the status of a griot whose craft is in less demand today. Finally, *Bouki cultivateur,* a film for children, portrays the adventures of Bouki the Hyena, the well-known trickster of countless West African tales.

SURVEY OF CRITICISM

Sarzan, which does not reflect any striking directorial skills, is remembered mainly for having been one of the very first fiction films made in Black Africa. Such views are shared by D'Dée (*L'Afrique Actuelle,* n. 15, 1967, p. 19), Jean-

René Debrix *(Afrique Contemporaine,* July-August, 1968, p. 12), Erik Maké-donsky *(L'Afrique Littéraire et Artistique,* n. 1, 1968, p. 57), and Guy Hen-nebelle *(L'Afrique Littéraire et Artistique,* 1st Quarter 1972, p. 210). Yves Alain remarks that *Sarzan* has "a very interesting subject matter which could have generated an excellent film. Unfortunately, Momar Thiam was at the time new to cinematography. This film resembles more a filmed theater play than a motion picture" *(Bingo,* December 1970, p. 60). Paulin Soumanou Vieyra* notes: "The film was a failure because of its bad technical quality and the poor interpretation of its actors who were performing as if on a stage" *(Le Cinéma africain,* 1975, p. 179).

After showing interest in its topic, Vieyra calls *N'Dakarou* "dull and boring." He is more favorably impressed by *La Malle de Maka Kouli,* which benefits from "a more assertive film language" *(Le Cinéma africain,* 1975, p. 180). Vieyra views *Luttes casamançaises* as a documentary which does not present any particular aesthetic concerns *(Le Cinéma africain,* 1975, pp. 179–80). Much the same could be said of *Simb, le jeu du faux lion.* Nevertheless, both films record for posterity ancestral customs which are vanishing in the modern world.

In his analysis of *Karim,* Vieyra finds that Thiam does not succeed in trans-ferring Ousmane Socé Diop's novel to a contemporary context, and that the filmmaker offers a rather pedestrian rendition of Diop's literary work *(Le Cinéma africain,* 1975, p. 180). Victor Bachy agrees in part with this viewpoint *(La Revue du Cinéma, Image et Son,* July 1979, p. 40). Guy Hennebelle terms *Karim* a "clumsy but sincere work" with unconvincing acting and faulty pho-tography *(L'Afrique Littéraire et Artistique,* 3rd Quarter 1978, p. 129).

For Ferid Boughedir, *Baks* presents the interest of attacking "the excessive Westernization of certain young people who drift into a life of drugs and crime" *(Young Cinema and Theatre,* n. 4, 1974, p. 18). Vieyra considers the film as Thiam's best work *(Le Cinéma africain,* 1975, p. 180), and Jean-René Debrix underscores its authenticity *(Afrique Contemporaine,* August-September 1975, p. 3). On the other hand, Guy Braucourt finds that *Baks* has an unsuccessful film style patterned after Western commercial filmmaking *Ecran 75,* February 1975, p. 10), and Hennebelle deplores its excessive didactism, accented by a poorly structured narrative *(L'Afrique Littéraire et Artistique,* 3rd Quarter 1978, p. 130).

FILMOGRAPHY

Sarzan, 35 mm, black and white, 35 min., 1963.
N'Dakarou, 16 mm, black and white, 40 min., 1964.
La Malle de Maka Kouli (The Maka Kouli Trunk), 16 mm, black and white, 20 min., 1967.
Luttes casamançaises (Casamance Wrestling), 16 mm, color, 18 min., 1968.
Simb, le jeu du faux lion (Simb, or the False Lion's Game), 16 mm, color, 12 min., 1969.

Karim, 16 mm, black and white, 70 min., 1971.
Baks (Cannabis), 35 mm, color, 120 min., 1974.
Sa Dagga-Le M'Bandakatt (The Griot), 16/35 mm, color, 80 min., 1981–82.
Bouki cultivateur (Bouki the Farmer), 16 mm, color, 16 min., 1983.

BIBLIOGRAPHY

Interviews of Momar Thiam

Beye, Ben Diogaye. "Le 3ème Congrès FEPACI aura-t-il lieu? Momar Thiam est pessimiste." *Unir Cinéma,* n. 16 (123), January-February 1985, pp. 7–9.
Hennebelle, Guy. "Thiam Momar." *L'Afrique Littéraire et Artistique,* n. 49, 3rd Quarter 1978, pp. 130–32.

Film Reviews and Studies of Momar Thiam

Alain, Yves. "Karim, film de Momar Thiam." *Bingo,* n. 215, December 1970, pp. 60–61.
Bachy, Victor. "Le Cinéma sénégalais." *La Revue du Cinéma, Image et Son,* n. 341, July 1979, pp. 38–43.
Binet, Jacques. "Cinéma africain." *Afrique Contemporaine,* n. 83, January-February 1976, pp. 27–30.
Boughedir, Ferid. "The Blossoming of the Senegalese Cinema." *Young Cinema and Theatre,* n. 4, 1974, pp. 14–20.
Braucourt, Guy. "Carthage." *Ecran 75,* n. 33, February 1975, pp. 9–11.
D'Dée. "Jeune cinéma d'Afrique noire." *L'Afrique Actuelle,* n. 15, 1967, pp. 1–40.
Debrix, Jean-René. "Le Cinéma africain." *Afrique Contemporaine,* n. 38–39, July-August 1968, pp. 7–12.
———. "Situation du cinéma en Afrique francophone." *Afrique Contemporaine,* n. 81, August-September 1975, pp. 2–7.
Diop, Mody. "Momar Thiam adapte Sa Dagga' de Birago Diop." *Le Soleil,* 19 July 1979, p. 2.
Haffner, Pierre. "Radiographie du cinéma sénégalais." *Filméchange,* n. 18, Spring 1982, pp. 41–48.
Hennebelle, Guy. "Momar Thiam." *L'Afrique Littéraire et Artistique,* n. 20, 1st Quarter 1972, pp. 210–16.
———. "Les Films africains en 1975." *Recherche, Pédagogie et Culture,* n. 17–18, May-August 1975, pp. 7–9.
———and Catherine Ruelle. "Thiam Momar." *L'Afrique Littéraire et Artistique,* n. 49, 3rd Quarter 1978, pp. 129–30.
Makédonsky, Erik. "Route étroite pour le jeune cinéma sénégalais." *L'Afrique Littéraire et Artistique,* n. 1, 1968, pp. 54–62.
Mbodj, Moustapha. "La Crise du cinéma sénégalais: les cinéastes s'expliquent." *Le Soleil,* 3–4 October 1981, p. 4.
Pedersen, Vibeke, and Viggo Holm Jensen. "Afrika, en kampande filmkontinent." *Chaplin 101,* n. 6, 1970, pp. 280–95.
Rouch, Jean. "Momar Thiam et les autres." *Jeune Afrique,* n. 551, 27 July 1971, p. 34.

Vieyra, Paulin Soumanou. *Le Cinéma africain*. paris: Présence Africaine, 1975.
————. "Les 5èmes Journées Cinématographiques de Carthage." *Présence Africaine*, vol. 93, 1st Quarter 1975, pp. 200–214.
————. *Le Cinéma au Sénégal*. Brussels: OCIC/L'Harmattan, 1983.

Mahama Johnson Traoré (1942–   )
Senegal

BIOGRAPHY

Of Muslim extraction and Malian origin (Traoré is a name commonly found among the Bambara, one of Mali's major ethnic groups), Mahama Johnson Traoré was born in 1942 in Dakar, Senegal's capital city, where he attended both primary and secondary schools.

After high school, Traoré went to France to study mechanical engineering. There, while working as a soundman on a set, he had his first practical encounter with cinema, and this led him to the decision of wanting to become a filmmaker himself. In order to carry out this ambition, he studied from 1964 to 1966 at the Conservatoire Indépendant du Cinéma Français, located in Paris, where he was trained as a film director. In 1966 Traoré acquired knowledge about educational radio and television by participating in a series of workshops offered at the time by the French Ministry of National Education. The following year, he worked with film crews in England, Italy, and Germany.

In 1968 Mahama Johnson Traoré went back to Senegal, where he started working as program coordinator for the Dakar ciné-clubs. As such, he organized film screenings (followed by public debates) in schools and various neighborhoods. Traoré recalls:

Returning to Senegal, I went to movie theaters quite often, sometimes also attending underground screenings. I was active in the cine-clubs at the time. . . . we would go to the movies and afterwards meet friends in front of the theater and discuss the films. It was during that time that I became aware of the importance of cinema. (*Cineaste*, vol. 6, n. 1, 1973, p. 33)

Shortly thereafter, Traoré succeeded in completing his first film, entitled *Diankha-bi* (The Young Girl). The director reminisces:

My first film was produced in 1969 by myself with the help of some friends. We cannot say—I say "we" because it was a collective work—that it was a normal production.

You see, I returned to Senegal in 1968, when the Senegalese cinema was at a turning point. I met a very nice person who doesn't want to be named—he wants to maintain his anonymity—and I told him my problems, that I had finished my studies and now I wanted to make a film. . . . So he gave me a thousand meters of 16 mm black and white raw stock. I got my friends together, a cameraman and some other technicians, and I told them, "Look, I've come back from Europe and I want to make a film." They asked me, "With what?"—I said, "With raw stock, a camera and a tripod." So we just dived in and made a short called *Diankha-bi. (Cineaste,* vol. 6, n. 1, 1973, p. 33)

Diankha-bi is based on a script written by Traoré in collaboration with friends. It was shot by a small technical crew including Momar Thiam* as cameraman. Except for Eddje Diop, a stage actor at the Dakar Daniel Sorano Theater, *Diankha-bi* was performed by nonprofessional actors. The year of its release, Traoré's motion picture (distributed by the Société d'Exploitation Cinémato-graphique Africaine, known as SECMA) won the Grand Prize at the Festival International du Film de l'Ensemble Francophone (FIFEF) in Dinard, France, and was screened at the First Pan-African Festival of Algiers, where it was well received by international film critics. After *Diankha-bi,* Mahama Johnson Traoré filmed *L'Enfer des innocents* (Hell of the Innocents) which, although presented at the Mannheim Film Festival (Germany, 1969) and in a few Tunisian ciné-clubs (the film was processed in Tunisia), has to date never been officially distributed.

Shot in Wolof (Senegal's main African language) and accompanied with French subtitles, *Diegue-bi* (The Young Woman, 1970), a sequel to *Diankha-bi,* was co-produced with SECMA (which provided half of its financing) and distributed by that same company. This well-publicized $20,000 color fiction film was seen by more than 200,000 viewers in Senegal, which was a significant number for an African film at the time. Also, *Diegue-bi* was shown in 1970 at the Carthage Film Festival and was featured three years later in Canada at "Le Sénégal à la Cinémathèque Québécoise" film series.

In 1972 Traoré completed his next film, *Lambaaye* (Graft), also shot in Wolof by the Senegalese cameraman Baidy Sow (who had worked on *Badou Boy* by Djibril Diop Mambety*). Like Traoré's previous motion picture, *Lambaaye* was co-produced by Sunu Films (Traoré's own company) and SECMA. The film is the screen adaptation of *Le Pot de vin* (Graft) a play written by the Senegalese author Sonar Senghor after one of Gogol's short stories entitled *Inspector General.* Because of its somewhat subversive overtones, *Lambaaye* received a partial ban from the government censors and was allowed to be seen for only six weeks in Dakar, where its commercial success equalled that of *Diegue-bi.* In 1972, *Lambaaye* received the Third Prize ("Tanit de Bronze") at the Carthage Film Festival, and was also presented at the Dinard Film Festival. The following year, the picture was also part of the Senegalese film series held at the Quebec Cinémathèque.

Also in 1972, Mahama Johnson Traoré single-handedly produced *Réouh-Takh*

(Big City), shot by Baidy Sow and performed by a cast of nonprofessional actors. Perceived by some as a pointed unilateral attack at the sociopolitical life in present-day Senegal, the film was completely banned in that country. Since then it has been seen primarily on the university and film festival circuit (among others at the Quebec Cinémathèque in 1973). Next, in 1973, Traoré became secretary of the Cinéastes Sénégalais Associés (Association of Senegalese Filmmakers).

In spite of his being adversely affected by censorship, Traoré continued his career as a filmmaker. In 1974 he filmed *Garga M'Bossé* (Cactus) with cameraman Georges Caristan (who has also worked on a number of films with Ousmane Sembene*). *Garga M'Bossé* was co-produced by Sunu Films and a Swedish television station (SR2), and does not appear to have been widely circulated outside of Africa. The following year saw the release of *Njangaan* (The Koranic School Student), an $80,000 film viewed by many as Traoré's major work. Based on a script by the young Senegalese writer Cherif Adramé Seck, and shot by Baidy Sow, this Wolof color feature was jointly produced by the now defunct Société Nationale de Cinéma (SNC) of Senegal and Sunu Films. *Njangaan* (also spelled Ndiongane) was shown at the 1974 Carthage Film Festival, where it won the third Prize ("Tanit de Bronze") but generated quite a few negative responses for its attack on the misuse of Islam; it was featured during the Directors' Fortnight at the 1975 Cannes Film Festival. In 1975 as well, *Njangaan* received the Jury's Grand Prize at the Taormina Festival (Italy), and in 1976 it was given an encouragement award at the Pan-African Film Festival of Ouagadougou (FESPACO) in Burkina Faso. Furthermore, this motion picture was screened at the Racines Noires (Black Roots) festival held in Paris in the spring of 1985 and at the 1986 Senegalese film series sponsored by the American Film Institute at the Kennedy Center in Washington, D.C.

In the spring of 1978, Mahama Johnson Traoré was honored at the fifth annual awards presentation of the Black Film Makers' Hall of Fame in Oakland, California, where he received the First International Award for achievement as film director. As he gave him the award, the African-American filmmaker Michael Schultz praised Traoré for having made films "through which we understand life in Senegal better, but also get a deeper insight into the human condition in all times and places" *(Africa,* May 1978, p. 36). That same year, several of Traoré's films *(Diankha-bi, Lambaaye, Réouh-Takh, Garga M'Bossé,* and *Njangaan)* were featured at a film series entitled "Senegal: Fifteen Years of an African Cinema, 1962–1977," which was held at the New York Museum of Modern Art (26 January-27 February). Also in 1978, the Senegalese director was made secretary general for the Fédération Panafricaine des Cinéastes (FEPACI), a post from which he resigned in November 1982 following various managerial problems. That same year, Traoré was appointed president of the newly created Société Nouvelle de Promotion Cinématographique (SNPC), subsidized by both government and private funds, whose goal is to facilitate the production and exhibition of Senegalese films. Again, Traoré found himself in the midst of controversy which led to his resignation in 1985. While he held the above functions, Mahama Johnson Traoré travelled widely to fulfill administrative responsibilities and attend film-related symposia. In the fall of 1983, for instance, he was invited to tour the United States as guest of the United States Information Agency's Bureau of Educational Affairs. This opportunity allowed him to meet with a number of independent Black American filmmakers and lecture on African film in several American universities.

Traoré views himself as a politically aware filmmaker at the service of his people. He emphasizes:

At the beginning I wanted to express myself and project my own thoughts onto the screen. Today it is no longer the same thing. My first films were dependent upon the "auteur" theory which had been taught to me in Europe. It was a very individualistic concept. I am henceforth engaged in a kind of filmmaking which is deliberately an integral part of a political process. It is no longer Mahama Traoré alone who expresses himself in my film, but also the social group to which I belong. This has not only an impact on my ideas but on my film style. (*L'Afrique Littéraire et Artistique,* 1st Quarter 1975, p. 92)

With regard to the role of the Senegalese director, Traoré offered the following description:

The Senegalese filmmaker must not be someone who is cut off from his people, or who lives solely in intellectual spheres. He must express the fears and aspirations of his compatriots. . . . Although a film or even a hundred films will never trigger a revolution . . . I personally feel that African and Third World cinemas must be political. I do not condemn people who make entertainment films provided they do not try to impose a vision of life that is alien to us. I am totally opposed to escapist movies of the James Bond type because we know that the lifestyle they reflect is not within our reach. One must not cheat people and have them believe in situations which are not true to life. (Traoré to author, Summer 1978)

Accordingly, Mahama Johnson Traoré disapproves of the bulk of foreign films which have for years inundated Senegalese screens. He states:

Distribution of films in Senegal does not reflect the needs of the people because what we receive are the latest commercial films from France, Italy, and America. It's really an imperialist and colonialist assault—those films are vehicles of violence, sex and a culture that is alien to us, a culture into which we are not integrated and into which we in fact refuse to be integrated because we want to remain ourselves. (*Cineaste,* vol. 6, n. 1, 1973, p. 33)

To help develop an authentic Senegalese popular cinema, Traoré joined the Foyer de Recherches d'une Ethique Négro-Africaine, a group including painters, musicians, and stage actors seeking an artistic style that would reflect their common cultural background. Furthermore, animated discussions with audiences in a ciné-club setting have also led him to chisel a film language with techniques customarily used in traditional African storytelling:

By participating in such debates I started to become interested in the relationship between the oral tradition and the aesthetics of African film. I realized, for instance, that repetition is often used in the oral tradition. . . . I think that African cinema can draw its verbal and visual expressions from the oral tradition. I also feel that African film could draw its inspiration from silent cinema inasmuch as the traditional storyteller makes ample use of pantomime and gestures: he does not always use words to express what he means. *(L'Afrique Littéraire et Artistique,* 1st Quarter 1975, p. 95)

For the sake of cultural authenticity, Traoré has used the Wolof language in most of his films—even in his first film, *Diankha-bi,* where the characters express themselves in Wolof while an off-screen voice (that of Haitian singer and actress Toto Bissainthe) comments in French upon the plot, and thus plays the role of an omniscient narrator/storyteller. Likewise, insisting on the naturalistic aspects of his motion pictures, the Senegalese director favors using nonprofessional actors.

Mahama Johnson Traoré maintains his residence in Dakar, where he owns a photo shop and continues to manage Sunu Films. He has been working for several years on the screen adaptation of *Le Revenant* (The Ghost) and *La Grève des Bàttu* (The Beggars' Strike), two novels by Aminata Sow Fall, a well-known Senegalese woman writer. Traoré points out:

We [Black African filmmakers] don't lack projects, we have a lot, we always have projects. The important thing for us, however, is not to have projects on a desk but to have the necessary funds to produce them. . . . But the essential thing is to have the will to struggle, the will to make films. *(Cineaste,* vol. 6, n. 1, 1973, p. 35)

MAJOR THEMES

Traoré describes his first three films as being essentially Senegalese through their themes and subject matter, whereas, starting with *Lambaaye,* his most recent works focus on issues crucial to Senegal as well as other developing countries *(Ecran 75,* March 1975, p. 18).

Both *Diankha-bi* and *Diegue-bi,* whose style wavers between docudrama and fiction film, focus on the changing status of contemporary Senegalese women portrayed at various stages of their evolution from a rural setting to that of a consumption-oriented society. Through such a thematic choice, Traoré wants to assert the significant role played by women in the course of his country's history. He stresses:

Their role may not be as visible in an urban African context, but as soon as you go to a rural environment, you meet women who are the true guardians of our sociocultural legacy. . . . they heal the sick by way of traditional medicine. . . . they raise children and transmit our traditional values to them. . . . even if some men would like to confine African women to a submissive role, nobody can deny the significant part they play in the development of our societies. . . . This is not only true of Senegal but of the entire world, and I am deeply convinced that the harmonious growth of any society will only take place with the emancipation and the active participation of women. (Traoré to author, Summer 1978)

Taking as an example the fate of three young Senegalese, *Diankha-bi* depicts the various antagonisms that exist between tradition and modernism in most African societies. Maimouna is illiterate and obedient, and she has been made to marry Doudou Seck, a well-off man whom she does not love. Her sister Seynabou, who has been sent to school, is Westernized, and her lifestyle is increasingly drifting away from traditional mores. In contrast, Assa, their mutual friend, has succeeded in assimilating both traditional and European cultures into a coherent symbiosis. She embodies Traoré's views of what a modern Senegalese woman should aspire to be.

Diegue-bi explores other aspects of the interrelationship between men and women in urban Senegal. Here the female protagonist appears as the femme fatale who leads men astray: in an attempt to quench a woman's insatiable thirst for material goods, a high-ranking civil servant sinks deeper and deeper into debt. Shortly thereafter, he is convicted of having embezzled a large sum of money from his office and is sent to jail.

In Traoré's terms, *L'Enfer des innocents*

concerns itself with Africa's braindrain. Students go to Europe to study and then return to Africa. But some wish to go back to Europe where salaries are much higher than in our developing countries. The film also depicts nepotism and class divisions within Senegalese society. (Traoré to author, Summer 1978)

''Politics is the art of trickery and hypocrisy,'' one of *Lambaaye*'s protagonists claims repeatedly. *Lambaaye* is a satire which denounces corruption, nepotism, and mismanagement, and offers a critical look at present-day government officials in a region of Senegal where the Commander (who is also an expert in electoral fraud) lives on the choice cuts of meat smuggled from the local hospital, while the sick are poorly fed. In that same institution, doctors resell for their own profit the hospital's supply of medicine, while cereals received as gifts from abroad end up being sold in grocery shops. One day, the postmaster, who routinely opens all letters, learns that a government inspector will soon come to town. Shortly thereafter another civil servant, who happens to travel through the area, is mistaken for the expected inspector. The former, who does not disclose his real identity, is subsequently showered with gifts and attention to distract him from the local government officials' fraudulent activities. At one point, encouraged by the diviner's predictions, and to satisfy his own political ambitions, the Commander even foresees giving his daughter's hand to the would-be inspector. But soon the postmaster announces the arrival of the real inspector, who will eventually discover the Commander's misdeeds and place him under arrest while the bogus inspector manages to escape.

Réouh-Takh (Wolof for "town of stone") follows the itinerary of a Black American who has gone to Senegal in search of his roots. While in Dakar, the protagonist visits the Island of Gorée, from which slaves were shipped to the New World. This visit unavoidably brings to his mind memories of his ancestors' destiny. Then, as he mingles with young Senegalese, the tourist is brought to a new awareness through direct contact with some of Senegal's present sociopolitical and economic realities. Traoré stresses:

Today you have a lot of African-Americans who are interested in Africa. They have read a lot of books about our continent and they sometimes come over here to see how things really are in Africa. . . . The film focuses on a Black-American tourist . . . he finds out that colonialism has left highly visible marks in Senegal (where, for instance, many streets still have French names). He is struck by the difference which exists between the city and the countryside, and also by the contrast between Westernized neighborhoods and the poorer areas of the city. He finds out that concepts such as that of "authenticity" are only meant for show-off, and that they do not have a direct relationship with true Negro-African culture. *Réouh-Takh* includes a very important flashback depicting Gorée's slave trade. (*L'Afrique Littéraire et Artistique,* 1st Quarter 1975, p. 94)

Garga M'Bossé concerns the issue of drought in the Sahel, which Traoré uses at the symbolic level to bring about new awareness among his viewers. He explains: "This drought is not only an atmospheric phenomenon but also a political and a cultural reality" (*L'Afrique Littéraire et Artistique,* 1st Quarter, 1975, p. 98).

Garga M'Bossé illustrates the various problems related to the displacement of people from village to town. Here drought forces a family of farmers out of their natural environment to Dakar. Their journey is tragically interrupted by the death of their son, who succumbs to dehydration. Once they reach town, the couple seeks shelter at the crowded home of a distant relative who is both a factory worker and a trade unionist. Faced with unemployment and the intricacies of bureaucracy, the disillusioned villagers will increasingly measure the distance that separates them from city living and their own relatives.

Njangaan denounces the misuse of Islam, a religion the filmmaker includes among the alien forces at work in Sub-Saharan Africa:

One must not forget that Islam was not a Black African religion in the beginning, it is a form of spiritual colonization which reached us through Arab countries, the same way political and economic colonization came from France. One can demonstrate that the new culture which derives from Islam is a form of alienation: the people who are supposed to disseminate this culture, the marabouts for example, are the first ones to make use of social comforts and exhibit bourgeois characteristics. (*Jeune Cinéma,* December 1976–January 1977, p. 3)

Traoré insists that *Njangaan* is based on real facts:

It is a film which deals with the education of children in Koranic schools where they are sometimes beaten and exploited by the marabout. It deals with the problems of the children and their parents. The children are forced to beg in the streets for their teachers to help pay for their education, and the parents strongly believe that the Koranic schools are best. My film does not attack religion. It denounces the exploitation of children in the name of religion. I do not denounce religion but how it is used. (Traoré to author, Summer 1978)

The film's protagonist, Mame, dies after being run over by a car while begging for his marabout. Mame's father, who had entrusted the boy to the marabout to "make a good Muslim out of him or else turn him into ashes," does not rebel at the news of the young boy's death, but accepts it as Allah's will.

SURVEY OF CRITICISM

Diankha-bi was one of the first Black African feature films to focus extensively on the condition of women in the midst of a patriarchal society undergoing significant mutations. And as such it is its theme rather than its technical qualities that have drawn critical attention. Guy Hennebelle notes:

Mahama J. Traoré devotes much attention in *Diankha-bi* . . . to the problems of the young Senegalese evolution. After raging against the unreliable products of "forced" emancipation, and also rejecting the subordination of traditionalist women, he opts prudently for a middle path. An interesting first attempt, but aesthetically incomplete. *(Young Cinema and Theatre, vol. 3, 1970, p. 30)*

As he analyzes *Diankha-bi*'s characters, Jacques Binet finds that "each of them is torn between a coercive social life and personal aspirations geared towards individual freedom. There is no communication . . . .the film is treated in a documentary fashion and one cannot identify with the characters: all in all this does nothing but strengthen the film's scope" *(Afrique Contemporaine,* January-February 1976, p. 30). For Louis Marcorelles, *"Diankha-bi* . . . sketches a portrait of the young traditional/modern Senegalese girl without coming to the heart of the matter" *(Le Monde,* 20 August 1969, p. 10). Likewise, Béatrice Rolland writes: "Johnson Traoré . . . wanted to make a realistic film on the young Senegalese girl. . . . he speaks of her position within the [Senegalese] nation, but . . . the social inclusion of the woman as a member of the labor force is totally neglected" *(Positif,* February 1970, p. 90). Paulin Soumanou Vieyra* feels that *Diankha-bi* has incoherent scenes and an unconvincing overall message. The critic finds the film well intentioned but superficial *(Le Cinéma africain,* 1975, p. 183).

Except for Vieyra's comments concerning *L'Enfer des innocents'* "mediocre technical quality" *(Le Cinéma africain,* 1975, p. 184), and Hennebelle's opinion that the film is "a complete technical failure" *(L'Afrique Littéraire et Artistique,*

3rd Quarter, 1978, p. 135), no other reviews seem readily available on Traoré's second motion picture.

Yves Alain likes *Diegue-bi* which, he says,

can be favorably compared with all the African feature length films produced to date. . . . Johnson Traoré's goal was not to make a touristic film about Senegal. Starting with his first shot, he deals with the core of his subject matter, the social life of his country seen through a Dakar couple. . . . But through this precise analysis of Senegalese society . . . Johnson Traoré seems to have a more profound and efficacious approach than that of some of his predecessors. . . . Traoré's images are self-explanatory . . . and many Senegalese may very well feel directly concerned. *(Bingo,* October 1970, pp. 38–39)

Hennebelle's views are less enthusiastic. He states:

Diegue-bi . . . looks like a sociological inquiry into the man/woman interrelationships in Dakar. . . . But a good topic is not enough to make a good film: the author's courage is harmed by a mise en scène which is not up to his intentions. Traoré drifts too often into a verbose and preaching tone. Moreover, his pictures are of bad quality and the construction of his film leaves much to be desired. *(L'Afrique Littéraire et Artistique,* n. 15, 1971, p. 70)

Vieyra likewise deplores the film's poor technical qualities and some weaknesses found in its scenario, but nonetheless prefers *Diegue-bi* to *Diankha-bi (Le Cinéma africain,* 1975, p. 184). Claude Michel Cluny considers *Diegue-bi* somewhat unconvincing as well *(Cinéma 72,* April 1972, p. 42).

Lambaaye prompted critiques not unlike those generated by Traoré's previous films. Jean-Loup Passek finds its theme interesting but expresses reservations concerning its construction *(Cinéma 72,* September-October 1972, p. 30). Lyle Pearson observes that "technique is often crude in a Traoré film—bad lighting, unbalanced compositions, awkward angles," and stresses that *Lambaaye*'s events and people tend to be more important than its plot *(Film Quarterly,* vol. 26, n. 3, 1973, pp. 44–45). Both Vieyra *(Le Cinéma africain,* 1975, p. 185) and Hennebelle *(L'Afrique Littéraire et Artistique,* 3rd Quarter 1978, p. 135) feel that *Lambaaye* is hampered by Traoré's unsuccessfully shifting from the theater devices used in the play from which the film is adapted. Victor Bachy finds Traoré's use of caricature exaggerated but seemingly well grounded *(La Revue du Cinéma, Image et Son,* July 1979, p. 42).

Vieyra believes that despite the lack of objectivity (the critic points out that positive and concrete governmental policies have been left out to stress Senegal's shortcomings) and rather elementary rhetoric, *Réouh-Takh* represents a decisive step in Traoré's burgeoning political consciousness *(Le Cinéma africain,* 1975, pp. 187–88). Hennebelle also calls *Réouh-Takh*'s story rudimentary *(L'Afrique Littéraire et Artistique,* 3rd Quarter 1978, p. 136), and Alain Ferrari terms the film an unstructured slap-dash characterized by poor acting and encroaching wordiness *(Téléciné,* January 1973, p. 5).

Guy Hennebelle and Ben Diogaye Beye *(Cinéma 77,* May 1977, p. 64) favor *Garga M'Bossé*'s slow pace which, they emphasize, fits perfectly the rural components of its story. Hennebelle concludes:

This disenchanted panorama of Senegalese society must, in the author's mind, bring about the viewers' will for change and incite them to get rid of the "cactus" [translation of the film's Wolof title] which prevents the nation's true emancipation. *(Recherche, Pédagogie et Culture,* May-August 1975, p. 8)

Njangaan, which remains Traoré's best known work, has generated primarily favorable reviews. For Mosk it is the

sharply-etched tale of a young boy sacrificed by deeply religious Musalman *[sic]* parents to a religious school that hides a ruthless treatment of the pupils and their use as beggars in an almost Dickensian sense of Fagin and his pickpockets.

But not Victorian or over-dramatized, this is directed with economy and force by Mahama Johnson Traoré who takes his place alongside such other noted countrymen filmmakers of his as Ousmane Sembene and Diop. *(Variety,* 4 June 1975, p. 18)

J. Hoberman finds *Njangaan* "forcefully and pragmatically assembled" *(Village Voice,* 6 February 1978, p. 42). Likewise, the Italian critic M.A. judges it a commanding pamphlet *(Rivista del Cinematografo,* July 1975, p. 327). For Mbye Baboucar Cham:

Traoré uses this film to launch a severe attack on the Senegalese Serigne-Marabout in his role as the prime guardian of the first phase of Islamic education. . . . the divergence between [the] true positive principle of Islam and its negative selfish practice and inter-pretation constitutes the focus of *Njangaan (American Journal of Islamic Studies,* August 1984, pp. 12, 14)

According to Kyalo Mativo, *Njangaan* "makes an important contribution . . . inasmuch as it reveals the exploitation and tyranny of those who hold positions of absolute power over the broad majority of the African people" *(UFAHAMU,* Fall 1983, p. 140). Guy Braucourt likes its straightforward narrative and praises its technical, ideological, and dramatic exactness *(Ecran 75,* February 1975, p. 10). André Pâquet favors its dialectics in spite of the film's occasional im-balance between style and content *(Cinéma-Québec,* April 1975, p. 38). Al-though he does not agree with what he calls *Njangaan*'s compliant ending, Vieyra recognizes that the motion picture is technically superior to Traoré's prior works *(Le Cinéma au Sénégal,* 1983, pp. 88–89). Guy Hennebelle also acknowledges Traoré's undeniable progress with *Njangaan (L'Afrique Littéraire et Artistique,* 3rd Quarter 1978, p. 136).

FILMOGRAPHY

Diankha-bi (The Young Girl), 16 mm, black and white, 55 min., 1969.
L'Enfer des innocents (Hell of the Innocent), 16 mm, black and white, 20 min., 1969.

Diegue-bi (The Young Woman), 16 mm, color, 80 min., 1970.
Lambaaye (Graft), 16 mm, color, 80 min., 1972.
Réouh-Takh (Big City), 16 mm, color, 45 min., 1972.
Garga M'Bossé (Cactus), 16 mm, color, 80 min., 1974.
Njangaan (The Koranic School Student), 35 mm, color, 100 min., 1975.

BIBLIOGRAPHY

Interviews of Mahama Johnson Traoré

Braucourt, Guy. "Brève rencontre . . . avec Mahama Traoré." *Ecran 75,* n. 34, March 1975, pp. 18–20.

Broullon, Marvis, and Gary Crowdus. "Cinema in Africa Must Be a School—An Interview with Mahama Traoré." *Cineaste,* vol. 6, n. 1, 1973, pp. 32–35.

Delati, Abu Achuba. "Mahama Johnson Traoré—sur la voie d'une éthique négro-africaine." *Cinéma 75,* n. 194, January 1975, pp. 93–96.

Delmas, Jean, and Ginette Delmas. "Mahama Traoré . . . au service du peuple." *Jeune Cinéma,* n. 99, December 1976–January 1977, pp. 3–7.

Diallo, A. B. "Mahama Johnson Traoré, secrétaire général du FePaCi: pas de conflit entre les J.C.C. et le FESPACO." *Le Soleil,* 25–26 April 1981, p. 7.

Hennebelle, Guy. "Côte d'ivoire, Sénégal, Guinée: six cinéastes africains parlent. . . . " *L'Afrique Littéraire et Artistique,* n. 8, 1969, pp. 58–70.

———. "Entretien avec Mahama Traoré: je suis pour le cinéma politique, contre un cinéma commercial, contre un cinéma d'auteurs." *L'Afrique Littéraire et Artistique,* n. 35, 1st Quarter 1975, pp. 91–99.

———. "Traoré Mahama." *L'Afrique Littéraire et Artistique,* n. 49, 3rd Quarter 1978, pp. 136–41.

Ndaw, Aly Kheury. "Entretien avec Mahama J. Traoré: Moins de politique, moins de démagogie mais beaucoup plus de films." *Le Soleil,* 11 November 1980, p. 4.

Pâquet, André. "Mahama Traoré: du rapport film/public." *Cinéma-Québec,* vol. 2, n. 6–7, March-April 1973, pp. 13–17.

Sow, Bachir. "Johnson Traoré, directeur général de la CNPC: option pour la coopération sud-sud dans la production de films." *Le Soleil,* 15 March 1985, p. 13.

Film Reviews and Studies of Mahama Johnson Traoré

A, M. "N'Diangane." *Rivista del Cinematografo,* n. 7, July 1975, pp. 326–27.

Alain, Yves. "Diegue-bi, le film de Johnson Traoré." *Bingo,* n. 213, October 1970, pp. 38–39.

Alavo, Yves. "Johnson Traoré: le revenant. Le cinéaste africain parle de son dernier film." *Bingo,* n. 320, July 1980, p. 64.

Bachy, Victor. "Le Cinéma sénégalais." *La Revue du Cinéma, Image et Son,* n. 341, July 1979, pp. 38–43.

Beye, Ben Diogaye. "Après le Festival de Royan, une réelle dialectique dans le dialogue des cultures." *Cinéma 77,* n. 221, May 1977, pp. 64–68.

Binet, Jacques. "Cinéma africain." *Afrique Contemporaine,* n. 83, January-February 1976, pp. 27–30.

————. "Le Cinéma africain." *Afrique Contemporaine*, n. 123, September-October 1982, pp. 5–8.

Boughedir, Ferid. "Dinard: le triomphe du cinéma africain." *Jeune Afrique*, n. 604, 5 August 1972, pp. 56–59.

————. "The Blossoming of the Senegalese Cinema." *Young Cinema and Theatre*, n. 4, 1974, pp. 14–20.

————. "1975, l'année des grandes victoires." *Jeune Afrique*, n. 782–783, 2 January 1976, pp. 60–61.

————. "Le Cinéma africain a quinze ans." *Filméchange*, n. 4, Fall 1978, pp. 75–80.

Braucourt, Guy. "Carthage." *Ecran 75*, n. 33, February 1975, pp. 9–11.

C, A. "Explorations africaines." *L'Humanité*, 1 July 1978, p. 8.

Cham, Mbye Baboucar. "Islam and the Creative Imagination in Senegal." *American Journal of Islamic Studies*, August 1984, pp. 1–22.

"Cinema in Africa." *Africa*, n. 42, February 1975, pp. 54–56.

Cluny, Claude Michel. "Dieg-bi [sic]." *Cinéma 72*, n. 165, April 1972, p. 42.

Daja, Allarabaye. "Effervescence dans le cinéma sénégalais." *Unir Cinéma*, n. 20–21 (127–128), September-December 1985, pp. 31–32.

"Diankha-bi, un film de Johnson Traoré ou du ciné-club à la mise en scène." *Bingo*, n. 197, June 1969, pp. 26–27.

Ferrari, Alain. "Le Second Souffle du cinéma africain." *Téléciné*, n. 176, January 1973, pp. 2–9.

Hennebelle, Guy. "Socially Committed or Exotic." *Young Cinema and Theatre*, vol. 3, 1970, pp. 23–33.

————. "Carthage." *Cinéma 71*, n. 154, March 1971, pp. 35–36.

————. "Diegue-bi et Badou-Boy (Sénégal)." *L'Afrique Littéraire et Artistique*, n. 15, 1971, p. 70.

————. "Mahama Traoré." *L'Afrique Littéraire et Artistique*, n. 20, 1st Quarter 1972, pp. 208–10.

————. "Des Cinémas d'Afrique noire depuis 1960." *Recherche, Pédagogie et Culture*, n. 17–18, May-August 1975, pp. 3–6.

————. "Les Films africains en 1975." *Recherche, Pédagogie et Culture*, n. 17–18, May-August 1975, pp. 7–9.

————. "Traoré Mahama." *L'Afrique Littéraire et Artistique*, n. 49, 3rd Quarter 1978, pp. 135–36.

Hoberman, J. "Inside Senegal." *Village Voice*, 6 February 1978, pp. 42, 48.

Kamphausen, Hannes. "Cinema in Africa: A Survey." *Cineaste*, vol. 5, n. 3, Summer 1972, pp. 29–37.

Lemaire, Charles. "FEPACI—s'unir ou mourir." *Afrique Nouvelle*, n. 1863, 20 March 1985, pp. 15–16.

Le Péron, Serge. "Lettre de Dakar: la 3ème génération." *Cahiers du Cinéma*, n. 322, April 1981, p. 11.

Makédonsky, Erik. "Route étroite pour le jeune cinéma sénégalais." *L'Afrique Littéraire et Artistique*, n. 1, 1968, pp. 54–62.

Marcorelles, Louis. "L'Afrique noire au rendez-vous d'Alger." *Le Monde*, 20 August 1969, p. 10.

Martin, Angela. *African Films: The Context of Production*. London: British Film Institute, 1982.

Mativo, Kyalo. "Resolving the Cultural Dilemma of the African Film." *UFAHAMU*, vol. 13, n. 1, Fall 1983, pp. 134–46.

Mosk. "N'Diangane." *Variety*, 4 June 1975, p. 18.

Pâquet, André. "Carthage et les cinémas africains—l'avance des cinémas arabes." *Cinéma-Québec*, vol. 4, n. 2, April 1975, pp. 34–39.

Passek, Jean-Loup. "Dinard." *Cinéma 72*, n. 169, September-October 1972, pp. 29–31.

Pearson, Lyle. "Four Years of African Film." *Film Quarterly*, vol. 26, n. 3, Spring 1973, pp. 42–47.

Pedersen, Vibeke, and Viggo Holm Jensen. "Afrika, en kampande film kontinent." *Chaplin 101*, n. 6, 1970, pp. 280–95.

Renaudin, N. "Notes sur l'enfant dans le cinéma." *Recherche, Pédagogie et Culture*, n. 44, 1979, pp. 101–7.

Rolland, Béatrice. "Alger, juillet 1969, ler festival panafricain." *Positif*, n. 113, February 1970, pp. 87–95.

Schoenberner, Gerhard. "Det svarta Afrikas filmer och deras regissörer." *Chaplin 166*, n. 1, 1980, pp. 10–15.

Vieyra, Paulin Soumanou. "Les 5èmes Journées Cinématographiques de Carthage." *Présence Africaine*, vol. 93, 1st Quarter 1975, pp. 200–214.

———. *Le Cinéma africain*. Paris: Présence Africaine, 1975.

———. *Le Cinéma au Sénégal*. Brussels: OCIC/L'Harmattan, 1983.

———. "Silence, on (dé) tourne!" *Africa*, n. 178, December 1985, pp. 36–38.

Paulin Soumanou Vieyra (1925–   )
Senegal

BIOGRAPHY

Paulin Soumanou Vieyra is not only one of the early figures of Black African cinema, but also one of its most diligent critics and historians. Of Yoruba origin, Vieyra was born into a Christian family comprising eight children on 30 January 1925 in Porto Novo, the capital of Benin. His father was a high-ranking civil servant of the French colonial administration who had studied and been trained in Gorée, Senegal. Paulin Soumanou Vieyra received his early education in Porto Novo, and at the age of ten was sent by his father to a boarding school in France. Vieyra recalls:

I would spend my vacation with a French family but I would stay at school most of the time. . . . There, I was considered an exotic individual and at first I felt totally disoriented because I had been cut off from Africa. . . . I was not discriminated against, and I had friends. The real problem was that, after a while, I did not feel any longer like an African. Everything I would see was white, and I had no mirror which would reflect my racial and cultural identity. I am sure that many Africans who have lived exclusively in a white environment have experienced that type of alienation. So, when I went back to Africa in 1950, I had problems adjusting to my prior surroundings and I could barely speak my own language. Maybe my father should not have severed me from my roots so soon, but he obviously believed France would provide me with better educational opportunities. (Vieyra to author, Ouagadougou, 1 March 1985)

Like his schoolmates, the young Vieyra followed a steady diet of Charlie Chaplin films and Westerns, and read books which familiarized him with the open spaces of the American West and quenched his adolescent thirst for vicarious escape and adventure. However, since he stayed in France throughout the Second World War, Vieyra endured hardship and food rationing like most people, and subsequently contracted tuberculosis. But, despite such health problems, he successfully completed high school and engaged in biological studies at the University of Paris. It was then, while seeking means to earn some money as a student, that Vieyra first entered the realm of filmmaking as an extra. He says:

One day, someone came to the African Student Center looking for a person to play the role of an African soldier in *Le Diable au corps* [Devil in the Flesh, 1949]. I decided that I would give it a try and this is how I became an extra in a number of films as well as on the stage. Since I could neither ride a horse nor swim, I was limited to very minor roles. Nonetheless, this kind of job offered a nice supplemental income and it introduced me to an entirely new world. (Vieyra to author, 1 March 1985)

Subsequently, because of recurrent illness, Vieyra was advised to interrupt his university studies and was sent to a sanatorium, where he received sustained medical treatment. There, while recovering, Vieyra mingled with film students who encouraged him to study cinema. In 1952, after preparing for the entrance examination on his own, Vieyra was admitted to the Institut des Hautes Etudes Cinématographiques (IDHEC) in Paris, where he studied mise-en-scène and production management. Vieyra graduated from the famous film school in 1955 after making a short student film entitled *C'était il y a quatre ans* (Four Years Ago, 1954).

After his formal film training, Paulin Soumanou Vieyra worked as assistant director to André Berthomieu during the filming of *Quatre jours à Paris* (Four Days in Paris, 1955). Then, with some friends, among them the Senegalese Mamadou Sarr, Vieyra shot *Afrique-sur-Seine* (Africa on the Seine, 1955), produced by Le Groupe Africain de Cinéma, an organization created by several students who had a serious interest in film. Thereupon, in 1957, he worked as film editor for Canadian television and received training as a television producer. That same year, Vieyra engaged in the making of *Mol* (Fishermen), a docudrama narrated by Med Hondo* and produced by the Groupe Africain du Cinéma and the French Ministry of Cooperation. Vieyra was not able to complete this work until nine years later for lack of sufficient funding. Also in 1957, Vieyra shot a documentary entitled *L'Afrique à Moscou*. In 1958 the aspiring filmmaker was hired by the French colonial administration to head its West African Bureau, which allowed him to produce *Le Niger d'aujourd'hui* (Niger Today). The following year, Vieyra made three short documentaries, namely, *Avec les Africains à Vienne* (Africans in Vienna), *Présence africaine à Rome* (African Presence in Rome), and *Les Présidents Senghor et Modibo Keita* (Presidents Senghor and Modibo Keita).

After West African countries had gained their independence, Vieyra directed the cinema services of the Mali Federation (a four-month federation which comprised Senegal and the former French Sudan). On the dissolution of the Mali Federation on August 22, 1960, Vieyra opted to reside in Dakar, where he was hired to work for the newsreel division of the Senegalese Ministry of Information. This occupation enabled him to witness many of the historical events taking place at the time in Francophone Africa and Madagascar, which he recorded for posterity in such short films as *Indépendance du Cameroun, Indépendance du Congo, Indépendance du Togo,* and *Indépendance de Madagascar,* produced and released in Senegal in 1960. In 1961 Vieyra shot *Une Nation est née* (A Nation Is Born), a government-funded documentary which was frowned upon by French authorities but widely shown and well received in Senegal. The following year *Une Nation est née* was awarded prizes at both the Locarno (Switzerland) and Karlovy Vary (Czechoslovakia) film festivals. Also in 1961, Paulin Soumanou Vieyra was appointed head of the Senegalese Film Bureau. At that time, he married Myriam Warner, a young Guadeloupean woman he had met while a student in Paris, and who was later to reveal herself as a gifted novelist.

From the early to the mid-1960s, Vieyra accompanied the Senegalese president, Leopold Sedar Senghor, on most of his official trips abroad. This resulted in a series of short films, sponsored by the Senegalese Ministry of Information, which depict President Senghor's visits to the USSR (1962), Italy (1962), Brazil and Trinidad-Tobago (1964), Canada (1966), and the United States (1966). Concurrently with the above, Vieyra also shot a number of other motion pictures (most of them government funded) pertaining to Senegal's sociocultural and political life. These include *Lamb* (Senegalese Wrestling, 1963), which was chosen to be featured at the 1964 Cannes Film Festival; *Ecrit du Caire* (A Letter from Cairo, 1964); *Sindiély* (1964); *Avec l'Ensemble National* (With the National Dance Troupe of Senegal, 1964), which received an award at the 1965 Saint-Cast Film Festival (France; *N'Diongane,* adapted from a story by the Senegalese writer Birago Diop and interpreted by drama students of the Dakar Art School (presented at the 1965 Moscow Film Festival); and *Le Sénégal et le Festival Mondial des Arts Nègres* (Senegal and the First International Festival of Negro Arts, 1966).

To enter a film competition at the 1967 Expo (a world fair which was held in Montreal, Canada), Vieyra in 1966 directed four one-minute films entitled *Le Rendez-vous* (whose Black male protagonist is interpreted by Ababacar Samb*), *La Bicyclette* (The Bike), *Le Marché* (The Market Place), and *Le Gâteau* (The Cake), which presented fictional vignettes of Dakar life. Subsequently, the filmmaker worked as production manager on a number of Senegalese motion pictures, among them *Mandabi* (1968), *Taw* (1970), *Emitai* (1971), *Xala* (1974), and *Ceddo* (1976) by Ousmane Sembene*, and *Kodou* (1971) by Ababacar Samb. Then, in 1971, Vieyra shot *Ecrits de Dakar* (Letters from Dakar). From 1972 to 1974, the filmmaker worked as program director and production manager for the newly created Senegalese television. In 1974 Vieyra made *Diarama* (Welcome), a film commissioned by Canadian television. Two years later, Vieyra shot *L'Habitat rural au Sénégal* (Rural Habitat in Senegal) and *L'Habitat urbain au Sénégal* (Urban Habitat in Senegal), which were produced by the Senegalese Ministry of Information. Moreover, in 1976, using his own financial resources, Vieyra engaged in the making of *L'Envers du décor* (Behind the Scenes), a documentary on Senegal's filmmaker Ousmane Sembene. Because of insufficient funding, however, the motion picture would only be completed in 1980. In 1978 *Afrique-sur-Seine, Une Nation est née,* and *N'Diongane* were selected to be featured at a retrospective of Senegalese cinema held at the New York Museum of Modern Art. The following year, Paulin Soumanou Vieyra retired from the Senegalese Ministry of Information, where he had worked for seven years as head of its film division. Nevertheless, this crucial change in his professional life by no means brought a halt to his career as a filmmaker. In 1981, with a $130,000 bank loan and some financial support from the Senegalese Film Fund (Fonds d'aide à l'industrie cinématographique), Vieyra completed his first feature length film, *En Résidence surveillée* (Under House Arrest), dedicated to the late Alioune Diop, the founder of the Présence Africaine publishing house, and starring the veteran Senegalese stage actor Douta Seck, with a musical score by the Cameroonian musician and writer Francis Bebey. Although the work was featured at the 1982 Berlin Film Forum and Carthage film festivals, *En résidence surveillée* received neither popular nor critical acclaim in Senegal or abroad.

Vieyra's most recent motion pictures are profiles of significant Senegalese figures in literature and the visual arts, including *Birago Diop, conteur* (Birago Diop, A Storyteller, 1982) and *Iba N'Diaye, peintre* (Iba N'Diaye, A Painter, 1984), which received the Second Prize ("Tanit d'Argent") in the documentary category at the 1984 Carthage Film Festival. In 1985 Vieyra's *Afrique-sur-Seine* was presented at the Racines Noires (Black Roots) festival in Paris, which attests to the film's now classic longevity. Vieyra is presently working on a film which highlights the accomplishments of Leopold Senghor as a poet. Says Vieyra:

This film on Senghor is really different from all the other films I have made until now. I show Senghor as he meets with heads of state, while excerpts of his poems are used in the soundtrack. Also, by way of a subjective camera, I show Senghor at Joal, his native village, as he walks through the places he knew as a child. He is subsequently seen at the French National Assembly, and then at the French Academy of which he has recently become a member. The film is also interspersed with personal interviews and will be 52 minutes long. (Vieyra to author, 1 March 1985)

Like *Birago Diop, conteur* and *Iba N'Diaye, peintre,* Vieyra plans to show this motion picture on Senghor on Senegalese television, in local movie theaters, and at French cultural centers throughout Francophone Africa.

Vieyra's next feature film will be *Wolle Wolle Voi Voi,* which he thematically envisions as a 105–minute sequel to *En résidence surveillée.* However, the completion of this project should not be expected in the near future since Vieyra is presently working as the production manager of *Samori,* Sembene's latest film, whose shooting had not yet started at the time of this writing.

To describe Paulin Soumanou Vieyra as solely a director would certainly be erroneous and unfairly restrictive. Besides making films, Vieyra is also leaving his mark in the area of Black African cinema as both a historian and a film reviewer. He has, through the years, attended an impressive amount of film festivals and has assiduously reported on these events in such publications as *Présence Africaine, Le Soleil, Afrique Nouvelle, Voix d'Afrique, L'Ouest Africain, Le Monde,* and *Africa.* Vieyra is also the author of several books, namely *Le Cinéma et l'Afrique* (1969), *Sembène Ousmane cinéaste* (1972), *Le Cinéma africain* (1975), and *Le Cinéma au Sénégal* (1983), all of which provide invaluable first-hand information concerning Black African cinema. Through the years, as well, Vieyra has lectured extensively on African cinema in Africa, Europe, the United States, and the Soviet Union. Moreover, Vieyra wrote a detailed thesis on the origins, growth, and aesthetics of African films for which he obtained a state doctorate (Doctorat d'Etat) from the University of Paris X in 1982. Here the filmmaker explains how he became a privileged chronicler of Black African film:

Since I had taken courses on film theory at IDHEC, I started writing articles for Présence Africaine, which documented the early striving of African filmmakers. I would concurrently write on the evolution of both French and world cinemas. Although I did not always have the leisure to write, I felt certain important things had to be recorded. Later on, as I was working for the Senegalese Ministry of Information, I would often spend half of my time travelling abroad, which considerably interfered with my personal career as a filmmaker. Thus, as I did not always have the time or the financial means to make films, I became further involved in film criticism. (Vieyra to author, Dakar, Summer 1978)

Although Vieyra feels that Black African films should not be studied solely in isolation from other cinemas, he also believes that such motion pictures should be judged primarily within the context of African aesthetics, hence the crucial role of the African film critic. Vieyra emphasizes:

For a long time, African films were reviewed mainly by Western critics according to Western criteria, which distorted the very notion of film criticism regarding Sub-Saharan African cinema. This is not to say that Western critics have no right to deal with African cinema, but their perspective may not always match the sociocultural and economic framework of Black African films. As most Western film critics do not understand African languages, they tackle African films through their French or English subtitles, and so these critics may miss a lot of the motion pictures' visual and cultural connotations. Until recently, most African film critics have been eager movie-goers, journalists who did not know much about film criticism, or people who were trained in film schools abroad. In the past years, however, I have personally taught a number of people involved in the area of journalism, so that they understand the mechanics of filmmaking, and how semiology and semantics should be applied to African films in order to formulate a precise and scientific judgment regarding the African motion pictures they may have to review later in their careers. (Vieyra to author, 1 March 1985)

For Paulin Soumanou Vieyra, "African cinema is made by Africans, for Africans, and deals with topics of interest to both Africa and the Black Diaspora" (Vieyra to author, Washington, D.C., Summer 1978). In agreement with the statements that were made in the 1975 Algerian Charter drafted by Black African filmmakers, Vieyra sees Black African cinema primarily as an instrument of education and information. He states:

The stereotyped image of the solitary and marginal creator spread through the Western capitalistic society must be rejected by the African cinematographer, who—on the contrary—must consider himself a creative artisan at his people's service. Moreover, commercial considerations should not be the preoccupation of African filmmakers.

The only criterion of diffusion to be considered is that of knowing that the film expresses the people's needs and aspirations and not those of groups with particular interests.

The engagement of the cinematographer will in no way mean his subordination. The state must play a promotional role in the building of a national cinema free from the hindrance of censorship and other controls which limit the cinematographer's free creation and the democratic and responsible exercise of his profession. *(First Mogadishu Pan-African Film Symposium,* 1983, pp. 16–17)

As he looks back over some thirty years of cinema production in Africa, Vieyra divides Black African filmmakers into three categories: the politically conscious directors, like Sembene, for whom film should have principally a sociopolitical function; the "image-makers," like Tidiane Aw of Senegal, who tend to use the standards of Western commercial cinema; and the "cinéastes-auteurs," such as Djibril Diop Mambety*, who are innovative creators in search of an original and personal film style.

A Senegalese citizen since 1972, Vieyra has now permanently settled in Dakar with his family (he has a daughter and two sons). Besides having been treasurer general for FEPACI (Fédération Panafricaine des Cinéastes) from 1970 to 1975, president of the Société des Réalisateurs Sénégalais (a Senegalese association of filmmakers); and president of the Association Sénégalaise des Critiques de Cinéma (ASSECCI), a Senegalese association of film critics, Paulin Soumanou Vieyra is also a representative of the Comité Africain des Cinéastes (African Committee of Filmmakers, also known as CAC). Furthermore, the filmmaker is a member of such associations as La Société Africaine de Culture, La Société des Gens de Lettres (a writers' organization), Pen Club International, l'Association des Ecrivains du Sénégal (a Senegalese writers' organization), and FIPRESCI (an international federation of film critics). Over the years, he has worked as consultant for UNESCO, the French Ministry of Cooperation, and L'Institut Culturel Africain (ICA). In 1985 Vieyra and such major directors as Ola Balogun*, Timité Bassori*, Souleymane Cissé*, and Ousmane Sembene founded the West African Film Corporation, a consortium for the production and distribution of African motion pictures. In addition to his administrative responsibilities, his writing, and his activities as both a filmmaker and a production manager, the indefatigable Vieyra has been teaching courses on Black cinema at the Centre d'Etudes Supérieures des Techniques de l'Information (CESTI) of the University of Dakar since 1983.

MAJOR THEMES

Vieyra's very first film, *C'était il y a quatre ans,* was made while he was a student at IDHEC. This five-minute black and white motion picture depicts the sociopsychological estrangement from which many Africans suffer when displaced in Western countries. *C'était il y a quatre ans* presents an African student in his exiguous Parisian room. While studying, he happens to hear a tune on his radio set, the same melody to which he danced just prior to leaving his country. He stands up and makes a few dance steps, and is interrupted by a knocking on his door. His French girlfriend comes to see him to talk about their introductory course to Western classical music. But, as soon as she leaves, his mind wanders back to Africa.

In spite of this early endeavor, it is Vieyra's second film, *Afrique-sur-Seine,* which is generally considered the genesis of Black African cinema. This work suffers from some technical deficiencies, but has nonetheless undeniable historical value because it offers an overview of Blacks as they were then living in the French metropolis, as well as a reflection of the hopes and frustrations commonly found amid uprooted youth in a foreign land. It features Marpessa Dawn, who was later to become the unforgettable female protagonist of Marcel Camus' *Orfeu Negro* (Black Orpheus, 1958).

A number of Vieyra's documentaries illustrate sociopolitical and cultural events related to Africa's history in the late 1950s and the 1960s. *L'Afrique à Moscou* focuses on the participation of Black Africans at a youth and student festival held in Moscow (1957). *Le Niger d'aujourd'hui* stresses recent technological and social progress in Niger; *Présence africaine à Rome* documents the Second Congress of Black Artists and Writers, held in Rome in 1959; *Les Présidents Senghor et Modibo Keita* presents viewers with portraits of the Senegalese and Malian heads of state as their respective countries were preparing to form the short-lived Mali Federation. Some of Vieyra's films record for posterity the independence celebrations of various former French colonies, while others focus on Leopold Sedar Senghor's official visits to a number of foreign nations. *Une Nation est née* mixes real life sequences, lyrical fictional episodes, and literary excerpts from the novel *Ambiguous Adventure* by Cheikh Hamidou Kane, to narrate Senegalese history from pre-colonial times to self-determination.

The cultural significance of traditional Senegalese wrestling is demonstrated by Vieyra in *Lamb* (in which Sembene makes a brief appearance). His *Ecrit du Caire,* made on the occasion of a summit meeting between the heads of member nations of the OAU (Organization of African Unity), offers interesting and often savory slices of Cairo life.

Sindiély, adapted from a ballet of Senegal's National Dance Troupe, tells the story of a young girl whose covetous father wants to marry her to a rich middle-aged merchant. She, however, is in love with a penniless suitor whom she will eventually wed after a succession of comical events. *Sindiély*'s plot, which is essentially expressed through dance and music, can easily be understood notwithstanding cultural and/or linguistical barriers. In *Avec l'Ensemble National,* Vieyra illustrates a number of folk dances from various regions of Senegal.

In *N'Diongane* a griot tells children the story of a young village boy named N'Diongane, whose father was killed by a lion while hunting. The boy now lives with his mother and sister, who affectionately call him "little husband," a nickname which soon generates mockery from his peers. At the age of twelve,

N'Diongane undergoes circumcision (the performer of the ritual is Ousmane Sembene). After this initiatory step toward adulthood, N'Diongane vehemently warns that he will run away if he is ever addressed as "little husband" again. His mother abides by his wish but, one day, his sister playfully calls him by his prior nickname. Consequently, N'Diongane leaves the village, and his mother and sister set out to find him. Subsequently, on seeing them, the young boy runs into the sea and drowns himself. Driven insane by grief, N'Diongane's mother strangles her daughter, and both are eventually engulfed by the sea. Since that time, it is said that the tide no longer covers the spot where the three died and that people picking up shells from the beach and holding them to their ear can hear a voice desperately repeating: "N'Diongane come back! N'Diongane come back!" Vieyra's film includes interesting scenes of the daily lives of Senegalese fishermen, and accurately documents the traditional ceremonial of circumcision. On several occasions (when adequately focused), *N'Diongane* offers sober and lyrical shots of great visual beauty.

Mol is set near Cayar (on the seashore north of Dakar) and centers around Ousmane, a young fisherman who wishes to modernize his trade by purchasing a motor for his boat. After consulting with the elders, who at first oppose his intentions, and the village diviner, the young man goes to Dakar, where he temporarily works as a longshoreman in order to earn the money necessary to carry out his project. After several months of hard work, Ousmane has accumulated some savings and is now able to buy his motor on an installment plan. Back in his village, he receives a warm welcome from his family and friends, in particular from his fiancée, who feared he would never return from the "big city." *Mol* is a didactic docudrama which calls for technical progress. Like *N'Diongane, Mol* has socioanthropological facets and offers a variety of beautiful scenes of collective fishermen's activities.

Paulin Soumanou Vieyra describes his sixty-second silent motion pictures as follows:

Le Rendez-vous features an attractive Senegalese woman going to and fro in front of Dakar's cathedral. A young African man stops walking to watch her. As she now comes towards him smiling, he feels inclined to accost her but then finds out that her smile is addressed to a European suitor walking up to her from behind him. The woman rushes to her friend. The young African man watches them as they embrace and walk away. *La Bicyclette* focuses on a brother and a sister playing together. They both ride bicycles. The brother (the older of the two) discovers he has a flat tire and waits for his sister. When she approaches, the boy drops his own bike, takes hold of hers and starts riding it. But, as he sees his sister cry, the boy comes back to her and takes her on the bike's luggage carrier. She stops crying, and the two happily ride away. In *Le Marché*, I show a French woman shopping at a Dakar market place. While bargaining with a vendor, she feels that someone is trying to steal from her bag. She quickly grasps a hand, which proves to be that of a visibly deprived Senegalese woman who carries a baby tied to her back. A policeman happens to walk by. What should she do? She looks insistently at the woman, especially at her infant, and decides to let her go. As the European woman walks away, one notices that she is limping. The way she looks at the baby may suggest her own childlessness. *Le Gâteau* starts in a pastry shop where a European woman buys a pastry for her young son. While his mother talks to a friend, the little boy goes out of the shop and sees two small Senegalese children enviously looking at him. The boy gives them his pastry and the two kids gratefully offer him a toy they made in return. The boy's mother will slap him in the face after she has noticed that he gave his pastry away. I should say that even many years later, I do feel the concise format of these films was in itself a worthwhile exercise. (Vieyra to author, 1 March 1985)

Vieyra's more recent pictures include *Ecrits de Dakar,* somewhat patterned after *Ecrit du Caire,* which illustrates the official visit of French president Georges Pompidou to Senegal; *Diorama,* a film on Canadian technical aid to Senegal; *L'Habitat rural au Sénégal* and *L'Habitat urbain au Sénégal,* documentaries which portray various aspects of rural and urban life in Senegal; *L'Envers du décor* which shows Ousmane Sembene at work during the making of *Ceddo; Birago Diop, conteur,* a tribute to the Senegalese writer whose tale-like stories (often drawn from the oral tradition) have inspired such filmmakers as Vieyra and Momar Thiam*; and *Iba N'Diaye, peintre,* which presents the figurative and abstract works of the Senegalese painter Iba N'Diaye.

En résidence surveillée provides a fictional account of the intricacies of political life. Mbye Baboucar Cham describes the film as a "satire of political and administrative intrigue in an imaginary African country whose President plots his own overthrow by a 'coup d'état' with the help of his foreign advisors and then returns to power, but this time as Emperor ruling over an empire" *(Présence Africaine,* 4th Quarter 1982, p. 182). Vieyra explains:

The idea for such a film came to me because of the frequency of political coups in Africa. . . . I simply wanted to demonstrate that those coups are not solely generated by Africans, but also by foreign powers who may want to destabilize a government whose views do not match theirs. . . . *En résidence surveillée* points out the mechanisms of such "coups d'état" in Black Africa. (Vieyra to author, 1 March 1985)

Although fictional, *En résidence surveillée* is a composite of events that actually occurred in various African nations. Never before had a Black African filmmaker dealt with such a sensitive topic. Thus, *En résidence surveillée* will probably be remembered more for its thematic audacity than for its stylistic and technical features.

SURVEY OF CRITICISM

Objective critical information pertaining to Vieyra's works is relatively scarce because he has been involved mainly in the making of documentaries which may have been seen on Senegalese television and in local movie theaters but have not enjoyed widespread distribution, and consequently lack extensive press coverage. Furthermore, since a film critic and historian must necessarily feel ill at ease providing subjective judgments concerning his own motion pictures, Vieyra has seldom reviewed his films, except to provide plot summaries, technical information, and/or rather laconic statements as to his likes and dislikes.

Thus, as he nostalgically looks back over the early stages of his career, Vieyra terms *C'était il y a quatre ans* one of his ''favorite films,'' but feels that *Afrique sur Seine* could have been better constructed *(Le Cinéma africain,* 1975, pp. 155–56). Interestingly enough, the film critic D'Dée also judges *Afrique sur Seine* as being poorly edited *(L'Afrique Actuelle,* n. 15, 1967, p. 21). Vieyra limits himself to calling *Une Nation est née* an ''allegory'' *(Le Cinéma africain,* 1975, p. 156), and *Lamb* ''an educational film'' *(Le Cinéma au Sénégal,* 1983, p. 58), but stresses the style of *Ecrit du Caire* because it espouses an epistolary format *(Le Cinéma africain,* 1975, p. 157). He reveals mixed feelings regarding the acting in *N'Diongane (Le Cinéma africain,* 1975, p. 159). Although he finds Senegalese wrestling sketchily presented, D'Dée finds *Lamb*'s topic interesting, but deplores the film's mediocre editing, though he favors the plastic beauty of some of its visuals *(L'Afrique Actuelle,* n. 15, 1967, p. 21). Then, after viewing *Avec l'Ensemble National,* the same critic declares:

The director does not appear to have been overly concerned with an original film language, he merely recorded a series of choreographic playlets. . . . The film's only merit is that it shows professional ballet dancers performing in outdoor settings. The image quality is quite satisfactory. *(L'Afrique Actuelle,* n. 15, 1967, p. 21)

D'Dée likes the thematic content and overall technical know-how of *Mol,* but dislikes its often redundant voice-over commentary as well as its deficient editing *(L'Afrique Actuelle,* n. 15, 1967, p. 20). Vieyra concurs that the film's narration is ill-adapted to its images *(Le Cinéma au Sénégal,* 1983, p. 54).

The Vieyra film that has perhaps received most critical attention is *En résidence surveillée.* Farida Ayari finds its theme worthwhile, but would have wished for more precise editing and cinematic spark *((Adhoua,* January-March 1981, pp. 22–23). A. Bamba Diallo calls the film a failure *(Le Soleil,* 25–26 April 1981, p. 5). Barthélémy Amengual notes:

Using both a serious and humorous tone, *En résidence surveillée* . . . denounces the single party system and the working of neo-colonialism in an imaginary African state. The film does not, however, turn to either parable or allegory, thus generating undeniable political impact in spite of a construction which often lacks forcefulness. *(Positif,* n. 256, July 1982, p. 46)

According to Biny Traoré, *En résidence surveillée* is a didactic motion picture which provides ''an autopsy of neocolonial African regimes'' *(Peuples Noirs, Peuples Africains,* May-June 1983, p. 59). Considering such critical appraisal of his cinematographic works, it is evident that Vieyra will probably be remembered more as a dutiful chronicler and documentary filmmaker than an artful creator.

FILMOGRAPHY

C'était il y a quatre ans (Four Years Ago), 35 mm, black and white, 5 min., 1954.
Afrique-sur-Seine (Africa on the Seine), 16 mm, black and white, 22 min., 1955.
A series of documentaries among which are *L'Afrique à Moscou* (Africa in Moscow, 1957), *Le Niger d'aujourd'hui* (Niger Today, 1958), *Avec les Africains à Vienne* (Africans in Vienna, 1959), *Présence africaine à Rome* (African Presence in Rome, 1959).
A number of newsreels, including *Les Présidents Senghor et Mobibo Keita* (Presidents Senghor and Modibo Keita, 1959), *Indépendance du Cameroun* (The Independence of Cameroon, 1960), *Indépendance du Congo* (The Independence of Congo, 1960), *Indépendance du Togo* (The Independence of Togo, 1960), *Indépendance de Madagascar* (The Independence of Madagascar, 1960), *Voyage présidentiel en URSS* (The Presidential Visit to the USSR, 1962), *Voyage du Président Senghor en Italie* (President Senghor's Visit to Italy, 1962).
Une Nation est née (A Nation Is Born), 35 min., color, 20 min., 1961.
Lamb (Senegalese Wrestling), 35 mm, color, 18 min., 1963.
Ecrit du Caire (A Letter from Cairo), 35 mm, color, 5 min., 1964.
Sindiély, 35 mm, color, 11 min., 1964.
Avec l'Ensemble National (With the National Dance Troupe of Senegal), 35 mm, color, 12 min., 1964.
Voyage du Président Senghor au Brésil et à Trinidad-Tobago (President Senghor's Visit to Brazil and Trinidad-Tobago), 35 mm, color, 10 min., 1964.
N'Diongane, 35 mm, color, 18 min., 1965.
Mol (Fishermen), 16 mm, color, 20 min., 1957–1966.
Visite officielle du Président Senghor au Canada (President Senghor's Official Visit to Canada), 35 mm, color, 9 min., 1966.
Le Sénégal et le Festival Mondial des Arts Nègres (Senegal and the First International Festival of Negro Arts), 35 mm, black and white, 35 min., 1966.
Visite officielle du Président Senghor aux Etats Unis d'Amérique (President Senghor's Official Visit to the United States), 35 mm, color, 9 min., 1966.
Le Rendez-vous, 35 mm, color, 1 min., 1966.
La Bicyclette (The Bike), 35 mm, color, 1 min., 1966.
Le Marché (The Market Place), 35 mm, color, 1 min., 1966.
Le Gâteau (The Cake), 35 mm, color, 1 min., 1966.
Ecrits de Dakar (Letters from Dakar), 35 mm, color, 6 min., 1971.
Diarama (Welcome), 16 mm, color, 26 min., 1974.
L'Habitat rural au Sénégal (Rural Habitat in Senegal), 16 mm, color, 13 min., 1976.
L'Habitat urbain au Sénégal (Urban Habitat in Senegal), 16 mm, color, 13 min., 1976.
L'Envers du décor (Behind the Scenes), 16 mm, color, 26 min., 1976–1980.
En résidence surveillée (Under House Arrest), 35 mm, color, 102 min., 1981.
Birago Diop, conteur (Birago Diop, A Storyteller), 16 mm, color, 26 min., 1982.
Iba N'Diaye, peintre (Iba N'Diaye, A Painter), 16 mm, color, 35 min., 1984.

BIBLIOGRAPHY

Writings by Paulin Soumanou Vieyra

Vieyra, Paulin Soumanou. "Quand le cinéma français parle au nom de l'Afrique Noire." *Présence Africaine*, n. 11, December 1956–January 1957, pp. 142–45.

————. "Où en sont le cinéma et le théâtre africains?" *Présence Africaine*, n. 13, April-May 1957, pp. 143–46.

————. "Réflexions sur le Premier Concours International du Film d'Outre-mer." *Présence Africaine*, n. 17, December 1957–January 1958, pp. 118–22.

————. "Propos sur le cinéma africain." *Présence Africaine*, n. 22, October-November 1958, pp. 106–17.

————. "Responsabilités du cinéma dans la formation d'une conscience nationale africaine." *Présence Africaine*, n. 27–28, August-November 1959, pp. 303–13.

————. "The cinema and the African Revolution." *Présence Africaine*, n. 34–35, October 1960–January 1961, pp. 66–77.

————. "A Montréal, les études africaines en question." *Présence Africaine*, n. 72, 4th Quarter 1969, pp. 214–19.

————. "Le Cinéma au Ier festival culturel panafricain d'Alger." *Présence Africaine*, n. 72, 4th Quarter 1969, pp. 190–201.

————. *Le Cinéma et l'Afrique*. Paris: Présence Africaine, 1969.

————. "Centres culturels et politiques de la culture en Afrique." *Présence Africaine*, n. 74, 2nd Quarter 1970, pp. 185–90.

————. "La création cinématographique en Afrique." *Présence Africaine*, n. 77, 1st Quarter 1971, pp. 218–31.

————. "Dinard 1971 ou le cinéma fait politique." *Présence Africaine*, n. 80, 4th Quarter 1971, pp. 139–42.

————. "Festival du film de Moscou 1971." *Présence Africaine*, n. 80, 4th Quarter 1971, pp. 143–49.

————. *Sembène Ousmane cinéaste*. Paris: Présence Africaine, 1972.

————. "Le 2ème Festival Cinématographique de Tachkent." *Présence Africaine*, n. 83, 3rd Quarter 1972, pp. 86–91.

————. "Le 3ème Festival Cinématographique de Dinard." *Présence Africaine*, n. 84, 4th Quarter 1972, pp. 109–16.

————. "L'Afrique et le cinéma." *Cinéma-Québec*, vol. 2, n. 6–7, March-April 1973, pp. 5–6.

————. "Les 4èmes Journées Cinématographiques de Carthage." *Présence Africaine*, n. 86, 2nd Quarter 1973, pp. 178–87.

————. "6ème Festival International de Films d'Expression Française." *Présence Africaine*, n. 92, 4th Quarter 1974, pp. 190–95.

————. "Les 5èmes Journées Cinématographiques de Carthage." *Présence Africaine*, n. 93, 1st Quarter 1975, pp. 208–14.

————. "Triomphe du cinéma africain à Genève." *Le Soleil*, 13 November 1975, p. 8.

————. *Le Cinéma africain*. Paris: Présence Africaine, 1975.

————. "Le Deuxième Congrès de la FEPACI (Fédération Panafricaine des Cineastes) à Alger (15–19 janvier 1975)." *Présence Africaine*, n. 97, 1st Quarter 1976, pp. 165–74.

————. "Le Cinquième FESPACO." *Présence Africaine*, n. 98, 2nd Quarter 1976, pp. 187–91.

————. "De l'idée à l'idéologie—le cinéma africain en question." Unpublished paper, 1977, pp. 1–10.

————. "Xème Anniversaire des Journées Cinématographiques de Carthage." *Présence Africaine*, n. 101–102, 1st and 2nd Quarter 1977, pp. 231–235.

————. "L'Afrique au 30ème Festival de Cannes." *Afrique Nouvelle*, 8 June 1977, pp. 16–17.

————. "Le Festival Cinématographique de Cannes et l'Afrique." *Présence Africaine*, n. 104, 4th Quarter 1977, pp. 143–51.

————. "Le critique africain face à son peuple." *Cinémarabe*, n. 7–8, January-April 1978, pp. 13–15.

————. "Le Cinéma au Sénégal en 1976." *Présence Africaine*, n. 107, 3rd Quarter 1978, pp. 207–16.

————. "Le 25ème Festival International du Film de l'Ensemble francophone." *Présence Africaine*, n. 108, 4th Quarter 1978, pp. 166–72.

————. "Critères critiques." *Le Monde Diplomatique*, March 1979, p. 29.

————. "Carthage 78." *Présence Africaine*, n. 110, 2nd Quarter 1979, pp. 157–66.

————. "Le Festival du Cinéma à Moscou: I—104 pays et 500 films." *Le Soleil*, 17 September 1979, p. 12.

————. "Le Festival du Cinéma à Moscou: II—l'Afrique était aussi présente." *Le Soleil*, 18 September 1979, p. 10.

————. "FESPACO 1979." *Présence Africaine*, n. 111, 3rd Quarter 1979, pp. 101–6.

————. "Carthage: d'un festival à un autre." *Le Soleil*, 29–30 November 1980, p. 12.

————. "Le Festival de Cannes 1981—les films africains." *Le Soleil*, 22 June 1981, p. 11.

————. "Le Douzième Festival du film de Moscou. I—un prix pour l'Algérie." *Le Soleil*, 4 September 1981, p. 17.

————. "Le Symposium Panafricain de Mogadiscio." *Afrique Nouvelle*, n. 1688, 11 November 1981, pp. 24–25.

————. "Présence africaine." *Le Soleil*, 24 June 1982, p. 19.

————. "FESPACO 83, avant première." *Afrique Nouvelle*, n. 1751, 26 January 1983, pp. 18–19.

————. "Ouagadougou, capitale du cinéma africain." *Le Soleil*, 27 January 1983, p. 21.

————. "FESPACO 83: au tournant de l'histoire." *Afrique Nouvelle*, 2 March 1983, pp. 20–21.

————. *Le Cinéma au Sénégal*. Brussels: OCIC/L'Harmattan, 1983.

————. "Festival de Moscou: Rencontre avec Alimata Salembéré." *Afrique Nouvelle*, n. 1780, 17 August 1983, pp. 18–19.

————. "Les Métaphores d'un conteur." *Le Soleil*, 1 March 1984, p. 6 (arts and lettres section).

————. "37ème Festival de Cannes: I—Une nouvelle mutation." *Le Soleil*, 20 June 1984, p. 21.

————. "37ème Festival de Cannes: II—Le retour de Bergman." *Le Soleil*, 21 June 1984, p. 22.

————. "37ème Festival de Cannes: III—La palme à Wim Wenders." *Le Soleil*, 22 June 1984, p. 22.

————. "Ombres et lumières." *Le Soleil*, 2 November 1984, p. 13.

———. "Fespaco 85: l'agonie du cinèma africain." *Le Soleil*, 9–10 February 1985, p. 10.

———. "Ouagadougou, mon amour." *Africa*, n. 169, February 1985, pp. 35–39.

———. "Silence, on (dé)tourne!" *Africa*, n. 176, December 1985, pp. 36–38.

———. "De l'adaptation cinématographique: réflexion faite." Unpublished paper, 1985, pp. 1–7.

———. "Pour une poignée de noirs." *Africa*, n. 185, July 1986, pp. 49–50.

———. "Le Rôle du critique et de l'historien africains dans le processus du développement de la production cinématographique en Afrique," in *FESPACO 1983*, pp. 43–48. Paris: Présence Africaine, 1987.

Interviews of Paulin Soumanou Vieyra

Haffner, Pierre. "Quatre entretiens avec Paulin Soumanou Vieyra (I)." *Peuples Noirs, Peuples Africains*, n. 37, January-February 1984, pp. 14–29.

———. "Quatre entretiens avec Paulin Soumanou Vieyra (II)." *Peuples Noirs, Peuples Africains*, n. 38, March-April 1984, pp. 27–49.

———. "Quatre entretiens avec Paulin Soumanou Vieyra (III)." *Peuples Noirs, Peuples Africains*, n. 39, May-June 1984, pp. 88–104.

———. "Quatre entretiens avec Paulin Soumanou Vieyra (IV)." *Peuples Noirs, Peuples Africains*, n. 43, January-February 1985, pp. 50–68.

Hennebelle, Guy. "Un Livre de Paulin Vieyra." *Afrique-Asie*, n. 96, 17 November 1975, pp. 49–50.

Film Reviews and Studies of Paulin Soumanou Vieyra

Amengual, Barthelemy, and Petr Kral. "Festival—Berlin 1982." *Positif*, n. 256, July 1982, pp. 42–46.

Awed, Ibrahim, et al., eds. *First Mogadishu Pan-African Film Symposium* (proceedings). Mogadishu, Somalia: MOGPAFIS Management Committee, 1983.

Ayari, Farida. "En résidence surveillée de Paulin Soumanou Vieyra (Sénégal)—satire politique." *Adhoua*, n. 3, January-March 1981, pp. 22–23.

Bachy, Victor. "Le Cinéma sénégalais." *Cinémaction*, n. 26, June 1983, pp. 28–30.

Bosséno, Christian. "A Carthage: l'entente arabo-africaine." *Afrique-Asie*, n. 283, 22 November 1982, pp. 52–53.

Boughedir, Ferid. "Le Cinéma sénégalais: le plus important d'Afrique noire." *Cinéma-Québec*, vol. 3, n. 9–10, August 1974, pp. 25–26.

———. "Le Cinéma en Afrique et dans le Monde." *Jeune Afrique Plus*, n. 6, April 1984, pp. 19–105.

Cham, Mbye Baboucar. "Film Production in West Africa: 1979–1981." *Présence Africaine*, n. 124, 4th Quarter 1982, pp. 168–87.

David, Colette. "La Danse, langage universel." *Jeune Afrique*, n. 1094, 23 December 1981, p. 61.

D'Dée. "Jeune cinéma d'Afrique noire." *L'Afrique Actuelle*, n. 15, 1967, pp. 1–40.

Diedhiou, Djib. "Paulin S. Vieyra a rencontré le cinéma africain." *Le Soleil*, 27 December 1982, p. 7.

Diallo, A. Bamba. "Silence . . . on ne tourne plus." *Le Soleil*, 25–26 April 1981, pp. 5, 7 (Magazine supplement).

Haffner, Pierre. "Radiographie du cinéma sénégalais." *Filméchange*, n. 18, Spring 1982, pp. 41–48.

Hennebelle, Guy. "Un Pionnier: Paulin Soumanou Vieyra." *L'Afrique Littéraire et Artistique*, n. 20, 1st Quarter 1972, pp. 201–2.

———. "Vieyra, Paulin Soumanou." *L'Afrique Littéraire et Artistique*, n. 49, 3rd Quarter 1978, p. 142.

Hennebelle, Monique. "Sembène Ousmane cinéaste—un livre de Paulin Soumanou Vieyra." *L'Afrique Littéraire et Artistique*, n. 27, February 1973, pp. 87–88.

Makédonsky, Erik. "Route étroite pour le jeune cinéma sénégalais." *L'Afrique Littéraire et Artistique*, n. 1, 1968, pp. 54–62.

Ndaw, Aly Kheury. "Cinéma: Tanit d'Argent pour un court métrage sénégalais."*Le Soleil,* 23 October 1984, p. 21.

N'Diaye, Malal. "Cinéma et tradition orale—une conférence de l'A.N.J.S. donnée vendredi par Paulin Vieyra." *Le Soleil,* 19 March 1973, p. 3.

Pedersen, Vibeke, and Viggo Holm Jensen. "Afrika, en kampande filmkontinent." *Chaplin 101,* n. 6, 1970, pp. 280–95.

Pfaff, Françoise. "Notes on Cinema." *New Directions,* vol. 6, n. 1, 1979, pp. 26–29.

"Portrait: Paulin Vieyra, au service du cinéma africain." *El Moudjahid,* 14 October 1983, p. 7.

Traoré, Biny. "Cinéma africain et développement." *L'Observateur,* n. 2524, 8 February 1983, pp. 6, 7, 12.

———. "Cinéma africain et développement." *Peuples Noirs, Peuples Africains,* n. 33, May-June 1983, pp. 51–62.

Traoré, Mahama. "Du rapport film-public." *Cinéma-Québec,* vol. 2, n. 6–7, March-April 1973, pp. xiii-xvii.

Bibliography

Adelugba, Segun. "We Need a Film Development Board." *Daily Times,* 25 March 1974, p. 32.

Agblemagnon, Ferdinand N'Sougan. "The Negro-African Socio-Cultural Condition and the Cinema." *Présence Africaine,* vol. 27, n. 55, 3rd Quarter 1965, pp. 34–44.

"African Films at the Cannes Film Festival." *West Africa,* n. 3279, 26 May 1980, pp. 918–919.

Aig-Imoukhuede, F. "The Film and Television in Nigeria." *Présence Africaine,* vol. 30, n. 58, 2nd Quarter 1966, pp. 89–93.

Akue, Miwonoui. "Togo: pour la promotion du cinéma africain." *Unir Cinéma,* n. 17 (124), March-April 1985, pp. 27–29.

Almeida, Ayi-Francisco. "Les Politiques de communication sociale au moyen du cinéma—le cas des pays africains." *Tiers-Monde,* vol. 24, n. 95, 1983, pp. 583–588.

Amara, Rokia, and Mouny Berrah. "Entretien avec Alkaly Kaba: quand on ne peut pas dire la vérité, on se tait." *Les 2 Ecrans,* n. 17, October 1979, pp. 24–25.

Armes, Roy. "Carthage Film Festival." *New African,* n. 207, December 1984, p. 34.

———. "Black African Cinema in the Eighties." *Screen,* vol. 26, n. 3–4, May-August 1985, pp. 60–73.

———. "Info FEPACI." *Unir Cinéma,* n. 23–24 (130–131), March-April and May-June 1986, pp. 19–21.

Aw, E. R. "Promotion du cinéma sénégalais: objectif de la SIDEC." *Le Soleil,* 16 March 1974, p. 5.

Awed, Ibrahim, et al., eds. *First Mogadishu Pan-African Film Symposium* (proceedings). Mogadishu, Somalia: MOGPAFIS Management Committee, 1983.

Ayari, Farida. "Ouagadougou 81—place aux jeunes." *Adhoua,* n. 4–5, April-September 1981, pp. 4–5.

———. "L'Oeil vert; collectif de cinéma." *Adhoua,* n. 4–5, April-September 1981, pp. 9–10.

———. "Carthage: la morosité." *Afrique-Asie,* n. 335, 19 November 1984, pp. 138–40.

Bachman, Gideon. "Afrique: une génération perdue de réalisateurs?" *Cinéma 75,* n. 194, January 1975, pp. 86–91.

———. "Afrikansk film—fel adjektiv?" *Chaplin 166,* n. 1, 1980, pp. 16–18.

Bachy, Victor. "Le Cinéma en république populaire du Congo." *La Revue du Cinéma, Image et Son*, n. 341, July 1979, pp. 44–46.

———. "La Distribution cinématographique en Afrique noire." *Filméchange*, n. 15, Summer 1981, pp. 31–44.

———. "Cannes—le cinéma africain au 36ème Festival de Cannes." *Unir Cinéma*, n. 7 (114), July-August 1983, pp. 19–20.

———. *Le Cinéma au Mali*. Brussels: OCIC/L'Harmattan, 1983.

———. *Le Cinéma en Côte d'Ivoire*. Brussels: OCIC/L'Harmattan, 1983.

———. *La Haute-Volta et le cinéma*. Brussels: OCIC/L'Harmattan, 1983.

Bakyono, J. S. "VIIIème FESPACO: une compétition serrée." *Ivoire-Dimanche*, n. 626, 6 February 1983, pp. 44–45.

Balogun, Françoise. *Le Cinéma au Nigéria*. Brussels: OCIC/L'Harmattan, 1984.

Bamouni, Babou Paulin, and B. Hubert Pare. "Regard rétrospectif sur le cinéma burkinabe et perspectives d'avenir." *Carrefour Africain*, n. 871, 22 February 1985, pp. 18–22.

Bassan, Raphael. "Vers une unité de la diaspora noire." *Afrique-Asie*, n. 347, 6 May 1985, pp. 54–56.

———. "Festival des Trois Continents—les mille et un regards." *Afrique-Asie*, n. 348, 20 May 1985, pp. 50–51.

———. "Oasis dans le désert. *"Afrique-Asie*, n. 388, 1 December 1986, p. 50–51.

Bassori, Timité. "Un Cinéma mort-né?" *Présence Africaine*, n. 49, 1st Quarter 1964, pp. 111–15.

Bataille. "Cinéma et acteurs noirs." *Présence Africaine*, n. 4, 2nd Quarter 1948, pp. 690–96.

Bebey, Francis. "Le Cinéma en Afrique—décoloniser l'image." *Le Courrier de l'U-NESCO*, May 1977, pp. 30–33.

Bellow, Ledji. "Du nouveau au Fespaco." *Jeune Afrique*, n. 1363, 18 February 1987, p. 61.

Benabdessadok, Cherifa. "C.I.D.C.: une drôle de gestion." *Afrique-Asie*, n. 341, 1 April 1985, pp. 56–57.

———. "10e FESPACO: Ouaga grand écran. *"Afrique-Asie*, n. 396, 23 March 1987, pp. 50–51.

———. "Entretien avec Tahar Chériaa. *Afrique-Asie* n. 396, 23 March 1987, pp. 51–53.

———. "CIDC/CIPROFILM, La Maladie honteuse." *Afrique-Asie* n. 397, 6 April 1987, pp. 56–57.

Bertin, Akaffou. "Le Cinéma et la télévision ivoirienne." *Unir Cinéma*, n. 23–24 (130–131), March-April and May-June 1986, p. 8.

Beye, Ben Diogaye. "Congrès Fepaci: Y aurait-il des pouvoirs parallèles." *Unir Cinéma*, n. 16, January-February 1985, pp. 9–11.

———. "IXème FESPACO—a moins d'une surprise. . . . " *Unir Cinéma*, n. 16, January-February 1985, pp. 5–6.

Binet, Jacques. "Le Cinéma africain à la Documentation Française." *Afrique Contemporaine*, n. 81, September-October 1975, pp. 7–8.

———. "Cinéma africain." *Afrique Contemporaine*, n. 83, January-February 1976, pp. 27–30.

———. "La Nature dans le cinéma africain." *L'Afrique Littéraire et Artistique*, n. 39, 1976, pp. 52–58.

———. "Classes sociales et cinéma africain." *Positif*, n. 188, December 1976, pp. 34–42.

———. "L'Argent dans les films africains." *L'Afrique Littéraire et Artistique*, n. 43, 1st Quarter 1977, pp. 90–93.

———. "Violence et cinéma africain." *L'Afrique Littéraire et Artistique*, n. 44, 2nd Quarter 1977, pp. 73–80.

———. "Le Cinéma africain." *Afrique Contemporaine*, n. 123, September-October 1982, pp. 5–8.

———, et al. "Cinémas noirs d'Afrique." *Cinémaction*, n. 26, 1983.

Bosséno, Christian. "Fêtes biennales de cinémas d'Afrique." *Recherche, Pédagogie et Culture*, n. 53–54, May-August 1981, pp. 69–73.

———. "Afrique, continent des origines." *Revue du Cinéma*, n. 424, February 1987, pp. 62–68.

Bouabib, Hamadi. "Entretien avec Louis Thombiano, secrétaire général du FESPACO." *Adhoua*, n. 3, January-March 1981, pp. 7–8.

Boughedir, Ferid. "Dinard: le triomphe du cinéma africain." *Jeune Afrique*, n. 604, 5 August 1972, pp. 56–59.

———. "Ouagadougou." *Ecran 73*, n. 15, May 1973, pp. 54–55.

———. "La Fepaci: pour la libération du cinéma en Afrique." *Cinéma Québec*, vol. 3, n. 9–10, August 1974, p. 49.

———. "Où vont les cinémas africains?" *Ecran 74*, n. 30, November 1974, pp. 36–48.

———. "1975, l'année des grandes victoires." *Jeune Afrique*, n. 782–783, 2 January 1976, pp. 60–61.

———. "Le Cinéma africain hors des ghettos." *Jeune Afrique*, n. 791, 5 March 1976, pp. 43–45.

———. "L'Image apprivoisée." *Jeune Afrique*, n. 914, 12 July 1978, pp. 185–88.

———. "L'Afrique à la une chez les "francophones' à Namur." *Jeune Afrique*, n. 926, 4 October 1978, pp. 44–45.

———. "Le Cinéma africain a quinze ans." *Filméchange*, n. 4, Fall 1978, pp. 75–80.

———. "FEPACI, fais pas ca." *Jeune Afrique*, n. 1107, 24 March 1982, pp. 58–59.

———. "Une Nouvelle Vague de cinéastes." *Jeune Afrique*, n. 1156, 2 March 1983, pp. 78–79.

———. "Derrière l'écran, l'apartheid . . . " *Jeune Afrique*, n. 1196, 7 December 1983, pp. 66–67.

———. "La Fin de l'amateurisme." *Jeune Afrique*, n. 1149, 12 January 1983, pp. 60–62.

———. "Fespaco: le 8ème festival panafricain du cinéma de Ouagadougou." *Recherche, Pédagogie et Culture*, n. 62, April-June 1983, pp. 89–92.

———. "Une Oasis en Somalie." *Jeune Afrique*, n. 1191, 2 November 1983, pp. 72–73.

———. "Où sont passés les films africains?" *Jeune Afrique*, n. 1220, 23 May 1984, pp. 54–55.

———. "Dix-huit bougies pour Carthage." *Jeune Afrique*, n. 1241, 17 October 1984, pp. 68–69.

———. "Fespaco—l'impossible décollage du cinéma africain." *Jeune Afrique*, n. 1262, 13 March 1985, pp. 50–51.

————. "A Cinema Fighting for Its Liberation," in Renee Tajima ed., *Journey Across Three Continents,* pp. 22–25. New York: Third World Newsreel, 1985.

————. "La Tunisie entre sectarisme et tolérance [Carthage Film Festival]." *Jeune Afrique,* n. 1350, 19 November 1986, pp. 82–83.

————. "Le Rôle de la presse et de la publicité dans la préparation du public à l'accueil du film africain," in *FESPACO 1983,* pp. 49–60. Paris: Présence Africaine, 1987.

Branco, Paulo. "Entretien avec Ruy Duarte de Carvalho." *Cahiers du Cinéma,* n. 274, March 1977, pp. 59–60.

Braucourt, Guy. "Carthage." *Ecran 75,* n. 33, February 1975, pp. 9–11.

Brossard, Jean-Pierre. "Brève histoire du cinéma au Mozambique (1975–1980)." *Les 2 Ecrans,* n. 33, April 1981, pp. 21–23.

Bureau, Patrick. "Le Premier Festival du Film Africain." *Les Lettres Françaises,* 6 June 1963, p. 6.

C, A. "Explorations africaines." *L'Humanité,* 1 July 1978, p. 8.

Caillens, J. "Sur le cinéma." *Présence Africaine,* n. 12, 4th Quarter 1951, pp. 233–34.

Casas, Arlette. "Images de femmes." *Afrique-Asie,* n. 386, 3 November 1986, pp. 54–55.

C.E.S.C.A. *Camera Nigra, le discours du film africain.* Brussells: C.E.S.C.A./OCIC, 1984.

Cham, Mbye Baboucar. "Film Production in West Africa: 1979–1981." *Présence Africaine,* n. 124, 4th Quarter 1982, pp. 168–87.

Chériaa, Tahar. "Policies, Politics and Films in the Arab and African Countries." *Young Cinema and Theatre,* n. 4, 1971, pp. 27–33.

————. "La Politique et le cinéma dans les pays arabes et africains." *Cinéma 71,* n. 154, March 1971, pp. 100–09.

————. "Une Prise de conscience." *Cinéma 72,* n. 165, April 1972, p. 37.

————. "Le Cinéma en Afrique noire francophone: structures, problèmes, perspectives." *Cinéma Québec,* vol. 1, n. 10, July-August 1972, pp. 23–27.

————. "1. La Fédération Panafricaine des Cinéastes. 2. La FePaci, instrument de promotion. 3. Le Canada et l'Afrique. 4. Les Journées Cinématographiques de Carthage." *Cinéma Québec,* vol. 2, n. 1, September 1972, pp. 35–36.

————. Ouagadougou—un cinéma africain libre s'affirme." *Cinéma 73,* n. 175, April 1973, pp. 22–29.

"Le Cinéma africain en 1974: longue marche et grandes manoeuvres." *Cinéma Québec,* vol. 3, n. 9–10, August 1974, pp. 46–48.

Cluny, Claude Michel. "Cinéma africain: le Festival de Ouagadougou." *Cinéma 72,* n. 165, April 1972, p. 36.

Coulibaly, Abdou Latif. "Tres Journées du cinéma africain au Canada." *Le Soleil,* 5 May 1987, p. 10.

————"Sénégal: une présence plutôt discrète." *Le Soleil,* 5 May 1987, p. 10.

Coulibaly, Oumar. "Devenir Cinéaste africain. . . . " *Fraternité Hebdo,* n. 113, 22 August 1980, p. 23.

Coustaut, Carmen. "Africans and Latins Lay Groundwork for Cooperation." *Black Film Review,* vol. 2, n. 2, Spring 1986, pp. 12–13.

Cressole, Michel. "Dans la chaleur de Ouaga." *Libération,* 15 March 1985, pp. 30–31.

Cyr, Helen W. *A Filmography of the Third World.* Metuchen, N.J.: Scarecrow Press, 1976.

————. *A Filmography of the Third World (1976–1983)*. Metuchen, N.J.: Scarecrow Press, 1985.

D, Philippe. "Naissance du cinéma en Guinée-Bissau." *La Revue du Cinéma, Image et Son*, n. 338, April 1979, pp. 15–17.

Dabia, Amévi. "Pour une production africaine rentable." *Filméchange*, n. 23, Summer 1983, pp. 45–54.

Dabla, Amévi. "Togo: week-ends du cinéma africain." *Afrique Nouvelle*, n. 1858, 13 February 1985, pp. 16–17.

Dadson, Nanabanyin. "Production and Co-production." *West Africa*, 22 December 1986, pp. 2649–50.

Daja, Allarabaye. "Fepaci—FESPACO: la fête de la réconciliation?" *Unir Cinéma*, n. 16 (123), January-February 1985, p. 4.

————. "CIDC—CIPROFILM ou la difficile reconquête du marché africain." *Unir Cinéma*, n. 17 (124), March-April 1985, pp. 23–24.

————. "FESPACO 85." *Unir Cinéma*, n. 17 (124), March-April 1985, pp. 15–22.

Daney, Serge. "Carthage, an 10." *Cahiers du Cinéma*, n. 272, December 1976, pp. 43–50.

————. "La (trop) longue marche du cinéma africain." *Libération*, 2 November 1981, p. 21.

————. "Off Mogadiscio." *Libération*, 2 November 1981, p. 22.

Debrix, Jean-René. "Le Cinéma africain." *Afrique Contemporaine*, n. 38–39, July-October 1968, pp. 7–12.

————. "Le Cinéma africain." *Afrique Contemporaine*, n. 40, November-December 1968, pp. 2–6.

————. "Situation du cinéma en Afrique francophone." *Afrique Contemporaine*, n. 81, September-October 1975, pp. 2–7.

Dia, Alioune Touré. "Cinema: Shadows over Senegalese Screens." *Afrika: Review of German-African Relations*, vol. 24, n. 1, 1983, pp. 24–25.

Diallo, A. Bamba. "Silence . . . on ne tourne plus." *Le Soleil*, 25–26 April 1981, pp. 5, 7 (magazine section).

Dialta, Esther. "Par le peuple et pour le peuple." *Jeune Afrique*, 19 August 1977, pp. 48–49.

Dia-Moukori, Urbain. "Intuition d'un language cinématographique africain." *Présence Africaine*, n. 61, 1st Quarter 1967, pp. 206–18.

Diawara, Manthia. "Images of Children." *West Africa*, 25 August 1986, pp. 1780–81.

Diedhiou, Djib. "VIIᵉ Festival Cinématographique de Ouagadougou: I—L'ombre d'Oumarou Ganda." *Le Soleil*, 3 March 1981, p. 8.

————. "VIIᵉ Festival Cinématographique de Ouagadougou: II—Des films de facture moyenne." *Le Soleil*, 12 March 1981, p. 7.

————. "VIIᵉ Festival Cinématographique de Ouagadougou: III—Un certain regard sur l'Afrique profonde." *Le Soleil*, 13 March 1981, p. 8.

————. "Des Cinéastes africains et antillais aux U.S.A." *Le Soleil*, 15–16 October 1983, p. 6.

Dieme, Fidèle. "Saint-Louis—le film africain et son public." *Unir Cinéma*, n. 7 (114), July-August 1983, pp. 25–27.

Diop, Baba. "Etre cinéaste en 1985." *Waarango*, n. 10, 1st Quarter 1985, pp. 21–36.

————. "Dans la Besace de Baba Diop: quelques films rapportés du FESPACO." *Waraango*, n. 11, 2nd Quarter 1985, pp. 14–15.

———. "Fepaci, fais pas ça! Elle ne l'a pas fait. . . . " *Waraango*, n. 11, 2nd Quarter 1985, pp. 16–18.

———. "Le Sourire de FESPACO." *Waraango*, n. 11, 2nd Quarter 1985, p. 13.

Diop, Mody. " 'Enfin l'Europe'—un project de film sénégalo-allemand." *Le Soleil*, 23 October 1981, p. 2.

Diop, Moustapha. "Nous tuons notre cinéma." *Jeune Afrique*, n. 1343, 1 October 1986, pp. 70–71.

Ewandé, F. "Causes du sous-développement africain en matière de cinéma." *Présence Africaine*, n. 61, 1st Quarter 1967, pp. 199–205.

Ewandé, Félix. "L'Afrique des caméras." *Jeune Afrique*, n. 386–87, 27 May 1968, p. 71.

Ferrari, Alain. "Le Second Souffle du cinéma africain." *Téléciné*, n. 176, January 1973, pp. 2–9.

Ferraton, Hubert. "Ouagadougou: la grande fête du cinéma africain." *Le Courrier* (Afrique-Caraibes-Pacifique-Communauté Européenne), n. 91, May-June 1985, p. 84.

Ford, Abiyi. "From the Fireside to the Screen: Toward the Synchronization of African Cinema with African Culture." Unpublished paper, 1981, pp. 1–30.

Gabriel, Teshome. *Third Cinema in the Third World: The Aesthetics of Liberation*. Ann Arbor, Mich.: UMI Research Press, 1982.

Gilliam, Angela. "African Cinema as New Literature," in Renee Tajima ed., *Journey Across Three Continents*, pp. 37–40. New York: Third World Newsreel, 1985.

Gnonlonfoun, Alexis. "Cinéma africain au présent." *Afrique Nouvelle*, 17 March 1982, p. 5.

Goffe, Anthony. "Cinéma—Racial Viewpoints." *West Africa*, 10 December 1984, pp. 2527–28.

Haffner, Pierre. *Palabres sur le cinématographe*. Kinshasa: Les Presses Africaines, 1978.

———. "Le Cinéma indien en Afrique noire." *Filméchange*, n. 21, Winter 1982–83, pp. 21–25.

———. "L'Adolescent africain et le cinéma." *Recherche, Pédagogie et Culture*, n. 62, April-June 1983, pp. 92–96.

———. "Les Films de la différence à Ouagadougou—une chronique du neuvième Festival Panafricain du Cinéma de Ouagadougou (23 février-2 mars 1985). "*Peuples Noirs, Peuples Africains*, n. 48, November-December 1985, pp. 97–131.

Hall, Susan. "African Women on Film." *Africa Report*, January-February 1971, pp. 15–17.

Hallis, Ron. "Movie Magic in Mozambique." *Cinema Canada*, n. 62, February 1980, pp. 18–24.

Hanou, Salima. "Pauvres mais beaux." *Jeune Afrique*, n. 1351, 26 November 1986, p. 84.

Head, Anne. "Africa: Towards a National Cinema." *Screen International*, n. 485, February 1985, p. 16.

Hennebelle, Guy. "Côte d'Ivoire, Sénégal, Guinée: six cinéastes africains parlent." *L'Afrique Littéraire et Artistique*, n. 8, 1969, pp. 58–70.

———. "Socially Committed or Exotic." *Young Cinema and Theatre*, vol. 3, 1970, pp. 23–33.

———. "Le Cinéma africain fait irruption." *Jeune Afrique*, n. 488, May 12, 1970, pp. 27–44.

————. "Africains, unissez-vous." *Cinéma 71*, n. 152, January 1971, pp. 19–20.

————. "Les Cinémas africains en 1972." *L'Afrique Littéraire et Artistique*, n. 20, 1st quarter 1972 (special issue).

————. "Rencontre à Dinard avec des responsables de la Fédération Panafricaine de Cinéastes." *L'Afrique Littéraire et Artistique*, n. 24, August 1972, pp. 92–96.

————. "Carthage: un festival ouvert à tous les cinémas." *L'Afrique Littéraire et Artistique*, n. 34, 1974, pp. 79–83.

————. "Des Cinémas d'Afrique noire depuis 1960." *Recherche, Pédagogie et Culture*, n. 17–18, May-August 1975, pp. 3–6.

————. *Guide des films anti-impérialistes*. Paris: Editions du Centenaire, 1975.

————. *Quinze ans de cinéma mondial*. Paris: Editions du Cerf, 1975.

————ed. "Cinémas de l'émigration." *Cinémaction*, n. 8, Summer 1979 (special issue).

————ed. "Le Tiers Monde en films." *Cinémaction Tricontinental*, January 1982 (special issue).

————, and Catherine Ruelle. "Cinéastes d'Afrique noire." *L'Afrique Littéraire et Artistique*, n. 49, 3rd Quarter 1978 (special issue).

Hennebelle, Monique. "Une Libération sans frontière." *Afrique-Asie*, n. 152, 9 January 1978, pp. 79–80.

Hill, Alan. "African Film and Filmmakers." *Essence*, July 1978, pp. 18, 23–24.

Houedanou, Lucien. "L'Exemple indien." *Afrique Nouvelle*, n. 1927, 25 June 1986, p. 17.

————. "La Grogne des cinéastes." *Afrique Nouvelle*, n. 1931, 23 July 1986, pp. 16–17.

Humblot, Catherine. "Conférence à Ouagadougou—le cinéma africain et les ministres." *Le Monde*, 6 May 1982, p. 17.

————. "Hollywood sur Volta." *Le Monde*, 6 May 1982, p. 17.

————. "Huis clos pour le cinéma africain." *Le Monde*, 12 January 1984, p. 20.

————. "Cinémas d'Afrique—impasse ou mauvaise passe?" *Le Monde*, 14 March 1985, p. 14.

Ibeabuchi, Aloysius. "Why Local Films Are Not Popular with African Audiences." *Daily Times*, 7 January 1984, p. 7.

Ilboudo, Patrick, and Jacob Olivier. "FESPACO, l'autre regard du cinéma." *L'Observateur*, 9 February 1983, pp. 1, 6–7.

————. "De la poule blanche au FESPACO." *Unir Cinéma*, n. 16, January-February 1985, pp. 13–23.

Jean-Bart, Anne. "Les cinéastes créent un groupement économique." *Le Soleil*, 22 November 1985, p. 8.

————. "L'Union ouest-africaine est née." *Le Soleil*, 29 November 1985, p. 6.

Johnson, Rudy. "African Film-Makers Seek Aid Here." *The New York Times*, 21 May 1973, p. 42L.

Journal du 8ème FESPACO, n. 1, 5 February 1983 (special issue).

Journal du 8ème FESPACO, n. 3, 13 February 1983 (special issue).

Jusu, K.K. Man. "Semaine du film africain—une belle initiative des cinéastes ivoiriens." *Fraternité Matin*, 7 April 1981, p. 18.

Kaboke, V. "Nuages noirs." *Unir Cinéma*, n. 23–24 (130–131), March-April and May-June 1986, p. 33.

Kaboré, Mouni Etienne. "Pourqoi ferme-t-on l'INAFEC?" *Carrefour Africain*, n. 975, 20 February 1987, pp. 27–29.

Kaissar, Abou. "Vers une libération totale des cinémas africains." *Ecran 74*, n. 30, pp. 37–38.

Kambou, Sansan. "A la découverte du cinéma ivoirien." *Sidwaya*, 25 February 1987, p. 6.

Kamphausen, Hannes. "Cinema in Africa—A Survey." *Cineaste*, vol. 5, n. 3, Summer 1972, pp. 29–41.

Khayati, Khémais. "Namur—présence en force de l'Afrique." *Cinéma 78*, n. 240, December 1978, pp. 71–73.

Kieffer, Maryse. "African Films in the U.S. Market." *Yaoundé Times*, Fall 1984, pp. 40–41.

Kitchener, Julie. "Africa's Poor Showing at London Film Festival." *New African*, January 1985, pp. 37–38.

Knight, Derrick. "African Films Turn On the Heat." *New African*, April 1983, pp. 42–43.

Leclercq, Pascal. "Une Politique de coopération cinématographique avec les pays en voie de développement." *Relais* (Bulletin des agents en coopération et à l'étranger), n. 3, May 1986, pp. 14–16, 23–24.

Lemaire, Charles. "9ème Festival Panafricain du Cinéma de Ouagadougou: histoire d'une rencontre." *Afrique Nouvelle*, n. 1862, 13 March 1985, pp. 14–17.

———. "Fepaci—s'unir ou mourir." *Afrique Nouvelle*, n. 1863, 20 March 1985, pp. 15–16.

———. "Credo libéral." *Unir Cinéma*, n. 20–21 (127–128), September-October 1985, pp. 14–15.

———. "Ecrire et informer." *Afrique Nouvelle*, n. 1911, 5 March 1986, pp. 16–17.

———. "Ils sont retombés sur la tête." *Afrique Nouvelle*, n. 1913, 19 March 1986, p. 19.

———. "Un Bilan trompeur." *Afrique Nouvelle*, n. 1921, 14 May 1986, pp. 16–17.

———. "Cinéma et information." *Unir Cinéma*, n. 23–24 (130–131), March-April and May-June 1986, pp. 22–24.

———. "Cinéma." *Afrique Nouvelle*, n. 1933, 6 August 1986, p. 19.

Le Péron, Serge. "Lettre de Dakar: la 3éme génération." *Cahiers du Cinéma*, n. 322, April 1981, p. 11.

McCaffrey, Kathleen. "African Women on the Screen." *Africa Report*, vol. 6, n. 2, March-April 1981, pp. 56–58.

Magill, Frank N. ed. *Magill Survey of Cinema: Foreign Language Films*. Englewood Cliffs, N. J.: Salem Press, 1985.

Malnic, Evelyne. "Propos sur le Festival de Cannes." *Jeune Afrique*, n. 806, 18 June 1976, pp. 50–51.

Malu, Kamba. "Zaire: la misère dorée." *Afrique-Asie*, n. 157, 20 March 1978, pp. 56–57.

Marcorelles, Louis. "Films afro-américains et négro-africains—le role des femmes." *Le Monde*, 28 October 1980, p. 27.

———. "L'Aide au cinéma africain." *Le Monde*, 4–5 January 1981, p. 7.

———. "Le Colloque de Niamey—une chance pour le cinéma africain." *Le Monde*, 21 January 1982, pp. 1, 12.

Martin, Angela. *African Films: The Context of Production*. London: British Film Institute, 1982.

———. "The Carthage Prizes." *West Africa*, 12 November 1984, p. 2272.

Mativo, Kyalo. "Resolving the Cultural Dilemma of the African Film." *UFAHAMU*, vol. 13, n. 1, Fall 1983, pp. 134–46.

Mativo, Wilson. "Cultural Dilemma of the African Film." *UFAHAMU*, vol. 1, n. 3, Winter 1971, pp. 64–68.

Meda, J. C. "IIIème Congrès de la FEPACI—une douloureuse renaissance." *Carrefour Africain*, n. 871, 22 February 1985, p. 11.

Meda, Yirzaola. "FESPACO et autres festivals: chroniques d'un cheminement." *Carrefour Africain*, n. 975, 20 February 1987, pp. 8–11.

———. "Ironu ou les intellectuels africains face aux responsabilités de leur pays." *Sidwaya*, 23 February 1987, p. 12.

Medeiros, Richard de. "L'Heure des bilans." *Le Monde Diplomatique*, September 1980, p. 12.

Medjigbodo, Nicole. "Afrique cinématographiée, Afrique cinématographique." *Canadian Journal of African Studies*, vol. 13, n. 3, pp. 371–87.

Minot, Gilbert. "Toward the African Cinema." *UFAHAMU*, vol. 12, n. 2, 1983, pp. 37–43.

Murcia-Capel, Pedro. "Les Caméras de l'Angola." *Afrique-Asie*, n. 322, 21 May 1984, pp. 56–57.

Nana, Hamado. "Vers un nouvel ordre du cinéma africain." *Carrefour Africain*, n. 766, 18 February 1983, p. 15.

———. "Desebagato—Propos sur la classe ouvrière." *Sidwaya*, 24 February 1987, p. 5.

———. "Nyamanton: un humour dérangeant." *Sidwaya*, 26 February 1987, p. 5.

Nana, Joanny. "Haute-Volta: condenser les interrogations." *Le Monde Diplomatique*, September 1978, p. 13.

Ndaw, Aly Kheury. "La SIDEC sur la voie du redressement—95 millions de plus sur l'année 1975." *Le Soleil*, 5–6 February 1977, p. 3.

———. "La SIDEC sur la voie du redressement—un lourd héritage légué par la SECMA et la COMACICO." *Le Soleil*, 7 February 1977, p. 3.

———. "La SIDEC sur la voie du redressement—400 nouveaux films dans le circuit chaque année." *Le Soleil*, 8 February 1977, p. 3.

———. "Le Cinéma africain à Ouagadougou: I—Un festival vraiment populaire." *Le Soleil*, 1 March 1979, p. 2.

———. "Le Cinéma africain à Ouagadougou: II—Emergence de jeunes talents." *Le Soleil*, 2 March 1979, p. 2.

———. "Le Cinéma africain à Ouagadougou: III—A propos de deux films." *Le Soleil*, 3–4 March 1979, p. 2.

———. "Le Cinéma africain à Ouagadougou: IV—Demain un jour nouveau." *Le Soleil*, 5 March 1979, p. 2.

———. "8ᵉ session des J.C.C.: trois tendances nouvelles du cinéma arabe et africain." *Le Soleil*, 29–30 November 1980, p. 12.

———. "D'une génération à l'autre." *Le Soleil*, 2 November 1984, pp. 12–13.

———. "Ouaga: un festival aux dimensions nouvelles." *Le Soleil*, 12 March 1985, p. 12.

———. "FEPACI, CIDC, CAC—trois structures mises en question." *Le Soleil*, 14 March 1985, p. 12.

———. "La Cinémathèque d'Alger: modèle unique en Afrique." *Le Soleil*, 13 February 1986, p. 9.

———. "Les Lampions sont allumés à Ouaga." *Le Soleil*, 23 February 1987, p. 10.

———. "Xᵉ FESPACO: la visite impromptue de Thomas Sankara." *Le Soleil*, 27 February 1987, p. 8.

N'Diaye, Catherine. "L'Afrique ne crève pas l'écran." *Jeune Afrique*, n. 1208, 29 February 1984, p. 51.

Nee-Owoo, Kwate. "Ghana—projets d'avenir." *Le Monde Diplomatique*, June 1981, p. 23.

Ngakane, Lionel. "The Cinema in South Africa." *Présence Africaine*, n. 80, 4th Quarter 1971, pp. 131–33.

———. "Film Makers Focus on African Problems." *Africa*, n. 116, April 1981, p. 70.

———. "Nigéria—l'influence du modèle américain." *Le Monde Diplomatique*, June 1981, p. 23.

———. "Cinema and the Liberation of People." *Africa*, n. 164, April 1985, pp. 88–89.

Nicolini, Elisabeth. "Un Grand Débat sur le septième art africain." *Jeune Afrique*, n. 1318, 9 April 1986, pp. 64–65.

Noel, Jean-Guy. "Clair de lune à Ouagadougou—5ème Festival Panafricain du Cinéma de Ouagadougou du 1er au 10 février 1976." *Cinéma Québec*, n. 42, 1976, pp. 40–42.

Otten, Rick. *Le Cinéma au Zaire, au Rwanda et au Burundi*. Brussels: OCIC/L'Harmattan, 1984.

Ouedraogo, B. Wole. "Symposium: cinéma africain—cinéma afro-américain." *Sidwaya*, 26 February 1985, special insert, p. I.

Ouedraogo, Isaac Rogomnoma. "Les Problèmes juridiques et fiscaux du cinéma en Afrique subsaharienne." *Carrefour Africain*, n. 870, 15 February 1985, pp. 26–30.

———. "Cinéma et littérature." *Carrefour Africain*, n. 873, 8 March 1985, p. 22.

Ousseini, Inoussa. "Vers une économie affranchie." *Le Monde Diplomatique*, March 1979, p. 29.

———. "La Fiscalité cinématographique en Afrique noire francophone." *Filméchange*, n. 17, Winter 1981–82, pp. 37–49.

———. "L'Évolution du marché cinématographique africain," in *FESPACO 1983*, pp. 61–70. Paris: Présence Africaine, 1987.

Oyekunte, Segun. "The Promises of Mogadishu." *West Africa*, 19 December 1983, pp. 2938–40.

Paquet, André. "The FESPACO of Ouagadougou—Towards Unity in African Cinema." *Cinéaste*, vol. 6, n. 1, 1973, pp. 36–38.

———. "L'Avance des cinémas arabes." *Cinéma Québec*, vol. 4, n. 2, April 1975, pp. 34–39.

———. "Kenya-Cinémas itinérants." *Le Monde Diplomatique*, June 1981, p. 23.

Pare, B. Hubert. "8ème FESPACO; symbole de l'unité africaine." *Carrefour Africain*, n. 765, 11 February 1983, p. 23.

———. "Clôture du 8ème FESPACO: le sacre de Souleymane Cissé, réalisateur de Finyé." *Carrefour Africain*, n. 766, 18 February 1983, pp. 10–11.

———. "L'Organisation du FESPACO: nouvelle approche." *Carrefour Africain*, n. 870, 15 February 1985, pp. 24–25.

———. "A nous la rue, Nyamanton: le public apporte un intérét aux débats." *Sidwaya*, 24 February 1987, p. 6.

———. "Débats-Forum: quatre films passés au crible." *Sidwaya,* 25 February 1987, pp. 5–6.

———. "Débats-Forum: Ironu, Duel sur la falaise, Mosebolatan, Moulin." *Sidwaya,* 26 February 1987, p. 7.

Pare, B. Hubert et al. "Special FESPACO." *Sidwaya,* 4 March 1985, special insert, pp. I-IV.

Passek, Jean-Loup. "Festivals et rencontres—Dinard." *Cinéma 72,* n. 169, September-October 1972, pp. 29–31.

Pauihan, Jean. "A la recherche de l'Afrique francophone." *French Review,* vol. 55, n. 6, May 1982, pp. 912–14.

Pearson, Lyle. "Four Years of African Film." *Film Quarterly,* vol. 26, n. 3, Spring 1973, pp. 42–47.

"Perspectives du cinéma en Afrique noire." *La Revue du Cinéma, Image et Son,* n. 185, June 1965, pp. 23–31.

Petion, Antoine. "Le Contrôle impérialiste de la production et de la distribution." *Le Monde Diplomatique,* April 1973, p. 21.

Pfaff, Françoise. "Hollywood's Image of Africa." *Commonwealth,* vol. 5, 1981–1982, pp. 99–116.

———. "Cinema in Francophone Africa." *Africa Quarterly,* vol. 22, n. 3, 1985, pp. 41–48.

———. "Researching Africa on Film." *Jump Cut,* n. 31, 1986, pp. 50, 57.

Prédal, René. "Jean Rouch, un griot gaulois." *Cinémaction,* n. 17, 1982 (special issue).

Ramonet, Ignacio. "Une Nécrose du colonialisme." *Le Monde Diplomatique,* April 1973, p. 21.

———. "Ecrans d'Afrique." *Le Monde Diplomatique,* September 1978, p. 13.

———. "Un Bilan africain." *Le Monde Diplomatique,* March 1979, p. 29.

———. "Marasme africain." *Le Monde Diplomatique,* September 1980, p. 12.

"Recommandations du Séminaire International sur le film africain et son public," in *FESPACO 1983,* pp. 91–94. Paris: Présence Africaine, 1987.

Relich, Mario. "Films of Struggle." *West Africa,* 13 August 1984, pp. 1632–33.

Rouch, Jean. "Le Cinéma africain." *Les Lettres Françaises,* n. 893, 21 September 1961, pp. 1–6.

———. "L'Afrique entre en scène." *Le Courrier de l'UNESCO,* n. 3, March 1962, pp. 10–15.

S, Elizabeth. "A la découverte du cinéma camerounais." *Sidwaya,* 26 February 1987, p. 8.

Sadoul, Georges. "Voyage au pays de la famine cinématographique." *Les Lettres Françaises,* n. 893, pp. 6–7.

Sail, Noureddine. "La Question du public dans la problématique du cinéma africain," in *FESPACO 1983,* pp. 71–82. Paris: Présence Africaine, 1987.

Salama, Mohand Ben. "Le Congrès de la Fepaci." *Ecran 75,* n. 35, April 1975, pp. 10–11.

Salambere, Alimata. "Festivals: New York." *Unir Cinéma,* n. 7 (114), July-August 1983, p. 17–18.

Sama, Emmanuel. "Amiens-FESPACO: la rencontre de deux festivals." *Carrefour Africain,* n. 811, 30 December 1983, pp. 26–28.

Sanou, Bernadette. "Discours de la camarade Bernadette Sanou, ministre de la culture, à l'occasion de l'ouverture de la Xᵉ édition du FESPACO." *Sidwaya*, 23 February 1987, p. 5.

Sarr, Mamadou. "Vers un cinéma africain." *Le Technicien du Film et le Cahier de l'Exploitant*, n. 32, 15 October 1957, pp. 8–9.

Sawadogo, Filippe. "3ème Symposium du Cinéma de Mogadiscio du 12 au 20 Octobre en Somalie." *Unir Cinéma*, n. 20–21 (127–128), September-October 1985, pp. 24–29.

———. "FESPACO–Information." *Unir Cinéma*, n. 23–24 (130–131), March-April and May-June 1986, pp. 12–16.

Schmidt, Nancy J. *Sub-Saharan African Films and Filmmakers—A Preliminary Bibliography*. Bloomington, Ind.: African Studies Program, 1986.

Seck, Papa O. "Cinéma Sénégalais: les leçons d'un débat." *Le Soleil*, 11 September 1985, p. 8.

"La Semi-Absence noire africaine au festival du tiers monde." *Bingo*, n. 332, September 1980, pp. 52–53.

"Seminar on the Role of the African Film-Maker in Rousing an Awareness of Black Civilization—Ouagadougou—8–13 April 1974 (report)." *Présence Africaine*, n. 90, 2nd Quarter 1974, pp. 3–204.

Senghor, Blaise. "Prerequisites for a Truly African Cinema." *Présence Africaine*, n. 49, 1st Quarter 1964, pp. 101–7.

Service de Psychologie et de Sociologie de 1'Institut National d'Education de Haute-Volta. "Qu'est-ce qui fait courir Nobila ou la psychologie du spectateur?" in *FESPACO 1983*, pp. 83–89. Paris: Présence Africaine, 1987.

Shirazi, Manny. "Burkina, Film Festival Host." *West Africa*, 23 March 1987, pp. 558–559.

S. I. "A la découverte du cinéma malien." *Sidwaya*, 24 February 1987, p. 8.

Somé, Sylvestre S. "9éme FESPACO: cinéma et libération des peuples—les exposés et les films n'ont pas démérité du théme." *Carrefour Africain*, n. 873, 8 March 1985, pp. 20–21.

Sourwema, Issaka. "FESPACO 87, la fête est finie." *Sidwaya*, 2 March 1987, p. 10.

Soyer, Chantal. "Afrique noire: un cinéma étranger à son propre monde." *Film-Action*, n. 2, February-March 1982, pp. 10–11.

Stern, Yvan. "L'Ame des peuples qu'on assassine." *Unir Cinéma*, n. 17 (124), March-April 1985, pp. 30–31.

———. "Festivals (Berlin, Cannes, Festival de Films du Tiers-Monde)." *Unir Cinéma*, n. 23–24 (130–131), March-April and May-June 1986, pp. 25–29.

Sy, Moulaye Abdoul Aziz. "Réflexion critique sur le cinéma africain." *Waarango*, n. 4, 3rd Quarter 1983, pp. 6–8.

Sylva, Evelyne. "Avec les fans du cinéma hindou." *Afrique Nouvelle*, n. 1919, 30 April 1986, pp. 16–17.

———. "L'Inde et L'Afrique." *Afrique Nouvelle*, n. 1927, 25 June 1986, pp. 16–17.

Tadros, Jean-Pierre. "Le Cinéma africain est en crise." *Le Devoir*, 5 August 1978, p. 23.

Tapsoba, Clément. "Le Public aura son mot à dire à ce 8ème FESPACO." *Carrefour Africain*, n. 764, 4 February 1983, pp. 16–17.

———. "Diversifier les genres cinématographiques." *Carrefour Africain*, n. 765, 11 February 1983, pp. 26–27.

———. "8ème FESPACO—Pari pour CINAFRIC." *Carrefour Africain*, n. 765, 11 February 1983, pp. 25–26.

———. "Quel avenir pour le cinéma africain? Beaucoup reste à faire." *Carrefour Africain*, n. 765, 11 February 1983, pp. 24–25.

———. "8ème édition du FESPACO—la Haute-Volta en sort auréolée." *Carrefour Africain*, n. 766, 18 February 1983, pp. 13–14.

———. "D'Alger à Ouagadougou: temps difficiles pour les cinémas arabe et africain." *Carrefour Africain*, n. 870, 15 February 1985, pp. 22–23.

———. "Concilier le public africain et son cinéma." *Carrefour Africain*, n. 767, 25 February 1983, pp. 19–20.

———. "Liquidation de CIDC-France—la fin d'une structure néo-coloniale." *Sidwaya*, 19 February 1985, p. 5.

———. "CIDC-CIPROFILM—grands maux, grands remèdes." *Carrefour Africain*, n. 871, 22 February 1985, pp. 24–26.

———. "Le Cinéma africain face aux tentatives de domination." *Carrefour Afrcain*, n. 871, 22 February 1985, pp. 16–17.

———. "FESPACO 85—un succès politique, les objectifs ont été largement atteints." *Carrefour Africain*, n. 873, 8 March 1985, pp. 18–19.

———. "La Co-production, seule voie viable." *Carrefour Africain*, n. 975, 20 February 1987, pp. 12–17.

———. "CIDC-CIPROFILM: la conférence de la dernière chance." *Carrefour Africain*, n. 975, 20 February 1987, pp. 25–26.

———. "Le choix'—un regard optimiste sur les problèmes de développement." *Sidwaya*, 25 February 1987, p. 6.

———. "10ᵉ FESPACO—conférence de presse du président du Faso: 'Le Fespaco est avant tout l'affaire des cinéastes.' " *Sidwaya*, 3 March 1987, p. 3.

———, and M. Etienne Kaboré. "Awa, Assita, Mariam: les nouvelles actrices du cinéma burkinabè." *Sidwaya*, 27 February 1987, p. 9.

Tapsoba, Clément, et al. "Special FESPACO." *Sidwaya*, 25 February 1985, special insert, pp. I-IV.

———. "Special FESPACO." *Sidwaya*, 27 February 1985, special insert, pp. I-IV.

Tarbagdo, Sita. "3ème Congrès de la FEPACI—la renaissance d'une institution." *Sidwaya*, 20 February 1985, p. 3.

———, Hubert Pare, and J. C. Meda. "Interview express—Que pensent les cinéastes présents au congrès de la FEPACI?" *Sidwaya*, 21 February 1985, p. 6.

Taylor, Clyde. "FESPACO 85 Was a Dream Come True." *Black Film Review*, vol. 1, n. 4, 1985, pp. 1, 6–9.

———. "Black Spirit in South Africa." *The Black Collegian*, September-October 1985, pp. 43–44.

———. "Africa, the Last Cinema," in Renee Tajima ed., *Journey Across Three Continents*, pp. 50–58. New York: Third World Newsreel, 1985.

Thiel, Reinold E. "Film in Afrika." *Filmkritik*, January 1961, pp. 11–15.

Tiao, Luc-Adolphe. "IIIème Congrès FEPACI: redynamiser une arme de combat du cinéma africain." *Carrefour Africain*, n. 870, 15 February 1985, pp. 19–20.

———. "Entretien: Brahim Babai président sortant de la FEPACI explique." *Sidwaya*, 21 February 1985, p. 6.

Tomaselli, Keyan. "Racism in South African Cinema." *Cineaste*, vol. 13, n. 1, 1983, pp. 12–15.

———. "Le Cinéma noir sud-africain—négociations idéologiques." *Unir Cinéma*, n. 10–11 (117–118), January-April 1984, pp. 5–24.

————ed. "Le Cinéma sud-africain est-il tombé sur la tête?" *Cinémaction*, n. 39, July 1986 (special issue).

Vaughan, J. K. "Africa South of the Sahara and the Cinema." *Présence Africaine*, n. 14–15, June-September 1957, pp. 210–21.

Vaughn, Jimmy. "Africa as Seen by European and American Film Makers." *Young Film*, n. 1, 1958, pp. 17–21.

Vencatachellum, Indrasen. "Cinéma et développement culturel en Afrique." *Filméchange*, n. 20, Fall 1982, pp. 55–61.

Vieyra, Paulin Soumanou. *Le Cinéma et l'Afrique*. Paris: Présence Africaine, 1969.

————. *Le Cinéma africain*. Paris: Présence Africaine, 1975.

————. *Le Cinéma au Sénégal*. Brussels: OCIC/L'Harmattan, 1983.

Villetard, Xavier. "Le Cinéma africain entre le fric et le troc." *Libération*, 5 November 1984, p. 33.

Vokouma, Francois. "Du rôle de nos cinéastes pour perpétuer nos valeurs." *Carrefour Africain*, n. 975, 20 February 1987, pp. 18–19.

Watamou, Lamien. "3ème conférence des ministres africains chargés du cinéma—une réelle volonté de redressement du CIDC-CIPROFILM." *Sidwaya*, 18 February 1985, p. 6.

Wiley, David S. *Africa on Film and Videotape 1960–1981—A Compendium of Reviews*. East Lansing, Mich.: African Studies Center, Michigan State University, 1982.

Zerbo, Salia. "A l'écoute du FESPACO: l'ère des premières compétitions 1972–1973." *Sidwaya*, 23 February 1987, p. 6.

————. "Journée d'ouverture du FESPACO 87: une ambiance de fête populaire." *Sidwaya*, 23 February 1987, p. 7.

————. "Réflexion à propos du film Ironu—Quelle méthode de lutte pour nos peuples?" *Sidwaya*, 24 February 1987, p. 5.

————. "A l'écoute du FESPACO: à l'approche de l'âge de raison: 1976–1979." *Sidwaya*, 24 February 1987, p. 10.

————. "A l'écoute du FESPACO: les périodes charnières 1981–1983." *Sidwaya*, 25 February 1987, p. 5.

Index

Abidjan-Niger, L' (Bassori), 35, 37
Abidjan, perle des lagunes (Bassori), 35, 38
Abusuan (Duparc), 88–89, 90–91, 92, 108
Adejume, Moses Olaiya, 21
Adjesu, Egbert, 14
African National Congress (ANC), 199
African Party for the Independence of Guinea and the Cape Verde Islands (PAIGC), 207, 212
Afrique à Moscou, L' (Vieyra), 290, 295
Afrique-sur-Seine (Vieyra), 290, 291, 292, 295, 298
After Winter: Sterling Brown (Gerima), 144, 148, 151
Agni, as film language, 89
Aiye (Balogun), 21, 24, 25, 28
Ajani-Ogun (Balogun), 20, 21, 26, 27–28
Akum (Kamwa), 187, 188, 190
Alassane, Moustapha: **1–9**, 116, 127, 209; bibliography, 8–9; biography, 1–4; criticism of, 6–8; filmography, 8; major themes, 4–6. Works: (films) *L'Arachide de Santchira*, 2, 4; *Aouré*, 2, 4, 7; *La Bague du Roi Koda*, 2, 4, 7; *Bon Voyage Sim*, 2, 6; *Les Contrebandiers*, 2, 6; *Deela*, 2, 5, 7; *Festival à Dosso*, 3; *F. V. V. A.—Femmes, villa, voiture, argent*, 3, 6; *Jamya*, 2, 4; *Kankamba*, 3, 6; *Kokoa*, 3, 6; *La Mort de Gandji*, 2, 6, 7; *La Pileuse de mil*, 2, 4; *Le Piroguier*, 2, 4; *Le Retour de l'aventurier*, 2, 5–6, 7; *Sakhi*, 3, 4; *Samba-le-Grand*, 3, 5; *Soubane*, 3, 4; *Toula ou le Génie des Eaux*, 3, 5, 7
Alea, Tomas Gutierrez, 140
Alexander Nevsky (Eisenstein), 254
Alpha (Balogun), 20, 21, 24, 27
Amadi (Balogun), 20, 24, 27
Ambassades nourricières (Faye), 117–18, 120–21, 122
Ambiguous Adventure (Kane), 295
Amédée Pierre (Bassori), 35, 38
Ames au soleil, Les (Faye), 117, 120
Amharic, as film language, 140
Ampaw, King, 14
Anderson, Georges, 20
Andrade, Mario de, 206, 207
Angela Davis (Nee Owo), 14
A. N. I. du Tassili, Les (Tadjer), 208
Annaud, Jean-Jacques, 36
A nous deux, France (Ecaré) 97, 99, 100–101, 102–3
Ansah, Kwaw: **11–18**, 117; bibliography, 17–18; biography, 11–14; criticism of, 16–17; filmography, 17; major themes, 14–16. Works (film): *Love Brewed in the African Pot*, 12, 13, 14–17. Works (plays): *The Adoption*, 12; *Mother's Tears*, 12
Araba: The Village Story (Sutherland), 14, 118

Arachide de Santchira, L' (Alassane), 2, 4

Aragon, Louis, 212, 239

Aryeti, Sam, 14

Ashes and Embers (Gerima), 143, 147–48, 151

Aspirant, L' (Cissé), 53, 58, 61

Aubert, Claude Bernard, 227

Augé, Simon, 79

Avec l'Ensemble National (Vieyra), 291, 295, 298

Avec les Africains à Vienne (Vieyra), 290

Aw, Tidiane, 294

Ayouma (Dong), 80, 82, 83–84

Ba, Amadou Hampaté, 43, 120

Baara (Cissé), 53–54, 55, 58–59, 61, 62

Badou Boy (Mambety), 218, 220, 223

Bague du Roi Koda, La (Alassane), 2, 4, 7

Bah, Cheikh Ngaido, 43, 109

Baks (Thiam), 268, 270, 271

Balade aux sources (Hondo), 159, 163

Balogun, Ola: **19–31**, 117, 162, 244, 294; bibliography, 29–31; biography, 19–23; criticism of, 27–29; filmography, 29; major themes, 24–26. Works (films): *Aiye*, 21, 24, 25, 28; *Ajani-Ogun*, 20, 21, 26, 27–28; *Alpha*, 20, 21, 24, 27; *Amadi*, 20, 24, 27; *Cry Freedom*, 21, 26, 28; *A Deusa Negra*, 21, 24, 27, 28; *Eastern Nigeria Revisited*, 20, 24; *Fire in the Afternoon*, 20, 24; *Ija Ominira*, 20, 26, 28; *In the Beginning*, 20, 24; *Money Power*, 21, 24, 26, 28, 29; *Musik Man*, 20, 26, 28; *Nigersteel*, 20, 24; *Nupe Mascarade*, 20, 24; *One Nigeria*, 19, 24; *Orun Mooru*, 21, 24, 26, 28; *Owuama, A New Year Festival*, 20, 24; *Les Ponts de Paris*, 20; *Thundergod*, 20, 24; *Vivre*, 20. Works (play): *Shango*, 23. Works (writings): *Nigéria, du réel à l'imaginaire*, 23; *The Tragic Years: Nigeria in Crisis, 1966–1970*, 23

Bambara, as a people, 60

Bambara, as film language, 53, 59, 91

Bamiléké, as a people, 189

Baraka, Imamu, 158

Barma, Kocc, 43

Basilique de Saint-Denis, La (Maldoror), 208, 212

Bassa, as film language, 72

Bassori, Timité: 15, **33–42**, 162, 205, 209, 221, 227, 244, 294; bibliography, 41–42; biography, 33–37; criticism of, 30–40; filmography, 40–41; major themes, 37–39. Works (films): *L'Abidjan-Niger*, 35, 37; *Abidjan, perle des lagunes*, 35, 38; *Amédée Pierre*, 35, 38; *Bondoukou, an 11*, 35, 38; Les Compagnons d'Akadi, 35, 38; *La Femme au conteau*, 35, 38–39, 40; *Feux de brousse*, 35, 37; *Les Forestiers*, 35, 37; *Kossou 1*, 35, 38; *Kossou 2*, 35, 38; *Odienné, an 12*, 35, 38; *Le Sixième Sillon*, 35, 38; *Sur la dune de la solitude*, 35, 38, 39. Works (writings): *Les Bannis du village*, 37; *Grelots d'or*, 37

Bathily, Moussa: **43–49**, 241; bibliography, 48–49; biography, 43–45; criticism of, 47–48; filmography, 48; major themes, 45–47. Works (films): *Le Certificat d'indigence*, 44, 47, 48; *Fidak*, 44; *Ndakarou, impressions matinales*, 44, 45; *Des Personnages encombrants*, 44, 45–46; *Siggi ou la poliomyélite*, 44; *Des Sites et des monuments au Sénégal*, 44, 45; *Tiyabu Biru*, 44, 46–47, 48

Battle of Algiers, The (Pontecorvo), 206

Bebey, Francis, 292

Belgrade Film School, 87

Bella, Thérèse Sita, 118

Bergman, Ingmar, 72

Berry, John, 227

Berthomieu, André, 290

Beti, Mongo, 239

Beye, Ben Diogaye, 43, 109

Bicots-nègres, vos voisins, Les (Hondo), 159–60, 162, 164, 166

Bicycle Thief, The (De Sica), 140

Bicyclette, La (Vieyra), 291, 296

Birago Diop, conteur (Vieyra), 292, 297

Bissainthe, Toto, 34, 205, 227, 279

Black Man Alive, 198
Blood of the Condor (Sanjines), 140
Bondoukou, an 11 (Bassori), 35, 38
Bongo, Josephine, 79
Bongo, Omar, 80
Bon Voyage Sim (Alassane), 2, 6
Borom Sarret (Sembene), 239, 240, 245, 247, 249
Boubou-Cravate (Kamwa), 186, 189, 190–91
Bouki cultivateur (Thiam), 268, 269, 270
Boukman, Daniel, 158, 160
Boulanger, Daniel, 208
Brachet, George, 219
Brecht, Bertold, 96, 158
Brierre, Jean, 45, 238
Brown, Sterling, 144, 148
Buñuel, Luis, 72, 140, 253
Burnett, Charles, 142, 143
Burton, Philip, 12
Bush Mama (Gerima), 142, 147, 148–49, 150

Cabascabo (Ganda), 126, 127, 128–29, 132–33
Cabral, Amilcar, 130, 206
Cam-Air, dix ans d'essor (Kamwa), 187, 190
Camus, Albert, 35
Camus, Marcel, 295
Capitaine Fracasse, Le, 33
Carcase for Hounds (Mwangi), 21
Caristan, Georges, 45, 228, 240, 241, 277
Carnaval dans le Sahel, Un (Maldoror), 208, 212
Carnet de voyage (Duparc), 88, 90
Carrefour humain (Dong), 79, 80, 83
Ceddo (Sembene), 44, 45, 234, 241–42, 246, 253–55, 291
Céline, 43
Centre d'Art Dramatique de la Rue Blanche, 34, 95, 205, 227
Certificat d'indigence, Le (Bathily), 44, 47, 48
Césaire, Aimé, 34, 57, 96, 158, 186, 205, 211, 212, 237, 238

C'était il y a quatre ans (Vieyra), 290, 294–95, 298
Chaplin, Charlie, 69, 289
Child of Resistance (Gerima), 140, 146–47, 148
Christian-Jaque, 35
Ciampi, Yves, 267
Cicatrice, La (Dikongue-Pipa), 71–72, 76
Cinq jours d'une vie (Cissé), 53, 58
Cissé, Souleymane: **51–67**, 99, 244, 294; bibliography, 64–67; biography, 51–57; criticism of, 61–63; filmography, 63–64; major themes, 57–60. Works (films): *L'Aspirant*, 53, 58, 61; *Baara*, 53–54, 55, 58–59, 61, 62; *Cinq jours d'une vie*, 53, 58; *Degal à Dialloubé*, 53, 58; *Den Muso*, 53, 58; *Dixième anniversaire de l'OUA*, 53; *Fête du Sanke*, 53, 58; *Finyé*, 54, 55, 59–60, 62–63; *L'Homme et les idoles*, 52; *Sources d'inspiration*, 52, 57; *Yeelen*, 54, 60
Cock, cock, cock, (Ganda), 127
Cocteau, Jean, 70
Coltrane, John, 40
Comité Africain de Cinéastes (CAC), 37, 72, 145, 162, 294
Commune, Louise Michel et nous, La (Maldoror), 207, 212
Compagnie d'Art Dramatique des Griots, 34, 205, 227
Compagnons d'Akadi, Les (Bassori), 35, 38
Concerto pour un exil (Ecaré), 87, 96–97, 99–100, 101, 102, 103
Conrad, Joseph, 43
Conservatoire d'Art Dramatique, 95
Conservatoire Indépendant du Cinéma Français, 70, 275
Consortium Interafricain de Distribution Cinématographique (CIDC), 89
Contras' City (Mambety), 217, 219–20, 222–23
Contrebandiers, Les (Alassane), 2, 6
Cornes, Les (Dikongue-Pipa), 70, 73
Costa-Gavras, Constantin, 158
Cours Simon, 34

Courte Maladie (Dikongue-Pipa), 71
Cry Freedom (Balogun), 21, 26, 28

Dadié, Bernard, 239
Dakar Festival of Negro Arts, 228
Damas, Léon, 239
Danse, automate, danse (Kamwa), 187, 188, 190
Davis, Angela, 146, 209
Death of a Bureaucrat (Alea), 250
De Beauvior, Simone, 239
Debrix, Jean-René, 2, 6, 75, 96, 223, 247, 271
Deela (Alassane), 2, 5, 7
Degal à Dialloubé (Cissé), 53, 58
Demain, un jour nouveau (Dong), 80, 82, 84
Den Muso (Cissé), 53, 58
Depestre, René, 158
De Sica, Vittorio, 140, 229
Dessert pour Constance, Un (Maldoror), 208, 211, 214
Deusa Negra, A (Balogun), 21, 24, 27, 28
Diable au Corps, Le (Autant-Lara), 290
Diagne, Blaise, 44
Diankha-bi (Traoré), 275–76, 277, 279, 280, 282, 283
Diarama (Vieyra), 291, 297
Dibango, Manu, 74, 89, 246
Diderot, 43
Diegue-bi (Traoré), 276, 279, 280, 283
Dikongue-Pipa, Jean-Pierre: 15, **69–78**, 189; bibliography, 76–78; biography, 69–72; criticism of, 75–76; filmography, 76; major themes, 72–74. Works (films): *La Cicatrice*, 71–72, 76; *Les Cornes*, 70, 73; *Courte Maladie*, 71; *Histoires drôles, drôles de gens*, 71; *Muna Moto*, 70–71, 73–74, 75–76; *Music and Music*, 71; *Le Prix de la liberté*, 71, 74, 76; *Rendez-moi mon père*, 70, 73; *Un Simple*, 70, 73
Diola, as film language, 240
Diop, Birago, 267, 268, 291, 292, 297
Diop, Cheik Anta, 238
Diop, David, 239
Diop, Ousmane Socé, 268

Dixième anniversaire de l'OUA (Cissé), 53
Djeli (Fadika), 108–12
Djerma, as a people, 4
Djerma, as film language, 127, 129
Doing Their Thing (Odjidja), 14
Dong, Pierre-Marie: **79–85**; bibliography, 84–85; biography, 79–80; criticism of, 83–84; filmography, 84; major themes, 80–83. Works (films): *Ayouma*, 80, 82, 83–84; *Carrefour humain*, 79, 80, 83; *Demain, un jour nouveau*, 80, 82, 84; *Gabon, pays de contraste*, 79, 80; *Identité*, 79, 80–81, 83; *Obali*, 79, 80, 81–82, 83; *Sur le sentier du requiem*, 79, 80, 82, 83
Donskoy, Mark, 206, 209, 239
Dos Passos, John, 43
Douala, as film language, 72
Douala, as a people, 189
Douglass, Frederick, 148
Dreyer, Carl Theodore, 99
Du Bois, W. E. B., 139, 148, 239
Duparc, Henri: 15, 36, **87–94**, 108; bibliography, 93–94; biography, 87–90; criticism of, 91–92; filmography, 92–93; major themes, 90–91. Works (films): *Abusuan*, 88–89, 90–91, 92; *Achetez ivoirien*, 88, 90; *Carnet de voyage*, 88, 90; *L'Herbe sauvage*, 89, 91, 92; *J'ai dix ans*, 88, 90; *Mouna ou le rêve d'un artiste*, 88, 89, 90, 91–92; *Obs*, 87; *Profil ivoirien*, 88, 90; *Les Racines de la vie*, 89, 90; *Récolte du coton*, 88, 90; *Tam-tam ivoire*, 88, 90

Eastern Nigeria Revisited (Balogun), 20, 24
Ecaré, Désiré: 87, **95–106**; bibliography, 104–6; biography, 95–99; criticism of, 102–3; filmography, 103–4; major themes, 99–102. Works (films): *A nous deux, France*, 97, 99, 100–101, 102–3; *Concerto pour un exil*, 96–97, 99–100, 101, 102, 103; *Visages de femmes*, 97–98, 99, 101–2, 103
École Supérieure d'Études Cinématographiques (ESE), 174

Écrits de Dakar (Vieyra), 291, 295
Écrits du Caire (Vieyra), 291
Eisenstein, Sergei M., 209, 254
Elles (Lallem), 206
Emitaï (Sembene), 240–41, 246, 250–52, 291
Empire Sonhraï, L' (Sembene), 239, 242, 245
End of the Dialogue (Mahomo), 197, 199–200, 201
Enfer des innocents, L' (Traoré), 276, 280, 282–83
English, as film language, 17, 20
En résidence surveillée (Vieyra), 292, 297, 298
Enrico, Robert, 158
Envers du décor, L' (Vieyra), 291, 297
Erneville, Annette M'Baye d', 228
Et la neige n'était plus (Samb), 227–28, 230–31, 232
Et les chiens se taisaient (Maldoror), 207, 211
Exception and the Rule, The (Brecht), 96
Exilé, L' (Ganda), 112, 127, 131–32, 133

Fadika, Kramo-Lanciné: **107–13**; bibliography, 113; biography, 107–9; criticism of, 111–12; filmography, 113; major themes, 109–11. Works (film): *Djeli*, 108–12
Fad'jal (Faye), 117, 120, 121, 122
Faleti, Adebayo, 20
Fanon, Frantz, 139
Faye, Safi: 71, **115–24**; bibliography, 122–24; biography, 115–18; criticism of, 121–22; filmography, 122. Works (films): *Ambassades nourricières*, 117–18, 120–21, 122; *Les Ames au soleil*, 117, 120; *Fad'jal*, 117, 120, 121, 122; *Goob na ñu*, 117, 120; *Kaddu beykat*, 116–17, 118, 119–20, 121–22; *Man Sa Yay*, 117, 120, 122; *La Passante*, 116, 118–19; *Revanche*, 116, 119; *Selbé et tant d'autres*, 117, 120; *3 Ans 5 mois*, 117, 120
Femme au couteau, La (Bassori), 15, 35, 38–39, 40, 221

Festival à Dosso (Alassane), 3
Fête du Sanke (Cissæ), 53, 58
Feux de brousse (Bassori), 35, 37
Fidak (Bathily), 44
Fille des dieux, La (Ka), 227
Film companies, African: Afrocult Foundation, 20, 21; Baobab Films, 229; DK7 Communications, 187, 188; Domirev, 239, 240, 241; Emebe Diffusion Films, 45; Les Films de la Lagune, 97; Mypheduh Films Inc., 145; Société Focale 13, 89; Sunu Films, 276, 277; West African Film Corporation (WAFCO), 23, 57, 162, 244, 294
Film festivals, African: Carthage Film Festival (Journées Cinématographiques de Carthage or JCC), 3, 36, 53, 54, 71, 88, 89, 96, 117, 127, 160, 161, 175, 187, 188, 198, 206, 208, 218, 224, 241, 276, 277, 292; Fédération Panafricaine de Cinéastes (FEPACI), 3, 54, 109, 176, 228, 244, 268, 277, 294; Festival Panafricain du Cinéma de Ouagadougou (FESPACO), 3, 14, 36, 44, 54, 71, 79, 80, 84, 88, 89, 97, 98, 108, 109, 111, 116, 127, 128, 143, 145, 159, 161, 162, 175, 186, 206, 208, 228, 229, 242, 277
Films, African: animated films/cartoons, 2, 3, 4, 6; audiences, 22, 53, 89, 127, 159, 218; censorship and, 98, 242, 276, 277; comedy, humor and satire, 6, 44, 46, 74, 99, 100, 109, 187, 190, 219, 220, 245, 246, 297; criticism of (theory), 293; distribution of, 13, 36, 37, 56, 188; epic in, 5, 133, 165, 246; ethnography in, 3, 4, 20, 24, 46, 73, 120; lyricism in, 4, 38, 47, 119, 178, 211, 295, 296; music/musical comedy in, 14, 20, 38, 40, 46, 57, 59, 74, 80, 89, 97, 99, 109, 119, 120, 128, 138, 143, 147, 161, 163, 164, 165, 175, 178, 189, 219, 220, 221, 246, 292, 295; nature and function of, 3, 14, 22, 36, 43, 56, 98, 107, 109, 128, 145, 161, 164, 176, 187, 188, 209, 219, 229, 230, 269, 278, 293, 294; poetry in, 119, 148, 178, 211; production of,

12, 13, 22, 23, 37, 45, 55, 70, 71, 72,
88, 108, 117, 141, 142, 145, 159,
176, 197, 207, 209, 243, 276; storytelling in, 3, 4, 5, 6, 22, 38, 109, 110,
120, 127, 130, 131, 148, 164, 175,
177, 188, 220, 222, 232, 243, 245,
268, 269, 270, 279, 295, 296, 297;
theater and, 20, 21, 25, 109
Finye (Cissé), 54, 55, 59–60, 62–63, 99
Fire in the Afternoon (Balogun), 20, 24
First Congress of African and Asiatic
Writers, 239
First Congress of Black Writers and Art-
ists, 34, 238
First International Festival of Negro Arts,
35, 240
Fleurs du terroir, Les (Kamwa), 187,
188, 190
Fogo, l'île de feu (Maldoror), 208, 212
Folayan, Ade, 20
Forestiers, Les (Bassori), 35, 37
French, as film language, 36, 40, 72, 82,
89, 90, 97, 186, 279
French Ministry of Cooperation, 2, 23,
53, 70, 96, 116, 117, 127, 186, 207,
228, 290, 294
Fritsch, Max, 186
Fugitive, The, 12
Fusils pour Banta, Des (Maldorod), 206–
7, 210
F.V.V.A. - Femmes, villa, voiture, argent
(Alassane), 3, 6

Gabon, pays de contraste (Dong), 79, 80
Ganda, Oumarou: 111, 112, **125–36**; bibliography, 134–36; biography, 125–28;
criticism of, 132–33; filmography,
133–34; major themes, 128–32. Works
(films): *Cabascabo*, 126, 127, 128–29,
132–33; *Cock, cock, cock*, 127;
L'Exilé, 127, 131–32, 133; *Saitane*,
127, 130–31, 133; *Le Wazzou polygame*, 127, 129–30, 133
Garga M'Bossé (Traoré), 277, 281, 284
Gâteau, Le (Vieyra), 291, 297
Gautier, Théophile, 33
Genêt, Jean, 34

Gentleman de Cocody, Le (Christian-Jaque), 35
Gerassimov, Sergei, 206, 239
Gerima, Haile: 117, **137–55**; bibliography, 152–55; biography, 137–46;
criticism of, 148–51; filmography, 152;
major themes, 146–48. Works (films):
After Winter: Sterling Brown, 144,
148, 151; *Ashes and Embers*, 143,
147–48, 151; *Bush Mama*, 142, 147,
148–49, 150; *Child of Resistance*, 140,
146–47, 148; *Harvest: 3,000 years*,
138, 140–42, 147, 149–50; *Hourglass*,
140, 146; *Wilminton 10–USA 10,000*,
143, 147, 150–51. Works (plays): *Aw-
ful Pit*, 139; *Chief*, 139
Godard, Jean-Luc, 99, 127, 209, 222,
223
Gods Must Be Crazy, The (Uys), 198
Gogol, Nicolas, 276
Goob na ñu (Faye), 117, 120
Goodman School of Drama, 138
Gorki Studios, 206
Goudiam, Ousmane, 269
Grève des Bàttu, La, (Sow Fall), 279
Griots-Shango, 158
Guevara, Che, 139, 164
Guillen, Nicolas, 34
Guirma, René, 178

Habitat rural au Sénégal, L' (Vieyra),
291, 297
Habitat urbain au Sénégal, L' (Vieyra),
291, 297
Hama, Boubou, 3, 5
Hanley, William, 158
Harvest: 3,000 Years (Gerima), 138,
140–42, 147, 149–50
Hausa, as a people, 5
Hausa, as film language, 127
Hello Children (Donskoy), 206
Herbe sauvage, L' (Duparc), 36, 89, 91,
92, 108
High Noon, 51
Hirszman, Leon, 234
Histoires drôles, drôles de gens, (Di-
kongue-Pipa), 71
Hogan's Heroes, 12

Hollywood, 12, 14, 16, 144, 244
Home Free (Wilson), 186
Homme de trop, Un (Costa-Gavras), 158
Homme, une terre: Aimé Césaire, Un (Maldoror), 208, 212
Hommes et les idoles, Les (Cissé), 52
Hondo, Med: 99, 140, **157–72**, 209, 290; bibliography, 168–72; biography, 157–63; criticism of, 165–68; filmography, 168; major themes, 163–65. Works (films): *Balada aux sources*, 159, 163; *Les Bicots-nègres, vos voisins*, 159–60, 162, 164, 166; *Nous aurons toute la mort pour dormir*, 160, 164, 166; *Partout ou peut-être nulle part*, 159, 163; *Polisario, un peuple en armes*, 160, 164, 166; *Sarraounia*, 162–63, 165, 168; *Soleil O*, 159, 160, 162, 163–64, 165–66; *West Indies*, 160–61, 162, 164–65, 166–68
Hôpital de Léningrad, L' (Maldoror), 208, 211
Hourglass (Gerima), 140, 146
Hour of the Blast Furnaces, The (Solanos), 140
Hughes, Langston, 144
Huston, John, 158

Iba N'Diaye, peintre (Vieyra), 292, 297
Ibo, as a people, 24
Ibo as film language, 20
Identité (Dong), 79, 80–81, 83
Ija Ominira (Balogun), 20, 26, 28
Il était une fois Libreville (Augé), 79
Iliad (Homer), 33
Indépendance de Madagascar (Vieyra), 290
Indépendance du Cameroun (Vieyra), 290
Indépendance du Congo (Vieyra), 290
Indépendance du Togo (Vieyra), 290
Inspector General (Gogol), 276
Institut Africain d'Études Cinématographiques (INAFEC), 174
Institut des Hautes Études Cinématographiques (IDHEC), 19, 35, 79, 87, 95, 290
In the Beginning (Balogun), 20, 24

Italian neorealism, 52
I Told You So (Adjesu), 14

J'ai dix ans (Duparc), 88, 90
Jamya (Alassane), 2, 4
Je viens de Bokin (Kaboré), 174, 177
Jom (Samb), 229, 231–32, 233–34

Ka, Abdou Anta, 227
Kaboré, Gaston: 99, **173–83**; bibliography, 181–83; biography, 173–77; criticism of, 178–80; filmography, 180–81; major themes, 177–78. Works (films): *Je viens de Bokin*, 174, 177; *Regard sur le VIème FESPACO*, 174, 177; *Stockez et conservez les grains*, 174, 177; *Utilisation des énergies nouvelles en milieu rural*, 174, 177; *Wend Kuuni*, 174–75, 177–80
Kaddu beykat (Faye), 71, 116–17, 118, 119–20, 121–22
Kamwa, Daniel, 20, 118, **185–94**; bibliography, 192–94; biography, 185–89; criticism of, 190–92; filmography, 192; major themes, 189–90. Works (films): *Akum*, 187, 188, 190; *Boubou-Cravate*, 186, 189, 190–91; *Cam-Air, dix ans d'essor*, 187, 190; *Danse, automate, danse*, 187, 188, 190; *Les Fleurs du terroir*, 187, 188, 190; *La Ligne de coeur*, 187, 190; *Messe à Melen*, 187, 188, 190; *Notre fille*, 187, 190, 191–92; *Nous les fous du volant*, 187, 188, 190; *Novotel*, 187, 190; *Pousse-Pousse*, 186–87, 189–90, 191
Kane, Cheikh Hamidou, 295
Kankamba (Alassane), 3, 6
Karim (Thiam), 268, 270, 271
King, Martin Luther, 57
Kodou (Samb), 15, 228, 232–33, 291
Kokoa (Alassane), 3, 6
Konté, Lamine, 59
Kossou 1 (Bassori), 35, 38
Kossou 2 (Bassori), 35, 38
Koula, Jean-Louis, 107
Kouyaté, S., 46
Kurosawa, Akira, 209, 254

Lacoste, Christian, 108
Lallem, Ahmed, 206
Lamb (Vieyra), 291, 295–96, 298
Lambaaye (Traoré), 276, 279, 280, 283
Lapido, Duro, 20
Lari, as film language, 207
Last Grave at Dimbaza (Mahomo), 197–
   98, 199, 200–201, 202
Laye, Camara, 239
Lemoine, Jacqueline, 46
Lemoine, Lucien, 46
Liberté 1 (Ciampi), 267
Ligne de coeur, La (Kamwa), 187, 190
Lingala, as film language, 207
Locke, Alan, 144
Louis Lumière Film School, 107, 116
Love Brewed in the African Pot (Ansah),
   12, 13, 14–17
Lucia (Solas), 140
Lumumba, Patrice, 57, 164
Luttes casamançaises (Thiam), 268, 270,
   271

MacLaren, Norman, 2
Mahomo, Nana: **195–204**; bibliography,
   203–4; biography, 195–99; criticism
   of, 201–2; filmography, 202; major
   themes, 199–201. Works (films): *End
   of the Dialogue*, 197, 199–200, 201;
   Last Grave at Dimbaza, 197–98, 199,
   200–201, 202
Makeba, Myriam, 57
Malcolm X, 139, 148, 164
Maldoror, Sarah: 34, 111, **205–16**, 227;
   bibliography, 215–16; biography, 205–
   10; criticism of, 212–14; filmography,
   214–15; major themes, 210–12. Works
   (films): *La Basilique de Saint-Denis*,
   208, 212; *Un Carnaval dans le Sahel*,
   208, 212; *La Commune, Louise Michel
   et nous*, 207, 212; *Un Dessert pour
   Constance*, 208, 211, 214; *Et les
   chiens se taisaient*, 207, 211; *Fogo,
   l'île de feu*, 208, 212; *Des fusils pour
   Banta*, 206–07, 210; *Un Homme, une
   terre: Aimé Césaire*, 208, 212; *L'Hôpital de Léningrad*, 208, 211; *Un Masque à Paris: Louis Aragon*, 208, 212;

Miro, 208, 212; *Monangambee*, 206,
   207, 210, 212; *Paris, le cimetiére du
   Père Lachaise*, 208, 212; *Le Passager
   du Tassili*, 208, 211, 214; *Portrait de
   Madame Diop*, 208; *Saint-Denis-sur-
   Avenir*, 207, 211–12; *Sambizanga*,
   207–8, 210–11, 212–13
Malinke, as a people, 109, 110
Malle de Maka Kouli, La (Thiam), 268,
   269, 271
Malraux, André, 35
Mamani, Abdoulaye, 165
Mambety, Djibril Diop: 209, **217–25**,
   294; bibliography, 224–25; biography,
   217–19; criticism of, 222–24; filmogra-
   phy, 224; major themes, 219–22.
   Works (films): *Badou Boy*, 218, 220,
   223; *Contras' City*, 217, 219–20, 222–
   23; *Touki-Bouki*, 218, 219, 220–22,
   223–24
Mandabi (Sembene), 47, 99, 112, 132,
   133, 240, 245, 249–50, 251, 291
Man Sa Yay (Faye), 117, 120, 122
Maran, René, 238
Marché, Le (Vieyra), 291, 296–97
Marker, Chris, 209
Martin du Gard, Roger, 239
Masque à Paris: Louis Aragon, Un (Mal-
   doror), 208, 212
Maury, Philippe, 79
M'Baye, Ousmane William, 43, 109, 241
McKay, Claude, 238
Memories of Underdevelopment (Alea),
   140
Merchant of Venice, The (Shakespeare),
   186
Messe à Melen (Kamwa), 187, 188, 190
Micheaux, Oscar, 142
Miro (Maldoror), 208, 212
Mizoguchi, Kenji, 99
Mor, un Noir (Rouch), 126, 128
Mol (Vieyra), 290, 296, 298
Monangambee (Maldoror), 206, 207,
   210, 212
Money Power (Balogun), 21, 24, 26, 28,
   29
Monga, Guy, 158
Montesquieu, 116

Moré, as film language, 174
Mort de Gandji, La (Alassane), 2, 6, 7
Mouna ou le rêve d'un artiste (Duparc), 15, 88, 89, 90, 91–92
Muna Moto (Dikongue-Pipa), 70–71, 73–74, 75–76, 189
Music and Music (Dikongue-Pipa), 71
Musik Man (Balogun), 20, 26, 28

National Council of the Church of Christ, 240
Nationalité immigrée (Sokhona), 71
Nation est née, Une (Vieyra), 290, 291, 295, 298
N'Dakarou (Thiam), 267–68, 269, 271
Ndakarou, impressions matinales (Bathily), 44, 45
N'Diongane (Vieyra), 291, 295, 296, 298
Nee-Owo, Kwate, 14
Nègres, Les (Genêt), 34
Négriers, Les (Boukman), 160
Négritude, 100
N'Gakane, Lionel, 199
Niaye (Sembene), 111, 239, 245, 247, 249
Niger d'aujourd'hui, Le (Vieyra), 290, 295
Nigersteel (Balogun), 20, 24
Njangaan (Traoré), 277, 281–82, 284
Noé (Obey), 95
No Exit (Sartre), 227
Noire de, La (Sembene), 111, 240, 245, 247–49
No Tears for Ananse (Aryete), 14
Notre fille (Kamwa), 187, 190, 191–92
Notre fille ne se mariera pas (Oyono-Mbia), 187
Nous aurons toute la mort pour dormir (Hondo), 160, 164, 166
Nous les fous du volant (Kamwa), 187, 188, 190
Novotel (Kamwa), 187, 190
Nupe Mascarade (Balogun), 20, 24

Obali (Dong), 79, 80, 81–82, 83
Obey, André, 95
Obs (Duparc), 87
Odets, Clifford, 234

Odienné, an 12 (Bassori), 35, 38
Odjidja, Bernard, 14
Odyssey (Homer), 33
Oeil Vert, L', 109
Ogunde, Hubert, 21
One Nigeria (Balogun), 19, 24
Open City (Rossellini), 149
Ophüls, Max, 99
Orfeu Negro (Camus), 295
Orun Mooru (Balogun), 21, 24, 26, 28
Othello (Shakespeare), 186
Ouedraogo, Idrissa, 109
Owuama, New Year Festival (Balogun), 20, 24
Oyono, Ferdinand, 239
Oyono-Mbia, Guillaume, 187

Pagnol, Marcel, 249
Pan-African Festival of Algiers, 35, 240
Pan-Africanist Congress (PAC), 196, 197
Papa Bon Dieu (Sapin), 95, 227
Paris, le cimetière du Père Lachaise (Maldoror), 208, 212
Parks, Gordon, 228
Partout ou peut-être nulle part (Hondo), 159, 163
Passager du Tassili, Le (Maldoror), 208, 211, 214
Passante, La (Faye), 116, 118–19
Persian Letters (Montesquieu), 116
Personnages encombrants, Des (Bathily), 44, 45, 46
Petit à petit ou Les Lettres persanes 1968 (Rouch), 2, 116
Pierrot-le-Fou (Godard), 223
Pileuse de mil, La (Alassane), 2, 4
Piroguier, Le (Alassane), 2, 4
Polisario, un peuple en armes (Hondo), 160, 164, 166
Pompidou, Georges, 297
Pons, Maurice, 208
Pontecorvo, Gillo, 206
Ponts de Paris, Les (Balogun), 20
Popular Movement for the Liberation of Angola (MPLA), 206, 207
Portrait de Madame Diop (Maldoror), 208
Portuguese, as film language, 21

Pot de vin, Le (Senghor), 276

Pousse-Pousse (Kamwa), 186–87, 189–
90, 191

Présence Africaine, 208, 239, 292

Présence africaine à Rome (Vieyra), 290,
295

Présidents Senghor et Modibo Keita, Les
(Vieyra), 290

Prix de la liberté, Le (Dikongue-Pipa),
15, 71, 74, 76

Procés du pilon, Le (Goudiam), 269

Profil ivoirien (Duparc), 88, 90

Pushkin, Aleksander, 34

Quatre Jours à Paris (Berthomieu), 290

Racines de la vie, Les (Duparc), 89, 90

Récolte du coton (Duparc), 88, 90

Regard sur le VIE FESPACO (Kaboré),
174, 177

Rendez-moi mon père (Dikongue-Pipa),
70, 73

Rendez-vous, Le (Vieyra), 291, 296

Réouh-Takh (Traoré), 276, 277, 281, 283

Resnais, Alain, 209

Retour de l'aventurier, Le (Alassane), 2,
5–6, 7

Revanche (Faye), 116, 119

Revenant, Le (Sow Fall), 279

Rocha, Glauber, 37, 254

Rose et Landry (Rouch), 126

Rossellini, Roberto, 149

Rouch, Jean, 2, 115, 116, 125, 126,
127, 247

Roumain, Jacques, 34

Sa Dagga-Le M'Bandakatt (Thiam), 268,
270

Saint-Denis-sur-Avenir (Maldorod), 207,
211–12

Saint-Exupéry, Antoine de, 43

Saison au Congo, Une (Césaire), 96, 186

Saitane (Ganda), 111, 127, 130–31, 133

Sakhi (Alassane), 3, 4

Samb, Ababacar: 15, 34, 205, **227–36**,
291; bibliography, 234–36; biography,
227–29; criticism of, 232–34; filmography, 234; major themes, 230–32.

Works (films): *Et la neige n'était plus*,
227–28, 230–31, 232; *Jom*, 229, 232–
32, 233–34; *Kodou*, 228, 232–33

Samba-le-Grand (Alassane), 3, 5

Sambizanga (Maldoror), 207–8, 210–11,
212–13

Sanjines, Jorge, 140

Sapin, Louis, 95, 227

Sarakholé, as film language, 44, 46

Sarraounia (Hondo), 162–63, 165, 168

Sartre, Jean-Paul, 34, 35, 205, 227, 239

Sarzan (Thiam), 15, 267, 269, 270–71

Schultz, Michael, 277

Second Congress of Black Artists and
Writers, 295

Selassié, Haile, 141

Selbé et tant d'autres (Faye), 117, 120

Sembene, Ousmane: 16, 37, 44, 45, 47,
51, 99, 111, 112, 127, 132, 133, 140,
162, 173, 199, 206, 209, 234, **237–66**,
277, 291, 292, 294, 296; bibliography,
256–66; biography, 237–44; criticism
of, 246–55; filmography, 255–56; major themes, 244–46. Works (films):
Borom Sarret, 239, 240, 245, 247,
249; *Ceddo*, 241–42, 246, 253–55;
Emitai, 240–41, 246, 250–51; *L'Empire Sonhrai*, 239, 242, 245; *Mandabi*,
240, 245, 249–50, 251; *Niaye*, 239,
245, 247, 249; *La Noire de*, 240, 245,
247–49; *Taw*, 240, 245–46, 250–52;
Xala, 241, 243, 246, 252–53. Works
(writings): *Les Bouts de bois de Dieu*,
238, 239, 242; *Le Dernier de l'Empire*, 242; *Le Docker noir*, 238; *L'Harmattan*, 239; *Niiwam*, 243; *O pays
mon beau peuple*, 238–39; *Vehi Ciosane ou Blanche Genèse, suivi du Mandat*, 239–40; *Voltaïque*, 239; *Xala*,
241, 243, 246

*Sénégal et le Festival Mondial des Arts
Nègres, Le*, (Vieyra), 291

Senghor, Léopold S., 34, 57, 100, 212,
219, 242, 276, 291, 292, 295

Serer, as a people, 120

Serge, Victor, 208

Serreau, Jean-Marie, 96, 158

Seven Samurai (Kurosawa), 254

Shakespeare, William, 186
Siggi ou la poliomyélite (Bathily), 44
Simb, le jeu du faux lion (Thiam), 268,
    271
Simple, Un (Dikongue-Pipa), 70, 73
Sindiely (Vieyra), 291, 295
Sites et des monuments au Sénégal, Des
    (Bathily), 44, 45
Sixième Sillon, Le (Bassori), 35, 38
Slim, Memphis, 97
Société d'Exploitation Cinématographique
    Africaine (SECMA), 268, 276
Sokhona, Sidney, 71
Solanas, Fernando, 140
Solas, Humberto, 140
Soleil O (Hondo), 99, 159, 160, 162,
    163–64, 165–66
Songhai, as film language, 127
Soubane (Alassane), 3, 4
Soulignac, Paul, 240
Sources d'inspiration (Cissé), 52, 57
Soviet sociorealism, 52
Sow, Baidy, 228, 276, 277
Sow, Pap Samba, 218
Sow Fall, Aminata, 279
Stevenson, Robert Louis, 33
Stockez et conservez les grains (Kaboré),
    174, 177
Struggle for a Free Zimbabwe (Nee-
    Owo), 14
Suicides (Tchuilen), 111
Sur la dune de la solitude (Bassori), 35,
    38, 39
Sur le sentier du requiem (Dong), 79, 80,
    82, 83
Sutherland, Efua, 14

Tadjer, Akli, 208
Tall, Papa Ibra, 268
Tamango (Berry), 227
Tam Tam à Paris (Bella), 118
Tam-tam ivoire (Duparc), 88, 90
Tams-Tams se sont tus, Les (Maury), 79
Tante Zita (Enrico), 158
Tarzan, 222
Taw (Sembene), 240, 245–46, 250–52,
    291
Tchecov, Anton, 158

Tchuilen, Jean-Claude, 111
Themes of African films: acculturation,
    6, 15, 38, 44, 81, 100, 121, 189, 230,
    231, 268; adultery, 59, 73, 91, 100,
    130; alienation, 5, 15, 24, 39, 80, 81,
    90, 96, 100, 111, 128, 146, 147, 163,
    164, 189, 210, 211, 220, 221, 222,
    230, 231, 244, 245, 269, 281, 294,
    295; apartheid, 199, 200, 201; ani-
    mism, 24, 25, 60, 81, 130, 190, 220,
    246; army, 60, 73, 128, 129, 143,
    147, 164, 245, 246, 269, 297; ar-
    ranged marriages, 6, 73, 74, 81, 82,
    129, 280, 295; arrivism, 6; art, 57, 80,
    90, 211, 229; black diaspora, 25, 57,
    80, 144, 146, 209, 281; beggars, 46,
    219, 246; bourgeoisie, 6, 15, 39, 58,
    91, 110, 246, 281; Brazil, 25; bu-
    reaucracy, 47, 81, 129, 244, 245, 270,
    280, 281; candomblé, 25; caste sys-
    tem, 109; children, 46, 47, 73, 74, 82,
    119, 120, 177, 200, 220, 245, 270,
    295, 296, 297; christianism, 46, 81,
    187, 190, 219, 242; circumcision, 46,
    296; class consciousness, 14, 15, 58,
    60, 280; colonialism, 14, 15, 71, 119,
    144, 163, 165, 177, 210, 211, 220,
    244, 245, 246, 281, 295; consumer-
    ism, 6, 146, 246, 279, 280; corrup-
    tion, 6, 47, 58, 59, 60, 81, 82, 232,
    244, 245, 246, 280, 282; cosmology/
    philosophy, 25; cowboys, 5; Dakar,
    45, 46, 219, 220, 221, 267, 269, 291;
    dance, 38, 46, 101, 160, 187, 189,
    190, 232, 295; deaf-mute, 58, 177; de-
    linquency, 6, 58, 81, 91, 220, 221,
    269, 270; development, 4, 5, 37, 38,
    44, 82, 88, 89, 90, 101, 119, 177,
    187, 190, 229, 295, 296, 297; divi-
    ners, 6, 15, 16, 91, 130, 270, 296;
    dowry, 73, 74, 82, 120, 130, 189,
    270; drought, 5, 120, 281; drugs, 146,
    270; education, 4, 14, 15, 58, 59, 99,
    110, 111, 190, 200, 280, 282, 294;
    emigration, 25, 99, 100, 101, 119,
    121, 160, 163, 164, 211, 245, 280,
    294, 295; excision, 91; exile, 24, 100,
    117, 118, 120, 131, 163, 164, 165,

230, 231; family, 14, 244; family solidarity (abuses of), 6, 90, 91; festivals,
4, 24, 46, 58, 73, 190, 212; France,
24, 55, 80, 87, 96, 100, 116, 118,
119, 160, 163, 211, 221, 245, 246,
294, 295; generation gap, 14, 60, 73,
74; griots, 3, 4, 109, 110, 127, 128,
129, 148, 158, 232, 245, 268, 270,
295; guerilla warfare, 57, 164, 165,
210; health, 45, 47, 58, 91, 120, 200,
201, 280, 281; history, 33, 88, 90,
109, 110, 120, 121, 127, 160, 161,
162, 165, 176, 177, 210, 212, 229,
232, 244, 245, 246, 281, 295; homi-
cide, 45, 58, 59, 74, 82, 91, 130, 132,
232, 246, 296; homosexuality, 220;
identity, 24, 57, 80, 81, 133, 164,
176, 190, 231, 281; illiteracy, 47, 244,
245, 280; impotence, 40, 177, 246;
imprisonment, 6, 73, 147, 210, 211,
269, 280; incest, 245; infant mortality,
47, 201; insanity, 14, 15, 39, 74, 90,
119, 231, 269, 296; Islam, 58, 129,
131, 219, 240, 242, 245, 246, 277,
282; jealousy, 91; justice (or lack
thereof), 6, 143, 147, 200, 210; love,
4, 5, 14, 15, 38, 39, 44, 58, 60, 73,
74, 81, 82, 90, 91, 101, 110, 111,
118, 119, 130, 131, 189, 190, 221,
231, 269, 270; Mamy Watta, 38; marriage, 4, 15, 82, 110, 111, 120, 130,
131, 178, 190, 246, 269, 270, 296;
money, 6, 73, 74, 109, 129, 130, 189,
245, 246, 268, 270, 280, 295; myths,
21, 24, 25, 38, 110, 246; neocolonialism, 81, 163, 244; nepotism, 280; police, 59, 81, 147, 220, 245; political
concerns, 5, 19, 24, 57, 59, 82, 119,
121, 128, 131, 146, 147, 176, 199,
200, 201, 218, 229, 230, 246, 280,
281, 295, 297; polygamy, 129, 130,
190, 209, 245, 246; prostitution, 129,
130, 146; racism, 163; rape, 15, 147;
religion, 244; rural African lifestyles,
4, 24, 37, 38, 39, 44, 46, 47, 58, 73,
74, 80, 81, 82, 90, 110, 119, 120,
130, 147, 177, 190, 221, 245, 246,
249, 270, 296, 297; rural migration,

90, 129, 177, 199, 220, 221, 269,
270, 279, 281; sex, 38, 73, 74, 101,
119, 221, 246; slavery, 25, 57, 144,
163, 164, 281; Soweto, 199; sports, 6,
241, 270, 295; suicide, 58, 110, 131,
163, 245, 296; tatooing, 231; Tarzan,
100; tourism, 38, 45, 80, 88, 90, 187,
190; traditional African healing, 15,
38, 58, 82, 120, 130, 231; traditional
African lifestyle, 4, 57; tradition vs.
modernity, 5, 14, 15, 38, 39, 46, 58,
60, 74, 80, 81, 90, 110, 111, 120,
177, 187, 189, 190, 219, 246, 268,
269, 280, 281; tribalism, 73; unemployment, 58, 90, 129, 281; unwed
mothers, 58; urban African lifestyles/
urbanization, 15, 24, 46, 47, 58, 60,
74, 80, 82, 91, 101, 110, 129, 175,
199, 200, 219, 220, 221, 231, 245,
246, 279, 280, 296, 297; urban poverty, 47, 244, 245, 281, 296; violence,
59, 199; women (modern African), 6,
14, 38, 47, 59, 74, 82, 90, 91, 100,
101, 177, 189, 190, 200, 244, 245,
246, 268, 279; women (traditional African), 73, 82, 90, 101, 120, 130, 190,
200, 211, 231, 245, 246, 279, 280,
296; working class, 14, 58, 59, 189,
200, 210, 211, 212, 245, 281; youth,
60, 81, 91, 99, 110, 220, 221, 222,
231, 232, 246, 268
They Call That Love (Ampaw), 14
They Don't Wear Black Tie (Hirszman),
234
Thiam, Momar: 15, **267–73**; bibliography, 272–73; biography, 267–69;
criticism of, 270–71; filmography,
271–72; major themes, 269–70. Works
(films): *Baks*, 268, 270, 271; *Bouki
cultivateur*, 268, 269, 270; *Karim*,
268, 270, 271; *Luttes casamançaises*,
268, 270, 271; *La Malle de Maka
Kouli*, 268, 269, 271; *N'Dakarou*,
267–68, 269, 271; *Sa Dagga-Le
M'Bandakatt*, 268, 270; *Sarzan*, 267,
269, 270–71; *Simb, le jeu du faux lion*,
268, 271
Thundergod (Balogun), 20, 24

Tiyabu-Biru (Bathily), 44, 46–47, 48
Touki-Bouki (Mambety), 218, 219, 220–
     22, 223–24
Toula ou le Génie des Eaux (Alassane),
     3, 5, 7
Tragédie du Roi Christophe, La (Cé-
     saire), 96, 158, 186, 205
Traoré, Mahama Johnson: 242, **275–87**;
     bibliography, 285–87; biography, 275–
     79; criticism of, 282–84; filmography,
     284–85; major themes, 279–82. Works
     (films): *Diankhabi*, 275–76, 277, 279,
     280, 282, 283; *Diegue-bi*, 276, 279,
     280, 283; *L'Enfer des innocents*, 276,
     280, 282–83; *Garga M'Bossé*, 277,
     281, 284; *Lambaaye*, 276, 279, 280,
     283; *Njangaan*, 277, 281–82, 284;
     Réouh-Takh, 276, 277, 281, 283
Traoré, Mory, 107
Treasure Island (Stevenson), 33
Tripes au soleil, Les (Aubert), 227
3 Ans 5 mois (Faye), 117, 120
Tropic and the North, The (Serge), 208
Truffaut, François, 99, 127
Tubman, Harriet, 148

UNESCO, 174, 242, 294
United Nations, 117
University of California at Los Angeles
     (UCLA), 139, 140, 142, 146
*Utilisation des énergies nouvelles en mil-
     ieu rural* (Kaboré), 174, 177
Uys, Jamie, 198

Varda, Agnès, 209
VGIK (State Institute of Cinema, Mos-
     cow), 52, 57
Victoire en chantant, La (Annaud), 36
Vida Verdadeira de Domingos Xavier, A
     (Vieira), 207
Vieira, Luandino, 206, 207
Vieyra, Paulin Soumanou: 7, 27, 61, 83,
     84, 92, 162, 179, 191, 213, 222, 223,
     232, 238, 244, 247, 248, 251, 271,
     282, 283, **289–303**; bibliography, 300–
     303; biography, 289–94; criticism of,
     297–99; filmography, 299; major
     themes, 294–97. Works (films): *L'Afri-

que à Moscou, 290, 295; *Afrique-sur-
     Seine*, 290, 291, 292, 295, 298; *Avec
     l'Ensemble National*, 291, 295, 298;
     Avec les Africains à Vienne, 290; *La
     Bicyclette*, 291, 296; *Birago Diop,
     conteur*, 292, 297; *C'était il y a quatre
     ans*, 290, 294–95, 298; *Diarama*, 291,
     297; *Ecrits de Dakar*, 291, 295; *Ecrits
     du Caire*, 291; *En résidence surveillée*,
     292, 297, 298; *L'Envers du décor*,
     291, 297; *Le Gâteau*, 291, 297; *Iba
     N'Diaye, peintre*, 292, 297; *Indépend-
     ance de Madagascar*, 290; *Indépend-
     ance du Cameroun*, 290; *Indépendance
     du Congo*, 290; *Indépendance du
     Togo*, 290; *L'Habitat rural au Sénégal*,
     291, 297; *L'Habitat urbain au Séné-
     gal*, 291, 297; *Lamb*, 291, 295–96,
     298; *Le Marché*, 291, 296–97; *Mol*,
     290, 296, 298; *Une Nation est née*,
     290, 291, 295, 298; *N'Diongane*, 291,
     295, 296, 298; *Le Niger d'aujourd'hui*,
     290, 295; *Présence africaine à Rome*,
     290, 295; *Les Présidents Senghor et
     Modibo Keita*, 290; *Le Rendezvous*,
     291, 296; *Le Sénégal et le Festival
     Mondial des Arts Nègres*, 291; *Sin-
     diely*, 291, 295; *Visite officielle du
     Président Senghor au Canada*, 291;
     *Visite officielle du Président Senghor
     aux États-Unis d'Amérique*, 291; *Voy-
     age du Président Senghor au Brésil et
     à Trinidad-Tobago*, 291; *Voyage du
     Président Senghor en Italie*, 291; *Voy-
     age présidentiel en URSS*, 291. Works
     (writings): *Le Cinéma africain*, 292; *Le
     Cinéma au Sénégal*, 292; *Le Cinéma et
     l'Afrique*, 292; *Sembene Ousmane, ci-
     néaste*, 292
Visages de femmes (Ecaré), 97–98, 99,
     101–2, 103
*Visite officielle du Président Senghor au
     Canada* (Vieyra), 291
*Visite officielle du Président Senghor aux
     États-Unis d'Amérique* (Vieyra), 291
Vivre (Balogun), 20
*Voyage du Président Senghor au Brésil et
     à Trinidad-Tobago* (Vieyra), 291

Voyage du Président Senghor en Italie
(Vieyra), 291
Voyage présidential en URSS (Vieyra),
291

Walk with Love and Death, A (Huston),
158
Warner-Vieyra, Myriam, 291
Wazzou polygame, Le (Ganda), 127,
129–30, 133
Welles, Orson, 98
Wend Kuuni (Kaboré), 99, 174–75, 177–
80
West Indies (Hondo), 160–61, 162, 164–
65, 166–68
Wilmington 10–USA 10,000 (Gerima),
143, 147, 150–51
Wilson, Lanford, 186
Wolof, as film language, 44, 119, 220,

228, 230, 240, 245, 276, 277, 279,
281
Woodson, Carter G., 144
Wright, Richard, 238

Xala (Sembene), 16, 44, 173, 241, 243,
246, 252–53, 291

Yacine, Kateb, 158
Yao, 35
Yeelen (Cissé), 54, 60
Yoruba, as a people, 24, 25
Yoruba, as film language, 20, 21, 26
You Hide Me (Nee-Owo), 14
Young and the Damned, The (Buñuel),
140

Zazouman de Treichville (Rouch), 125

About the Author

FRANÇOISE PFAFF is a Professor of French at Howard University. She is the author of a book entitled *The Cinema of Ousmane Sembene, A Pioneer of African Film* (Greenwood Press, 1984). Her articles have appeared in *Africa Quarterly*, *Black Art*, *CLA Journal*, *Commonwealth*, *Jump-Cut*, *Positif*, and other French- and English-language publications. She has also lectured on African film at various universities and cultural institutions in the U.S. and abroad.